The Constitutional Law Dictionary

THE CONSTITUTIONAL LAW DICTIONARY

VOLUME 2: GOVERNMENTAL POWERS

Ralph C. Chandler
Richard A. Enslen
Peter G. Renstrom

ABC·CLIO

Santa Barbara, California
Oxford, England

Library of Congress Cataloging in Publication Data
(Revised for vol. 2)

Chandler, Ralph C., 1934–
  The constitutional law dictionary.

  (Clio dictionaries in political science; 8)
  Includes indexes.
  Contents: v. 1. Individual rights—v. 2. Governmental powers.
  1. United States—Constitutional law—Terms and phrases. 2. United States—Constitutional law—Cases.
I. Enslen, Richard A., 1931–   . II. Renstrom,
Peter G., 1943–   . III. Title. IV. Series.
KF4548.5.C47 1985   342.73'003   84–12320
                    347.302'003

ISBN 0-87436-031-5 (v. 1: alk. paper)
ISBN 0-87436-440-X (v. 2: alk. paper)

10 9 8 7 6 5 4 3 2

ABC-Clio, Inc.
2040 Alameda Padre Serra
Santa Barbara, California 93103–1788

Clio Press Ltd.
55 St. Thomas' Street
Oxford, OX1 1JG, England

This book is printed on acid-free paper ∞.
Manufactured in the United States of America

Clio Dictionaries in Political Science

The African Political Dictionary
Claude S. Phillips

The Asian Political Dictionary
Lawrence Ziring and C. I. Eugene Kim

The Constitutional Law Dictionary, Volume 1: *Individual Rights*
Ralph C. Chandler, Richard A. Enslen, and Peter G. Renstrom

The Constitutional Law Dictionary, Volume 1: *Individual Rights,*
Supplement 1
Ralph C. Chandler, Richard A. Enslen, and Peter G. Renstrom

The Constitutional Law Dictionary, Volume 2: *Governmental Powers*
Ralph C. Chandler, Richard A. Enslen, and Peter G. Renstrom

The Dictionary of Political Analysis, second edition
Jack C. Plano, Robert E. Riggs, and Helenan S. Robin

The European Political Dictionary
Ernest E. Rossi and Barbara P. McCrea

The International Law Dictionary
Robert L. Bledsoe and Boleslaw A. Boczek

The Latin American Political Dictionary
Ernest E. Rossi and Jack C. Plano

The Middle East Political Dictionary
Lawrence Ziring

The Presidential-Congressional Political Dictionary
Jeffrey M. Elliot and Sheikh R. Ali

The Public Policy Dictionary
Earl R. Kruschke and Byron M. Jackson

Clio Dictionaries in Political Science

The Soviet and East European Political Dictionary
Barbara P. McCrea, Robert E. Riggs, and Helenan S. Robin

Forthcoming

The Arms Control, Disarmament, and Military Security Dictionary
Jeffrey M. Elliot and Robert Reginald

The International Relations Dictionary, fourth edition
Jack C. Plano and Roy Olton

The Public Administration Dictionary
Ralph C. Chandler and Jack C. Plano

The State and Local Government Political Dictionary
Jeffrey M. Elliot and Sheikh R. Ali

This book is dedicated to

WILLIAM JEFFREY CHANDLER
whose loyalty to his father
is a spring of clear water

DAVID, SUSAN, SANDRA,
THOMAS, JANET, and JOSEPH ENSLEN
whose courage and fortitude
have served as their father's inspiration

BOBBI RENSTROM
whose love, support, and companionship
sustain her husband

SERIES STATEMENT

Language precision is the primary tool of every scientific discipline. That aphorism serves as the guideline for this series of political dictionaries. Although each book in the series relates to a specific topical or regional area in the discipline of political science, entries in the dictionaries also emphasize history, geography, economics, sociology, philosophy, and religion.

This dictionary series incorporates special features designed to help the reader overcome any language barriers that may impede a full understanding of the subject matter. For example, the concepts included in each volume were selected to complement the subject matter found in existing texts and other books. All but one volume utilize a subject-matter chapter arrangement that is most useful for classroom and study purposes.

Entries in all volumes include an up-to-date definition plus a paragraph of *Significance* in which the authors discuss and analyze each term's historical and current relevance. Most entries are also cross-referenced, providing the reader an opportunity to seek additional information related to the subject of inquiry. A comprehensive index, found in both hardcover and paperback editions, allows the reader to locate major entries and other concepts, events, and institutions discussed within these entries.

The political and social sciences suffer more than most disciplines from semantic confusion. This is attributable, *inter alia,* to the popularization of the language, and to the focus on many diverse foreign political and social systems. This dictionary series is dedicated to overcoming some of this confusion through careful writing of thorough, accurate definitions for the central concepts, institutions, and events that comprise the basic knowledge of each of the subject fields. New titles in the series will be issued periodically, including some in related social science disciplines.

— Jack C. Plano
Series Editor

CONTENTS

A NOTE ON HOW TO USE THIS BOOK

The Constitutional Law Dictionary: Governmental Powers focuses on concepts of constitutionalism, biographical sketches of leading justices of the United States Supreme Court, words and phrases common to American constitutional law, and landmark case decisions rendered by the Supreme Court. Several techniques have been utilized to help the reader locate entries with ease.

The materials in Chapters 1, 10, and 11 are arranged alphabetically. The terms in Chapter 1 develop the major elements of constitutionalism and provide the conceptual framework around which the other chapters are organized. Chapter 1 should be reviewed in its entirety for an understanding of the fundamental characteristics of constitutional law. Chapter 10 lists 35 leading justices of the Supreme Court and briefly describes their careers and judicial philosophies. Chapter 11 closely resembles a traditional dictionary. It contains definitions standing alone but also words and phrases that appear in other entries in the volume. The terms in Chapter 11 do not constitute an exhaustive listing of legal words and phrases, however. The closest this book comes to that kind of treatment is in the comprehensive Index.

Chapters 2 through 9 are organized around topical issues—judicial power, executive power, legislative power, federalism, the commerce power, the federal taxing and spending power, state economic regulation and due process, and the contract clause—with older cases preceding more recent ones. The reader may locate a case or concept in his or her area of interest by scanning the summary of entries at the beginning of each chapter. The summary shows the page number of each entry.

A complete alphabetical listing of all case entries and their respective page references is provided at the front of the book.

The reader can explore the implications of a topic by using the cross-references provided at the end of each definitional paragraph. The references point to related materials included in the same chapter or to relevant discussions in other chapters. Page numbers are provided for all cross-references.

If the reader is unsure about which chapter to consult for a particular case or concept, he or she may consult the comprehensive Index at the end of the book. It includes every case or concept contained in the dictionary, either as a major entry or as a reference within an entry. Various permutations of entries are also provided in the Index to aid in the reader's search. All indexed terms include page numbers.

The authors have designed the format of the book to offer the student or general reader a variety of useful approaches to locating information. The book may be used as (1) a *dictionary* and *reference guide* to the language and major decisions of the United States Supreme Court in the field of governmental powers; (2) a *study guide* for students enrolled in law school or in political science classes in colleges and universities; (3) a *handbook* for use by lawyers; (4) a *supplement* to a textbook or a book of readings in the field of constitutional law; (5) a source of *review materials* for the attorney, judge, professor, or student of constitutional law; and (6) a *social science aid* for use in cognate fields, such as business and commercial law, economics, history, and sociology.

PREFACE

The series of which this book is a part takes as its organizing idea the fact that precise language is the primary tool of every intellectual discipline. This is particularly true in the field of law. We undertook to write *The Constitutional Law Dictionary: Governmental Powers* in pursuit of clear and precise legal language.

The authors have assembled a book that explains the fundamental ideas of constitutionalism in general and American constitutional law in particular. The task involved the integration of many elements reflective of the multidimensional character of the subject matter. We hoped to reach both general readers and specific audiences of academics and practitioners. A major objective is to introduce students considering a career in law to some of the operational concepts in the field. We also intend to reach the legal community, including lawyers who may find themselves removed by the circumstances of their lives from easy access to the essential elements of constitutional law.

The concepts, justices, terms, and cases selected here represent our best judgment about how to advance the understanding of constitutional law in the area of governmental powers. We learned something about how to do that from our similar effort in the area of individual rights. A large number of terms and cases could have been selected. We did not intend, however, for this book to be an exhaustive reference source. A number of such volumes already exist. Our selections were guided by such questions as: Does this term, concept, or case enhance the ability of the reader to communicate in the fundamental language of the field? Will a biographical sketch of this justice facilitate the reader's understanding of definitional processes and his or her appreciation for how constitutional standards evolved? Will the volume complement and supplement materials commonly used in courses in constitutional law? By limiting our dictionary to fundamental concepts, we believe a more thorough description and analysis was made possible.

Two considerations were important in the selection of Supreme Court cases. One was that certain cases should be included because they are generally regarded as landmark cases. *Marbury v. Madison* is one such example. No discussion of judicial power can be complete without it. The second consideration was that we thought a conscious effort should be made to emphasize *recent* decisions, both to present the current thinking of the Court and to provide a sense of how the evolution of a particular line of cases has taken place. The Burger and Rehnquist Courts are therefore heavily represented. Citations for recent cases are sometimes referred to in the text using references to the Lawyer's Editions of the United States Reports series. The obvious reason for this is that, at the time of publication of this volume, the complete United States Reports series was not available from the publisher.

Although all dictionaries tend to resemble one another, *The Constitutional Law Dictionary*, Volume 2: *Governmental Powers* has several unique features. First, entries have been selected to reflect the major issue areas of the field. The book has a subject-matter chapter format in which key cases are grouped for study and review purposes. This allows the dictionary to be used both in and out of class as a teaching and learning tool by professors, students, and practitioners. The chapters are linked through their subject-matter chapter format to leading textbooks. A second unique feature is the inclusion of a paragraph of *Significance* following the definitional discussion. The authors have sought to provide historical perspective through this paragraph. We offer comments that underscore why we think the case is important. A third feature is the inclusion of cross-references that function as suggestions about how to seek additional information within the volume. A fourth distinctive element of the book is its attention to the biographies of Supreme Court justices in Chapter 10. Finally, the book incorporates a comprehensive Index to facilitate the location of entries.

We wish to acknowledge the large number of scholars who have contributed to the volume by their elaboration of the language of constitutional law. We are greatly indebted to them. We also wish to acknowledge with deep gratitude the intellectual stimulation of our students. We want to express our sincere appreciation for the inspiration provided by Professor Jack C. Plano, series editor of the ABC-CLIO Political Dictionary Series. Professor Plano has spent many hours with our manuscript. There likely would never have been a *Constitutional Law Dictionary* without his years of labor in the development of the art of lexicography. A hearty thanks is extended to Janet T. Lawing, who assisted substantially in the production processes of the book. These colleagues and friends made the enterprise possible. The authors accept full responsibility for errors, and we invite readers to communicate with us about any matter of mutual interest.

— Ralph C. Chandler
Professor of Political Science
Western Michigan University

— Richard A. Enslen
United States District Judge
Western District of Michigan

— Peter G. Renstrom
Professor of Political Science
Western Michigan University

ALPHABETICAL LIST OF CASE ENTRIES

The Constitutional Law Dictionary

1. Constitutionalism

Articles of Confederation   The first constitution of the United States of America. The Articles of Confederation governed the united colonies from 1781 until 1789, when they were superseded by the new federal Constitution. The drafting of the Articles of Confederation by the Second Continental Congress began on June 7, 1776, the same day the first formal motion was introduced to declare independence from Great Britain. The battles of Lexington and Concord in April had made it clear to all but the staunchest loyalists that a war of independence was inevitable. A formal government for the united colonies was needed, if only for military purposes. The Second Continental Congress rejected John Dickenson's first draft because it created too strong a central government. Congress approved Dickenson's second draft on November 15, 1777. The required ratification by all the states was not completed until Maryland's approval was given on March 1, 1781. Maryland's price of ratification was Virginia's agreement on a controversial western territories land question.

The general issue in congressional debate had been what kind of union was best for the thirteen colonies. Although there was a spectrum of opinion from monarchist to fervent state sovereignty, historians have distinguished two main groups in opposition to each other. The original Federalists wanted a weak central government. They were led in the Second Continental Congress by Thomas Burke and included Richard Henry Lee, John Witherspoon, and George Mason. Thomas Jefferson, Patrick Henry, and Thomas Paine were sympathetic to that position but were not present at the Congress. The Nationalists, called Federalists in the subsequent debate in the 1787 Constitution, wanted a strong central government. The Nationalists were led in the Second Continental Congress by John Dickenson and later by James Wilson. The party included John Adams, Charles Carroll, James Duane, Joseph Galloway, John Jay, James Madison, Gouverneur Morris, John Rutledge, and George Washington. A combination of hatred for the tyranny of the British government, strong patriotic feelings for individual states, distrust of politicians and rulers generally, and the self-interest of groups and regions won the day for the old Federalists.

In its thirteen articles, the final version of the Articles of Confederation laid out a loose confederation of sovereign states over which the central government had only the limited powers enumerated in the document. Since there was provision only for a weak executive and no judiciary, most of the powers of the central government were vested in the Congress. It was to meet at least every six months. Each state, represented by from two to seven persons elected and reimbursed by the state legislature, had just one vote in the Congress. Any important issue required the consent of nine states, and any amendment to the

Articles had to be unanimous. When Congress was not in session, the daily business of the United States was to be conducted by a Committee of the States. The Committee was composed of one representative from each state, with one of the thirteen members elected president for a one-year term. The Articles also permitted the establishment of any necessary congressional committees. The government was soon run by the four committees regulating finance, the army, the navy, and foreign affairs.

The enumerated powers of Congress included the determination of each state's share of the confederation's common expenses, although Congress had no power actually to collect taxes or to compel individual states to do so. Congress was given procedural and moral authority to settle disputes between individual states, but it had no authority to enforce compliance with the settlements. Congress had the exclusive power to declare war and peace; conduct foreign diplomacy (except for commercial treaties that limited the rights of individual states to impose tariffs and embargoes); regulate currency, weights, and measures; run the postal service; appoint the highest officers in the army and navy; and set limits of size for the armies and navies of the individual states.

Three specific issues occupied much of the debate over the Articles. They were the formula of representation in the Congress, the formula for the sharing by the states of the confederacy's common debts, and jurisdiction over the lands west of the Alleghenies. Representation was finally set at one vote per state. The larger states' desire for representation in proportion to population was defeated. The more populous but underdeveloped southern states finally won the common-debt debate, with the stipulation that a state's share would be proportionate to the improved value of its land. On the western land question, Maryland's dogged refusal to ratify the Articles finally won the concession of the eight states with western land claims, especially Virginia. The jurisdiction of that land was turned over to Congress. The Articles of Confederation contained no bill of rights. Many anti-Nationalists would later criticize the Constitution of 1787 because it had the same defect. *See also* CONSTITUTIONALISM, HISTORICAL DEVELOPMENT OF, p. 15; CONSTITUTION OF THE UNITED STATES OF AMERICA, p. 19; CONTINENTAL CONGRESS, p. 23.

Significance   The Articles of Confederation created the thirteen United States of America from thirteen British colonies and enabled the new government to survive both a war with Great Britain and the war's aftermath. The perennial question regarding the Articles has been whether they represented a noble but necessarily transitional form of government that was legitimately replaced by the 1787 Constitution, or whether they were the sole authentic governmental embodiment of the Declaration of Independence and the Revolution. In the latter view the Articles were illegitimately supplanted by the Constitution. Today historians admit that many of the alleged weaknesses of government under the Articles have been exaggerated. There is also general agreement that refusal to establish a stronger central government under the Articles was the reason for the confederation's inability to make individual states share the $60 million national debt after the Revolutionary War. The Articles were also the reason for the young nation's inability to overcome British, French, and Spanish interference with American commerce. Historian Merrill Jensen maintains that accounts of such weaknesses are based on the shoddy historical reports of John Fiske. Jensen argues that the supplanting of the Articles in 1787 reflected the conservatives' successful interruption of an internal sociopolitical revolution that had been the real inspiration for the external revolution against Great Britain. Whatever one's view of this historical debate, there can be little doubt that the centralization-decentralization issue has continued to be a prime source of disagreement throughout the history of the United States. From the debate over the Articles, through Jefferson's conversion from the old Federalist to the new Federalist position, through New England's strong states' rights position during the War of 1812 and the Webster-Calhoun debates before the Civil War, all the way to the debates over the New Deal and Ronald Reagan's New Federalism, the United States has continued to search for the proper balance between an adequate central government and the rights of states and individuals.

Bill of Rights   The enumeration of the rights of individuals legally protected against violation by government. The American Bill of Rights is found in the federal Constitution and its amendments, especially the first ten. The Bill of Rights is broader than the first ten amendments, with which it has traditionally been identified. The protection of many individual rights was included in the body of the original Constitution of 1787: (1) the prohibition of suspension of *habeas corpus* except in wars and rebellions and the prohibition of bills of attainder or *ex post facto laws* (Article I, Section 9); (2) trial by jury for all crimes except impeachment (Article III, Section 2); (3) limitations concerning indictments, trials, and punishments of accused traitors (Article III, Section 3); and (4) the prohibition of religious tests for public officeholders (Article VI). Moreover, there are many personal rights protected by amendments subsequent to the first ten: (1) the prohibition of slavery (the Thirteenth Amendment, ratified 1865); (2) the prohibition of racial bars to voting rights (the Fifteenth Amendment, ratified 1870); (3) the prohibition of gender bars to voting rights (the Nineteenth Amendment, ratified 1920); (4) the right to drink alcohol (the Twenty-first Amendment, ratified 1933); (5) the prohibition of tax payment as a condition for voting (the Twenty-fourth Amendment, ratified 1964); and (6) the prohibition of age bars to voting rights for those over 18 years of age (the Twenty-sixth Amendment, ratified 1971). Although it does not enumerate any new personal rights, the Fourteenth Amendment (ratified 1868) played a crucial role in broadening the enforcement of all personal rights in American constitutionalism.

The first ten amendments themselves guarantee the following personal rights: (1) the freedom of religion, speech, press, assembly, and peaceful protest; (2) the right to bear arms in order to maintain a well-regulated militia; (3) freedom from having soldiers quartered in one's home; (4) freedom from search and seizure without probable cause; (5) the requirement of grand jury indictment for all but military crimes, freedom from double jeopardy and judicial self-incrimination, and the guarantee of legal due process, as well as just compensation for publicly appropriated private property; (6) the right to a speedy, public, and impartial trial, with the right to know the charge against one, the right to compel witnesses for the defense, and the right to have legal counsel; (7) the right to jury trial for civil matters concerning $20 or more, and the prohibition of judicial review of such trials except in accordance with civil law; (8) prohibition of excessive bails or fines and of cruel and unusual punishment; (9–10) of those rights not enumerated in the Constitution or its amendments, individuals enjoy all other rights except those delegated to the central government, reserved to individual states, or forbidden by the states.

The history of the federal Bill of Rights can be traced in five stages: (1) its British and philosophical antecedents; (2) early colonial enumerations of personal rights; (3) the bills of rights of states during the Revolutionary period; (4) the actual drafting of the federal Bill of Rights; and (5) the extension of federal enforcement of the Bill of Rights to prevent violations by the states. The two primary sources of the Bill of Rights were British statutory and common law on the one hand and natural law theory on the other. During the colonial period Americans stressed the protection of their rights by British law, especially as found in Magna Carta (1215), the Petition of Rights (1628), the Bill of Rights (1689), and as expounded in Blackstone's *Commentaries*. As the American desire for independence from Great Britain increased, the colonists became more and more assertive of the natural law basis of their rights, especially as found in Locke, Montesquieu, and Beccaria. Many of the colonies adopted an enumeration of individual rights in their charters or in separate statutes. Maryland's Act for the Liberties of the People (1639) was the first. Rhode Island's charter

(1663) was the first to allow broad religious freedom. The most developed charters were West New Jersey's Great Charter of Fundamentals (1676), the Pennsylvania Frame of Government (1683), the New York Charter of Liberties and Privileges (1683), and especially the Pennsylvania Charter of Privileges of 1701.

When the inevitability of the war for independence became clear, the Revolutionary leaders urged colonial legislatures to draft autonomous constitutions. Sensitive to governmental abuses in these documents, the legislatures sought guarantees for personal rights in the new state constitutions. The most influential document of this period was the Virginia Declaration of Rights (June 12, 1776), drafted by George Mason. Six other states followed Virginia's example in drafting a bill of rights separate from their new constitutions: Pennsylvania, Delaware, Maryland, and North Carolina in 1776, Massachusetts in 1780, and New Hampshire in 1784. New Jersey, Georgia, New York, and South Carolina drafted new constitutions between 1776 and 1778 with guarantees of personal rights embodied in the constitution itself rather than in a separate bill of rights. Only Connecticut and Rhode Island continued to operate under their colonial charters, which contained what they considered adequate provisions for individual rights. The Articles of Confederation (drafted 1777, ratified 1781) contained no individual rights guarantees either in the body of the document or in an appendix.

When the federal Constitution was drafted in 1787, it contained various guarantees in the body of the text but lacked a separate bill. The omission received more public criticism from opponents of ratification than did any other aspect of the Constitution. Among the proponents of ratification, Alexander Hamilton considered a separate bill of rights unnecessary because he said the states already had the power to protect individual rights. He believed an enumeration of rights to be dangerous because any listing might be considered exhaustive. Hamilton argued that social diversity and watchfulness were the ultimate guarantees of personal rights. Although James Madison originally agreed with Hamilton, he eventually came to support the drafting of a separate bill of rights. Madison was persuaded by his friend Thomas Jefferson and perhaps convinced by political necessity as well. Two months after Congress convened in 1789, Madison therefore proposed a federal bill of rights. He became the document's primary author, relying heavily on the Virginia Declaration of Rights and Jefferson's Virginia Statute for Establishing Religious Freedom. On September 25, 1789, Congress gave final approval to an American Bill of Rights containing twelve amendments. All but two were subsequently ratified by the states, Virginia completing the process on December 15, 1791.

The final phase in the development of the Bill of Rights came in the

Reconstruction Era following the Civil War. The Thirteenth Amendment added to the content of the Bill of Rights, while the Fourteenth Amendment increased its scope. Until the Thirteenth Amendment, the Bill of Rights was understood to forbid only federal violations of personal rights. The Fourteenth Amendment required the federal government to ensure that individual states guaranteed individuals due process of law and equal protection of the laws in matters concerning life, liberty, or property. Still, it was not until the 1920s that the Supreme Court began to incorporate the specific rights contained in the federal Bill of Rights in decisions directly affecting the states. Eventually the position of Justice Benjamin N. Cardozo in *Palko v. Connecticut* (302 U.S. 319: 1937) prevailed: Although the Fourteenth Amendment does not incorporate the whole federal Bill of Rights, it does include all those federally guaranteed rights implicit in the concept of "ordered liberty." *See also* BLACKSTONE'S *COMMENTARIES*, p. 11; COMMON LAW, p. 13.

Significance   If the ultimate purpose of constitutionalism is the protection of individual rights against the encroachments of government, the full fruit of any constitution is the enforcement of its bill of rights. Separation of powers and the specified rights of states within a federal system are the constitutional root, trunk, and branches meant to ensure the rights of persons. The key structural elements of a bill of rights are an enumeration of personal rights, a statement of the government's obligation to protect them, and effective provisions for their enforcement. Whether and how federal governments guarantee these elements determines the authenticity of their bills of rights. Great Britain, for example, has no single-document bill of rights, just as Great Britain has no written constitution. It does have a long tradition of protecting the rights of individual citizens, however, a tradition contained in centuries of common and statutory law such as the Bill of Rights Act of 1689. On the other hand, the Soviet Union's single-document constitution of 1936 has a highly developed bill of rights. But given the Communist party's unlimited power, the document does not have the enforcement provisions that would qualify it as an authentic bill of rights. For different reasons the United Nations Universal Declaration of Human Rights of 1948 also lacks the enforcement provisions of a genuine bill of rights. How well does the American Bill of Rights meet the criteria of legitimacy? Its enumeration of rights was the most complete of its era, adding rights of speech, press, peaceful protest, and religion then unheard of in England. Yet the original Bill of Rights failed to abolish slavery despite the deep qualms of Jefferson and Washington. Today some would insist that the enumeration of the rights of American citizens should include the right to education, the right to be employed, and the Equal Rights Amendment. Implicit in such argumentation is the question of the grounds for including new rights in a bill of rights. Is the right to education a natural right? Are there utilitarian reasons for enumerating new rights such as employment? Does popular opinion suffice to establish the Equal Rights Amendment? Perhaps more crucial is the issue of effective provisions for enforcement. The Supreme Court has established itself as the ultimate guarantor of individual rights in the United States. While the institution of judicial review has generally worked well as a vehicle for the Court to monitor compliance with the Bill of Rights, there are glaring examples of the Court's willingness to sacrifice individual rights to the prevailing national *Zeitgeist* or to the will of the other two branches of government. In *Dred Scott v. Sandford* (19 How. 393: 1857), for example, the Court actually quoted the Fifth Amendment to oppose the abolition of slavery. In World War I the Court upheld federal convictions of persons who merely criticized the draft. In *Korematsu v. United States* (323 U.S. 214: 1944), the Court justified the federal government's indiscriminate internment of Japanese Americans during World War II. When the Supreme Court overturned state abortion laws in *Roe v. Wade* (410 U.S. 113: 1973), critics accused it of simply yielding to the social prejudices of the times. Such alleged or real weaknesses in the enforcement of the Bill of Rights have led political scientist Robert A. Dahl to repeat Alexander Hamilton's thesis that extraconstitutional mechanisms, especially a widespread grass-roots sensitivity to justice, are far more important guarantees of human rights than are constitutional norms. Perhaps Dahl and Hamilton are correct. If they are not, however, and if a societal passion for justice is in fact a fragile if not a utopian idea, the Bill of Rights enforced through judicial review remains an irreplaceable protection for individual freedom in the United States.

Blackstone's *Commentaries* An eighteenth-century compilation of English common law. Blackstone's *Commentaries on the Laws of England* was the most influential body of common law in the early modern era. Sir William Blackstone was born in 1723. He served one term as an elected member of Parliament, then was appointed Vinerian Professor of Law at Oxford University in 1758. His appointment was the first time anyone had been given an academic chair to teach English law exclusively, rather than English law as related to Roman law. Blackstone wrote the *Commentaries* between 1765 and 1769. In 1770 he became a judge in the Court of Common Pleas of England, and he died ten years later. Blackstone's *Commentaries* consist of four volumes totaling 2,000 pages. The volumes are entitled (1) *Of the Rights of Persons;* (2) *Of*

the Rights of Things; (3) *Of Private Wrongs;* and (4) *Of Public Wrongs.*
Blackstone believed that English common law could be discovered
through the study of English history and that knowledge of the law
should be made available to people at all levels of society, especially to
members of Parliament. He said, for example, "How unbecoming must
it appear for a member of the legislature to vote for a new law while
being utterly ignorant of the old." Blackstone presented the law as the
perfection of reason. His emphasis on logic and principle popularized
his work, and he became something of an involuntary law reformer.
Blackstone wrote that man's actions are subject to the laws of nature
and that no human law could be considered valid if it contradicted the
laws of nature. He said that common law is in fact a secondary law of
nature with principles that are fixed and unchangeable. Blackstone
opined about such specific areas as a prisoner's right to counsel when
his life is at stake. He said that no one should be forced to incriminate
himself, or be tried twice for the same crime. He presented these kinds
of concepts as maxims, or universal rules of nature. They were said to
be simultaneously part of the law of nature and examples of the
common law of England. No one successfully challenged Blackstone's
legal theory or his reading of English history. *See also* BILL OF RIGHTS,
p. 7; COMMON LAW, p. 13; MAGNA CARTA, p. 45.

Significance   Blackstone's *Commentaries* were decisive in the development of constitutional government both because they were the best
law books of their time and because they appeared when the struggle
between the American colonies and the British Crown was at its zenith.
The legal theory of Blackstone largely shaped the political attitudes of
the American colonists. They had long cherished elements of the
common law of England, especially its forms of civil and criminal
procedure. When the *Commentaries* were published, American lawyers
made them popular and undertook to write American law in a manner
similar to the language of the *Commentaries.* The idea that law is rule-
permanent, uniform, and universal is a permanent legacy from
Blackstone, as is the concept that law is an entity separate from society,
which it in fact controls. Blackstone's maxims were affirmed by the
inclusion of most of them in the American Bill of Rights. The First
Amendment, for example, is an extension of Blackstone's discussion in
Book IV, Chapter 11, where he adds to his discussion of freedom of the
press. "If one publishes what is improper, mischievous, or illegal, he
must take the consequences of his own temerity." The Fifth Amendment's holding that no person can be held to answer for a capital crime
except by the indictment of a grand jury is taken almost verbatim from
the *Commentaries.* The restriction against the taking of private property
for public use without just compensation is an institutionalization of

Blackstone's maxim that the possession of property is an inherent right of every man. Yet the American legal system also has unique characteristics not found in the *Commentaries*. In *Marbury v. Madison* (1 Cranch 137: 1803), for example, the Supreme Court broke with the English common law tradition, which maintained that judges or justices must remain interpreters of the law and never become makers of new law. The Court's claim of the right to declare acts of Congress unconstitutional was a radical departure from the basic conservatism of Blackstone. The *Commentaries* made their contribution to American constitutionalism primarily as textbooks for late eighteenth-century legal philosophy and as a comprehensive reference source for the writers of American state constitutions, the federal Constitution of 1787, and especially the Bill of Rights of 1789.

Common Law   The tradition that a single body of law represents valid judicial interpretations of customary rules of action. Common law is a peculiarly English institution because it preserves and promulgates principles of law based on judicial decisions rather than on rules resulting from legislative enactments. France and Germany, in contrast, pursue a jurisprudential system founded on codified statutory law in the Roman tradition. Common law is judge-made law as opposed to statutory law. Soon after the Norman Conquest, in an attempt to establish and administer the King's Justice, Henry III authorized a circuit commission that charged circuit judges from the King's Bench with the responsibility of selecting the best of English county laws and transforming them into the common law of the kingdom. The process by which the justice of the king was defined, and his subjects controlled, created the common law. It was an astute and prudent sovereign who recognized the practical usefulness of adopting the best features of the county administration of justice, and who also was willing to chance that what was effective at the county level would also be effective throughout the realm. The circuit judges also sat on the royal courts at Westminster, where discussions shaped the rendering of local decisions and created the corpus of English common law. One law was made applicable to all disputes before the bar, set apart from ecclesiastical law and equity pleadings. Common law was therefore very much a statement of royal law as it was interpreted through the central royal courts. Those who found themselves pleading before a court on a common law issue were most often members of the aristocracy. Only infrequently were the lower classes affected by the principles of early English common law, for nonlandowners were governed by manor law.

The tradition of common law evolved in large part because the English legal profession strongly resisted the establishment of a statutory system. Students of law in England were trained more in the pragmatic applications of the law than they were in documentary systems of law enforcement. The legal profession was not so much interested in anticipating the adjudication of infractions of the law, such as those anticipated by statutory proscriptions, as it was in maintaining the precedent-setting value of actual controversies settled. This reliance on the value of precedent is perhaps the greatest legacy of the English common law system. Judges were placed in the position of either following the established precedent or distinguishing it, and in either case, they became the arbiters of the existing law. No decision was made unless an actual dispute existed. Much that was fundamental to common law was recorded only in the opinions rendered by judges.

From 1765 to 1769, Sir William Blackstone undertook the task of reducing to writing what he considered to be the essence of the common law. He said that common law was "nothing else but custom, arising from the universal agreement of the whole community," and that common law judges were "the depositories of the law—the living oracles who must decide all cases of doubt, and who are bound by an oath to decide according to the [precedent] law of the land." Blackstone's four-volume *Commentaries on the Laws of England* were not without their flaws and misrepresentations, however. Utilitarian philosopher Jeremy Bentham condemned them as worthless because they were not succinctly reasoned expositions of the law and could not, therefore, be scientifically accurate. Nonetheless, the *Commentaries* represented the first concerted attempt to commit to writing the evolving patterns of the common law. They served as a textbook and as a legal tool for students of law both in England and in the American colonies. The *Commentaries* became an indispensable guide in articulating the common law origins of both English and American jurisprudence. Another chronicler and advocate of the common law was Sir Edward Coke, the Chief Justice of the Royal Court. He reacted to Bentham's criticism of Blackstone by arguing that the common law was identical to natural law and was inherently the very embodiment of reason. *See also* BLACKSTONE'S *COMMENTARIES*, p. 11; ENGLISH CONSTITUTION, p. 26; SOCIAL CONTRACT, p. 59.

Significance   Common law in England represents the oldest corpus of jurisprudence administered by a central court and made applicable to an entire country. As originally conceived, it assigned powers to the king and clearly delineated the rights and privileges accruing to the king's subjects. Coke maintained that by the seventeenth century the common law also limited royal prerogatives. Chief Justice Coke said from the bench that "the king cannot create any offense by his prohibition or proclamation which was not an offense before." It is ironical that the impetus for the common law should have come from the king who would eventually be called to task for abuses of it. English common law found its way into the Constitution and the Bill of Rights of the United States. The framers were determined to maintain Blackstone's and Coke's legal theory in the new republic. It was in fact a reaction to English departures from the position of Blackstone and Coke that precipitated the events of the American Revolution. The federal Constitution is replete with barely disguised language from Blackstone, including that concerning indictment by a grand jury in the Fifth Amendment, trial by jury in the accused's vicinage in the Sixth Amendment, the prohibition against cruel and unusual punishment in the Eighth Amendment, the right to writs of *habeas corpus,* and the principle of stare decisis. Indeed, one of the fundamental doctrines of constitutionalism in the United States is its adherence to the tradition of stare decisis. Despite the fact that the United States is governed in the twentieth century by more and more statutory law, common law continues to be highly influential in American legal circles. The judiciary is concerned to remember its legacy. In *Bishop v. United States* (334 F. Supp. 415: 1971), a U.S. District Court consciously deviated from a holding on strict statutory construction to credit once again the ultimate source of much of its decision making.

> The common law is generally described as those principles, usage, and rules of action applicable to the government and security of persons and property which do not rest for their authority upon any express and positive declaration of the will of the legislature.

Thus custom continues to be as important as statute in the definition of American legal standards.

Constitutionalism, Historical Development of The growth of constitutional theory and practice through human history. The historical development of constitutionalism begins in a technical sense when the English term *constitution* was first used in its current political science context in the late seventeenth century. *Constitutionalism* was introduced in the mid-eighteenth century. The concept itself antedates use of either term, however. Political scientist Carl Friedrich notes six senses of the idea of constitutionalism. The first five of them are (1) philosophical, including Aristotle's definition of *politeia*; (2) structural, including the general organization of any actual government; (3) legal, including the basic law of a political entity; (4) documentary, including written constitutions; and (5) procedural, requiring more intricate amendment procedures for constitutions than for ordinary statutes. This entry traces the history of constitutionalism in its sixth sense, which Friedrich calls its modern and normative sense, including the theory and practice of effective, systematic, and institutionalized restraints on political and governmental power in order to prevent the violation of individual rights. Most constitutional scholars divide the history of constitutionalism into an ancient, a medieval, a modern, and a contemporary period.

The roots of modern constitutionalism, both its theory and practice, stretch back to Greece, Rome, and the Judeo-Christian religions. Plato advanced the theory of constitutionalism by stressing that government must be guided by law (*nomos*). But he also insisted that the law-making power be concentrated in wise men. Aristotle distinguished between a nation's basic governmental structure, its laws, and its changeable policies (*politeia*). He helped to clarify the fundamental and semipermanent nature of constitutions. Aristotle's description of the "mixed constitution" foreshadowed modern constitutionalism's separation of powers and its doctrine of the balance of power. Whatever their theories, however, Plato and Aristotle's Athens was not a constitutional democracy, if only because it denied women, foreigners, and slaves the rights of citizenship. The Roman stoics advanced constitutional theory by emphasizing the equality of all human beings, despite the widespread practice of slavery in Rome, and by formulating a natural law theory that would be further developed in the medieval period. The Roman jurists—notably the authors of the *Institutes*, the *Digests*, and the *Code of Justinian*—moved the practice of constitutionalism forward by giving "government by law" a written and codified foundation. Together with Roman natural law theory, the Judeo-Christian belief in the inviolable dignity of the individual constituted the most important inspiration for modern constitutionalism. Less important roots are found in certain ancient tribal practices of the early Germans, such as the division of power between dual kings, and in the egalitarian temperament and social practices of the first residents of the British Isles.

Building on an ancient heritage, thinkers in the medieval period added important new dimensions to the developing theory of constitutional government. Canon lawyers, especially Gratian in his *Decrees*, underscored the importance of written and codified laws. Thomas Aquinas worked out a fully developed natural law theory, on the basis of which he subordinated all government to good law. The proponents of conciliarism, notably William of Ocham, Nicholas of Cusa, and Marsilius of Padua, were unsuccessful in replacing papal absolutism with a more participative form of church government, but they did develop an influential body of governmental theory based on the consent of the governed. Despite its authoritarian internal governmental practices, the church exercised considerable restraint on would-be absolute rulers in the secular realm. The church maintained a constitutionalism "from the outside" that broke down only with the Reformation. Medieval Europeans sponsored movements demanding charters of royal privileges. The best known of these charters, Magna Carta (1215), gave a new impulse to the development of common law in England. Henry de Bratton (d. 1268), also known as Bracton, completed a *Treatise on the Laws of England* that served as the most complete codification of English law until Blackstone's *Commentaries*. Another English author, John Fortescue (d. ca. 1479), developed a theory of legal restraints upon government based on the work of Thomas Aquinas.

A number of authors helped provide the theoretical transition from the medieval to the modern period. Richard Hooker (1553–1600) kept Aquinas's natural law theory alive and further developed the ideas of consent of the governed and social contract. The latter two traditions were elaborated fully by Johannes Althusius (1557–1638) and Hugo Grotius (1583–1645). The classical development of social contract theory was then achieved by Thomas Hobbes (1588–1679), John Locke (1632–1704), and Jean-Jacques Rousseau (1712–1778), Locke and the Baron de Montesquieu (1689–1755) also helped to define the doctrine of separation of powers. American writers such as Thomas Jefferson (1743–1826), Alexander Hamilton (1755–1804), and James Madison (1751–1836) wrote penetrating analyses of the American experiment in putting constitutionalism into practice. The modern development of constitutionalism came about as much through events as by the elaboration of ideas. The fragmentation of the church's secular influence through the Reformation removed the foremost obstacle to the royal absolutism that had begun in the fifteenth and sixteenth centuries. Yet the increasingly powerful commercial class, having outgrown its need for government-supported mercantilism, plotted to reduce the power of its former royal patrons. The first phase of constitutionalism in the modern period was England's development of a constitutional monarchy. It began with Sir Edward Coke's successful defense of common law as superior to royal prerogative and subject only to Parliament. Gradually as the supremacy of Parliament was established Parliament itself became absolutist, until the role of the opposition and of regular popular elections was secured. Through all of these events, England never had a unitary constitutional document, except for Cromwell's short-lived *Instrument of Government* (1653). After England's constitutional monarchy, the next phase in the development of modern constitutionalism was the American Revolution and constitutional movement (1776–1789), which founded the first constitutional republic since Athens. The American Revolution began a widespread push to develop written constitutions throughout the civilized world. The American experiment was followed by the French Revolution (1789) and France's own constitutional experiments. The constitutional movement then spread to the other countries of Continental Europe. The final phase of modern constitutionalism was its democratization, beginning in the United States with Andrew Jackson and Abraham Lincoln and in Great Britain with the Reform Act of 1832.

The contemporary phase of constitutionalism includes five trends, all of which throw the future of constitutionalism into question. The first trend is the "negative revolutions" in France, Italy, and West Germany, where weakened forms of constitutionalism were adopted in reaction against a recent fascist past (Petain-Laval, Mussolini, and Hitler). All of the negative revolutions have failed to guarantee constitutional restraints on government power. The second trend is that toward supranational constitutionalism, as seen in the United Nations and especially in the European Common Market. Many constitutionalists see this as a positive and necessary development. They say that intranational constitutionalism is not secure without an international counterpart. The third trend is the generally unsuccessful attempt to constitutionalize emerging nations. Although virtually every new nation hastens to draft a constitution, the written document frequently lacks social institutionalization and is quickly set aside in times of crisis. The fourth trend is the appearance of constitutions in communist countries, which proclaim themselves to be both democratic and constitutional. Most constitutional lawyers say they are neither, while communist writers in turn consider many aspects of Western constitutionalism, such as the independent judiciary and the separation of powers, to be aberrations that pander to bourgeois individualism. The fifth trend is toward anarchy. Although anarchy is frequently overlooked as an alternative outcome to totalitarianism and constitutionalism, it continues to be a possible choice, if only by default. Anarchy has increased in the modern world, not only in the instability of emerging nations, but also in sociopolitical breakdowns in such developed nations as the United States, France, West Germany, and Italy during the 1960s and 1970s. *See also* CONSTITUTION OF THE UNITED STATES OF AMERICA, p. 19; ENGLISH CONSTITUTION, p. 26; CARL FRIEDRICH, p. 33; REPUBLICANISM, p. 55.

Significance   The historical development of constitutionalism gives the reader an important sense of the contingency of the social institutions he or she may consider eternal and unchanging. Constitutionalism is neither a historical nor a logical necessity. Were it not for a very contingent historical sequence of ideas and events, it would not have arisen at all. Constitutionalism also embodies a practical and theoretically troublesome logical paradox—self-limiting absolute power—that its rival, unrestrained absolutism, neatly avoids. Constitutionalism's future direction is not at all clear. There are unresolved questions. Will greater socialization and centralization usher in new phases of constitutionalism, as republicanism and democratization did in the past? Will international federalism and constitutionalism increase? What will be the effects of international federalism on intranational constitutionalism? It appears that constitutionalism's future is not guaranteed. In emerging countries it is frequently overwhelmed by totalitarian regimes. Traditional constitutional governments are frequently tempted to adopt unconstitutional measures to protect their constitutionalism. The first step in guaranteeing the future existence of constitutionalism is the development of consensus on whether and how it should exist. The consensus necessarily involves a reaffirmation of the inviolability of the individual person's rights and the basis for that inviolability, whether Judeo-Christian religion, natural law, or some alternative ground of argument. It may also involve a realization that respect for the person does not necessarily imply unchecked individualism and that there may be important truths in the Marxist critique of Western institutions. Constitutionalism's continuing task is to achieve the proper balance between the rights of the community and the rights of the individual.

Constitution of the United States of America   The federal Constitution of the United States was completed by the Constitutional Convention on September 17, 1787. It was ratified by the requisite ninth state, New Hampshire, on June 21, 1788, and put into effect on March 4, 1789. The document consists of a preamble of purpose, a body of articles, and a series of amendments. The body of articles regulates the following subjects: (I) the legislative branch; (II) the executive branch; (III) the judicial branch; (IV) the relation of the states to each other and to the central government, the admission of new states, and the regulation of territories; (V) the methods of amending the constitution; (VI) provisions for the national debt, the oath required of all state and federal officials to support the federal Constitution, laws, and treaties as "the supreme law of the land," and the prohibition of religious tests for officeholders; and (VII) provisions for ratification of the Constitution. Through 1983, 26 amendments, technically called "articles," had been ratified. Further, there is a "living Constitution" that includes developments and interpretations not included in the document itself.

The federal Constitution of 1787–1789 is really the second constitution of the United States. The first was the Articles of Confederation, drafted in 1777 and ratified in 1781. Because the Articles deprived the central government of any real power over the individual states, a host of problems arose concerning domestic and foreign commerce, the national debt, and internal and external security. Consensus developed that the central government had to have more power. After the successful Mount Vernon Convention to resolve commercial and boundary disputes between Virginia and Maryland in 1785, representatives from five states met at Annapolis in 1786 to discuss interstate trade conflicts. The Annapolis delegates soon abandoned their original purpose and instead called for a convention of all the states in Philadelphia to work out the measures "necessary to cement the Union of the United States." The Continental Congress gave its approval to the proposed meeting on the condition that the Philadelphia convention limit itself to amending the Articles of Confederation.

The Philadelphia convention met from May 25 to September 17, 1787. By the time of its adjournment, it bore the descriptive title Constitutional Convention, because it proposed not amendments to the Articles of Confederation but rather the constitution for a very different government. A total of 73 delegates were elected by the states to attend the Philadelphia convention, of whom 55 actually did attend, and 39 signed the finished document. Many of the delegates were widely read in political theory and had played leading roles in the drafting of their state constitutions. Since the convention's official secretary, William Jackson, kept such poor records, the best guides to the proceedings are the notes of Robert Yates and James Madison. George Washington was elected unanimously to the chair, but the dominant figure at the convention was Madison, later called the "Father of the Constitution." Although there was a wide range of opinion among the delegates, the combination of strong and moderate Nationalists far outnumbered the proponents of state sovereignty. The strong Nationalists included Washington, Madison, Benjamin Franklin, Alexander Hamilton, Rufus King, Gouverneur Morris, Edmund Randolph, John Rutledge, and James Wilson. The moderate Nationalists included Oliver Ellsworth, Elbridge Gerry, George Mason, and Roger Sherman. Among the strong state sovereignty delegates were Gunning Bedford, John Lansing, William Peterson, and Robert Yates. Near the outset of the convention, Governor Edmund Randolph of Virginia presented the Virginia Plan, which proposed a strongly centralized parliamentary form of government. On June 15, William Patterson countered with the New Jersey Plan, which called for a somewhat stronger central government but stayed within the framework of the Articles of Confederation. The rest of the convention was devoted to working out compromises between these positions and conflicts related to them.

The first was the Connecticut Compromise, which attempted to balance the interests of small and large states. While representation in the House of Representatives would be set in proportion to population, thus favoring the larger states, representation in the Senate was set at two for each state, thus favoring the smaller states. Another successful compromise guaranteed to the commercial North the federal protection of all trade, while to the agrarian South it guaranteed freedom from export taxes and the right to continue the slave trade until at least the year 1808. The nature and the method of election of the executive presented some of the convention's thorniest problems. The insistence of Madison, James Wilson, and Gouverneur Morris on a clear separation of powers defeated the proposal for a parliamentary executive and won approval for a presidential office. In a compromise between direct popular election, considered dangerously populist, and election by state legislatures, considered too great a concession to state sovereignty, the convention approved the election of the president by an electoral college. The Supremacy Clause of Article VI was introduced by the states' rights delegates as preferable to the proposed congressional veto power over state legislation. The states' rights group also successfully insisted on the powers of Congress being enumerated rather than broad and unspecified. To win this concession, however, they had to agree on the Necessary and Proper Clause (Article I, Section 8), which did in fact give Congress wide discretionary powers. The Constitution approved by the convention was a tremendous victory for those favoring a strong central government. The ensuing ratification debate, best preserved in the opposing viewpoints of *The Federalist* and Richard Henry Lee's *Letters of the Federal Farmer*, was long and furious. North Carolina and Rhode Island were the last two states to ratify, North Carolina in November of 1789, and Rhode Island in May of 1790.

The Constitution was never an inert document. Immediately it began to grow through amendments, interpretations, and other developments. Constitutional lawyer Paul Murphy has grouped the amendments into four historical phases: (1) early amendments (Amendments 1–12); (2) Reconstruction Era amendments (Amendments 13–15); (3) progressive era amendments (Amendments 16–19 and Amendment 21); and (4) later procedural amendments (Amendment 20 and Amendments 22–25). The Twenty-sixth Amendment and the attempts to pass an Equal Rights Amendment and a Right to Life Amendment reflect a new social reform phase of American constitutional history. The Constitution has also grown through interpretation. This includes presidential, congressional, and judicial interpretations, as well as the theories of influential statesmen. One example is President Madison's broad interpretation of the pocket veto, an interpretation that has persisted despite strong congressional opposition. Another example is the case of *Marbury v. Madison* (1 Cranch 137: 1803), in which the Supreme Court declared itself the final interpreter of constitutional matters, a claim that was generally accepted by the 1860s. The interpretations of the Supreme Court have rarely reflected a neutral reading of the Constitution, especially regarding such distinctions as strict versus broad construction of it. The Court has passed through various phases of interpretation: John Marshall's defense of federal supremacy and of inviolate property rights; Roger B. Taney's emphasis on community rights as a limitation on property rights; Salmon P. Chase's defense of local sovereignty against federal legislation; the return to Marshall's interpretation by Stephen J. Field, Joseph P. Bradley, and Melville W. Fuller; permission for broad federal regulation granted by the Court in the progressive era; and the property-oriented opposition to New Deal legislation that lasted until 1937, when the Court began to concentrate on guarantees of personal rights. The final way the Constitution has grown is vague to describe but fundamental in importance. It includes sociopolitical developments such as the two-party system and the aggrandized power of the presidential office. It embraces the changing economic and moral climate of the country as these factors influence the interpretation and enforcement of the documentary Constitution. As it allows for continuing citizen input, the Constitution becomes more and more a living document. *See also* ARTICLES OF CONFEDERATION, p. 5; ENGLISH CONSTITUTION, p. 26; SEPARATION OF POWERS, p. 56; STATE CONSTITUTIONS, p. 61; VIRGINIA PLAN, p. 64.

Significance   The federal Constitution of the United States is the oldest documentary constitution in force in the modern world. Aside from its other merits, the Constitution's longevity has won widespread respect for it and frequent imitation of it on the part of other nations. It is held in near religious reverence by Americans. Still, the Constitution has faced severe criticisms, four of which are summarized here. The first, dating from the time of the Constitutional Convention, but also implicit in the works of modern historians, is that the convention itself was unconstitutional for two reasons. The convention exceeded the mandate given to it by the Continental Congress as well as the mandates the state legislatures had given their delegates, and it violated the amendment procedures defined in the Articles of Confederation. Constitutional lawyer Benjamin F. Wright has conceded the technical extralegality of the convention and its Constitution. He argues, however, that it was a necessary solution to the constitutional impasse created by the requirement of the Articles that the states be unanimous on any major question. Wright also maintains that the Constitution was far more democratic than either the Declaration of Independence or the Articles of Confederation. The Declaration had not been submitted to either the states or the people for approval. The Articles were drafted by the Continental Congress and ratified by the state legislatures, but none of the principals had been elected by the people for that purpose. The Constitution, by contrast, was drafted by delegates elected by their legislatures specifically for that purpose, was widely reported upon, was subjected to a long public debate, and was ratified by state conventions selected by the people specifically for that purpose. The second criticism of the Constitution concerns the motives of the drafters. Historian Merrill Jensen argues that the new Constitution aborted the internal socioeconomic revolution that was the real inspiration of the external revolution against Great Britain. The new government's strong centralism protected the interests of the big landowners and merchants against the small landowners, tradesmen, and businessmen. Historian Charles A. Beard advanced a similar position in his seminal *An Economic Interpretation of the Constitution of the United States* (1913). The motivation of the framers remains a contested issue. The third criticism concerns the written document's omissions and ambiguities. Its fuzziness about the role of the Supreme Court in constitutional interpretation and about the implied powers of Congress caused decades of debate. The Constitution's initial omission of a bill of rights was soon corrected, but the new Bill of Rights refused to deal with the problem of slavery. The conflicts between the rights of the central government and state governments came to be fought not just in the halls of government but finally with great bloodshed on the battlefields of the Civil War. The final criticism concerns the interpretations and developments that have guided the growth of the living Constitution. The frontier and its disappearance, industrialization, immigration, the Great Depression, America's emergence as a major world power after two world wars, the civil-rights movement of the 1960s, and the tragedy of Vietnam are just some of the forces that have shaped the American character and thus the living Constitution. Some conservatives argue that the central government has become dangerously strong and expensive, that individual rights and enterprise are being stifled, and that the nation is degenerating into a welfare collectivity. Some liberals argue that the Constitution's provisions for procedural justice are often a cloak for the denial of substantive justice for the powerless and that the government is a pawn if not an accomplice of the domestic and foreign imperialism of American business. If there is substance to any of these criticisms, the Constitution is still an unfinished work. Each generation of Americans is required to provide new framers of the Constitution.

Continental Congress The assembly serving as the collective voice and advisory forum for the thirteen colonies from 1774 until

1781, and then as the central government of the thirteen states from 1781 until 1789. The Continental Congress, whose official name was simply "Congress," is usually divided into four historical periods: (1) the First Continental Congress, September 5 to October 26, 1774; (2) the Second Continental Congress, May 10, 1775, to December 12, 1776; (3) the sessions from late December 1776 until the end of February 1781; and (4) the sessions under the Articles of Confederation, also called the Congress of the Confederation, from March 1, 1781, to March 4, 1789. On the latter date the Continental Congress was replaced by the three branches of the new federal government. The First Continental Congress met in Philadelphia's Carpenter's Hall at the urging of groups from Massachusetts, Virginia, New York City, Philadelphia, and Providence. Although the Congress had no legal status, its conveners were convinced that the colonies had to present a united front against the "Intolerable," or "Coercive," Acts passed by the British Parliament in 1774. Those acts, especially the Boston Port Act and the Massachusetts Government Act, threatened the commercial interests and the self-rule of the Massachusetts Bay Colony and, by implication, of all the colonies. Fifty-six representatives from 12 colonies attended the First Continental Congress, Georgia alone refusing to participate. The main achievements of the first Congress were the Suffolk Resolves opposing the Intolerable Acts, the Declaration of Rights, and the establishment of the Continental Association. The Continental Association agreed on the nonimportation and nonconsumption of British goods and on the nonexportation of colonial goods to Great Britain. The Second Continental Congress met at the Statehouse in Philadelphia, later called Independence Hall. Planned by the first Congress in view of Great Britain's likely refusal to redress American grievances, the second Congress found its real urgency in the battles of Lexington and Concord, which had occurred just three weeks earlier. Twelve colonies were represented from the beginning, and Georgia finally sent representatives in the fall of 1775. Like its predecessor, the second Congress had no legal status. But it soon became the provisional government when hopes died for reconciliation with Great Britain. On June 7, 1776, Richard Henry Lee of Virginia presented a revolutionary dual motion; that the united colonies were and had the right to be independent states, and that Congress should draft articles of confederation for the new political entity. Events moved fast after that. On June 12, a drafting committee was established to write the Articles of Confederation. On June 15, George Washington was appointed Commander-in-Chief of the Army, although the Continental Army itself was not created until October 13. On July 2, Congress passed a resolution of independence. The resolution was formally announced to the colonies and the world two days later. From the end of its second session until early 1781, Congress met several times, focusing on the war and its aftermath. The Second Continental Congress also devoted a good deal of time to debating the Articles of Confederation. On November 15, 1777, the Articles were approved, and Congress referred them to the state legislatures for ratification. With the ratification of the Articles, Congress was reorganized according to the Articles' provisions and became the first central government of the United States. In fact the Articles created a very limited central government, little more than an instrument of state sovereignty. All governmental authority resided in the Congress. When it was not in session, the business of government was handled by a Committee of the States and the four congressional committees in charge of finance, the army, the navy, and foreign affairs. One of the main achievements of the Congress of the Confederation, the fourth phase of the Continental Congress, was the Northwest Ordinance (1787). This ordinance regulated the establishment of governments in the lands north of the Ohio River and west of the Alleghenies and made provisions for the eventual statehood of those lands. The severe limitations on central power under the Articles hindered government from dealing with some of the other major issues of the day, such as the United States' mounting debt and poor foreign credit, growing disunity among the states, Shays' Rebellion (1786–1787), and commercial pressures from Britain, France, and Spain. A number of attempted amendments to the Articles that would have strengthened the central government were blocked by small and varying groups of states. Finally, a commercial convention in Annapolis (1786) issued a call for a major convention in Philadelphia in 1787 "to consider the exigencies of the Union." Congress cautiously endorsed the convention, with the proviso that it have the "sole and express purpose of revising the Articles of Confederation." Within four months, however, Philadelphia's Constitutional Convention had approved a federal Constitution that would replace the Continental Congress in 1789 with a new and stronger form of central government. *See also* ARTICLES OF CONFEDERATION, p. 5; NATURAL LAW AND NATURAL RIGHTS, p. 50; REPUBLICANISM, p. 55; SEPARATION OF POWERS, p. 56.

Significance The Continental Congress was an attempt to unify the American colonies, but it was not the first attempt. As early as 1696 William Penn had formulated a plan for colonial unification. From 1643 through 1684, the Puritans of Connecticut, Massachusetts, New Haven, and Plymouth joined together in the United Colonies of New England, also called the New England Confederation, for their mutual defense and for the spread of their common religion. From 1686 through 1689, Great Britain grouped Massachusetts, Plymouth,

Rhode Island, Connecticut, New Hampshire, Cornwall County in north Maine, and King's Province into the Dominion of New England, an administrative grouping the British hoped to replicate in the other colonies. In 1754, Benjamin Franklin proposed the Albany Plan, with "one general government" for all the colonies as its purpose. Great Britain rejected the plan because it undercut royal authority, and the colonies rejected it because it weakened each colony's independence. In 1765, representatives from nine colonies met in New York City for the Stamp Act Congress, whose collective protest helped force Great Britain's repeal of the Stamp Act. In the First Continental Congress, loyalist Joseph Galloway proposed a "General Council" that would have established a colonial branch of the British Parliament. Despite these precedents, the Continental Congress was unique because it included all the colonies and because its authority was totally indigenous. The Continental Congress provided the necessary transition from a loose grouping of British colonies to the United States of America.

English Constitution   The foremost example of a "living" constitution, drawing its authority not from a written document but from the promulgation of statutes, the evolving interpretations of common law, and faith in custom and convention. The English constitution represents an unbroken legal tradition reaching across 14 centuries. It is highly adaptive to political changes and conditions, and it provides a strong and effective system of governance because it depends on the application of logic by those charged with the constitution's interpretation. Stability depends on the commonsense interpretation of law by the monarch, Parliament, and the judiciary. The living constitution also relies heavily on the British people, assuming, for example, that in the event of a crisis that could threaten civil liberties, public outrage in opposition to the threat would preserve the common law. The English constitution recognizes at least three different sources of its authority: (1) statutes; (2) the common law; and (3) conventions.

Among the historic statutes and charters it considers important is Magna Carta. The Great Charter was the consequence of an attempt by English barons at Runnymede to articulate a constitutional basis for ensuring a balanced relationship between the sovereign and his subjects. Magna Carta is not unlike the American Declaration of Independence in that it serves as a focal point for the living tradition of a government. Several statutes spanning many centuries are also considered fundamental to the English constitutional tradition. The Statute of York of 1322 established the basis for the House of Commons. The Petition of Right of 1628 was passed to denounce the abuses of royal prerogatives by Charles I and to reassert intrinsic common law liberties. In fact many of the statutes that found their way into the tradition of the English constitution were designed to limit abuses of royal power, but at the same time to maintain recognition of the propriety of the monarchy. Another part of the constitutional tradition is the consequence of struggles for power among the Crown, Parliament, and the arbiters of the common law. A typical statute in this regard is one resulting from the Tudor reign of absolutism and the Revolution of 1688–1689: the Bill of Rights of 1689. This act assured the legislative authority of Parliament, forbade the Crown from imposing any tax or duty without the consent of Parliament, mandated the regular convening of Parliament, and incorporated and effected specific common law civil liberties. The Act of Settlement of 1701, as modified by the Abdication Act of 1936, altered the order of royal succession and mandated that the monarch be a member of the Church of England. The Act of Settlement also incorporated Protestant Scotland into Great Britain. By the beginning of the eighteenth century, the constitutional dynamic between the monarch and Parliament can be characterized as a kind of harmonic dissonance. This dissonance became the model for the system of checks and balances favored by the authors of the United States Constitution. What it meant in England was that the Crown had the power to dissolve Parliament at any time, while Parliament could bring the Crown's governing processes to a halt by refusing to legislate financial support and/or by disbanding the King's Army. It was understood by both institutions that such a constitutional deadlock would precipitate anarchy. Such a fundamental dislocation of English government was clearly unacceptable to either party, the Crown or Parliament. The Reform Act of 1832 is yet another historic statute in the tradition of the living English constitution. This act significantly altered the balance of power within Parliament. The assumption that the Lords would dominate both houses ended, and the franchise was extended to include greater numbers of British citizens. The Reform Act of 1832 was also significant in that it marked the beginning of parliamentary considerations of party rather than dependence on patronage as an instrument of royal prerogative. Important twentieth-century statutes are the Parliament Acts of 1911 and 1949, which delineate the relationships between the House of Lords and the House of Commons. The statutory basis of the English constitution also recognizes that the monarch must always respond positively to the cabinet because the cabinet represents the inherent power of Parliament. The cabinet in turn must depend on the support of the House of Commons. In such a system there is little room for the kinds of conflict frequently seen between the executive and legislative branches of government in the United States. Parliament is able to exercise supreme legal power in Great Britain. The potential abuses inherent in such power make Parliament constantly aware of the need for self-restraint. A constitutional principle in Great Britain is that no act of Parliament can be declared unconstitutional because only Parliament can repeal its own statutes. While the heritage of the English constitution supports the vesting of all legal authority in Parliament, at the same time it acknowledges that ultimate political authority rests with the people.

The English constitutional tradition also looks to the common law as a source of its authority. Indeed, the most important principles of the constitution are those decisions ordered and reported by the courts applying the principles of the common law. Most of the civil liberties and rights that inure to a British citizen are not to be found in statutes passed by Parliament. They are found rather in the corpus of the common law. Trial by jury and the writ of *habeas corpus* are but two of these constitutional rights that emanate from the heritage of the common law. Common law courts have been vigilant in protecting individual rights against arbitrary government actions. The English constitutional tradition rests on the public consciousness that Parliament will not defy the common law by passing legislation contrary to it.

The living constitution also relies on customs, conventions, and usages considered practical for the efficient operation of government that have no foundation in either statutory or common law. Ministers in the cabinet, for example, are expected to resign immediately after defeat in a general election. The Crown, at least since the reign of Queen Anne, will not refuse its assent to legislation passed in good faith by the House of Commons and the House of Lords. A prime minister will hold his or her office only so long as he or she retains the trust of a majority of the members of the House of Commons. Such customs and conventions form an unquestioned part of the consensus of English constitutionalism. *See also* BLACKSTONE'S *COMMENTARIES*, p. 11; COMMON LAW, p. 13; MAGNA CARTA, p. 45.

Significance   The English constitution is a "living" constitution because the people of Great Britain have never felt compelled to commit their governing agreements and processes to paper. The government of Great Britain is a remarkably stable system that has not undergone any significant upheaval in at least three centuries. It certainly has not experienced in recent times the kind of drama that concluded with the Constitution of the United States in 1789. The English Civil War of 1642–1649 was the last such national trauma in Great Britain. It resulted in the execution of Charles I, and it also produced the only written constitution Great Britain has ever had. An *Instrument of Government* was promulgated by Oliver Cromwell as self-appointed Lord Protector. By 1658, however, the *Instrument of Government* had disappeared. The English constitution is amended in a subtle process that is quite unlike the amendment procedure through which additions to the United States Constitution must pass. In England it is done simply by legislation and by decisions of the courts of common law. The maintenance of the United States Constitution relies on the Supreme Court as its ultimate arbiter, but the survival of the English constitution depends on the infrastructural governing processes of both executive and legislative apparatuses as well as on the political awareness and strength of those governed. To observe the evolution of the English constitution is to appreciate certain fundamental characteristics of English history. To understand fully the unwillingness of the English people to adopt a document into which they incorporate their constitutional precepts, one must appreciate the English penchant for tradition and the tradition's reliance on acts of Parliament to correct perceived inequities in the distribution of political power. The English people have reposited a great deal of faith in their governors, knowing their governors are prisoners of the common law and imperial custom.

Federalism   The theory and practice of joining several political entities into a larger political unity while preserving the basic political integrity of each entity. Federations and federal principles are found in many different kinds of organizations, such as labor unions (e.g., the American Federation of Labor–Congress of Industrial Organizations [AFL-CIO]), church bodies (e.g., the World Council of Churches), and supranational political associations (e.g., the European Common Market). There is also an economic version of federalism called fiscal federalism, which claims superiority over both economic centralization and decentralization. But the term *federalism* is usually reserved for federations at the national political level. Strictly speaking, "federal government" refers to an overall system containing both central and state governments. Common usage, however, equates "federal government" with "central government." Political scientists generally have continued to affirm the classical problem of federalism as formulated in the sixteenth and seventeenth centuries: the proper balance between local sovereignty and the requirements of centralization. Some political unions remain weak because none of their members are willing to forego any of their sovereignty. Weak unions are commonly called associations, leagues, or confederations. Other political unions are so dominant that they destroy the real sovereignty of their members. These are empires and unitary states. Even though 17 countries claimed to have federal governments in the early 1980s, political scientists question the authenticity of many. Because of the dominance of the

Russian Soviet Federated Socialist Republic, for example, the Union of Soviet Socialist Republics, the USSR, is more an empire than a federated state.

There were prototypes of federal states in the ancient and medieval world. Ancient Israel and the Delphic League were *amphictyonies*, or federations of tribes or cities united around a common religious center. The Achaean League (280–146 B.C.) was a defensive league of Greek cities. A number of medieval commercial towns joined in leagues for mutual assistance. In 1291, the Swiss cantons formed a defensive confederation that still exists today as the world's oldest uninterrupted federal government. A young federal system was growing in Aragon until Ferdinand and Isabella imposed a unitary system on the united kingdoms of Aragon and Castille. Reformation ecclesiology and the beginnings of national unification encouraged the growth of federal principles in Scotland, England, parts of France and Germany, and especially Switzerland and the Netherlands in the sixteenth century. These developments gave rise to the first theories of federalism by Jean Bodin, Hugh Grotius, Samuel Pufendorf, and Johannes Althusius. Since they viewed state sovereignty as absolute, these early writers on federalism tended to consider only looser forms of political union such as leagues and confederations. Federalist theory took a qualitative leap with the American Revolution. Alexander Hamilton, John Jay, and James Madison gave modern federalism its classical exposition in *The Federalist*. Federalism became the territorial version of the separation of powers and the bulwark of constitutional democracy. In contrast, the French Revolution's emphasis on the centralized rule of the majority left no room for federalism. Since the nineteenth century, federalism, or the use of federal principles, has grown in Europe, Latin America, and Asia. Important theoretical advances were made by J.K. Bluntschli and Otto von Gierke. In the twentieth century federalism has been used to create political unities out of hitherto independent cultural, political, and tribal groups, often in the wake of war or decolonialization. Such was the origin of the USSR, Yugoslavia, India, and many African nations. *See also* THE FEDERALIST, p. 31; REPUBLICANISM, p. 55; SEPARATION OF POWERS, p. 56.

Significance   Federalism is an essential element in constitutional democracy. Like the functional separation of powers (legislative, executive, and judicial), federalism's territorial separation of powers protects individual and local rights by discouraging the concentration of power in any individual or group. A number of issues continue to dominate both the practice and theory of federalism. Among them is the question of sovereignty. How can the constituent members of a federal union simultaneously keep their individual sovereignty intact and yet give a measure of it to a central government? Political scientist Carl Friedrich argues that sovereignty is a red herring because strict sovereignty, i.e., absolute independence, is a fiction in both personal and political life. Friedrich says the issue is not sovereignty versus unity but "autonomy in community." In this view the crucial question is not which powers a smaller unit decides to share or forego in order to join a larger community, but whether the smaller unit fully and freely participates in the decision. Others maintain that the classical attempt to distinguish various classifications of political centralization (e.g., leagues, confederations, and federal governments) incorrectly makes discrete categories out of what is really a continuous process. "Federalizing" is a common trait of all human life. While the balance between centralization and decentralization may shift back and forth, the overall tendency of personal and corporate life is toward more inclusive unions. Finally, not all political thinkers agree that federalism is absolutely essential for constitutional democracy. The "federalists" say it is, but the "pluralists" say it is not. Using the centralized government of Great Britain as an example, the pluralists argue that other forms of separation of powers can secure the foundations of constitutional democracy even in the absence of federalism. In *Constitutional Government and Democracy* (1968) Friedrich is not frightened by the prospect that "the pressures and exigencies of a compact and highly industrialized national economy may eventually force the United States to abandon federalism."

The Federalist   The title of the 1788 edition of a collection of essays by Alexander Hamilton, James Madison, and John Jay aimed at winning support for state ratification of the federal Constitution of 1787. *The Federalist* contained 85 essays in two volumes, all but the last 8 essays having previously appeared as letters in various New York newspapers between October 1787 and April 1788. Bearing the collective penname "Publius," reminiscent of republican Rome, the essays were begun by Hamilton, who soon enlisted the help of Madison and Jay. Hamilton also appealed to William Duer and Gouverneur Morris, but they were unable to oblige. Jay wrote only 5 essays, none of them exceptionally important. Hamilton and Madison wrote the remaining 80, usually alone but sometimes jointly, with Hamilton the author of the majority. Scholars still disagree about the authorship of a small number of the essays. Although he hoped the essays would influence the ratification process in other states as well, Hamilton's immediate concern was to convince his native state of New York. He had been the sole member of the New York delegation to the Constitutional Convention who supported the new document. The other two, Robert Yates and

John Lansing, were avid supporters of New York's strong states' rights governor, George Clinton. Because of Clinton's great popularity, Hamilton knew that only a massive public education effort could win New York for the Constitution. As it turned out, New York's ratifying convention voted overwhelmingly against the Constitution and ratified it only after learning that one more than the necessary nine states had already done so.

There was general agreement among opponents of the proposed Constitution about its main defects. First, it violated the true federalism authorized by the Articles of Confederation and created a unitary and national government that usurped state sovereignty. Second, the federated states were territorially too large to be governed as a whole. Third, the proposed Constitution permitted the central government to maintain a peacetime army and navy, a power that could be easily abused. Fourth, the proposed Constitution did not include a bill of individual rights. Fifth, the separation of powers proposed in the new Constitution was not clear enough and thus was antidemocratic. In response to the first three objections, Hamilton and Madison conceded that the new Constitution did create an unprecedented form of federalism in which the central government had real sovereignty of its own and was not a mere instrument of the confederated states. Madison's Essay 39 contained the most comprehensive discussion of the new federalism, arguing that it in no way destroyed the sovereignty of the individual states. Hamilton and Madison insisted that a strong central government was necessary for the defense of the states against foreign and domestic foes, especially the British and Indians. A strong central government would also be necessary in resolving disputes among the states concerning boundaries, trade, and shares in the national debt. Finally, they held that while a "democracy" (a direct democracy) was not possible for such a large area, a "republic" (a representative democracy) was possible. Such a representative form of government was well suited to mitigate the destructive influence of the factions that typically plague democracies. The first 46 essays state and restate the necessity of a strong central government. *The Federalist* spent little time defending the omission of a bill of rights. Hamilton and Madison, like the other drafters of of the Constitution, assumed that the case for individual rights was secure enough through the Declaration of Independence and the bills of rights of the individual states. Moreover, they were convinced that the bill of rights issue was a cover for the real issue, the reluctance of powerful groups to share or relinquish part of their sovereignty to a central government. The new Constitution was more democratic than most state constitutions, which still contained property requirements for voters and officeholders. Hamilton and Madison argued that the proposed separation of powers was adequate to ensure democracy. Madison explained how the bicameral legislature furthered that end, while Hamilton distinguished the roles played by the executive and the judiciary. In the course of this discussion, in Essays 78 and 81, Hamilton anticipated Marshall's *Marbury v. Madison* ruling of 1803, which established the Supreme Court as the ultimate interpreter of the Constitution and of the constitutionality of federal laws. Many individual essays of *The Federalist* have been the focus of scholarly interest, such as Madison's Essay 10, which some have claimed to be an anticipation of the Marxist theory of economic class struggle. The main purpose of the essays is quite clear, however. Their authors wanted to convince their fellow citizens that, if the United States were to survive and flourish, a stronger form of union was necessary and that form was aptly developed in the Constitution of 1787. *See also* CONSTITUTION OF THE UNITED STATES OF AMERICA, p. 19; FEDERALISM, p. 29; SEPARATION OF POWERS, p. 56.

Significance   *The Federalist* is a political classic although it is in no sense a systematic treatise on government. It provides the best access we have to the original intent of the authors of the federal Constitution, the oldest unitary written constitution and the basis for the first modern federated republic. *The Federalist*'s primary authors, Hamilton and Madison, put aside their personal differences and the differences they had with a document crafted through compromise in Philadelphia, in order to defend it and win its ratification. Privately, both were for a more centralized government than was provided for by the Constitution. Hamilton later questioned whether the American version of democracy was acceptable to him. A sharp split between Hamilton and Madison did not occur until 1791, but even in their *Federalist* collaboration Hamilton could not win Madison over to his view on the supremacy of the Supreme Court. Still, both were so convinced of the value of the Constitution that they borrowed time from their busy lives to join forces in its defense. As with the other drafters of the Constitution, their underlying view of human nature was pessimistic. They were convinced that neither individuals nor the majority itself could be trusted with absolute power. In designing a government that had enough power to function as a modern state while dividing the functions of that power sufficiently to avoid tyranny, they gave birth to a new era of constitutionalism.

Carl Friedrich (b. 1901)   German-born American political scientist and contemporary scholar of constitutionalism. Carl Friedrich came to Harvard University as an undergraduate transfer student after World War I. After finishing his doctorate at Heidelberg, he returned to Harvard in 1926 and taught there until retiring in 1971. Some fifteen of Friedrich's published works deal with issues central to constitutionalism. The most important is *Constitutional Government and Democracy: Theory and Practice in Europe and America* (4th ed., 1968), which has been translated into five foreign languages. His "Constitutions and Constitutionalism" in the *International Encyclopedia of the Social Sciences* (1968) summarized the main points of that seminal work. His *Transcendent Justice: the Religious Dimensions of Constitutionalism* (1964) analyzes the religious roots of constitutionalism, especially in the Judaeo-Christian tradition. His most recent work is *Limited Government: A Comparison* (1974). Friedrich writes not only out of immense scholarly research but also out of rich practical experience in government. He helped train United States military government officers in postwar West Germany and served as a consultant for the restoration of constitutional democracy there. He also served as an adviser in setting up the Puerto Rican commonwealth and in writing the constitution of the Virgin Islands. Friedrich stresses the importance of functional definitions of constitutionalism, by which he means effectiveness of regularized restraints upon political and governmental powers. He has a very normative approach to constitutionalism, although his writing brims with historical and comparative analyses of governments. He ultimately measures them all by the purpose he sees as central to genuine constitutionalism, and that is the protection of individual rights against the tyranny of government. Friedrich maintains that a government must first be effective before it can be constitutional, arguing that a well-developed bureaucracy is central to any good government. To achieve its ultimate purpose, however, a constitutional government must allow for a division of power, functionally by separation of branches of government, and territorially throuh federalism. Friedrich says that not all democracies with a constitution are constitutionalist. The constitution of the Roman Republic before Christ, for example, was merely a facade for the aristocratic control of the Senate. The "people's democracy" found in the Union of Soviet Socialist Republics is a facade for the oligarchy of the Communist Party. And an absolute democracy can be a facade for the tyranny of the majority.

Significance   Friedrich's analysis of constitutionalism follows closely that of earlier scholars, notably Charles McIlwain and Francis Wilmuth, but the notable difference in Friedrich's approach is that it is "functional-political." It is functional because it studies the actual workings of government, not just its legally mandated structure. It is political because it considers not just the governmental aspects of constitutionalism but also the effects of the political environment on constitutional practices. The reader of *Constitutional Government and Democracy* becomes aware that all the details packed into its 700 pages constitute a single thesis: that a country's living constitution is determined not only by the documentary constitution and its governmental structures but also by its political parties; lobbies; mass media; educational, military, and economic systems; and by its international relations. Friedrich says that federalism is best described as a *process*, which he calls "federalizing." Federalizing is the process of increasing the unity between several previously separate political entities, and Friedrich believes federalizing is the major constitutional trend of the modern world. The growing social and economic interdependence of the United States may eventually so unify the nation that its federal structure may become obsolete, says Friedrich. Since nations are independent only in a legal sense, world federalism can be expected to grow as well. Indeed, Friedrich considers world federalism a necessary safeguard for national constitutionalism. He declares sovereignty to be an illusion, since it overlooks the essential interdependence of persons and nations. Following his favorite "philosopher of freedom," Immanuel Kant, Friedrich focuses finally on the autonomy of constituent members of a political union. After carefully distinguishing planning, socialization, and socialism, Friedrich asserts that modern constitutional democracy is compatible with, and even requires, a high degree of planning and social control.

The Fundamental Orders of Connecticut (1639)   The basic laws for self-government adopted by the early settlers of Connecticut in 1639. The Fundamental Orders of Connecticut were the first constitution written in the Anglo-American world. In 1635, under the leadership of Roger Ludlow and the Puritan minister Thomas Hooker, inhabitants of several Massachusetts Bay towns set out to find more land in the Connecticut River Valley. There they founded the towns of Hartford, Wethersfield, and Windsor. The Massachusetts legislature, called the General Court, gave the Connecticut towns legitimacy by appointing eight commissioners to govern them from 1636 to 1638. The commissioners convened several sessions of a General Assembly, also called a General Court, between 1637 and 1638. Although there is no solid historical information about the precise origins of the Fundamental Orders, we know they were drafted in 1638 and approved on January 14, 1639. Most historians assume they were requested and approved by the local General Court and written by Roger Ludlow.

The document consists of a preamble and eleven "orders." The preamble portrays the document as setting up "an orderly and peaceful government established according to God," the purpose of which is "to maintain the peace and union of such a people." The document makes no mention of either the king or natural law requiring or authorizing the government. The only authority mentioned is "the word of God." The document itself derives its name from the opening words of each of the eleven orders: "It is ordered, sentenced, and decreed that. . . ." The orders outline the government of the confederated towns and of any towns that might later be allied with them. There were to be two General Assemblies each year, attended by four deputies elected from each town. One of the assemblies would be a Court of Elections, at which a governor and six magistrates would be elected. Governors and magistrates could hold office only in alternate years. There were no religious requirements for voting, but the governor had to belong to "an approved congregation." Should the governor and magistrates refuse to call a General Assembly at the required time, the freemen of the three towns retained the ultimate authority to do so. The Connecticut towns were governed by the Fundamental Orders from 1639 until 1662. The General Assemblies became bicameral, the deputies being distinguished from the magistrates. The governor had no vote, except in the case of a tie, and no veto. It soon became the custom for the governor and the deputy governor to alternate years of service as governor until, in 1660, the General Assembly amended the Fundamental Orders so that Governor John Winthrop, Jr., could be reelected indefinitely. There were two levels of suffrage: "freemen" and "admitted inhabitants." The freemen had the right to elect officials at all levels—governor, magistrates, deputies, and town officials. The admitted inhabitants, who lacked the required property holdings to be freemen but who were approved by a majority of the freemen, could vote for only deputies and town officials.

The Fundamental Orders had no legal standing with the king of England. When Charles II assumed the throne under the Restoration, John Winthrop, Jr., went to England and returned with a royal charter for Connecticut in 1662. Although the charter superseded the Fundamental Orders, it changed very little. The only major difference was that it barred approved inhabitants from voting for deputies. The citizens of Connecticut were so pleased with their charter, and with the Fundamental Orders upon which it was based, that they, along with Rhode Island, were the only colonies that did not draft new constitutions during the revolutionary period. Connecticut did not draft a new state constitution until 1818. *See also* MAYFLOWER COMPACT, p. 47; SOCIAL CONTRACT, p. 59; STATE CONSTITUTIONS, p. 61.

Significance   The Fundamental Orders of Connecticut paved the way for constitutionalism in the United States. Connecticut still proclaims on its automobile license plates that it is the "constitution state." American historian Benjamin F. Wright agrees with the citizens of Connecticut that the Fundamental Orders were the first constitution of America, but other historians such as Robert J. Taylor consider it an anachronism to call the Fundamental Orders a constitution. Taylor says constitutionalism was an idea that did not develop in America for several generations after 1639. The language of the document may indeed mark it more as a religious covenant than a political charter. Perhaps the same aspirations that grasped for Biblical foundations in seventeenth-century Hartford grasped for political foundations in eighteenth-century Philadelphia. If constitutionalism is more a process than an accomplishment, Connecticut's Fundamental Orders are one of the early mountain streams that would flow together to form a mighty torrent of constitutionalism a century later. An assessment of the Fundamental Orders would not be complete without some comment on the role of the Reverend Thomas Hooker, not to be confused with Richard Hooker, a near-contemporary philosopher of constitutionalism. Earlier historians have called Thomas Hooker "the father of American democracy," basing their opinion largely on his insistence in 1638 that a popularly elected assembly was best suited to conduct important public business. The context of his remarks concerned negotiations about the New England Confederation, not the Fundamental Orders of Connecticut. His democratic principles were less consistently applied to local government than they were to rhetoric about the theory of intercolonial cooperation. Modern historians are more modest in their claims for Hooker's role in the democratization of America.

Jurisprudence   The science of law. Jurisprudence has evolved to include the examination and classification of legal ideas, theories, and analyses based on lines of inquiry developed in anthropology, philosophy, politics, psychology, and sociology. Jurisprudence as a mode of thought has its genesis in Plato and Aristotle, neither of whom distinguished between legal and social theory. They said that without law there could be no polity. Later Roman writers summarized jurisprudence in the phrase, "Jurisprudentia est divinarum atque humanarum rerum notitia, justi atque injusti scientia," or "Jurisprudence is the knowledge of things divine and human, the science of what is right and what is wrong." Jurisprudence can be considered, therefore, the repository of thoughts and the body of sources from which the law emanates. Many Western philosophers have devoted attention to expositions of legal theory, by which they typically mean the rules which should govern the behavior of individuals in relationship to each other and to the state. Analytical jurisprudence seeks answers to the following questions, for example: "What is law?" "What is a state?" "What is a right?" "What is property?" and "What determines a contractual obligation?" From such questions evolved an understanding of the makeup of the legal order. The contribution of Aristotle (384–322 B.C.) includes the *Nicomachean Ethics*, especially Book V, in which he develops and discusses theories of commutative and distributive justice. *The Summa Theologica: Treatise on Law* of Thomas Aquinas (1225–1274) was published as a theological work, but it also made a major effort to organize the science of law as it existed in the thirteenth century. The *Leviathan* (1651), the political philosophy of Thomas Hobbes, contains many discourses on natural law, expressed by Hobbes as "justice, equity, modesty, mercy, and, in sum, doing to others as we would be done to...." The American Founding Fathers assumed the legacy of John Locke. His *Two Treatises of Government* (1759) is acknowledged to be the first modern philosophic defense of government and property based upon the consent of the governed. Locke's arguments provided the theoretical justification for the Declaration of Independence and the United States Constitution. Jeremy Bentham (1748–1832) said that social reforms could best be effected through the legal, not the political, order, and Immanuel Kant substantially added to the force of Bentham's arguments in 1796 with publication of his *Philosophy of Law*. Kant said that law is pure reason and cannot be subject to political manipulation. Kant's thesis is consistent with and antecedent to George Wilhelm Friedrich Hegel's *Philosophy of Right* (1831). Jurisprudence is typically divided into three schools of thought: historical, sociological, and realist. Each school is discussed below.

Friedrich Carl von Savigny (1779–1861) founded the historical school in 1814 with the publication of his *Of the Vocation of Our Age for Legislation and Jurisprudence*. Savigny wrote, "Law grows with the growth, and strengthens with the strength, of the people, and finally dies away as the nation loses its nationality." He maintained that the substance of the law is derived from a subtle national development that eventually concludes in a national legal identity. He acknowledged that law must originate in legislative enactments, but philosophically he eschewed codified law such as Roman law. He argued that since law is construed in direct relationship to the particular social milieu in which it develops, it would be presumptively irrational to assume that what is proper or lawful at one point in time could be equally valid in another. "An age has no need of a code for itself. It would merely compose one for a succeeding and less fortunate age, as we lay up provisions for winter. But an age is seldom disposed to be so provident for posterity." Savigny said the basis of the legal order is the history of a nation's social cognition rather than in the individual's abstract relationship to the state. He therefore emphasized the common spirit of the people, or *Volksgeist*. In founding the historical school, Savigny also contributed substantially to the sociological jurisprudence movement, easily the most pervasive interpretation in American constitutional law.

Many of the early contributors to sociological jurisprudence were Europeans. Among the most important are the Baron de Montesquieu, who suggested in *The Spirit of the Laws* (1748) that a good law was the result of its conscious adaptation to the spirit and volition of a group of people. A good law must be seen as the product of the interaction between governmental structures and the physical environment of a particular society. "[Laws] should have a relation to the degree of liberty which the constitution will bear, to the religion of the inhabitants, and to their inclinations, riches, numbers, commerce, manners, and customs." Eight years earlier, David Hume had suggested a similar approach to jurisprudence in his *Treatise on Human Nature*. Hume considered law a developing social institution that owed its origins not to individual natures but to accepted social conventions. Other philosophers making important contributions to the early discussion of sociological jurisprudence were Rudolf von Inhering (1818–1892), Max Weber (1864–1920), and Eugen Ehrlich (1862–1922). In 1913 Ehrlich wrote in his *Principles of the Sociology of Law:* "At the present as well as at any other time, the center of gravity of legal development lies not in legislation, nor in juristic science, nor in judicial decision, but in society itself." Sociological jurisprudence came to full flower in the work of Roscoe Pound (1870–1964), for 20 years the dean of the Harvard University Law School. His most extensive discussion of the subject, *My Philosophy of Law*, was published in 1941. "The legal order," Pound said, "is a regime of social control through politically organized society." The science of law must always be more concerned with an empirical analysis of the law than with law in its abstract form. Rather than being conceived as a theoretical construct, law is more properly conceived as an institution of social control. Sociological jurisprudence became interested in incorporating sociological techniques and research methods in the pursuit of social justice. As a by-product of the industrialism and economic expansion of the late nineteenth and early twentieth centuries, it emphasized law as a partner in social progress. Proponents of the movement rejected abstract law because abstract law recognized no solutions to the problems and challenges inherent in twentieth-century technology. Sociological jurisprudence also rejected the natural law position that an ultimate theory of value can be discovered. There can be no *natural* guide to the resolution of conflict and proscribed behavior, said the movement, and legal rules and precepts must necessarily be only flexible directives rather than rigid restrictions and sanctions envisioning entirely just outcomes. Sociological jurisprudence stressed the social objectives of law, regarding the science of law as merely a means of accomplishing the multivariant purposes of society. Thus the rules of law of a given society are a balancing of competing interests. Each legal decision or opinion is the equalizing of perceived social alternatives. Sociological jurisprudence did demonstrate interest in justice for the individually oppressed person, and it did embrace this principle as a purpose of the law, but more generally it attempted to order conduct in which group action and dynamics were determinative of the public good. This ordering of relations can best be brought about in a society which is homogeneous, static, and cohesive, and one in which there are shared values and traditions. Roscoe Pound issued a challenge to teachers as well as practitioners of the law when he urged lawyers to pursue social rather than legal justice in its narrowest sense. He said that justice may very well be consistent with prevailing societal values and public standards. In summarizing his views Pound wrote in his *Introduction to the Philosophy of Law* (1954):

> For the purpose of understanding the law of today I am content with a picture of satisfying as much of the whole body of human wants as we may with the least sacrifice. I am content to think of law as a social institution to satisfy social wants, so far as such wants may be satisfied or such claims given effect by an ordering of human conduct through politically organized society. For present purposes, I am content to see in legal history the record of a continually wider recognizing and satisfying of human wants or claims or desires through social control and a more embracing and more effective elimination of waste and precluding of friction in human enjoyment of the goods of human experience—in short, a continually more efficacious social engineering.

Some legal writers have argued that sociological jurisprudence is not a philosophy of law at all but is rather an attempt to associate the empiricism of sociological methods with the legal order. This identification has come to be known as the sociology of law. Other authorities say the sociology of law is correctly understood as a general science of society of which considerations of law are a part. Whatever its definition, the sociology of law has received significant attention in modern American legal practice, much of it the result of the etiology of the Brandeis Brief. In 1908, as a practicing attorney, Louis D. Brandeis filed a brief on behalf of the defendant in the case of *Muller v. Oregon* (208 U.S. 412: 1908). Brandeis argued that an Oregon law that set the maximum number of hours per day during which women could work was legal. He looked beyond traditional legal parameters and based his position on supporting sociological data. The data said long working hours were detrimental to the health and morals of working women. Through the employment of such research, Brandeis helped to bring about social reforms that historically had been considered only the purview of legislators. The introduction of sociological evidence thus interjected a normative analysis to aid in the clarification of legal doctrine. The history of Supreme Court interpretations of the due process and equal protection clauses of the Fourteenth Amendment provides a paradigm for the application of the sociological approach to legal reasoning. *Muller v. Oregon* is but one example of the Court's application of accepted societal norms prevailing at the time in which the decision was rendered. A more dramatic example is Justice Henry B. Brown's opinion in *Plessy v. Ferguson* (164 U.S. 537: 1896). It is fraught with theories of Social Darwinism when it posits racial suprem- acy, "in this instance the white race," as an absolute social norm. The *Plessy* principle of "separate but equal" established a new standard of racial inequality based on the social science hypotheses of Herbert Spencer and Charles Darwin. Since empirical evidence demonstrated the black race was inferior to the white, it was presumed irrational to grant the black race equal recognition in constitutional law. When Thurgood Marshall, as lawyer for the National Association for the Advancement of Colored People (NAACP), argued the NAACP posi- tion in *Brown v. Board of Education* (347 U.S. 483: 1954), he also relied on social science literature. Rather than Spencer and Darwin, however, Marshall used Gunnar Myrdal's *An American Dilemma* (1941). Marshall maintained as an empirically verifiable sociological fact that segregated educational institutions had an inherently harmful effect on black children. Noted social psychologist Kenneth Clark testified in the *Brown* case that tests administered by him to black children demon- strated that these children tended to develop a negative awareness of themselves at an early age. Marshall therefore concluded that separate could never be equal. This application of sociological jurisprudence was frequently cited in footnotes explaining the unanimous decision overturning *Plessy*. In *Goesaert v. Cleary* (335 U.S. 464: 1948), the Court sustained the constitutionality of a Michigan statute that prohibited the granting of a bartender license to a woman unless she was the wife or daughter of the male owner of the bar. Justice Felix Frankfurter, writing for the majority in a decision consistent with the preponderant social norms of the time, reasoned that Michigan had a legitimate interest in protecting women against "the moral and social problems" that would accompany bartending by women. The state could protect against these problems by "the oversight assumed through ownership of a bar by a barmaid's husband or father ... [and] minimize the hazards that might confront a barmaid without such protecting over- sight." In *Roe v. Wade* (410 U.S. 113: 1973), Justice Harry A. Blackmun devoted an extensive section of his opinion to the positions on abortion held by the American Bar Association (ABA), the American Medical Association (AMA), and the American Public Health Association

(APHA). Clearly, the opinions of the AMA and the APHA had more to do with medical evidence than they did with legal standards, but Blackmun chose to emphasize their extralegal authority to lend validity and substance to his legal reasoning.

Legal realism is interested in articulating and demonstrating the marked differences between legal theory and legal practice. Legal realists say the study of law is only an empirical exercise. It is best understood in terms of what is discovered in the courtroom and not necessarily what is discovered in an abstract study of the legal order. Realists are skeptical of those who adopt antiquated or traditional legal theories. Realists such as Kurt Llewellyn and John Dewey are noted for their insistence on the use of logic to guide legal decisions, while other realists such as Glendon Schubert are known for their systematic statistical analyses and mathematical formulae that predict the outcomes of judicial decision making. Jurist and realist Jerome Frank has suggested that the unpredictability of court decisions resides primarily in the elusiveness of the facts of a given case. He argues that the clearest law to follow is that found at the appellate court level since the facts of a particular case have already been established in lower court proceedings. Legal realists maintain that the courts not only find the law but create it as well. In his compendium of lectures, *The Common Law* (1881), the preeminent realist of them all, Oliver Wendell Holmes, Jr., articulated his conception of legal realism as follows:

> The life of the law has not been logic; it has been experience. The felt necessities of the time, the prevalent moral and political theories, intuitions of public policy, avowed or unconscious, even the prejudices which judges share with their fellowmen have had a good deal more to do than the syllogism in determining the rules by which men should be governed. The law embodies the story of a nation's development through many centuries and it cannot be dealt with as if it contained only the axioms and corollaries of a book of mathematics.

Jurisprudence is the science of law. It is an amalgam of philosophic thought, historical analysis, sociological evidence, and legal experience. *See also* COMMON LAW, p. 13; JOHN LOCKE, p. 43; NATURAL LAW AND NATURAL RIGHTS, p. 50.

Significance   The study of jurisprudence allows students of the law to appreciate the fact that ideas about law do not develop in an intellectual or legal vacuum. Rather they evolve from rich sources of thought in other disciplines. Especially in the United States, sociology has helped to shape impressions about law and its impact on those it seeks to serve, protect, and discipline. Jurisprudence enables one better to understand the complex history of the legal ordering of behavior and institutions, and more properly value the heavy responsibility held by those persons society must trust to make the law and render equitable decisions.

John Locke (1632–1704)   British philosopher whose political thought, especially as found in his *Second Treatise of Government* (1690), provided the theoretical base for the American Revolution and constitutionalist movement. John Locke was educated in medicine and philosophy at Oxford. Aside from brief periods of teaching at Oxford, however, he spent most of his working life as an aide to government officials and as a minor official himself. He lived a number of years in Brandenburg, France, and Holland, as well as in his native England. Perhaps the most formative influence on Locke's political thought was Anthony Ashley Cooper, the first Earl of Shaftesbury. Locke was his aide for a number of years. Shaftesbury was a leader of the Whig party, a supporter of religious tolerance for all except Catholics, and a pioneer of British commercial imperialism and colonialism. Locke's *Essay Concerning Human Understanding* (1690) presented a moderate empiricism that inspired the more radical empiricism of Berkeley and Hume. Its representationalist theory of knowledge, which held that we know our ideas of things rather than things themselves, paved the way for Hume's skepticism and Kant's critical philosophy. Locke's most influential political work was his *Two Treatises of Government* (1690), although *A Letter Concerning Toleration*, published in Latin in 1689, was also important. His Preface to the *Treatises* says the work was meant to justify the Glorious Revolution of 1688 that brought William of Orange to the British throne. Scholars now believe, however, that the work was actually written almost a decade earlier and was intended to justify a revolution against the Catholic King James II. The *First Treatise* was simply a refutation of the theory of the divine right of kings. The *Second Treatise* outlined Locke's own political theory. Like Hobbes, Locke believed that human beings start out in a state of nature. But while Hobbes believed that persons in the state of nature were lawless and warlike, Locke believed they are endowed by God with knowledge of the law of nature. He borrowed that concept from Richard Hooker. The main precepts of the law of nature concern the individual's rights to life, liberty, and property. These rights did not prevent Locke from considering slavery legitimate in the case of captives from a just war, however. Locke is preoccupied with defending the right to property, even though he admits this is not an unlimited right. While he defends the right of inheritance, Locke holds that the primary title to property comes from the labor we invest in the property. In order to guarantee that everyone obeys the law of nature, people enter into an "original compact" that inaugurates civil society. Their consent to majority rule limits their personal freedom to some extent, but they thereby gain the protection of written law and the enforcing power of political authority. Locke considered the founding of Rome, Venice, and certain American colonies to have been historical instances of such original compacts. He maintained that the establishment of a particular form of government is a secondary step founded on trust of rulers. It is a more conditional form of consent than is the original compact among the people. Locke insists upon a separation of governmental powers, with the legislature having supreme authority over the executive, which includes the judiciary, and the federative, which supervises relations with other states. The people retain the ultimate right to rebel against a government that has unjustly infringed upon their rights. Locke was a devout Christian, although of a decidedly rationalist bent. In *A Letter Concerning Toleration*, written at the request of Jean le Clerc, a Christian minister in Amsterdam, Locke argues that the "unhappy agreement that we see between the church and state" is the cause of the religious intolerance that injures both civil society and true religion. Religious authorities should restrict their concerns to religious and moral matters and should not try to control political life. Civil authorities should not meddle in religious or moral matters, unless certain religious practices injure the rights of others or disturb the public peace. Locke thus argued that civil toleration should be extended to all religious persuasions—Christian, Jewish, Muslim, and pagan—but with the exception of Roman Catholics and atheists. Roman Catholics were excluded because of their doctrinaire intolerance of other religions and their allegiance to the Pope as their primary earthly sovereign. Atheists were excluded because of their rejection of the religious basis for public morality. *See also* CONSTITUTIONALISM, HISTORICAL DEVELOPMENT OF, p. 15; NATURAL LAW AND NATURAL RIGHTS, p. 50; SOCIAL CONTRACT, p. 59.

Significance   John Locke's philosophy decisively influenced political thinkers in England, France, and the American colonies. Among those most influenced were Voltaire, Montesquieu, the French Encyclopedists, Hamilton, and Jefferson. Locke's *Second Treatise* contained the philosophy underlying Jefferson's Declaration of Independence, especially the Declaration's appeal to self-evident laws of nature, the natural equality of human beings, popular consent as the basis of government, and the right of a people to rebel against an unjust government. Indeed, the final words of the Declaration are an echo of Locke's original compact theory. The *Second Treatise* and *A Letter Concerning Toleration* also bore upon the framing of the Constitution, with its insistence on the separation of church and state, majority rule, the primacy of the legislative branch, and, by way of Montesquieu's refinements, the separation of powers. Locke also influenced American developments in more subtle ways. His tendency to equate the common good with the will of the majority and his emphasis on the rights of private property tended to justify both the neglect of minority rights and the pursuit of economic individualism. The fact that Locke justified revolution not as a path toward an ideal society, as in the French and Russian revolutions, but only as a restoration of the majority's elemental political and economic rights, is reflected in the basically conservative nature of the American Revolution and American political history. John Locke is the single most important figure in the founding of American constitutionalism.

Magna Carta   The "Great Charter" issued by King John at Runnymede on June 15, 1215. Magna Carta became the statutory basis for English liberties while it simultaneously reflected the gradual maturation of secular law in Europe. During the twelfth and thirteenth centuries, there were many instances in France, Germany, Hungary, Italy, and Spain of towns and nobles winning royal charters of liberties because of their developing economic and military strength. William the Conqueror had been powerful enough to resist such charters, but all of his successors to the English throne were forced to grant them to ecclesiastical and baronial lords. The charters were *privilegia*, or laws for particular groups, and were not in any sense laws for the entire realm. King John came to the throne in 1199 inheriting heavy debts from his brother Richard's crusade to the Holy Land and Richard's war with France. John was forced to press his barons for greater and greater financial contributions to the royal treasury. John's position was considerably weakened when he received an interdict and eventual excommunication from Pope Innocent III for his refusal to recognize Stephan Langton's election as Archbishop of Canterbury, an issue on which John eventually relented. Finally in 1215, Langton and William Marshall, the Earl of Pembroke and the most influential of the English barons, convinced the angry secular and ecclesiastical lords to demand a charter of liberties from John rather than fight him in a civil war. They presented John with the *Articles of the Barons*, which served as the basis for Magna Carta. Magna Carta was divided into 63 clauses and covered a large number of issues among which were the rights of the church, of higher nobles, of lesser nobles and freemen, and of towns, tradespeople, and merchants. Rules were laid down for royal officials, especially local ones. Disagreements concerning use of the forests were settled, a clause of Magna Carta that in 1217 was expanded into a separate *Charter of the Forest*. Certain crucial juridical questions were regulated, such as the trial of nobles and freemen by their peers and according to the law of the land; prompt justice; specific locations for trials; and restrictions of writs of *praecipe* as well as writs of inquiry concerning life and limb. One of the most interesting parts of Magna Carta was Clause 61. In that clause the king authorized the establishment of a committee of 25 barons who, in the event of a royal violation of the charter that was not rectified within 40 days, would lead the whole kingdom in confiscating the king's possessions. Despite Magna Carta, however, the barons soon waged war on John. After John's defeat at the Battle of Lewes in 1215, he reissued the charter in its original form. After John's death in 1216, the regent council of the young Henry III issued a revision of the charter in 1217, which served as the basis of Henry's own charter of 1225. It is the Magna Carta of 1225, not the preceding versions, which was included in subsequent English statute rolls and expounded by its classic commentator, Sir Edward Coke. *See also* COMMON LAW, p. 13; CONSTITUTIONALISM, HISTORICAL DEVELOPMENT OF, p. 15; ENGLISH CONSTITUTION, p. 26.

Significance   Magna Carta came to have an importance for constitutionalism that far outweighed its literal and historical meaning. Although its use of "freeman" was broader than any other European document of its time, the rights of freemen still fell within the category of privilege. Yet by the fourteenth century, the English Parliament had universalized a number of Magna Carta's fundamental provisions, so that nine chapters of the 1225 charter still stand in the *English Statute Book*. Some of the language of Magna Carta was incorporated into the constitutions of the early American states and into the federal Constitution of 1787. More influential than the words of Magna Carta, however, was its spirit. It stands as permanent testimony to the human belief in the importance of written law, the limits of absolute monarchy, and the right of rebellion against tyranny. These ideas become fundamental guiding principles in the development of constitutional government in both England and the United States. Yet Magna Carta has not been venerated by everyone. Hobbes and Locke felt that statutory law should be based on natural law rather than on precedent law such as that found in the charter. Petit-Dutaillis (1894) and Edward Jenks (1904) rejected Magna Carta as a throwback to an earlier feudalism. They said it presented an obstacle to the growth of constitutionalism in England. Current discussions of Magna Carta center on the question of whether a precedent legal system is inherently more or less responsive to social need than a natural law system. Whatever the outcome of the continuing debate, Magna Carta stands unassailed as the most influential statement of early English constitutionalism.

Mayflower Compact   The social covenant signed by the first settlers of Plymouth Plantation in 1620. The Mayflower Compact reads as follows:

> In ye name of God, Amen. We whose names are underwritten, the loyall subjects of our dread soveraigne Lord, King James, by ye Grace of God, of Great Britaine, France, & Ireland king, defender of ye faith, &c, haveing undertaken, for ye glorie of God, and advancemente of ye Christian faith, and honour of our king & countrie, a voyage to plant ye first colonie in ye Northerne parts of Virginia, doe by these presents solemnly & mutually in ye presence of God, and one of another, covenant & combine our selves togeather into a civill body politick, for our better ordering & preservation & furtherance of ye ends aforesaid; and by vertue hereof to enacte, constitute, and frame such just & equall lawes, ordinances, acts, constitutions, and offices, from time to time, as shall be thought most meete & convenient for ye general good of ye Colonie, unto which we promise all due submission and obedience. In witnes whereof we have hereunder subscribed our names at Cap-Codd ye 11 November, in ye year of ye raigne of our soveraigne lord, King James, of England, France, & Ireland ye eighteenth, and of Scotland ye fiftie-fourth. Ano: Dom. 1620.

The main force behind the settlement of Plymouth Plantation, or New Plymouth, were the Separatists, also called Brownists. While the Puritans were content to try to reform the Church of England from within, the Separatists set up independent congregations that embodied their more primitive Christian ideals of doctrine, ritual, and church government. Following the lead of the Reverend Robert Browne, the Separatists insisted that each congregation enter into a convenant providing for the democratic election of ministers and officials and for congregational discipline based on majority rule. Despised by Anglicans and Puritans alike for their "gathered church" doctrine, many Separatists fled to Holland, where their leader there, Henry Ainsworth, gave them the name Pilgrims. William Brewster the Younger formed a Separatist congregation in the Village of Scrooby in Nottinghamshire, with John Robertson as minister and the orphaned William Bradford as one of its members. In 1608, to escape religious persecution, Brewster moved his congregation to Amsterdam and then to Leyden in 1609. Because of the congregation's hardships there, they then decided to move to the New World. After considering agreements with the Virginia Company and the Dutch New Netherlands Company, the Pilgrims finally signed with Thomas Weston's London-based Adventurers to set up a fishing industry in Northern Virginia. Our sole records of the journey are William Bradford and Edward Winslow's *Mourt's Relation* (1622) and Bradford's *Of Plimouth Plantation*, published posthumously in 1856. Having sailed from Holland to England in their own ship, the *Speedwell*, the Pilgrims were joined by the rented

Mayflower, which contained more Pilgrims and other non-Separatist settlers who had been recruited by the Adventurers Company. After the *Speedwell* proved unseaworthy on two attempted sailings, a reduced contingent of 102 settlers and a crew of 47 finally left Plymouth, England, on September 17, 1620, all aboard the *Mayflower*. Of the settlers embarked, only 40 were Pilgrims. The rest were "strangers," i.e., other freemen, hirelings, and indentured servants. All were lower-middle class in economic status. A few of the strangers, notably Miles Standish and John Alden, had been hired by the Pilgrims in England as "strongmen." When the travelers sighted land at what is now Provincetown, some of the strangers asserted they did not have to abide by the agreements signed in England, since they were landing not in Northern Virginia but in New England. To avert turmoil before landing, therefore, the Pilgrims, probably the Cambridge-educated William Brewster, drafted the Mayflower Compact. Forty-one of the men aboard signed the Compact on November 21, 1620 (Gregorian calendar). The only men who did not sign were one stranger, three hirelings, and two indentured servants. At the same meeting, the Pilgrim John Carver was elected governor with total legislative, executive, and judicial powers. On December 26, the settlers began building their permanent home in the New World, which they named Plymouth. Aided by the English-speaking Indian, Squanto, they made a peace treaty with Massasoit, chief of all the local Indians except the Massachusetts tribe, and began farming, fishing, and trading with the Indians. They set up a strictly communistic economic system, but gradually abandoned it as unworkable beginning in 1623. When Carver died in 1621, Bradford became governor, holding the position until 1656. Because he was weakened by an injury, Bradford asked for the election of an assistant governor. The assistant became seven assistants by 1633, and together the assistant governors formed the Governor's Council, later called the General Court. The governor and his council were elected yearly. By 1623 there was already a limitation on suffrage, and by the mid-1600s, with 232 freemen among the 3,000 inhabitants of Plymouth Plantation, only those freemen who met stringent property qualifications could vote. In 1626, the Pilgrims bought out their English partners, the Adventurers, but despite their concerted efforts, they never received a royal charter. Between 1636 and 1640, five new towns were founded within Plymouth Plantation—Duxbury, Sandwich, Scituate, Taunton, and Yarmouth. In 1636, the General Court, together with representatives from each of the colony's then-existing towns, Plymouth, Duxbury, and Scituate, adopted the Great Fundamentals, the colony's first constitution. Plymouth's towns used town meetings from the beginning of the settlement, although Sandwich did not establish a formal town government until 1651. The history of Pilgrim Plymouth was closely tied to that of the Puritan Massachusetts Bay Colony. The latter, founded at Salem in 1628, adopted the Pilgrims' organization for its religious congregations, while Plymouth modeled its General Court after that of Massachusetts Bay. In general, however, no love was lost between the two colonies. Plymouth was much more democratic and religiously tolerant than Massachusetts. There were no executions of religious dissenters and no witch convictions in Plymouth. Massachusetts Bay did finally absorb Plymouth Plantation in 1691, when Plymouth was unable to purchase a new charter after the fall of the Stuarts in England. *See also* CONSTITUTIONALISM, HISTORICAL DEVELOPMENT OF, p. 15; FUNDAMENTAL ORDERS OF CONNECTICUT, p. 35; SOCIAL CONTRACT, p. 59.

Significance   The Mayflower Compact was rediscovered in the mid-eighteenth century by historians who idealized it as the foundation of American liberties and the first written constitution. In fact, it was neither. Jefferson did not consult it in drafting the Declaration of Independence, and there is no record of its being mentioned at the Constitutional Convention. Nor was the Mayflower Compact a constitution. The Pilgrim constitution, the Great Fundamentals, was not drafted until 1636. The Compact was rather a social contract, or, in Bradford's words, "a combination made by the Pilgrims before they came ashore, being the first foundation of their government in this place." Although Richard Hooker's theories of social contract and consent of the governed would have been available to the Pilgrims, their more immediate inspiration was Robert Browne's notion of religious covenant. The central ideal of the Mayflower Compact was the consensual formation of a civil society to be governed by "just and equal laws," which the covenanters would later enact. Despite their democratic beginning, however, at least for male freemen, the government became a benevolent dictatorship by the governor. The freemen eligible to vote decided only the matters the governor chose to set before them. Nor were the laws completely equal, for it was recommended that punishments vary "according to the nature and quality of the person." Plymouth's compact became a model for several other foundations, however. Roger Williams was expelled from Plymouth for his radical democratic views and founded Providence in 1636 with a similar social contract. Rhode Island became the most democratic and religiously tolerant colony of the original thirteen. The same compact idea underlay the founding of the New England Confederation in 1643. The United Colonies of New England, disrupted by England's creation of the short-lived Dominion of New England, inspired Benjamin Franklin's proposal for an all-colony confederation in 1775. Perhaps the most important legacy of the Mayflower Compact was the institution of the town meeting of Plymouth Plantation's member towns. Thomas Jefferson called the town meeting "the wisest invention ever devised by the wit of man for the perfect exercise of self-government and for its preservation." Given this tradition of active self-government, it was not a coincidence that the first active steps toward American independence were taken near the original home of the Pilgrims, at Lexington and Concord.

Natural Law and Natural Rights   Terms from the vocabulary of moral and political philosophy used to counter positivistic theories of private and public morality. Natural law and natural rights philosophy asserts that the fundamental rules governing human behavior derive from basic characteristics of a human nature common to all. This is true for both our moral obligations (natural law) and for the moral authority to do certain acts (natural rights). Natural law and natural rights are common to all persons of all times and places. As a corollary, if a legislator creates a rule that violates one of the fundamental natural rules, the new rule is immoral and not a valid law. Positivistic moral theories, on the other hand, deny that there is a universal basis for the fundamental rules of human conduct. Instead, positivists say that such rules derive from historical circumstances or simply from arbitrary choice. Thus fundamental rules may vary widely among times and places, groups and individuals. As a corollary, there is no moral basis for distinguishing between morally valid and morally invalid laws. A law is a law. While various natural law and natural rights theories agree on their rejection of positivism, they differ markedly among themselves. The development of these theories can be viewed in four stages: (1) cosmological, (2) juridical, (3) theological-anthropological, and (4) rationalist. In the first three stages, the term *natural rights* is rarely mentioned explicitly. It is implicit in the theories' treatment of justice, i.e., my rights are the correlatives of the obligation of others to be just toward me. In rationalist theory, the term *natural rights* becomes both explicit and dominant.

Socrates, Plato, and Aristotle formulated the key moral concepts that would be incorporated into the classic medieval natural law theories. Given the nature-law split they accepted from their Sophist opponents, however, "natural law" would have seemed a contradiction in terms to them. Natural law in the moral sense was first used by the Greek Stoics of the fourth and third centuries B.C., who in turn greatly influenced Roman thinkers such as Cicero. For the Stoics, the moral life consisted in living harmoniously with the cosmic law of nature established by God or fate.

The next interpretation of natural law and natural rights was formulated by the Roman jurists. Reinterpreting the tripartite division of law introduced by Ulpian, both Isadore of Seville and Gratian distinguished between civil law and natural law. Civil law was proper to each nation, although there was a *jus gentium*, "the law of nations," common to all nations. Natural law was common to human beings wherever they lived, and was superior to civil law, the latter drawing its authority from proper interpretations of the natural law.

The most systematic natural law theory is the theological-anthropological theory developed by Thomas Aquinas. He distinguished three kinds of law: eternal law (God's plan of creation and providence), natural law (the eternal law as embodied in the strivings of human nature and as known by human reason), and human law (human legislation). Aquinas's concept of natural law synthesized juridical theory with Aristotle's doctrine of moral virtue as the habitual and properly integrated exercise of human capacities in pursuit of their natural goals. Aquinas also held that human legislation was authentic law only if it was consonant with the eternal and natural law. Aquinas's theory was weakened by the voluntarism of late medieval scholasticism, but it survived intact in sixteenth-century thinkers such as Richard Hooker. Grotius's seventeenth-century version of the *jus gentium*, in which he applied natural law to international relations, was built upon Aquinas's theory.

Concerned that Catholicism had ignored the central role of grace in Christian life, the Reformation held that human nature was so radically perverted by original sin that nature alone could not be the basis of morality. Enlightenment thinkers, especially after Hume's empiricism and skepticism, cast doubt upon our ability to know human nature, even if it were an adequate basis for morality. Thus a new view of natural law began to emerge. This rationalist view rejected the Aristotelian-Thomistic conception of human nature as teleological, and instead portrayed it as a set of physical capacities and needs governed by rationality and freedom. These capacities and needs lacked any particular natural orientation except self-interest. One's moral obligation was simply to live and let live in accordance with self-interest. John Locke reflects the transition from the theological-anthropological stage to the rationalist stage. While he is definitely in the rationalist tradition, he is also influenced by the natural law theory of Richard Hooker. Under rationalist theory, the emphasis of moral philosophy shifted to natural rights. By the nineteenth century, reference to natural law had generally disappeared except in pockets of ecclesiology where Thomism survived. It was a short step from the rationalist doctrine of natural rights to utilitarianism's rejection of the very idea of natural rights. Bentham called the concept "nonsense upon stilts" and led the modern world into a consideration of individual liberties dictated by social utility. Since the Thomistic revival of the late nineteenth century, and especially since the *reductio ad absurdum* of moral positivism under the Nazis, Aquinas's natural law doctrine has received renewed attention. As Protestant-Catholic polemics have receded, interest in natural law theory has been rekindled among Protestant scholars such as Brunner, Althaus, and Wendland. But natural law doctrine is far from the dominant moral philosophy of the 1980s. The most important modern statement of contractarian natural rights theory, John Rawls's *A Theory of Justice*, makes no reference to natural law. *See also* COMMON LAW, p. 13; JURISPRUDENCE, p. 37; JOHN RAWLS, p. 52.

Significance   The development of natural law and natural rights theories was an attempt to clarify how mankind should deal with unjust human laws and behavior, both within and between states. These theories provided the moral rationale for the English Bill of Rights (1689), the American Declaration of Independence (1776), the American Bill of Rights (1789), the French Declaration of the Rights of Man and Citizen (1789), and the United Nations Universal Declaration of Human Rights (1948). They also underlay many acts of civil disobedience in the modern world, not to mention revolutions and such circumscribed discussions of natural law and natural rights as the Nuremberg War Crime Trials. There is universal agreement today that all human beings have certain inalienable rights, whether these rights are grounded in nature or not. The question remains whether and how this belief can be justified. Purely theological arguments aside, the main contemporary justifications for human rights are Kantian, utilitarian, contractarian, and Thomistic. Of these, only the Thomistic view appeals to natural law. The utilitarians have been highly successful in basing individual rights on simple considerations of social usefulness. An adequate theoretical justification of human rights is crucial not only in securing their existence but also in determining their content. Human rights can otherwise degenerate into a distorted version of civil liberties, according to which people have a right to do anything they please, regardless of how what they do affects the common good. Such an extreme view of the content of human rights can eventually provoke a reaction strong enough to threaten the existence of all human rights.

John Rawls (b. 1921)   Contemporary Harvard University moral philosopher who systematically restated the natural rights contractarian theory of justice. John Rawls painstakingly wrote the 600 pages of his definitive *A Theory of Justice* (1971) over a 12-year period. He defends the view that human beings have certain natural rights and that the most secure grounding of both public and private morality is in the idea of social contract. Rawls conceives the ideal social contract more along the lines of Kant than of other contractarians such as Hobbes, Locke, and Rousseau, and he vigorously opposes the utilitarians. The latter deny natural rights by speaking instead of civil liberties meted out according to calculations of social utility. Rawls believes that social justice is more fundamental than individual justice. Most of his book is spent explaining the four stages through which social justice is brought about: (1) the establishment of the principles of social justice in the "original position"; (2) the establishment of constitutional justice in the "constitutional convention"; (3) the establishment of legislative justice in the "legislative stage"; and (4) administrative and judicial application of relevant rules, along with citizen compliance with them in concrete and particular cases. Rawls emphasizes that these four stages and their corresponding principles describe not how people actually do establish and apply the principles of justice but how they ought to do so. Rawls says repeatedly that he wants to achieve a parsimony of assumptions in order to achieve the fullest possible consensus on the principles he derives. He assumes that people are driven only by a desire to maximize their own self-interest, and that they take no interest in the interests of others. To make self-interest work in the cause of fairness, for justice is fairness, Rawls requires the first three stages of choice to be performed behind what he calls a "veil of ignorance." A brief elaboration of Rawls's four stages in the development of social justice follows.

In the first stage, the "original position," people know nothing particular about themselves, whether they are geniuses or idiots, rich or poor, black or white, male or female, American or Russian. Neither do they know anything about their society. Without this ignorance, people who know that fate has given them a greater share of natural and social assets would be tempted to push for a less-than-fair contract, to their own advantage. Rawls says that in such an original position, all self-interested people would choose his "two principles of justice" and the "two priority rules." The two principles of justice are (1) basic liberties such as freedom of conscience and freedom of opportunity must be distributed with absolute equality; and (2) other social goods such as wealth and political power may be distributed unequally only if the inequalities are to the advantage of the least advantaged members of society. The priority rules tell us how to solve conflicts of principle. The first rule says that the first principle of justice is more fundamental than the second principle. The second rule says that the two principles of justice taken together are more important than any other consideration.

In the constitutional convention and the legislative stage the veil of ignorance is partly drawn back so that, while the participants still know nothing about their own individual conditions, they know the relevant facts about their own society. Building on this knowledge and on the principles of justice and priority rules, the participants now establish just political procedures, by which Rawls means a constitution and just laws. The first principle of justice is more important in the constitutional phase; the second principle is more important in the legislative phase. Rawls assumes that the outcome of stages 2 and 3 will be a constitutional democracy with just laws.

In the administrative and judicial application stage, the veil of ignorance is completely removed. Particular cases are judged on the basis of full factual knowledge, the principles of justice and the priority rules, the constitution, and the laws. Good citizens follow the judgments indicated by these combined natural rights forces, and social justice is achieved. *See also* CONSTITUTIONALISM, HISTORICAL DEVELOPMENT OF, p. 15; NATURAL LAW AND NATURAL RIGHTS, p. 50; SOCIAL CONTRACT, p. 59.

Significance   John Rawls is a moral philosopher who enjoys the deep respect of his peers. One measure of the importance of his *A Theory of Justice* is the enormous body of secondary literature it generated almost immediately upon publication in 1971. In its twentieth annual *Nomos* Yearbook, entitled *Constitutionalism* (1979), the American Society for Political and Legal Philosophy included two detailed articles on Rawls. But Rawls has not been without his critics. Robert Nozick's *Anarchy, State, and Utopia* (1974) questions the fairness of the redistributive effects of Rawls's second principle of justice. Other moral philosophers have questioned whether Rawls's hypothetical veil of ignorance can guarantee the moral objectivity he is seeking. Rawls's reliance on rational self-interest as the spring of his moral theory is as questionable for him as it was for earlier contractarians. It is unlikely that moral obligation can ever be reduced to calculations of self-interest. Rawls's initial assumption that human beings are devoid of interest in the interests of others is similar to basing a theory of human physiology on the assumption that humans have no heart. It is an interesting intellectual exercise, but it is contrary to the facts, and it leads to false conclusions about the real human body. Rawls's theory has a noble purpose. Many of his conclusions about the redistribution of social goods and about sacrificing one's life in the cause of justice are worthy of the best traditions in moral philosophy. It is not clear, however, that his assumptions are strong enough to support his conclusions.

Republicanism   The doctrine of government by the people through majority rule or by consent. A republic is a political system based on representation in government by delegates chosen by the people. The principle of representation makes government a reflection of a given culture or society, and limits the power that any individual or group may wield over others. Republicanism forces citizens to work together and compromise, theoretically avoiding extremism by broadening and softening points of view. The doctrine first appeared in the Greek city-states, where the political good was defined in representational and majoritarian terms. It reappeared in medieval constitutional theory in the fourteenth century as the idea of a selected individual acting as an attorney for his fellow citizens. Late medieval political theorists believed that government should act as a balancer and/or mixer of interests for the benefit and satisfaction of the majority. Republicanism flourished in English society with the rise of liberal economic thought and mercantilism in the sixteenth century, with a concomitant mistrust for the king and his ability to govern effectively. Although the living English constitution required that law making be carried out by both the Crown and the Houses of Parliament, the Whig principle of legislative supremacy became so popular that by 1649 Parliament had been established as the supreme law-making body.

There are three theories of representation in the application of republicanism: the mandate theory, the independence theory, and the mandate and independence theories combined. In mandate theory, the representative does only what his or her constituents say they want done. In independence theory, once a representative is chosen the representative is free to do what he or she feels is right. In mandate and independence theory combined, an attempt is made to balance both the constituents' and the representative's interests for reasons of political stability. In mandate theory the representative is a delegate or agent chosen merely to look after the interests of the attentive public. In independence theory it is assumed the representative is typical of those he or she represents, shares their characteristics, but may lead individual interested parties to less parochial opinions. Both mandate and independence theory are concerned about the means by which a representative is chosen, whether it is by election, for example, or by lot, or by a pattern of succession. Republicanism continuously debates the question of what constitutes true and just representation. *See also* ENGLISH CONSTITUTION, p. 26; JOHN LOCKE, p. 43; NATURAL LAW AND NATURAL RIGHTS, p. 50; VIRGINIA PLAN, p. 64.

Significance   Republicanism provides the theoretical basis for the American constitutional system. The writers of the federal Constitution combined the thought of John Locke with their own experience under the English constitution and common law to form the concept of limited government by consent of the governed. The framers had experienced many different types of government in the several colonies. They had suffered under the weak and ineffective government of the Articles of Confederation. They were convinced, therefore, that the best model for government was one in which legislative supremacy, majority rule, popular sovereignty, and representation prevailed. Any federal government should have at least these characteristics, they reasoned, but how much power relative to the states should a central government have? Obviously, to be efficient and effective the central government must have more power than it had under the Articles of Confederation. Yet federal power should be limited to the extent it would not encroach upon local and individual rights. Representation should be maximized, but small groups or factions should be prevented from gaining too much power. The framers were thus attracted to the Virginia Plan, which established a bicameral legislature. The Virginia Plan combined a larger house with greater or more direct representation (smaller groups, specific interests) with a smaller house with less direct representation (larger groups, diversified interests). Small states felt they were disadvantaged because of their small populations. The Connecticut Compromise addressed this concern by establishing equal representation for all states in the Senate, giving the upper house a point of view based on broader and more national interests. The Constitution also guaranteed every state a republican form of government in Article IV, Section 4. The first Supreme Court case concerned with this clause was *Luther v. Borden* (7 Howard 1: 1849), in which the Court said through Chief Justice Roger B. Taney that the issue of which of two rival governments in Rhode Island was the proper one should be decided by Congress, not by the Court. The Court held that representation was a political question that should be decided by the people through their representatives. Although the Court has since intervened in the electoral process to ensure the approximate equal value of each citizen's vote, the purpose of the intervention has consistently been to maintain the basic principle of republicanism: government by the people through majority rule.

Separation of Powers   The doctrine and practice of dividing the powers of government among several of its constituent parts in order to prevent the abusive concentration of power in any one part. The separation of powers embodied in the federal Constitution has two dimensions: a *functional* distinction between government and people, and between legislature, executive, and judiciary; and a *territorial* distinction between central and state governments. A related doctrine and practice is that of checks and balances. Sometimes the framers used checks generically for any type of block against absolute power, of which the separation of powers was one example, but more typically they used checks specifically for a device that simultaneously softened and implemented the separation of powers. Checks softened the separation of powers because they allowed, indeed they required, the concurrence of one branch in the work properly assigned to another branch, and they implemented the separation of powers because they specified the controls each part of government had over other parts. In what was hardly an exhaustive list, John Adams counted eight checks and balances in the Constitution: central government vs. states, House vs. Senate, Congress vs. President, Senate vs. President (in treaties and appointments), the people vs. their elected representatives, the Senate vs. the state legislatures (in the original formula for electing United States Senators), and the people vs. the Electoral College.

The territorial separation of powers is discussed in this Dictionary under Federalism. This entry concentrates on the functional separation of powers, specifically the division of government into legislative, executive, and judicial branches. The functional separation found in the federal Constitution had both theoretical and practical origins. The first discussion of separation of power theory is found in Greek thought. Plato's distinction between guardians, auxiliaries, and craftsmen in the *Republic* is a division of social functions, however, and not of governmental power. Aristotle's "mean" forms of government, i.e., polity and aristocracy, and his distinction between the deliberative, magistrative, and judicial functions of government (*Politics*, Book IV, Chapters 9–11 and 14–16) were the first true governmental applications of separation theory. In his attempt to analyze the way the Roman Republic combined the power of the consuls, the senate, and the people, Polybius in about 118 B.C. coined the term "mixed" government. His analysis, continued by Cicero in 43 B.C., reappeared in modern form in Sir Thomas Smith's *De Republica Anglorum* (1583) and in James Harrington's *Oceana* (1656). Harrington recommended a division between senate, people, and magistracy. Despite his absolutist practices, Oliver Cromwell three years earlier had written into his *Instrument of Government* a separation of power between the executive (the Lord Protector) and Parliament. John Locke's *Second Treatise of Government* (1690) championed a distinction between the legislative, executive, and federative branches, although he thought the legislature should dominate. Charles de Secondat, better known as the Baron de Montesquieu, is usually credited with having first formulated in his *The Spirit of Laws* (1748) the legislative-executive-judicial separation theory later embodied in the federal Constitution. In fact, however, the Constitution differs from Montesquieu's theory in many essential respects, such as an elected executive, Congress's power to impeach, and the absence of estates. Sir William Blackstone's *Commentaries on the Laws of England* (1765) insisted upon a separation between the executive and the legislative branches. One other author deserves mention, even though his separation theory appeared after the federal Constitution was drafted. In the first part of his *Metaphysics of Morals* (1797), Immanuel Kant elaborated a philosophical justification for Montesquieu's tripartite scheme. More names could be added. In his *Defense of the Constitution* (1786), John Adams claimed to find at least a dozen authors who advocated the doctrine of separation of powers.

Historian Benjamin F. Wright, Jr., has argued that early American governmental experience was at least as important as theory was in shaping the separation of powers in the federal Constitution. The separation between the executive and the legislature had begun with the establishment of the House of Burgesses in Virginia in 1619, especially with its strengthening in 1624. This pattern was substantially copied in all the colonies except Rhode Island and Connecticut, even though the dominance of royal governors hardly made separation an equal division of power. Bicameralism first appeared in Massachusetts in 1644 and eventually spread to all the other colonies except Pennsylvania. Even though its origins are more obscure, a separate judiciary had been established in several colonies by the mid-seventeenth century, and in all the colonies before the Revolution. In the period between 1776 and 1784, all the states except Rhode Island and Connecticut wrote new constitutions, and all of them except Pennsylvania asserted the importance of separation of powers, especially Virginia, North Carolina, and Georgia. Yet only New York, New Hampshire, and Massachusetts refused to put the executive under the domination of the legislature. This reluctance was because of the hatred the states had for abusive royal governors. All the states except Pennsylvania and Georgia adopted bicameral legislatures. The Articles of Confederation, ratified in 1781, was not influenced by the separation of powers doctrine because of the pervasive distrust of a strong executive and because of the insistence of the individual states upon their autonomy. The few powers allowed to the central government were dominated by the unicameral Congress, with no judicial system and with an executive council so weak it disbanded after its first meeting. It was the inadequacies of government under the Articles that created a consensus in favor of a strong separation of powers in the Constitutional Convention. Benjamin Franklin and Roger Sherman—and, outside the Convention, Thomas Paine—were the sole dissenting voices. Still, the exact shape of the separation of powers in the new government emerged only after extended debate on the convention floor. *See also* CONSTITU-

TION OF THE UNITED STATES OF AMERICA, p. 19; FEDERALISM, p. 29; CARL FRIEDRICH, p. 33.

Significance   Separation of powers is the necessary structural support for the functional division of governmental power that is the foundation of constitutional democracy. It prevents government from obtaining tyrannical power over groups and individuals. The critiques of the federal Constitution's separation of powers doctrine fall into three categories. (1) Totalitarian theorists reject it because they reject any separation of power, favoring instead the concentration of power in an enlightened single authority such as the Philosopher-King, *le Roi-Soleil, il Duce, der Führer*, or the Party. (2) Some proponents of the separation of powers argue that the American version is so extreme as to be inefficient. This group of critics includes many British writers and the American historian J. Allen Smith. (3) Other proponents of the separation of powers argue that the American version is ineffective. They point out that each period of American history has been marked by the unchecked power of one branch or another. In the early years, it was Congress; then came a powerful Supreme Court under John Marshall; in the modern era the nation has a strong presidency, culminating in the imperial presidency of the 1970s and 1980s. Several crucial factors in the recent growth of presidential power were clearly unforeseen by the framers. They include the extraconstitutional role of the president as the head of his party in Congress, the president's ability to appeal directly to the people through the electronic media, and the need of government to deal instantaneously with nuclear attack. Despite the changing fortunes of each functional division of the federal government, the doctrine of separation of powers continues to be the chief structural cornerstone of American constitutionalism.

Social Contract   A theoretical justification for the consensual basis of human society and government. Social contract theory involves two concepts, the governmental contract and the social contract proper, each of which has a history extending back into antiquity. The concept of a governmental contract (*pactum subjectionis*) holds that the relation between a people and its rulers arises from a mutual agreement between both parties. This notion is found in the Old and New Testaments; Roman law; ancient German and Frankish law; feudalism; medieval thought, particularly in Manegold of Lautenbach and Thomas Aquinas; conciliarism, especially in Nicholas of Cusa and Marsilius of Padua; the development of bourgeois economic interests; the Reformation, notably the Huguenots; the Counter-Reformation

(Bellarmine, Suarez, and Mariana); modern thinkers (Hobbes, Locke, Hume, Rousseau, Pufendorf, Althusius, Grotius, Kant, and Fichte); and in the constitutional phase of Rawls's *A Theory of Justice* (1971). While the concept of governmental contract was usually invoked as a limitation on governmental authority, including the rights of rebellion and regicide, Hobbes and Spinoza used it also as a justification for absolute monarchy. But most defenders of absolute sovereignty have avoided the dangers of governmental contract theory and instead held theories of the divine right of kings, as in Barclay and Filmer, or papal absolutism.

The concept of a social contract proper (*pactum unionis*) holds that the establishment of any society greater than the family or clan arises from a mutual agreement, historical or hypothetical, among all the individuals of the society. This theory has three main versions, each distinguished by its account of the relationship between the social contract and morality. The first version states that individuals in the state of nature preceding the contract are already subject to a moral natural law. Representatives of this position include Cicero, Richard Hooker, Vitoria, Molina, Locke, and Grotius. The second version states that individuals in the state of nature are not yet under a moral law of any sort. Indeed, the social contract is the foundation of morality, rather than vice versa. Representatives of this position include the Greek Sophists and Epicureans, Hobbes, Spinoza, and Rousseau. Despite his explicit rejection of a social contract, Hume's foundation of both morality and society built upon an informal utilitarian agreement among individuals is not easily distinguished from social contract theory. The third version, held mainly by Kant and those influenced by him, especially Fichte and Rawls, holds that the social contract is preceded by and founded on moral law. But the moral law itself, as seen in the formulation of Kant's categorical imperative, is the result of an ideal original contract with all other human beings. *See also* JOHN LOCKE, p. 43; MAYFLOWER COMPACT, p. 47; NATURAL LAW AND NATURAL RIGHTS, p. 50; JOHN RAWLS, p. 52.

Significance   Social contract theory as a legitimating idea for government enjoys almost universal recognition today, even in those totalitarian regimes where it is violated in practice. The American colonists felt an urgent need for such a legitimating idea. It is seen in the Mayflower Compact of 1620 through the federal Constitution of 1787. Yet the theory of a social contract proper, with the exception of its Kantian and neo-Kantian (Rawlsian) version, has been discarded for several reasons. First, the existence of a state of nature has been discredited by both historians and anthropologists. Second, political thinkers such as Marx and McPherson have exposed the economic individualism that fed the growth of social contract theory. Third, Aristotelians and most twentieth-century Catholic social thinkers have insisted that human sociability and morality are based in human nature itself and are not the creations of arbitrary choice. It is instructive to compare Locke's version of the social contract with Rousseau's. For Locke, individuals who enter into the social contract retain their own wills, even though they are limited by the will of the majority. For Rousseau, individuals abandon their own will to the general will. This difference is reflected in the American and French revolutions respectively, the former concentrating on individual economic freedoms, the latter accelerating into a program for total social reform, often at the expense of individual liberties.

State Constitutions   The fundamental laws of the respective states within the United States of America. State constitutions are not required by the federal Constitution, which provides merely for a "republican form of government" in each state. However, there is a universal tradition of state constitutions antedating the Constitutional Convention and serving as one of its main inspirations. The history of state constitutions can be divided into three phases: colonial charters, revolutionary constitutions, and subsequent developments. Each of the thirteen colonies except New Jersey and Delaware had a charter. Most of these charters were land grants to companies or individuals and included no provisions for self-government by the colonists. Virginia's second charter (1609) required that the London Company's legislation conform with British law and be subject to review by the king in council, a stipulation found in later charters as well. This was not a completely empty requirement because historian E. B. Russell calculated that 5.5 percent of the 8,563 colonial laws were ruled invalid on review. This meant, of course, that company law was limited by a more fundamental law, which laid the foundation for judicial review. It was under the third Virginia charter (1618) that the General Assembly was established, the first instance of representative government in America. The Fundamental Orders drafted by the towns in the Connecticut valley (1639) was the first citizen-drafted constitution in Anglo-American history. William Penn's first version of the Frame of Government for Pennsylvania (1682) contained a closely reasoned statement of the nature of constitutionalism, the first formula for amending a constitution, and the first suggestion of a constitutional convention.

The Revolutionary period of state constitutions began on May 15, 1776, when the Continental Congress began to prepare for independence from Great Britain. New Hampshire and South Carolina had drafted temporary constitutions earlier that year, and Congress now informed them and the other colonies that reconciliation with Great Britain was hopeless and that permanent constitutions were needed. At the same time, Congress began work on the Articles of Confederation, which were approved by Congress in 1777 but not ratified until 1781. The Virginia constitution was completed in June 1776 and served as a model for the others. New Jersey, Delaware, Pennsylvania, Maryland, and North Carolina completed their statements of fundamental law before the end of that year. Georgia and New York (and Vermont, even though it was not yet a state) completed their constitutions in 1777, Massachusetts in 1780, and New Hampshire in 1784. Massachusetts and New Hampshire took longer because their town meetings were determined that the drafting and ratification process would be as democratic as possible. This concern was not so apparent in the other states. Massachusetts is the only state of the original thirteen still operating under its original constitution. The only states that did not draft new constitutions were Connecticut and Rhode Island. They simply revised their colonial charters. Of the Revolutionary era constitutions, only those of New York and Massachusetts provided for an executive who was popularly elected and endowed with broad administrative powers. In all the other states, distrust of kings and royal governors led constitution writers to put the executive and judiciary under the domination of a strong legislature. A number of states, most notably Maryland, set property requirements for voters and officeholders. Few of the state constitutions had well-developed bills of rights, and several had no provisions for amendments.

Subsequent developments in state constitution writing give one an overwhelming impression of constant change. Fourteen states have adopted new constitutions since World War II. Discounting Rhode Island, only 19 states have kept their original constitutions, and even those have been thoroughly revised. By the end of 1979, there had been 4,603 state constitutional amendments. Why this general instability in state constitutions, as compared with the stability of the federal Constitution? One factor is the increasing dominance of the central government, which obviously has limited the powers of the states. Another is faulty governmental structures in state governments that the federal Constitution has been able to avoid. For example, the states eventually decided that total legislative dominance hindered efficient government. They then moved to establish separation of powers among the legislative, executive, and judicial branches. A third factor is that state constitutions have included many laws of a nonfundamental nature. The Louisiana constitution of 1921, for example, contained almost 250,000 words. The current Georgia constitution contains over 600,000 words. The main reasons for such long documents are no doubt that normal legislative processes will adequately regulate certain state and local issues, and the successful struggle of many groups to have their special interests given constitutional protection. A fourth and final reason for instability in state constitutions, dependent in part upon the first three, is that few state constitutions have the sacred aura attached to the federal document. The states use four methods to change their constitutions: (1) legislative proposals (used by all the states); (2) popular initiatives for limited changes (used by 17 states); (3) constitutional commissions (required by statute in 16 states); and (4) constitutional conventions. Constitutional commissions, which study the current constitution and make recommendations for change, were used in 21 states during the 1970s. Constitutional conventions, which adopt proposals for constitutional change, were held in 10 states during the 1970s. In all states but Delaware, the proposals adopted by a constitutional convention must be ratified by the voters. Of all the amendments adopted between 1972 and 1979, most were concerned with taxation and financing (20.2 percent), various state functions (12.1 percent), changes in the legislative branch (11.4 percent), and changes in the judicial branch (11.4 percent). A number of resources for improving state constitutions are available. Beginning with its first edition of the *Model State Constitution* (1921), the National Municipal League has provided numerous publications and other services. Also helpful in the process of streamlining state constitutions are the Council of State Governments, the United States Advisory Commission on Intergovernmental Relations, and the League of Women Voters. *See also* CONSTITUTIONALISM, HISTORICAL DEVELOPMENT OF, p. 15; CONSTITUTION OF THE UNITED STATES OF AMERICA, p. 19; FEDERALISM, p. 29; SEPARATION OF POWERS, p. 56.

Significance   State constitutions have a proud past. They are a clear witness to the deep-rooted American belief in written law. The earliest state constitutions were also the schools in which the framers of the federal Constitution learned their trade. State constitutions guided their citizens through most of the nation's rapid territorial, economic, and population expansion. The present condition of many state constitutions is less shining, however. The modern tendency is to make the state constitution an extended piece of omnibus legislation or a set of guarantees for special interest groups. The state constitution reform movement has attempted to address such problems and foster improvements, maintaining that better state government cannot be worked out by the individual states in isolation. The social, political, and economic problems inherent in contemporary American federalism must be solved before thoroughgoing state constitutional reform can be accomplished.

Virginia Plan   A set of fifteen resolutions or proposals presented to the Constitutional Convention on May 29, 1787, by Edmund Randolph, governor of Virginia. The Virginia Plan, also referred to as the Randolph Plan, although it was written largely by James Madison, proposed the creation of a strong central government. In fact the central government would have virtually unlimited powers, which the Virginia Plan described as "national." The plan said the Articles of Confederation should be "corrected and enlarged" so as to provide for the "common defense, security of liberty, and general welfare" of the nation. The proposal offered by Governor Randolph went far beyond the initial vision of many of the delegates to the convention. They thought the purpose of the meeting was to amend the Articles of Confederation. The Articles had created a federal government with few powers relative to the states. The Virginia Plan provided for a national government with power *over* the states. In the end, much of the plan was included in the Constitution. The Virginia Plan suggested the replacement of the unicameral Continental Congress with a legislature consisting of two houses. It called for the legislature to have the power to legislate "in all cases to which separate states are incompetent, or in which the harmony of the United States may be interrupted by the exercise of individual legislation." The national legislature would also have the power to negate any law passed by the states that it determined to be contrary to the best interests of the union. The proposal included the creation of an executive branch of government to oversee the administration of the laws and a national judiciary of one or more supreme tribunals, along with a system of lower national courts, to interpret the laws. The most controversial part of the Virginia Plan was a proviso that made the voting power of both houses of Congress proportional to "quotas of contribution, or number of free inhabitants, or by the amount of property or population" in each state. Small states rebelled against this idea since they would obviously be disadvantaged in such a system. New Jersey countered with a plan of its own, charging that the Virginia Plan would totally usurp state sovereignty. The debate over proportional versus equal representation was resolved through a compromise approved on July 16 that gave states proportional representation in the House and equal representation in the Senate. The Virginia Plan set the agenda for the entire Constitutional Convention. Its brilliant and innovative propositions captured the imagination of the delegates and forced them either to agree or amend. *See also* CONSTITUTION OF THE UNITED STATES OF AMERICA, p. 19; *THE FEDERALIST*, p. 31; SEPARATION OF POWERS, p. 56.

Significance   The Virginia Plan of union provided both foundation and substance for the federal Constitution. It provided the impetus behind the arguments and decisions concerning what type of government the United States was to establish, whether it was to be federal, meaning at this time a confederation of sovereign states, or national. The old Federalists said nationalism would be fatal to liberty. The Nationalists said federalism had proven itself to be incompetent under the Articles of Confederation. The Nationalists finally won the argument, and a central governmental system was established. To make that decision palatable, however, the Senate was converted from a representation of formal property interests to a protection of the interests of the separate states. In summary, the Virginia Plan proposed a bicameral legislature, the power of the legislature to pass laws directly related to individuals, the creation of an executive branch with authority to enforce national laws, and a national judiciary with a Supreme Court. It gave the nation Article IV, Section 3 of the Constitution, which says that the legislature, executive, and judiciary are all bound by the same oath to support the Constitution. It successfully established the Guarantee Clause of Article IV, Section 4, which mandates a republican form of government in every state. The idea of taking a national census from which the allotment for representatives for each state would be derived also came from the Virginia Plan. The success and longevity of the United States Constitution is in no small way indebted to this set of proposals from a remarkable group of men living within a few miles of each other in the Virginia Tidewater. They successfully challenged the Constitutional Convention to share their vision of ordered liberty.

2. Judicial Power

Overview, 69

Article III, 73

OVERVIEW

The judicial power of the United States is conveyed by Article III of the Constitution. Among other things, this article sets forth the requisites of the exercise of federal judicial power; it defines the jurisdiction of the federal courts. Federal jurisdiction extends to matters in the form of a bona fide case or controversy, and is divided between cases making a first appearance before the courts (cases on original jurisdiction) and those cases that have been heard by other courts previously (appellate jurisdiction). Federal jurisdictional requirements are met if a case involves a federal constitutional issue or involves a federal statute or treaty. Cases having an interstate character also qualify for the exercise of federal judicial power. Cases based on diversity of citizenship, cases where the parties are citizens of two or more different states, fall under federal jurisdiction. In *Erie Railroad Company v. Tompkins* (304 U.S. 64: 1938), the Court held that federal courts must apply the governing law of the state in diversity cases. Citizen suits against states are also permitted under certain conditions. In *Maine v. Thiboutot* (448 U.S. 1: 1980), the Court held that civil suits may be filed against state and local governments for actions which violate any federal statute.

In order for judicial power to be properly exercised, the question dealt with in a case must be "judicial" in nature. Court decisions may not be made subject to the "review and revision" of the other branches of government. This "finality of judgment" requirement was asserted in the opinions submitted in *In Re Hayburn's Case* (2 Dallas 409: 1792). Article III also discusses the appellate jurisdiction of the United States Supreme Court. This power is subject to the regulation of Congress. The Court upheld congressional restriction of appellate jurisdiction in *Ex Parte McCardle* (7 Wallace 506: 1869). In deference to the shared power between the federal and state levels, the abstention doctrine has been developed. This doctrine requires that federal courts defer to state proceedings at least until they are concluded. The applicability of this doctrine was recently reiterated in *Middlesex County Ethics Commission v. Garden State Bar Association* (457 U.S. 423: 1982). Article III also contains a compensation clause that prohibits reduction of judicial salaries. The intent of this provision is to ensure the independence of the courts by freeing them from reprisal in the form of salary reduction for controversial decisions. A recent case examined a legislative attempt to withhold salary increases previously set by law. The Court held in *United States v. Will* (449 U.S. 200: 1980) that while judges are not entitled to increases, once any increase has taken effect, it cannot be withdrawn or diminished. Another aspect of protecting judicial independence involves immunity of judges from civil law suits against actions taken while performing their official duties. The Court held that this immunity is virtually absolute in *Stump v. Sparkman* (435 U.S. 349: 1978).

A major judicial power issue is not addressed by Article III. This is the power of judicial review, which would permit the courts to invalidate legislative and executive actions if those actions are found to be incompatible with the Constitution. The power of judicial review was first asserted by the Court in *Marbury v. Madison* (1 Cranch 137: 1803). The extent to which the Court might use this power to negate legislative initiatives could be seen in *Dred Scott v. Sandford* (19 Howard 393: 1857). The question of the scope of judicial review and the standards by which courts should conduct review have been addressed on numerous occasions. In *United States v. Carolene Products Company* (304 U.S. 144: 1938), for example, the Court indicated that regulation affecting individual liberties might be subject to a more scrutinizing review. On the other hand, *Carolene* suggested that the Court ought to generally defer to legislative enactments aimed at regulating economic activities. At least in more recent years, the Court has adopted such a position. In *Federal Power Commission v. Natural Gas Pipeline Company* (315 U.S. 575: 1942), the Court held that rate-making decisions of regulatory agencies would not be substantively reviewed. More recently, the Court said in *Motor Vehicle Manufacturers Association v. State Farm Mutual Insurance Company* (463 U.S. 29: 1983) that while agency decisions must be supported by "reasoned analysis," the role of the courts was not to substitute its policy preferences for those adopted by the agency. Judicial review of actions of municipal officials may occur, but it is subject to the limitations stemming from principles of federalism. In *Rizzo v. Goode* (423 U.S. 362: 1976), the Court found federal court intervention into local police practices inappropriate without a showing of a direct linkage between the officials actually named in the suit and specific violations of protected rights.

As mentioned earlier, before federal jurisdiction can be accessed, a matter must take the form of a bona fide case or controversy. In other words, the parties must be truly "adverse." In *Muskrat v. United States* (219 U.S. 346: 1911), the Court refused to respond to a suit where

Congress had literally designated the parties for the sole purpose of getting the Court to respond to the constitutional questions contained in a legislative act. For the Court to respond to hypothetical or contrived issues would put it in the position of rendering advisory opinions, a role incompatible with the concept of separation of power. Before the courts may be accessed, parties must possess standing to sue. The parties must have a legal interest in the outcome of the litigation, have suffered some kind of direct injury, and be legitimately contending with one another. The interests of a large group of litigants may be represented through a class action. In *Gulf Oil Company v. Bernard* (452 U.S. 89: 1981), the Court examined the nature of federal court discretion in supervising such actions. The standing issue has produced a number of interesting decisions. The first important case was *Frothingham v. Mellon* (262 U.S. 447: 1923), which held that a federal taxpayer had insufficient injury from that status to permit challenge to the way Congress had chosen to spend tax revenues. The *Frothingham* decision remained virtually unaltered until late in the Warren Court period, with the case of *Flast v. Cohen* (392 U.S. 83: 1968). In *Flast,* the Court permitted a taxpayer challenge provided it was closely enough connected to a specific constitutional violation. Litigant Flast had created a close enough "nexus" between the taxpayer status and the First Amendment establishment clause to achieve standing to challenge a federal spending program that made public monies available to nonpublic schools. The Court diminished the need to demonstrate injury to a specific legally protected right in *Association of Data Processing Service Organizations v. Camp* (397 U.S. 150: 1970). So long as an injury falls within a "zone of interests" touched by a statute, access to courts may occur. Two years later, the Court upheld the need to show injury "in fact" in *Laird v. Tatum* (408 U.S. 1: 1972). Allegations of a "substantial" chilling of a right is not a sufficient substitute for a specific and present or future injury. In *United States v. Students Challenging Regulatory Agency Procedures* (412 U.S. 669: 1973), the Court relaxed the direct injury standing requirement for "public interest" litigants by permitting a suit alleging aesthetic and environmental injury. In *Singleton v. Wulff* (428 U.S. 106: 1976), the Court held that a group of physicians could not only sue for their own losses of Medicaid reimbursements for performing abortions, but could also seek relief based on third-party assertion of their patients' rights. Finally, the Court held in *Warth v. Seldin* (422 U.S. 490: 1975) that a group could not satisfy standing requirements with only "generalized" claims of injury. Suits brought by organizational litigants must still show a direct injury just as individuals must. Standing can also be lost because a case becomes moot. A moot case is one for which the courts can no longer provide relief to a party because the dispute on which the case is based no longer exists. An example of the Court's refusal to allow judicial power to be exercised in a moot case can be seen in *DeFunis v. Odegaard* (416 U.S. 312: 1974).

The last set of cases in this chapter involves the "political question" doctrine. A political question is one in which the substance of the issue is primarily political or involves a matter clearly assigned to one of the other two branches of government. A political question is therefore one not appropriate for judicial consideration. In other words, political questions are not justiciable issues. The first statement of the doctrine came in *Luther v. Borden* (7 Howard 1: 1849), in which the Court refused to make a determination about whether a state had a "republican" form of government. Rather, the Court held that enforcement of the guaranty clause had been committed to the Congress, not to the courts, by the Constitution. The issue of legislative appportionment was considered for many years to be a political question until the Warren Court held otherwise in *Baker v. Carr* (369 U.S. 186: 1962). Soon after, the Court held that House exclusion of a duly elected member did not constitute a political question in *Powell v. McCormack* (395 U.S. 486: 1969). Two more recent Burger Court decisions demonstrate that the doctrine is occasionally appropriate. In *O'Brien v. Brown* (409 U.S. 1: 1972), the Court invoked the doctrine in holding that federal court intervention in the proceedings of a national party nominating convention constitutes a nonjusticiable political question. And in *Goldwater v. Carter* (444 U.S. 996: 1979), the Court refused to review a case brought against the president for his termination of a defense treaty without congressional approval. In deciding not to review this case, several members of the Court indicated that foreign relations matters, such as treaty termination, come under the political question doctrine.

Article III   Defines federal judicial power. Article III is the shortest of the articles dealing with the three branches of the national government. It contains three sections, the first two of which are devoted to the structure, jurisdiction, and personnel of the federal judiciary. Section 1 provides that the "judicial power of the United States shall be vested in one Supreme Court." Thus, by constitutional mandate, the federal judiciary must contain a court structured to operate atop any other constituent courts that might be created. Those other courts are handled indirectly, however, as Section 1 continues, "and in such inferior courts as the Congress may from time to time ordain and establish." Courts created under this authority are known as Article III courts and may properly exercise federal judicial power. Courts may also be created by Congress under its Article I, necessary and proper clause authority. These courts, known as "legislative" courts, may be given nonjudicial functions as well. Judges of these courts are selected through processes set by Congress and serve under conditions that may be different from those of Article III courts. Article III court judges "both of the supreme and inferior courts, shall hold offices during good behavior." This effectively grants federal judges life tenure. Section 1 continues by saying that federal judges "shall, at stated times, receive for their services, a compensation which shall not be diminished during their continuance in office." This language provides political insulation for judges such that their independence cannot be threatened through manipulation of salaries.

Section 2 defines the jurisdiction of the federal courts. Section 2 provides that the "judicial power shall extend to all cases, in law and equity, arising under this Constitution, the laws of the United States, and treaties made ... under their authority." This defines federal jurisdiction in terms of subject matter. Any cases dealing with the mentioned substantive matters are able to access federal courts. Section 2 goes on to specify particular parties who qualify for the exercise of federal judicial power. Federal jurisdiction extends to cases involving ambassadors, other "public ministers and consuls," and international parties in admiralty and maritime cases, and where the United States itself is a party. Federal jurisdictional requirements are also satisfied by cases with an interstate character covering questions between two or more states, a state and citizens of another state (subsequently redefined by the Eleventh Amendment), citizens of different states, citizens of the same state claiming lands under grants of different states, and controversies between a state or its citizen and foreign states, citizens, or subjects.

Section 2 then distinguishes between the original and appellate jurisdiction of the Supreme Court. The Supreme Court has original jurisdiction (the power to be the first court to hear a particular case) in all matters "affecting ambassadors, other public ministers and consuls, and those in which a state shall be party. . . ." Original jurisdiction in all kinds of federal cases is left to whatever lower courts Congress designates. Appellate jurisdiction extends to the Supreme Court in all cases "both as to law and equity, with such exceptions, and under such regulations as the Congress shall make." The law and equity reference reflects an English concept that distinguishes cases where damages are sought (cases in law) from cases seeking injunctive relief (cases in equity). The provision on appellate jurisdiction at least theoretically subjects the Supreme Corut to substantial control by the Congress.

Section 2 concludes by guaranteeing jury trial to persons charged with federal crimes and that trials will be held in the state within which the crime was allegedly committed. Section 3 defines the crime of treason, establishes some conditions that must exist in order to convict anyone of that crime, and limits the Congress from the Old English practices of "attainders of treason" that shall produce "corruption of blood" or inability of a traitor's heirs to inherit from him or her. *See also* ARTICLE I, p. 183; ARTICLE II, p. 139; COURT OF APPEALS, p. 669; DISTRICT COURT, p. 671; JUDICIAL REVIEW, p. 627; LEGISLATIVE COURTS, p. 630.

Significance   Article III establishes the Supreme Court, creates the process by which additional courts may be established, and defines federal judicial power. Article III establishes some intriguing political dynamics. It grants to the legislative branch the authority to establish additional courts and define their jurisdiction. The Congress also has the power to determine the size of the Supreme Court. Indeed, the Supreme Court has functioned with as few as five or six justices early in our constitutional history and with as many as ten justices at one point during the Civil War. Clearly, the power to add justices of the Supreme Court could be used to influence decisional outcomes. While the Congress resisted what would have been the most blatant political pressure through the change in court size when it refused to adopt Roosevelt's "court-packing" scheme in 1937, power over the size of the Court brings with it some leverage. Similarly, Article III vests Congress with authority over the Supreme Court's appellate jurisdiction. Since the Court operates almost exclusively as an appeals court, this congressional power is substantial. Our constitutional history reveals a number of occasions when Congress has attempted to influence the direction of the Court by alteration of appellate jurisdiction. For example, fearing judicial invalidation of Reconstruction, the Congress withdrew appeals access to the Court for any case stemming from Reconstruction. In the case of *Ex Parte McCardle* (7 Wallace 506: 1869), the Court held that its power had been constitutionally restricted. At least theoretically, Congress has the power to remove all appellate jurisdiction from the Court.

Furthermore, the judicial selection process is highly political. Article II empowers the president to nominate all federal judges with the advice and consent of the Senate. To a certain extent, the political vulnerability of the Court is mitigated by the "good behavior" tenure provision, which allows federal judges to withstand changing political tides, and the protection from being subjected to decreases in compensation. One other mechanism which would have provided the Supreme Court with additional capacity to counteract political pressures was the power of judicial review. Article III is silent on the matter, although such review was considered by the Constitutional Convention. The judicial review function was established for the Court by its own decision in *Marbury v. Madison* (1 Cranch 137: 1803).

Article III also sets out the scope of federal judicial power. It requires that all courts operating from a source in Article III deal only with bona fide cases or controversies. This requirement creates a particular form for the exercise of judicial power. The courts known as constitutional courts are created under Article III, and are precluded from rendering advisory opinions by the cases and controversies language. Those courts created by Congress under provisions of Article I are known as legislative courts, and are not similarly limited. Legislative courts do not share the independence of Article III courts. They are generally established not only to function in a judicial or at least quasi-judicial fashion, but also to perform quasi-legislative and administrative functions. Article III refers to both original and appellate jurisdiction. While retaining original jurisdiction over the categories of cases enumerated in Article III, the Supreme Court is essentially an appellate court reviewing cases that have previously been heard by other courts. Pursuant to provisions of Section 1, Congress established the District Court as the principal federal court of original jurisdiction. Provided the substantive or party criteria for federal jurisdiction are present, most federal cases begin with the district court. Federal appellate power was lodged by Congress in the court of appeals, typically the first level of appeals review for federal cases. The Supreme Court has appellate jurisdiction over all cases coming from the Article III courts as well as cases from state courts of last resort, provided that an important enough federal issue is contained.

Diversity of Citizenship Jurisdiction

Erie Railroad Company v. Tompkins, **304 U.S. 64, 58 S.Ct. 817, 82 L.Ed. 1188 (1938)** Held that federal courts are bound to apply principles of state law in diversity of citizenship cases not governed by federal law. The Court's holding in *Erie Railroad Company v. Tompkins* reversed the policy on diversity cases that had been in place since virtually the passage of the Judiciary Act of 1789. Tompkins, a Pennsylvania citizen, was injured by an Erie Railroad Company train while walking along the right of way. He sued Erie Railroad, incorporated in New York, in a federal district court in New York. He claimed negligence on the part of the railroad, arguing that he was on a footpath frequently used by pedestrians, and that he was wrongfully struck by something projecting from the train. The railroad responded by asserting that under a holding of the highest court of Pennsylvania, Tompkins was no more than a trespasser and, therefore, that the railroad could have no liability. Tompkins disputed that interpretation of Pennsylvania law, but also argued that in the absence of definitive treatment of the matter by statute at the state level, the federal courts must independently determine the question of liability. In a 6–2 decision, the Supreme Court held for the railroad (with Justice Cardozo not participating).

In deciding as it did, the Court expressly overruled the precedent of *Swift v. Tyson* (16 Peters 1: 1842). The opinion of the Court was authored by Justice Brandeis, who framed the principal question as whether the "oft-challenged doctrine of *Swift v. Tyson* shall now be disapproved." The railroad contended that the Judiciary Act of 1789 required application of state common law. The obstacle was *Swift,* which had held that in diversity cases, federal courts could exercise "independent judgment as to what the 'common law' of the state is—or should be." Brandeis noted that criticism of this doctrine "became widespread." Further, he said that experience in using the doctrine "revealed its defects, political and social." The benefits expected from the doctrine simply "did not accrue." The uniformity that had been expected failed to materialize. The line between the "province of general law and that of local law developed a new well of uncertainties." Equal protection was prevented because "grave discrimination by non-citizens against citizens" was introduced and rights enjoyed under the "unwritten 'general law'" varied depending on whether enforcement was sought in a federal or a state court. The "injustice and confusion" stemming from *Swift v. Tyson* was "repeatedly urged" as a rationale for "abolishing or limiting diversity of citizenship jurisdiction." Indeed, Brandeis concluded that the "unconstitutionality" of the *Swift v. Tyson* doctrine "has now been made clear and compels" abandonment of it. He then articulated the new doctrine. Excepting matter stemming from the federal Constitution or federal law, "the law to be applied in any case is the law of the State." He went further and said that it is immaterial whether the applicable state law had been passed by a legislature or determined by its highest court. There is, Brandeis concluded, "no federal general common law." Congress may not declare "substance rules of common law applicable in a State. . . ." Though *Swift v. Tyson* had been the doctrine for almost a century, Brandeis suggested that "no lapse of time" should make the Court "hesitate" to correct the "unconstitutional assumption of power by courts" represented by that decision. Justices Butler and McReynolds concurred in finding for the railroad, but they felt the Court had impermissibly restricted congressional authority to prescribe rules governing diversity jurisdiction. *See also* ARTICLE III, p. 73; JURISDICTION, p. 629.

Significance   The Court held in *Erie Railroad Company v. Tompkins* (304 U.S. 64: 1938) that applicable state law will govern diversity of citizenship cases. The problem confronted by the Court in *Erie Railroad* was serious. *Swift v. Tyson* had held that in conferring diversity jurisdiction to federal courts, the Judiciary Act of 1789 had intended that the applicable "laws of the several states" was confined to statutory law. The effect of *Tyson* was to give federal courts independence to resolve diversity cases in the absence of formally controlling state statutes. It generated great nonuniformity because virtually every state had different federal and state common law to apply to commercial diversity cases. The intent of *Erie* was to create some greater likelihood of comparable decisions in federal and state courts through the use of the same procedural and substantive law. However, the track record of *Erie Railroad* did not live up to expectation. The independent federal influence is still seen in diversity cases. *Erie* did not create an easily applicable formula, certainly not one that requires mechanical utilization of state common law. While *Erie Railroad* reshaped policy on diversity jurisdiction, it has not precluded federal courts from moving outside state law. It is also important to note that *Erie* only applies to actions involving legally protected interests at the state level. The *Erie* restrictions on the exercise of federal judicial power do not apply where a case is based on any aspect of federal law.

Citizen Suit against State Government

Maine v. Thiboutot, **448 U.S. 1, 100 S.Ct. 2502, 65 L.Ed. 2d 555 (1980)**   Held that Section 1983 of Title 42 of the United States Code entitles persons to bring suit against state and local governments for denial of rights under any federal law. *Maine v. Thiboutot* expanded the right to sue state and local governments. The Thiboutots were notified by a state agency that they would lose certain benefits under the Aid to Families with Dependent Children (AFDC) portion of the Social Security Act. After exhausting administrative remedies, the Thiboutots brought suit in state court seeking review of the action. They also claimed violation of Section 1983 for deprivation of benefits under the Social Security Act. Section 1983 allows civil action against officials acting under "color" of law to deprive a citizen of rights secured "by the Constitution and laws of the United States." Prior to this case, suits could be brought only for claimed violations of constitutional or civil rights. The state court enjoined implementation of the benefit change. The Thiboutots also claimed recovery of their attorney fees under the Civil Rights Attorney's Fees Awards Act, but were denied. The state Supreme Court subsequently found the Thiboutots eligible for the attorney costs.

In a 6–3 decision, the U.S. Supreme Court held that Section 1983 provides remedy for such a case as this, and that litigants are entitled to recovery of attorney fees. The opinion of the Court was delivered by Justice Brennan. The decision hinged on an interpretation of the phrase "and laws" as used in Section 1983. Did it really apply to "all laws" or was it "limited to some subset of laws"? The Court used the plain language approach. The Congress "attached no modifiers" to the phrase, and the language was unambiguous. Even if some ambiguity could be said to exist, any "doubt" as to the meaning "has been resolved" by various judicial interpretations indicating, "explicitly or implicitly," that the remedy under Section 1983 "broadly encompasses violations of federal statutory law as well as constitutional law." Despite the "plain language," it was urged that the phrase "and laws" should be limited to "civil rights or equal protection laws." The Court examined the "scanty legislative history" concerning the addition of the phrase, and the conclusion "which emerges clearly" is that the legislative history "does not permit a definitive answer." That history certainly did not "demonstrate that the plain language was not intended." The Court then turned to the matter of whether the claims were covered by the Civil Rights Attorney's Fees Act of 1976. Again, through use of the "plain language" approach, the Court held that the statute covered fees for "any" Section 1983 action. The legislative history was "entirely compatible" with the "plain language" interpretation. The Court also rejected the contention that, even if all claims alleging deprivation of statutory rights were covered, the act did not apply to state courts. The Court saw the fee provision as part of the remedy available under Section 1983 "whether the action is brought in federal or state court."

Justice Powell, joined by Chief Justice Burger and Justice Rehnquist, dissented. He said the majority had "dramatically" expanded the liability of state and local officials to suit without giving sufficient consideration to the "consequences of its judgment." The reading given to Section 1983 is "anything but 'plain'" and runs counter to historical evidence. Powell criticized the "plain language" approach as "too simplistic a guide to the construction of Section 1983." He saw the practical effect of the decision as expanding the liability of state and local governments and their officials to suit whenever a person thinks he or she has been injured by the "administration of any federal-state cooperative program," whether or not it was related to equal protection or civil rights. This creates a "major new intrusion into state sovereignty under our federal system." The decision "makes new law with far-reaching consequences," and the Court did so without sufficient consideration of the critical issues of "congressional intent, national policy, and the force of past decisions." *See also* EQUITY JURISDICTION, p. 629; JUDICIAL REVIEW, p. 627; *RIZZO V. GOODE* (423 U.S. 362: 1976), p. 99.

Significance   The Court held that Section 1983 suits may be brought for alleged denial of rights under any federal statute in *Maine v. Thiboutot* (448 U.S. 1: 1980). The decision opened the prospect of a broader range of lawsuits that might be brought by citizens claiming injury under federal law. The Court depended on several precedents it viewed as leading to the decision in *Thiboutot*. In *Rosado v. Wyman* (397 U.S. 397: 1970), the Court held that Section 1983 suits were appropriate to "secure compliance" with the provisions of the Social Security Act on the part of "participating States." In *Scheuer v. Rhodes* (416 U.S. 232: 1974), a case arising out of the shootings at Kent State University in 1970, the Court held that officials responsible for calling out the National Guard were not immune from civil damages suits filed under Section 1983. In *Monell v. Department of Social Sciences* (436 U.S. 658: 1978), the Court extended *Scheuer* by holding that municipalities and local governing bodies were not immune from Section 1983 suits. The decision in *Thiboutot* to allow Section 1983 suits alleging violation of any federal law may prove to have a substantial impact on federal-state relationships. Given the extent to which federal statutes, especially those involving entitlement programs, intertwine with state governmental activities, state officials now become subject to direct legal action as a result of *Thiboutot*. Thus state governments and their officials have become subject to a greater degree of federal court power.

Finality of Judgment

In Re Hayburn's Case, **2 Dallas 409, 1 L.Ed. 436 (1792)** Established the principle that finality of judgment is an essential component of judicial power. *Hayburn's Case* involved a motion for mandamus filed by the attorney general asking the Circuit Court of Pennsylvania to act in a pension matter. A 1792 federal statute had authorized federal district courts to determine pension claims of invalid Revolutionary War veterans. The circuit courts were then required to submit their opinions to the secretary of war, who was empowered to accept or reject these judgments. After the case was argued before the Supreme Court, the Court postponed its decision. In the interim, Congress amended the process by which pensioners could obtain relief. Thus the Supreme Court never rendered a decision as such on the matter. Since this question had been considered by the circuit courts, the Supreme Court reporter included the opinion of the circuit courts of New York, Pennsylvania, and North Carolina. Sitting on the Circuit Court of New York at this time were Chief Justice Jay and Justice Cushing. Justices Wilson and Blair were members of the Circuit Court of Pennsylvania, and Justice Iredell served on the Circuit Court of North Carolina. The justices' views were contained in the circuit court opinion (part of which included comments in letter form directed to the president).

Hayburn's Case, though not a formal Supreme Court decision, did reflect the thinking of five of the six members of the Supreme Court at the time if one aggregates the individual opinions from the circuit court level. Thus the case is of value in representing the Court's position on the matter of finality. Chief Justice Jay and Justice Cushing referred to separation of our government into three "distinct and independent" branches. Encroachment on the "duty of each" was not to occur. Accordingly, neither the legislature nor the executive branch may assign duties to the judiciary except those that are "properly judicial" and that can be "performed in a judicial manner." The duties assigned in this situation were "not of that description." The decisions of the circuit court were first subject to the "consideration and suspension" of the secretary of war and then to the "revision" of the legislature. The Constitution does not permit the secretary of war or even the legislature to "sit as a Court of errors on the judicial acts or opinions of this court." Justices Wilson and Blair also spoke of the need for judicial independence. Key in their view was maintenance of separation of power. Courts and the legislature must remain distinct. The people, in forming the Constitution, "placed their judicial power not in Congress, but in 'courts.'" They saw assignment of the pension under the original statute as "not of a judicial nature." It "forms no part" of the power vested by the Constitution. They saw the statute as inappropriately allowing court judgments to be "revised and controlled" by the other branches. Such revision and control was "radically inconsistent with the independence of that judicial power which is vested in the courts," and consequently, with that "important principle" so "strictly observed" in the Constitution. Justice Iredell also expressed the view that the statute was unconstitutional "inasmuch as the decision of the court is not made final." *See also* ARTICLE III, p. 73; CASE OR CONTROVERSY, p. 583; JUDICIAL REVIEW, p. 627.

Significance   The Supreme Court indicated in *Hayburn's Case* (2 Dallas 409: 1792) that the Congress could not assign to the judiciary any functions that were not "judicial" in character. The members of the Court commenting on this case said that finality of judgment is an essential element of judicial power and its exercise. That condition is a natural outgrowth of the separation of power concept. The independence of the courts requires that their decisions not be subject to review and possible revision by the other branches. Similarly, the courts are not to provide counsel to the other branches through the rendering of advisory opinions. *Hayburn's Case* established from the outset of our constitutional history that federal judicial power extends only to situations outlined in Article III. Assignment of the pension claims as attempted here was viewed as wholly incompatible with the Constitution. Indeed, had the Congress not altered the claim process on its own, and had the Court eventually rendered a decision, this case would likely have established the power of judicial review, as there can be little doubt, from the opinions submitted by the justices acting in their role as circuit judges, that they would have found the statute unconstitutional.

Appellate Jurisdiction

***Ex Parte McCardle*, 7 Wallace 506, 19 L.Ed. 264 (1869)**
Upheld congressional authority to withdraw or withhold appellate jurisdiction from the U.S. Supreme Court. *Ex Parte McCardle* was one of a number of cases aimed at getting the Supreme Court to examine the constitutionality of Reconstruction. McCardle was a Southern newspaper editor who had been convicted by a military commission of sedition for publishing libelous articles. He appealed to the Supreme Court following denial of his petition for *habeas corpus* by the circuit court. The Supreme Court found that it possessed power to hear the case and took arguments. In an effort to prevent the Court from holding Reconstruction unconstitutional, Congress repealed the law authorizing jurisdiction to hear McCardle's case. The Court waited until the legislative activity had concluded before deciding on the effect of the repeal of jurisdiction. The Court then held unanimously that its jurisdiction had been constitutionally withdrawn by Congress.

The opinion of the Court was authored by Chief Justice Chase. The principal question was "necessarily" the matter of jurisdiction. Discussion of any other matter was seen as "useless, if not improper." While appellate jurisdiction is conferred by the Constitution, it is conferred with "such exceptions" and under "such regulations" as the "Congress shall make." Chase indicated that the Court had never existed without such exceptions and regulations, indicating presence of proscriptions on the Court flowing from the Judiciary Act of 1789. While that initial act may have described appellate jurisdiction in "affirmative" terms, it has been understood to "imply a negation of all such jurisdiction as not comprehended within it," even though the affirmative character of such legislation would naturally stand out. Here, however, the exception to appellate jurisdiction is not inferred. Rather, it is made in specific terms. The Habeas Corpus Act, which affirmed appellate jurisdiction, is "expressly repealed." It is "hardly possible to imagine a plainer instance of positive exception." Having established a clear absence of jurisdiction, Chase went on to say that the Court is "not at liberty to inquire into the motives of the legislature" on this point. Instead, the Court is confined to an examination of "power under the Constitution." The power to make exceptions to the appellate jurisdiction of the Supreme Court is "given by express words." Since jurisdiction is "power to declare the law," when jurisdiction "ceases to exist," the "only function remaining to the Court is that of announcing the fact and dismissing the cause." *See also* JUDICIAL REVIEW, p. 627; JURISDICTION, p. 629.

Significance   Ex Parte McCardle (7 Wallace 506: 1869) affirmed congressional power to define the appellate jurisdiction of the Supreme Court. The Court felt that any alternative interpretation had been foreclosed at the outset of our constitutional history. Two early cases were cited by the Court in *McCardle* as controlling precedents. The Judiciary Act of 1789 contained provisions on appellate jurisdiction, and in the case of *Wiscart v. Dauchy* (3 Dallas 321: 1796), the Court held that without such legislation, the Court would not have had power. In *Durousseau v. United States* (6 Cranch 307: 1810), the Court extended *Wiscart,* holding that affirmative legislative action on appellate jurisdiction also implied withholding or denial of jurisdiction where positive grants do not exist. The consequence of these decisions was that Congress's power to remove or alter Supreme Court appellate jurisdiction at will was acknowledged. In addition to the action taken in *McCardle* to insulate Reconstruction from Court review, there have been a number of congressional attempts to restrict Court access to particular issues. After a series of controversial decisions by the Warren Court in the late 1950s, a proposal known as the Jenner-Butler Amendment would have withdrawn appellate jurisdiction from the Supreme Court for various national security issues. The initiative failed, but the Court could not have mistaken the message sent by the attempt. More recently, bills seeking to "curb" the appellate power of the Supreme Court have been introduced on such issues as abortion, prayer in public schools, and busing. Clearly the power to make "exceptions" to the appellate jurisdiction of the Surpeme Court creates the possibility of political vulnerability for the Court.

Abstention

***Middlesex County Ethics Commission v. Garden State Bar Association* 457 U.S. 423, 102 S.Ct. 2515, 73 L.Ed. 2d 116 (1982)** Employed the abstention doctrine to limit federal court intervention into a pending state disciplinary proceeding. *Middlesex County Ethics Commission v. Garden State Bar Association* involved charges brought against an attorney by a local attorney ethics committee. The committee had been appointed by the state supreme court to examine violations of disciplinary rules stemming from the attorney's public statements, which were critical of a particular criminal trial and the presiding trial judge. Instead of responding to the charges, the attorney and three organizations, including the Garden State Bar Association, filed suit in a federal court attacking the disciplinary rule as vague, overbroad, and violative of free speech protections. The United States district court dismissed the action on the grounds that it should abstain from intervening in a state proceeding. The court of appeals, however, reversed, saying that the disciplinary proceeding was unlike state proceedings to which federal courts usually defer, and that it did not seem to afford an adequate opportunity to assess the constitutional issues involved. The court of appeals maintained its position on reconsideration despite an affidavit from the state supreme court that the disciplinary proceeding was judicial in nature, and that the constitutional issues would be fully and directly considered. In a unanimous decision, the Supreme Court held that the federal courts should abstain from intervening in such cases.

The opinion of the Court was authored by Chief Justice Burger. He said that the rationale for abstention had been "frequently reiterated." Included is the notion of "comity," which reflects a "proper respect for state functions" and the belief that the national government will "fare best" if the states and their institutions are "left free to perform their separate functions in their separate ways." "Minimal respect" for state processes precludes assuming that state courts "will not safeguard federal constitutional rights." The doctrine of abstention is "fully applicable" to other than criminal proceedings when "important state interests are involved." Where such interests exist, federal courts should abstain unless state law "clearly bars the interposition of the constitutional claims."

This case presented three issues: whether the Garden State Bar Association disciplinary hearing constituted an "ongoing state judicial proceeding"; whether important state interests were involved; and if there was adequate opportunity in the state proceeding to "raise constitutional challenges." Under New Jersey law, filing a complaint against an attorney with a local committee is "in effect a filing with the Supreme Court of the state," which has the authority to oversee the practice of law in the state. From the beginning, the disciplinary process is "judicial in nature." Thus, these are proceedings that "warrant federal court deference." The state interest in maintaining professional conduct by attorneys was seen as "extremely important." Finally, the Court responded to the contention that the disciplinary proceeding afforded "no opportunity" to make a federal constitutional challenge to the disciplinary rules. Burger noted that the defendant attorney failed to respond to the complaint at all and made no attempt to lodge any constitutional objections. Abstention is based on the proposition that a person should first "set up" and "rely upon his defense" in the state courts unless it "plainly appears" that this course would not afford adequate protection." In light of the "unique relationship" between the state supreme court and the local ethics committee, the Court concluded that the attorney would have an "adequate" and "abundant" opportunity to present his constitutional challenges. *See also* ABSTENTION, p. 575; FEDERALISM, p. 29; *YOUNGER V. HARRIS* (401 U.S. 37: 1971), p. 271.

Significance   The Court held that federal courts ought not intervene in state disciplinary proceedings in *Middlesex County Ethics Commission v. Garden State Bar Association* (457 U.S. 423: 1982). The Court based its decision on the abstention doctrine. This policy is designed to reduce conflict between federal and state courts by instructing that a federal court should not intervene in a state court case until the appropriate state courts have addressed the matter. The contemporary character of the abstention doctrine was substantively defined in *Younger v. Harris* (401 U.S. 37: 1971). The case involved a state prosecution of a socialist for violation of a state law making it a crime to belong to an organization advocating use of force to achieve its political objectives. A court decision two years earlier had overturned a similar statute, and Harris contended that the statute on which his prosecution was based was also unconstitutional on First Amendment grounds. He obtained a federal court injunction against the prosecution. The Supreme Court reversed, however, holding that considerations of federalism should generally preclude a federal intervention to interrupt a state prosecution. *Younger* represents a broader application of the abstention doctrine than had existed under the Warren Court, and accordingly, access to federal courts has become more difficult for state litigants, as seen in the *Middlesex* case.

Judicial Immunity from Salary Reductions

United States v. Will, 449 U.S. 200, 101 S.Ct. 471, 66 L.Ed. 2d 39 (1980)   Held that the compensation clause prevented Congress from reducing previously authorized cost of living adjustments for federal judges. *United States v. Will* was a lawsuit brought by a number of federal judges challenging four laws, passed by Congress, which were designed to interrupt the effect of earlier legislation calling for annual cost of living salary increases for various federal officials including judges. These salary adjustments were to have become effective automatically on October 1 of each year beginning in 1976. In 1976, Congress stopped the scheduled 4.8 percent increase with a statute signed by the president on October 1. The law nullifying the 1977 increase was signed into law the July prior to the effective date. In 1978, the act withholding the increase was signed the day before the effective date. The act passed to reduce the scheduled increase for fiscal 1979 was signed 12 days after the effective date. The challenge to these laws was based upon the compensation clause found in Article III, Section 1. It provides that the compensation of federal judges "shall not be diminished during their continuance in office." The Court, in an 8–0 decision (Justice Blackmun not participating), held that the two laws passed and signed prior to the effective date were permissible, but that the two signed after the effective date violated the compensation clause.

The opinion of the Court was delivered by Chief Justice Burger. Before getting to the compensation clause issue, the Court first had to address the matter of jurisdiction and disqualification. Noting that the lower court judge as well as all the members of the Supreme Court had "an interest in the outcome" of these cases, the court's jurisdiction was not in doubt. The disqualification matter was handled through invocation of the rule of necessity. The rule, a "well-settled" principle of common law, held that while it might be preferred that a judge not take part in a case, because of a personal interest, he or she may have to if the case cannot be heard otherwise. A litigant is entitled to a right adjudicated, and that takes precedence over disqualification. As for the compensation clause claim, the Court explored the origin of the provision. A "long-standing" Anglo-American tradition is that of an "independent judiciary." The courts were seen as needing to be "free from control" by the other branches of government. Such independence is "essential" if there is a "right to have claims decided by judges who are free from political domination" by the other branches. The Court cited Hamilton's observation in *The Federalist* that the "power over a man's subsistence amounts to a power over his will." The Court noted that the relationship of judicial compensation was well established by the time of the Constitutional Convention, and its inclusion was a natural consequence of an understanding of English history. The Court also suggested the clause guarantees a prospective judge, who may be leaving a more lucrative private practice for the judiciary, that compensation in that position will not be decreased.

Burger then moved to the specific statutes involved here. The question as he saw it was whether Congress could repeal salary increases that would otherwise take effect under previously established formulas. The question turned on when the increase "vests" or becomes "irreversible." Put another way, did the compensation clause offer protection at the point the formula was enacted or when the increases were to take effect? The Court chose the effective date. Accordingly, the 1976 and 1979 enactments diminished the compensation of judges because they were not signed, and thus did not become law, until the formula increases were "already in force." The repeal of the increases was aimed at officials in all three branches and did not single out or "discriminate" against judges only. This was not sufficient to save these statutes because the inclusion of officials not protected by the compensation clause "does not insulate a direct diminution of judges' salaries from the clear mandate of the clause." The statutes applying to 1977 and 1978 were signed before the effective date of the increase. This was a crucial difference. The compensation clause "does not erect an absolute ban on all legislation that conceivably could have an adverse effect on compensation of judges." The framers of the Constitution struck a balance by insulating judges from decreases in salary but delegating to Congress the discretion to fix salaries and make salary adjustments to "meet economic changes" such as inflation. Congress used this discretion when it adopted the formula contained in the original act. A subsequent decision to abandon the formula for these two years "in no sense diminished the compensation" the judges were receiving. Burger concluded by saying that not to allow Congress to alter a method of calculating salaries would mean that the judicial branch "could command Congress to carry out an announced future intent as to a decision the Constitution vests exclusively in the Congress." *See also* COMPENSATION CLAUSE, p. 587; *O'MALLEY V. WOODROUGH* (307 U.S. 277: 1939), p. 401.

Significance   The Court held in *United States v. Will* (449 U.S. 200: 1980) that a scheduled judicial salary increase could only be interrupted before the effective date of the adjustment. Otherwise, such interference was prohibited by the compensation clause of Article III.

The clause is aimed at ensuring judicial independence. Early tests of the clause involved imposition of an income tax. After ruling in *Evans v. Gore* (253 U.S. 245: 1920) that even a nondiscriminatory general tax on incomes was contrary to the compensation clause, the Court reversed itself in *O'Malley v. Woodrough* (307 U.S. 277: 1939). The Court in *O'Malley* said that to argue that a general income tax threatens judicial independence "trivializes" the objectives of the clause. Imposition of a general tax was seen as nothing more than a recognition that "judges are also citizens," and that their judicial functions did not immunize them from sharing the cost of government with their fellow citizens. As for the matter of actually setting salaries, *Will* clearly indicates that Congress has discretion to make any and all adjustments upward. Judges are not entitled to increases even to offset the impact of inflation. Once salaries have taken effect, however, those salaries are protected by the compensation clause. So too with salary increases. Once they are "in force," they may not be withdrawn.

Judicial Immunity

***Stump v. Sparkman*, 435 U.S. 349, 98 S.Ct. 1099, 55 L.Ed. 2d 331 (1978)**   Held that judges are immune from civil suits for actions done in performance of their judicial function. *Stump v. Sparkman* involved a judge-approved sterilization of a minor. Stump, a judge of a state general jurisdiction court, was approached by the minor's mother with a petition requesting the sterilization. The mother stated that her fifteen-year-old daughter was "somewhat retarded" and was "associating with" men to the extent that she wished to prevent "unfortunate circumstances." After the judge approved the petition, a tubal ligation was performed. The minor was told she was undergoing an appendectomy. The daughter subsequently married and discovered after unsuccessful attempts at becoming pregnant that she had been sterilized. She and her husband brought suit against the judge and others under 42 USCS Section 1983, seeking damages for violation of her constitutional rights. The district court dismissed the complaint, finding the judge to be immune from suit. On review, the court of appeals reversed. The Supreme Court reversed again in a 5–3 decision (Justice Brennan not participating) and held that the judge was immune.

The opinion of the Court was delivered by Justice White. The pivotal question was whether the judge "had jurisdiction over the subject matter before him." White indicated that the "scope of jurisdiction must be construed broadly" where the issue is judicial immunity. Immunity exists even if the action taken by the judge was "in error, was done maliciously, or was in excess of his authority" so long as he or she has not acted in "clear absence of jurisdiction." Judge Stump was a judge of a general jurisdiction court, and while the court was not expressly given power to grant parental petitions for sterilization of minor children, no state law prohibited consideration of such petitions. The Court then turned to the lower court's conclusion that, jurisdiction aside, the judge's failure to "comply with elementary principles of due process" left him liable. White said this "misconceives" what judicial immunity is. A judge must be immune from liability for his "judicial acts," and no flaw in the judge's performance makes the judgment "any less a judicial act." The Sparkmans argued that Stump's action lacked judicial character because he approved the petition without its having been assigned a docket number or formally being placed on file, that the proceeding was ex parte with no notice given to the daughter and no appointment of counsel to represent her interests. The Court used two criteria to determine that Stump's action was a judicial one. Responding to petition was a function "normally performed by a judge," and it was handled consistent with the "expectation of the parties," that is, Sparkman's mother was dealing with the judge in his "judicial capacity." Finally, the Court responded to the argument that there are actions of a judicial nature that a judge "even when exercising general jurisdiction is not empowered to take." Here, it was contended that Stump's action was "so totally devoid of judicial concern" for the interests of the minor as to "disqualify it as a judicial act." The Court said that "disagreement" with an action cannot justify depriving a judge of immunity. "Despite the unfairness . . . that sometimes results," judicial immunity is seen as critical to the administration of justice because it allows a judicial officer to act "without apprehension of personal consequences to himself." The fact that the issue before a judge is "controversial" is "all the more reason" that a judge "should be able to act without fear of suit."

Justices Stewart, Powell, and Marshall dissented. Stewart said that "what Judge Stump did . . . was beyond the pale of anything that could sensibly be called a judicial act." Stewart disputed that what the judge did was an act "normally performed by a judge." Certainly judges do not normally approve parental decisions for surgery on children in general. And in the instance of sterilizations, state statutes set out certain procedures, at least for institutionalized persons, which had to be completed. No less could be expected here. Neither was Stewart satisfied with the "expectations" criterion. Simply because Sparkman's mother approached the judge thinking he had authority cannot be conclusive. "False illusions" as to a judge's power can hardly "convert a judge's response to those illusions into a judicial act." Similarly, if the judge represented to her that he was acting in his judicial capacity, "merely his own say-so" cannot in itself make his conduct judicial.

Stewart concluded by saying that a judge is "not free, like a loose cannon, to inflict indiscriminate damage whenever he announces he is acting in his judicial capacity." Stewart acknowledged an "aura of deism" that "surrounds the bench." But that "aura" cannot be maintained by "exonerating ... such lawless conduct" as occurred here. If that constitutes the kind of 'intimidation' of judges that the immunity doctrine was to prevent," the deterrent effect would be "in the public interest." *See also* COMPENSATION CLAUSE, p. 587; JUDICIAL IMMUNITY, p. 626.

Significance   The Court reiterated a very broad judicial immunity doctrine in *Stump v. Sparkman* (435 U.S. 349: 1978). The doctrine was intended to protect judges from having to fear that unsatisfied litigants "may hound him with litigation." The imposition of "such a burden" on judges would "contribute not to principled and fearless decision-making, but to intimidation." The doctrine was aimed at serving the public interest of having judges who could function "with independence and without fear of consequences." The Court first spoke to the immunity doctrine in *Bradley v. Fisher* (13 Wallace 335: 1872) and said that immunity from civil actions exists even when the actions are "in excess of their jurisdiction," and are allegedly "maliciously or corruptly" motivated. Only nonjudicial acts are not immunized, and stem only from situations where the judge acts in "clear absence of all jurisdiction." In a case much more proximate to *Stump,* the Court held in *Pierson v. Ray* (386 U.S. 547: 1967) that the doctrine of immunity applied to suits brought under 42 USC Section 1983. After examining the legislative history of the statute on which Section 1983 was based, the Court concluded that the record gave "no indication that Congress intended to abolish this long-established principle."

Judicial Review

***Marbury v. Madison,* 1 Cranch 137, 2 L.Ed. 60 (1803)**   The case in which the United States Supreme Court asserted itself as being *the* institution that logically must be the ultimate authority in interpreting the federal Constitution. *Marbury v. Madison* was the first case in which the Supreme Court in a published opinion invalidated an act of Congress on the ground that it violated the Constitution. Thus the Court enunciated the doctrine of judicial review, and formally established its policy-making function.

Marbury v. Madison raised the question of whether the secretary of state could choose not to deliver a justice of the peace commission once the designate of that commission had been confirmed by the Senate, and his commission signed and sealed. The designate in question, William Marbury, applied to the Supreme Court for a writ of mandamus to compel the president to show cause why his commission had not been delivered, basing his appeal on a 1789 act of Congress that gave the judiciary authority to issue writs of mandamus to "persons holding office under the authority of the United States."

Chief Justice John Marshall's opinion said that the Court had jurisdiction to consider Marbury's case. Although the president had unlimited discretion to appoint federal officials, he could not arbitrarily remove them once appointed. The executive should therefore show cause why the commission had not been delivered. Nevertheless, the Supreme Court lacked power to issue the writ of mandamus, because the 1789 act violated the section of Article III in the Constitution conferring original jurisdiction on the Court.

In the course of his argument Marshall decided at least three political questions: (1) that the president had discretion to appoint federal officers at his will; (2) that once appointed, he could not arbitrarily remove them; and (3) that the Court had the authority to decide that an act of Congress violated the Constitution.

Marbury v. Madison made use of the following syllogism:

Major Premise: The laws of a nation are to be interpreted by its courts.

Minor Premise: The Constitution is a law of the United States.

Conclusion: The Constitution is to be interpreted by the federal courts, the Supreme Court being the ultimate interpreter.

The two principal propositions of *Marbury* are the supremacy of the Constitution over statutory law, and the fundamental role of the courts to safeguard that supremacy. Marshall cast the first issue in categorical terms. The Constutition is "either a superior paramount law, unchangeable by ordinary means," or it is "on a level with ordinary legislative acts," and alterable when the legislature "shall please to alter it." For Marshall, the answer was obvious. If the Constitution is supreme, then a legislative act "contrary to the constitution, is not law." Otherwise, constitutions are "absurd attempts" to limit power, "in its own nature, illimitable." The second proposition focused on judicial review. Here Marshall said that it is "emphatically the province and duty of the judicial department" to "say what the law is." Resolving a situation where a law "be in opposition to the constitution . . . is of the essence of judicial duty." If the Constitution is superior to legislative enactments, the Constitution rather than statute, "must govern the case to which they both apply." *See also* ARTICLE III, p. 73; JOHN MARSHALL, p. 530; JUDICIAL REVIEW, p. 627.

Significance   *Marbury v. Madison* was not the first use of the principle of judicial review in the United States. The principle had been widely used by state courts to invalidate state legislation prior to the adoption of the federal Constitution in 1789, and between 1789 and the *Marbury* decision in 1803, there were at least 20 cases in which state laws were struck down as being contrary to state constitutions. Judicial review was a respectable intellectual position in the climate of late eighteenth-century jurisprudence. If the theoretical framework of the Constitution was one of natural rights, and if the Constitution was not the exclusive source of those rights, but merely an important one, then the lines between law, philosophy, and politics were not always clear.

Marbury's lasting importance for American jurisprudence is that it blurred the distinction between political and legal questions, thereby suggesting that the Constitution was an exclusively legal rather than a political document. Many of John Marshall's contemporaries, Thomas Jefferson among them, strongly disagreed with this premise. They pointed out that judicial review was not explicitly mentioned in the Constitution, and that the president and Congress, no less than the Supreme Court, were required in their oath of office to uphold the Constitution of the United States. Perhaps the most celebrated of the anti-*Marbury* judicial statements was that of Justice Gibson of the Pennsylvania Supreme Court, who contended in 1825 that each branch of government was ultimately responsible to the people for the constitutionality of its own acts (*Eakin v. Raub*, 12 Sergeant and Rawle 330).

Nevertheless *Marbury v. Madison* occupies a unique place in American jurisprudence. It set the precedent for the convenient mechanism by which Congress and the president can escape the political liability of final decisions on tough constitutional issues. The constitutional escape valve *Marbury* provided makes it possible to sometimes shift the burden of final decision from elected officials to appointed judges. Judicial review has also proved to be a critical check upon vast governmental power in an ever-expanding, increasingly complex, and impersonal system of government.

Dred Scott v. Sandford, 19 Howard 393, 15 L.Ed. 691 (1857)   Held that blacks, their slave status notwithstanding, were not citizens of the United States. *Dred Scott v. Sandford* was one of the Supreme Court's first major rulings on civil liberties. It explored the nature of citizenship, the institution of slavery, and it was a factor in precipitating the Civil War. It also prompted the policies embodied in the Fourteenth Amendment. Dred Scott was a black slave from Missouri who had been taken by his master to the free state of Illinois and then to the Louisiana Territory, an area designated "free" under terms of the Missouri Compromise of 1820. Scott ultimately returned to the slave state of Missouri, where he brought suit claiming his residency in free areas had altered his status as a slave. The Missouri Supreme Court held that Missouri law governed despite Scott's residence elsewhere. Scott then pressed his suit in federal court. The case could have been resolved by a court holding that Scott's status was a matter of Missouri law, but the Supreme Court chose to address the substance of the case, largely because two justices wanted to make it an occasion to examine slavery critically. The remainder of the Court decided against Scott in a 7–2 decision, with each member of the Court entering a separate opinion.

In what is viewed as the Court's prevailing sentiment, Chief Justice Taney opined that Scott was not entitled to sue because he was not a citizen. He was not a citizen because he was black and a slave. The Chief Justice contended that at the time the Constitution was written, the blacks were regarded as "beings of an inferior order and altogether unfit to associate with the white race, either in social or political relations." Blacks were property. Chief Justice Taney invoked the concept of dual citizenship to foreclose Scott's claims. Federal citizenship is conferred only through federal action, he said, and no matter how extensive the privileges and immunities conferred elsewhere, they neither carried over to Missouri nor could they affect Scott's ineligibility for federal citizenship. The chief justice said no state can "introduce a new member into its political community created by the Constitution of the United States. It cannot make him a member of this community by making him a member of its own." Neither can a state "introduce any person, or description of persons, who were not intended to be embraced in this new political family, which the Constitution brought into existence, but here intended to be excluded from it." Scott's noncitizen status also flowed from his still being a slave. Chief Justice Taney asserted that Scott had never achieved free status under provisions of the Missouri Compromise because that enactment was unconstitutional. In the Court's view, Congress did not have the authority to designate certain territories as free. To do so would deprive slaveholders of their due process property rights.

The two dissenters, Justices Curtis and McLean, split from the majority on every issue in the case. Justice Curtis in particular disputed Chief Justice Taney's proposition that blacks were not citizens at the time the Constitution was ratified. He noted that there were several states where those "descended from African slaves were not only citizens of those States, but such of them had the franchise of electors, on equal terms with other citizens." To Justice Curtis, "it would be strange if we were to find in that instrument anything which deprived of their citizenship any part of the people of the United States who were among those by whom it was established." *See also* JUDICIAL REVIEW, p. 627; PRIVILEGES AND IMMUNITIES CLAUSE, p. 647.

Significance   The citizenship questions of *Dred Scott v. Sandford* (19 Howard 393: 1857) were rendered moot by adoption of the Fourteenth Amendment in 1868. Indeed, the first sentence of Section 1 reversed *Dred Scott*. Although the Fourteenth Amendment was very narrowly interpreted initially, its provisions have since become the foundation for civil liberties and civil rights protections in modern America. *Dred Scott* provided the political impetus for a tragic Civil War fought over the extent to which federal authority could be brought to bear on the issue of slavery. Eventually it paved the way for public policy adjustments that gave the descendents of Dred Scott equal protection of the laws. *Dred Scott* also constituted a substantial expansion of the scope of judicial review. In this case, the Court invalidated a major legislative policy statement. Not only had the Missouri Compromise been in effect for 37 years prior to the Court's striking it down, it represented the principal legislative attempt to handle the major political issue of the period. *Dred Scott* raised the Court to a position of playing a critical, sometimes decisive, policy-making role at the national level through the use of the judicial veto.

Standards of Judicial Review

United States v. Carolene Products Company, **304 U.S. 144, 58 S.Ct. 778, 82 L.Ed. 123 (1938)**   Upheld a federal regulation that prohibited interstate shipment of skimmed milk "compounded with any fat or oil other than milk fat." The real importance of *United States v. Carolene Products Company* comes from the expression of a "preferred position" doctrine when due process rights are affected by legislation. Carolene Products Company was indicted for violation of the act because it shipped interstate packages of "Milnut," a combination of condensed skimmed milk and coconut oil "made in imitation or semblance of condensed milk or cream." The indictment asserted that Milnut was an "adulterated article of food which was injurious to the public health." The trial court found the indictment insufficient," and the United States appealed. The Supreme Court, in a 6–1 decision with Justices Cardozo and Reed not participating, reversed and upheld the "filled" milk regulation.

Justice Stone delivered the opinion of the Court. He first offered a broad interpretation of the commerce power. The power is "complete in itself, may be exercised to its utmost extent," and "acknowledges no limitations other than are prescribed by the Constitution." If Congress wishes to exclude articles from commerce, it is free to do so provided the Congress is convinced the public health and welfare are threatened. Neither did the Court find such regulation precluded by the Tenth Amendment. The most important aspect of the opinion was the discussion of how the Court ought to approach the judicial review function. Stone referred to the description in the statute of what the Congress saw as "adulteration" of food that might cause "injury" to the public. This legislative characterization was designed to aid "informed judicial review." But "even in the absence of such aids," the Court said the "existence of facts supporting the legislative judgment is to be presumed" for enactments "affecting ordinary commercial transactions." Unless otherwise demonstrated, such legislation must be presumed to rest upon some rational basis within the knowledge and experience of the legislators. Stone added a footnote to this statement suggesting that legislation affecting individual rights needs to be examined more carefully by the courts. He said "there may be a narrower scope for operation of the presumption of constitutionality" when legislation "appears on its face" to be within a "specific prohibition" of the Constitution, such as those of the "first ten amendments," which are "deemed equally specific when held to be embraced within the Fourteenth." Stone also posed the question of whether legislation "which restricts those political processes which can ordinarily be expected to bring about repeal of undesireable legislation" is to be "subjected to more exacting judicial scrutiny" under the "general prohibitions of the Fourteenth Amendment." Finally, he wondered whether statutes directed at particular "religious, or national, or racial minorities" which may have the effect of curtailing the operation of "those political processes ordinarily relied upon to protect minorities" may call for a "correspondingly more searching judicial inquiry." Having said that, Stone left the matter to later decisions and reiterated the validity of the "Filled Milk" Act. Justice Black dissented from Stone's opinion regarding the nature of judicial review although he concurred in the result of the decision. *See also* JUDICIAL REVIEW, p. 627.

Significance   The Court upheld a congressional prohibition on the interstate shipment of "filled" or supplemented milk in *United States v. Carolene Products Company* (304 U.S. 144: 1938). More importantly, the Court took the case as an opportunity to comment on the nature of the Court's function in reviewing challenged legislation. While the due process clauses had previously been generally effective in forestalling state and federal regulation, the Court here revealed a substantial change in philosophy. Stone announced in *Carolene* that sufficient supporting facts for legislative judgments in the area of economic regulation were to be "assumed" by the courts. Presumption of a rational basis for such regulation was to become the starting point of departure for the consideration of suspect legislation. But Stone did not stop there. Instead, he fashioned a different thrust for the courts. He focused on safeguarding of the Bill of Rights. He raised, in his often-cited footnote, the possibility that the Court scrutinize legislation affecting personal freedoms more closely than commercial legislation. His suggestion clearly expressed something commonly referred to as the "favored position" or "preferred freedoms" doctrine. Because such freedoms are at the very core of our political system, the Court is obligated to demand a compelling justification for infringement of those liberties. Thus, the doctrine poses a presumption of constitutionality that varies with the substantive content of the legislation under review.

Judicial Review of Rate Making

Federal Power Commission v. National Gas Pipeline Company, **315 U.S 575, 62 S.Ct. 736, 86 L.Ed. 1037 (1942)**   Limited the extent to which federal courts would review rate decisions of regulatory agencies. In *Federal Power Commission v. Natural Gas Pipeline Company,* the Court considered Federal Power Commission (FPC) authority to set prices of natural gas transported interstate for distribution. The case involved rates charged by Natural Gas Pipeline Company and Texoma Natural Gas Company, two companies "engaged in business as a single enterprise," for the production, interstate transportation, and ultimate wholesale distribution of natural gas. Following investigation of the companies' rates, the FPC issued an interim order characterizing the existing rates as "unjust, unreasonable, and excessive." The FPC required the companies to file new and reduced rates. The companies appealed to the court of appeals. While the court of appeals acknowledged the authority of the FPC to issue such an order, it vacated the order because it differed with the FPC computation of the base rate. The FPC was granted certiorari by the Supreme Court because of the "novelty and importance" of the questions presented by the FPC challenge to the basis on which the court of appeals struck down the order. The companies also filed a cross-petition attacking the constitutionality of the Natural Gas Act upon which the FPC had based its action. The Supreme Court reversed the court of appeals and sustained the interim order in a unanimous decision.

The opinion of the Court was delivered by Chief Justice Stone. The Court first rejected the contention that the statute as applied here was unconstitutional as being "without merit." The interstate character of the companies' operations brought them fully within congressional power to regulate interstate commerce. In addition, the act empowered the FPC to investigate rates charged and, after a hearing, "determine just and reasonable rates." The Court next addressed the validity of the interim order. The Court found that the order had been preceded by a full hearing affording the companies full opportunity to "offer all their evidence." Further, the Court held that in fulfilling its function of rate setting, the commission may choose not to establish a specific rate schedule, but rather only order that rate reductions take place. The Court then moved to consideration of whether the FPC had required rates that were too low by ordering the reduction. This issue involved consideration of the scope of judicial review for commission rate-making decisions. The statute permitted the FPC to order rate decreases where rates were found to be unjust or unlawful or "not the lowest reasonable rates." By "long standing usage" in the field of rate regulation, the "lowest reasonable rate" is one that is not "confiscatory." The Court said that the congressional standard established in the statute "coincides with that of the Constitution" and that courts are "without authority ... to set aside as too low any 'reasonable rate' adopted by the Commission which is consistent with constitutional requirements." Stone said that the Constitution "does not bind" rate-making bodies to the "service of any single formula or combination of formulas." When an agency like the FPC has been delegated rate-making power, it may, within the limits of its statutory authority, make "pragmatic adjustments" that are necessary under particular circumstances. Once "fair hearing" has been given, "proper findings" made, and any other obligations fulfilled, the courts "cannot intervene in the absence of a clear showing that the limits of due process have been overstepped." If any rate-making order, as "applied to the facts before it" and taken in "its entirety," produces no "arbitrary result," the Court's "inquiry is at an end." Justices Black, Douglas, and Murphy concurred, saying that this decision returned to the "constitutional principles which prevailed for the first hundred years of our history." In their view, the Court properly held that rate making is a "constitutional prerogative of the legislative branch, not subject to judicial review or revision." *See also* JUDICIAL REVIEW, p. 627; *MOTOR VEHICLE MANUFACTURERS ASSOCIATION V. STATE FARM MUTUAL INSURANCE COMPANY* (463 U.S. 29: 1983), p. 97; *MUNN V. ILLINOIS* (94 U.S. 113: 1877), p. 420; *UNITED STATES V. CAROLENE PRODUCTS COMPANY* (304 U.S. 144: 1938), p. 93.

Significance The Court redefined the scope of judicial review for administrative rate-making decisions in *Federal Power Commission v. Natural Gas Pipeline Company* (315 U.S. 575: 1942). The decision reflected a change in the Court's posture toward legislative initiatives in regulating the economy generally and utilities specifically. Prior to this case, the operative standard was established in such cases as *Smyth v.*

Ames (169 U.S. 466: 1898). *Smyth* was decided at the height of the substantive due process period, and it held that the judiciary ought to be free to fully examine the reasonableness of rates fixed by legislative agencies. *Smyth* produced many years of uncertainty about the way such review would occur. As the Court abandoned its substantive due process orientation, greater deference was displayed toward economic regulation, and *Federal Power Commission v. Natural Gas Pipeline Company* is representative of that change in philosophy. Of primary importance was the Court's willingness to permit rate-making agencies some latitude in determining criteria by which rates would be evaluated. Accordingly, this case explicitly limits the scope of court review to the reasonableness of the "total effect of the rate order." Two years later, the Court directly overruled *Smyth* in *Federal Power Commission v. Hope Natural Gas Company* (320 U.S 591: 1944) and indicated that it had no authority at all to review rates set by a regulatory commission.

Judicial Overrule of Administrative Agency

Motor Vehicle Manufacturers Association v. State Farm Mutual Insurance Company, **463 U.S. 29, 103 S.Ct. 2856, 77 L.Ed. 2d 443 (1983)**   Held that federal courts can require regulatory agencies to justify their actions with adequate rationale. The Court held in *Motor Vehicle Manufacturers Association v. State Farm Mutual Insurance Company* that the National Highway Transportation Safety Administration (NHTSA) had acted arbitrarily when it withdrew its earlier requirement that all cars be equipped with passive safety restraints: airbags or detachable or undetachable seat belts. The NHTSA, pursuant to provisions of the National Traffic and Motor Vehicle Safety Act, established the passive restraint requirement in 1977 for all cars by 1982 or 1984, depending on the model. Before the effective date of the regulation, however, the agency rescinded the requirement as no longer reasonable or practical. State Farm and a number of independent insurers petitioned for review of the change of standard. The court of appeals found the order to rescind deficient, and the Supreme Court concurred in a unanimous decision. It should be noted that Chief Justice Burger and Justices Rehnquist, Powell, and O'Connor felt that the NHTSA rescission of the detachable seat belt had been adequately supported, thus the Court was split 5–4 on this component of the case.

The opinion of the Court was expressed by Justice White. He indicated that the scope of judicial review was clearly spelled out in the statute. Under provisions of the Motor Vehicle Safety Act and its amendments, the safety standards are to be promulgated under procedures established by the Administrative Procedure Act. Standards may be "set aside" if found to be "arbitrary, capricious, an abuse of discretion, or otherwise not in accordance with law." He said that "rescission or modification" of a standard is "subject to the same test." The Motor Vehicle Manufacturers Association (MVMA) argued that rescission of an agency rule should be judged by the same standards a court would use to review an agency's "refusal to promulgate a rule in the first place." This standard was seen as "narrower than the traditional arbitrary and capricious test and 'close to the borderline of nonreviewability.'" The Court rejected the approach, saying it would "render meaningless Congress' authorization for judicial review of orders revoking safety rules. The Court said "revocation of an extant regulation" was "substantially different" from failure to act. White said that there is "at least a presumption" that the policies committed to the agency will be "carried out best" by adhering to the settled or established course. Consequently, when an agency changes its course by rescission, it is "obligated to supply a reasoned analysis for the change beyond that which may be required when an agency does not act in the first instance." Acknowledging that regulatory agencies do not establish rules "to last forever," the Court said that if Congress "established a presumption" from which judicial review should start, that presumption is "not against safety regulation, but against changes in current policy that are not justified by the rulemaking record." The Court then turned to the "ultimate question" of whether NHTSA's rescission of the passive restraint requirement was "arbitrary and capricious." The Court concluded that it was. The "most obvious" reason was that the NHTSA "apparently gave no consideration whatever" to modifying the standard to "require that airbag technology be required." The Court would not accept the "post hoc rationalizations" from other sources. An agency's action must be upheld, "if at all, on the basis articulated by the agency itself." The Court rejected the contention that to compel the agency to consider airbags was dictation of the procedures an agency was to follow. The Court saw the airbag as "more than a policy alternative." Rather, it was a "technological alternative within the ambit of the existing standard." Given that airbags were initially seen as effective and cost-beneficial by the NHTSA, the Court required that the original passive restraint standard "not be abandoned without any consideration whatsoever of an airbag-only requirement." An agency must "explore the evidence" available, and must offer a "rational connection between the facts found and the choice made." In this instance, the agency's explanation for rescission of the standard was "not sufficient to enable us to conclude that the recision [sic] was the product of reasoned decisionmaking." See also JUDICIAL REVIEW, p. 627; FEDERAL POWER COMMISSION V. NATURAL GAS PIPELINE COMPANY (315 U.S. 575: 1942), p. 95; UNITED STATES V. CAROLENE PRODUCTS COMPANY (304 U.S. 144: 1938), p. 93.

Significance   The Court held the National Highway Transportation Safety Administration's rescission of the passive restraint requirement for new automobiles to be "arbitrary and capricious" in *Motor Vehicle Manufacturers Association v. State Farm Mutual Insurance Company* (463 U.S. 29: 1983). Since the 1930s, the Court had withdrawn itself from the examination of the substance of regulatory agency decisions. That deference was based on the proposition that fashioning such regulations was primarily a legislative rather than a judicial function. At the same time, cases such as *State Farm* indicate that the Court has at least a threshold expectation that agency actions be based on reasoned analysis. Agencies must provide adequate support for an explanation of their decisions. Absent this support and explanation, an agency judgment will be seen as "arbitrary and capricious" even if the agency decision might ultimately be justified. The Court is authorized by provision of the Administrative Procedures Act to extend review to agency decision making, and the "arbitrary and capricious" standard has evolved into the primary test. The explicitly stated principle in *State Farm* is that in the conduct of review, the intent of the Court is not to "substitute its judgment" or preference for that of the agency. Rather, after examining the relevant data, the agency needs to "articulate a satisfactory explanation for its actions." That explanation must include a "rational connection" between the facts found and the choices made. In this case, the NHTSA could proceed with the original airbag requirements or attempt to adequately support a decision to modify or even abandon the passive restraint requirement. Even this final option was not foreclosed so long as the explanation and support for the decision were sufficient.

Review of Municipal Police Practices

***Rizzo v. Goode*, 423 U.S. 362, 96 S.Ct. 598, 46 L.Ed. 2d 561 (1976)**   Held that a federal district court did not have authority to order municipal officials to act in a particular way to remedy unconstitutional police misconduct toward minority citizens. *Rizzo v. Goode* was a suit brought under Section 1983 of Title 42 of the United States Code. This section allows civil action against anyone acting under "color" of state authority who deprives anyone else of civil rights. The suit (actually two class actions) was brought in federal district court against the mayor (Rizzo) and various supervisory police officials of Philadelphia. The suit sought relief from an allegedly "pervasive pattern" of police misconduct, particularly against the city's minorities. The district court concluded from the evidence presented that the defendants should be held responsible for an unacceptably high number of incidents of police misconduct. The Court ordered the defendants to submit to the court a plan for addressing the matter of adequate response to citizen complaints about the police. A plan was negotiated and made part of the district court's final order. The court of appeals affirmed the judgment, but the Supreme Court reversed in a 5–3 decision with Justice Stevens not participating.

Justice Rehnquist wrote the opinion of the Court. He characterized the issue as whether the district court order constituted an "unwarranted intrusion" by a federal court into an area of discretionary authority committed to local officials by state and local law. Rehnquist began by examining the district court's findings leading to the issuance of the challenged order. The lower court found evidence that the named defendants in the suit had not directly violated any legal rights of the plaintiffs. It was found that individual police officers, none of whom were named as parties, had committed such violations. Rehnquist called this a "central paradox" that "permeates" the lower court's conclusions. There was no "affirmative link" between the police misconduct found and formal action of the defendants. The "sole causal connection" between those named as defendants and the plaintiffs was that "in absence of a change in police disciplinary procedures, the incidents were likely to continue to occur." The Court saw the suit as having evolved into an "attempt by the federal judiciary to resolve a 'controversy' between the entire citizenry of Philadelphia" and the named officials on how to prevent future police misconduct. The Court had "serious doubt" that such a situation had the requisites of an Article III case between named plaintiffs and defendants. The plaintiffs' claim to future injury did not so much depend on what the named defendants would do, but "upon what a small, unnamed minority of policemen might do to them in the future" because of that "unknown policeman's perception of departmental disciplinary procedures." The situation was too hypothetical to constitute a bona fide case. Rehnquist characterized the District Court judgment as based on an "unprecedented theory of § 1983 liability."

Rehnquist then turned to one final matter: a claimed "right" to protection from police misconduct and whether "mandatory equitable relief" is appropriate when "those in supervisory positions do not take steps to reduce the incidence of unconstitutional police misconduct." This included consideration of the extent to which federal equity power "should be extended to the fashioning of prophylactic procedures for a state agency" designed to reduce such conduct. Such a claim is "at odds" with the "settled rule" in federal equity cases that the "nature of the violation determines the scope of the remedy." Rehnquist also indicated that "considerations of federalism" weighed against such use of federal judicial power. The court order "significantly" revised the "internal procedures" of the Philadelphia police department and was "indisputably a sharp limitation" on the "department's latitude" in the handling of its "own internal affairs." Given our system where federal courts operate "side by side" with state governments, "appropriate consideration must be given to principles of federalism in determining the availability and scope of equitable relief." The district court "departed from these precepts" when it granted injunctive relief and "inserted itself" into the "internal disciplinary affairs of this state agency." Justices Blackmun, Brennan, and Marshall dissented, saying that the violations were "patterned" and that federal relief must be "available against persistent deprival of federal constitutional rights." *See also* EQUITY JURISDICTION, p. 600; INJUNCTION, p. 622; *MAINE V. THIBOUTOT* (448 U.S. 1: 1980), p. 77.

Significance   The Court restricted the intervention of federal courts into the internal disciplinary matters of local police departments in *Rizzo v. Goode* (423 U.S. 362: 1976). Federal protection of civil rights was not frequently before the courts until the 1950s. Despite a flurry of federal legislation immediately following the Civil War, civil rights policy was tied to the proposition that only overt state action that violated specific federal rights could be reached by federal law. Like actions based on other civil rights laws, civil suits under Section 1983 were relatively infrequent. This law allows civil suit against persons violating, under "color" of law, the constitutional rights of others. Long dormant, Section 1983 cases began to be successfully litigated in the early 1960s. In *Monroe v. Pape* (365 U.S. 156: 1961), for example, the Court held that police brutality constituted deprivation of civil rights and could be reached by Section 1983 action. From this decision on, civil rights actions seeking damages or other relief became more numerous. Reaching the conduct of state and local officials under Section 1983 has serious implications for the federal-state relationship. The trend has been generally to bring state and local levels of government under closer federal scrutiny (see *Maine v. Thiboutot* (448 U.S. 1: 1980). In *Rizzo,* however, the Court deferred to the "principles of federalism" to limit federal court intervention where named municipal officials could not be linked tightly enough to the civil rights violations. While Section 1983 has become a meaningful avenue to litigate alleged injury to legally protected rights, success is not guaranteed.

Test Case

Muskrat v. United States, 219 U.S. 346, 31 S.Ct. 250, 55 L.Ed. 246 (1911)   Held that a "friendly suit" brought under specific congressional authorization did not present a valid case or controversy. *Muskrat v. United States* involved a law that altered the distribution of Indian property following admission of the Cherokee tribe to citizenship. The effect of the law was to diminish the lands and monies to which certain tribe members were entitled; thus the validity of the enactment was in doubt. To provide a test for the statute, Congress included in the law specific provisions for Muskrat and others to bring suit in the Court of Claims with right of appeal to the Supreme Court. In addition to requiring that the courts give priority to these cases, the statute provided that the Indians would be reimbursed for all costs associated with the litigation. The U.S. attorney general was also directed to defend the suits. A unanimous Court held that the case presented an abstract or hypothetical question because the parties were not truly adverse.

The opinion of the Court was delivered by Justice Day. The controlling issue was whether or not the jurisdiction conferred by the Congress was proper, given the constitutional limitations on judicial power. Day drew heavily from the language attached to *Hayburn's Case* (2 Dallas 409: 1792). It was said in that case that neither the legislative nor the executive branches "can constitutionally assign to the judicial any duties but such as are properly judicial, and to be performed in a judicial manner." The Constitution requires in Article III that the exercise of judicial power be "limited to 'cases and controversies.'" Beyond this point, judicial power "does not extend." Day then explored the nature of a "case." A claim of a party under federal law that "takes such a form that the judicial power is capable of acting upon it" is a case. The term "implies the existence of present or possible adverse parties, whose contentions are submitted to the court for adjudication." The jurisdiction conveyed here was intended to gain a "determination of the constitutional validity of certain acts of Congress." Is such a determination permissible? The Court said, "We think it is not." The power of judicial review "arises because a congressional act relied upon by one party is in conflict with the fundamental law." The exercise of judicial review, which the Court called "its most important and delicate duty," is not to allow the Court to revise legislation, but to resolve "justiciable controversies." The *Muskrat* case did not present a case per se because the parties are artificially contending. The federal government "has no interest adverse to the claimants." Rather, the "only judgment required is to settle the doubtful character of the legislation in question." If the Court were permitted to deal with questions in this way, it would exceed the constitutional limits on the judicial power and "be required to give opinions in the nature of advice concerning legislative action." This was seen as a function never intended by the Constitution and "against the exercise of which this court has steadily set its face from the beginning." *See also* ADVISORY OPINION, p. 577; CASES AND CONTROVERSIES, p. 583; *IN RE HAYBURN'S CASE* (2 Dallas 409: 1792), p. 79; JUDICIAL REVIEW, p. 627; STANDING, p. 655.

Significance   The Court held in *Muskrat v. United States* (219 U.S. 346: 1911) that Congress may not create a "case" by statute merely by defining an issue and designating parties to contest one another. The courts are available to examine legal disputes, and the development of an appropriate "test" is a basic strategy. These cases are bound, however, by the Article III requirement that an actual case or controversy exist before federal judicial power can be exercised. A contrived suit, one between parties who are not really adversaries, has two principal effects. First, because bona fide adversaries most fully develop the legal arguments pertaining to each interest, courts are able to most fully administer justice. Arguments advanced by parties who are not truly adverse detract from that process. Second, exercising power in cases where the parties are not really contending essentially places courts in the position of rendering advisory opinions. An advisory opinion is precluded by Article III as a means of preserving separation of power and keeping the courts from political entanglements that might do damage to the judicial branch. Fully cognizant of these factors, the Court had little alternative in *Muskrat* but to strike down the legislation at issue here.

Class Actions

***Gulf Oil Company v. Bernard*, 452 U.S. 89, 101 S.Ct. 2193, 68 L.Ed. 2d 693 (1981)**   Limited the discretion of federal courts to restrict communications among members of a class action. *Gulf Oil Company v. Bernard* grew out of an employment discrimination claim filed by a class of Gulf Oil employees and rejected employment applicants. The suit was brought claiming violation of Title VII of the Civil Rights Act of 1964, which prohibits employment discrimination. Prior to the filing of the class action, an agreement had been reached between Gulf and the Equal Employment Opportunity Commission (EEOC), an agency established by the same Title VII. The agreement provided for payment of back wages to those having been discriminated against. Gulf was actively pursuing eligible persons, informing them of the agreement, the amounts they would be paid under terms of the agreement, and, in exchange, requesting release from all discrimination claims. Gulf sought and received an order from a U.S. district court prohibiting all communications relating to the class action between the parties, their counsel, or potential class members without prior approval of the court. The order was revised by the court of appeals, and the Supreme Court unanimously concurred.

The opinion of the Court was delivered by Justice Powell. Class actions are governed by provisions of the Federal Rules of Civil Procedure. Rule 23(d) contains language covering orders that may be issued in connection with class actions. The Court saw the issue of this case as whether the order limiting communication was consistent with the "general policies embodied in Rule 23." Powell acknowledged the "important function" served by class actions in our system of civil justice. They are, however, subject to abuse and create management problems; thus they need some protective monitoring. A district court provides this monitoring as it possesses "broad authority to exercise control over a class action," but this discretion is "not unlimited." Indeed, it is "bounded by the relevant provisions of the Federal Rules." In addition, exercise of discretion by the district court is subject to appellate review. In this case, the order was seen to create at least "potential difficulties" to the initiators of the class action. The order "interfered with their efforts to inform potential class members of the existence of this lawsuit." The order was also seen as especially problematic to the "class as a whole" since they were being "pressed" to decide whether or not to accept the back pay settlement offer. The order also made it more difficult for representatives of the class to "obtain information about the merits of the case from the persons they sought to represent." Under these circumstances, an order limiting communications between class members and potential members must be based "on a clear record" with "specific findings" that reflect a "weighing of the need for a limitation and the potential interference with the rights of the parties." Only in this way can a court ensure that it is "furthering rather than hindering" the policies contained in the Federal Rules of Civil Procedure. This approach should also result in a "carefully drawn order" that limits free speech "as little as possible." In this case, one "looks in vain" for "any" indication of a "careful weighing of competing factors." The record revealed "no grounds" on which the lower court had determined that the order was "necessary and appropriate." As a result, the imposition of the order was seen as an "abuse of discretion." *See also* CLASS ACTION, p. 586.

Significance   The Supreme Court prevented a federal court from limiting communications between members and potential members of a class action in *Gulf Oil Company v. Bernard* (452 U.S. 89: 1981). A class action is a suit brought by a number of persons on behalf of a group whose members have a common legal interest. Class actions have been used frequently in recent years as a means of litigating civil rights, consumer questions, and environmental questions. This kind of litigation provides some efficiency and economy in the adjudication of an issue. Some limitations apply. For example, if access is sought to federal courts through diversity of citizenship jurisdiction, each member of the class must demonstrate an individual injury of at least $10,000 in value. In addition, those initiating a class action must bear the costs associated with notifying class members of the litigation. Notwithstanding these limitations, the class action is a reasonably well protected entity. Provisions in the Federal Rules of Civil Procedure govern class actions in federal courts, and trial judges possess substantial discretion to monitor these actions. Cases such as *Gulf Oil* indicate that the Supreme Court will review the exercise of that discretion. Reflected in *Gulf Oil* is the Court's commitment to having class actions develop as free of restrictions as possible. The capacity of class members and prospective members to freely and fully communicate is essential to the development of class action. *Gulf Oil* indicates that a district court order that interferes with the communications process must be based on a demonstrable and powerful need for the restriction.

Standing: Taxpayer

***Frothingham v. Mellon,* 262 U.S. 447, 43 S.Ct. 597, 67 L.Ed. 1078 (1923)** Held that a taxpayer did not have sufficient direct injury to challenge federal expenditures. *Frothingham v. Mellon* was actually one of two cases (the other being *Massachusetts v. Mellon*) that were combined to examine two aspects of the issue of who has sufficient interest to challenge the constitutionality of a federal statute. The enactment under attack was the Maternity Act of 1921, which appropriated federal monies to those states complying with its provisions to "reduce maternal and infant mortality and protect the health of mothers and infants." Frothingham sought injunction against implementation of the act on the ground that she was deprived of property "under the guise of taxation." Massachusetts also sought an injunction claiming federal usurpation of state powers. The Court disposed of both cases without considering the merits of the constitutional questions. In a unanimous decision, the Court found that Frothingham had no interest or injury either "inflicted or threatened" to enable her to sue. Similarly, Massachusetts was seen as presenting no "justiciable controversy" either in "its own behalf" or as a "representative of its citizens."

Justice Sutherland authored the opinion of the Court. He characterized Frothingham's interest in municipal taxing and spending as "direct and immediate," but her status as a federal taxpayer was "very different." The taxpayer's interest is "shared with millions of others" and is "comparatively minute and indeterminable." Future effects on tax levels are "so remote, fluctuating, and uncertain" that there is no basis for activating the "preventive powers of a court of equity." Given the vast number of taxpayers involved, administration of such statutes as the Maternity Act is a "matter of public, and not of individual, concern." If single taxpayers may litigate such issues, then every other taxpayer may challenge any and all other enactments. To make the courts a continuous location of such challenges would interfere with the apportionment of functions under the American system of government. Rather, courts are to be reserved for cases where a party can not only demonstrate invalidity of a statute, but also show he or she has "sustained or is in immediate danger of sustaining some direct injury" and not merely suffers in some "indefinite way in common with people generally."

In response to the Massachusetts suit, the Court said that Article III does not automatically confer jurisdiction simply because the state is a party to an action. Rather, jurisdiction extends to suits where a state is a party "to a proceeding of judicial cognizance." The Court found the state without injury here. The burden of taxation falls to the state's inhabitants, and the statute did not "require the states to do or yield anything." As a result, the question presented "is political and not judicial in character, and therefore is not a matter which admits of the exercise of the judicial power." Thus, Massachusetts could not bring the suit on its own behalf. The Court also rejected the attempt of Massachusetts to bring suit "as the representative of its citizens." The only way that a state may afford protection to its citizens is "through the enforcement of its own criminal statutes," or by "opening its courts to the injured persons for the maintenance of civil suits or actions." Citizens must bring suit themselves. The state may not act as *parens patriae* (reference to a traditional state role as "parent of the country" or legal guardian) in a federal case because the United States, not the states, stands in that capacity. Thus, Massachusetts was determined to have no justiciable interest in this situation. *See also* FLAST V. COHEN (392 U.S. 83: 1968), p. 107; JUSTICIABILITY, p. 630; STANDING, p. 655.

Significance   *Frothingham v. Mellon* (262 U.S. 447: 1923) provided the Court with its first opportunity to examine whether taxpayer status provided sufficient standing to sue. The Court's answer in *Frothingham* was that taxpayer status in itself did not satisfy the standing requirement. To have standing, a party must demonstrate a direct injury and not merely that he or she "suffers in some indefinite way in common with people generally." Frothingham's interest was simply too "minute and indeterminable" as well as "remote, fluctuating, and uncertain" to warrant judicial intervention. Clearly the Court was fearful that allowing the status of taxpayer to satisfy the standing requirements would trigger judicial examination of virtually every federal enactment appropriating public funds. To a substantial degree, separation of power arguments permeate Sutherland's opinion in *Frothingham*. He reviewed the functions of each branch, and said that the courts were not to "invade" the legislative domain of appropriations as a "general rule."

The *Frothingham* case served as an effective barrier to taxpayer suits challenging federal expenditures until the late 1960s, when the Court allowed challenge of the federal funding of certain activities in non-public schools in *Flast v. Cohen* (392 U.S. 83: 1968). Key to the modification of *Frothingham* in *Flast* was the connection or "nexus" between taxpayer status and a specific constitutional violation. As a general proposition, however, the *Frothingham* position that a taxpayer must show a personal and direct injury remains, and taxpayers may not challenge federal expenditures simply because they are taxpayers per se.

Standing: Taxpayer Challenging Constitutional Violation

Flast v. Cohen, **392 U.S. 83, 88 S.Ct. 1942, 20 L.Ed. 2d 947 (1968)** Held that a taxpayer had standing to challenge specific constitutional violations. *Flast v. Cohen* was brought to examine the validity of the Elementary and Secondary Education Act of 1965. The act appropriated federal funds to underwrite cost of instructors and textbooks for such subjects as reading and math in nonpublic schools. Flast and others brought suit in federal court seeking an injunction against Cohen, the secretary of the Department of Health, Education, and Welfare, to prevent expenditure of the authorized federal funds. They claimed that the act subsidized religion and was, thus, a violation of the establishment clause of the First Amendment. Their suit was dismissed on the grounds that they lacked standing. In an 8–1 decision, the Supreme Court reversed the lower court.

Chief Justice Warren issued the opinion of the Court. The Court's decision hinged on interpretation of *Frothingham v. Mellon* (262 U.S. 447: 1923), a case in which taxpayer status in itself was held insufficient to establish standing. Flast argued that the *Frothingham* decision was not a "constitutional bar" to taxpayer suits, but rather expressed "no more than a policy of judicial self-restraint" that could be disregarded where "compelling reasons for assuming jurisdiction over a taxpayer's suit exist." Federal judicial power is "constitutionally restricted" to "cases" and "controversies," but, according to Warren, those words have an "iceberg quality," having beneath their "surface simplicity submerged complexities which go to the very heart of our constitutional form of government." The cases and controversies requirement embodies two "complementary but somewhat different limitations." They limit courts to questions in an "adversary context" and in a form "capable of resolution through the judicial process." In addition, they "define the role assigned to the judiciary" to assure that the federal courts "will not intrude into areas committed to the other branches of government." The term *justiciability* gives "expression to this dual limitation." Justiciability is a concept of "uncertain meaning and scope." It is not a "legal concept" with a "fixed content or susceptible of scientific verification." Rather, its utilization is the "result of many subtle pressures." Here Warren examined the government's position that taxpayer suits challenging the validity of federal spending programs were absolutely barred. Spending decisions, according to the argument, were committed to branches other than the judiciary; thus "mere disagreement by a taxpayer" ought not to be sufficient to make them justiciable questions. Accordingly, standing to sue should not be conferred under any circumstances. Warren responded by saying that "analysis of the function served by standing limitations compel a rejection of the Government's position." Standing "is an aspect of" justiciability. The basic question of standing is whether the person is a proper party to request an "adjudication of a particular issue and whether the issue itself is justiciable." A taxpayer "may or may not have the requisite personal stake in the outcome." It depends on circumstances, but Article III does not absolutely bar taxpayer suits challenging federal taxing and spending programs.

The problem is to determine when standing exists for a federal taxpayer. The question "turns on whether they can demonstrate the necessary stake as taxpayers in the outcome of the litigation to satisfy Article III requirements." In order to establish standing, a taxpayer must show two things. First, a "logical link" must be established between the taxpayer status and the "type of legislative enactment attacked." A taxpayer could challenge Article I, Section 8 taxes and expenditures, but not "incidental expenditures" coming from administration of an "essentially regulatory statute." Second, the taxpayer must establish "a nexus between that status and the precise nature of the constitutional infringement alleged." Here, the taxpayer must show that the law "exceeds specific constitutional limitations imposed upon the exercise of the congressional taxing and spending power." When both "nexuses" are established, the litigant will have shown a taxpayer's stake sufficient to invoke federal court jurisdiction.

Justice Harlan dissented because the Court's decision granted standing to a taxpayer who had a public rather than private interest in the outcome. This materially altered the direct interest element previously required to establish standing, and, in his view, unnecessarily broadened access to the federal courts by taxpayers as an additional category of litigants over and above those who would otherwise have standing to challenge enactments like the one involved in this case. *See also FROTHINGHAM V. MELLON* (262 U.S. 447: 1923), p. 105; JUSTICIABILITY, p. 630; STANDING, p. 655.

Significance   *Flast v. Cohen* (392 U.S. 83: 1968) held that a taxpayer has standing to challenge federal appropriations provided there exists a connection between taxpayer status and a specific constitutional violation. *Flast* was thus a more permissive definition of standing than had been established in *Frothingham v. Mellon* (262 U.S. 447: 1923), where the Court categorically rejected standing based on taxpayer status alone. The Burger Court, however, soon made it clear that *Flast* was not quite so inviting as initially thought. In *United States v. Richardson* (418 U.S. 166: 1974), the Court held that a taxpayer could not challenge the secrecy of the CIA budget. The Court held that the plaintiff suffered no concrete injury, and that the federal courts could not function as a "forum in which to air . . . generalized grievances about the conduct of government." This trend was seen more recently in *Valley Forge Christian College v. Americans United for Separation of Church and State, Inc.* (454 U.S. 464: 1982). Here, the government disposed of surplus public property by giving it to a religious college. The Court noted that *Flast* seemed to allow virtually unrestricted access when making an establishment clause challenge, but found standing absent because no direct personal injury was shown nor was there a specific exercise of the appropriation power by Congress.

Standing: Legal Right Requirement

***Association of Data Processing Service Organizations v. Camp,* 397 U.S. 150, 90 S.Ct. 827, 25 L.Ed. 2d 184 (1970)** Distinguished legal interest from considerations of standing to sue. Prior to *Association of Data Processing Service Organizations v. Camp,* it was necessary to show a violation of a legal right to establish standing. In this case, the Court considered a less restrictive standard for standing. The association brought suit against Camp, comptroller of the currency, challenging his ruling that national banks could make data processing services available to their own customers as well as other banks. Since the association was in the business of selling such data processing services, the banks were positioned to become competitors. The district court dismissed the suit for lack of standing, and the court of appeals affirmed. The association was granted certiorari, and the issue was reviewed by the Supreme Court. The Court reversed the lower courts in a unanimous decision and held that the association indeed had standing to sue.

The opinion of the Court was delivered by Justice Douglas. He began by suggesting that "generalizations about standing to sue are largely worthless as such." Nonetheless, one necessary generalization is that standing in federal courts is to "be considered in the framework of Article III where judicial power is confined to 'cases' and 'controversies'." Any dispute seeking to be adjudicated must be "presented in an adversary context" and in a form "historically viewed as capable of judicial resolution." The "first question" is whether a plaintiff alleges that a particular action "has caused him injury in fact, economic or otherwise." That condition was satisfied in this case because national banks would now be in direct competition with the association and this "might entail some future loss of profits." The court of appeals, however, had held that standing was contingent on demonstrating the infringement of a legal right. A legal right was defined as "one of property, one arising out of contract, one protected against tortious invasion, or one founded on a statute which confers a privilege." The association members may have suffered some economic loss, but the injury did not constitute an invasion of a legal right, thus the court of appeals denied standing. Douglas said the "'legal interest' test goes to the merits." The question of standing is "different." In addition to the case or controversy consideration, standing involves whether the interest "sought to be protected" is arguably within the zone of interest to be protected or regulated by a statute or constitutional guarantee in question. The Administrative Procedure Act grants standing to anyone "aggrieved by agency action." Thus the association members have standing through the statute regardless of whether they fulfilled the legal right condition. Douglas went on to describe interests for which protection might be sought as a reflection of "'aesthetic, conservational, and recreational' as well as economic values." He mentioned the noneconomic values to emphasize that standing may stem from them as well as from the economic injury on which the Association relied in this case. Douglas stressed that apart from Article III conditions, standing issues are subject to congressional action as illustrated by the Administrative Procedure Act. The statutory trend "is toward enlargement of the class of people who may protest administrative action." The "whole drive" for expanding the category of "aggrieved" persons is "symptomatic of that trend." Accordingly, the Court remanded the case for hearing. Justices Brennan and White concurred in the result of this decision, but offered a partial dissent on the opinion in a companion case, *Barlow v. Collins* (397 U.S. 159: 1970). They would have found the standing requirement satisfied so long as the plaintiff's alleged injury was related to the challenged action. It was an even more permissive definition of standing, and it would have discarded the majority's inquiry into whether the interests asserted were protected or regulated by statute or constitutional guarantees. *See also* JUSTICIABILITY, p. 630; STANDING, p. 655.

Significance   The Court's decision in *Association of Data Processing Service Organizations v. Camp* (397 U.S. 150: 1970) diminished the relevance of the legal right standing requirement. For years prior to this decision, litigants were unable to access federal courts because they could not demonstrate a legally protected interest such as a right protected by contract or statute. Many actions of federal administrative agencies were insulated from judicial review by failure to establish violation of a legal right. In 1946, Congress passed the Administrative Procedure Act, which opened the possibility of accessing federal courts by persons "adversely affected or aggrieved" by any agency action. The *Camp* case fits this category, and the Court's decision became part of a general pattern of softening the technical requirements of standing. In a case decided the same day as *Camp, Barlow v. Collins* (397 U.S. 159: 1970), the Court held that tenant farmers had sufficient personal stake to challenge regulations promulgated by the secretary of agriculture relating to payment assignments under the Food and Agriculture Act of 1965. The Court found the farmers had demonstrated "injury in fact" and that they, like the data processing services in *Camp,* were within the "zone of interests" protected by the statute.

Standing: Direct Injury Requirement

***Laird v. Tatum,* 408 U.S. 1, 92 S.Ct. 2318, 33 L.Ed. 2d 154 (1972)** Held that allegations of a "subjective chill" are not a sufficient substitute for a specific present or future injury to establish standing to sue. Suit was brought in *Laird v. Tatum* by a number of plaintiffs, largely antiwar activists, to restrain the United States Army from conducting surveillance of civilian political activities. The army engaged in surveillance after being asked to assist local law enforcement authorities in handling civil disorders. The plaintiffs brought a class action claiming that the "mere existence" of the army intelligence-gathering system imposed a "chilling effect" on the exercise of their First Amendment rights. The plaintiffs argued that the chilling effect stemmed from the inappropriate use of the army for such surveillance and the potential or future misuse of information gathered by the Army. The district court dismissed the action finding no justiciable claim for relief, but the court of appeals reversed. In a 5–4 decision, the Supreme Court held that the plaintiffs failed to establish standing to sue.

The opinion of the Court was delivered by Chief Justice Burger. He identified the central issue as whether the jurisdiction of a federal court may be accessed by a complainant who alleges that the "exercise of his First Amendment rights is being chilled by the mere existence, without more, of a governmental investigation and data-gathering activity" that is allegedly "broader than reasonably necessary for the accomplishment of a valid governmental purpose." He examined the situations where constitutional violations may arise from the "deterrent, or 'chilling' effect" of governmental regulations that "fall short of a direct prohibition against the exercise of First Amendment rights." In none of these situations did a chilling effect arise "merely" from knowledge of governmental activities. Rather, chilling effect violations were found when the exercise of governmental power was "regulatory, proscriptive, or compulsory in nature," and the complainant was "either presently or prospectively subject to the regulations, proscriptions or compulsions." Tatum and the others failed to show even an indirect effect on the exercise of First Amendment rights. The Court saw their claim as merely a disagreement with executive branch judgments with respect to army data gathering. Simply because one perceives that involvement in such data gathering is inappropriate or that it places the military in an improper relationship with civilian activities does not produce a constitutional violation or even a chilling effect. Allegations of a "subjective 'chill' are not an adequate substitute for a claim of specific present objective harm" or a "threat of specific future harm." If such an approach were permitted, the federal courts would become "continuing monitors of the wisdom and soundness of Executive action." Burger indicated that monitoring was not the role of the judiciary, "absent actual present or immediately threatened injury resulting from unlawful governmental action."

Justices Douglas, Marshall, Brennan, and Stewart dissented. Douglas referred to the issue as a "cancer in our body politic." He argued that Congress had passed no law directing the Army surveillance, and such authority could not exist merely by implication. Since the plaintiffs were subjects of the surveillance, he felt they had standing to challenge the entire intelligence mechanism. He saw a clear inhibition on the exercise of First Amendment rights flowing from the surveillance. Brennan's dissent also represented the view that the claim was sufficient for judicial relief and that a chilling effect on First Amendment rights existed. *See also* JUSTICIABILITY, p. 630; STANDING, p. 655.

Significance   The Court refused to find a claimed "chilling effect" sufficient to satisfy the direct injury standing requirement in *Laird v. Tatum* (408 U.S. 1: 1972). *Laird* is characteristic of a general tendency of the Burger Court to be quite demanding regarding the direct injury standing requirement. The Court refused to find the mere presence of the army intelligence system in itself sufficient to produce enough injury to justify judicial intervention. Allegations of a "subjective chill" were not seen as a satisfactory substitute for a "claim of specific present objective harm or a threat of specific future harm." Two similar decisions followed soon thereafter. In *United States v. Richardson* (418 U.S. 166: 1974), the Court rejected a taxpayer suit aimed at making public the CIA budget and expenditure records. The Court held that taxpayers may not turn courts into a "forum in which to air . . . generalized grievances" about governmental policies. In the Court's view, Richardson had failed to demonstrate how he would have suffered injury from the secrecy of the CIA budget. In another case decided on the same day as *Richardson,* the Court held in *Schlesinger v. Reservist's Committee to Stop the War* (418 U.S. 208: 1974) that a group of reserve officers did not have standing to challenge the membership of some congressmen in the reserves. It was argued that their military obligations construed "holding an office" while in Congress, something prohibited by Article I, Section 6. The Court denied standing, saying that no "concrete injury," either "actual or threatened," flowed from this dual membership of congressmen. In addition, the Court said that the plaintiff's injury was "undifferentiated from the generalized interest of all citizens" and presented injury only in the "abstract."

Standing: Noneconomic Injury

United States v. Students Challenging Regulatory Agency Procedures, **412 U.S. 669, 93 S.Ct. 2405, 37 L.Ed. 2d 254 (1973)** Held that aesthetic and environmental injury may be sufficient to satisfy standing requirements. *United States v. Students Challenging Regulatory Agency Procedures* (SCRAP) involved a challenge to a proposed surcharge on all freight rates filed by all the nation's railroads with the Interstate Commerce Commission (ICC). When the ICC failed to suspend the increase, various environmental groups including SCRAP filed suit in the District of Columbia seeking to enjoin collection of the surcharge. The environmental groups challenged the ICC failure to suspend the surcharge, claiming "economic, recreational and aesthetic harm." SCRAP and the others asserted that the new rate structure would "discourage" use of "recyclable" materials and "promote the use of new raw materials that compete with scrap," which would adversely affect the environment by "encouraging unwarranted mining, lumbering, and other excavative activities." The groups also asserted that the adverse environmental impact would disturb their members' recreational use of the forests, streams, and other resources in the area of the district. Finally, SCRAP challenged the propriety of the ICC decision refusing to suspend the surcharge because it did not include an environmental impact statement as required under the National Environmental Policy Act. A three-judge district court held that SCRAP had standing and granted a preliminary injunction forbidding collection of the surcharge. The Supreme Court held 5–3 (Justice Powell not participating) that SCRAP had established standing. The Court also held in a 6–2 decision with Justices Douglas and Marshall dissenting that the District Court was without jurisdiction to issue an injunction against collection of the surcharge.

Of principal importance to this chapter is Justice Stewart's treatment of the standing matter. He said that standing exists in cases involving the Administrative Procedures Act (applicable here) when challengers could show "injury in fact," and where the injury was within a "zone of interest" protected by statutes allegedly violated by a federal administrative agency. Standing was "not confined" to those who could show "economic harm," but "aesthetic and environmental well-being" were sufficiently "important ingredients of the quality of life in our society" to deserve legal protection through the judicial process. Accordingly, just because SCRAP claimed "only" a harm to their "use and enjoyment of the natural resources of the Washington area, or the fact that all those using these resources "suffered the same harm" was not sufficient to deprive them of their standing. Their injury was somewhat "attenuated," but the action of the ICC potentially created sufficient harm to permit judicial consideration. In addition, the challenged agency action in this case was applicable to virtually all the nation's railroads and arguably had an adverse environmental impact on "all the resources of the country." Standing cannot be denied "simply because many people suffer the same injury." To deny standing on that ground "would mean that the injurious and widespread governmental actions could be questioned by nobody."

Justice White, joined by Chief Justice Burger and Justice Blackmun, dissented, saying that the allegations did not satisfy the "threshold requirement of injury constituting a judicial case or controversy." They saw the alleged injuries as "so remote, speculative and insubstantial" that they failed to confer standing. Those allegations become "no more concrete, real or substantial" when combined with claims of cost increases in the marketplace or "somehow" increased air pollution. The general "right" to have government administer laws wisely or most effectively "does not confer standing to litigate in federal courts. *See also* JUSTICIABILITY, p. 630; STANDING, p. 655.

Significance   The Court relaxed the direct injury standing requirement for "public interest" plaintiffs in *United States v. Students Challenging Regulatory Agency Procedures* (412 U.S. 669: 1973). Specifically, the plaintiff in *SCRAP* was an environmental group seeking to challenge an ICC action it believed would create injury to the public at large through adverse environmental impact. The Court made it clear in *SCRAP* that "aesthetic and environmental" values were sufficiently important to American quality of life to permit access to the judicial process. As important, the Court said that standing determinations are not to be a function of the number of people affected. As distinct from taxpayer groups, environmental groups have generally been accorded standing. One exception was *Sierra Club v. Morton* (405 U.S. 727: 1972), where the Court held that an environmental organization had failed to demon-

strate direct enough personal injury from a proposed resort development in a national forest. The Court distinguished *Sierra Club* in the
SCRAP holding, saying that the alleged injury was "very different."
While pleadings must be "something more than an ingenious academic
exercise in the conceivable," it could not be said that SCRAP could not
have demonstrated their allegations, and they should have been permitted to try. Had the allegations been supportable, SCRAP members
would be placed "squarely among those persons injured in fact" by the
ICC action and entitled to seek review even under the less permissive
Sierra Club standard.

Standing: Third-Party Assertion

***Singleton v. Wulff*, 428 U.S. 106, 96 S.Ct. 2868, 49 L.Ed. 2d 826
(1976)**   Held that physicians had standing to sue for loss of
Medicaid abortion reimbursement and that the physicians had third-
party standing to assert relief based on their patients' rights. *Singleton v.
Wulff* involved a number of physicians challenging a state statute
excluding other than "medically necessary" abortions from Medicaid
eligibility. In response to a motion to dismiss, the doctors argued
immediate loss of reimbursement for performing the procedure. They
also cited the impact on their ability to practice medicine as each
considered most beneficial for the patients. Finally, they asserted that
the policy deprived the patient of a fundamental right "to make the
abortion decision herself" as well as depriving her of equal protection
guarantees. The district court dismissed the physicians' suit, finding
insufficient "nexus" between their status and the claim they sought to
have adjudicated. The court of appeals reversed the district court and
went on to hold the statute unconstitutional. The Supreme Court
unanimously held that the physicians had standing to sue. Five members of the Court held that under the circumstances of this case, the
physicians had standing to seek relief based, at least in part, on the
rights of their patients. The Court was unanimous that the court of
appeals erred in dealing with the merits of the constitutional issue and
remanded the case.

The opinion of the Court was delivered by Justice Blackmun. He
noted two "distinct" standing questions. The first was whether the
physicians had a "sufficiently concrete interest" in the outcome of the
case to fulfill the Article III jurisdiction requirements for the federal
courts. The Court had "no doubt" that the physicians' injury was
sufficiently concrete. Were it not for the statutory limitation on
Medicaid abortion reimbursements, the physicians would continue to
perform the operations and be compensated for their services.
Further, it would be the government that would "be out of pocket" the

amount of the payments. The relationship between the parties is, thus, "classically adverse," and there "clearly" exists between them a "case or controversy in the constitutional sense." The second question was more difficult, and divided the Court virtually in half. This question involved what rights the physicians may assert. Included was the question of whether the physicians could assert rights of their patients. Blackmun cautioned that federal courts must "hesitate" before resolving cases, even those "within their constitutional power to resolve," on the basis of rights of "third persons not parties to the litigation." He developed two reasons for such hesitancy. Courts should not "unnecessarily" adjudicate such rights. There is the possibility that the right-holder may not wish to assert the right, or the right-holder may not benefit from litigation of those rights. Second, Blackmun saw the third parties themselves as the "best proponents of their own rights." Having offered these cautions, he indicated that, "like any general rule," this proposition should not be "applied where its underlying justifications are absent." Two "factual elements" are used to determine whether the rule should apply. The first is the relationship of the litigant to the party whose rights are asserted. If the "enjoyment" of the right is "inextricably bound up with" the activity of the litigant, the Court can be sure that its "construction of the right is not unnecessary." In addition, the relationship between the two may be such that the litigant is nearly "as effective proponent of the right" as the third party. The other element is the ability of the third party to "assert his own right." Applying these criteria, the Court found a sufficiently close relationship between doctor and patient. The "constitutionally protected abortion decision is one in which the physician is intimately involved." Thus, the physician is "uniquely qualified to litigate the constitutionality of the State's interference with . . . that decision." The Court also found several "obstacles" to a woman's asserting her own rights, such as preservation of privacy and imminent mootness. For those reasons, the Court found it appropriate to allow a physician to assert these rights.

Justice Stevens concurred on this point, but only because it was so tightly linked with the constitutional interest otherwise shown by the physicians themselves. Chief Justice Burger and Justices Powell, Stewart, and Rehnquist dissented on the third-party issue. Justice Powell suggested that more than the elements posed by the majority were necessary to permit third-party assertion. To Powell, litigation would have to be a practical impossibility before it would justify third-party assertion of rights. Neither did the dissenters see the relationship between the physician and patient as merging the interest of the two. The woman was not precluded from having an abortion. The "only impact" is that because of the way Missouri chose to structure its

Medicaid payments, it "causes these doctors financial detriment." *See also* JUSTICIABILITY, p. 630; STANDING, p. 655; *WARTH V. SELDIN* (422 U.S. 490: 1975), p. 117.

Significance   The Court held in *Singleton v. Wulff* (428 U.S. 106: 1976) that physicians had standing to challenge a policy excluding abortions from Medicaid coverage. Their standing was based on their own economic interest in being compensated for performing the procedure. But the Court also recognized standing based on the right of their patients to obtain abortions without interference from the government. It was on the matter of third-party assertion that the Court divided. The split was caused by a difference of view on the applicability of certain precedents. The plurality felt this case should be governed by such decisions as *Barrows v. Jackson* (346 U.S. 249: 1953), where a third party was permitted to assert rights that would have been "difficult if not impossible" to assert directly. The Court extended that language in *Singleton* to those cases where a "genuine obstacle" exists to the third party's own litigation. The dissenters felt that such a principle was an "understatement" of decisions like *Barrows*, and that the "obstacles" in women's asserting their own rights were "chimerical." They saw the case as "much closer" to *Warth v. Seldin* (422 U.S. 490: 1975), where third-party standing was denied because there were no obstacles to the right-holders' bringing their own suit.

Group Standing

Warth v. Seldin, **422 U.S. 490, 95 S.Ct. 2197, 45 L.Ed. 2d 343 (1975)**   Held that a group must show more than a generalized injury to establish standing. *Warth v. Seldin* was a challenge by various groups and individuals from Rochester, New York, to a zoning ordinance passed by Penfield, an adjacent suburban town. The ordinance allocated 98 percent of the town's vacant land to single-family detached housing and established requirements relating to lot size, setback, floor area, and habitable space. The plaintiffs came from several categories of persons, and each claimed a different kind of injury from the Penfield ordinance. One group of plaintiffs was low- and middle-income ethnic minorities who claimed that the ordinance excluded them from living in Penfield by making housing they could afford unavailable. A second group of plaintiffs was local builders who claimed they had been denied profits because they could not build low- and middle-income housing in Penfield. A third group of plaintiffs was two nonprofit organizations dedicated to bettering housing opportunities in the Rochester area. Finally, some of the plaintiffs were taxpayers from Rochester who asserted that the exclusive Penfield policy forced their city to provide more low- and middle-income housing, thus increasing their property taxes. The suit was dismissed in the lower courts on absence of standing grounds. The Supreme Court affirmed the lower courts in a 5–4 decision.

The opinion of the Court was delivered by Justice Powell. Inquiry into standing involves consideration of both "constitutional limitations on federal-court jurisdiction" and "prudential limitations on its exercise." The former involves the "threshold" question of whether a plaintiff has presented a "case or controversy" between himself and the defendant "within the meaning" of Article III. As an aspect of justiciability, standing reflects a sufficient personal stake in the outcome of the litigation to warrant a plaintiff's "invocation of federal court jurisdiction" and to "justify exercise of the Court's remedial powers on his behalf." The "prudential" limitations are "apart from this minimum constitutional mandate." When asserted harm is a "generalized grievance" shared by a large class of citizens, that "harm alone normally does not warrant exercise of jurisdiction." In addition, even when the plaintiff has met the case or controversy requirements, the rights asserted must be the plaintiff's own and generally cannot be grounded on interests of third parties. Without such limitations as these, the courts would be drawn into deliberation of "abstract questions of wide public significance even though other governmental institutions may be more competent to address the questions" and court intervention "may be unnecessary to protect individual rights." Having established these parameters, Powell turned to the specific claims in this case. The low- and moderate-income plaintiffs failed to show any direct relationship to the "ordinance's strictures," such as having been denied a variance from the ordinance. Rather, the plaintiffs asserted indirect injury. This did not preclude standing, but "may make it substantially more difficult" to establish that the asserted injury was the "consequence of the defendant's actions," or that "prospective relief will remove the harm." The Court also denied standing to the home builders associations. The association could have standing as representative of its members "only if it has alleged facts sufficient to make out a case or controversy had the members themselves brought suit." The association demonstrated no project denied to any of its members and thus failed to "show the existence of any injury" to its members of "sufficient immediacy and ripeness to warrant judicial intervention." The claims presented by the nonprofit associations were seen as attempts to "raise putative rights of third parties" without any of the "exceptions which allow such claims" to be made. Though these associations satisfied the Article III case or controversy threshold, prudential considerations led the Court to resist exercising judicial power on behalf of those plaintiffs. Finally, the plaintiffs asserting standing as taxpayers were rejected because of the "conjectural nature of the asserted injury" and because the "line of causation" was "not apparent." Their arguments were regarded as an "ingenious academic exercise." Powell concluded by saying that the rules of standing are "threshold determinants of the propriety of judicial intervention." The Court found that none of the plaintiffs met this threshold requirement.

Justice Douglas dissented, saying the Court read the complaint with "antagonistic eyes." He suggested standing had become a "technical barrier" often keeping the courts from being the forum "where justice is dispensed." Justices Brennan, White, and Marshall also dissented. They saw the various plaintiffs as ones whose "interests are intertwined" rather than as separate litigants. Standing of "any one group must take into account its position vis-a-vis the others." *See also* JUS-TICIABILITY, p. 630; *SINGLETON V. WULFF* (428 U.S. 106: 1976), p. 115; STANDING, p. 655.

Significance   The Court held that groups could not establish standing with only "generalized" grievances in *Warth v. Seldin* (422 U.S. 490: 1975). Crucial to the Court's holding was that none of the plaintiffs actually showed "injury in fact." *Warth* is characteristic of the Burger Court practice of reinstating relatively strict standing criteria, especially when considering "prudential limits" on judicial power. In *Simon v. Eastern Kentucky Welfare Rights Organization* (426 U.S. 26: 1976), the Court refused to permit a challenge to the IRS policy of granting tax-exempt status to hospitals as charitable organizations despite the hospitals' unwillingness to treat indigents. More recently, the Burger Court failed to find sufficient personal injury for a plaintiff seeking to challenge the practice of disposing of surplus government property by giving it to a religious college (see *Valley Forge Christian College v. Americans United for Separation of Church and State, Inc.*, 454 U.S. 464: 1982). Clearly, suits brought by organizational plaintiffs must show that a "personal injury" has occurred. It will not suffice that the injury asserted by such organizations has been inflicted on "other, unidentified members of the class to which they belong and which they purport to represent."

Mootness

***DeFunis v. Odegaard*, 416 U.S. 312, 94 S.Ct. 1704, 40 L.Ed. 2d 164 (1974)**   Sidestepped consideration of reverse discrimination issues relating to a law school's admission policies by holding the plaintiff's case to be moot. *DeFunis v. Odegaard* involved a challenge to the University of Washington Law School's use of a special admissions process for minority applicants. DeFunis graduated magna cum laude from the University of Washington and sought admission to the law school. He was denied admission even though his academic credentials were superior to 38 minority students who were admitted under the special procedures. DeFunis brought suit against various officials at the university including Odegaard, the president. The trial court found for DeFunis and ordered that the university start him with their next first-year class. The university successfully appealed to the Washington Supreme Court. DeFunis petitioned the U.S. Supreme Court, but also obtained a stay from the state court judgment until the case had been heard at the Supreme Court level. By the time the Court heard oral arguments on his case, DeFunis was in his last year of law school. In a 5–4 decision, the Supreme Court held that since DeFunis was about to graduate anyway, a decision would have no direct bearing on his interests, thus it held his case to be moot.

In a *per curiam* opinion, the majority started by offering the "familiar" proposition that "federal courts are without power to decide questions that cannot affect the rights of litigants of the federal judiciary." The inability of the courts to review "moot" cases derives from the Article III requirement of a bona fide "case or controversy." Despite "great public interest in the continuing issues" raised in the case, the Court was satisfied that DeFunis would remain a student "for the duration" of the term for which he was enrolled. Since he was enrolled in his final term, the controversy between the parties had "clearly ceased to be 'definite and concrete' and no longer 'touches the legal relations of parties having adverse legal interests.'" The majority indicated that had the university unilaterally changed its admissions procedures, it might have entertained the issues of this case, but the mootness question here turned on DeFunis's status for his final term of study. Since DeFunis had already registered for his final term, he would not again be required to run the "gantlet" of the admission process; thus the question was not "capable of repetition" so far as DeFunis was concerned. This freed the case from the established exception to the mootness limitation.

Justice Brennan's dissent was joined by Justices Douglas, White, and Marshall. First, Brennan felt that DeFunis's need to deal with the university's policy may not necessarily be over if, for some reason, DeFunis did not graduate. Despite the law school's assurance that DeFunis "will be allowed to complete this term's schooling regardless of our decision," Brennan suggested that these promises "have not dissipated the possibility" that petitioner might again have to "run the gantlet of the University's allegedly unlawful admissions policy." Second, Brennan commented on the Court's unwillingness to respond to the merits of the issue. In "endeavoring to dispose of this case as moot," the Court "clearly disserves the public interest." The questions "avoided today" concern "vast numbers of people, organizations, and colleges and universities." Few recent issues, observed Brennan, "have stirred as much debate and they will not disappear." In his view, the Court should have decided this case and put an end to such inevitable repetition. *See also* ADVISORY OPINION, p. 577; JUSTICIABILITY, p. 630; MOOTNESS, p. 634; STANDING, p. 655.

Significance The Court held that the reverse discrimination issues raised in *DeFunis v. Odegaard* (416 U.S. 312: 1974) were moot because the plaintiff was no longer in a position to be adversely affected by the challenged policy. A moot case is one for which the Court can no longer provide relief to a party because the dispute on which the suit is based is no longer alive. Such a suit thus fails the Article III requirement that judicial power extend only to bona fide cases or controversies. The Court mentioned exceptions to the mootness concept in *DeFunis,* but held that none applied there. Typically, exceptions involve situations where time is far too limited to litigate an issue fully, and where a likelihood exists that the issue will reoccur. The abortion issue qualifies for an exception because no appellate court can respond to it prior to a pregnancy completing its term. The Court said in *Roe v. Wade* (410 U.S. 113: 1973) that appellate review would always be foreclosed by mootness in abortion cases, and that the law should not be that rigid. The Court suggested that exceptions should be granted if issues are "capable of repetition, yet evading review." The courts are particularly cautious about granting exceptions or responding to cases that are moot. Otherwise, courts would be extensively involved in rendering advisory opinions.

Political Question Doctrine: Guaranty Clause

Luther v. Borden, **7 Howard 1, 12 L.Ed. 581 (1849)** Held that the determination of whether a state had a "republican" form of government was a "political question" and thus inappropriate for judicial consideration. *Luther v. Borden* arose out of the Dorr's Rebellion, which took place in Rhode Island in 1841 and 1842. At this time, the state was using as its constitution the old colonial charter. Among its alleged defects was a serious limitation on the right to vote. Dorr and others called a convention and adopted a new state constitution. Under provisions of the new document, elections were held, and a second government was established. Dorr was elected governor in the process.

Meanwhile, the government operating under the old charter continued to function. Officials of the charter government viewed the actions of the new government as rebellion, and they sought to resist. Borden, acting as an agent of the charter government, tried to arrest Luther, who was a supporter of the Dorr government. Borden was supported at the trial level, and Luther sought review to have the Supreme Court consider, among other issues, whether the old charter government satisfied conditions of the guaranty clause of Article IV. The clause requires the federal government to "guarantee to every state in the Union a republican form of government." The Supreme Court, with only Justice Woodbury dissenting, affirmed the lower courts by holding that a guaranty clause finding was a nonjusticiable "political question."

The opinion of the Court was offered by Chief Justice Taney. He said that the question posed in this case "has not heretofore been recognized as a judicial one in any of the state courts." Rather, the "political department" has generally determined the content of state constitutions, and the "judicial power has followed in its decision." While federal courts have some powers not extended to state courts, the power to determine that a state government has been "lawfully established . . . is not one of them." This is especially true when the issue has already been decided by a state court. Taney posed the question of how a federal court would make such a determination. He saw it as a matter beyond judicial competence to resolve. Rather than a judicial matter, the Constitution treated the subject as "political in its nature," and placed authority to handle "an emergency of this kind" in the hands of "that [the political] department." The guaranty clause authorizes Congress to "decide what government is the established one in a state," a determination that necessarily precedes consideration of whether that government is republican or not. Congress's decision on such a matter is "binding on every other department of the government, and could not be questioned in a judicial tribunal." While Congress was itself not called on to resolve this case, "the right to decide is placed there, and not in the courts." In fulfilling this responsibility, the Congress put in place a mechanism by which the guaranty clause could be given effect. Through an act passed in 1795, Congress designated the president to act in this situation. In the event of a rebellion or insurrection, a state legislature or governor may request federal intervention. The president will the "call forth such numbers of the militia . . . as he may judge sufficient to suppress such insurrection." The power to decide whether the exigency requires federal intervention was thus delegated to the executive. In making such a decision, the president must, "of necessity, decide which is the government, and which party is unlawfully arrayed against it." The Court commented that this choice by Congress was sound, saying that it "would be difficult . . . to point out any other hands in which this power would be more safe, and at the same time equally effective." In this case, the president had recognized the charter government as legitimate and acted accordingly. Taney concluded by saying that the Supreme Court ought to "be the last" to overstep this limit. While it must address questions "confided to it by the Constitution," it is "equally its duty" not to "pass beyond its appropriate sphere of action." The Court must "take care not to involve itself in discussions which properly belong to other forums." *See also* BAKER V. CARR (369 U.S. 186: 1962), p. 123; JUDICIAL REVIEW, p. 627; JUSTICIABILITY, p. 630; POLITICAL QUESTION, p. 644.

Significance   The "political question" doctrine had its origin in *Luther v. Borden* (7 Howard 1: 1849). The doctrine is a limitation on the exercise of judicial power. It permits the Court to shift responsibility for decisions on an issue to one of the other branches. Generally, these issues require political rather than legal responses. A political question is not easily defined, but several contemporary cases such as *Baker v. Carr* (369 U.S. 186: 1962) have offered guidance. Among the characteristics of a political question is the absence or lack of "judicially discoverable or manageable standards." While not expressing it quite that way, Taney had suggested this kind of problem in handling guaranty clause claims. Taney also saw certain questions as more appropriately resolved if not "textually committed" to the "political departments." Similar to guaranty clause issues are those involving the constitutional amendment process. In *Coleman v. Miller* (307 U.S. 433: 1939), the Court used the political question doctrine to opt out of deciding how long the amendment ratification process should last. The case also raised the issue of whether a state may change its mind on a ratification vote, but the Court considered that matter political as well and subject to the judgment of Congress. Until 1962, the issue of legislative apportionment was viewed as a political question, but the Court abandoned that position in *Baker*, holding apportionment to be a justiciable question.

Political Question Doctrine: Legislative Apportionment

***Baker v. Carr*, 369 U.S. 186, 82 S.Ct. 691, 7 L.Ed. 2d 663 (1962)**   Held that legislative apportionment was a matter properly before federal courts. *Baker v. Carr* abandoned the position that apportionment was a political question not subject to resolution by the judicial branch. By the middle of the twentieth century, gross malapportionment existed for most state legislative districts as well as for

Congress. Years of inattention to shifting populations had produced highly inequitable representation. Baker and others brought suit in federal district court in Tennessee, claiming that despite significant growth and shifts in the population of Tennessee, legislative districts were still apportioned on the basis of a 1901 statute. The Court through Justice Brennan said the federal courts possessed jurisdiction in the case because the equal protection claim was not "so attenuated and unsubstantial as to be absolutely devoid of merit." Precedent would seem to have foreclosed the Court from adjudicating *Baker* by virtue of the political question doctrine in *Colegrove v. Green* (328 U.S. 549: 1946). The *Colegrove* decision held that the enjoining of an election because of malapportionment was beyond the Court's competence. Apportionment was of a "peculiarly political nature and therefore not meet for judicial determination." Thus the Court viewed the matter in separation of power terms. For the judiciary to involve itself would "cut very deep into the very being of Congress. Courts ought not to enter this political thicket."

Justice Brennan traced the history of the doctrine and concluded that its application revealed a definite pattern. "Prominent on the surface of any case held to involve a political question is found a textually demonstrable constitutional commitment of the issue to a coordinate political department." Guaranty clause claims and the conduct of foreign affairs were especially reflective of this category. A second category of political question issues involved cases where there was a lack of judicially discoverable and manageable standards for resolving such cases, or where it was impossible to decide without an initial policy determination clearly outside judicial discretion. Justice Brennan said the apportionment question fit neither of those categories. It was rather an equal protection problem containing claims of arbitrary and capricious action by the state of Tennessee.

Justices Frankfurter and Harlan dissented. Justice Frankfurter, who had written the Court's opinion in *Colegrove,* felt the *Baker* case was controlled by the political question doctrine and that the decision was a "massive repudiation of the experience of our whole past in asserting destructively novel judicial power." The Court must, in Justice Frankfurter's view, maintain "complete detachment, in fact and in appearance, from political entanglements and by abstention from injecting itself into the clash of political forces in political settlements." Justice Harlan remarked that those who consider the Court's authority as based on wise exercise of self-restraint and discipline in constitutional adjudication "will view the decision with deep concern." *See also* JUSTICIABILITY, p. 630; *LUTHER V. BORDEN* (7 Howard 1: 1849), p. 121; POLITICAL QUESTION, p. 644; STANDING, p. 655.

Significance   *Baker v. Carr* (369 U.S. 186: 1962) held that the issue of legislative apportionment was a justiciable cause of action. Prior to *Baker,* the Court had avoided the apportionment question because it posed a "political question," a matter better resolved by another branch of government. The political question doctrine had, since *Luther v. Borden* (7 Howard 1: 1849) restricted the exercise of judicial power under certain circumstances. *Baker,* however, minimized the applicability of the doctrine, which obliges the Court to defer to appropriate executive and congressional prerogatives. By focusing on the equal protection aspects of the apportionment question, the Court broke reapportionment away from the guaranty clause in *Baker,* which freed the justices from a line of cases holding that determination of what constitutes a republican form of government is necessarily a political question. *Baker* redefined the political question doctrine, and is generally regarded as the Court's most useful contemporary discussion of the subject. As far as the matter of reapportionment is concerned, *Baker* had an immediate effect. While it did not develop particular standards for reapportionment, it left in its wake a great deal of activity directed toward relieving malapportionment. The Court's first indication of a standard that could guide redistricting came in *Gray v. Sanders* (373 U.S. 368: 1963). The voting practice at issue was the unit system, a technique by which statewide officials were nominated in Georgia. While the Court distinguished this process from legislative districting, it held that the equal protection clause required persons to have an equal vote. Specific reference to "one man, one vote" was made in *Gray.* The following year, the Court applied the one man, one vote standard to apportionment of congressional districts in *Wesberry v. Sanders* (376 U.S. 1: 1964). Soon thereafter, the Court extended the standard to both houses of state legislatures and all local units of government, including educational boards with elective, single-member district representation.

Political Question Doctrine: Legislator Qualifications

***Powell v. McCormack*, 395 U.S. 486, 89 S.Ct. 1944, 23 L.Ed. 2d 491 (1969)**   Held the U.S. House could not exclude a person elected to Congress and possessing all the constitutional qualifications to serve. *Powell v. McCormack* involved an attempt by the House of Representatives to exclude a long-standing member, Congressman Adam Clayton Powell, for misconduct. The Constitution says in Article I, Section 1 that a House member must be at least 25 years of age, a U.S. citizen for at least seven years, and a resident of the district from which he was elected. Section 5 goes on to say that Congress is to "be the judge" of the "elections, returns and qualifications of its own members." Powell met the constitutionally enumerated qualifications, but a House committee recommended excluding Powell because of various actions such as wrongful diversion of House funds, filing false financial reports, and misuse of legislative immunity from state court processes. The Speaker of the House, Congressman John McCormack, ruled that Powell's exclusion could occur by House resolution, an action requiring only a majority vote. Such a resolution was passed, and Powell's seat was declared vacant. Powell unsuccessfully sought to enjoin the exclusion, but failed because the federal courts held they had no jurisdiction over this kind of issue. In the meantime, two things occurred. First, Powell was reelected to the House in a special election, but beyond submitting his certification of election, Powell "did not again present himself to the House or ask to be given the oath of office." More important, the 90th Congress from which Powell was excluded terminated, and Powell was then elected to the 91st Congress. The House adopted a resolution allowing him to sit, but fining him and stripping him of his seniority. Powell persisted in his appeal of the initial exclusion, and in an 8–1 decision, the Supreme Court held that Powell had been wrongfully excluded from the 90th Congress.

The opinion of the Court was delivered by Chief Justice Warren. The case hinged on the justiciability of the issue, but several questions had to be resolved prior to addressing that matter. First, the Court held that Powell's back pay claim "remains viable." Though some issues in the original suit had become moot, the "live issues" satisfied the case and controversy requirement. Next, the Court set aside the speech and debate clause as prohibiting judicial review. Third, the Court held that the congressional resolution excluded Powell from membership, an action that could not be treated as the "equivalent of expulsion." Finally, the Court rejected the contention that it lacked jurisdiction because the action was not a "case 'arising under' the Constitution within the meaning of Article III." It was argued that this was a matter committed exclusively to the House for determination, but the Court disagreed.

The justiciability issue was more difficult and involved two components. First, was Powell's claim and the relief he sought "of a kind which admits of judicial resolution"? The Court said it was. Second, was the issue presented a "political question," and thus inappropriate for federal courts on separation of power grounds? The Court held that it was not a political question. Among other things, a political question is one where there is "textually demonstrable constitutional commitment" of the issue to a coordinate branch. The principal question here was whether Article I, Section 5, which gives Congress the power to "judge the qualifications of its members," was a "textual commitment" of the function to the Congress exclusively. The Court concluded that the framers had not intended to vest the Congress with the "discretionary power to deny membership by a majority vote." Thus, Article I only committed judgments to the Congress on those qualifying criteria set forth there. Thus, the "textual commitment" element of the political question doctrine does not preclude consideration of Powell's case. It was also argued that a political question existed because judicial resolution would produce a "politically embarrassing confrontation between coordinate branches." The Court held this case presented a constitutional interpretation, a determination that "falls within the traditional role accorded courts to interpret the law." No "lack of respect" for a coordinate branch was found to exist here. Neither were any of the other elements of the political question doctrine. Justice Stewart dissented on grounds of mootness. He characterized the "essential purpose" of Powell's suit to be reinstatement in the 90th Congress. That purpose "became impossible" when the 90th Congress adjourned and the 91st Congress was convened. See also CASE OR CONTROVERSY, p. 583; JUDICIAL REVIEW, p. 627; JUSTICIABILITY, p. 630; POLITICAL QUESTION, p. 644.

Significance   The Court held that House exclusion of a duly elected person from membership did not constitute a nonjusticiable political question in *Powell v. McCormack* (395 U.S. 486: 1969). The case provided useful discussion of two interesting issues, the political question doctrine and legislative qualifications. In the course of his opinion. Warren set out the several criteria or elements of a political question. In addition to the "demonstrable textual commitment," potential for embarrassment stemming from multibranch treatment of the same issue, and reflection of "lack of respect" for another branch, Warren mentioned three other situations that might require invocation of the doctrine. First, the courts ought refrain from dealing with issues that "lack judicially discoverable or manageable standards" for resolving the matter. Second, the courts must avoid cases that cannot be decided without policy guidance from the other coordinate branches or elsewhere outside the courts. Finally, a political question exists when there is an "unusual need for unquestioning adherence to a political decision already made." While these elements did not pertain to the *Powell* case, the opinion in this decision nicely represented the characteristics of the doctrine. The *Powell* case also spoke to the matter of legislative qualifications. So long as a person has been duly elected and satisfies the age, citizenship, and residency requirements expressly set out in the Constitution, the Congress (or state legislative body) was without the authority to add or alter these membership qualifications. Thus, exclusion from membership was prohibited even on misconduct grounds. Three years earlier, in *Bond v. Floyd* (385 U.S. 116: 1966), the Court had held that a state legislature could not deny membership because of antiwar statements made by a person (Julian Bond in this case) who had been duly elected to the state senate. Such exclusion was seen as a fundamental violation of Bond's First Amendment rights. As distinct from exclusion, legislative bodies are generally free to censure or even expel members for misconduct. That the Court saw the House as excluding rather than expelling Powell was a critical distinction. This procedure, by provisions of Article I, Section 5, requires "concurrence of two thirds" of the House membership.

Political Question Doctrine: Party Convention Credentials

O'Brien v. Brown, 409 U.S. 1, 92 S.Ct. 2718, 34 L.Ed. 2d 1 (1972)   Used the political question doctrine to hold that federal courts ought not interfere with proceedings of a national political convention. *O'Brien v. Brown* developed out of the 1972 Democratic National Convention and involved challenges to delegate seating decisions made by the Convention Credentials Committee. As an outgrowth of the struggle between those supporting the candidacy of Senator George McGovern and those who opposed his nomination, the committee determined that certain Illinois and California delegates had been selected in violation of party guidelines. The committee recommended that these delegates not be seated. Actions were filed by the unseated delegates. The U.S. district court dismissed the complaints, finding no justiciable issue. The court of appeals found the matter justiciable, however, and sustained the committee's recommendation regarding the Illinois delegation while invalidating the recommendation pertaining to the California delegates. Petitions for certiorari and applications for a stay of the court of appeals judgment were filed with the Supreme Court. In a 6–3 decision, the Court granted the stays.

The *per curiam* opinion first noted that the certiorari petitions presented "novel and important" questions, but the Court delayed action on them because of the severe time constraints involved. The application for stay called for consideration of "three basic factors": whether "irreparable injury" would occur without a stay; the "probability" that the lower court had wrongly held these issues appropriate for federal court decision; and the "public interests" that may be affected by the court of appeals judgment. The Court noted that without stay of the court of appeals decision, the convention was denied "its traditional power to pass on . . . credentials." Granting a stay, on the other hand, will "not foreclose" the convention's giving the delegates the relief they sought in court. The Court then looked at the authority of the court of appeals to render a decision on the matter. The Court found no precedent to support judicial intervention under these circumstances. Such a case involves relationships of "great delicacy" that are essentially "political in nature." Judicial intervention in this kind of case "has been approached with great caution and restraint." The Court said it had been "understood" from their origin that political parties were voluntary associations, and that their conventions were the "proper forum for determining intra party disputes." Though not undertaking "final resolution" of the important issues involved in this case without full argument and deliberation, the Court expressed "grave doubts" about the court of appeals judgment. Finally, the Court recognized the "large" public interest in "allowing the political processes to function free from judicial supervision." Coupled with the availability of the convention itself to serve as a forum for consideration of the Credentials Committee recommendations, and the lack of precedent support for the court of appeals action, the Court granted the stay. In doing so, it recognized that judicial review of the convention's final action may not be possible. This, however, was compatible with nearly 150 years in which the national political parties had handled these matters for themselves. That practice ought not be altered through the exercise of "extraordinary equity powers" under the circumstances and time pressures present here.

Justice Brennan concurred in granting the stays pending action on the certiorari petitions. Justices Douglas, Marshall, and White dissented. Douglas said the stay "presupposes an ultimate decision on the merits," and characterized the granting of the stay as an "oblique and covert way" of deciding the merits. Marshall argued that the Court ought to consider the merits immediately. He rejected the suggestion that the issue was nonjusticiable because it involved the "internal decision-making of a political party." The "political question" doctrine was "fashioned to deal with a very different problem." It was intended to keep the Court from rendering a decision that would put the Court "into conflict with one or more of the coordinate branches of government." Neither of the other branches had jurisdictional claims here. Neither could it be asserted, in Marshall's view, that "judicially manageable standards" were lacking. The questions presented were seen as "well within" the range of questions "regularly presented to courts" and "capable of judicial resolution." *See also:* JUDICIAL REVIEW, p. 627; JUSTICIABILITY, p. 630; POLITICAL QUESTION, p. 644.

Significance   The Court invoked the "political question" doctrine in *O'Brien v. Brown* (409 U.S. 1: 1972) to find that federal courts had no authority over national political conventions. The Court used the doctrine to examine the propriety of the lower court's intervention in the "deliberative processes" of the party convention procedure. The Court noted the absence of precedent for such intervention. Situations such as this were seen as "essentially political" and involving "relationships of great delicacy." Accordingly, judicial involvement must be approached with "great caution and restraint." As long as the convention itself could resolve these disputes, the "large public interest" was best served by allowing the political processes of the convention to "function free of judicial supervision." In a related situation, the Court held in *Democratic Party of the United States v. LaFollette* (450 U.S. 107: 1981) that a state cannot require its national convention delegates to vote for the state's primary winner. The decision deferred to the convention's own rules governing the nomination process and emphasized the associational rights of the delegates as well as the traditional detached role of courts from such political processes.

Political Question Doctrine: Foreign Policy

Goldwater v. Carter, **444 U.S. 996, 100 S.Ct. 533, 62 L.Ed. 2d 428 (1979)** Dismissed a suit brought against the president for termination of a treaty without congressional approval. Despite the dismissal, *Goldwater v. Carter* provided an occasion for several members of the Court to consider the "political question" doctrine as it applies to the conduct of foreign affairs. Various members of Congress including Senator Barry Goldwater brought suit against President Carter after he gave notice of termination of the Mutual Defense Treaty with Taiwan. He had not sought counsel of Congress before taking this action, much less secured their approval. The Court refused to grant a writ of certiorari by a 6–3 margin.

Several useful statements on the justiciability of this issue were offered in individual concurring and dissenting opinions. Justice Rehnquist's concurrence was joined by Chief Justice Burger and Justices Stewart and Stevens. He characterized the principal issue in the case as "political" and therefore "nonjusticiable" because it involved the "authority of the President in the conduct of our country's foreign relations" and the degree to which the "Senate or the Congress is authorized to negate the action of the President." He noted no constitutional provision governing this process and suggested the possibility that "different termination procedures may be appropriate for different treaties." Treaty termination then "must surely be controlled by political standards." He added that "justifications for concluding that the question here is political" are even more compelling because the case involves "foreign relations," specifically a "treaty commitment to use military force in the defense of a foreign government if attacked." Furthermore, Rehnquist saw this case as a request to have the Court settle a dispute between "coequal branches" of our government "each of which has resources available to protect and assert its interests in ways private litigants could not." He urged dismissal of the case because to use Article III power to resolve a political question would create substantial "disruption among the three coequal branches of government."

Justice Powell concurred with the dismissal, but took issue with Rehnquist's treatment of political questions. Powell would have dismissed the case as "not ripe for judicial review" given that no official action had been taken by President Carter. In the "present posture" of the case, the Court was uncertain "whether there ever will be an actual confrontation between the Legislative and Executive Branches." He went on, however, to take issue with Rehnquist's characterization of a nonjusticiable political question. Powell said the doctrine "incorporates three inquiries." The first is whether the case involves resolution of issues "committed by the text of the Constitution." He did not feel a "textually demonstrable" commitment of treaty termination to the president alone existed in this case. The second inquiry is whether the case "would demand that a court move beyond areas of judicial expertise." The case here was not lacking for "judicially discoverable and manageable standards." While resolution of the issue may not be easy, "it only requires us to apply normal principles of interpretation." Though the case involved foreign relations, the questions presented only concern the "constitutional division of power between Congress and the President." The third inquiry is whether "prudential considerations counsel against judicial intervention." Powell found no such prudential considerations that would call for limiting the exercise of judicial power.

Justice Blackmun, with Justice White, dissented in part, saying that the question of whether a president possesses the unilateral power of treaty termination ought to be set for argument to "give it the plenary consideration it so obviously deserves." Justice Brennan also dissented. He argued that the plurality view "profoundly misapprehends" the political question principle. The doctrine "restrains" courts from reviewing an "exercise of foreign policy judgment by the coordinate political branch" to which that judgment has been committed. The doctrine does not apply, however, when a court examines the "antecedent question" of whether a particular branch has been "constitutionally designated as the repository of political decision-making power." The issue of decision-making authority must, he felt, be resolved "as a matter of constitutional law, not political discretion." Brennan then offered an observation on the merits of the case. Abrogation of the treaty was a "necessary incident to Executive recognition of the Peking government," and the Constitution commits to the "President alone" the power to "recognize, and withdraw recognition from, foreign regimes." *See also* BAKER V. CARR (369 U.S. 186: 1962), p. 123; JUDICIAL REVIEW, p. 627; JUSTICIABILITY, p. 630; POLITICAL QUESTION, p. 644.

Significance   The Court refused to interfere with the president's announcement of intent to terminate unilaterally a foreign defense treaty in *Goldwater v. Carter* (444 U.S. 996: 1979). In dismissing the suit, four members of the Court saw the treaty termination matter as a nonjusticiable political question. Since the inception of the political question doctrine in *Luther v. Borden* (7 Howard 1: 1849), certain matters have generally been viewed as "political" in nature. Determination of what constitutes a "republican form of government" is such an issue. Issues stemming from the conduct of foreign affairs have also generally been held to fit the political category. Though the treaty ratification process requires Senate participation, presidents have typically enjoyed broad discretion in the foreign policy arena. That position is reflected not only in the judgment of the Court to dismiss, but even in the opinion of Justice Brennan, who disagreed with the dismissal. A fuller discussion of executive prerogatives in foreign affairs can be found in Chapter 3.

3. Executive Power, Foreign Affairs, War Powers, and Citizenship

Overview, 135

Article II, 139

War Powers, 163

Citizenship, 173

OVERVIEW

Executive power is conveyed to the president by Article II. The powers conferred are extensive and have increased over our constitutional history. Some of the powers discussed in this chapter are specifically enumerated, while others are implied. Implied power has been the most troublesome for the Court, especially where presidents claim broad prerogative or inherent power. Such power gives a president the capacity to act at his discretion on behalf of the public interest without even implicit authorization.

The Court's responses to the inherent power argument have been mixed. In *In Re Neagle* (135 U.S. 1: 1890), the Court found that a president need not have specific legislative authorization to act to protect the safety of a Supreme Court justice. Rather, he might act to preserve the "peace of the United States." The Court rejected, however, President Truman's assertion of inherent power as sufficient to allow him to seize privately-owned steel mills in order to end a national steel strike. The Court held in *Youngstown Sheet and Tube Company v. Sawyer* (343 U.S. 579: 1952) that Congress had set forth the means by which such situations were to be handled, thus precluding alternative action by the president. In *New York Times v. United States* (403 U.S. 713: 1971), the Nixon Administration sought an injunction to prevent the *New York Times* from publishing the Pentagon Papers. The administration argued that the publication would jeopardize national security. The Court's decision to deny the injunction was, in part, based on the inherent power issue.

The Constitution heavily involves the president in the conduct of foreign policy. Over the years, this function has expanded, and the Court's decisions have generally supported presidential initiatives.

In *United States v. Curtiss-Wright Export Corporation* (299 U.S. 304: 1936), the Court clearly distinguished external affairs from domestic policy activity and held that the president has "plenary" power as the "sole organ" of the government in international relations. Consistent with this view, the Court, in *United States v. Belmont* (301 U.S. 324: 1937), recognized that executive agreements entered into without Senate approval and foreign treaties were comparable. In a more recent decision, the Court upheld executive authority to revoke, on national security grounds, the passport of an American citizen in *Haig v. Agee* (453 U.S. 280: 1981).

The president has more specific powers allowing him to act as the chief executive officer of the United States, such as broad powers of appointment. This permits the president to exercise administrative control. The issue of whether this appointing power carries with it a comparable removal power was first addressed in *Myers v. United States* (272 U.S. 52: 1926), which permitted almost absolute removal authority. Subsequent cases such as *Humphrey's Executor v. United States* (295 U.S. 602: 1935) confined unilateral removals to executive branch appointees. It has also been established that the president's executive function generally confers immunity from judicial interference. In *Mississippi v. Johnson* (4 Wallace 475: 1867), the Court held that a president could not be enjoined from enforcement of a federal statute. The Court based its decision on the view that executing the law is a "purely executive and political" task requiring substantial executive discretion. The Court has also held in *Nixon v. Fitzgerald* (457 U.S. 731: 1982) that a president is comprehensively immune from civil damage suits brought against actions taken in the performance of his official duties. In the wake of the Watergate scandal, the Court examined the issue of executive privilege, the capacity of a president to withhold information from the other two branches. In *United States v. Nixon* (418 U.S. 683: 1974), the Court recognized a limited privilege, but rejected the assertion that it was absolute in scope. In this case, the Court unanimously held that the privilege could not prevail in the face of a criminal investigation. A president's power of pardon, on the other hand, is virtually full. In *Ex Parte Grossman* (267 U.S. 87: 1925), the Court upheld a presidential pardon from criminal contempt, thus extending pardons to common law offenses.

Over the years, the president has acquired greater initiative in the area of budget preparation and supervision. While this generally remains the case, the Court limited the president's ability to withhold or impound funds once specifically appropriated by the Congress in *Train v. City of New York* (420 U.S. 35: 1975).

The most demanding circumstance faced by any government is the emergency of war. The president possesses substantial military power under his authority as commander in chief. The Court has generally deferred to the exercise of executive authority during wartime. In *The Prize Cases* (2 Black 635: 1865), the Court upheld Lincoln's blockade of Confederate ports without prior congressional authorization. Citing military exigency, the Court also upheld a presidential order compelling the relocation of persons of Japanese ancestry in *Korematsu v.*

United States (323 U.S. 214: 1944). The Court did find in *Ex Parte Milligan* (4 Wallace 2: 1866) that the president does not possess the power to create military tribunals with authority to try civilians. A president may, however, establish military commissions to try enemy military personnel, as held in *In Re Yamashita* (327 U.S. 1: 1946). The existence of war also permits Congress to exercise powers in response to the demands of the emergency. In *Bowles v. Willingham* (321 U.S. 503: 1944), the Court upheld the rent control provisions of the Emergency Price Control Act. In *Woods v. Miller* (333 U.S. 138: 1948), the Court permitted Congress to extend those same rent controls even after formal cessation of hostilities.

The chapter also includes two cases dealing with the issue of citizenship. The Fourteenth Amendment provides that persons "born or naturalized in the United States" are citizens. The principle of "jus soli" or citizenship based on place of birth was established in *United States v. Wong Kim Ark* (169 U.S. 649: 1898). While Congress possesses comprehensive authority over naturalization, the Court, because of international relations implications, has imposed limits on the removal of citizenship. In *Afroyim v. Rusk* (387 U.S. 253: 1967), the Court struck down a statute that required automatic forfeiture of citizenship if the person participated in a foreign election. Now a citizen may lose citizenship only if it is voluntarily relinquished.

Article II　Places executive power in the office of the president and enumerates specific aspects of presidential power. The article is broken into four sections. Section 1 provides that "the executive Power shall be vested in a President of the United States of America." The character and scope of this executive power is not fully clear from this language, and extensive debate has occurred on the issue. The prevailing view is that the executive power includes not only the specified grants and power directly implied from express provisions, but also that a president has the capacity to respond to emergencies with powers over and above those conveyed explicitly or implicitly. This latter kind of power is called inherent or prerogative power. The remainder of Section 1 describes the presidential selection process, eligibility requirements, and presidential succession. Section 1 also contains the presidential oath, which requires the president to "protect and defend the Constitution," a provision cited in support of the broad executive power. The last portion of Section 1 establishes the electoral college, although much of the original language has been modified or replaced by the Twelfth and Twenty-fifth Amendments.

Section 2 begins the enumeration of particular powers assigned to the president. He is to be "Commander in Chief" of the military, which guarantees civilian control over the military. The commander-in-chief provision serves as the heart of the "war powers" that may be drawn upon by the president in times of national emergency. He is given full control over the executive departments and their officers. The president may grant reprieves and pardons for any federal offense. Section 2 also contains the treaty-making language requiring Senate concurrence before a treaty is made effective. Despite the ratification requirement, substantial foreign policy initiative flows from the president's role in treaty making. Finally, Section 2 contains the appointment power. The president is responsible for nominating all "Ambassadors, other public Ministers and Consuls, Judges of the Supreme Court, and all other officers of the United States." Such appointments are subject to the "advice and consent" of the Senate. Section 2 does permit the president to make temporary appointments to fill vacancies existing while the Senate is recessed.

Section 3 includes three elements that have become important over the course of our constitutional history. First, the president is required to inform the Congress as to the "State of the Union." The president may also make legislative proposals to the Congress for its consideration, and he may convene both houses of Congress on "extraordinary occasions." This plus the legislative veto power provided in Article I places the president directly into the legislative process. Second, Section 3 gives the president power to "receive Ambassadors and other public Ministers." This authority has become critical to the president's capacity to conduct foreign relations as the principal representative of the United States. The power to receive ambassadors permits the president to recognize new governments or regimes. Section 3 concludes by instructing the president to "take Care that the laws be faithfully executed. . . ." This clause permits the president to effectively pursue enforcement of the laws, including through the use of force. This language, in addition to the more open-ended initial clause conveying executive power, provides the presidency with relatively comprehensive authority. This includes absolute control over those executive officers who are engaged in enforcing laws.

Section 4 of Article II deals with the matter of impeachment. The section provides that the president, vice president, or any other civil officer of the United States "shall be removed from office on impeachment for and conviction of treason, bribery, or other high crimes and misdemeanors. The actual process by which the impeachment would take place is described in Article I, Section 3. *See also* EXECUTIVE IMMUNITY, p. 601; EXECUTIVE PRIVILEGE, p. 603; IMPLIED POWER, p. 618; INHERENT POWER, p. 622; WAR POWERS, p. 673.

Significance   Article II represents an attempt by the framers of the Constitution to strengthen the extremely weak executive found under the Articles of Confederation. Article II grants to the president a substantial array of authority and responsibility. There are four kinds of powers that may be exercised by the executive. First, there are the specifically enumerated powers. These are quite broad in that they vest the president with the authority to execute the laws and protect our constitutional system. Beyond the enumerated powers, the president possesses powers derived or implied from those expressed. It has generally evolved that the executive has the power required to fulfill the enumerated functions, a kind of implicit necessary and proper power. The Court's recognition of such concepts as presidential privilege and immunity, even though not absolute, reflects the existence of implicit presidential power.

Second, the Constitution authorizes the president to undertake policy initiatives. With respect to domestic policy, the president is the proposer of legislation to the Congress. While congressional action is ultimately required, the president's legislative proposals are the catalyst of the legislative process. Third, the president plays a role in the legislative process through the veto mechanism. Fourth, in the foreign policy sphere, the president has become the personification of American sovereignty, and as such, possesses the authority to shape foreign policy. This, of course, is augmented by his role as commander-in-chief of the military.

Finally, there is the matter of inherent power. Inherent or prerogative power allows the president to act in the public interest when circumstances dictate, even in the absence of explicit or implied authorization. Though certain attempts to exercise this inherent power have been struck down, there seems to be consensus that certain situations pose such threats to the system itself that the president is obligated to do whatever is required to meet the threat. This inherent power comes from outside the Constitution or statutes, but when combined with the grants of power contained in or implicit from Article II, it is clear that the president plays the pivotal role in the governance structure.

Scope of Executive Power

In Re Neagle, **135 U.S. 1, 10 S.Ct. 658, 34 L.Ed. 55 (1890)**
Ruled that a president may act even in the absence of explicit constitutional or statutory authority. *In Re Neagle* raised fundamental inherent power questions despite its unusual fact setting. Neagle was a federal marshal assigned to protect the safety of United States Supreme Court Justice Stephen J. Field. The need for security precautions arose out of a case presided over by the justice sitting as a circuit judge in California. A civil litigant, represented by her husband, lost a judgment in a case with considerable financial stakes. At the conclusion of the case, the litigant made accusations that led to a broader conflict in the courtroom. The woman and her husband were both sentenced to jail for contempt as a result. They threatened to kill Justice Field if he ever returned to California, which he did regularly to fulfill his circuitriding responsibilities. The attorney general was apprised of the situation and assigned Neagle to protect Field. Soon thereafter, Neagle shot and killed the lawyer husband when he appeared to be commencing an attack on the justice. Neagle was arrested and charged with murder before a state court. He was subsequently released under provisions of a statute that permitted issuance of a writ of *habeas corpus* for acts done under federal law. The problem in this case was that there was no federal law covering the assignment of Neagle as a bodyguard. The Supreme Court upheld the release nonetheless in a 6–2 decision (Justice Field did not participate).

Justice Miller's opinion of the Court fully embraced the view that presidents must possess certain prerogatives or inherent power to allow response to particular situations. The Court presumed no statute covered the situation, and based its holding on Article II, Section 3, which requires that the president "take care that the laws be faithfully executed." The Court chose not to limit the executive only to the "express terms" of statutes or treaties. Rather, the executive function includes the "rights, duties, and obligations growing out of the Constitution itself, our international relations, and all the protection implied by the nature of the government under the Constitution." The Court suggested that there exists a "peace of the United States" that is violated by a person attacking a federal judge. The Court concluded that the marshal must be able to keep that peace, and the executive branch has the authority to "set in motion the necessary means" to do so.

Chief Justice Fuller and Justice Lamar dissented, arguing that the executive does not have prerogatives that go beyond the laws enacted by Congress. They referred to the "necessary and proper" clause of Article I as the "germ of all the implication of powers" to be drawn from the Constitution. The executive has no such implicit authority and may not proceed without explicit permission of statute. *See also* IMPLIED POWER, p. 618; INHERENT POWER, p. 622; *YOUNGSTOWN SHEET AND TUBE COMPANY V. SAWYER* (343 U.S. 579: 1952), p. 146.

Significance   The Court's decision in *In Re Neagle* (135 U.S. 1: 1890) recognized inherent power residing within the executive branch. Such power has no explicit source, but rather emanates from the function of the executive. Soon after *Neagle,* the Court reiterated this view in *In Re Debs* (158 U.S. 564: 1895). The *Debs* case arose out of the Pullman railway strike. In response to the strike, the president dispatched federal troops and sought a court injunction against the striking workers including Debs, the union president. The union continued its activities, and Debs was cited for contempt. The Court upheld the enforcement initiatives taken by the executive even in the absence of authorizing legislation. The executive must be able to "command obedience" to law by drawing upon whatever power is required to "keep the peace." According to this view, the president possesses inherent power that permits virtually any response to national needs so long as the action is not expressly forbidden. Inherent power simply provides the president with the capacity to discharge the executive function. The inherent power concept raises serious concerns about the limits of executive power. A less supportive view can be found in *Youngstown Sheet and Tube Company v. Sawyer* (343 U.S. 579: 1952), where the Supreme Court invalidated President Truman's seizure of the steel industry to end a national strike.

Immunity from Injunction

Mississippi v. Johnson, **4 Wallace 475, 18 L.Ed. 437** (1867)
Held that a president is immune from judicial injunctions aimed at restraining enforcement of legislation. *Mississippi v. Johnson* arose out of the Reconstruction and was an attempt to have the Court rule on the basic constitutionality of the enactments. Just prior to the scheduled implementation of the policy, Mississippi sought to have the Supreme Court "perpetually enjoin and restrain" President Andrew Johnson from "executing, or in any manner carrying out" the Reconstruction Acts on the grounds that they were unconstitutional. In a unanimous decision, the Court refused to issue such an injunction. The issue, according to Chief Justice Chase, was whether the president can be "restrained by injunction from carrying into effect an act of Congress alleged to be unconstitutional."

The Court's decision rested on the nature of the executive responsibilities involved. The Court acknowledged that the judiciary might compel certain executive conduct, but only where purely "ministerial" duties were involved. Such a duty is one where "nothing is left to discretion." A ministerial duty is a "simple, definite duty arising under conditions admitted or proved to exist, and imposed by law." Carrying out the Reconstruction Acts, however, was not a ministerial duty, but rather an executive duty. The Court enumerated the various judgments the president needed to make in order to execute the Reconstruction policy. The need for broad discretion made the enforcement duty upon the president "purely executive and political." The judiciary has no role to play in the performance of this kind of duty. Even where legislation is alleged to be invalid, the Court failed to see any justification for "judicial interference with the exercise of Executive discretion." For the judiciary to have such capacity would be "an absurd and excessive extravagance." The chief justice concluded by considering the possible consequences of improper interference by the judiciary. If a court issued such an injunction like that sought here, it would be "without power to enforce its process" if the president refused to comply. If, however, the president did comply and failed to execute an enactment of Congress, he could be subject to impeachment for such conduct. Under these circumstances, would the Court be expected to intervene on behalf of the complying president and attempt to enjoin an impeachment? Referring to the foregoing as a "strange spectacle," the Court refused to allow the possibility of these consequences by withholding the injunction against President Johnson. *See also* EXECUTIVE IMMUNITY, p. 601; INHERENT POWER, p. 622; SEPARATION OF POWERS, p. 56; *UNITED STATES V. NIXON* (418 U.S. 683: 1974), p. 153; *YOUNGSTOWN SHEET AND TUBE COMPANY V. SAWYER* (343 U.S. 579: 1952), p. 146.

Significance *Mississippi v. Johnson* (4 Wallace 475: 1867) established that a president is immune from judicial orders to withhold enforcement of federal statutes. The decision was based upon the fundamental character of separation of power. Each of the three branches must remain free from interference of the others in the performance of its respective functions. Thus the judiciary may not command Congress to enact particular legislation, nor may it attempt to forestall the executive branch from the discharge of its constitutional responsibilities. The position of the Court in this case was consistent with a long-held view of presidential immunity. Beyond considerations of separation of power, the judiciary simply does not have the capacity to enforce court orders directed at the president, a reality clearly recognized by Chief Justice Marshall in *Marbury v. Madison* (1 Cranch 137) in 1803. There are limits on presidential immunity, however. In *United States v. Nixon* (418 U.S. 683: 1974), the Court rejected assertions of executive privilege and required a sitting president to surrender recordings of White House conversations for use as evidence in a criminal proceeding. While recognizing an absolute presidential immunity from civil suits in *Nixon v. Fitzgerald* (457 U.S. 731: 1982), the Court did not extend that immunity to presidential aides in *Harlow and Butterfield v. Fitzgerald* (457 U.S. 800: 1982). The Court has also confronted presidents occasionally on the matter of exercising inherent power, such as in *Youngstown Sheet and Tube Company v. Sawyer* (343 U.S. 579: 1952). On balance, however, the Court has seldom sought to curtail the exercise of executive enforcement power.

Inherent Power: Foreign Affairs

United States v. Curtiss-Wright Export Corporation, 299 U.S. 304, 57 S.Ct. 216, 81 L.Ed. 255 (1936) Recognized that the president possesses broad discretionary authority to conduct foreign affairs. *United States v. Curtiss-Wright Export Corporation* established that presidents possess an inherent power, even in the absence of express or implied authority, that allows response to emergency situations. The *Curtiss-Wright* case developed out of a congressional initiative to limit the sale of arms and war materials to belligerent nations in South America. Congress adopted a resolution that permitted the president to issue a declaration specifically prohibiting arms sales. The Curtiss-Wright Export Corporation violated the declared prohibition and challenged the executive declaration as an exercise of unconstitutionally delegated legislative power. The Supreme Court upheld the arms sale restriction in a 7–1 decision with Justice Stone not participating. Curtiss-Wright contended that the resolution was an impermissible delegation of power and focused on defects traditionally asserted in delegation challenges. Included was that the president needed to make substantive judgments that were left to his "unfettered discretion" and "controlled by no standard" established by Congress.

The opinion of the Court was delivered by Justice Sutherland and was governed throughout by the factor that the resolution had been intended to "affect a situation entirely external to the United States, and falling within the category of foreign affairs." Even if the Congress could not have delegated comparable discretion for a domestic policy matter, the delegation of power may be sustained here because of its foreign policy focus. Indeed, the Court concluded that domestic and foreign affairs involved "two classes of powers," different in both "their origin and their nature." This is "categorically true" because sovereignty passed directly to the federal government and did not "depend upon affirmative grants of the Constitution," as is the case with the exercise of power in domestic matters. Not only did the Court find that power over external and internal affairs is different in its "origin and essential character," but that "participation in the exercise of the power is significantly limited." In the "vast external realm," with its "important, complicated, delicate and manifold problems," the "President alone has the power to speak or listen as a representative of the nation." At issue in this case was not only power directed to the president through the congressional resolution, but also the "very delicate, plenary and exclusive power of the president as the sole organ of the federal government in the field of international relations." This latter power "does not require as a basis for its exercise an act of Congress." The president's prohibition of arms sales, therefore, could not be challenged on delegation of legislative power grounds since his capacity to conduct foreign affairs permitted the action even without congressional resolution. *See also* DELEGATION OF LEGISLATIVE POWER, p. 591; IMPLIED POWER, p. 618; INHERENT POWER, p. 622; *NEW YORK TIMES V. UNITED STATES* (403 U.S. 713: 1971), p. 148; *YOUNGSTOWN SHEET AND TUBE COMPANY V. SAWYER* (343 U.S. 579: 1952), p. 146.

Significance   The Court's decision in *United States v. Curtiss-Wright Export Corporation* (299 U.S. 304: 1936) established that a president must be accorded a "degree of discretion and freedom from statutory restriction" in the conduct of foreign affairs. The exercise of such power would clearly not be permissible if "domestic affairs alone" were involved. The *Curtiss-Wright* decision recognized inherent executive power that is a direct outgrowth of sovereignty located with the federal government. As such, inherent power in the conduct of foreign affairs is not dependent on "affirmative grants" from the Constitution. Rather, the power to wage and end war, maintain diplomatic relations, and generally function in the international sphere are contained in the federal government as "necessary concomitants of nationality." This power is bounded by specific limitations on executive power as set forth in the Constitution; it cannot supersede or suspend those limitations. In addition, this inherent power may not permit encroachment upon individual liberties protected by the Constitution. On balance, however, the effect of *Curtiss-Wright* was to firmly establish that the president possesses inherent power in the field of foreign affairs, a power more extensive than any enumerated constitutional power.

Inherent Power: Seizure

Youngstown Sheet and Tube Company v. Sawyer, **343 U.S. 579, 72 S.Ct. 863, 91 L.Ed. 1153 (1952)**   Struck down a presidential order directing the seizure and government operation of privately-owned steel mills. The Court was asked in *Youngstown Sheet and Tube Company v. Sawyer* to permit an extensive exercise of inherent or aggregate executive power. A six-member majority of the Court was unpersuaded that the president possessed such authority under these circumstances. The seizure order was precipitated by a labor dispute in the steel industry. After failing to achieve resolution of the problem through certain administrative means, President Truman ordered Commerce Secretary Sawyer to "take possession of a number of steel mills and keep them operating." The action was taken because Truman believed that a steel strike would immediately jeopardize our "national defense." The steel companies sought to enjoin the seizure, and the Supreme Court reviewed the matter within days of the original seizure order.

Each of the majority's six members authored an individual opinion. Justice Black noted the absence of statutory authorization for seizure. Indeed, he pointed out that the Congress had "refused to adopt that method of settling labor disputes" when considering the Taft-Hartley Act. Black felt that authority to order the seizure must "be found in some provisions of the Constitution," and he rejected the contention that power can be implied from the "aggregate of his powers." In addition Black did not feel that the order could be sustained as an exercise of the president's military command authority. The Court, said Black, "cannot with faithfulness to our constitutional system" allow even the Commander-in-Chief the "ultimate power . . . to take possession of private property in order to keep labor disputes from stopping production." Such an action might be a "job for the Nation's lawmakers," but "not for its military authorities." Justice Frankfurter acknowledged that the president's constitutional authority is not as "particularized" as that of Congress, but "unenumerated powers do not mean undefined powers." Authority is governed by the separation of powers mechanism, which "gives essential content to undefined provisions." Accordingly, seizure could not occur without legislative authorization and certainly not when such action directly contradicts legislative judgment on such a technique. Justice Douglas's concurring opinion was also grounded on separation of powers. Emergencies do not "create" power or suspend checks and balances. The separation doctrine was not intended to "promote efficiency, but to preclude the exercise of arbitrary power." That may produce stalemate and lack of "harmonious, reciprocal action" between the president and Congress, but that is both the "risk" and the "price" of the system. Justice Jackson more directly rejected the inherent power arguments as based on the "unarticulated assumption . . . that necessity knows no law." Jackson felt that constitutional authors consciously withheld such emergency power because crises are a "ready pretext for usurpation" and that possession of emergency power "would tend to kindle emergencies." The concurrences of Justices Burton and Clark also noted the lack of legislative authorization for seizure, but they suggested that procedures under the Taft-Hartley Act were still available to Truman. Seizure certainly could not be considered in the absence of congressional authorization when legislative options were still to be utilized by Truman. Clark did acknowledge, however, that emergency power may be exercised at some point to preserve the nation itself.

A dissent was written by Chief Justice Vinson that was joined by Justices Reed and Minton. Vinson urged that "flexibility as to mode of execution to meet critical situations is a matter of practical necessity." Presidents must possess sufficient prerogative authority to respond to emergencies. He disagreed with the majority that unlimited executive authority was involved in this case and indicated that Truman's action was only temporary and subject to subsequent action by Congress. Vinson also cited historical precedent for the action and placed the seizure wholly within the bounds of executive action previously established. *See also* IMPLIED POWER, p. 618; INHERENT POWER, p. 622; *UNITED STATES V. CURTISS-WRIGHT EXPORT CORPORATION* (299 U.S. 304: 1936), p. 144.

Significance   *Youngstown Sheet and Tube Company v. Sawyer* (343 U.S. 579: 1952) voided President Truman's seizure of the steel mills as an impermissible encroachment into the legislative sphere. The decision also responded unsympathetically to assertions of inherent or aggregate executive power as made in this case. At the same time, several members of the majority plus the three dissenters felt that inherent executive power may be drawn upon under appropriate circumstances. Many of the members of the Court stressed the practical necessity of inherent executive power and rejected the view of rigidly fixed functional lines for the three branches. Rather, most of the Court seemed to prefer a view of separation of powers that would continually redefine or rebalance checks on power created by separation. Truman's problem in *Youngstown* was not the Court's unwillingness to support the exercise of inherent power by a president, but rather that inherent power may not be exercised when it attempts to achieve an end incompatible with established congressional policy. Congress had set forth procedures by which Truman could handle the steel strike. In doing so, Congress had rejected seizure as an option open to a president. Invocation of inherent power may not be used to nullify that judgment. To have allowed such a use of inherent or prerogative power would have placed the president "above the law." *Youngstown* clearly demonstrates that such inherent power cannot be indiscriminately exercised and is always subject to judicial review.

Inherent Power: National Security

New York Times v. United States, **403 U.S. 713, 91 S.Ct. 2140, 29 L.Ed. 2d 822 (1971)**   Struck down an executive attempt to suppress publication of the Pentagon papers. *New York Times v. United States* examined the press's protection from "prior restraint" as well as considering the dimensions of executive authority to protect national security interests. Two prominent newspapers, the *New York Times* and the *Washington Post*, had come into possession of copies of Defense Department documents detailing the history of American involvement in the Vietnam conflict. After failing to prevent publication by direct request to the newspapers, injunctions were sought by the Nixon Administration in federal court against the two newspapers to stop publication on grounds of threat to the national security. An injunction was obtained against the *Times,* but not the *Post.* The Supreme Court determined in a 6–3 decision that injunctive restraint against the *Times* was unwarranted. In a brief *per curiam* opinion, the Court suggested that there is a "heavy presumption" against prior restraint or censorship of the press, and that in this instance, the burden of proof had not been carried by the government.

Each member of the Court entered an individual opinion in the case. The Pentagon papers cases raised substantial issues of regulation of the press through prior restraint and inherent power of the executive to protect national security. The majority, fragmented as individuals, were drawn to one or the other of these issues. Justices Black and Douglas both focused on the free press aspects of the case and categorically rejected prior restraint. In Justice Black's view, the injunction constituted a "flagrant, indefensible and continuing violation of the

First Amendment." Justice Douglas suggested that the free press case of *Near v. Minnesota* (283 U.S. 697: 1931) had "repudiated" the doctrine of inherent executive power to seek an injunction to protect national security interests. Justice Brennan allowed that prior restraint might be possible in the most extreme circumstance, but the demands of this situation were not sufficiently compelling. The other members of the majority, Justices Stewart, White, and Marshall, focused on the authority of the executive to seek injunctions in the absence of explicit statutory authority. Each, however, recognized "enormous power" located in the executive to deal with national defense and international relations. This power, in the words of Stewart, is "largely unchecked" by the other branches with the "only effective restraint" residing in an "informed citizenry." Given the role of the press in serving that condition, the inherent power implications involved here had to be subordinated to the free press interests. Marshall also acknowledged some measure of inherent executive power. He noted, however, that Congress had rejected the use of judicial power to enjoin certain conduct, including this kind of prior restraint. Accordingly, it would be "utterly inconsistent with the concept of separation of power" for the Court to assist the executive branch to accomplish something already rejected by Congress. To that extent, the inherent power arguments advanced by the president must yield in this case. Chief Justice Burger and Justices Harlan and Blackmun dissented, though none took the position that the inherent power rationale supported issuance of the injunctions. Rather, the dissenters felt that the case was handled too hastily to allow adequate response on the merits. *See also* INHERENT POWER, p. 622; INJUNCTION, p. 622; *UNITED STATES V. CURTISS-WRIGHT EXPORT CORPORATION* (299 U.S. 304: 1936), p. 144; *YOUNGSTOWN SHEET AND TUBE COMPANY V. SAWYER* (343 U.S. 579: 1952), p. 146.

Significance   *New York Times v. United States* (403 U.S. 713: 1971) rejected executive power arguments to support an attempt to enjoin publication of the Pentagon Papers. This case probably has greater importance as a free press decision limiting the power of the government to impose prior restraint on publication. Nonetheless, the case represented the first federal attempt to seek judicial injunctions against publishers. The heart of the Court's opinion on the executive power dimension was that, notwithstanding certain prerogative or inherent power in the area of foreign affairs, the president may not, without prior congressional authorization, seek to enjoin publication. As in the *Youngstown* case, Congress had specifically rejected such authorizing legislation. The Court did not categorically rule out exercise of inherent power of prior restraint, but exercising that power would require the president to carry the burden of demonstrating that publication would create "grave and irreparable" damage to the national security. In this instance, the heavy presumption of unconstitutionality that exists in any prior restraint situation could not be countered.

Appointment and Removal

***Myers v. United States*, 272 U.S. 52, 47 S.Ct. 21, 71 L.Ed. 160 (1926)**   Held that presidents possess virtually unlimited power to remove appointed officials. *Myers v. United States* raised the issue of whether the president has exclusive removal power over executive officers. Myers had been appointed, with the advice and consent of the Senate, a first-class postmaster with a term of four years as provided by federal statute. President Wilson sought to remove Myers before the end of his term without Senate concurrence. Myers claimed salary for the balance of his term, arguing that he had been removed in a manner that violated the statute. The Supreme Court ruled the statute unconstitutional in a 6–3 decision.

The opinion of the Court was authored by Chief Justice Taft, a former president. He focused on the nature of the executive function. The president was granted the authority to "execute the laws." The president, however, cannot perform that function "alone and unaided." The president must be able to select appropriate persons to act "under his direction in the execution of the laws." By implication, given the "absence of any express limitation respecting removals," if a president may select subordinates to assist in the execution of laws, he must have the power of "removing those for whom he cannot continue to be responsible." Taft distinguished appointment from removal. While the Senate may be reasonably able to assess the fitness of a nominee at the appointment stage, it is not able to assess actual performance. The president or his subordinates are best able to make that judgment. Thus, the "power of removal is incident to the power of appointment, not to the power of advising and consenting to appointment." The removal power is "in its nature an executive power." Because the Constitution made the president responsible for law enforcement, he must possess the "disciplinary influence upon those who act under him of a reserve power of removal" as an "indispensible aid." To require Senate concurrence would "make impossible that unity and co-ordination in executive administration essential to effective action."

Justices Brandeis, Holmes, and McReynolds dissented. Justice Brandeis argued that the setting of a four-year term had established a condition the president could not alter unilaterally. Brandeis did not see removal power as "inherent," but rather as a power which "comes immediately from Congress." Congress has the power to create the office and prescribe its tenure. The latter power includes "prescribing the conditions under which incumbency shall cease." Similarly, Holmes saw the postmastership as an office that "owes its existence to Congress and that Congress may abolish tomorrow." Holding such power over the existence of the office, Holmes had no difficulty believing Congress could define conditions of tenure. *See also* APPOINTMENT POWER, p. 581; *HUMPHREY'S EXECUTOR V. UNITED STATES* (295 U.S. 602: 1935), p. 151.

Significance Had *Myers v. United States* (272 U.S. 52: 1926) confined itself to exclusively executive officers, it may not have been a particularly noteworthy decision. But Chief Justice Taft, himself a former president, seized the *Myers* case as an opportunity to offer *obiter dictum* on the broader question of executive removal power. Not only had Congress impermissibly limited the president's power to remove exclusively executive officers such as Myers, but Taft suggested that even quasi-judicial officers may be removed at the pleasure of the president if such officers render decisions with which a president disagrees. Such disagreements are themselves cause for removal on the ground that "discretion regularly entrusted to that officer by statute has not been on the whole intelligently or wisely exercised." For a president to ignore such differences would amount to failure to "discharge his own constitutional duty of seeing that the laws be faithfully executed." The implications of such broad removal power raised fundamental questions about quasi-judicial agencies and statutory language that restricted removal to situations of inefficiency, neglect, or malfeasance. The *dictum* offered by Taft in *Myers* was challenged and reversed in *Humphrey's Executor v. United States* (295 U.S. 602: 1935).

Humphrey's Executor v. United States, 295 U.S. 602, 55 S.Ct. 869, 79 L.Ed. 1611 (1935) Limited presidential removal power for nonexecutive officers. *Humphrey's Executor v. United States* reviewed provisions of the Federal Trade Commission Act, which established terms for commissioners and defined the causes for removal. The act allowed removal of commissioners only for "inefficiency, neglect of duty, or malfeasance." Humphrey had been nominated for a second term on the Federal Trade Commission (FTC) by President Hoover in 1931. The nomination was confirmed by the Senate, and Humphrey was officially commissioned. In 1933, President Roosevelt sought Humphrey's resignation in order to replace him with a person of more compatible political views. Humphrey refused to resign and was subsequently removed by Roosevelt. Humphrey brought suit claiming his removal was improper. While the suit was in the courts, Humphrey died. The executor of his estate continued to press the legal action, seeking back salary for the period following the challenged removal. The Supreme Court, in a unanimous decision, found for Humphrey.

The Court's opinion was authored by Justice Sutherland, who emphasized the quasi-judicial and quasi-legislative function of the commission. It was created to be "nonpartisan" with duties that were neither "political nor executive." The intention of Congress in creating the commission was to keep it "free from 'political domination or control'" and "'separate and apart from any existing department of the government—not subject to the orders of the President.'" In attempting to create independence for the FTC, it is "clear" that Congress intended that "length and certainty of tenure would vitally contribute." The Court then rejected the argument, based largely on the case of *Myers v. United States* (272 U.S. 52: 1926), that the statutory limitation was an unconstitutional interference with executive prerogatives. The Court stressed that *Myers* applied only to purely executive officers. The postmastership involved in *Myers* was seen as "so essentially unlike the office now involved that the decision in the Myers case cannot be accepted as controlling." A postmaster has no duties related to "legislative or judicial power" and is clearly a subordinate of the chief executive. As such, he is subject to "exclusive and unlimitable" removal discretion. The FTC, on the other hand, "occupies no place in the executive department" and "exercises no part of the executive power vested by the Constitution in the President." Rather, the "power exists for Congress, when creating quasi-legislative or quasi-judicial agencies, to address conditions of tenure, if Congress believes that will ensure independence." It is "quite evident" that "one who holds his office only during the pleasure of another cannot be depended upon to maintain an attitude of independence against the latter's will." Thus, Humphrey could only have been removed for one or more of the causes specified by Congress. *See also* APPOINTMENT POWER, p. 581; *MYERS V. UNITED STATES* (272 U.S. 52: 1926), p. 150.

Significance   Humphrey's Executor v. United States (295 U.S. 602: 1935) established limits on presidential removal power by holding that Congress could define conditions of tenure for officers not exclusively within the executive branch. The *Humphrey* decision hinged on what constituted executive duties. The effect of the Court's decision was to legitimize a congressional role in defining conditions of tenure for some federal positions. More important, *Humphrey* enabled the Congress to create entities to perform various quasi-legislative and/or quasi-judicial functions free from the threat of removal. In other words, *Humphrey* preserved the option of structured independence for nonexecutive officers. The Court expanded the *Humphrey* holding in *Wiener v. United States* (357 U.S. 349: 1958), when it held that if an agency has a quasi-judicial function, its members may not be removed by a president whether Congress defines conditions of tenure or not. *Wiener* noted that "sharp line of cleavage" between executive officers and others drawn by *Humphrey*, and held that even in the absence of explicit provisions, it must be "inferred that Congress did not wish to have the Damocles sword of removal by the President for no reason other than that he preferred to have . . . men of his own choosing." Presidents do, however, have virtually unlimited power to nominate any "officer" of the United States. The Court emphasized this initiative in *Buckley v. Valeo* (424 U.S. 1: 1976), as it struck down the provisions of the Federal Election Campaign Act under which Congress appointed four of the six members of the Federal Election Commission.

Executive Privilege

United States v. Nixon, **418 U.S. 683, 94 S.Ct. 3090, 41 L.Ed. 2d 1039 (1974)**   Ruled that presidents cannot withhold information from a grand jury proceeding. *United States v. Nixon* is the Supreme Court's major ruling on the matter of executive privilege. The privilege would allow a president to refuse legislative or judicial requests for information. This case arose out of the Watergate scandal and the subsequent legislative and judicial inquiries into the affair. In addition to the investigations conducted by the Ervin Committee in the Senate and the House Judiciary Committee in its impeachment role, information was sought by a special prosecutor named by the Justice Department to investigate criminal violations. The special prosecutor, Leon Jaworski, to enable prosecution of those involved in the cover-up of the Watergate break-in, subpoenaed some tape recordings and other materials relating to White House conversations. The subpoenas were reinforced by an order from U.S. District Court Judge John Sirica. While some materials were surrendered, others were withheld on the grounds of executive privilege. Judge Sirica denied the claim, and the Supreme Court, with Justice Rehnquist not participating, unanimously upheld Judge Sirica's ruling against the claimed privilege.

The opinion of the Court was delivered by Chief Justice Burger. The discussion of executive privilege began with consideration of an absolute privilege. President Nixon's counsel had argued for comprehensive privilege to ensure full and free discussion among the president and his advisers. Nixon had also asserted absolute privilege on separation of power grounds. The Court rejected their arguments, however, indicating that neither the doctrine of separation of powers, nor the need for confidentiality of high-level communications, by themselves sustain an "absolute, unqualified" presidential privilege. Only if the president could show a need to protect "military, diplomatic, or sensitive national security secrets" could the claim of privilege prevail. An absolute privilege would place an "impediment" on the courts' discharge of their constitutional function. The Court acknowledged that a president should be extended some degree of privilege, but the competing interests of the judicial process might outweigh that privilege. In cases where the judicial branch is involved, the privilege must be "considered in light of our historic commitment to the rule of law." If privilege were to prevail, the "ends of criminal justice would be defeated" because the "very integrity" of the judicial system depends on "full disclosure" of all relevant facts. Accordingly, it is "imperative" that the courts be able to compel the production of evidence. To allow a president to withhold evidence germane to a criminal proceeding would "cut deeply into the guarantee of due process of law and gravely impair the basic function of the courts." *See also* INHERENT POWER, p. 622; SEPARATION OF POWERS, p. 56; SPEECH OR DEBATE CLAUSE, p. 654.

Significance   *United States v. Nixon* (418 U.S. 683: 1974) severely limited the presidential claim to executive privilege. Executive privilege is not an express power, and its status as an implied power had been uncertain prior to this decision. The rationale for the privilege is that presidents must be able to engage in unrestrained discussions with advisers when considering policy options. In addition, vital national security interests might be compromised by compelled disclosure of information. *United States v. Nixon* acknowledged that privilege should extend to certain information. At the same time, the *Nixon* case determined that the demands of the criminal justice process must take precedence. The limited view of executive privilege also prevailed when the Court considered the matter of presidential records and documents. Following the resignation of President Nixon, Congress enacted a statute requiring screening of all Nixon presidential materials, with those judged personal or private to be retained by Nixon. The remainder were to be retained by the government and ultimately opened to the public. Nixon asserted executive privilege, but the Court rejected the claim in *Nixon v. Administrator of General Services* (433 U.S. 425: 1977). By rejecting claims to absolute privilege, these decisions of the Court substantially confined the circumstances under which executive privilege can be effectively claimed by a president.

Executive Immunity

Nixon v. Fitzgerald, **457 U.S. 731, 102 S.Ct. 2690, 73 L.Ed. 2d 349**
1982   Ruled that a president is immune from civil suits for actions taken in the course of performing his official duties. *Nixon v. Fitzgerald* involved a suit by a former employee of the Department of the Air Force. Fitzgerald had appeared before a congressional subcommittee and testified about development problems and cost overruns associated with a particular aircraft. Subsequently he was dismissed during the course of a reorganization of the department. Fitzgerald contended unsuccessfully before the Civil Service Commission that his dismissal had occurred because his testimony had brought embarrassment to the department. The Commission rejected Fitzgerald's allegations, though it did cite "personal" factors as having a bearing on the termination. Fitzgerald commenced a suit against President Richard M. Nixon and those in the department involved in his dismissal. The suit was dismissed by the lower federal courts on grounds that the president is immune from such suits. The Supreme Court agreed in a 5–4 decision.

The opinion of the Court was written by Justice Powell and was joined by Chief Justice Burger and Justices Rehnquist, Stevens, and O'Connor. The Court held that President Nixon was entitled to absolute immunity as a "functionally mandated incident of the President's unique office." Such immunity was seen as "rooted in the constitutional tradition of the separation of powers and supported by our history." The president possesses a "unique status under the Constitution" that distinguishes him from any other executive officer. The opinion then turned to some more focused reasons for presidential immunity. The president cannot be subjected to lawsuits that create "diversion of his energies" from his vital duties. Given that presidents deal with issues that arouse "intense feelings," he must be able to "fearlessly and impartially" tend to "sensitive and far-reaching" decision making. Without immunity, the president would be an "easily identifiable target" for many civil damage suits. This vulnerability could easily become a "detriment not only to the President and his office but also the Nation." The Court also refused to define narrowly the functions to which presidential immunity would extend. Rather, the Court noted the "special nature" of the office and thought it "appropriate" to recognize absolute immunity to the "outer perimeter" of a president's official duties.

Justices White, Brennan, Marshall, and Blackmun dissented. Their principal difference from the majority was the scope of the immunity. Justice White was critical of the failure to distinguish "categories of presidential conduct" that should or should not be entitled to immunity. White characterized the Court's opinion as permitting a president to engage in any action, "however contrary to the law he knows his conduct to be without fear of liability." In the view of the dissenters, the Court departed from a functional approach to the question of immunity by focusing on the office itself. *See also* EXECUTIVE PRIVILEGE, p. 603; INHERENT POWER, p. 622; SPEECH OR DEBATE CLAUSE, p. 654; *UNITED STATES V. NIXON* (418 U.S. 683: 1974), p. 153.

Significance   *Nixon v. Fitzgerald* (457 U.S. 731: 1982) extended absolute immunity from civil damage suits to the president. The Court sought to shield the president from becoming a frequent target of lawsuits which, in turn, would interfere with the need to devote full attention to the demands of the office. Some saw this decision as placing the president "above the law." Justice Powell's opinion noted remaining safeguards against abusive presidential conduct. He specifically mentioned the impeachment process, various "formal and informal checks" that apply generally to executive officers, press vigilance, the desire to "earn re-election," the need to "maintain prestige as an element of presidential influence," and a "President's traditional concern for his historical stature." In Powell's view, possession of absolute immunity "will not place the President 'above the law.'" The absolute immunity "merely precludes a particular private remedy for alleged misconduct." In a companion decision, *Harlow and Butterfield v. Fitzgerald* (457 U.S. 800: 1982), the Court refused to extend immunity from civil suits to aides and advisers of the President. The Court cited decisions involving legislative aides and rejected an absolute "derivative" immunity extending to aides. Rather, any immunity enjoyed by aides must be drawn from a functional source.

Executive Agreements

United States v. Belmont, **301 U.S. 324, 57 S.Ct. 758, 81 L.Ed. 1134 (1937)**   Upheld the presidential use of executive agreements as a means of entering into international agreements. The issue in *United States v. Belmont* was whether an executive agreement, a covenant that does not have to go through the Senate treaty approval process, has comparable legal status to a ratified treaty. The Belmont case developed out of the Russian Revolution of 1918. The Soviet government nationalized a number of properties, including an enterprise with assets in Belmont's bank located in New York. The United States broke diplomatic relations with the new regime immediately after the revolution, and the foreign assets remained in the American bank. Some fifteen years later, President Roosevelt formally recognized the Soviet government. Restoration of diplomatic contact led to, among other things, negotiation and settlement of the dispute involving assets like those in Belmont's bank. Agreements known as the Litvinov Assignments granted title to the assets to the United States. The assignment of title took place within diplomatic channels, and the agreement was not reviewed by the Senate. A lower federal court refused to honor the assignment of title to the United States because it viewed the initial nationalization action as a confiscation of private property prohibited by federal and New York law. The Supreme Court reversed the lower court in a unanimous decision.

The opinion of Justice Sutherland emphasized that the conduct of foreign relations belongs to the "political departments of government" and that what may be done in the "exercise of this political power" is not properly "subject to judicial inquiry." The determination of who is sovereign over a particular territory "conclusively binds" the courts. When Roosevelt recognized the Soviet government, his action governed the courts and "validates all actions and conduct of the government so recognized." That act of recognition had the effect of validating the assignment of assets because recognition, establishing diplomatic relations, negotiating the assignment, and the associated agreements "were all parts of one transaction resulting in an international compact between the two governments." Entering into the negotiations and acceptance of the assignments was "within the competence of the President." Sutherland reiterated that power to deal with foreign affairs lies exclusively with the national government. With respect to conducting foreign policy, as in this instance, the "Executive had authority to speak as the sole organ of that government." Accordingly, the agreements produced in the negotiations conducted here "did not require the advice and consent of the Senate." Sutherland went on to suggest that certain international compacts are not always treaties. Nonetheless, a compact such as the assignment here has status as a treaty for legal purposes and is insulated from "curtailment or interference on the part of the several states" as a treaty. *See also* TREATY POWER, p. 661; *UNITED STATES V. CURTISS-WRIGHT EXPORT CORPORATION* (299 U.S. 304: 1936), p. 144.

Significance   *United States v. Belmont* (301 U.S. 324: 1937) recognized the legal status of executive agreements. Several important consequences resulted. Executive agreements were viewed as having comparable legal status to treaties. At the same time, executive agreements are not subject to Senate review and approval. Thus, the approach allows presidents substantial initiative and flexibility as they use executive agreements in the conduct of foreign affairs. The recent pattern shows a continuing increase in the use of such agreements, with a corresponding decline in the conclusion of new treaties. In addition, because executive agreements are similar to treaties, both treaties and executive agreements may nullify any state law incompatible with them. The holding in *Belmont* was reiterated by the Court in *United States v. Pink* (315 U.S. 203: 1942), a case that also involved the Litvinov Assignments. The Court reversed a state court dismissal of an action by the United States to recover assets of a nationalized Russian company that were located in a New York bank. The Court held that the supremacy clause requires state law to yield to treaties where conflicts exist, and executive agreements such as the Litvinov Assignments "have a similar dignity." A more recent decision on executive agreements is *Weinberger v. Rossi* (456 U.S. 25: 1982). Like cases before it, the *Weinberger* decision maintains the comparability of treaties and executive agreements. A provision of federal statute prohibited employment discrimination against American citizens, but noted exemptions coming by "treaty." The Court in the *Weinberger* case held that executive agreements were included in the term "treaty" for purposes of the exemption. As a result, the Court upheld an agreement providing preferential employment of Filipino citizens on American military installations in the Philippines.

Passport Regulation

Haig v. Agee, **453 U.S. 280, 101 S.Ct. 2766, 69 L.Ed 2d 640 (1981)** Upheld executive revocation of a passport because the holder's actions threatened national security and foreign policy interests. *Haig v. Agee* involved a campaign on the part of a former Central Intelligence Agency (CIA) employee to undermine the operations of the agency. Agee repeatedly identified and exposed CIA personnel located in various foreign countries and caused their expulsion in several cases. The secretary of state revoked Agee's passport because his activities were causing "serious damage" to the "national security" or foreign policy of the United States. Agee filed suit alleging that the Passport Act of 1926 did not confer the authority to revoke his passport in this manner. The Supreme Court upheld the revocation, however, in a 7–2 decision.

The opinion of the Court was delivered by Chief Justice Burger, who framed the issue in the case as whether the Passport Act authorizes the secretary of state's action. Burger began by examining the language of the statute, and he acknowledged that the act did not "in so many words confer upon the Secretary of State a power to revoke a passport." At the same time, the statute did not "expressly limit those powers." The act granted what Burger characterized as "broad rule-making authority" to the executive, and such construction of the statute must be followed by the Courts, unless there are "compelling indications" to the contrary.

This is "especially so in the areas of foreign policy and national security, where congressional silence is not to be equaled with congressional disapproval." Burger then examined the characteristics of a passport. He concluded that whatever else it may be, a passport is a travel control document, a document that proves identity and "allegiance to the United States," and through which the government "vouches for the bearer and for his conduct." The history of passports and passport control have, since "the earliest days of the Republic," reflected "congressional recognition of Executive authority to withhold passports on the basis of substantial reasons of national security and foreign policy." The Court also rejected Agee's arguments that the revocation impermissibly burdened his right to travel, and that action was aimed at penalizing him for the exercise of his right to free speech. While interstate travel is "virtually unqualified," the freedom to travel internationally is fundamentally different. The latter may be regulated based upon foreign policy considerations. As for Agee's free speech claims, the Court found that Agee's speech was intended to obstruct intelligence operations and hamper agency personnel recruitment and, thus, unprotected expression. Burger said, "The mere fact that Agee is also engaged in criticism of the government does not render his conduct beyond the reach of the law." Justices Brennan and Marshall dissented and expressed concern that the implied executive authority exercised here was "potentially staggering" and may possibly be directed against citizens who "merely disagree with government foreign policy."

Significance   Executive control over passports was substantially strengthened by the Court in *Haig v. Agee* (453 U.S. 280: 1981). Early legislation on passports extended broad discretion to the secretary of state at least insofar as issuance was concerned. Subsequently, Congress authorized the executive to regulate international travel by means of passports. During the "Red scare" of the post–Second World War period, Congress passed legislation denying passports to political "subversives." This policy was struck down by the Court in *Aptheker v. Secretary of State* (378 U.S. 500: 1964). Despite the *Aptheker* decision, the State Department continued to use passports to limit travel to particular locations. This practice was upheld in *Zemel v. Rusk* (381 U.S. 1: 1965), a case involving denial of passports to travel to Cuba. This approach was subsequently discontinued for lack of effective means of enforcement. *Haig v. Agee* represents a change of direction by the Court on this matter. It is the first case in which a revocation was upheld on national security grounds, and it invests the executive with substantial capacity to regulate foreign travel as incident to the conduct of foreign affairs.

Impoundment of Funds

***Train v. City of New York*, 420 U.S. 35, 95 S.Ct. 839, 43 L.Ed. 2d 1 (1975)**   Rejected an attempt by the president to withhold or impound funds formally allocated by statute. *Train v. City of New York* examined portions of the Federal Water Pollution Control Act that provided federal financial support for municipal sewer and sewage treatment facilities. Section 207 of the Act established appropriation levels for particular years with a "not to exceed" cap on specified project expenditures. Section 205 directed that the funds be allotted to the states by the administrator of the Environmental Protection Agency (EPA) by the dates specified in the enactment. Train, the administrator of the EPA, withheld portions of these allotments to various municipalities at the direction of President Richard M. Nixon. The City of New York sought a declaratory judgment that obligated the administrator to distribute the full amounts authorized by Congress. The Supreme Court unanimously held that the administrator may not impound any funds authorized by the act.

The opinion of the Court was authored by Justice White, who carefully limited the decision to funding under the Pollution Control Act. The "sole issue" in White's view was whether Section 205 permitted allotment of anything less than the entire amounts authorized for appropriation by Section 207. In support of the impoundment, it was argued that Section 205 directed that funds be allotted, not necessarily all the funds authorized; that Congress had "intended to provide wide discretion in the Executive to control the rate of spending under the Act." It was argued that the deletion of the word "all" by the congressional conference committee in reference to sums to be allotted to qualifying projects conveyed wide discretion in implementation of the act. The Court disagreed. Simply striking the term "all" was held to be an "inadequate means" of conferring discretion. The Court viewed deletion of the word "all" as having no effect on the "sums" mandated for distribution. Certainly that change could not be interpreted as fundamentally altering the grant program. The act was aimed at providing a "firm commitment" of funds to be used in addressing an "urgent problem." The Court was not convinced that Congress "at the last minute scuttled the entire effort by providing the Executive with the seemingly limitless power to withhold funds from allotment and obligation." If Congress wished to confer such executive discretion, it needed to do so explicitly. White observed that "legislative intention, without more, is not legislation." *See also* DELEGATION OF LEGISLATIVE POWER, p. 591.

Significance   Control over federal expenditures was at issue in *Train v. City of New York* (420 U.S. 35: 1975). The Budget Act of 1921 made presidents responsible for developing federal budgets for presentation to the Congress. The Budget Act had the effect of locating substantial budget prerogatives in the executive branch. It also gave rise to the view that, while Congress has constitutional power to appropriate, such appropriations only broadly establish spending priorities. Over the years, presidents have occasionally withheld some portion of authorized funds from programs for which they were not themselves supportive. These infrequent impoundment actions did not prompt direct confrontations with Congress. President Nixon, however, sought to withhold funds more extensively than his predecessors, and a number of court actions were commenced. The *Train* decision held that Congress had left the president no discretion to impound funds appropriated under the Water Pollution Control Act, but carefully confined the decision to that particular statute. The question of presidential impoundment more generally was not resolved. Nixon's impoundments also prompted legislation to require presidents to expend any impounded funds unless Congress concurs with the withholding. The invalidation of the legislative veto in *Immigration and Naturalization Service v. Chadha* (462 U.S. 919: 1983) leaves the power of Congress to effectively counteract the impoundment technique in doubt.

Pardon Power

***Ex Parte Grossman*, 267 U.S. 87, 45 S.Ct. 332, 69 L.Ed. 527 (1925)**   Held that the president may pardon a person cited for contempt of court. The question in *Ex Parte Grossman* was whether the power to grant pardons given the president in Article II, Section 2 permitted exempted persons from judicially imposed penalties for contempt of court. Grossman owned a speakeasy during Prohibition and was enjoined from operation of the establishment. Grossman violated the injunction and was found in contempt of court. He was both fined and imprisoned. Grossman was pardoned by the president insofar as the imprisonment was concerned. The pardon was challenged as going beyond the power granted in Article II. The Supreme Court unanimously upheld the pardon of the judicial contempt.

The Court, in an opinion by Chief Justice Taft, rejected the argument that the pardon power was confined to federal legislative offenses only. Rather, the Court felt it appropriate to view the power as it existed in British law at the time the Constitution was written. Thus, common law offenses such as contempt of court were to be included in addition to statutory criminal convictions. The Court also rejected the argument that to allow presidential pardon for contempt would "destroy the independence of the judiciary and violate the primary constitutional principle of separation of the legislative, executive and judicial powers." Chief Justice Taft responded by suggesting that there is no explicit constitutional mandate providing for such independence. Neither is "complete independence and separation" a status "attained" or "intended." In other words, the independence is "qualified." Taft then moved to the pardon power itself, indicating that it exists to "afford relief from undue harshness or evident mistake in the operation or enforcement of the criminal law." It is to be used by the executive in "special cases" and "whoever is to make it useful must have full discretion to exercise it." To use it frequently "to the extent of destroying the deterrent effect of judicial punishment would be to pervert it." But the Court noted that presidential pardons for contempts "had been practiced for more than three quarters of a century," and "no abuses" had occurred in that time to warrant limitation. *See also* PARDON POWER, p. 642.

Significance   *Ex Parte Grossman* (267 U.S. 87: 1925) reinforced the position that the presidential power to pardon is extensive. The power to pardon allows a president to exempt persons or groups from penalties of law, and Grossman extended that power to common law offenses like contempt of court. The effect of a pardon is to fully negate any consequences of particular criminal conduct. In the case of *Ex Parte Garland* (4 Wallace 333: 1867), the Court upheld a pardon granted to a Confederate legislator who had been barred from the practice of law. Garland's pardon was "full" such that it "blots out the existence of the guilt, so that in the eye of the law the offender is as innocent as if he had never committed the offense." Pardons may also be limited or conditional. In *Schick v. Reed* (419 U.S. 256: 1974), the Court upheld the commutation of a death penalty conviction to a sentence of life imprisonment with the stipulation that parole could never be obtained. The presidential pardon power of Article II is limited to federal offenses and may not be utilized for impeachment. Neither can pardons be secured in situations of civil contempt. Civil contempt is different from criminal contempt in that it is intended to bring about compliance with a court order rather than punishment as such. As the Grossman case pointed out, for civil contempt, punishment is "remedial and for the benefit of the complainant, and a pardon cannot stop it."

WAR POWERS

Military Tribunals

Ex Parte Milligan, **4 Wallace 2, 18 L.Ed. 281 (1866)**   Struck down a presidential proclamation ordering trial of civilians by military commissions. *Ex Parte Milligan* arose out of actions of President Abraham Lincoln during the Civil War. The use of military tribunals to try citizens even in areas removed from the hostilities was the most controversial of all Lincoln's war measures. Milligan, a civilian and a sympathizer of the Confederacy, was arrested and tried for disloyalty by a military tribunal in Indiana. At the time, no state of hostility existed in Indiana, and the civilian courts were operating. Milligan was convicted, and he appealed, claiming that the military tribunal had no jurisdiction to try him. The Supreme Court agreed with Milligan in a unanimous decision.

Justice Davis began the opinion of the Court with the broad pronouncement that the Constitution is a "law for rulers . . . equally in war and in peace, and covers with the shield of its protection all classes of men, at all times, and under all circumstances." To allow suspension of constitutional provisions would involve "more pernicious consequences" than tolerable; it would lead "directly to anarchy or despotism." Suggesting that the Constitution empowers sufficient authority to "preserve the existence" of the government, Davis turned to the more specific question of jurisdiction of the military tribunals. Clearly, no portion of judicial power was conveyed through Article III. Neither was it "pretended that the commission was court ordained and established by Congress." Nor could creation of the tribunals be justified on the "mandate of the President because he is controlled by law, and has his appropriate sphere of duty," which does not include initiating law. Finally, jurisdiction cannot be derived under the "laws and usages of war." Such law can "never be applied to citizens in States which have upheld the authority of the government, and where the courts are open and their process unobstructed." The Court categorically rejected that any "usage of war could sanction a military trial . . . for any offense whatever of a civilian in civil life, in nowise connected with military service." Going further, the Court opined that even the Congress was without the power to authorize creation of military tribunals with jurisdiction over civilians. The Court held that Milligan should have been tried, after indictment by grand jury, by the civil courts of Indiana and given a trial by jury. Even if a special tribunal could have been properly established, it would have needed to fulfill constitutional obligations to safeguard the accused so long as a state of martial law did not exist. The entire Court agreed that Lincoln was without authority to create the military commissions; thus Milligan's conviction could not stand. Four members of the Court, Chief Justice Chase, and Justices Wayne, Miller, and Swayne, were of the opinion that Congress might possess the power to establish the kind of military tribunal involved here. *See also IN RE YAMASHITA* (327 U.S. 1: 1946), p. 171.

Significance   The Court's decision in *Ex Parte Milligan* (4 Wallace 2: 1866) was restrictive of presidential power in wartime. The Court held that governmental powers are not to be affected by emergencies; limits on authority are equivalent in "war and in peace." Accordingly, Lincoln was found to have violated the Habeas Corpus Act and overextended himself in creating military tribunals in areas where civil courts could still function. While *Milligan* struck down Lincoln's actions, it did not do so until the conclusion of the Civil War, at a time when the political environment had changed substantially. During the war itself, the Court had upheld Lincoln's blockade of Southern seaports even though war had not been formally declared (see *The Prize Cases*, 2 Black 635: 1865, p. 000). It could have been inferred from that decision that the Court viewed war power as whatever power is needed to successfully conduct a war. That same view can be seen in *Ex Parte Vallandigham* (1 Wallace 243:1864), a Milligan-like case, and the Court's only occasion to examine the military tribunals during the war itself. Unlike the restrictive decision in *Milligan,* the Court dismissed in Vallandigham, holding that it had no authority to review such cases. Not only did *Milligan* depart from that view, but its five-justice majority held that even Congress was without power to create the military tribunals that tried Milligan. The principle of *Milligan* was reiterated in *Duncan v. Kahanamoku* (327 U.S. 304: 1946), where the Court held that the territorial governor of Hawaii could not suspend constitutional guarantees through a declaration of martial law.

Military Authority

Korematsu v. United States, **323 U.S. 214, 65 S.Ct. 193, 89 L.Ed. 194 (1944)**   Upheld the presidential order to evacuate all persons of Japanese ancestry from designated "Military Areas." *Korematsu v. United States* called upon the Court to examine executive power in its most far-reaching form, the authority to act during an emergency. The executive order at issue in *Korematsu* was issued by President Franklin D. Roosevelt several weeks after the Pearl Harbor attack. The order permitted creation of "areas" of military sensitivity from which persons could be removed as military demands required. Shortly after the enabling order was issued, military authorities designated all of the

West Coast to a distance of 40 miles inland to be such an area. A curfew was initially imposed on all persons of Japanese ancestry. This was followed by an evacuation of all those of Japanese ancestry to "war relocation centers" away from the coast. A subsequent act of Congress made it a crime to violate any military order issued under the authority conferred by Roosevelt's executive order. Korematsu refused to leave his home after his evacuation had been ordered, and he appealed his conviction for noncompliance. The Supreme Court upheld the order in a 6–3 decision.

The opinion of the Court was authored by Justice Black, who concentrated on the military emergency. Only the "gravest imminent danger to the public safety" could justify the evacuation. The prevention of espionage and sabotage was sufficiently urgent and closely enough related to the evacuation to be constitutionally permissible. The Court deferred to the judgment of the military authorities as to the severity of the threat. The Court also spoke of the "hardships" of war and how the "burdens" of citizenship become "heavier" during time of war. While exclusion is "inconsistent" with our political history, the "power to protect must be commensurate with the threatened danger." The circumstances here represented the "direst emergency and peril." Black rejected the assertion that the evacuation had been racially inspired. The Court concluded that to "cast this case into outlines of racial prejudice, without reference to the real military dangers which were presented, merely confuses the issue." Korematsu was not excluded because of racial hostility, but because military authorities "feared an invasion" and had been given authority to respond to that threat. Given that evidence existed pointing to the disloyalty of some citizens of Japanese ancestry, the military needed to be able to respond quickly.

Justices Roberts, Jackson, and Murphy each wrote strong dissents. Roberts and Murphy in particular emphasized the racially discriminatory character of the evacuation. Roberts felt that the exclusion orders could not be upheld unless some evidence of disloyalty could be shown against particular individuals. Murphy characterized the policy as "going over the very brink" of permissible action and falling into the "ugly abyss of racism." Murphy would have required the military to demonstrate before a court that such pressing public danger existed to warrant evacuations rather than to simply proceed based upon presumptions of "racial guilt." *See also* EXECUTIVE ORDER, p. 602; *THE PRIZE CASES* (2 Black 635: 1865), p. 166; WAR POWERS, p. 673.

Significance   *Korematsu v. United States* (323 U.S. 214: 1944) upheld an order issued under the authority of the constitutional provision establishing the president as commander-in-chief. The conduct of war is probably the most demanding of all presidential responsibilities, and the Court has been reluctant to impose restrictions on a president's military authority. The Court's handling of the Japanese evacuation is illustrative. Despite the severity and unprecedented character of the evacuation, the Court upheld the orders against claims that the treatment of the Japanese violated basic due process and equal protection safeguards. The Court's first opportunity to examine the evacuation program came in *Hirabayashi v. United States* (320 U.S. 81: 1943). The Court chose to confine itself to the curfew aspects of the order and upheld the curfew as a justified emergency measure prompted by the military exigency. By the time the Court heard the *Korematsu* case, almost two years had passed since the order had been issued. In *Ex Parte Endo* (323 U.S. 283: 1944), the Court did hold that persons whose loyalty had been established could not be detained any longer under the evacuation program. The injustices inflicted by the evacuation have been acknowledged, and minimal compensation was directed toward some of the Japanese-American citizens subjected to relocation. At the same time, the unfortunate episode reflects the comprehensive authority that resides in the presidency during times of war.

The Prize Cases, 2 Black 635, 17 L.Ed. 459 (1865) Upheld President Abraham Lincoln's use of military authority in the absence of a formally declared war. The lawsuits collectively known as *The Prize Cases* stemmed from actions taken by President Lincoln early in 1861 to establish a blockade of southern ports. The owners of various ships damaged while carrying cargo to Confederate ports sought to recover damages inflicted by the United States Navy in their enforcement of the blockade. The question before the Court was whether a state of war existed such that Lincoln could utilize his war powers, among other things, to impose a legal blockade. In a 5–4 decision, the Court held that Lincoln possessed such power.

The controlling question in this case was whether a "state of war existed which would justify a resort to these means of subduing the hostile force." The Court determined that a war need not be declared to constitute a situation within which war powers may be exercised. In the Court's view, an insurrection is inevitably a precursor to civil war, and a civil war is one that is "never solemnly declared." Nonetheless, while never "publicly proclaimed, . . . its actual existence is a fact." And while Congress "alone has the power to declare a national or foreign war," it cannot "declare war against any State, or any number of States." Thus, the Civil War situation is a special case of belligerency and does not require formal action by Congress. As for the prerogatives existing for a president, the Court held that no president can initiate a war, but he is "bound to accept the challenge without waiting for any special legislative authority." Indeed, the president's discretion in such situations is extensive. The president may determine whether the military authority he possesses is being used to counter an insurrection or a "civil war of such alarming proportions as will compel him to the character of belligerents." The Court felt that the president "must determine what degree of force the crisis demands," and the Court "must be governed by the decisions and acts of the political department of government to which this power was entrusted." Lincoln's proclamation of the blockade was "official and conclusive evidence" that a "state of war" existed, which "demanded and authorized" use of such a measure under these circumstances. Having found that Lincoln possessed the authority to institute the blockade, the Court held that "neutrals" are bound to recognize the blockade and are liable to capture or damage if they do not.

Justice Nelson issued a dissent which was joined by Chief Justice Taney and Justices Catron and Clifford. The minority insisted on a formal congressional declaration of war as a necessary condition of the exercise of executive war power. In their view, "civil war can exist only by an act of Congress" and thus reflects assent of both the legislative and executive branches. A president may not unilaterally "declare war or recognize its existence." *See also* INHERENT POWER, p. 622; *UNITED STATES V. CURTISS-WRIGHT EXPORT CORPORATION* (299 U.S. 304: 1936), p. 144; WAR POWERS, p. 673; *YOUNGSTOWN SHEET AND TUBE COMPANY V. SAWYER* (343 U.S. 579: 1952), p. 146.

Significance   The Prize Cases (2 Black 635: 1865) recognized that a president may respond to a state of war whether or not it is formally declared. The Court held that the insurrection by the Confederacy constituted a war by any criterion, and that Lincoln was not only empowered, but obligated to respond. The authority comes from the president's inherent power as commander-in-chief to protect the nation's security. While the exercise of such power is subject to judicial review, the Court has been deferential when actual warfare exists. Indeed, the Court in *The Prize Cases* indicated that circumstances may "compel" response that includes whatever "degree of force the crisis demands." *The Prize Cases* did not alter the congressional power to formally declare war. The effect of the decision was to reduce the significance of that power. As commander-in-chief, and possessing ever-increasing discretion over the conduct of foreign relations, the president has become the principal participant in determining when to commence military action. This has been borne out several times since World War II when presidents have initiated military actions without the prior approval of Congress. These events, especially the prolonged engagement in Southeast Asia in the 1960s, led Congress to enact the

War Powers Act of 1973. The act limits the length of time troops may be committed to foreign military action without authorization by Congress. A portion of the act was voided as an unconstitutional legislative veto in 1983, which leaves the president with essentially unlimited options with regard to initiating military response.

Rent Controls

***Bowles v. Willingham*, 321 U.S. 503, 64 S.Ct. 641, 88 L.Ed. 892 (1944)**   Upheld rent control provisions of the Emergency Price Control Act of 1942. *Bowles v. Willingham* was one of several cases that challenged the constitutionality of wartime regulations. The act permitted the administrator of the Office of Price Administration to order reduction in housing rents in locations designated as "defense-rental areas." Willingham was ordered to reduce rents for her properties and successfully sought an injunction from a state court barring execution of the rent control order on the grounds that the statute was unconstitutional. Bowles, administrator of the Office of Price Administration, brought suit in a federal court seeking to restrain Willingham from further state proceedings and for violations of the rent control order itself. The U.S. district court agreed with Willingham that the statute was unconstitutional and dismissed Bowles's suit. The Supreme Court reversed, however, in an 8–1 decision.

The Court responded to three challenges of the statute. It first dealt with the constitutionality of the rent control provisions. The controls Congress chose to adopt were thought "necessary 'in the interest of national defense and security'" and for the "effective prosecution of the present war." The provisions were aimed at protecting "price structures against the forces of disorganization and the pressures created by war and its attendant activities." Congress was found to have authority to legislate against these problems. The act was then attacked as an improper delegation of legislative power. The Court disagreed, saying that the "policy of the Act is clear." The statute supplied "sufficient criteria for its application" such that the administrator could reasonably proceed with the setting of maximum rents. The act did not "grant unbridled administrative discretion." Rather than being free to fix rents "whenever and wherever he might like and at whatever level he pleases," the act specifically directed that maximum rents be fixed in areas where "defense activities" have created inflated rentals incompatible with the objectives of the legislation. The act also supplied the "standard and the base period to guide . . . in determining what the maximum rentals should be." The Court concluded by saying that the

Congress does not "abdicate its functions when it describes what job must be done, who must do it, and what is the scope of his authority." Finally, the Court responded to the assertion that the statute violated Fifth Amendment due process protections by not providing hearings to landlords before rent orders became effective. The Court pointed out that Congress was attempting to deal with the "exigencies of wartime conditions and the insistent demands of inflation control." Congress intentionally selected a procedure allowing elimination of lengthy and costly proceedings. For the Congress to have required hearings for "thousands of landlords" before a rent control order might become effective "might have defeated the program of price control." Under the circumstances, the "national security might not have been able to afford the luxuries of litigation and the long delays which preliminary hearings have traditionally entailed." Justice Roberts dissented, finding that Congress "had delegated the lawmaking power in toto to an administrative officer." *See also* DELEGATION OF LEGISLATIVE POWER, p. 591; WAR POWERS, p. 673; *WOODS V. MILLER* (333 U.S. 138: 1948), p. 170.

Significance   The Court held in *Bowles v. Willingham* (321 U.S. 503: 1944) that Congress has the power to impose rent restrictions on private property during wartime. While the power to do so is not specifically provided in the Constitution, it is implicit from the power of Congress to declare war. Generally, the Court has found that war powers are as broad as necessary for the government to effectively contend with the demands of war. A companion case to *Bowles* was *Yakus v. United States* (321 U.S. 414: 1944), which upheld price restrictions of the Emergency Price Control Act. The act also had provisions that removed jurisdiction over any aspect of the statute from existing federal or state courts. It created a special court with exclusive authority to review pricing regulations produced under the act. The Court upheld this assignment of exclusive jurisdiction to the Emergency Court of Appeals in *Yakus*. During the First World War, the Court was presented with the question of whether Congress had the authority to draft persons for military service. In the *Selective Draft Law Cases* (245 U.S. 366: 1918), the Court unanimously upheld the draft law as an exercise of authority to "raise and support armies." The Court was "unable to conceive" any reason by which the government could not exact service of a citizen in order to prosecute a declared war. Drawing from the power provided by the necessary and proper clause, the power to declare war, and the authority to raise and support army and naval forces, congressional war power is extensive. The Court made it clear in *Bowles* that the exigencies of war permit regulation that might not be allowed otherwise. When Willingham claimed the rent controls on her property were an unconstitutional "taking" of that property, the Court responded by saying that while the country can place people's lives at risk during military service, it is under no constitutional obligation to assure landlords "fair return" on their property.

Woods v. Miller, 333 U.S. 138, 68 S.Ct. 421, 92 L.Ed. 596 (1948)
Upheld a rent control regulation enacted by Congress after the Second World War had ended as a proper exercise of war power. *Woods v. Miller* involved a challenge to the Housing and Rent Act, a statute passed by Congress some six months after President Truman had declared by proclamation that hostilities had officially ceased. The act essentially embraced the rent control features of the Emergency Price Control Act enacted during the war, and it maintained those regulations during the postwar period. The issue in this case was whether the war power of Congress extended beyond the formal cessation of hostilities, and, if so, what the limits of such power were. The case was brought to the Court because Miller increased rental charges in violation of the act. The U.S. district court dismissed the case on the ground that Congress had no authority to regulate rents under the war power after Truman's proclamation. The Supreme Court reversed in a unanimous decision.

Justice Douglas delivered the opinion of the Court and indicated that the war power was sufficient to sustain the legislation. The Court held that the war power includes the power to "remedy the evils which have arisen from its rise and progress" and such power "continues for the duration of the emergency." In addition, the Court said that "whatever may be the consequences when war is officially terminated, the war power does not necessarily end with the cessation of hostilities." When the Court examined the legislative history of the act, the Court found it "abundantly clear" that there existed a "deficit in housing." Since the war "contributed heavily to that deficit, Congress has the power even after cessation of hostilities to act to control the forces that a short supply of the needed article created." To hold otherwise would too drastically limit the effect of the necessary and proper clause and would "render Congress powerless" to counteract the effects of war mobilization. Such an interpretation would be "paralyzing" and "self-defeating." Having said this, the Court noted that the war power was not open-ended. The effects of war may continue for "years and years," but the war power cannot be "used in days of peace to treat all the wounds which war inflicts on our society." If so, the war power would "swallow up" other powers of Congress and "largely obliterate" the Ninth and Tenth Amendments. The Court cautioned that upholding the Housing and Rent Control Act did not sanction unlimited peacetime use of the war powers. The safeguards rest in Congress's own awareness of its "constitutional responsibilities" and that the use of it is "open to judicial inquiry" as in this case. *See also* BOWLES V. WILLINGHAM (321 U.S. 503: 1944), p. 168; WAR POWERS, p. 673.

Significance   *Woods v. Miller* (333 U.S. 138: 1948) held that a formal state of war is not required for the exercise of war powers. Such a proposition did not originate with *Woods*. The Court had found it permissible for the government to maintain its preparedness for national defense in cases such as *Ashwander v. Tennessee Valley Authority* (297 U.S. 288: 1936). The Court had also addressed the exercise of war power following World War I. In *Hamilton v. Kentucky Distilleries and Warehouse Company* (251 U.S. 146: 1919), the Court upheld a wartime prohibition statute passed after the armistice. The Court found support for the enactment because war activities had not come to a conclusion and peace had not been restored. While the Court would probably restrain use of war power far removed from an actual conflict, a point noted in *Woods*, the Court has generally deferred to the other branches to determine when war emergencies are over. In *Ludecke v. Watkins* (335 U.S. 160: 1948), the Court allowed a postwar deportation under a statute limiting such actions to the period of declared war. The Court ignored the "fiction" that formal war still existed because bringing the state of war to an end is a "political" judgment.

War Trials

***In Re Yamashita*, 327 U.S. 1, 66 S.Ct. 340, 90 L.Ed. 499 (1946)**
Upheld a war crimes conviction of a Japanese general rendered by a special military commission established by the president. The principal question in *In Re Yamashita* was whether constitutional protections extended to members of an enemy's military. General Yamashita had commanded a unit of the Japanese Army in the Philippines. At the conclusion of the war, the president appointed a special commission of American military officers to try Yamashita for alleged war crimes committed by troops under his command in the Philippines. Although Yamashita was provided legal counsel, he was not afforded other constitutional rights such as trial by jury. After a lengthy trial, Yamashita was convicted and sentenced to death. He appealed, arguing that the commission had been improperly created and was, as a result, without authority to conduct his trial. Yamashita also contended that the charges lodged against him failed to specifically cite any violation of the law of war. The Supreme Court rejected Yamashita's claims in a 6–2 decision with Justice Jackson not participating.

The opinion of the Court was delivered by Chief Justice Stone, and it first established the scope of what the Supreme Court could appropriately review. Military tribunals, sanctioned under articles of war, are "not courts whose rulings and judgments are made subject to review by this Court." Accordingly, the Supreme Court can consider only the "lawful power of the commission to try the petitioner for the offense charged" through its *habeas corpus* review. If properly established, military commissions may render decisions that are "not subject to judicial review." In this instance, the Court found that the order creating the commission was "authorized by military command," and was in "complete conformity to the Act of Congress sanctioning the creation of such commissions." In addition, the Court held that the commission could be convened even though hostilities had ceased. Generally, the "practical administration of the system of military justice under the law of war would fail if such authority were thought to end with the cessation of hostilities." The Court then turned to the charges themselves. While not appraising the evidence upon which Yamashita was convicted, the Court concluded that the charge of failure to control those in his command was a charge properly before the commission because it involved performance of a duty imposed on him "by the law of war." Finally, the Court refused to require that the commission's proceedings be governed by the same due process protections afforded those accused of criminal conduct in civilian courts. The "mode of conducting those proceedings . . . is not reviewable by the courts, but only by the reviewing military authorities."

Justices Murphy and Rutledge offered vigorous dissents. Murphy argued that due process guarantees of the Fifth Amendment apply to "any person" accused of a crime without exception. Those rights are "immutable" and "belong not alone to members of those nations that excel on the battlefield or that subscribe to the democratic ideology." Justice Rutledge shared those sentiments, saying that due process safeguards must be available to all persons, "whether citizens, aliens, alien enemies or enemy belligerents." *See also* EX PARTE MILLIGAN (4 Wallace 2: 1866), p. 168; WAR POWERS, p. 673.

Significance   The decision in *In Re Yamashita* (327 U.S. 1: 1946) focused on two issues. First, it examined the establishment of the military commission by which Yamashita was tried. The Court concluded that Congress may statutorily authorize such a commission or that the president can do so under his authority as commander-in-chief. The Court also determined that the proceedings conducted by such military tribunals were not reviewable by established civilian courts. Rather, the commissions were subject only to review by military authorities. The conclusion led to the second issue in Yamashita, the matter of applicability of constitutional protections to enemy military defendants on trial for war crimes. The Court held that safeguards such as grand jury indictment, trial by jury, or evidentiary rules in civil courts were not required in trials of enemy military personnel. This aspect of *Yamashita* simply restated the Court's holding in *Ex Parte Quirin* (317 U.S. 1: 1942), which examined the military trial of eight German saboteurs. The effect of both these decisions is that the Court usually finds it inappropriate to intervene in matters directly related to war emergencies, be it in the conduct of the war itself or in formally prosecuting those charged with violations of the law of war.

CITIZENSHIP

Birthplace

United States v. Wong Kim Ark, 169 U.S. 649, 18 S.Ct. 456, 42 L.Ed. 890 (1898) Held that the Constitution confers citizenship to a child born in the United States to noncitizen parents. *United States v. Wong Kim Ark* clarified the citizenship provisions of the Fourteenth Amendment and established that American citizenship was contingent on a person's birthplace regardless of the citizenship status of the parents. Wong Kim Ark was born in California. His parents were Chinese citizens although they had become permanent residents of the United States. At the age of 21, Wong Kim Ark went to China and attempted to return to the United States the following year. He was not considered to be a citizen and was denied entry under immigration quotas established by Congress in the Chinese Exclusion Acts. He sought a writ of *habeas corpus* claiming American citizenship because of his birth on American soil. The Supreme Court held that he was a citizen by virtue of his birthplace in a 6–2 decision (with Justice McKenna not participating).

The opinion of the Court was offered by Justice Gray, who framed the issue as determining whether the citizenship clause of the Fourteenth Amendment established Wong Kim Ark's citizenship. The clause reads: "All persons born or naturalized in the United States and subject to the jurisdiction thereof, are Citizens of the United States." Key to resolving the questions was examination of the "condition" and "history of the law as previously existing," in which "light" the Exclusion Acts must be "read and interpreted." Since the Constitution did not provide precise definition of what was meant by the terms "citizen" and "natural born citizen," the Court turned to the established principles of common law that were "familiarly known" to the constitutional authors. English common law, settled for the "last three centuries" on this point at the time of settlement in the United States, held that children of aliens under protection of the English sovereign were considered "natural born" subjects. This principle, known as *jus soli*, was "in force" in English colonies in North America through the time of the Declaration of Independence and "continued to prevail under the Constitution as originally established." The words themselves as well as the weight of history indicated to the Court no intention to restrict citizenship. Rather, the language is "declaratory in form, and enabling and extending in effect." The conclusion of the Court was that the Fourteenth Amendment had affirmed the "ancient and fundamental rule of citizenship by birth within the territory."

Chief Justice Fuller and Justice Harlan dissented. They rejected the argument that passage of the Fourteenth Amendment necessarily brought with it the common law rule adopted by the Court in this case. Rather, both dissenters felt that Congress retained authority to regulate citizenship in situations such as this. *See also AFROYIM V. RUSK* (387 U.S. 253: 1967), p. 174; CITIZENSHIP, p. 585.

Significance   *United States v. Wong Kim Ark* (169 U.S. 649: 1898) established the rule of *jus soli* as the basis of American citizenship. The effect of the *Wong Kim Ark* decision was to strike down legislative policy set in the Chinese Exclusion Acts and to reverse the Court's first construction of the citizenship clause in the *Slaughterhouse Cases* (16 Wallace 36: 1873). According to the *Wong Kim Ark* holding, birth on American soil and naturalization are the two routes by which citizenship is obtained. *Wong Kim Ark* does note some exceptions to the *jus soli* rule. For example, not included are children of "foreign sovereigns" or "their ministers." Neither are children of "enemies" present on American soil during "hostile occupation" of American territory. Subsequently, the Congress established the rule of *jus sanguinis* (or the "law of blood") to apply to situations where children of American citizens are born abroad. The citizenship through naturalization process is regulated exclusively by federal statute. As a result, the Court's judgments in this area have generally validated congressional enactments.

Loss of Citizenship

***Afroyim v. Rusk*, 387 U.S. 253, 87 S.Ct. 1660, 18 L.Ed. 2d 757 (1967)**   Struck down an enactment that provided that citizenship is forfeited by participation in a foreign election. *Afroyim v. Rusk* involved Section 401(e) of the Nationality Act of 1940, which required loss of citizenship if an American citizen votes in an election in a foreign country. Afroyim was a naturalized citizen of some twenty-five years when he voted in an Israeli election, which terminated his American citizenship under the act. Afroyim appealed to the Supreme Court and prevailed in a 5–4 decision.

The majority opinion was authored by Justice Black, and it categorically rejected the position that Congress has "any general power, express or implied, to take away an American citizen's citizenship without his assent." Such power is simply not an "implied attribute of sovereignty possessed by all nations." In the United States, the "people are sovereign," and the government "cannot sever its relationship to the people by taking away their citizenship." There is no language that empowers Congress "to strip" persons of their citizenship, nor is there any power derived from the exercise of "implied power to regulate foreign affairs" that could be used to the end of expatriation. It seemed clear to the Court that those who proposed the Fourteenth Amendment wanted to "put citizenship beyond the power of any government unit to destroy." Citing further the history surrounding the passage of the Fourteenth Amendment, Black suggested that there had been "strong feeling" in the Congress that the "only way" citizenship could be lost was by the "voluntary renunciation or abandonment by the citizen himself."

Justices Harlan, Clark, Stewart, and White dissented and characterized the striking down of Section 401(e) as occurring through a "remarkable process of circumlocution." Harlan contended that the majority argued by unsubstantiated assertion and "arcane" observations. The dissenters did not view either history or the citizenship clause of the Fourteenth Amendment as comprehensively denying Congress the authority to "deprive a citizen of his nationality." The dissenters' position was that the Fourteenth Amendment "neither denies nor provides to Congress any power of expatriation." The dissenters clearly did not read the Fourteenth Amendment as creating "additional, and entirely unwarranted, restriction upon legislative authority." *See also* CITIZENSHIP, p. 585; *UNITED STATES V. WONG KIM ARK* (169 U.S. 649: 1898), p. 173.

Significance   The decision in *Afroyim v. Rusk* (387 U.S. 253: 1967) imposed restrictions on the capacity of the secretary of state to revoke citizenship. Prior to *Afroyim*, the governing precedent on expatriation had been *Perez v. Brownell* (356 U.S. 44: 1958), which had also decided on the Nationality Act provision regarding participation in foreign elections. Unlike *Afroyim*, the *Perez* case had seen expatriation on this basis a reasonable exercise of federal power pursuant to the capacity to conduct foreign relations. The *Perez* rationale presumed that anyone participating in a foreign election did so voluntarily and with cognizance of the consequences. The Court has generally been less receptive to involuntary expatriation. For example, the Court struck down loss of citizenship as a reasonable penalty for wartime desertion from the military. Revocation of citizenship of persons who have been naturalized generally hinges on willful misrepresentation that occurred at the time of naturalization. In *Fedorenko v. United States* (449 U.S. 490: 1981), for example, the Court upheld a revocation of citizenship of a former concentration camp guard who had concealed those activities at the time he applied for a visa. Policy governing naturalization and denaturalization rests fully with the Congress and is thus distinguishable from expatriation.

4. Legislative Power

Overview, 179

Article I, 183

OVERVIEW

The Congress is granted legislative power by Article I of the Constitution. This chapter focuses on the scope and limits of legislative power, excluding the power to regulate interstate commerce and the power to tax and spend. These two specific powers have been of paramount policy significance and are separately discussed in Chapters 6 and 7.

Article I conveys extensive powers both expressly and implicitly. The power to investigate is an implied power necessary for Congress to gain information to exercise its legislative function. In *McGrain v. Daugherty* (273 U.S. 135: 1927), the Court allowed Congress to investigate any subject in which it has a legitimate legislative interest. *Watkins v. United States* (354 U.S. 178: 1957) limited inquiries about personal political beliefs to areas pertaining to subjects over which Congress had legislative authority. *Barenblatt v. United States* (360 U.S. 109: 1959) eased the standards of legislative purpose and pertinency, returning to Congress the broad investigative power initially defined in *McGrain*. To ensure free debate over controversial public issues, Article I provides that legislators are not accountable for anything said in the course of official business. *Gravel v. United States* (408 U.S. 606: 1972) held that a Senator's aide is covered in this immunity, but certain acts, such as arranging for the private publication of committee records, are outside the scope of the protection. Similarly, in *Hutchinson v. Proxmire* (443 U.S. 111: 1979), the Court limited immunity by holding that even congressional members are not protected from libel actions if statements made in protected speeches are disseminated to the public via newsletters or other releases.

The operational necessities of governance also allow the Congress to delegate some authority to the executive branch, despite seeming prohibitions stemming from separation of power considerations. Such delegation may only occur, however, if the legislative objective has been carefully defined. *J. W. Hampton, Jr. and Company v. United States* (276 U.S. 394: 1928) permitted the use of a flexible tariff rate to allow periodic adjustment based on industry production costs. More contemporary delegation was upheld in *American Textile Manufacturers Insti-*

tute, Inc. v. Donovan (452 U.S. 490: 1981), where the Congress was permitted to have the secretary of labor set cotton dust standards. In permitting administrative agencies to exercise some discretion in the implementation of laws, Congress must not leave such latitude that the policy decisions themselves are left to the executive branch. *Schechter Poultry Corporation v. United States* (295 U.S. 495: 1935), on the other hand, struck down the code-making mechanism of the National Industrial Recovery Act because it excessively delegated such policy judgments.

Most legislative authority is specifically granted in Article I. Congress, for example, is authorized to conduct the census. *Baldridge v. Shapiro* (455 U.S. 345: 1982) upheld the authority of Congress to protect the confidentiality of census data. *Oregon v. Mitchell* (400 U.S. 112: 1970) upheld the statutory lowering of the voting age for federal elections based on power granted in Section 4 of Article I. Additional power is also available to Congress to protect the integrity of the electoral process as seen in *Buckley v. Valeo* (424 U.S. 1: 1976) and *California Medical Association v. Federal Election Commission* (453 U.S. 182: 1981). Those two cases examined various financial disclosure requirements and ceilings on individuals' contributions to campaigns and multicandidate political action committees. The section of the Federal Election Campaign Act limiting campaign expenditures was struck down in *Buckley* on First Amendment grounds.

Congressional power is also found outside Article I. The Thirteenth, Fourteenth, and Fifteenth Amendments provided a substantial legislative power source. The Voting Rights Acts of 1965, an enactment based on the Fifteenth Amendment, was upheld in *South Carolina v. Katzenbach* (383 U.S. 301: 1966). In *Jones v. Alfred Mayer Company* (392 U.S. 409: 1968), the Court allowed Congress to use the Thirteenth Amendment as a means to eliminate such "badges" of slavery as housing discrimination. The nature of the Fourteenth Amendment as a means of legislatively protecting civil rights was examined in *United States v. Guest* (383 U.S. 745: 1966), while legislation to combat sex discrimination in educational employment was upheld in *North Haven Board of Education v. Bell* (456 U.S. 512: 1982).

The exercise of legislative power is also limited by specific provisions of Article I. *United States v. Brown* (381 U.S. 437: 1965) struck down a federal statute because it directly imposed a penalty on an identifiable group, which is a prohibited bill of attainder. Legislatures are not permitted to pass laws that retroactively cause disadvantage in a criminal context. *Weaver v. Graham* (450 U.S. 24: 1981) finds a state enactment in violation of this *ex post facto* prohibition. Finally, the exercise of legislative power must be seen in the broader context of separation of power. Congress is the legislative body, and that function may not be usurped nor abdicated. Nor may the legislative branch encroach on executive or judicial functions. Accordingly, the Court struck down the device known as the legislative veto in the case of *Immigration and Naturalization Service v. Chadha* (462 U.S. 919: 1983), a case of major significance.

The principal definitional cases on legislative power excluding the substantive areas of interstate commerce and taxation follow.

Article I   Assigns legislative authority to the Congress. Article I contains ten sections describing and defining the nature of and limits upon legislative power. The primary elements of Article I will be highlighted. Section 1 confers the basic legislative power with the words, "All legislative powers herein granted shall be vested in a Congress of the United States." A bicameral legislature is established by specifying that the Congress "shall consist of a Senate and a House of Representatives." Sections 2 and 3 provide for the membership qualifications, election procedures, and apportionment of seats for the House and Senate. These sections also assign respective roles in the impeachment process for each of the two chambers. Sections 4 and 5 establish the timing of congressional elections, the supervision of the counting, and certification of results, and grants discretion to each house to create its own internal rules. Section 5 also requires a published journal of congressional proceedings and the means by which members can compel recorded roll call votes. Section 6 allows Congress to establish its own compensation and conveys immunity from arrest while engaged in official business. Section 6 contains the speech or debate clause, which shields members of Congress from being "questioned in any other place" for anything said during the course of official duties, including liability for libelous, slanderous, or seditious speech. Section 7 describes the process by which legislation and resolutions are to be handled. Included is the specified requirement that all revenue measures commence in the House. The presidential veto and override process is also set forth.

Section 8 sets out the specific powers that may be exercised by Congress. Several of these powers stand out. First, Congress is empowered to "lay and collect Taxes, Duties, Imposts and Excises, to pay the Debts and provide for the Common Defence and general Welfare of the United States." Second, the Congress may "regulate Commerce with foreign Nations, and among the several States." Third, Congress has the power to establish any courts inferior to the Supreme Court and define their jurisdiction. Fourth, Section 8 gives Congress the power to "declare war," "raise and support Armies," "provide and maintain a Navy," and "call for the Militia to execute the laws of the Union, suppress insurrections and repel Invasions." Fifth, Congress can "make all laws which shall be necessary and proper for carrying into Execution the foregoing powers." Also contained in Section 8 are specific grants of power to deal with such other issues as naturalization, bankruptcy, international law, patents, coining money, the post office, and the borrowing of money.

Sections 9 and 10 enumerate limitations on legislative power at the federal and state levels, respectively. Section 9 precludes Congress from suspension of the writ of *habeas corpus* except under emergency circumstances; passing bills of attainder or *ex post facto* laws; imposing a direct tax or taxing articles exported from a state; preferring one state over another through the exercise of the commerce power; and granting titles. Section 10 prohibits states from entering into treaties, coining money, passing bills of attainder or *ex post facto* laws, granting titles, or "impairing the obligation of contracts." *See also* ARTICLE II, p. 139; ARTICLE III, p. 73; COMMERCE CLAUSE, p. 291; CONTRACT CLAUSE, p. 465; GENERAL WELFARE CLAUSE, p. 377; NECESSARY AND PROPER CLAUSE, p. 637; SEPARATION OF POWERS, p. 56; SPEECH OR DEBATE CLAUSE, p. 654.

Significance   The framers of the Constitution consciously chose to use Article I to convey the legislative power. It reflects the priority the framers placed on the legislative function in several ways. First, the framers had a fundamental trust in the governmental power distributed among a large number of elected representatives as compared with a general distrust in power lodged in the executive. Second, the framers were committed to the concept of government by law, and they wished to have the legislative branch play the pivotal role in establishing national policy. Third, the framers sought to create a governmental structure that contained safeguards against abusive and arbitrary behavior. Article I vests certain powers in the legislative branch that are aimed at achieving a "checks and balances" relationship among the three principal branches. Finally, the framers desired to provide in Article I that the national legislature would possess power sufficient to ensure survival of the constitutional government. This reflected a recognition that the government created under the Articles of Confederation was too severely limited to achieve viability.

Three kinds of powers are allocated in Article I. The first conveys specific authority to address particular matters. The enumerated powers that have evolved to primary importance in the contemporary United States are the power to regulate interstate commerce and the power to tax. Through these two expressed powers, Congress has extensive authority to fashion regulations. Chapters 6 and 7 examine these two powers in detail. The second kind of power comes from the necessary and proper clause. Unlike the enumerated powers, power conveyed by this clause is of a general kind. The nature and scope of implied powers that may be exercised by Congress derive from interpretation of the necessary and proper clause. This is a source of considerable legislative power and has been since Chief Justice Marshall's permissive interpretation of the clause in *McCulloch v. Maryland* (4 Wheaton 316: 1819). The final group of powers are those related to the manner in which Congress may perform the legislative function.

Auxiliary powers of this kind provide for such things as legislative information gathering and immunity from civil liability while engaged in official business.

Investigations

***McGrain v. Daugherty*, 273 U.S. 135, 47 S.Ct. 319, 71 L.Ed. 580 (1927)**   Held that Congress possessed extensive investigative power. A Senate committee began an investigation of the Justice Department, largely to inquire into the possible relationship of the department to the Teapot Dome scandal. The brother of the attorney general, Mally Daugherty, was subpoenaed to appear and bring certain documents. McGrain, a Senate sergeant-at-arms, arrested Daugherty after he refused to honor the subpoenas. Daugherty successfully sought *habeas corpus* relief and gained his release. McGrain appealed to the Supreme Court on behalf of the committee, and he prevailed in a unanimous decision (with Justice Stone not participating).

There is no express provision authorizing Congress to investigate or demand information from witnesses. The question addressed by the Court was whether such power is "so far incidental to the legislative function as to be implied." The Court determined that the power to obtain information, even from unwilling persons, is an "attribute of the power to legislate." The Court noted that such a view prevailed relative to the British Parliament and colonial legislatures, and today exists for most state legislatures. The power to gather information is an "auxiliary" power that is "necessary and appropriate" to make expressly conveyed powers effective. The power to investigate is limited, however. Neither the House nor the Senate possesses a general power to "inquire into private affairs." At the same time, the Court held that Congress was entitled to gather information on any issue upon which it could legislate. The "only legitimate object" upon which the Senate could base an inquiry is that which would directly "aid it in legislating." In this instance, the Court concluded that, given the subject matter, the "presumption should be indulged" that the Senate's purpose was to aid it in legislating. *See also* BARENBLATT V. UNITED STATES (360 U.S. 109: 1959), p. 187; LEGISLATIVE INVESTIGATIONS, p. 631; *WATKINS V. UNITED STATES* (354 U.S. 178: 1957), p. 186.

Significance   *McGrain v. Daugherty* (273 U.S. 135: 1927) established very permissive standards for reviewing legislative investigations. The investigatory power is implied, and prior to *McGrain*, the Court had set relatively confining boundaries. A leading early case is *Kilbourn v.*

Thompson (103 U.S. 168: 1881), which held that congressional investigations were limited by the principle of separation of powers. In other words, legislative inquiries could not be made into areas reserved to the executive and judicial branches. In addition, *Kilbourn v. Thompson* limited investigations to matters over which Congress held the power and the interest to legislate. *McGrain* dramatically extended those boundaries by broadening the definition of what constituted a permissible legislative objective. As important, McGrain suggested that it should be presumed that inquiries undertaken by Congress are within its authority and reflect its intention to legislate. The *McGrain* decision defined an investigative power as one limited only by protections afforded witnesses called by the investigating committee. *McGrain* did require that investigating committees set forth objectives in the form of authorizing resolutions, and that inquiries stay within those defined objectives. Since the Teapot Dome investigation had not exceeded such limits, that boundary was not developed substantially in *McGrain*. This standard was, however, to become central in the 1950s.

Watkins v. United States, 354 U.S. 178, 77 S.Ct. 1173, 1 L.Ed. 2d 1273 (1957)   Held that Congress could not inquire into the personal political beliefs of citizens without establishing that the questions are pertinent to a valid legislative objective. *Watkins v. United States* involved a union organizer who was subpoenaed to testify before a subcommittee of the House Committee on Un-American Activities (HUAC). Watkins agreed to answer all questions about both his own association with the Communist Party as well as about persons he knew to be current party members. He refused, however, to respond to questions about persons who were no longer affiliated with the Communist Party. Watkins claimed that such information was beyond the authority of the committee to demand. Watkins was convicted of contempt of Congress. The Supreme Court reversed the conviction in a 6–1 decision with Justices Burton and Whittaker not participating.

Chief Justice Warren authored the opinion of the Court and articulated several premises about which there was "general agreement." He suggested the investigatory power is "inherent in the legislative process," and that such power is "broad." But as broad as it is, there are limits. There is "no general authority to expose the private affairs of individuals without justification in terms of the functions of Congress." In addition, congressional investigations are subject to First Amendment limitations, and Warren recognized that the investigative process "may imperceptibly lead to abridgement of protected freedoms." Congress may not simply use the power to investigate "to expose for the sake of exposure." The possible negative consequences befalling a witness are clearly too great. At this point, the Court offered some guidelines. Compelled testimony must only occur to further a legislative purpose clearly set forth in the committee's authorizing resolution. Committees are restricted to the "missions delegated to them," and compelled disclosures outside that sphere are impermissible. Questions posed to witnesses must be pertinent to the authorized inquiry. If the authorizing resolution is broad or "uncertain," it becomes particularly difficult to assess pertinency. As in the definition of criminal conduct, the "vice of vagueness" must be avoided. Warren concluded by stating that this decision would not keep Congress from "obtaining any information it needs for the proper fulfillment of its role." It simply must take a "measure of added care" in authorizing the use of the investigatory power.

The sole dissenter was Justice Clark, who characterized the requirements imposed by the decision as both "unnecessary and unworkable." He argued that the Court ought not sit as the "grand inquisitor and supervisor of congressional investigation." The effect, in Clark's view, of the *Watkins* holding was to "bring all inquiries ... to a 'dead end'. " *See also BARENBLATT V. UNITED STATES* (360 U.S. 109: 1960), p. 187; *MCGRAIN V. DAUGHERTY* (273 U.S. 135: 1927), p. 185.

Significance   *Watkins v. United States* (354 U.S. 178: 1957) used the pertinency test to define the scope of reasonable legislative investigations. Earlier cases reviewing the boundaries of the power to investigate had confined their considerations to the "inherent limitations of the sources of that power." *Watkins*, on the other hand, shifted the emphasis to balancing government interests with Bill of Rights protections of witnesses. Use of the pertinency test to determine the jurisdictional authority of legislative investigations substantially toughened the legislative purpose criterion. In a parallel case, *Sweezy v. New Hampshire* (354 U.S. 234: 1957), the Court imposed the *Watkins* requirements on state legislative investigations. The Court was extensively criticized for the *Watkins* decision, and Congress sought to negate its effect legislatively. The Court, however, softened the impact of *Watkins* within two years in such decisions as *Barenblatt v. United States* (360 U.S. 109: 1959).

Barenblatt v. United States, **360 U.S. 109, 79 S.Ct. 1081, 3 L.Ed. 2d 1115 (1959)**   Held that Congressional investigations of subversive political associations were proper. In *Barenblatt v. United States*, a former university professor was subpoenaed to appear before a subcommittee of the House Committee on Un-American Activities (HUAC). Barenblatt refused to respond to questions about his own political associations, claiming that the committee had no authority to inquire into that subject. Barenblatt appealed his conviction for contempt of Congress. The Supreme Court upheld the conviction in a 5–4 decision.

The opinion of the Court was authored by Justice Harlan. A central issue for the majority was the meaning of the decision rendered in *Watkins v. United States* (354 U.S. 178: 1957) just two years prior. Barenblatt argued that *Watkins* had found the authorizing resolution for HUAC irreparably vague. The Court rejected that interpretation of the *Watkins* case, suggesting instead that *Watkins* had only allowed refusal to answer questions for which the pertinency had not been established. While *Watkins* "was critical" of HUAC's authorizing resolution, it was not the "broad and inflexible holding" Barenblatt claimed. The pertinency of the questions asked Barenblatt was made with "indisputable clarity." Barenblatt was "sufficiently apprised" of the topic under inquiry and the relationship of questions posed to the broader topic. The record, in short, left "no room for a pertinency objection."

As to the more fundamental issue of congressional inquiry into subversive political associations, the Court found that to be a legitimate subject of legislative concern. Congress has "wide power to legislate in the field of Communist activity," and the legitimacy of information gathering in pursuit of such legislation is "hardly debatable." Once the legitimacy of the inquiry is established, it is not the Court's function to "pass judgment upon the general wisdom or efficacy" of the investigation in a field as "vexing and complicated" as subversive activities. If Congress is investigating a subject that is not constitutionally precluded, the judiciary "lacks the authority to intervene on the basis of the motives which spurred the exercise of that power." A balance must be struck between the interests of the individual and the government. The Court chose the latter interest in this case.

Chief Justice Warren and Justices Douglas, Black, and Brennan disagreed emphatically. Justice Black's dissent focused on the vagueness of the authorizing resolution and the impropriety of a congressional inquiry into political beliefs as distinguished from actions. Black was critical of the way the majority balanced the competing interests, and he characterized HUAC as a committee that pursued objectives of "exposure and punishment," the latter imposed by "humiliation and public shame." *See also* LEGISLATIVE INVESTIGATIONS, p. 631; *MCGRAIN V. DAUGHERTY* (273 U.S. 135: 1927), p. 185; *WATKINS V. UNITED STATES* (354 U.S. 178: 1957), p. 186.

Significance   *Barenblatt v. United States* (360 U.S. 109: 1959) returned to a broad and relatively unrestricted interpretation of the legislative purpose test. Indeed, *Barenblatt* was most deferential in that the Court seemed willing to presume the sufficiency of an investigation if the target of the inquiry fell within legislative purview. Through the use of the balancing test, *Barenblatt* weighted the interests of information gathering more than had the *Watkins* decision. In a related case, the Court also permitted state legislative inquiries into subversive activities in *Uphaus v. Wyman* (360 U.S. 72: 1959). As the composition of the Court changed, the Court intervened more often, although legislative authority to conduct investigations was never doubted. The focus tended to be procedural in most of these cases. Nonetheless, the First Amendment was used in the case of *Gibson v. Florida Legislative Investigating Committee* (372 U.W. 539: 1963) to limit a state inquiry into NAACP activities. Currently, Congress is able to gather information without substantial interference from the courts. A later decision, *Eastland v. United States Servicemen's Fund* (421 U.S. 491: 1975), protected legislative subpoena power for investigations subject only to the legislative purpose test. At the same time, congressional contempt is handled through the federal courts, which allows the judiciary to directly monitor investigative practices.

Delegation of Authority

Schechter Poultry Corporation v. United States, 295 U.S. 495, 55 S.Ct. 837, 79 L.Ed. 1570 (1935)   Struck down the National Industrial Recovery Act because it impermissibly delegated legislative power. *Schechter Poultry Corporation v. United States* reviewed the use of industry codes, which were a favored regulatory approach of some of the New Deal economic recovery legislation. The National Industrial Recovery Act (NIRA) was passed in 1933 and was intended to create codes covering wages and trade practices within various industries. The substantive provisions of the codes for each industry came in the form of proposals from representative groups within that industry. Proposals meeting the approval of the president became industry-wide regulation through executive order. Schechter Poultry Corporation was convicted of violations of the Live Poultry Code and appealed to the Supreme Court. The Court unanimously found the code-making provisions of the NIRA to be excessive and unconstitutional.

The Court, through Chief Justice Hughes, first rejected the argument that the national economic crisis provided cause to alter constitutional limits. Hughes said, "Extraordinary conditions do not create or enlarge constitutional power." There are limits on power granted by the Constitution, and those exercising such power are "not at liberty to transcend the imposed limits because they believe that more or different power is necessary." Even though the legitimate power is not to be supplemented by emergency circumstances, Article I conveys the legislative power to Congress along with authority to do what is "necessary and proper" in exercising that power. The Court has "repeatedly recognized the necessity of adapting legislation to complex conditions involving a host of details with which the national legislature cannot deal directly." At the same time, Congress cannot be "permitted to abdicate or to transfer to others the essential legislative functions with which it is vested."

The question in *Schechter* was whether the industry "codes of fair competition" constitute an improper transfer of the legislative task. The Court found the NIRA to be vague and imprecise in establishing its objectives. Fair competition was not defined, and the codes ranged too extensively. The codes "may cover conduct which existing law condemns, but they are not limited to conduct of that sort." The Court held Congress could empower a group of industry representatives to promulgate codes compatibly with the Constitution. However, Congress could not extend to the president "unfettered discretion" to make "whatever law he thinks may be needed or advisable for the rehabilitation and expansion of trade or industry." Justice Cardozo was even more outspoken in his concurring opinion. He suggested that delegation manifest in the codes is "not canalized within banks that keep it from overflowing." The delegation here was "unconfined and vagrant." Cardozo saw no limit to economic regulation through codes and referred to the process as "delegation run riot." *See also* AMERICAN TEXTILE MANUFACTURERS INSTITUTE, INC. V. DONOVAN (452 U.S. 490: 1981), p. 192; DELEGATION OF LEGISLATIVE POWER, p. 591; *J. W. HAMPTON, JR. AND COMPANY V. UNITED STATES* (276 U.S. 394: 1928); p. 388; LEGISLATIVE VETO, p. 632; SEPARATION OF POWERS, p. 56.

Significance   The code-making approach of the NIRA was struck down in *Schechter Poultry Corporation v. United States* (295 U.S. 495: 1935) as an excessive delegation of legislative power. It was representative of a historical period where several enactments were found to have left both objectives and implementation standards too vague and indefinite. In addition to *Schechter*, the Court also struck down portions of the NIRA which allowed the president to prohibit interstate shipments of oil in *Panama Refining Company v. Ryan* (293 U.S. 388: 1935). The statute did not establish "any criterion to govern the President." No specific finding was required to trigger presidential action, thus the president had "unlimited authority to determine the policy." The Court also struck down the code provisions of the Bituminous Coal Conservation Act of 1935 in *Carter v. Carter Coal Company* (298 U.S. 238: 1936). Delegation in the field of foreign affairs, however, has never been subjected to the same degree of scrutiny (see *United States v. Curtiss-Wright Export Corporation*, 299 U.S. 304: 1936). Since the flurry of cases in the 1930s, federal statutes have typically not experienced problems on delegation grounds.

J. W. Hampton, Jr. and Company v. United States, **276 U.S. 394, 48 S.Ct. 348, 72 L.Ed. 624 (1928)**   Upheld delegation of power allowing the president to raise or lower tariff rates. *J. W. Hampton, Jr. and Company v. United States* examined the delegation of power issues stemming from provisions of the Tariff Act of 1922. The act was aimed at equalizing production costs of items made in the United States and competing foreign countries. Section 315 of the act allowed the president, through a special commission, to monitor production cost differentials and raise or lower the tariff by up to 50 percent to create price parity between foreign and domestic items. J. W. Hampton, Jr. and Company imported a certain product that was subjected to an increased duty under authority of a presidential proclamation issued under the flexible tariff policy. Hampton and Company challenged the enactment on the ground that only Congress could lay and collect taxes; it could not delegate to the president that legislative function. The Court unanimously upheld the constitutionality of Section 315.

The opinion of the Court was issued by Chief Justice Taft, and it focused upon congressional intent. It was clear to the Court that in addition to generating revenue, Congress had intended to "enable domestic producers to compete on terms of equality with foreign producers in the markets of the United States." Since the tariff was to be based on the continually changing difference between foreign and domestic production costs, calculation of the difference would be complex, but what the statute sought to accomplish was "clear and perfectly intelligible." The difficulty of Congress gathering the necessary data required to adjust the tariff itself was apparent, but Section 315 provided a plan by which the executive branch could carry out the intended policy. While the Constitution divides governmental authority into three spheres, it does not intend that the "three branches are not co-ordinate parts of one government" and that each of the branches may not "invoke the action of the other branches in so far as the action invoked shall not be an assumption of the constitutional field of action of another branch." In reviewing the limits on constitutionally seeking assistance from another branch, the "extent and character of that assistance must be fixed accordingly to common sense and the inherent necessities of the governmental co-ordination." The Court concluded that the "same principle" that enables Congress to delegate its complex rate-making power to the Interstate Commerce Commission by "declaring the rule which shall prevail in the legislative fixing of rates" justifies the procedure established in the flexible tariff policy. *See also*

AMERICAN TEXTILE MANUFACTURERS INSTITUTE, INC. V. DONOVAN (452 U.S. 490: 1981), p. 192; DELEGATION OF LEGISLATIVE POWER, p. 591; *SCHECHTER POULTRY CORPORATION V. UNITED STATES* (295 U.S. 495: 1935), p. 189; SEPARATION OF POWERS, p. 56.

Significance   Delegations of legislative power may be constitutional as seen in *J. W. Hampton, Jr. and Company v. United States* (276 U.S. 394: 1928). There is a maxim applicable to the law of agency that says *delegate potestas non potest delegati* meaning that power that has been delegated cannot be redelegated. Nonetheless, it has been recognized since the outset of our constitutional history that some delegation of Article I power is required from a practical standpoint. Generally, this delegation takes the form of permitting the executive branch some discretion in implementation of general laws. In an earlier case, *Brig Aurora v. United States* (7 Cranch 382: 1813), the Court permitted the president to impose an embargo if particular conditions were found to exist. The Court held that statutes could be designed to apply conditionally. In *Wayman v. Southard* (10 Wheaton 1: 1825), the Court held that the judiciary could be delegated the responsibility for generating rules relating to the conduct of judicial business. Chief Justice Marshall suggested that to delegate the task of filling in the "details" was clearly distinct from delegating broad policy judgments, which are exclusively the domain of the legislative branch. The critical determination that must be made in cases involving delegation is whether an enactment clearly sets forth its policy objectives and the standards by which implementation of that policy is to occur.

American Textile Manufacturers Institute, Inc. v. Donovan, **452 U.S. 490, 101 S.Ct. 2478, 69 L.Ed. 2d 185 (1981)**   Upheld health standards established by an administrative agency for cotton dust standards against a delegation of legislative power challenge. *American Textile Manufacturers Institute, Inc. v. Donovan* reviewed provisions of the Occupational Safety and Health Act of 1970 that sought, among other things, to eliminate the threat of "brown lung" disease, a respiratory disability suffered by many employees of cotton mills and causally connected to exposure to cotton dust. Section 6 of the act authorized the secretary of labor to establish health standards that would, "to the extent feasible," assure that no employee would suffer impairment of health. Standards were established and set for a four-year phase-in to achieve the acceptable exposure levels. In the interim, employees were to be provided respirators. Employees unable to wear respirators were to be transferred with no reduction in wage. The cotton industry challenged the standards on the grounds that the labor secretary had not considered cost-benefit in fashioning the standards. The Court held 5–3 (Justice Powell not participating) that economic feasibility was not a required element in the process of creating exposure standards. The Court did strike down the wage guarantee provision as beyond the scope of the secretary's authority to establish exposure standards.

The primary question in this case was whether the secretary was free to set standards without determining that the "costs of the standard bear a reasonable relationship to its benefits." Key to reaching a conclusion was construction of the words "to the extent feasible." The manufacturers argued that standards set without cost-benefit analysis were not feasible, and thus outside the secretary's authority. The Court held that Section 6 directed that a standard be set that "most adequately" protects employee health limited only by the "extent to which this is 'capable of being done'." In the Court's view, the Congress had thus defined the relationship of cost of benefits by placing the "benefit" of worker health above all other considerations save for those making attainment of this "benefit" unachievable. If the secretary had based the standard on a cost-benefit balance, it would have been different from and inconsistent with the command of Section 6. Had Congress wanted to include cost-benefit, it would have indicated so in the statute. Use of the cost-benefit method "imposes an additional and overriding requirement" that would "eviscerate the 'to the extent feasible' requirement." The act placed "pre-eminent value on assuring employees a safe and healthful working environment," and the validity of the secretary's actions must be measured against that priority. The Court did hold that OSHA is not authorized to "repair general unfairness to employees that is unrelated to achievement of health and safety goals" such that it has no power to issue wage guarantee requirements.

Chief Justice Burger, Justice Stewart, and Justice Rehnquist dissented, saying that the "'feasibility standard' is no standard at all." That standard made the statute "so vague and precatory as to be an unconstitutional delegation of legislative authority." While legislation need not "resolve all ambiguities," Rehnquist felt this statute, resulting from legislative compromise, was an abdication by Congress of its responsibility for making a fundamental and difficult policy choice. *See also* DELEGATION OF LEGISLATIVE POWER, p. 591; *J. W. HAMPTON, JR. AND COMPANY V. UNITED STATES* (276 U.S. 394: 1928), p. 388; *SCHECHTER POULTRY CORPORATION V. UNITED STATES* (295 U.S. 495: 1935), p. 189; SEPARATION OF POWERS, p. 56.

Significance   American Textile Manufacturers Institute, Inc. v. Donovan (452 U.S. 490: 1981) is reflective of the contemporary position on delegation of power. Since the Court invalidated several New Deal enactments on grounds of improper delegation in the 1930s, the Congress has been more careful in circumscribing the discretion delegated to the executive branch. As shown in *American Textile*, the Court is most interested in whether Congress has established a basic policy and reasonably set forth standards by which it is to be achieved. It is apparent that Congress may exercise legislative power that does not intricately detail each provision of each enactment. The Constitution has not been viewed as making impractical demands in this regard. When the Court upheld the Fair Labor Standards Act in *Opp Cotton Mills v. Administrator of the Wage and Hour Division* (312 U.S. 126: 1941), Justice Stone suggested that the core of the legislative function is the determination of policy and the fashioning of that policy into a "rule of conduct." This function is constitutionally fulfilled when Congress "specifies that basic conclusions of fact upon ascertainment of which, from relevant data by a designated administrative agency, it ordains that its statutory command is to be effective." That view has prevailed since.

Speech or Debate Clause

Gravel v. United States, **408 U.S. 606, 92 S.Ct. 2614, 33 L.Ed. 2d 583 (1972)**   Held that private publication of material placed into the official record of a congressional committee was not protected by the speech or debate clause. *Gravel v. United States* involved an attempt by a member of the United States Senate to heighten the visibility of the Pentagon Papers. Gravel obtained a copy of the classified documents and placed them into the record of his Senate subcommittee. He then arranged for private publication of the documents through a commercial publisher. A federal grand jury, investigating possible criminal violations in the release of the documents, called an aide of the senator to testify. The senator claimed that the speech and debate clause found in Article I, Section 6 provided immunity for the activities an aide performed for a member of Congress. The Supreme Court held against the senator in a 5–4 decision.

The *Gravel* case raised two issues as to the scope of the speech and debate clause. First, did the clause extend beyond members of Congress to include aides and other staffers; and, second, what kinds of activities are protected? Justice White's opinion of the Court approached the matter of staff coverage by examining the immunity of the congressional member. A member is shielded from "criminal or civil liability and from questioning elsewhere than in the Senate."

Gravel's claim of immunity was "incontrovertible" because the speech and debate clause was designed to protect members "against prosecutions that directly impinge upon or threaten the legislative process." White then extended the coverage, saying it would be "literally impossible" given the "complexities of the modern legislative process" for members of Congress to "perform their legislative tasks without the help of aides and assistants." So crucial is such assistance to the basic legislative function that aides must be seen as members' "alter egos." To view aides otherwise would be to diminish and frustrate the role of the speech or debate clause. While supporting Gravel on the issue of immunity of his aide, the Court found against him on the question of whether arranging private publication was a protected activity. Historically, the Court suggested, the privilege did not include "protecting republication of an otherwise immune libel on the floor of the House." The clause only reaches matters that are an "integral part of the deliberative and communicative processes" by which the legislative function is discharged. The Court found that the private publication of the classified Pentagon Papers was "in no way essential to the deliberations of the Senate." Justices Brennan, Douglas, Marshall, and Stewart dissented, claiming that the majority took "too narrow a view of the legislative function." A legislator has the "duty" to inform the public on matters of public importance. *See also* HUTCHINSON V. PROXMIRE (443 U.S. 111: 1979), p. 196; SPEECH OR DEBATE CLAUSE, p. 654.

Significance   *Gravel v. United States* (408 U.S. 606: 1972) provided some clarification on the applicability of the speech or debate clause shield to legislative aides and staffers. Such immunity had not always been extended to such persons. In *Dombrowski v. Eastland* (387 U.S. 82: 1967), for example, the Court held that legal counsel to a congressional committee could be sued in a civil rights action even though the committee chair could not. Immediately following *Gravel*, the Court sharpened the boundaries of protected persons in *Doe v. McMillan* (412 U.S. 306: 1973). The Court held in *McMillan* that persons who were involved in the preparation of a report that libeled schoolchildren could not be sued. The Court went on to point out, however, that any personnel such as Government Printing Office employees involved in distributing the "actionable material" beyond the "reasonable bounds of the legislative task" were not shielded. Finally, there is the matter of the speech or debate clause impact on criminal prosecutions of congressional members. In *United States v. Brewster* (408 U.S. 501: 1972), the Court held that, while motivation for protected speeches may not be introduced, criminal conduct such as bribery is not part of the protected legislative process.

Hutchinson v. Proxmire, 443 U.S. 111, 99 S.Ct. 2675, 61 L.Ed. 2d 411 (1979)   Held that a newsletter containing defamatory statements was not protected by the speech or debate clause. *Hutchinson v. Proxmire* involved a defamation action brought by a federally funded research scientist against a member of the United States Senate. The senator has a practice of awarding a "Golden Fleece of the Month Award" to governmental agencies he felt were misusing or wasting federal tax money. One of the monthly awards was given to the agency that had supported Hutchinson's research. The award was announced during the course of a speech on the Senate floor and thus was immune from suit under the speech or debate clause. The text of the speech, however, was included in a press release from the senator's office, referred to in newsletters distributed by the senator, and mentioned by the senator in television interviews. The Supreme Court, with only Justice Brennan dissenting, held against the Senate member in this case.

The crucial question involved a definition of legislative business or protected activity. The Court held that "whatever imprecision there may be in the term 'legislative activities,' it is clear that nothing in the explicit language of the Clause suggests any intention to create an absolute privilege from liability or suit for defamatory statements made outside the Chamber." The objective of the speech or debate immunity was to ensure legislator independence, but the framers understood that abuse could occur if the privilege was too broad. The clause does not shield more than what is necessary to "preserve the integrity of the legislative process." Republication of defamatory statements initially made in the Congress has not been protected, and the Court found "no basis for departing from that long-established rule." While Senator Proxmire's speech was "wholly immune," the newsletters and press releases were not because neither was "essential to the deliberations of the Senate." The Court acknowledged that the clause was an extensive grant of privilege. It constituted a "conscious choice" of the framers to "enable reckless men to slander (by speech or debate) and even destroy others with impunity." Nonetheless, the Court could not "discern any 'conscious choice' to grant immunity for defamatory statements scattered far and wide by mail, press, and the electronic media." Justice Brennan dissented, feeling that Proxmire's newsletters and press releases were covered. In Brennan's view, "public criticism by legislators of unnecessary governmental expenditures, whatever its form, is a legislative act shielded by the Speech and Debate Clause." *See also* GRAVEL V. UNITED STATES (408 U.S. 606: 1972), p. 194; SPEECH OR DEBATE CLAUSE, p. 654.

Significance   *Hutchinson v. Proxmire* (443 U.S. 111: 1979) held that protected floor speeches cannot maintain that status if widely circulated outside the Congress. Senator Proxmire had argued that the speech or debate clause was intended to give congressional members a right to fully criticize spending policies. He also contended that most contemporary debate actually occurs not on the floor, but through such techniques as media releases. Finally, Proxmire asserted a legislative duty to keep constituents fully informed. The Court rejected these contentions in favor of a narrower definition of shielded legislative activity. This is the main impact of the Hutchinson case. Beyond the issue of speech and debate, the *Hutchinson* decision had consequences on libel litigation more generally. Proxmire had sought to have Hutchinson called a "public figure," a status that would have made a libel judgment against Proxmire more difficult. Public figures can be libeled only when statements are made with "actual malice" which the Court defines as "actual knowledge of falsity" or "reckless disregard of the truth." The Court held that Hutchinson had neither "thrust himself or his views into public controversy to influence others" nor did he have "regular and continuing access to the media," which conditions are necessary to constitute a "public figure" for purposes of a libel action.

Voting Discrimination

South Carolina v. Katzenbach, 383 U.S. 301, 86 S.Ct. 803, 15 L.Ed. 2d 769 (1966)   Upheld the Voting Rights Act of 1965. *South Carolina v. Katzenbach* explored how the Fifteenth Amendment protects the right to vote and provides Congress with authority to enact appropriate legislation to further that objective. The Voting Rights Act of 1965 abolished devices to disqualify citizens from voting, such as the literacy test and accumulated poll taxes. The act also provided for extensive federal supervision of elections and required that any new conditions of voter eligibility be reviewed by the attorney general before implementation. Provisions of the act were triggered if less than 50 percent of citizens of voting age were registered to vote or where fewer than 50 percent of the voting age population had participated in the 1964 presidential election.

Chief Justice Warren wrote the opinion of the Court. He noted that the purpose of the act was "to banish the blight of racial discrimination in voting, which has infected the electoral process in parts of our country for nearly a century." The Court accorded great deference to an act dedicated to such a purpose even if Congress had exercised power in an inventive manner. Referring to the stringent remedies and their implementation without prior adjudication, the Court said that litigation was inadequate when discrimination was widespread and persistent. Following nearly a hundred years of systematic resistance to the Fifteenth Amendment, Congress might well decide to shift the advantage of time and inertia from the perpetrators of the evil to its victims. The targeted nature of the act's coverage was a reasonable legislative option. Congress determined that voting discrimination "presently occurs in certain sections of the country. In acceptable legislative fashion, Congress chose to limit its attention to the geographic areas where immediate action seemed necessary." In sum, the Court viewed the act as an array of potent weapons marshalled to combat the evil of voting discrimination. They were weapons that constitute "a valid means for carrying out the commands of the Fifteenth Amendment." *See also* BUCKLEY V. VALEO (424 U.S. 1: 1976), p. 200; CALIFORNIA MEDICAL ASSOCIATION V. FEDERAL ELECTION COMMISSION (453 U.S. 182: 1981), p. 202; FIFTEENTH AMENDMENT, p. 606; OREGON V. MITCHELL (400 U.S. 112: 1970), p. 199.

Significance   *South Carolina v. Katzenbach* (383 U.S. 301: 1966) allowed the Congress to aggressively seek to use power conveyed by the Fifteenth Amendment to protect the election process from discrimination. The Voting Rights Act of 1965 was an unprecedented attempt to invoke federal authority to regulate voting practices, a policy area that had previously resided exclusively with the states. The Voting Rights Act also allowed the targeting of voting practices involving non–English-speaking voters for the first time. The act had provisions intended for the large Spanish-speaking Puerto Rican population in New York City. These provisions were upheld on equal protection grounds in *Katzenbach v. Morgan* (384 U.S. 641: 1966). The act had a five-year limitation but was extended in 1970, 1975, and 1982. The 1970 extension banned the use of literacy tests. The same extension also set the minimum voting age at 18 throughout the country. The Court held in *Oregon v. Mitchell* (400 U.S. 112: 1970), however, that Congress could only establish age qualifications for federal elections. States retained control over state and local elections. Ratification of the Twenty-sixth Amendment in 1971 superseded the Court's decision in *Oregon v. Mitchell*. Primary elections have also attained constitutional status, although the Court has based some of these decisions on the equal protection clause of the Fourteenth Amendment. After several decisions to the contrary, the Court held in *United States v. Classic* (313 U.S. 299: 1941) that the federal government could regulate primaries because of their integral role in the overall election process. In *Smith v. Allwright* (321 U.S. 649: 1944), the Court found that political parties conducting racially exclusive primaries were acting as an agent of the state and thus were in violation of the Fifteenth Amendment. The Court also outlawed the poll tax for state elections in *Harper v. Virginia State Board of Elections* (383 U.S. 663: 1966), holding that such a tax discriminated in an invidious fashion.

Regulation of Elections

***Oregon v. Mitchell*, 400 U.S. 112, 91 S.Ct. 260, 27 L.Ed. 2d 272 (1970)** Upheld congressional power to lower the voting age to 18 for federal elections. *Oregon v. Mitchell* was the case through which the Court reviewed the Voting Rights Act of 1970. The 1970 version of the act retained federal supervision mechanisms aimed at combating racially discriminatory voting practices used in the original 1965 act. The 1965 act was based on power conveyed to Congress by the Fifteenth Amendment, a power source recognized by the Court in *South Carolina v. Katzenbach* (383 U.S. 301: 1966). The 1970 act, however, contained three new elements. It prohibited literacy tests and severely limited state residency requirements for presidential elections. The act also lowered the minimum age for both federal and state elections to 18. The federal government and several states filed suits attempting to enjoin, on the one hand, states from noncompliance, and, on the other hand, the United States attorney general from enforcing the act's provisions. The Supreme Court heard the case on original jurisdiction. The Court split differently on the component elements but upheld bans on literacy requirements and residency requirements by 9–0 and 8–1 votes, respectively. The 18-year-old vote question was more complex. By a 5–4 vote, the Court held that Congress had power to lower the voting age through statute, but only for federal elections. The provision lowering the voting age for state elections was voided, also by a 5–4 vote.

Justice Black was part of both five-member majorities. He was joined by Justices Douglas, Brennan, Marshall, and White to uphold lowering the age for federal elections, and he combined with Chief Justice Burger and Justices Harlan, Stewart, and Blackmun to strike down adjustment of minimum age for state elections. Justice Black's opinion of the Court accorded the Congress plenary power in regulating federal elections. From the outset of our constitutional history, Congress has been empowered to initiate regulations or alter any regulations set by the states regarding federal elections. This power was provided in Article I, Section 4, which delegates authority to set voter guidelines to the states, but Congress "may at any time by law make or alter such regulations." In addition, congressional power over national elections is "augmented by the Necessary and Proper Clause." Black noted that Congress has been given the power to "lay out or alter boundaries" in congressional districts. In Black's view, there could be no doubt that the power to alter district boundaries is "vastly more significant in its effect than the power to permit 18-year-olds to go to the polls and vote in all federal elections." By similar reasoning, the Court held that Congress has the power to oversee presidential elections. Black said that it "cannot be seriously contended that Congress has less power over the conduct of presidential elections than it has over congressional elections." The limitation on congressional power utilized in *Oregon v. Mitchell* was that the voting age could not be statutorily lowered for state elections. The Court held that the Constitution intended to "preserve to the States the power that even the Colonies had to establish and maintain their own separate and independent governments" unless specifically provided. Justice Black indicated that "no function is more essential" to that end than the power "to determine the qualifications of their own voters for state, county and municipal offices and the nature of their own machinery for filling local public offices." *See also BUCKLEY V. VALEO* (424 U.S. 1:1976), p. 200; *CALIFORNIA MEDICAL ASSOCIATION V. FEDERAL ELECTION COMMISSION* (453 U.S. 182: 1981), p. 202; NECESSARY AND PROPER CLAUSE, p. 637; *SOUTH CAROLINA V. KATZENBACH* (383 U.S. 301: 1966), p. 197; TWENTY-SIXTH AMENDMENT, p. 667.

Significance   *Oregon v. Mitchell* (400 U.S. 112: 1970) said several things about congressional power to regulate the electoral process. First, it reinforced the Court's holding in *South Carolina v. Katzenbach* (383 U.S. 301: 1966) that the Fourteenth and Fifteenth Amendments could be used extensively to eliminate any discriminatory voting practices. Second, *Mitchell* said that Congress has unconditional power to regulate federal elections based on Article I. Third, the decision vigorously protected state policy preferences in the area of state and local electoral processes except in those instances where the Constitution expressly authorizes federal intervention. In other words, *Oregon v. Mitchell* struck a balance between federal legislative power and state authority. The practical effect of the decision was to make it necessary to conduct the 1972 election with separate registration and balloting procedures, at least for 18- to 20-year-olds. The prospect of such an administrative nightmare prompted the Twenty-sixth Amendment, which lowered the voting age to 18 for all elections.

Buckley v. Valeo, 424 U.S. 1, 96 S.Ct. 612, 46 L.Ed. 2d 659 (1976)   Examined the constitutionality of the Federal Election Campaign Act of 1974. Regulation of the electoral process impinges upon individual and group expression or at least has that potential. *Buckley v. Valeo* considered the 1974 act against various First Amendment–based challenges. The act, passed in the wake of Watergate, sought to protect the electoral process by (1) limiting political campaign contributions, (2) establishing ceilings on several categories of campaign expenditures, (3) requiring extensive and regular disclosure of campaign contributors and expenditures, (4) providing public financing for presidential campaigns and (5) creating a Federal Election Commission to administer the act. Suit was filed by a diverse collection of individuals and groups that included a United States senator (James Buckley), the Eugene McCarthy presidential campaign, the Libertarian Party, the American Conservative Union, and the New York Civil Liberties Union, among others. By differing majorities, the Court upheld those portions of the act that provided for campaign contribution limits, disclosure, public financing, and the Federal Election Commission. The sections imposing limits on campaign expenditures and the appointment mechanism for the Election Commission were invalidated.

The Court upheld the contribution and disclosure regulations and, through a *per curiam* opinion, acknowledged the legitimate congressional interest in protecting the "integrity of our system of representative democracy" from quid pro quo arrangements on their appearance that might arise from financial contributions. The act's contribution and expenditure ceilings did create serious First Amendment problems because they reduce the "quality of expression . . . because virtually every means of communicating ideas in today's society requires the expenditure of money." The Court distinguished, however, between the limits on contributions and the things for which contributions might be spent. Contributions involve "little direct restraint," while expenditure limits represent "substantial restraint" on the "quality and diversity of political speech." Even though the contribution ceiling might deter some person from financially supporting political campaigns, the Court viewed this approach as a "least restrictive means of curbing the evils of campaign ignorance and corruption." The Court also upheld the public financing provisions of the act. The Court held that the general welfare clause is an expansive grant of power that provides Congress with authority to regulate presidential elections and campaigns. The option to use public financing as a "means to reform the electoral process" was clearly conveyed. "It is for Congress to decide which expenditures will promote the general welfare." The Federal Election Commission was also upheld as a reasonable means of monitoring elections, although the Court struck down the selection provisions contained in the act because they violated the appointments clause of Article II, Section 1. The appointments clause requires the president to make all appointments of federal agencies, although Congress may advise and consent. *See also* CALIFORNIA MEDICAL ASSOCIATION V. FEDERAL ELECTION COMMISSION (435 U.S. 182: 1981), p. 202; GENERAL WELFARE CLAUSE, p. 377; OREGON V. MITCHELL (400 U.S. 112: 1970), p. 199; SOUTH CAROLINA V. KATZENBACH (383 U.S. 301: 1966), p. 197.

Significance   The Court's ruling in *Buckley v. Valeo* (424 U.S. 1: 1976) struck a balance between individual rights of association and expression, and the congressional interest in protecting the integrity of the electoral process. While the expenditure provisions were invalidated on First Amendment grounds, the Court recognized extensive congressional power to restrict political contributions and move to a system of public financing. It can generally be concluded that *Buckley* was deferential to congressional efforts to legislate in this sphere. The *Buckley* decision also generated some important followup questions regarding electoral regulation at the state level. In *First National Bank of Boston v. Bellotti* (435 U.S. 765: 1978), the Court struck down a state statute prohibiting the use of corporate funds for the purpose of influencing a referendum question. Absent a showing that the corporation's advocacy "threatened imminently to undermine democratic processes," the state has no interest sufficient to limit a corporation's expression of views on a public issue. In *Citizens Against Rent Control/ Coalition for Fair Housing v. City of Berkeley* (454 U.S. 290: 1981), the Court struck down a municipal ordinance limiting contributions to organizations formed to support or oppose ballot issues. With only Justice White dissenting, the Court drew heavily on *Buckley* and concluded that the ordinances impermissibly restrained individual and associational rights of expression.

California Medical Association v. Federal Election Commission, 453 U.S. 182, 101 S.Ct. 2712, 69 L.Ed. 2d 567 (1981)

Upheld provisions of the Federal Election Campaign Act that placed limits on contributions to multicandidate political committees. *California Medical Association v. Federal Election Commission* focused upon political action committees (PACs) and refined the Court's earlier holding in *Buckley v. Valeo* (424 U.S. 1: 1976). A section of the Federal Election Campaign Act prohibited contributions of more than $5,000 annually to PACs from individuals and unincorporated associations. The statute also forbade PACs from knowingly accepting contributions beyond the established limit. An unincorporated medical association (CMA) formed a committee (CALPAC) and subsequently received notification from the Federal Election Commission that enforcement proceedings were under way for alleged violations of the Campaign Act. CALPAC and several individual members challenged the constitutionality of the act on First Amendment grounds. The Supreme Court found the PAC limitation constitutional in a 5–4 decision.

The majority did not agree on a rationale for the First Amendment issue, but Justice Marshall wrote a plurality opinion on behalf of himself and Justices Brennan, White, and Stevens. The *Buckley* decision struck down expenditure limitations on campaigns, CALPAC attempted to extend this reasoning to remove PAC contribution limitations, claiming the act unconstitutionally restricted the ability of the association to "engage in political speech through a political committee." The majority found these contentions "unpersuasive." The plurality opinion suggested that "'speech by proxy'" sought by the CMA by virtue of its contributions is "not the sort of political advocacy that this Court in *Buckley* found entitled to First Amendment protection." Because CALPAC receives contributions from several sources, it cannot be viewed as identical with CMA. While CMA is likely to be in general agreement with the political position of CALPAC, "this sympathy of interests alone does not convert CALPAC's speech into that of CMA." As in *Buckley*, its transformation of contributions into political expression requires speech by other than the contributor. The plurality noted that Congress had a legitimate concern that the contribution limits upheld in *Buckley* would not be circumvented. Such concerns prompted enactment of the PAC limitation, and the provision is "an appropriate means by which Congress could seek to protect the integrity of contribution restrictions" as upheld in *Buckley*.

Justice Blackmun concurred in the judgment, but disagreed with the plurality opinion and its reliance on the limited First Amendment protection of contributions as a form of political advocacy. Rather, Blackmun viewed the limit as a "means of preventing evasion" of previously upheld limits. Congress must be able to act to prevent "actual or potential corruption" so long as the limitation is "no broader than necessary" to achieve that objective. The provision under review satisfied that narrow test in Blackmun's view.

The minority of Chief Justice Burger and Justices Stewart, Powell, and Rehnquist focused upon procedural issues including what they felt was an improper certification of the case to the court of appeals by the district court. *See also* BUCKLEY V. VALEO (424 U.S. 1: 1976), p. 200; OREGON V. MITCHELL (400 U.S. 112: 1970), p. 199; SOUTH CAROLINA V. KATZENBACH (383 U.S. 301: 1966), p. 197.

Significance   California Medical Association v. Federal Election Commission (453 U.S. 182: 1981) upheld a section of the Federal Election Campaign Act targeting contributions to multicandidate political committees. While Congress is clearly not free to regulate comprehensively in the area in deference to First Amendment interests, the Court has recognized protection of the integrity of the electoral process as a substantial competing interest. This case touches upon the most problematic contemporary campaign element, the PAC. The Court will likely continue to struggle with balancing regulatory and First Amendment interests. In *Common Cause v. Schmitt* (453 U.S. 129: 1982), the Court split 4–4 (Justice O'Connor not participating), thus allowing a lower court ruling permitting unlimited PAC expenditures in presidential campaigns. Clearly, the basic holding in *Buckley v. Valeo* (424 U.S. 1: 1976) remains as the main force.

Power to Protect Civil Rights

United States v. Guest, **383 U.S. 745, 86 S.Ct. 1170, 16 L.Ed. 2d 239 (1966)**   Upheld congressional power to punish individual conspiracies that violate Fourteenth Amendment rights. *United States v. Guest* permitted the application of provisions of the Enforcement Act of 1870 (currently referred to as Section 241 of Title 18 of the U.S. Code) against violations of a person's civil rights. Section 241 provides for fine and imprisonment of persons who conspire to "injure, oppress, threaten, or intimidate any citizen in the free exercise or enjoyment of any right or privilege secured to him by the Constitution or laws of the United States." The *Guest* case involved the murder of a black citizen on a Georgia highway. Guest was one of two persons allegedly involved in the conspiracy who was acquitted in a state murder proceeding. Subsequently, Guest and others were indicted for conspiracy to violate Section 241. The United States District Court dismissed the indictment, and the federal government appealed. The Supreme Court reversed and held, in an 8–1 decision, that the indictments should not have been dismissed.

The principal issue in this case was whether Congress possessed the authority to protect more than a narrow range of "secured" rights that flow directly from national citizenship against infringement by private persons. Prior to *Guest*, it was required that the state be shown to be a party to any acts of discrimination to be within the legislative reach of the Fourteenth Amendment. A majority of the Court felt such state action was present in this case. Part of the conspiracy involved private parties causing the false arrest of blacks. The Court determined that the state was drawn into the conspiracy sufficiently to allow the indictments to stand. The majority also cited the right of travel as one of those fundamental rights of federal citizenship to be secure from violation even by private parties. Thus, under a liberal construction of state action, the Court found the conspiracy involved in this case to be within reach using traditional Fourteenth Amendment standards.

Two groups of three justices each wished to go further and indicate some rather far-reaching conclusions about the need to demonstrate state action in the conspiracy. The common thrust of both of these concurring groups was that Section 5 of the Fourteenth Amendment provided Congress with the power to penalize any conspiracy, public or private, that violates Fourteenth Amendment rights. Justice Harlan concurred insofar as indictments for state-aided interference with the right to travel were concerned. He disagreed, however, that state action was no longer a required component of Fourteenth Amendment violations. *See also* FOURTEENTH AMENDMENT, p. 612; *JONES V. ALFRED MAYER COMPANY* (392 U.S. 409: 1968), p. 205; RIGHT TO TRAVEL, p. 661; STATE ACTION, p. 657.

Significance   *United States v. Guest* (383 U.S. 745: 1966) held that Congress had the power to punish private conspiracies to deprive persons of their right to travel interstate. The utility of Section 241 as a means of preventing conspiracies was limited because it was felt that the provisions only applied to a narrow class of civil rights. *Guest* dramatically broadened the scope of Section 241. The effect of the Court's holding in *Guest* needs to be seen in a broader context of Warren Court decisions affecting congressional power to protect civil rights. In a companion case to *Guest, United States v. Price* (383 U.S. 787: 1966), the Court upheld indictments allowing federal prosecution for the murders of three civil rights workers in Mississippi. These indictments were brought under Section 242 of Title 18 of the U.S. Code, provisions growing out of the Civil Rights Act of 1866. Section 242, while requiring actions committed "under color" of state authority, protected an extensive range of rights, not just those derived from federal citizenship. The holding in *Price* allowed the federal government to intervene if civil rights were violated and state prosecutions were unsuccessful. Coupled with the decision in *Jones v. Alfred Mayer Company* (392 U.S. 409: 1968), which acknowledged comprehensive legislative power through the Thirteenth Amendment, the Warren Court's decisions in aggregate left Congress with substantial authority to protect civil rights. Indeed, the Civil Rights Act of 1968 prohibits "willful" interference with various civil rights whether the conspirator acts "under color" of law or privately.

Jones v. Alfred Mayer Company, 392 U.S. 409, 88 S.Ct. 2186, 20 L.Ed. 2d 1189 (1968)   Held that private discrimination in the sale or rental of property could be legislatively prohibited under authority conveyed by the Thirteenth Amendment. *Jones v. Alfred Mayer Company* examined "open housing" protections incorporated as Section 1982 of the U.S. Code that were portions of the Civil Rights Act of 1866. The section protected the rights of "all citizens" to "inherit, purchase, lease, sell, hold, and convey real and personal property." Jones sought to invoke the section when he encountered racial discrimination in his attempt to purchase a home. The lower federal courts dismissed Jones's complaint, determining that Congress was not empowered to regulate private discriminatory conduct. The Supreme Court reversed in a 7–2 decision.

Justice Stewart began the opinion of the Court by examining what Congress had intended by the original enactment. The act attempted, in his view, to protect all citizens from discrimination "not only by 'state or local law,' but also by 'custom or prejudice.'" The act "plainly meant to secure" the right to purchase or lease property against "interference from any source whatever, whether governmental or private." Stewart then moved to the issue of whether "Congress has power under the Constitution to do what Section 1982 purports to do." The Court concluded that the enabling language of Section 2 of the Thirteenth Amendment provided Congress with the power to "eliminate all racial barriers to the acquisition of real and personal property." The Court's language seemed to offer limitless possibilities for the Thirteenth Amendment as a legislative power source. Stewart said, "Surely Congress has the power . . . rationally to determine what are the badges and incidents of slavery," and the power to "translate that determination into effective legislation." Any burden or disability that restrains exercise of a fundamental right constitutes a badge or incident of slavery sufficient to justify federal intervention. "At the very least," Congress has authority to guarantee that any citizen may buy and live anywhere. If Congress cannot protect at least that, "then the Thirteenth Amendment made a promise that the Nation cannot keep."

Justice Harlan, joined by Justice White, issued a dissent. Neither felt that Section 1982 could apply to "purely private action." In addition, their historical analysis yielded the conclusion that the majority was departing from what the Congress really had intended with the Civil Rights Act of 1866. More important, Harlan and White doubted that the Thirteenth Amendment provided sufficient authority to support the Civil Rights Act of 1866. *See also* FOURTEENTH AMENDMENT, p. 612; NORTH HAVEN BOARD OF EDUCATION V. BELL (456 U.S. 512: 1982), p. 207; THIRTEENTH AMENDMENT, p. 660; UNITED STATES V. GUEST (383 U.S. 745: 1966), p. 204.

Significance   *Jones v. Alfred Mayer Company* (392 U.S. 409: 1968) established the Thirteenth Amendment as a potentially extensive legislative power source for Congress to deal with racial inequality. *Jones* permitted the Congress to exercise authority over virtually all forms of discriminatory conduct so long as it was regarded as a "badge" of slavery. In addition, the Thirteenth Amendment was not directed at official conduct as is the case with the Fourteenth. Thus, the public-private distinction limiting the reach of the Fourteenth Amendment did not apply to the Thirteenth. The broad potential of this power is further reflected in *Griffin v. Breckenridge* (403 U.S. 88: 1971), which upheld a federal statute authorizing use of the federal courts for civil rights violation damage suits against private citizens. The Court said that there "has never been any doubt" that the Thirteenth Amendment gives Congress power to "impose liability on private persons." Congress was "wholly within its powers" to create a means for black citizens who have been the "victims of conspiratorial, racially discriminatory private action aimed at depriving them of the basic rights that the law secures to all free men." The matter of fair housing was addressed by the Congress in the Civil Rights Act of 1968, a law that emerged almost simultaneously with the *Jones* decision. The fair housing provisions of 1968 superseded the enactment at issue in *Jones*, but the Court's ruling on the character of the Thirteenth Amendment as a power source remains.

North Haven Board of Education v. Bell, 456 U.S. 512, 102 S.Ct. 1912, 72 L.Ed. 2d 299 (1982)

Held that statutorily mandated regulations prohibiting sex discrimination in federally funded educational programs were constitutional. *North Haven Board of Education v. Bell* examined Department of Health, Education, and Welfare (HEW) employment regulations developed under force of Title IX of the Educational Amendments of 1972. Section 901 of Title IX bars gender discrimination in any educational program that receives federal funding. Section 902 requires funding agencies to establish rules to ensure that recipients comply with Section 901. The enactment provides that funds may be terminated for any program found in noncompliance. The regulations promulgated by HEW prohibited sex discrimination in the employment practices of recipients. The North Haven (Connecticut) Board of Education sought to enjoin enforcement of the regulations on the ground that Title IX was not intended to apply to employment. The Supreme Court disagreed in a 6–3 decision.

The central issue for the Court in this case was the scope of Title IX language dealing with sex discrimination. The prohibition is that "No person . . . shall, on the basis of sex, be excluded from participation in, be denied the benefits of, or be subjected to discrimination under any education program or activity receiving Federal financial assistance."

The Court's opinion was delivered by Justice Blackmun, and it supported the employment regulations on three grounds. First, the language itself. The broad directive that "no person" may be discriminated against was seen as use of a word that was most inclusive—the word *person*. Congress could easily have chosen a more restrictive term, such as *student* or *beneficiary*. Second, the Court considered the legislative history of Title IX to determine whether "Congress meant somehow to limit the expansive language of Section 901." The Court cited statements by the Senate sponsor of Section 901 during the congressional debate. The senator's remarks indicated clear intent to cover the area of employment. Because Section 901 originated as a floor amendment, no committee report addressed its provisions; thus the sponsor's remarks were used as an "authoritative guide to the statute's construction." Finally, the Court looked at the "postenactment history" of Title IX and noted that Congress had "not seen fit to disturb" the regulations as applied to employment or pass bills that would have "amended Section 901 to limit its coverage of employment discrimination."

Justice Powell dissented and was joined by Chief Justice Burger and Justice Rehnquist. They disagreed that Title IX was intended to reach employment, arguing that the Court had altered the statute by interpretation. Their view was that the absence of specific reference to employment discrimination was significant. They also disputed that the legislative history of Title IX supported inclusion. They pointed out that "Only when legislative history gives clear and unequivocal guidance" as to what Congress intended should a "court presume to add what Congress failed to add." *See also* FOURTEENTH AMENDMENT, p. 612; *JONES V. ALFRED MAYER COMPANY* (392 U.S. 409: 1968), p. 205; *UNITED STATES V. GUEST* (383 U.S. 745: 1966), p. 204.

Significance When the Court upheld the use of Title IX to reach employment discrimination in *North Haven Board of Education v. Bell* (456 U.S. 512: 1982), it approved another in a series of legislative enactments aimed at gender discrimination in employment. In addition to decisions from the Court that brought gender classification more closely under equal protection clause scrutiny, the Court has consistently supported congressional efforts to proscribe many discriminatory bases, including gender, through legislation. In 1963, Congress passed the Equal Pay Act, which amended the Fair Labor Standards Act. The Court upheld this enactment in *Corning Glass Works v. Brennan* (417 U.S. 188: 1974). Title VII of the Civil Rights Act of 1964 also prohibited gender discrimination by employers. Title VII was upheld in *Phillips v. Martin Marietta Corporation* (400 U.S. 542: 1971). In *County of Washington v. Gunther* (452 U.S. 161: 1981), the Court ruled that actions brought under Title VII may go beyond claims of unequal pay for equal work, a decision that meant that women bringing wage discrimination suits need only show that gender was used in a discriminatory way in setting pay rates.

Bill of Attainder

United States v. Brown, **381 U.S. 437, 85 S.Ct. 1707, 14 L.Ed. 2d 484 (1965)** Held Section 504 of the Labor-Management Reporting and Disclosure Act to be an unconstitutional bill of attainder. Section 504 made it a crime for a member of the Communist party to serve as an officer or employee of a labor union. Brown, an "open and avowed" Communist, was elected to the executive board of a local of the International Longshoreman's and Warehouseman's Union. Brown was charged with violation of Section 504 and convicted. He appealed on First and Fifth Amendment as well as bill of attainder grounds. The Supreme Court found Section 504 to be a prohibited bill of attainder in a 5–4 decision.

Chief Justice Warren reviewed the reason for the prohibition, which appears in Sections 9 and 10 of Article I, in his majority opinion. The bill of attainder clause was intended not as a "narrow, technical (and therefore soon to be outmoded) prohibition, but rather as an implementation of the separation of powers, a general safeguard against legislative exercise of the judicial function, or more simply—trial by legislature." The clause reflected a belief that legislatures are "not so well suited as politically independent judges and juries" to the task of ruling upon the "blame-worthiness of, and levying appropriate punishment upon, specific persons." Having developed the general character of the prohibition, the Court faced the question of whether Section 504 actually constituted a bill of attainder. The government argued that the language of Section 504 neither named Brown specifically nor did it punish as such, and that the statute was preventative rather than punitive or retributive. The Court, however, found that Section 504 disqualified not only present Communist party members, but also those who had been members within the past five years. The section did not, thus, permit persons to resign their memberships to take union office or employment. As a result, the Court held Section 504 to inflict the kind of "punishment" forbidden by the bill of attainder language. Punishment, in the Court's view, was more comprehensive than only retribution. The deprivation of Section 504 was aimed at the membership of the Communist party, which the Court felt was sufficiently specific to constitute a bill of attainder.

A dissent, joined by Justices Clark, Harlan, and Stewart, was entered by Justice White. The dissent argued that Congress had taken a reasonable course to prevent undesired future conduct, and that Congress may legitimately focus on a group for regulation without punitive intent "even when some of its members are unlikely to engage in the feared conduct." In the dissenters' view, the majority posed a "too narrow view of the legislative process." *See also* EX POST FACTO, p. 604; *WEAVER V. GRAHAM* (450 U.S. 24: 1981), p. 210.

Significance   United States v. Brown (381 U.S. 437: 1965) rejected legislation attempting to preclude Communist party members from service as union officers or employees. Cases like *Brown* represent a view that the legislative function is one of rule making, the prescription of general laws for the governing of society. The bill of attainder prohibition ensures that application of such general laws to specific individuals rests with the other branches of government. The first bill of attainder challenges to legislation came soon after the Civil War. In *Cummings v. Missouri* (4 Wallace 277: 1867), the Court struck down a state constitutional amendment requiring an oath from persons of specified professions stating that they had not sympathized with the cause of the Confederacy. A similar oath at the federal level required lawyers to swear that they had not "aided the Confederacy." The statute was invalidated in *Ex Parte Garland* (4 Wallace 333: 1867). A classic bill of attainder was found in *United States v. Lovett* (328 U.S. 303: 1946), where Congress had legislatively denied pay to three named federal employees found by the House Un-American Activities Committee to be "subversives." At the same time, a bill of attainder challenge to the noncommunist oath provisions of Taft-Hartley was unsuccessful in *American Communications Association v. Douds* (339 U.S. 382: 1950), *Brown* was distinguished from *Douds* in that Communist party members could "escape from the class of persons specified by Congress simply by resigning from the Party," an option that removed any punitive tone from the regulation.

Ex Post Facto

Weaver v. Graham, 450 U.S. 24, 101 S.Ct. 960, 67 L.Ed. 2d 17 (1981)   Held a state reducing good conduct deductions from a prisoner's criminal sentence to be an *ex post facto* law prohibited by Sections 9 and 10 of Article I. An *ex post facto* law retroactively disadvantages an individual or a group. Weaver pled guilty to second-degree murder and was sentenced to 15 years imprisonment. The state statute operating at the time of the offense and at the time of Weaver's sentencing contained a formula by which "gain time" credits could be deducted from sentences if a prisoner committed no rule infraction and had performed all duties and tasks assigned to him. While Weaver was serving his sentence, a statute was passed replacing the earlier deduction or credit formula with a less generous one. The change was estimated at depriving Weaver of the possibility of lessening his sentence by more than two years. Weaver's appeal to the Florida Supreme Court was denied on the grounds that the statute did not affect a "vested" right and was therefore not within the scope of the *ex post facto* limitation. The United States Supreme Court reversed unanimously.

Justice Marshall's opinion of the Court indicated that *ex post facto* laws were prohibited in Sections 9 and 10 of Article I because the authors of the Constitution wished to "assure that legislative acts give fair warning of their effect and permit individuals to rely on their meaning until explicitly changed." The Court also saw the prohibition as a safeguard against "arbitrary and potentially vindictive" legislation. According to Marshall, two "critical elements" must be present for a statute to be *ex post facto*. First, it must be retroactive, applying to "events occurring before its enactment." Second, such a retroactive law must "disadvantage the offender affected by it." A statute need not "impair a 'vested right'" to qualify for *ex post facto* limitations. The "presence or absence of an affirmative, enforceable right is not relevant" to the *ex post facto* prohibition. Weaver was not entitled as such to less punishment, but the policy change did constitute an *ex post facto* because of the "lack of fair notice and governmental restraint" when the legislature increased punishment beyond what it was when Weaver committed his crime. Even a statute that "merely alters penal provisions accorded by the grace of the legislature," such as the "gain time" policy involved here, violates the *ex post facto* prohibition if it is both "retroactive and more onerous than the law in effect on the date of the offense." *See also* BILL OF ATTAINDER, p. 582; *UNITED STATES V. BROWN* (381 U.S. 437: 1965), p. 209.

Significance   *Weaver v. Graham* (450 U.S. 24: 1981) held the statutory alteration of good behavior credit policy to be an unconstitutional *ex post facto* law. An *ex post facto* law imposes criminal law disadvantages retroactively. In a very early decision, *Calder v. Bull* (3 Dallas 386: 1798), the Court confined *ex post facto* limits to the criminal context. Generally, administrative proceedings including those involving denaturalization are viewed as civil and outside the scope of the *ex post facto* prohibition. In addition to bill of attainder flaws, the oaths involving "aid" to the Confederacy as a condition of pursuing specified professions were held to have impermissibly imposed "criminal" class penalties in *Cummings v. Missouri* (4 Wallace 277: 1867) and *Ex Parte Garland* (4 Wallace 333: 1867). The *ex post facto* limitation does not preclude procedural changes from being instituted. In *Dobbert v. Florida* (432 U.S. 282: 1977), the

Court upheld a change in Florida's death penalty statute that changed the jury's role in capital cases from binding to advisory. Dobbert was sentenced to death by a judge despite a jury recommendation of life imprisonment. Formerly, the jury judgment of a life sentence would have precluded the death penalty. The Court, however, saw the change as dealing with "modes of procedure which do not affect matters of substance." A procedural change, even a disadvantageous one, is not subject to *ex post facto* limits. In this case, the change only altered the "methods employed in determining whether the death penalty was to be imposed; there was no change in the quantum punishment attached to the crime."

Census Confidentiality

Baldridge v. Shapiro, **455 U.S. 345, 102 S.Ct. 1103, 71 L.Ed. 2d 199 (1982)**   Upheld the power of Congress to protect the confidentiality of the census. *Baldridge v. Shapiro* rejected attempts by localities claiming undercounting in the 1980 census to access raw census data. Access was sought through the Freedom of Information Act (FOIA) and discovery means contained in the federal court rules. Acting pursuant to Article I, Section 2, which mandates a decennial census, Congress enacted the Census Act of 1976. The act contained language in Sections 8(b) and 9(a) that exempted census material from disclosure under either the FOIA or the discovery provisions. Two of the communities found to have lost population in the 1980 census were Denver, Colorado, and Essex County, New Jersey. These two localities challenged the census count and sought to compel disclosure of the "master" address lists. The Court unanimously held that Congress could absolutely protect the confidentiality of census data.

Chief Justice Burger delivered the opinion of the Court and addressed the Freedom of Information Act claim first. The FOIA contains an exemption provision for incorporation where an agency is given no discretion for disclosure. The Court found the language of Sections 8(b) and 9(a) of the Census Act to fall within the disclosure exemption. Burger cited the broad power possessed by Congress in the matter of the census and noted the legislative objective in protecting census data. Congress must provide assurances of confidentiality if the public cooperation vital to an accurate census is to be fostered. Pursuit of this objective is a reasonable use of congressional power, and withholding census data clearly qualifies for the exemption provided under the FOIA. Such an interpretation was strongly reinforced by the legislative history surrounding the census. That history clearly reflected "congressional intent to protect the confidentiality of the raw census data." Over and above protecting individual confidentiality, the data itself required protection in its own right.

As for the use of discovery procedures, the Court indicated that information must be disclosed where relevant to a pending legal action unless that information is privileged. Privilege may be granted by statute, however, and the Court held that Sections 8(b) and 9(a) "embody explicit congressional intent to preclude all disclosure." The Court saw this "strong policy of nondisclosure" as constituting the creation of a privilege within the federal court rules. The prohibition on disclosure in Sections 8(b) and 9(a) are "within congressional discretion." Burger went on to say that the wisdom of the policy "is not for us to decide in light of Congress' 180 years experience within the census process." Congress also possesses the authority to permit disclosure, but until Congress rescinds Sections 8(b) and 9(a), its "mandate is to be followed by the courts." *See also* ARTICLE I, p. 183.

Significance   *Baldridge v. Shapiro* (455 U.S. 345: 1981) affirmed a comprehensive power of Congress to govern the census process. The *Baldridge* ruling makes raw census data virtually inaccessible and makes it extremely difficult for any local unit of government to demonstrate undercounts in populations. Such undercounts, if they exist, have serious practical consequences. The census data is used as the basis for legislative redistricting, and alteration of district boundaries may be quite disadvantageous to any underrepresented area. More important in some respects, funding formulas for most federal programs are affected substantially by population. The *Baldridge* decision clearly shows that Congress possesses a virtually unconditional authority over the census, which includes maintaining its inaccessibility.

Legislative Veto

Immigration and Naturalization Service v. Chadha, **462 U.S. 919, 103 S.Ct. 2764, 77 L.Ed. 2d 317 (1983)**   Held the legislative veto to be unconstitutional. *Immigration and Naturalization Service v. Chadha* involved review of a provision of the Immigration and Naturalization Act that allowed Congress to invalidate executive branch decisions affecting deportation of aliens. Chadha, who had entered the country under a student visa, unlawfully remained in the United States after expiration of the visa. He sought suspension of deportation proceedings under the provisions of the act that conveyed discretionary authority to the attorney general to grant such relief. The House, acting unilaterally, then passed a resolution pursuant to Section 244(c) (2) of the act vetoing the suspension and reopening the deportation proceedings. Chadha was subsequently ordered deported. Chadha appealed to the court of appeals, which held the legislative veto to be unconstitutional. The Supreme Court affirmed with only Justice White dissenting on the veto question. Two members of the Court, Justices Powell and Rehnquist, would have preferred to resolve the case on narrower issues than the legislative veto.

Chief Justice Burger authored the opinion of the Court and focused on the separation of powers defect of the legislative veto. The decisive issue in the case was whether the veto was itself a legislative action, thus triggering the constitutional requirement that both houses of Congress approve with the president being provided an opportunity to sign or veto. The chief justice created a general framework for the review by observing that, while powers delegated to the three branches are not "hermetically sealed from one another," actions of each branch are usually "functionally identifiable." Thus, when an action is taken by all or part of the Congress, it is "presumptively acting within its assigned sphere." In this case, the House overruled the deportation suspension and altered Chadha's status. The action was "essentially legislative in purpose and effect." Further, the Court viewed the overrule of the attorney general as "no less" a policy decision than the original decision to delegate authority. Finally, if the framers had intended this kind of unilateral action, it would have been explicitly provided, as in the case of impeachment or treaty ratification. The Constitution requires that when the Congress engages in legislating, both houses must concur and legislation must be sent or "presented" to the president. This makes law making a shared function to protect the people from laws that may be "improvident" even if such a process has "flaws of delay, untidiness, and potential for abuse."

Justice White viewed the legislative veto as a productive means of ensuring executive accountability. Without it, Congress is faced with a "Hobson's choice" of the "hopeless task" of anticipating all contingencies and not delegating any authority, or "abdicating its lawmaking function to the executive branch and independent agencies." White felt the Court's decision was "destructive" in scope and took from Congress the authority it needed to "fulfill its designated role under Article I as the nation's lawmaker." *See also* DELEGATION OF LEGISLATIVE POWER, p. 591; SEPARATION OF POWERS, p. 56.

Significance   The Supreme Court's decision in *Immigration and Naturalization Service v. Chadha* (462 U.S. 919: 1983) substantially altered the power relationship between the Congress and the president by invalidating the legislative veto. The legislative veto had been utilized in more than 200 federal statutes since its introduction in the 1930s. Many, as in the instance of Chadha, permitted a single chamber of the

Congress to employ a veto. As pointed out by Justice White in dissent, the decision "strikes down in one fell swoop provisions in more laws enacted by Congress than the Court had cumulatively invalidated in its history." The *Chadha* decision substantially alters the balance of legislative and executive power in favor of the latter. All recent presidents have strongly felt that the veto was an invasion of the executive enforcement function, and the Court agreed in *Chadha*. Given the extent to which Congress had come to use the mechanism, it can be expected that Congress will attempt to recover a role in the implementation and oversight of federal policy. This may take the form of an increasing reluctance of Congress to delegate administrative discretion to the executive in the future.

Separation of Powers

Bowsher v. Synar, **478 U.S. 000, 106 S.Ct. 000, 92 L.Ed. 2d 583 (1986)** Invalidated a federal law establishing an "automatic" spending reduction mechanism as a means for forcing the federal budget deficit down. *Bowsher v. Synar* examined provisions of the Balanced Budget and Emergency Deficit Control Act of 1985, more commonly known as the Gramm-Rudman-Hollings Act. The act fixed maximum deficits for each fiscal year as it moved toward a zero deficit in 1991. If in any year the deficit exceeded the established limit, the act required across-the-board spending cuts to achieve the targeted deficit levels. These cuts were to be accomplished through the "reporting" provisions contained in Section 251, which required the director of the Office of Management and Budget and the Congressional Budget Office to send deficit estimates and reduction calculations to the comptroller general. Upon review of these data, the comptroller general was to send his conclusions to the president. The president was required to issue a "sequestration" order mandating the reductions specified by the comptroller general unless Congress legislated other reductions to obviate the need for the order. The act was challenged by several members of Congress and a federal employees' union. In federal district court, a three-judge panel ruled the reporting provisions unconstitutional. On direct appeal, the Supreme Court affirmed the lower court in a 7–2 decision.

Chief Justice Burger spoke for the majority. The question revolved around the doctrine of separation of powers. Specifically, the case turned on whether the comptroller general was perceived as a legislative or executive officer. Burger reviewed Montesquieu's thesis on checks and balances as well as a number of applicable precedents involving appointment and removal of "officers of the United States."

This review indicated that the Constitution "does not contemplate an active role for Congress in the supervision of officers charged with the execution of the laws it enacts." If an officer controlled by Congress has a role in executing the laws, it would in essence permit a "congressional veto." Congress could simply remove (or threaten to remove) an officer for executing the laws found unsatisfactory to Congress. This kind of "congressional control over the execution of the laws . . . is constitutionally impermissible." The office of comptroller general was created by the Budget and Accounting Act of 1921. While it was argued that the comptroller general "performs his duties independently and is not subservient to Congress," the Court concluded that it was "clear that Congress has consistently viewed the Comptroller General as an officer of the Legislative Branch." His functions under the reporting provisions of Gramm-Rudman are executive in nature, however. Once Congress makes its initial policy choice in enacting the laws, its participation ends. Congress can thereafter control execution of its policy "only indirectly—by passing new legislation." In this instance, when Congress placed responsibility for execution of the act "in the hands of an officer who is subject to removal only by itself," Congress retained control over the law's execution and "intruded into the executive function." The Constitution "does not permit such intrusion." Burger concluded by saying that the budget deficit presented problems of "unprecedented magnitude." Nonetheless, the fact that a given law or procedure is "efficient, convenient and useful in facilitating functions of government, standing alone, will not save it if it is contrary to the Constitution." Convenience and efficiency are "not the primary objectives—or the hallmarks—of democratic government."

In a separate opinion, Justice Stevens said that when Congress makes "binding policy, it must follow the procedures prescribed in Article I." Neither the "unquestioned urgency" of the deficit problem or the comptroller general's "proud record of professionalism and dedication" provides a justification for allowing a congressional agent to set policy that binds the nation.

Justices White and Blackmun dissented, saying that the reality of the situation was that Congress could not unilaterally remove the comptroller general. White was also critical of the majority's "distressingly formalistic view" of separation of powers, which led to invalidation of a "novel and far-reaching" legislative initiative. He asserted that the Court had "conjured up" the threat to separation of power and noted that the president must concur in any resolution calling for the removal of the comptroller general. This requirement reduces, said White, to "utter insignificance" the potential that threat of removal will "induce subservience to Congress." Justice Blackmun said he could not see the wisdom of striking down legislation of this "magnitude in order to preserve a cumbersome, 65-year-old removal power that has never been exercised and appears to have been all but forgotten until this litigation." Preserving the close to "deadwood" removal provision of the 1921 act "certainly pales in importance beside the legislative scheme the Court strikes down today." The separation of power defect found by the majority, he concluded, "cannot justify the remedy it has imposed." *See also* DELEGATION OF LEGISLATIVE POWER, p. 591; *IMMIGRATION AND NATURALIZATION SERVICE V. CHADHA* (462 U.S. 919: 1983), p. 213; LEGISLATIVE VETO, p. 632.

Significance   The Supreme Court invalidated the self-executing spending cuts of the Gramm-Rudman-Hollings Act in *Bowsher v. Synar* (92 L.Ed. 2d 583: 1986). The statute's process for implementing deficit-reducing expenditure cuts through the comptroller general reporting mechanism had been a politically appealing approach because members of Congress did not have to vote for specific program cuts. This political insulation ultimately was the act's undoing on separation of power grounds. Chief Justice Burger drew heavily from the Court's reasoning in *Immigration and Naturalization Service v. Chadha* (462 U.S. 919: 1983). The *Chadha* case ruled the legislative veto unconstitutional. The legislative veto is a technique by which Congress can review and possibly abort executive branch orders issued to implement legislation. The legislative veto allowed Congress to directly supervise executive enforcement. In *Chadha*, the Court held that the veto preempted executive participation in policy making. Article I requires that the president be presented with all legislation for consent or rejection. Since the president or administrative agency was not presented with items subjected to the legislative veto, the practice was held to violate separation of power. A similar intrusion into the executive domain was found in *Bowsher v. Synar*. The decision did leave intact a "fallback" provision that would take effect in the event the reporting procedure was defective. It remains to be seen whether this fallback procedure will be effective in achieving deficit-reducing targets.

5. Federalism

Overview, 221

Article IV, 225

Supremacy Clause, 227

Tenth Amendment, 229

OVERVIEW

The American Constitution was designed to divide power between a national level of government and the states. The powers of the national government were specified in the document itself, while powers not assigned to the federal level were reserved to the states in the Tenth Amendment. Conflicts between the levels were addressed in Article VI, where the supremacy clause resolved collisions of legitimately exercised power by the national government by providing that such law is "supreme." Various aspects of interstate relations were defined in Article IV.

A number of early Supreme Court decisions examined the relationship of federal and state power. In *Chisholm v. Georgia* (2 Dallas 419: 1793), the Court ruled that federal courts could entertain suits against states brought by citizens of other states. Substantial negative reaction to this decision prompted adoption of the Eleventh Amendment. This amendment prohibited such citizen suits against states in federal courts. Notwithstanding the amendment, the Court held in *Fitzpatrick v. Bitzer* (427 U.S. 448: 1976) that Congress could authorize suits against states and state officials to enforce provisions of the Civil Rights Act of 1964.

A central issue early in our constitutional history was the manner in which the supremacy clause was to be given effect. In *Martin v. Hunter's Lessee* (1 Wheaton 304: 1816) and *Cohens v. Virginia* (6 Wheaton 264: 1821), the Court examined the role of the federal judiciary in maintaining national supremacy. In both *Martin* and *Cohens*, the Court held that state court decisions are subject to review by the United States Supreme Court if a question of federal law is involved. Legislative supremacy was established in the landmark decision of *McCulloch v. Maryland* (4 Wheaton 316: 1819) when the Court invalidated a state tax levied against the Bank of the United States. More recently, in *Blum v. Bacon* (457 U.S. 132: 1982), the Court held that the supremacy clause precluded a state from establishing strict eligibility requirements for accessing emergency assistance programs subsidized by the federal government through the Social Security Act. In *Jefferson County Pharmaceutical Association, Inc. v. Abbott Laboratories* (460 U.S. 150: 1983), the

Court held that federal antitrust applied to the purchase and sale of pharmaceutical products by hospitals operated by state and local governments. The strongest formulation of the federal legislative supremacy concept is contained in the preemption doctrine. This doctrine holds that certain policy areas are exclusively federal, and that federal law supersedes or preempts any conflicting state law in that field. The principal criteria by which the supersession issue is assessed were defined in *Pennsylvania v. Nelson* (350 U.S. 497: 1956). The preemption doctrine was used in *Nelson* to invalidate state prosecutions for sedition. In 1983, the Court held in *Pacific Gas and Electric Company v. State Energy Resources Conservation and Development Commission* (461 U.S. 190: 1983) that the doctrine did not prohibit a state from making certification of new nuclear power facilities contingent upon the finding of safe ways to dispose of the nuclear waste. At the same time, the Court ruled in *New Mexico v. Mescalero Apache Tribe* (462 U.S. 324: 1983) that state hunting and fishing regulations imposed on nontribe members while on Indian reservations were preempted by federal law.

One policy that facilitates the effective operation of the American federal system is intergovernmental tax immunity. The immunity doctrine had its origin in *McCulloch*, and holds that the taxing power of one level cannot be used to impair or disrupt functions of the other. Since the late 1930s, the Court has essentially held that the application of the doctrine is limited to those activities and entities essential to the survival of the governmental level itself. In *Helvering v. Gerhardt* (304 U.S. 405: 1938), the Court ruled that a federal income tax imposed on all citizens could be levied against employees of a state agency. The general tax was not an impermissible burden on the state government itself. In *United States v. New Mexico* (455 U.S. 720: 1982), the Court upheld a state tax on federal contractors doing business in the state. The question of applicability of the federal Bill of Rights to the states was first addressed in *Barron v. Baltimore* (7 Peters 243: 1833). There the Court held that the provisions of the Bill of Rights limited only the federal government, not the states. Following adoption of the Fourteenth Amendment, the Bill of Rights was gradually extended to the states and is presently applicable in its entirety. A recent example of state policy found unconstitutional on First Amendment grounds is *Minneapolis Star and Tribune Company v. Minnesota Commissioner of Revenue* (460 U.S. 575: 1983). In this case, the Court held that a state could not level a special or differential tax against publishers.

The fundamental and permanent character of the Union was seen in the decision of *Texas v. White* (7 Wallace 700: 1869), rendered just after the Civil War. In this case, the Court held the Union to be perpetual, and that once a state was formally admitted, that state could not constitutionally secede. In *Missouri v. Holland* (252 U.S. 416: 1920), the

Court held that a federal law enacted pursuant to a lawfully executed treaty may reach subjects otherwise reserved to the states. The Court argued that it was necessary to retain greater federal discretion where international matters were involved. Using much the same reasoning, the Court held in *United States v. California* (332 U.S. 19: 1947) that states did not possess ownership rights to coastal waters and the marginal lands under them. Congress subsequently ceded title to those lands to the states.

The history of American federalism has been marked with frequent conflicts over authority to regulate particular behaviors. Several representative examples are included in this chapter. In 1875, Congress attempted to regulate private acts of racial discrimination. The Court held in the *Civil Rights Cases* (109 U.S. 3: 1883) that the Fourteenth Amendment only empowered the federal government to intervene where the state was an actual party to the discriminatory conduct. Federal regulation of discrimination, even in the private sector, has increased over the years. In *McDonald v. Santa Fe Trail Transportation Company* (427 U.S. 273: 1976), the Court held that the job discrimination language of the Civil Rights Act of 1964 reaches conduct of private employers and applies to white persons as well as nonwhites. The Fifteenth Amendment has also given the federal government greater authority to regulate elections, an area traditionally reserved to the states. In *Allen v. Board of Elections* (393 U.S. 544: 1969), the Court upheld provisions of the Voting Rights Act of 1965 that required federal approval of changes in state election law. In *Oregon v. Mitchell* (400 U.S. 112: 1970), the Court permitted the federal government to lower the voting age in federal elections, but refused to allow the lowered age requirement for state and local elections without a constitutional amendment. Restriction of residency requirements and prohibition of literacy tests as a condition for voting was also upheld in *Oregon v. Mitchell*. Federal regulatory power presently reaches even the employment practices of state and local governments. Provisions of the Age Discrimination in Employment Act were held applicable to state employees in *Equal Employment Opportunity Commission v. Wyoming* (460 U.S. 226: 1983). Exercise of the federal commerce power has also generated numerous issues relating to the federal system. Using reasoning similar to that in *EEOC v. Wyoming*, the court, in *Garcia v. San Antonio Metropolitan Transit Authority* (469 U.S. 528: 1985), held that minimum wage and overtime requirements of federal law could be applied to a public mass transit authority. Both of these recent cases were decided by a 5–4 margin, and they represent an extremely volatile federalism issue.

Several other doctrines or constitutional provisions apply to federalism issues. The abstention doctrine governs the relationship between state and federal courts. Citing considerations of federalism and the abstention doctrine, the Court held in *Younger v. Harris* (401 U.S. 37: 1971) that federal court intervention into state criminal prosecutions should occur in only the most extraordinary situations. In *Baldwin v. Montana Fish and Game Commission* (436 U.S. 371: 1978), the Court held that the privileges and immunities clause did not preclude a differential hunting license fee for residents and nonresidents. The Court here said that the clause is reserved for those situations where differential state policies interfere with an "essential activity" or the exercise of a "basic right."

Article IV also contains provisions for the interstate rendition of fugitives and requires states to accord each other "full faith and credit" for official acts. In *Pacileo v. Walker* (449 U.S. 86: 1980), the Court ruled that the rendition clause was essentially "summary and mandatory" in nature, and that it did not permit a state to make inquiry into various questions such as prison conditions in another state as a condition for the return of a fugitive. In *Allstate Insurance Company v. Hague* (449 U.S. 302: 1981), the Court ruled that the full faith and credit clause did not prevent a state from applying its own insurance laws to a suit involving an accident in another state provided the first state could show a "legitimate interest" in the outcome of the action.

Article IV   Contains provisions that govern the relationships of the states to one another. Article IV is comprised of four sections, each of which deals with a different aspect of interstate relations. Section 1 is primarily aimed at recognition of court judgments. It provides that "full faith and credit shall be given in each state to the public acts, records, and judicial proceedings of every other state." The section also gives Congress the authority to enact legislation providing for the authentication and implementation of documents and records. Congress passed such legislation immediately upon ratification of the Constitution. As a result, court decisions and records are recognized in any court.

Section 2 deals with the nature of protections accruing to citizenship at the state level, and the rendition of fugitives. The section begins by saying that the "citizens of each state shall be entitled to all privileges and immunities of citizens in the several states." The objective of this provision is to establish comparability of treatment between state citizens and out-of-state residents. The section also requires that when a fugitive charged with any state offense is found in another state, "on demand of the executive authority of the State from which he fled," the person shall be "delivered up, to be removed to the state having jurisdiction for the crime." This language on rendition is given effect by federal legislation. Section 2 also contains provisions requiring the return of fugitive slaves, but this language was nullified by the abolition of slavery under terms of the Thirteenth Amendment.

Section 3 is devoted to the way in which new states may be added to the Union. The process operates at the discretion of Congress. The process created by Congress requires that the territory petitioning for statehood develop and approve a state constitution. This proposed constitution is then submitted to Congress for approval. A resolution of statehood, subject to presidential approval or veto, is passed by Congress. Section 3 does limit congressional discretion on this issue. Congress cannot admit a state "formed or erected within the jurisdiction of any other state" or one "formed by the junction of two or more states, or parts of states" without the consent of the affected states. Section 3 concludes by assigning power over any territories to the Congress.

Section 4 contains language known as the guarantee (sometimes guaranty) clause. It says that the United States "shall guarantee to every state in this Union a Republican form of government." The federal government is also required to protect each state "against Invasion" and "domestic violence." The guaranty clause is triggered by a state legislature, or state executive if the legislature cannot be convened, formally requesting federal intervention. *See also* CITIZENSHIP, p. 585; FEDERALISM, p. 29; FULL FAITH AND CREDIT CLAUSE, p. 615; GUARANTEE CLAUSE, p. 616; INTERSTATE RENDITION, p. 625; PRIVILEGES AND IMMUNITIES CLAUSE, p. 647.

Significance   Article IV addresses interstate relations as well as the relationship between the federal and state levels. Under provision of Article IV, Congress governs admission of new states. The process is political in character, and Congress may act accordingly. Since the outset, Congress has established that any state added to the union enjoys "equal footing" with the original states. Once a statehood resolution has been adopted and signed by the president, it may not be repealed. The language governing admission was critical early in our history with so much territory to the west of the original states. The opportunities for contemporary utilization of this process appear limited to possible statehood for Puerto Rico. Article IV also provides that the federal government ensure or guarantee that the states retain a "republican form of government." The federal government has not frequently intervened under this clause. While the Constitution does not define what constitutes a "republican form" of government, it seems reasonable to conclude that a threat to a state's electoral processes would prompt federal intervention. The Court held in *Luther v. Borden* (7 Howard 1: 1849) that guarantee clause issues are "political questions" and not appropriate for judicial determination. Rather, determinations of this kind are to be made by the legislative branch. Congress has, in turn, formally delegated to the president the function of determining whether a republican form of government has been breached.

Article IV also established three basic conditions for interstate relations. First, it requires a state to extend "full faith and credit" to certain kinds of actions of other states. Principal impact falls in the area of recognition of court judgments. Generally, judgments rendered in one state are regarded as conclusive and binding in other states. This presumes that the court rendering the judgment had jurisdiction to decide the matter. Such judgments may require authentication before they can be enforced against persons in another state, but the merits of the issue are not reargued. This clause has acted to protect legal rights and obligations as people move from state to state. The clause does not require states to enforce each other's criminal laws, and in *Nevada v. Hall* (440 U.S. 410: 1979), the Court held that the clause does not require a state "to apply another state's law in violation of its own legitimate public policy." Second, Article IV obligates a state to return fugitives to states from which they have fled. Rendition occurs when the executive authority of the state from which the fugitive fled "demands" return of the individual. Compliance with this request is virtually automatic, but the Court held in *Kentucky v. Dennison* (24 Howard 66: 1861) that, while it is a governor's duty to return a fugitive, there are no legal means by which execution of this duty can be compelled. Third, Article IV contains a privileges and immunities clause designed to keep a state from discriminating against citizens of other states in favor of its own. The impact of this provision has been somewhat limited. The Court placed most key civil and political rights within the category of state citizenship in the *Slaughterhouse Cases* (16 Wallace 36: 1873). This decision had the effect of limiting privileges and immunities of federal citizenship to such things as the right to interstate travel, protections while traveling abroad, and the right to participate in federal elections. This provision was aimed at guaranteeing equality of treatment to citizens of one state coming under the jurisdiction of another. This function is more effectively performed through use of the equal protection clause.

Supremacy Clause   Declaration that all federal laws and treaties enacted or entered pursuant to the Constitution have legal superiority over conflicting provisions of state constitutions or laws. The supremacy clause is the featured element of Article VI, which has three sections. Section 1 transferred the contracted indebtedness under the Articles of Confederation to the new federal government. Such transfer would likely have occurred anyway, and the provision has no contemporary significance. Section 2 contains the supremacy clause and states that "this Constitution" and the laws made in "pursuance thereof" as well as "all treaties made" under authority of the United States "shall be the supreme law of the land." It concludes by saying that judges "in every state shall be bound thereby, anything in the Constitution or laws of any state to the contrary notwithstanding." The framers of the Constitution sought to fashion a governmental structure that would provide a viable central government while preserving some state autonomy. What emerged was a federalism in which power was divided between the central government and the constituent states. The nature of the line of division was a major, if not the dominant, political issue at the Constitutional Convention. The functions and powers ultimately were divided and assigned, but it was understood that disputes over these lines of division would necessarily occur. The supremacy clause provided the principle by which such disputes were to be resolved. When a conflict arises between federal and state law, the federal law must prevail so long as it is within the reach of federal authority. Section 3 provides that all governmental officials, regardless of branch, at both the federal and state levels "shall be bound by oath or affirmation to support the Constitution." The section concludes by prohibiting any "religious test" as a condition of holding public office or "trust." *See also* MCCULLOCH V. MARYLAND (4 Wheaton 316; 1819), p. 238; PREEMPTION DOCTRINE, p. 645; TENTH AMENDMENT, p. 229.

Significance The supremacy clause is sometimes called the "linchpin" of the Constitution. The national government possesses powers that are limited, but the supremacy clause establishes that these powers are supreme when in the appropriate field of power. If national and state laws come into conflict, state law must give way so long as the federal law was based upon power expressly or implicitly conveyed to Congress. The role of the courts in administering the supremacy clause is to determine whether federal-state incompatibility exists and if the federal policy is legitimately federal in nature. The importance of the clause was dramatically demonstrated in *McCulloch v. Maryland* (4 Wheaton 316: 1819). The state of Maryland had levied a tax on the Bank of the United States, a chartered entity of the federal government. The Supreme Court held that the state tax could not be imposed. Chief Justice Marshall, a strong Federalist, resolved the issue on supremacy clause grounds. He said if any single proposition could "command the universal assent of mankind," it is that the "government of the Union," though otherwise limited, is "supreme within its sphere of action."

A more aggressive statement of this view is contained in the preemption doctrine. This doctrine holds that when Congress enters a domain in which it is empowered to act, then its policies supersede any incompatible state policies. The Court set out three criteria to be used to determine whether the federal government has preempted the field in *Pennsylvania v. Nelson* (350 U.S. 497: 1956). First, is the "scheme" of federal regulation "so pervasive" as to allow a reasonable inference that Congress "left no room" for states to act? Second, does the federal policy "touch a field" in which the federal interest is "so dominant" that the federal system precludes enforcement of state laws on the same subject? Third, is enforcement of state law a potential obstacle to "administration of the federal program"? Full development of the national security principle in the *Nelson* case was found to require federal authority to preempt state actions in the same field. Although provision for judicial review of such situations was contained in the Judiciary Act of 1789, judicial supremacy evolved through a series of decisions rendered by the Marshall Court. In *Martin v. Hunter's Lessee* (1 Wheaton 304: 1816) and *Cohens v. Virginia* (6 Wheaton 264: 1821), the Court reiterated its right to review decisions of state courts. Many feel that the principle of national supremacy is the critical integrative element that has allowed the American federalism to survive. While it has withstood various challenges over the years, the broad construction of the supremacy clause by the early Court has become settled doctrine.

Tenth Amendment   Retains powers not assigned to the federal government for the states. The Tenth Amendment was added to the Constitution to diminish the concerns of the states' rightists that the federal government established by the new Constitution would substantially curtail state authority. The states had, of course, possessed often decisive power under the Articles of Confederation, and the new division of powers between the federal and state levels redefined that balance. The Tenth Amendment was not necessarily intended to alter this redistribution. Rather, it was aimed at reiterating that the federal government could only exercise assigned powers. The Tenth Amendment states that the "powers not delegated to the United States by the Constitution, nor prohibited by it to the states, are reserved to the states respectively, or the people." *See also* DUAL FEDERALISM, p. 594; FEDERALISM, p. 29; JOHN MARSHALL, p. 530; SUPREMACY CLAUSE, p. 227; ROGER B. TANEY, p. 560.

Significance   The Tenth Amendment reserves to the states those powers not conveyed to the federal government. This amendment, the final element of the constitutional additions comprising the Bill of Rights, was included largely to alleviate concerns of the antifederalists. The amendment was intended to reiterate and confirm the original understanding regarding division of power between the national and state levels. The amendment was not an effort to redistribute power. Early attempts to use the Tenth Amendment to limit federal authority were unsuccessful. In *McCulloch v. Maryland* (4 Wheaton 316: 1819), for example, the Marshall Court rejected the contention that the Tenth Amendment could limit exercise of Congress's necessary and proper clause powers.

Marshall was succeeded as chief justice by Roger B. Taney, a strong advocate of dual federalism. Under this doctrine, the Court withdrew many substantive policy areas from the reach of Congress. Initially developed to protect state initiatives that arguably entered the domain of the federal government, the Court later adopted the proposition that the "reserved" powers of the states were immune from powers exercised by the federal government (see, for example, *Collector v. Day* 11 Wallace 113: 1871, where the Court held that a federal income tax could not be levied on the salary of a state judge). The most far-reaching interpretation of the Tenth Amendment came between 1918 and 1937. In *Hammer v. Dagenhart* (247 U.S. 251: 1918), the Court struck down a federal law prohibiting the interstate shipment of any item produced with child labor. Invoking the reserve clause, the Court said that regulation of child labor had been "reserved" to the states. In this case, the Court actually inserted the word "expressly" into the

Tenth Amendment to produce the desired effect of limiting the exercise of power at the national level. Throughout much of the 1930s, this interpretation prevailed as the Court struck down many federal initiatives including the agricultural production limitations of the Agricultural Adjustment Act (*United States v. Butler*, 297 U.S. 1: 1936), and the coal code established under the Guffey Act (*Carter v. Carter Coal Company*, 298 U.S. 238: 1936).

By the 1940s, the Court returned to the interpretations of the clause during the time of the Marshall Court. Having already upheld use of the commerce power and taxing power as sufficient bases for the National Labor Relations and Social Security acts, respectively, the Court expressly reiterated Marshall in *United States v. Darby Lumber Company* (312 U.S. 100: 1941). In a decision that directly overruled *Hammer*, the Court referred to the "truism" stated by the Tenth Amendment, that "all is retained which has not been surrendered." One of the few departures from this position since 1941 occurred in *National League of Cities v. Usery* (426 U.S. 833: 1976), where the Court held that the Tenth Amendment provided some immunity for states from federal interference. In holding that the minimum wage and overtime provisions of the Fair Labor Standards Act did not apply to state and local government employees, the Court said in *Usery* that the federal government could not interfere with such "traditional" and "integral" state and local government functions as employee relations. This decision was essentially reversed, however, in *Garcia v. San Antonio Metropolitan Transit Authority* (469 U.S. 528: 1985). While certainly not dead letter, the Tenth Amendment is no longer an effective means by which to confine the exercise of federal power.

State Immunity from Citizen Suits

***Chisholm v. Georgia*, 2 Dallas 419, 1 L.Ed. 440 (1793)**   Held that a state was subject to suit in federal court by a citizen of another state. *Chisholm v. Georgia* developed out of the Revolutionary War. Supplies were purchased from a private party on credit, but the debt was not paid. Some 15 years later, the merchant's estate unsuccessfully sought payment from the state of Georgia. Suit was subsequently brought in the U.S. circuit court. Georgia argued that as a sovereign entity, it could not be subject to such a suit. The circuit court agreed and dismissed the case. Chisholm sought review from the Supreme Court, however, and the Court accepted the case for argument. Georgia refused to participate in the proceeding, claiming the Supreme Court had no authority to review such a case. The Supreme Court rendered a decision nonetheless and, by a 4–1 margin, held that the suit was properly brought and that a state could be sued by a citizen of another state without the state's consent.

Justice Wilson called the case one of "uncommon magnitude," because the core question was whether the "people of the United States form a nation." For Wilson, the issue turned on Georgia's claims of sovereignty. When the people acted to establish the Union, they did not "surrender" sovereign power to the states, but rather "retained it to themselves." As a result, Georgia is not a "sovereign state." Further, Wilson concluded that because no state possessed sovereignty, the people could legitimately bind the states by the legislative, executive, and judicial power vested by the Constitution. He then turned to the question of whether this is what the people had meant to do. He concluded that it was, pointing out that the new constitution was aimed primarily at relieving "defects" of the Articles of Confederation that had operated "only upon states." The new constitution "has an operation on individual citizens." He felt it could not be contended that the legislative power of the national government was meant to "have no operation on the several states." To do so would be to "balance by a defect," the defect remedied by replacing the Articles. Having established that legislative power may bind the states, he used the same principle to reach the executive and judicial powers. If legislation is to have effect, it must be enforced. "Nothing could be more natural" than to intend that legislative power "should be enforced by powers executive and judicial."

Chief Justice Jay drew the same conclusions regarding sovereignty. In addition, he embraced the explicit language of Article III as extending federal judicial power to cases "between a state and citizens of another state." If the Constitution had only meant cases where the state is a plaintiff, it is "inconceivable" that it would not have explictly said so. He saw "not even an intimation of such intention" in the Constitution. Justice Iredell saw sovereignty as having been placed, at least in part, with the states. As a result, he did not feel a sovereignty could be sued by a citizen without its consent. *See also* ELEVENTH AMENDMENT, p. 598; FEDERALISM, p. 29; SOVEREIGNTY, p. 654.

Significance   The Court held in *Chisholm v. Georgia* (2 Dallas 419; 1793) that federal courts had authority to entertain suits brought against states by citizens of other states. The *Chisholm* decision was nullified almost immediately by the Eleventh Amendment. The amendment said that federal judicial power "shall not be construed to extend to any suit in law or equity, commenced or prosecuted against one of the United States by citizens of another State, or by citizens or subjects of any Foreign State." Notwithstanding Article III language, the states fiercely (and successfully) contested the *Chisholm* decision as a major assault on states' rights. They argued that as a sovereign entity, a state could only be sued with its consent. These sentiments prevailed in the amendment process. Although overruled by this process, *Chisholm* represents an important recognition that the Court is the final authority on the Constitution. By resorting to the formal amendment process, the Court's capacity to render authoritative interpretation of the Constitution was reflected. As for the subsequent impact of the Eleventh Amendment, such recent decisions as *Fitzpatrick v. Bitzer* (427 U.S. 445: 1976) and *Maine v. Thiboutot* (448 U.S. 1: 1980) clearly hold that the states are not immune from suits claiming violations of federal constitutional or statutory provisions.

Fitzpatrick v. Bitzer, **427 U.S. 445, 96 S.Ct. 2666, 49 L.Ed. 2d 614 (1976)**　　Held that Congress has authority to require a state to pay damages to employees who have suffered discrimination at the hands of the state. *Fitzpatrick v. Bitzer* was a class action filed by current and retired employees of Connecticut claiming discrimination in the state retirement plan. They sought relief in the federal courts, asserting violations of the 1972 Amendment to Title VII of the Civil Rights Act of 1964. The district court enjoined prospective implementation of the plan, but refused to award retroactive benefits, citing the Eleventh Amendment. The district court also ruled that the plaintiffs were not entitled to recover legal fees. The court of appeals agreed with respect to damages, but held that the plaintiffs were entitled to attorney fees. The Supreme Court unanimously held that Congress had the power to make states liable for damages. The Court also affirmed the lower court decision allowing recovery of legal fees.

The opinion of the Court was delivered by Justice Rehnquist. The 1972 amendments to Title VII, enacted by Congress under authority of Section 5 of the Fourteenth Amendment, authorized federal courts to award money damages in favor of a private individual against a state government found to have subjected that person to "employment discrimination on the basis of race, color, religion, sex or national origin." The central issue in *Bitzer* was whether Congress could authorize federal courts to enter such awards as a means of enforcing the Fourteenth Amendment "against the shield of sovereign immunity afforded the state by the Eleventh Amendment." Rehnquist began by saying that the states limited their own powers through adoption of the Fourteenth Amendment. As ratified by the states, the amendment "quite clearly contemplates limitations on their authority. The provisions of the amendment are "by express terms directed at the States," and "standing behind the imperatives is Congress' power to 'enforce' the amendment 'by appropriate legislation'." From the outset, it has been recognized that the Civil War amendments limit state power and are "enlargements" of the power of Congress. Addition of power to the federal government involves a "corresponding diminution" of the state power. It is "carved out of them." Early recognition of the "shift in the federal-state balance" by the Civil War amendments has been "carried forward" to the present, and there "can be no doubt" that congressional intrusions under these amendments into the "judicial, executive, and legislative spheres of autonomy previously reserved to the States" have been sanctioned. Accordingly, the Court concluded that the Eleventh Amendment, and the "principle of state autonomy which it embodies" are "necessarily limited" by the enforcement provisions of Section 5 of the Fourteenth Amendment. When Congress acts pursuant to this section, it is exercising plenary power "within the terms of the constitutional grant," but also exercising power under one section of an amendment whose other sections "by their own terms embody limitations on state authority." As a result, the Court concluded that Congress may, in determining what is "appropriate legislation" for enforcing provisions of the Fourteenth Amendment, permit private suits against states or state officials "which are constitutionally impermissible in other contexts." *See also* CHISHOLM V. GEORGIA (2 Dallas 419: 1793), p. 230; ELEVENTH AMENDMENT, p. 598; FEDERALISM, p. 29; *MAINE V. THIBOUTOT* (448 U.S. 1: 1980), p. 77.

Significance   The Court held in *Fitzpatrick v. Bitzer* (427 U.S. 445: 1976) that the Congress could authorize suits against states and state officials to enforce provisions of Title VII of the Civil Rights Act of 1964 notwithstanding the general immunity provided by the Eleventh Amendment. Article III of the Constitution says that federal judicial power shall extend to controversies between a state and citizens of another state. It was presumed that this applied to suits where the state was a plaintiff, but not a defendant. In *Chisholm v. Georgia* (2 Dallas 419: 1793), the Court interpreted Article III to mean that states could be sued by citizens of other states. The *Chisholm* decision prompted adoption of the Eleventh Amendment, which provided that federal judicial power shall not extend to suits commenced by citizens of one state against other states. This seemed to convey a broad immunity against suit without a state's consent. This immunity has not proven to be absolute. Federal laws may establish legal rights that can be enforced against states as seen in *Fitzpatrick*. This authorization must be expressed by Congress, however. In *Edelman v. Jordan* (415 U.S. 651: 1974), the Court held that the Eleventh Amendment barred monetary relief for claims by welfare recipients because the Social Security Act relied on by the claimants did not "authorize suits against anyone." In *Fitzpatrick*, on the other hand, the "threshold fact of congressional authorization" was present and legitimately based on Section 5 of the Fourteenth Amendment. Thus, authorization for private parties to sue the state as employer was "clearly present." This interpretation was broadened by the Court in *Maine v. Thiboutot* (448 U.S. 1: 1980). This decision expanded the possibility of private parties to sue state and local governments where violations of rights under any federal statute as well as any constitutional provision were involved. This had the effect of removing the limitation present in *Edelman* and was the most extensive expansion defined by the Court.

Federal Judicial Supremacy

Martin v. Hunter's Lessee, **1 Wheaton 304, 4 L.Ed. 97 (1816)** Held that the U.S. Supreme Court had authority to review state court decisions on matters of federal law. Martin, a British subject, inherited extensive land in Virginia from his uncle, a Lord Fairfax. Virginia common law prohibited enemy aliens from inheriting, and a law enacted following Fairfax's death sought to confiscate the property devised to Martin. A portion of that property was subsequently sold to Hunter. Suit was brought two years later, and the matter resided in the Virginia courts until 1810, when the Virginia Court of Appeals sustained Hunter's title to the property. The U.S. Supreme Court reversed this decision in *Fairfax's Devisee v. Hunter's Lessee* (7 Cranch 603: 1813), ruling that Martin's property was protected from confiscation under provision of the Treaty of 1794. Reacting to what it felt was unwarranted extension of federal power over state laws, the Virginia Court declared unconstitutional the portion of the Judiciary Act of 1789 that granted the Supreme Court this power. The refusal to obey the decision in *Fairfax's Devisee* precipitated this case. A unanimous Court reiterated that the Supreme Court has appellate jurisdiction to review state decisions affecting federal law.

The opinion of the Court was delivered by Justice Story. He saw the questions raised by the case as ones of "great importance and delicacy." Upon their "right decision rest some of the most solid principles which have hitherto been supposed to sustain and protect the Constitution itself." As a "preliminary consideration," Story stated that there "could be no doubt" that it was "competent to the people" to establish a general government with "all the powers which they might deem proper and necessary." Accordingly, the people could prohibit the states from exercising power "incompatible with the objects of the general compact." Story then focused on construction of Article III, and the "nature and extent of federal appellate jurisdiction." This power may include every case enumerated in the Constitution not decided by way of original jurisdiction. This jurisdiction may be assigned by Congress to other than the Supreme Court. The appellate power "is not limited by the terms of the third article to any particular court." The judicial power extends to "cases"; thus it is the case and not the court that "gives the jurisdiction." The framers anticipated that "cases within the judicial cognizance of the United States" would necessarily arise in state courts as those courts exercised their "ordinary jurisdiction." It is for this reason that Article VI contains the supremacy clause and directs that judges in every state "shall be bound thereby" notwithstanding state laws to the contrary. The language of the Judiciary Act of 1789 granting concurrent jurisdiction must be seen in this context. Similarly, any cases arising under the Constitution, laws, and treaties of the United States addressed by state courts must be subject to the appellate jurisdiction of the Supreme Court. The federal courts may "revise the proceedings" of state executives and legislative authorities if they are contrary to the Constitution. "Surely, the exercise of the same right over judicial tribunals is not a higher or more dangerous act of sovereign power." Such review does not "impair the independence of state judges."

With regard to powers granted by the United States, "they are not independent; they are expressly bound to obedience by the letter of the Constitution." In addition, there is the need to maintain "uniformity of decisions throughout the United States." If there were no revising authority to "control . . . jarring and discordant judgments, and harmonize them into uniformity," the federal Constitution and laws would be different in different states, possibly never having "precisely the same construction, obligation, or efficacy in any two states." The "public mischief" that would result would be "truly deplorable." Appellate jurisdiction "must continue to be the only adequate remedy for such evils." *See also* COHENS V. VIRGINIA (6 Wheaton 264: 1821), p. 236; FEDERALISM, p. 29; *McCULLOCH V. MARYLAND* (4 Wheaton 316: 1819), p. 238; SUPREMACY CLAUSE, p. 227.

Significance   The role of the Federal courts in maintaining national supremacy was examined in *Martin v. Hunter's Lessee* (1 Wheaton 304: 1816). The most lasting impact of the Court under John Marshall was the establishment of the principle of national supremacy. Through the exercise of judicial review, the Court was able to withstand serious challenges to federal power from the states, especially the state judiciary. The authority for the Court to engage in review of state court decisions came from Section 25 of the Judiciary Act of 1789. It authorized review of state judgments where state courts had questioned the validity of federal laws, upheld a state law challenged as incompatible with the Constitution, or as failing to recognize a right or privilege derived from the federal Constitution. Many states felt that this provision of the Judidiary Act unconstitutionally impinged on state judicial independence. They preferred shared jurisdiction as the means of best safeguarding state sovereignty. The first confrontation over the Judiciary Act occurred in *Fairfax's Devisee v. Hunter's Lessee* (7 Cranch 603: 1813). When the Court reversed the state courts in this case, the Virginia Court claimed the Judiciary Act to be unconstitutional and refused to implement the Supreme Court's decision regarding Fairfax's estate. It was this failure to implement that prompted *Martin v. Hunter's Lessee*. The struggle over federal judicial supremacy continued for several years and was ultimately resolved in *Cohens v. Virginia* (6 Wheaton 264: 1821). *Martin*, however, was a major intermediate step in arriving at judicial supremacy for the federal courts.

Cohens v. Virginia, **6 Wheaton 264, 5 L.Ed. 257 (1821)**   Held that state court decisions are subject to review by the United States Supreme Court if a question of federal law is involved. *Cohens v. Virginia* ruled this to be so even in cases where a state is itself a party to the lawsuit. In 1802, Congress passed a law enabling the District of Columbia to conduct lotteries. The city subsequently passed an ordinance establishing a lottery. The state of Virginia had a law prohibiting lotteries unless authorized by the state. The Cohens were convicted of selling tickets for the District Lottery in Virginia. They appealed to the Supreme Court, claiming immunity from prosecution at the state level by virtue of the federal law permitting the lottery. In a unanimous decision, the Court held that the federal courts had jurisdiction to review this kind of case notwithstanding the existence of the state as a party. The Court also held that the Cohens were not protected from prosecution outside the boundaries of the District of Columbia.

The opinion of the Court was delivered by Chief Justice Marshall. The case, in his view, raised questions of "great magnitude," and these "vitally . . . affect the Union." Virginia contended that the Constitution "has provided no tribunal for the final construction of itself" or federal laws and treaties. Rather, this power may be exercised "in the last resort by courts of every state of the Union." Marshall began his response by examining the nature of federal jurisdiction as provided by Article III. Judicial power extends to two categories of controversies. The first is defined by the substantive character of the case. Cases arising under federal laws or treaties are of this kind. The second category stems from the character of the parties. Enumerated in this category are suits between a state and citizens of another state. Virginia argued that it could not be sued without its consent, citing its own sovereignty and the Eleventh Amendment. The Court ruled, however, that some portion of sovereignty was relinquished at the time the national government was established under the Constitution. Federal jurisdiction must be exercised in a manner that maintains national supremacy. To do otherwise would have "mischievous consequences." "It would prostrate" the federal government and its laws "at the feet of every state in the Union." Neither did the Court see the Eleventh Amendment as insulating the state from federal jurisdiction. Here, Virginia had initiated the action by prosecuting the Cohens, and thus the immunity from becoming an unwilling defendant in a suit did not apply. Marshall then returned to the principle of national supremacy to put aside Virginia's contention that cases could not be appealed from state courts to the United States Supreme Court. The United States, Marshall said, "has chosen to be . . . a nation," and for this purpose, has established a government that is "complete" and "supreme" within its sphere of competence. Accordingly, the state and federal courts cannot be wholly autonomous. Rather, the federal judiciary must be able to maintain compatibility of state laws to the federal Constitution and federal laws. To do so, the Supreme Court must be empowered to hear appeals from state courts. While Virginia did not prevail on the fundamental federal-state issue contained in this case, the conviction of the Cohens was upheld. The Court held that the congressional lottery law was confined to the District of Columbia and could not authorize sale of lottery tickets in Virginia in the face of the state prohibition on such activity. *See also* FEDERALISM, p. 29; *MARTIN V. HUNTER'S LESSEE* (1 Wheaton 304: 1816), p. 234; *McCULLOCH V. MARYLAND* (4 Wheaton 316: 1819), p. 238; SUPREMACY CLAUSE, p. 227.

Significance   *Cohens v. Virginia* (6 Wheaton 264: 1821) represents the conclusion of a long conflict over federal judicial supremacy. For a number of years previous, states' rightists had claimed that the portion of the Judiciary Act of 1789 that conveyed appellate jurisdiction over certain state decisions to the Supreme Court was unconstitutional. The states' rights position was most forcefully advanced by members of the Virginia judiciary. This states' rights position even manifested itself in the Virginia courts' refusal to implement the Supreme Court's decision in *Fairfax's Devisee v. Hunter's Lessee* (7 Cranch 603: 1813). This refusal prompted reiteration of the position that the Supreme Court possessed jurisdiction to review state cases in *Martin v. Hunter's Lessee* (1 Wheaton 304: 1816). After five more years of resistance by the states' rightists, the Court again responded in *Cohens*. Virginia argued that cases such as this might fall within the original jurisdiction language of Article III, but federal appellate jurisdiction could not be supreme. The magnitude of this question is clear. If states possessed concurrent jurisdiction, then decisions of state courts on the federal Constitution, laws, and treaties would prevail within the respective state. This would create a situation comparable to that which was fatal to the governmental structure under the Articles of Confederation—a central government operating at the pleasure of the states. It would also have destroyed any possibility of federal law being uniformly applied in every state. Marshall, however, rejected these contentions in *Cohens*, and held that the Supreme Court had appellate jurisdiction over state court decisions on any matters involving federal power. These decisions created the necessary integration of the exercise of judicial power and contributed substantially to the survival of the American federal system.

Federal Legislative Supremacy

McCulloch v. Maryland, 4 Wheaton 316, 4 L.Ed. 579 (1819) Established the principle of national supremacy that requires federal law to prevail over conflicting state law. *McCulloch v. Maryland* also contains a powerful articulation of the implied power doctrine. The case had its origin in 1816, when Congress established the second Bank of the United States. Two years later, the state of Maryland attempted to impose a tax on all banks not chartered by the state. McCulloch, a cashier at the Baltimore branch of the Bank of the United States, refused to pay the state tax (a $15,000 annual fee) or require the bank to affix state tax stamps on notes issued by the bank. Maryland sought to impose penalties, an action upheld in the Maryland courts. McCulloch sought review by the United States Supreme Court. In a unanimous decision, the Supreme Court invalidated the state tax, at least as it applied to the Bank of the United States.

The opinion of the Court was issued by Chief Justice Marshall. The decision broke into two major components. The first revolved around the question of whether Congress had the power to establish the bank. In addressing this question, Marshall developed two propositions. One was that the Constitution "proceeds directly" from the people. The conventions that ratified the Constitution were instruments of the people, and from these conventions the federal government "derives its whole authority." This conclusion allowed Marshall to fully reject Maryland's contention that the powers of the federal government were derived from the states as sovereign entities. While recognizing sovereignty residing with the states, Marshall developed a strong national supremacy argument from the Constitution's popular base. If "any one proposition could command the universal assent of mankind," it would be that "the government of the Union, though limited in its powers, is supreme within its sphere of action." He then turned to the second component of this question and offered his view that the

Constitution must be interpreted broadly. The national government must be allowed to exercise not only those powers expressly conveyed, but those reasonably implied as well. Legislative bodies, Marshall concluded, must be able to adopt the means through which to fulfill their assigned functions. A government that possesses such "ample powers" on which the "happiness and prosperity" of the nation depends "must also be intrusted with ample means to their execution." In addition, Marshall pointed to the necessary and proper clause as a broad mandate for congressional discretion. In determining what is necessary and proper, Marshall suggested some latitude. The words did not mean "absolutely" necessary. Rather, the clause was a means for "carrying into execution all sovereign powers," and may be used "although not indispensably necessary." The clause, in other words, was broadly enabling of legislative prerogatives. Marshall provided some guidance for assessing the exercise of implied power. "Let the end be legitimate" and within the "scope of the Constitution," and "all means plainly adopted to that end" that are not prohibited "consistent with the letter and spirit of the Constitution" are constitutional.

The second major issue posed in this case was whether Maryland could levy a tax on the bank. Maryland claimed exclusive power to charter corporations and to regulate them even to the point of prohibiting corporations established by other than state authority. Marshall rejected these arguments on national supremacy grounds. Since the bank had been established through lawful exercise of power implied from the Constitution, the federal law had to prevail over the state law attempting to tax the bank. This outcome was also dictated by the nature of our federation. We created two levels of representative government. The federal government might impose taxes on state activities since the people of each state were represented in Congress. No state, however, could tax a federal instrument because a state legislature cannot be made accountable to a national constituency. The power to tax "is the power to destroy," and the taxing power cannot be exercised at the state level if its intent or effect is detrimental to a federal institution. *See also* COHENS V. VIRGINIA (6 Wheaton 264: 1821), p. 236; FEDERALISM, p. 29; IMPLIED POWER, p. 618; *MARTIN V. HUNTER'S LESSEE* (1 Wheaton 304: 1816), p. 234; SUPREMACY CLAUSE, p. 227.

Significance   Chief Justice John Marshall established the supremacy of federal law over conflicting state laws in *McCulloch v. Maryland* (4 Wheaton 316: 1819). In doing so, Marshall also advocated giving the Constitution very broad construction. He utilized the doctrine of implied powers as advanced by Alexander Hamilton, a position antithetical to the views held by the states' rights advocates. This aspect of *McCulloch* created the flexibility necessary for the Constitution to evolve as an integrating structure of government. Once past the question of implied powers, Marshall rejected the concept of dual federalism in favor of national supremacy. While sovereignty was seen as divided between the federal and state levels, Marshall forcefully established that points of conflict between the two levels must be resolved in favor of the national government. The Constitution is of "paramount" character such that it has the capacity to prevail in conflict situations. While Marshall claimed that he was only intending to protect the exercise of granted federal powers, the practical effect of decisions like *McCulloch* and *Cohens v. Virginia* (6 Wheaton 264: 1821) was to define the federal-state balance in a decidedly national direction. This more than anything else ensured that government under the Constitution would not resemble in any way our experience under the Articles of Confederation.

***Blum v. Bacon*, 457 U.S. 132, 102 S.Ct. 2355, 72 L.Ed. 2d 728 (1982)**   Held a state emergency assistance provision not extending coverage to Aid to Families with Dependent Children (AFDC) recipients to be invalid under the supremacy clause. The state of New York had established an Emergency Assistance Program. The program depended heavily on federal funding under Title IV-A of the Social Security Act. The New York program excluded recipients of AFDC from emergency cash assistance and excluded public assistance recipients and AFDC recipients from reimbursement for lost or stolen checks. Such reimbursement was extended to recipients of other public benefit programs. A class action was brought by a number of AFDC recipients seeking injunction against enforcement of the no-cash and loss-or-theft policies. They argued that the law was in conflict with the Social Security Act as well as incompatible with the equal protection clause. The district court eventually invalidated the no-cash provision, but upheld the loss-or-theft provision. The court of appeals found both provisions constitutionally defective. New York sought appeal to the Supreme Court, which unanimously affirmed the court of appeals.

The opinion of the Court was delivered by Justice Marshall. The specific question in this case was whether the "complete and automatic exclusion" of AFDC recipients from the emergency assistance program was permissible under provisions of the Social Security Act. The Court indicated that prior cases had ruled that the emergency assistance provisions establish "only permissive, not mandatory eligibility standards." But despite the recognition that states "retain considerable flexibility" in determining which emergencies to cover, the Court held that the secretary of health, education, and welfare had authority to review and regulate plans that may "arbitrarily or inequitably" exclude a class of recipients. In this instance, the secretary had previously issued a regulation that prohibited the establishment of eligibility conditions on a basis incompatible with the purposes of the Social Security Act. The Court found the New York rules to be inconsistent with those regulations as well as the broader purposes of the act. The Court examined the legislative history of the act and determined that it was "unmistakably clear" that AFDC recipients were expected to benefit from the emergency assistance program. In looking at the House and Senate debates on this aspect of subsequent amendments to the act, the Court found "many statements" that even reflected a belief that the emergency assistance element "would be principally an AFDC program." Accordingly, the secretary's decision to apply the "equitable treatment" regulation is "eminently reasonable" and "deserves judicial deference." Since AFDC recipients were seen as the "core" of this program, and the "principal group of beneficiaries under federally-assisted state welfare programs," the contrary state rules relating to eligibility were invalid under the supremacy clause. *See also* FEDERALISM, p. 29; *STEWARD MACHINE COMPANY V. DAVIS* (301 U.S. 548: 1937), p. 391; SUPREMACY CLAUSE, p. 227.

Significance The court held in *Blum v. Bacon* (457 U.S. 132: 1982) that the supremacy clause prohibited a state from establishing restrictive eligibility conditions for access to emergency assistance programs subsidized under Title IV-A of the Social Security Act. The supremacy clause was included in the Constitution as the means of resolving disputes between the federal and state levels. The role of this language was graphically demonstrated in *McCulloch v. Maryland* (4 Wheaton 316: 1819), as Chief Justice Marshall established the legislative supremacy of the federal government. So long as Congress has acted in a constitutional manner, no state can interfere with the implementation of those laws. It is against this broad backdrop that cases like *Blum* are reviewed by the Court. In 1937, the Court upheld the Social Security Act in *Steward Machine Company v. Davis* (301 U.S. 548: 1937). The Court ruled that the taxing and spending provisions of the enactment were compatible with the general welfare clause of Article I and not an invasion of the reserve powers of the states. A number of assistance programs including AFDC have subsequently been umbrellaed under the Social Security Act. New York's emergency assistance program contained restrictive qualification conditions. Not only was the funding for the emergency program subsidized by the federal government, but the eligibility policy imposed disabilities on a group of persons already receiving benefits through the Social Security Act. The Court concluded that the restrictive state conditions were incompatible with the objectives of the lawfully established federal program, and had to be invalidated on grounds of federal legislative supremacy.

***Jefferson County Pharmaceutical Association, Inc. v. Abbott Laboratories*, 460 U.S. 150, 103 S.Ct. 1011, 74 L.Ed. 2d 882 (1983)**   Held that a federal antitrust law applied to the purchase and sale of pharmaceutical products by hospitals operated by state and local governments. The practice targeted in this suit was the resale of these products by the hospitals in competition with private pharmacies. A trade association of retail pharmacists and pharmacies claimed the practice violated the price discrimination provisions of the Robinson-Patman Act. A U.S. district court dismissed the complaint, holding that the hospitals were governmental entities and therefore outside the reach of the Robinson-Patman Act. The court of appeals affirmed, but on certiorari the Supreme Court reversed in a 5–4 decision.

The opinion of the Court was authored by Justice Powell. The specific issue presented was whether the sale of pharmaceutical products to government-run hospitals for resale in competition with private retail pharmacies is exempt from the regulatory provisions of the Robinson-Patman Act. The Court saw this issue as "narrow," limited to state purchases "for the purpose of competition against private enterprise—with the advantage of discriminatory prices—in the retail market." The Court found it compelling that the act did "not exempt state purchases." The only exemption was for nonprofit institutions, and the statutory references to "persons" and "purchasers" was viewed as "sufficiently broad to cover governmental bodies." The Court noted several prior decisions in which the definition of "person . . . embraces both cities and states." In short, the Court found the "plain language" of the act provided no exception for "state purchases to compete with private enterprise." The plain language "is controlling" unless there is a "different legislative intent" apparent from the purpose and history of the legislation. The Court then reviewed the history of federal antitrust legislation including Robinson-Patman. Antitrust laws are a comprehensive and "carefully structured attempt" to regulate activities that might "restrain or monopolize commercial intercourse among the states." As such, there is a "heavy presumption" against "implicit exemptions" from antitrust laws. Specifically, Robinson-Patman was enacted to "curb and prohibit" all means by which large buyers gain "discriminatory preferences" over smaller ones "by virtue of greater purchasing power." Because the act is "remedial," it is to be "construed broadly to effectuate its purposes." After examining the legislative history, the Court found no intention to "enable a State" by an "unexpressed exemption" to enter "private competitive markets with congressionally approved price advantages." The Court concluded by noting that the act had been "widely criticized" both for its "effects" as well as the "policies it seeks to promote." Congress, though cognizant of these criticisms, has chosen to retain the policy. The Court felt it was certainly not its function to "indulge in the business of policy making in the field of antitrust legislation." Application of Robinson-Patman to "all combinations . . . organized to suppress commercial competition" is "in harmony" with the "spirit and impulses of the times which gave it birth." The Court saw "no reason" in the absence of an explicit exemption to think that congressmen who "feared these evils" intended to deny to small businesses like the associated pharmacies involved here "protection from the competition of the strongest competitor of them all."

Justice O'Connor, joined by Justices Brennan, Rehnquist, and Stevens, dissented, saying Congress rather than the Court ought to further delineate the coverage of the act. In a separate dissent, Justice Stevens argued that neither the purchases or sales of the state-operated hospitals were the kind of "competition" addressed by Robinson-Patman. *See also* ANTITRUST LAWS, p. 579; FEDERALISM, p. 29; *UNITED STATES V. E. C. KNIGHT COMPANY* (156 U.S. 1: 1895), p. 302.

Significance   The Court upheld the application of federal antitrust laws to state and local government hospitals in *Jefferson County Pharmaceutical Association, Inc. v. Abbott Laboratories* (460 U.S. 150: 1983). Antitrust regulation is designed to preserve competition through federal regulation. Most often, antitrust legislation is aimed at combinations or monopolies and trusts that gain unfair market advantage in one way or another. The federal power to regulate business competition is based on congressional authority over interstate commerce. The primary antitrust laws are the Sherman Act of 1890 and the Clayton Act of 1914. The former is directed at monopolies that restrain trade through control of market supplies of particular goods and services. The Clayton Act reinforces the Sherman Act and targets price fixing and the development of interlocking directorates that might impair competition. Robinson-Patman was enacted in 1936 and was designed to prohibit price discrimination. By the time Robinson-Patman was passed, federal regulation was relatively well established in the antitrust field despite a somewhat uneven history prior to the mid-1930s. Certainly the enactment of antitrust laws was viewed as an appropriate exercise of the commerce power by 1936. Application of Robinson-Patman to hospitals operated by state and local governments in the *Jefferson County* case is compatible with other decisions of the 1980s coming from a narrowly divided Burger Court. In *Equal Employment*

Opportunity Commission v. Wyoming (460 U.S. 226: 1983), the Court held that the Age Discrimination in Employment Act applied to state employees. Similarly, the minimum wage and overtime provisions of the Fair Labor Standards Act were ruled to apply to state and local government employees in *Garcia v. San Antonio Metropolitan Transit Authority* (469 U.S. 528: 1985). Each of these cases reflects the principle of federal legislative supremacy.

Preemption Doctrine: Subversive Activities

***Pennsylvania v. Nelson*, 350 U.S. 497, 76 S.Ct. 477, 100 L.Ed. 640 (1956)** Held that sedition was a policy field in which federal law superseded or preempted incompatible state law. The decision in *Pennsylvania v. Nelson* was based on the doctrine of preemption. Nelson, a member of the Communist party, was convicted of violation of the Pennsylvania Sedition Act. On appeal, the Pennsylvania Supreme Court reversed Nelson's conviction, ruling that prosecution for seditious conduct against the United States was governed by federal law. The operative federal statute was the Alien Registration Act of 1940, an enactment more commonly known as the Smith Act. This statute prohibited the "knowing advocacy" of the overthrow of the government of the United States by force or violence. Pennsylvania appealed the state court decisions to the United States Supreme Court. The Court held that the federal statute preempted the field in a 6–3 decision that precluded Pennsylvania from prosecuting Nelson.

The opinion of the Court was delivered by Chief Justice Warren. He began by observing that, when Congress does not express a clear intent to fully occupy a policy field, there is "no one crystal clear, distinctly marked formula" that the Court may use. Warren then set forth those tests of supersession he thought appropriate in cases such as *Nelson*. The first was whether the "scheme of federal regulation" was "so pervasive" as to "make reasonable the inference that Congress left no room for the states to supplement it." In this instance, the conclusion was "inescapable" that Congress intended to fully occupy the field of sedition. The various enactments, "taken as a whole . . . evince a congressional plan" that leaves no room for the states to act, even in supplement. The second test asks whether the federal laws "touch a field in which the federal interest is so dominant" that the federal system precludes enforcement of state laws on the same subject. Warren cited the "all-embracing program" devised by Congress to resist the "various forms of totalitarian aggression." With Congress having treated seditious conduct "as a matter of vital national concern," the Court concluded that sedition was "in no sense a local enforcement problem."

Thirdly, the Court considered whether enforcement of state acts endangered administration of the federal sedition program. The Court noted the federal government had "urged" local authorities not to intervene in matters involving subversive activities. The problem, said Warren, must "be handled on a nation-wide basis." The national security interest is "best served" by letting the FBI exclusively handle sedition. Without this, matters could get ensnared in "red tape" and even be handled in an "amateur" fashion. Furthermore, it was seen as critical that "punitive sanctions for sedition against the United States" be established by the central government and administered under the supervision of the federal judiciary. This will most effectively balance national security and free expression interests. If the states had concurrent jurisdiction in this area, conflict would develop around the nonuniformity of the state laws and criteria for substantive offenses. Finally, the Court said that concurrent jurisdiction raises the possibility of "double or multiple punishment," something the Court should not "assume" Congress intended to permit.

Justices Reed, Burton, and Minton dissented. They argued that Congress had not explicitly precluded state action here, and that the Court ought not invalidate state initiatives without legislative mandate. They disagreed that the federal program was so pervasive as to leave the states no room. Finally, they felt that state and local enforcement efforts could productively supplement federal activity. *See also* FEDERALISM, p. 29; PREEMPTION DOCTRINE, p. 645; SUPREMACY CLAUSE, p. 227.

Significance   The Court used the preemption doctrine in *Pennsylvania v. Nelson* (350 U.S. 497: 1956) to void state prosecutions for sedition. The Court ruled that the various federal laws, most notably the Smith Act, exclusively committed this policy field to the federal level. The doctrine of preemption is grounded in the supremacy clause of Article VI, and it represents the strongest formulation of federal legislative supremacy. The Court's decision in the *Nelson* case was far-reaching and directly affected virtually every state since laws like Pennsylvania's were common. At the same time, there are limits to the *Nelson* decision. The Court explicitly said that for the doctrine to have effect, Congress must act. States are not precluded from action in the absence of federal legislation. In *Nelson*, the Court said that states have the power to enforce "sedition laws at times when the Federal Government has not occupied the field." Thus, states are not necessarily permanently preempted in a particular policy field. Further, *Nelson* did not remove the right of a state to "protect itself at any time against sabotage or attempted violence of all kinds." Finally, the Court clarified the double jeopardy issue. *Nelson* was not to be read as preventing a state from "prosecuting where the same act constitutes both a federal offense and a state offense under the police power." So while supersession or preemption represents an extremely powerful concept of federal legislative supremacy, states are not left without any power in its wake.

Preemption Doctrine: Nuclear Power Plants

Pacific Gas and Electric Company v. State Energy Resources Conservation and Development Commission, **461 U.S. 190, 103 S.Ct. 1713, 75 L.Ed. 2d (1983)** Upheld a state law that made certification of new nuclear plants contingent upon the finding of safe ways to permanently dispose of nuclear waste. California has attempted to regulate development of nuclear power plants in two ways. A statute provided that construction of new nuclear power plants was contingent on the state energy commission's determining on a plant-by-plant basis that there would be adequate capacity for storage of spent fuel rods. Another provision of the same statute established a moratorium on certification of new plants until the state energy commission was satisfied that the United States, through its authorized agency, had approved of means for safe disposal of high-level nuclear waste. Two utilities brought suit, claiming the California law to be invalid because it was preempted by the Atomic Energy Act. A U.S. district court held the California law void on preemption grounds. The court of appeals held that the provision dealing with determination of the adequacy of storage capacity for spent fuel rods was not ripe for review. The certification moratorium was viewed as ripe, however, and the court of appeals held the provisions were not preempted by the federal law. In a unanimous decision, the Supreme Court affirmed the court of appeals.

The opinion of the Court was delivered by Justice White. The case, said White, "emerges from that intersection" of the federal government's efforts to "ensure that nuclear power is safe" and the exercise of the "historic state authority over the generating and sale of electricity." While the interrelationship of federal and state authority in the nuclear energy field has not been "simple, the federal regulatory structure has been frequently amended to optimize the partnership." The preemption challenge made here had to be reviewed in that context. White reviewed the general principles of preemption. Congress may preempt state authority by "so stating in express terms." If such language is not contained in legislation under review, intent to supersede or preempt may be found from a "scheme" of federal regulation "so pervasive as to make reasonable the inference that Congress left no room to supplement it." Preemption can also occur where state law conflicts with federal law or where the state regulation "stands as an obstacle" to the accomplishment of the "full purposes and objectives of Congress." The utilities contended the certification moratorium was preempted on three grounds. First, they claimed the California law was a safety regulation and encroached on the exclusive federal authority in that field. Second, the utilities asserted the state law conflicted with federal law concerning nuclear waste disposal. Third, it was argued that the state law "frustrates the federal goal of developing nuclear technology as a source of energy. The Court rejected these contentions. The Atomic Energy Act has preserved "dual regulation" on nuclear-powered energy generation in the Court's view. The states retained authority over economic issues under terms of the federal law, and the Court deferred to California's "avowed economic rather than safety purpose" for its certification moratorium. This placed the California law "outside the federally occupied field" of nuclear safety regulation. Second, the Court held that the state regulation did not conflict with the Nuclear Waste Policy Act of 1982 or a decision of the Nuclear Regulatory Commission (NRC). Indeed, the Court found the regulatory objectives to be separable. NRC regulations are aimed at ensuring plant safety, not that the plants are economical. Finally, the Court did not see the California regulation as frustrating the national policy objective of development of commercial use of nuclear power. The Court said that development of nuclear power is "not to be accomplished at all costs." Congress preserved state authority to determine "as a matter of economics," whether nuclear power plants are feasible. California's choice to exercise that authority did not "in itself constitute a basis for pre-emption." *See also* CONCURRENT POWER, p. 588; FEDERALISM, p. 29; *NEW MEXICO V. MESCALERO APACHE TRIBE* (462 U.S. 324: 1983), p. 248; *PENNSYLVANIA V. NELSON* (350 U.S. 497: 1956), p. 244; SUPREMACY CLAUSE, p. 227.

Significance   The Court upheld a state moratorium on certification of new nuclear plants in *Pacific Gas and Electric Company v. State Energy Resources Conservation and Development Commission* (461 U.S. 190: 1983). When the federal government enters a policy area where it has authority to act, the supremacy clause of Article VI provides that the federal regulation supersedes all state regulation that may conflict. This is known as the preemption doctrine. The utilities argued in this case that the federal government so fully occupied the field of nuclear power plant regulation that states were precluded from additional regulation. In this case, there was federal regulation—the Atomic Energy Act and the Nuclear Waste Policy Act. Had these statutes expressly provided, preemption of any and all state regulatory activity could have been achieved. Absent explicit preemption, the Court must assess the extent to which there is conflict between federal and state policies. Without conflict, the state regulation cannot be superseded. In this case, the Court saw the focus of the state regulation as derived from traditional state authority to examine economic feasibility. This was outside the field occupied by the federal government. The Court also interpreted the federal statutory language as tolerating dual or concurrent regulation. In a related case, however, the Court held in *Metropolitan Edison v. People Against Nuclear Energy* (460 U.S. 766: 1983) that the Nuclear Regulatory Commission need not examine the risk of psychological harm to persons in communities near nuclear plants as a condition of approval of operating plans for those plants. This case had arisen out of NRC proceedings examining possible resumption of operations at Edison's nuclear plant at Three Mile Island.

Preemption Doctrine: Indian Reservation Regulations

New Mexico v. Mescalero Apache Tribe, **462 U.S. 324, 103 S.Ct. 2378, 76 L.Ed. 2d 611 (1983)** Held that application of a state's hunting and fishing regulations to nontribe members on an Indian reservation is preempted by federal law. Under federal supervision, the Mescalero Apache Tribe developed a comprehensive management plan for the fish and wildlife resources of the reservation. New Mexico, however, sought to apply its own laws to nonmembers of the tribe on the reservation. The state regulations were generally more restrictive, and the tribe filed suit, trying to prevent New Mexico from regulating on-reservation hunting or fishing by tribal members and nonmembers. The U.S. district court and court of appeals both ruled in favor of the tribe. In a unanimous decision, the Supreme Court affirmed.

The opinion of the Court was delivered by Justice Marshall. He started by pointing out that in "demarcating the respective state and tribal authority" over Indian reservations, prior cases had stressed that Indian tribes "are unique aggregations possessing attributes of sovereignty over both their members and their territory." Because of their sovereign status, tribes and their reservations "are insulated in some respects by an 'historic immunity from state and local control.'" The sovereignty retained by Indian tribes includes authority to regulate "their internal and social relations" so long as they do not conflict with the "overriding interests of the National Government." While acknowledging that "under some circumstances" a state may exercise concurrent jurisdiction over nontribe members on reservations, this kind of state authority "may be asserted only if not pre-empted by the operation of federal law." The Court went on to say that the preemption doctrine is applied a little differently when dealing with the "unique historical origins of tribal sovereignty." The federal commitment to "tribal self-sufficiency and self-determination" makes it "treacherous to import . . . notions of pre-emption that are properly applied to other contexts." State authority is preempted if it "interferes or is incompatible" with federal or tribal interests" reflected in federal law. The exercise of state authority must pursue a substantial regulatory interest in order to overcome a presumption that a state regulation interferes with the accomplishment of a federal objective where Indian tribes and reservations are involved. The Mescalero Apache Tribe lawfully exercises "substantial control" over the lands and resources of its reservation. Concurrent jurisdiction between the state and tribe "would effectively nullify" the tribe's authority in this field. Concurrent jurisdiction would allow New Mexico "wholly to supplant tribal regulations." The tribe would be able to exercise its authority "only at the sufferance of the State." Assertion of concurrent jurisdiction would not only "threaten to disrupt the federal and tribal regulatory scheme," but would also threaten Congress's "overriding objective of encouraging tribal self-government and economic development." For these reasons, the Court disallowed New Mexico's application of its own hunting and fishing laws to nontribe members. *See also* CONCURRENT POWER, p. 588; FEDERALISM, p. 29; *PACIFIC GAS AND ELECTRIC COMPANY V. STATE ENERGY RESOURCES CONSERVATION AND DEVELOPMENT COMMISSION* (461 U.S. 190: 1983), p. 246; *PENNSYLVANIA V. NELSON* (350 U.S. 497: 1956), p. 244; PREEMPTION DOCTRINE, p. 645; SUPREMACY CLAUSE, p. 227.

Significance   The Court used the preemption doctrine in *New Mexico v. Mescalero Apache Tribe* (462 U.S. 324: 1983) to uphold tribal hunting and fishing regulations for nontribe members while on the reservation. The preemption doctrine is derived from the supremacy clause of Article VI. The doctrine holds that when Congress legitimately acts, its laws and regulations supersede or preempt any incompatible state policies. In the Mescalero Apache case, there were two factors that led to the supersession of the state attempt to regulate nontribal members on Indian reservations. First, Indian tribes possess a sovereign status that does not attach to other groups in the population. This provides some "historic immunity" from certain state and local controls. Second, the federal government had a well-established policy of attempting to foster tribal "self-sufficiency" and "self-determination." If state regulation is incompatible with the federal or tribal interests represented by this policy, it necessarily triggers the preemption doctrine.

Intergovernmental Tax Immunity

Helvering v. Gerhardt, 304 U.S. 405, 58 S.Ct. 969, 82 L.Ed. 1427 (1938)　　Ruled that state immunity from federal taxation must be limited to those state activities and entities seen as essential to the existence of the state. *Helvering v. Gerhardt* was one of many cases examining the issue of intergovernmental tax immunity. The specific question raised in this case was whether the federal government could collect an income tax on the salaries of employees of the Port of New York Authority, a bi-state (New York and New Jersey) corporation created by interstate compact. The Court ruled, in a 5–2 decision (Justices Cardozo and Reed did not participate), that collection of this tax did not impose an unconstitutional burden on the two states.

The opinion of the Court was delivered by Justice Stone. He began by noting no explicit constitutional limitation on either the state or federal levels from taxing each other. There is an implied limitation, however, and it stemmed from Chief Justice Marshall's opinion in *McCulloch v. Maryland* (4 Wheaton 316: 1819), where the Court struck down a state tax on the Bank of the United States. In that case, the Court "recognized a clear distinction" between state taxation of federal instrumentalities (like banks), and the national government's taxing state instrumentalities. In levying a federal tax, the people of the states, acting through their respective representatives, "are laying a tax on their own institutions" and are consequently subject to the political restraints that curtail or prevent abuse. State taxation on national instrumentalities "is subject to no such restraint." There is a safeguard present in the one case, but not in the other. Stone then went on to state that restriction of the national taxing power should be kept to a minimum. One reason is that the "people of all the states" have created the national government and are represented in Congress. The political process provides the best safeguard against misconduct, and it affords the best means by which to secure "accommodation of the competing demands for national revenues." Secondly, to allow immunity for the protection of state sovereignty "is at the expense of the nation to tax." Stone suggested that "enlargement of the one involves diminution of the other." If every federal tax levied on some "new form of state activity" were to be invalidated as an encroachment of state sovereignty, this would become a "ready means for striking down the taxing power of the nation."

After review of numerous cases involving immunity issues, Stone identified two "guiding principles of limitation for holding the tax immunity of state instruments" to only those involving a state's "proper function." First, excluded from immune activities are those thought "not to be essential to the preservation of state governments." Even if the tax is collected from the state government itself, immunity will not extend to the privilege of, for example, carrying on the state's liquor business. The second principle is that immunity cannot be recognized where the impact on the state is so "speculative and uncertain" that even with immunity, no "tangible protection to the state government" would be afforded. A nondiscriminatory tax on income was seen as fitting this latter category. By "no reasonable probability" could this be considered to "preclude the performance" of the state governmental functions.

Justices Butler and McReynolds dissented, expressing the view that application of *McCulloch* was reciprocal and should provide immunity in this case. *See also* FEDERALISM, p. 29; INTERGOVERNMENTAL TAX IMMUNITY, p. 623; *McCULLOCH V. MARYLAND* (4 Wheaton 316: 1819), p. 238.

Significance   The Court upheld a federal income tax on employees of a state agency in *Helvering v. Gerhardt* (304 U.S. 405: 1938). The Court held that immunity from federal taxation should only occur if necessary to ensure the continued existence of the state government. This constituted an extremely narrow interpretation of the intergovernmental tax immunity doctrine, and marked the end of the doctrine as an effective limitation on federal taxing power. This was not always so. State immunity from federal taxation was most extensively advanced by the Court in *Collector v. Day* (11 Wallace 113: 1871). Here the Court held that a state judge's salary could not be subject to a federal income tax. The Court based its judgment on *McCulloch v. Maryland* (4 Wheaton 316: 1819), and simply argued that self-protection of state independence required reciprocal immunity. The position taken in *Collector v. Day* was subsequently extended without limit through the early 1930s. Soon thereafter, a number of decisions like *Helvering v. Gerhardt* reduced the immunity doctrine to more reasonable proportions. Furthermore, the federal and state levels no longer have parity in the application of the doctrine. Congress is currently less limited by the doctrine than the states, as it shields only fundamental state functions and property.

Intergovernmental Tax Immunity: Private Contractors

***United States v. New Mexico*, 455 U.S. 720, 102 S.Ct. 1373, 71 L.Ed. 2d 580 (1982)**   Upheld imposition of state taxes on federal contractors doing business in the state. Three contractors doing work for the Department of Energy operated under contracts that included an "advance funding" procedure. This technique allowed contractors to pay all obligations out of a special account into which federal funds had been deposited. New Mexico imposed a gross receipts and compensating use tax on persons doing business in the state. The gross receipts tax operated directly upon the sale of goods and services, while the compensating use tax functioned as an enforcement feature for the gross receipts tax by imposing a levy on the use of all property not already taxed. The United States brought suit seeking a declaratory judgment against the state's imposition of the gross receipts tax on the "advanced" funds, and the application of the compensating use tax on use of government-owned property. The district court held that the contractors were procurement agents of the government and thus immune from taxation. The court of appeals reversed the district court, finding the contractors were sufficiently outside the governmental structure such that they did not become instruments of the federal government. In a unanimous decision, the Supreme Court agreed that the contractors were not entitled to immunity.

The opinion of the Court was delivered by Justice Blackmun. He suggested that, since *McCulloch v. Maryland* (4 Wheaton 316: 1819), the question of federal immunity from state taxation has become a "much litigated and often confused field." Indeed, the area is one that has been "marked . . . by inconsistent decisions and excessively delicate distinctions." But since the 1930s, the Court has generally concluded that it is not necessary to "cripple" a state's capacity to tax by "extending the constitutional exemption from taxation" to those subjects that "fall within the general application of non-discriminatory laws" and where "no direct burden" is laid upon the governmental instrumentality and the effect (if any) upon governmental functions is "remote." While the supremacy clause does not permit a state to lay a tax "directly upon the United States," there are limits to the immunity doctrine. Immunity cannot be conferred "simply because the tax has an effect on the United States," or even because the federal government "shoulders the entire burden" of the tax. Neither can immunity be conferred simply because the tax falls on the earnings of a contractor providing services to the federal government. Nor can immunity be conferred simply because the state is levying a tax on the use of federal property in private hands. And immunity cannot be conferred merely because the tax is paid with federal funds. In short, immunity was seen as appropriate only when the tax levy falls "on the United States itself," or an agency or instrumentality "so closely connected" to the government that the two "cannot realistically be viewed as separate entities," at least as far as the taxed activity is concerned.

The Court said that immunity must be conferred narrowly, giving "full range" to each sovereign's taxing authority. Applying these principles to this case, the Court found that the contractors were not instrumentalities of the United States, but rather privately owned corporations. The "congruence" of professional interests between the contractors and the United States was "not complete." As for the sales tax, the Court saw the contractors as having an "independent role" in making purchases, and that sales to the contractors were "in neither a real or a symbolic sense sales to the United States itself." The Court concluded by saying that if a broader immunity doctrine was appropriate, such issues "are ones which Congress is best qualified to resolve." *See also* FEDERALISM, p. 29; *HELVERING V. GERHARDT* (304 U.S. 403: 1938), p. 250; INTERGOVERNMENTAL TAX IMMUNITY, p. 623; *McCULLOCH V. MARYLAND* (4 Wheaton 316: 1819), p. 238; SUPREMACY CLAUSE, p. 227.

Significance The Court refused to invoke the supremacy clause to invalidate a state tax on federal contractors in *United States v. New Mexico* (455 U.S. 720: 1982). The Court held in *McCulloch v. Maryland* (4 Wheaton 316: 1819) that states could not subject the federal government or any of its instrumentalities to taxation. This element of the *McCulloch* decision became known as the intergovernmental tax immunity doctrine. It was strongly believed that such immunity from taxation was imperative, otherwise the states would use their taxing power to impair operations of the federal government. Eventually this doctrine was extended to federal taxation of state governments, and through the 1930s was applied to any governmental activity no matter how far removed from basic governmental functions. This view has largely been abandoned, as reflected in this case. The Court now holds that the immunity doctrine is to be very narrowly interpreted and infrequently applied in deference to the taxing authority of the two levels of government. Only those taxes levied against the federal government itself or those entities so fully integrated with the government that they cannot be reasonably viewed as separate are presently invalidated on immunity grounds. Since the 1930s, the Court has recognized the authority of Congress to extend the immunity doctrine by legislative means to virtually any subject or activity.

State Tax on Newspaper Materials

***Minneapolis Star and Tribune Company v. Minnesota Commissioner of Revenue*, 460 U.S. 575, 103 S.Ct. 1365, 75 L.Ed. 2d 295 (1983)** Held that a state use tax assessed against the cost of ink and paper used in the production of publications violated the First Amendment. The tax statute exempted publications from the state's general sales tax and also exempted the first $100,000 of such costs each year from the use tax. The Minneapolis Star and Tribune Company began an action in state court seeking to recover part of the taxes paid. It claimed the use tax violated the free press guarantees of the First Amendment and the equal protection clause of the Fourteenth. The tax was upheld against federal constitutional challenge by the Minnesota Supreme Court. In a 7–2 decision, the U.S. Supreme Court reversed the state court and invalidated the tax.

The opinion of the Court was delivered by Justice O'Connor. She reiterated that the First Amendment protection of the press was not absolute. She said it is "beyond dispute" that both the states and the federal government can subject newspapers to "generally applicable economic regulations without creating constitutional problems." In examining the Minnesota tax, the Court found no legislative history or "any indication" beyond the structure of the tax itself of "any impermissible or censorial motive on the part of the legislature." The legislature, however, chose not to apply its general sales and use tax to newspapers. Rather, it created a "special tax" that applies only to "certain publications protected by the First Amendment." The Court found Minnesota's use tax "facially discriminatory" by "singling out" publications for treatment "unique" to Minnesota tax law. The Court then needed to determine whether the First Amendment "permits such special taxation." A tax that "burdens rights protected by the First Amendment" cannot stand unless the "burden is necessary to achieve an overriding governmental interest." The Court said that there was "substantial evidence" that differential taxation of the press "would have troubled the Framers of the First Amendment." The power to tax differentially "gives a government a powerful weapon against the taxpayer selected." When a state imposes a generally applicable tax, there is "little cause for concern." But when the state singles out the press, the "political constraints" that prevent a legislature from passing "crippling taxes of general applicability are weakened," and the threat of "burdensome taxes becomes acute." That threat can "operate as effectively as a censor to check critical comment by the press." In addition, differential treatment, unless justified by some "special characteristic" of the press, suggests that the objective of the regulation was not "unrelated to suppression of expression," and such a goal is "presumptively unconstitutional." The differential tax was seen as placing such a burden on interests protected by the First Amendment that a state can only sustain it by showing an "interest of compelling importance" that it cannot achieve without the tax. The principal interest offered by Minnesota in this case was raising revenue. While that interest is "critical" to a government, "standing alone" it cannot justify the "special treatment" of the press because "alternative means" of achieving the same interest are "clearly available." Without raising First Amendment concerns, a state could generate revenue by "taxing businesses generally," thus avoiding the "censorial threat implicit in a tax that singles out the press." The Court also found the Minnesota tax defective because it not only singled out the press, but because it "targets a small group of newspapers."

Justices White and Rehnquist dissented, feeling that the press had not really been disadvantaged by the differential tax. They argued that a state had the power to choose one method of taxation over another provided the press benefited or at least was not disadvantaged. *See also* FEDERALISM, p. 29; FIRST AMENDMENT, p. 609.

Significance   The Court found First Amendment defects in a state tax against certain publications in *Minneapolis Star and Tribune Company v. Minnesota Commissioner of Revenue* (460 U.S. 575: 1983). Prior to the Civil War, the states were not bound by any provisions of the Bill of Rights. Through a process known as incorporation, the Bill of Rights guarantees were gradually drawn through the due process clause of the Fourteenth Amendment. One by one, applicable amendments became the basis for invalidating incompatible state actions. The First Amendment provision covering free press was applied to the states by the Court in *Near v. Minnesota* (283 U.S. 697: 1931). *Near* involved the basic press freedom from prior restraint. Soon after, the Court examined the matter of targeted taxation of the press in *Grosjean v. American Press Company* (297 U.S. 233: 1936). The Court struck down a state tax, finding the levy to be punitive in character. The Minneapolis *Star* had based its challenge of the Minnesota use tax on the *Grosjean* decision, but the Court found the impermissible censorial motive lacking. Nonetheless, the Court held that differential taxation of the press was suspect and could be justified only by demonstrating a compelling state need. The First Amendment, however, has not been used to preclude states from subjecting publishers to general regulations including taxation.

Application of the Federal Bill of Rights to States

***Barron v. Baltimore*, 7 Peters 243, 8 L.Ed. 672 (1833)**   Held that provisions of the Bill of Rights did not limit actions of state governments. Barron owned a wharf that was rendered useless by certain actions of the city of Baltimore. To accomplish certain public improvements such as street paving, the city diverted streams that caused sand and gravel to be deposited around Barron's wharf, thus preventing ships from docking. Barron unsuccessfully sought compensation within the state courts, whereupon Barron turned to the U.S. Supreme Court. He argued that Baltimore's action violated the Fifth

Amendment, which prohibits the "taking" of private property without "just compensation." He claimed this provision ought to be interpreted as a restraint not only on the federal government, but the states as well. In a unanimous decision, the Court refused to apply the Fifth Amendment to the states.

The opinion of the Court was delivered by Chief Justice Marshall. He referred to the question posed by the case as one of "great importance, but not of much difficulty." The Constitution, he said, was ordained and established by the people of the United States for themselves, for their own government, and not for the government of the individual states. Each state, in turn, established its own constitution with provisions restricting that particular government "as its judgment dictated." When the federal Constitution was created, powers were conferred on the federal government to be exercised "by itself," and the limitations on power were "naturally, . . . necessarily applicable to the government created by the instrument." These were limitations on power granted by the instrument, not of "distinct government, framed by different persons and for different purposes." Barron argued that elements of the federal constitution applied to the states and pointed to the restrictions on state power found in Article I, Section 10. Marshall found this argument to support the opposite conclusion. He pointed to the prohibitions against bills of attainder and *ex post facto* laws. Section 9 of Article I precludes such actions by Congress. No language can "be more general," Marshall observed, but it obviously only applied to the federal government, since the same language can be found in Section 10 as restraint against state legislatures. The clear conclusion is that the provisions in Section 9, "however comprehensive its language," do not apply to the states. Marshall's conclusion was that no limitation of federal power would apply to the states "unless expressed in terms" such as the limits contained in Section 10. If the original constitution drew such a line between limits on the general government and on the states, "some strong reason must be assigned for departing from this safe and judicious course in framing the amendment." Marshall said, "We reach in vain for that reason." Had the framers of the amendments intended them to restrain the states, "they would have declared this purpose in plain and intelligible language." Given no such declaration, "this court cannot so apply them." Since the Fifth Amendment is not applicable to state actions, Barron could find no relief from the Supreme Court, and the case was dismissed. *See also* FEDERALISM, p. 29; FOURTEENTH AMENDMENT, p. 612; INCORPORATION, p. 620.

Significance   *Barron v. Baltimore* (7 Peters 243: 1833) held that the Bill of Rights only applied to the federal government. The Court's ruling was clear and compelling, and the decision in *Barron* has never been overruled. Its impact, however, was dramatically muted by the adoption of the Fourteenth Amendment in 1868. The Fourteenth reopened the issue (known as "incorporation") because it directed itself to state governments. The Fourteenth Amendment contains a due process clause that prohibits a state from denying liberty without due process of law. The prevailing view has been that the due process clause requires states to provide fundamental fairness to citizens. Due process is assessed by criteria of immutable principles of justice or elements implicit in the concept of "ordered liberty." If Bill of Rights provisions are adjudged to be of a "fundamental" nature, they are incorporated or absorbed through the Fourteenth Amendment and made applicable to the states. Over the years, virtually all of the Bill of Rights provisions have been incorporated and operate at the state as well as federal levels. Without the Fourteenth Amendment, the *Barron* ruling would still pertain. With no explicit language extending the Bill of Rights to the states, the limitations contained there would still apply only to the federal government.

Secession from the Union

Texas v. White, **7 Wallace 700, 19 L.Ed. 227 (1869)**   Held that, once admitted to the Union, a state could not constitutionally secede. *Texas v. White* had its origin in 1851, when Congress authorized transfer of United States bonds to the state of Texas. The bonds, redeemable in 1864, were payable to either the state or bearer. At the time of receipt, Texas enacted a law requiring endorsement of the bonds by the governor if they were to be valid for individual holders. The confederate legislature repealed this law in 1862 and authorized use of the bonds for supplies to use in the Civil War. After the war, the Reconstruction government of Texas attempted to reclaim the bonds in the hands of White and others. It was argued by White and the other defendants that the Supreme Court had no jurisdiction in this case because Texas was no longer a state. The Court disagreed, and in a 6–3 decision, held the Union to be "perpetual" and "indissoluble."

The opinion of the Court was delivered by Chief Justice Chase. The central issue in the case was whether Texas, through "her ordinance of secession," disengaged from the Union in a way that "so far changed her status" as to be "disabled" from bringing suit in federal court as a state. Chase reviewed actions taken by members of the Confederacy during the Civil War and acknowledged that there was no recognition of national authority by Texas during that period of time. Nonetheless, these actions did not change Texas's status as a state or cause its membership in the Union to cease. Chase said the Union was never "a purely artificial and arbitrary relation." The Union grew out of a "common origin, mutual sympathies, kindred principles, similar interests, and geographical relations." These led to federation under the Articles, where the Union was "solemnly declared to be 'perpetual.'" The Constitution was subsequently ordained to "form a more perfect Union." Chase said it was "difficult to convey the idea of indissoluble unity more clearly than by these words." The Constitution, "in all its provisions," Chase continued, "looks to an indestructible Union, composed of indestructible States." When Texas became one of the United States, "she entered into an indissoluble relation." The act of admitting Texas into the Union was "something more than a compact." It was "incorporation of a new member into the political body. And it was final." Against this background, the ordinance of secession and all legislative acts "intended to give effect to that ordinance were absolutely nil." They were "utterly without operation in law." During this period, her obligations as a member of the Union and her citizens as citizens of the United States "remained perfect and unimpaired." The state "did not cease to be a state" nor did her population "cease to be citizens."

Chase then examined whether Texas had a government "competent to represent the State" in its relations with the federal government, and to be party to a suit in federal court. While Texas's statehood had remained unimpaired, its relation to the Union "greatly changed." This new relation "imposed new duties upon the United States." The first was to "suppress the rebellion." The second was "reconstructing the broken relations" with Texas. The first was accomplished by the war, and the second with restoration of state government under Reconstruction. The latter was undertaken in the exercise of the guarantee clause, and Congress must be permitted broad discretion in the selection of means to achieve restoration of relations. The Reconstruction government of Texas was "recognized . . . as provisional, as existing, and as capable of continuance." That was sufficient for the Court, and accordingly, the Reconstruction government of Texas was seen as having the right to bring suit.

Justice Greer offered a dissent that was joined by Justices Swayne and Miller. They regarded Texas as a territory without capacity to bring suit. They saw the majority decision as a "legal fiction" that ignored the political realities of the Civil War. They said the Court is "bound to know and notice the public history of the nation." Citing the previous eight years as the "truth of history," they did not see Texas "as one of the United States." *See also* FEDERALISM, p. 29; GUARANTEE CLAUSE, p. 616; INTERPOSITION, p. 624.

Significance   *Texas v. White* (7 Wallace 700: 1869) held that the Union was "perpetual" and "indissoluble," and one from which no state could withdraw. The decision marked a technical and legal response to the questions effectively resolved by the outcome of the Civil War. The act of secession is the most extreme means of attempting to preserve states' rights and is a logical extension of the concepts of interposition and nullification. The theory of interposition holds that a state may interpose itself between its citizens and the federal government to preclude enforcement of federal law. Interposition is a strong states' rights concept and is based upon the assertion of state sovereignty as a shield against the exercise of federal power. If the states feel that the federal government has assumed powers not formally conveyed or abused its authority, the states have the remedial option of nullification. Advocacy of nullification surfaced during the bitter conflict over the Alien and Sedition Laws. In the most extreme instances, nullification may be insufficient to protect the interests of state sovereignty. As a final remedy, some states' rightists argued that secession from the Union was justified. The Court issued an unequivocal negative response in *Texas v. White*.

Federal Regulation of Private Property

Civil Rights Cases, **109 U.S. 3, 3 S.Ct. 18, 27 L.Ed. 835 (1883)**
Limited the applicability of the equal protection clause to situations where the state is an actual party to the discriminatory conduct. The *Civil Rights Cases* were an aggregation of suits that challenged the constitutionality of the Civil Rights Act of 1875, passed on the authority conferred by the Fourteenth Amendment. The cases specifically challenged the power of Congress to regulate private acts of racial discrimination. The Civil Rights Act provided that all persons "shall be entitled to the full and equal enjoyment of the accommodations, advantages, facilities and privileges of inns, public conveyances and theaters." In addition to its prohibitions of private discriminatory behavior in public accommodations, the act also assumed federal control over situations where state and local governments failed to protect citizens from discrimination by other private citizens. Over the vigorous dissent of Justice Harlan, the Court struck down the act.

Justice Bradley's opinion for the Court stressed that the Fourteenth Amendment did not extend to Congress an unlimited source of legislative power. The Fourteenth Amendment was intended to "provide modes of relief against State legislation, or State action." This amendment did not "invest Congress with power to legislate upon subjects which are within the domain of State legislation" or "authorize Congress to create a code of municipal law for the regulation of private rights." The Fourteenth Amendment authorized Congress to enact corrective rather than general legislation that "may be necessary and proper for counteracting such laws as the States may adopt or enforce, and which, by the amendment, they are prohibited from making or enforcing." The Civil Rights Act of 1875 was defective in that it was not corrective, it referred to no State violation, and it impermissibly reached into the domain of local jurisprudence and laid down rules for the conduct of individuals. Justice Bradley expressed the fear that if Congress had authority to pass such legislation it would be difficult "to see where it is to stop." Nor did Justice Bradley think that the Thirteenth Amendment authorized such legislation. He indicated that "mere discrimination on account of race or color was not regarded as a badge of slavery."

Justice Harlan felt that the Thirteenth Amendment was a sufficient power source, saying that "such discrimination practiced by corporations and individuals in the exercise of their public or quasi-public functions is a badge of servitude the imposition of which Congress may prevent under its power." Critical for Justice Harlan was the "public convenience" or accommodations nature of the enterprises covered by the Civil Rights Act. *See also* FEDERALISM, p. 29; FOURTEENTH AMENDMENT, p. 612; *HEART OF ATLANTA MOTEL V. UNITED STATES* (379 U.S. 241: 1964), p. 343.

Significance   The Court held in the *Civil Rights Cases* (109 U.S. 3: 1883) that the federal government could not regulate private acts of discrimination. The Court ruled that Section 5 of the Fourteenth Amendment did not permit Congress to more than redress state discrimination. The Civil Rights Act of 1875, which was the focal point of these suits, was seen as going substantially further. As an enactment focusing on private rather than public conduct, the statute entered a regulatory domain traditionally belonging to the states. The act also reflected a congressional assumption that it possessed comprehensive power to enforce the Fourteenth Amendment. For a Court already sympathetic to the concept of dual federalism, the act represented a major redistribution of authority in the federal-state relationship. It was not surprising that the Court of this period resolved the *Civil Rights Cases* with the most restrictive interpretation possible of the Fourteenth Amendment, especially as it related to the exercise of legislative power to enforce the amendment. The decision, then, left the Congress limited by the state action concept (able only to correct state, rather than private, affirmative acts of discrimination).

The state action requirement established in the *Civil Rights Cases* (109 U.S. 3: 1883) remains in force, but discrimination in privately owned public accommodations is now regulated. The Court eventually became receptive to assertions that a close relationship exists between state authority and discriminating activity. In *Burton v. Wilmington Parking Authority* (365 U.S. 715: 1961), the Court found that the state had become a party to discrimination by a restaurant that leased space in a municipal parking facility. The state had not required equal access to all patrons. Granting a liquor license to a racially exclusive private club, however, was held not to alter the club's private character in *Moose Lodge #107 v. Irvis* (407 U.S. 163: 1972). Congress was also able to bypass the state action requirement by regulating access to public accommodations through the commerce clause in the Civil Rights Act of 1964. The Court upheld the public accommodations title of the statute, provisions of which looked very much like those of the Civil Rights Act of 1875. In *United States v. Guest* (383 U.S. 745: 1966), the Court upheld a federal indictment of private individuals for the violation of a murder victim's civil rights. While the Court found state action present, six members of the Court said Congress has the power to reach wholly private acts that violate Fourteenth Amendment protections. The Burger Court has yet to take the indicated final step and abandon the state action requirement altogether.

Federal Regulation of Private Employment Discrimination

***McDonald v. Santa Fe Trail Transportation Company*, 427 U.S. 273, 96 S.Ct. 2574, 49 L.Ed. 2d 493 (1976)** Held that the job discrimination provisions of the 1964 Civil Rights Act forbid all racial discrimination including that imposed on white persons. *McDonald v. Santa Fe Transportation Company* involved the discharge of two white employees (L. W. McDonald and a Raymond Laird) from their jobs for "misappropriating private property from their employer." A black employee was similarly charged with participating in the crime, but he was not dismissed. After unsuccessfully seeking relief from the Equal Employment Opportunity Commission (EEOC), McDonald and Laird brought suit against their employer as well as their union in a U.S. district court, claiming violation of Title VII of the Civil Rights Act of 1964. This statute (42 USCS Section 2000e) prohibits discriminatory employment practices. 42 USCS Section 1981 provides that "all persons" shall have the same right to make and enforce contracts "as is enjoyed by white citizens." The suit was dismissed because no claim was made upon which Title VII relief could be granted. The district court also ruled that Section 1981 did not apply to racial discrimination against whites. The court of appeals affirmed this judgment. The Supreme Court, however, reversed. A unanimous Court held the Title VII claim applicable to whites upon the same standards as nonwhites. By a 7–2 margin, the Court also ruled that Section 1981 afforded protection to white persons as well as nonwhites in private employment.

The opinion of the Court was delivered by Justice Marshall. He began with consideration of Title VII. The law prohibits discharge of "any individual" on the basis of race. Both prior court decisions and Equal Employment Opportunity Commission interpretations concur that Title VII proscribes racial discrimination in private employment "against whites on the same terms as racial discrimination against nonwhites." He then turned to Santa Fe's contention that the dismissal of the employees was based on their criminal conduct. While Title VII cannot compel an employer to absolve and rehire a person who has engaged in unlawful conduct, the inquiry for reviewing courts "must not end there." Although it cannot compel rehiring, neither does Title VII permit the employer to use previous conduct "as the pretext for the sort of discrimination" prohibited by the Civil Rights Act. The company is free to determine that participation in cargo theft "renders a person unqualified for employment," but this criterion must be applied "alike to members of all races," and Title VII is violated if it is not. Misconduct may be a legitimate basis for discharge, but it is "hardly one for racial discrimination." And for the same reasons, the Court found the union had joined Santa Fe's discrimination and "shirked its duty" to "properly . . . represent" McDonald and Laird. Marshall then addressed the question of whether 42 USCS Section 1981 affords a remedy against discrimination in private employment. Santa Fe contended that the section was limited to protection of only nonwhite citizens. Marshall allowed that a "mechanical reading" of the section "would seem to lend support to Santa Fe's contention, but he said that previous decisions have characterized the language "simply as emphasizing the racial character of the rights being protected." In addition, Marshall cited "cumulative evidence" of legislative history that shows the original congressional intent in 1866 was to apply the law to all races. While the language has been "streamlined" in reenactment and codification, Marshall saw nothing that indicated change in that intent. Justices White and Rehnquist did not feel Section 1981 was applicable in this case. *See also* FEDERALISM, p. 29; THIRTEENTH AMENDMENT, p. 660.

Significance   The Court held in *McDonald v. Santa Fe Transportation Company* (427 U.S. 273: 1976) that the job discrimination provisions of Title VII of the Civil Rights Act of 1964 apply to whites as well as nonwhites. As seen in the *Civil Rights Cases* (109 U.S. 3: 1883), the Court was reluctant to permit the exercise of federal power to address discrimination except where "state action" existed. The reach of federal power based on the Thirteenth and Fourteenth Amendments incrementally increased as time passed, but discriminatory conduct by private parties remained generally insulated. Since most employers are private, the equal protection clause was relatively ineffective in combating job discrimination. Indeed, such recent cases as *Washington v. Davis* (426 U.S. 229: 1976) require demonstration of discriminatory intent in order to establish a constitutional violation. In 1964, the Congress enacted the Civil Rights Act. Title VII prohibited employment discrimination. As distinct from constitutional violations, statutory violations did not require a showing of discriminatory motive. Through the act, the federal government became effectively involved in responding to claims of job discrimination. The impact of Title VII became evident in *Griggs v. Duke Power Company* (401 U.S. 424: 1971), where the Court set aside discriminatory job qualification requirements under the act. *McDonald* reflected even broader federal power in that it upheld not only use of Title VII to prohibit the discriminatory discharge of the two nonblack employees by a private employer, but the Court also ruled that provisions of an 1866 statute enacted under the Thirteenth Amendment afforded the two employees protection as well.

Treaties and State Power

Missouri v. Holland, **252 U.S. 416, 40 S.Ct. 382, 64 L.Ed. 641 (1920)** ~ Held that federal law passed pursuant to a treaty may regulate subjects otherwise reserved to the states. *Missouri v. Holland* involved a treaty between the United States and Great Britain (for Canada) designed to protect migratory birds. The treaty provided that both the United States and Canada would enact legislation prohibiting the "killing, capturing or selling" of birds except in accordance with regulations set forth by the federal government. The state of Missouri brought suit attempting to enjoin enforcement of the federal regulations, arguing that its reserve powers under the Tenth Amendment had been invaded. In a 7–2 decision, the Supreme Court upheld implementation of the regulations promulgated pursuant to the treaty.

The Court's opinion was delivered by Justice Holmes. The question in this case was whether the treaty and statute were "void as an interference with the rights reserved to the states." The answer required, in Holmes's view, more than a reference to the Tenth Amendment. Article II, Section 2 expressly delegates the treaty power, and under provisions of Article VI, treaties made under the authority of the United States are the "supreme law of the land." If a treaty is valid, there then follows the legitimate exercise of the necessary and proper clause from Article I, Section 8. Key to resolving this issue was the nature of the treaty power. Missouri argued that a treaty cannot be valid if it "infringes the

Constitution." They saw the treaty-making power as limited. One limit, they argued, was that if an act of Congress cannot do something directly because it would derogate "powers reserved to the states," a treaty cannot accomplish the same thing. Holmes distinguished between laws and treaties. While there are qualifications to the treaty-making power, they "must be ascertained in a different way" from statutes. It is "obvious," Holmes suggested, that there may be "matters of sharpest exigency for the national well-being" that an act of Congress could not deal with, but that a "treaty followed by such an act could." It is for this reason that laws and treaties were distinguished in language found in Article VI. Federal statutes are supreme law of the land "only when made in pursuance of the Constitution," while treaties are declared supreme when "made under authority of the United States."

Holmes then offered an observation that recognized the concept of inherent power. "It is not lightly to be assumed that, in matters requiring national action, 'a power which must belong to and somewhere reside in any civilized government' is not to be found." In this case, the matter requiring national attention could be reached by the treaty power. The only question was whether this was precluded "by some invisible radiation from the general terms of the 10th Amendment." In reaching a judgment, Holmes said "we must consider what this country has become in deciding what that amendment has reserved." While the state may regulate the killing and sale of migratory birds, "it does not follow that its authority is exclusive to paramount powers." To claim state title to such birds is to "lean on a slender reed." These migratory birds are "not in the possession of anyone." Furthermore, the birds are only present in a given state for a brief time; they certainly have no permanent habitat in any state. Rather, what is involved here is a matter of "national interest of very nearly the first magnitude." This interest can be protected only by "national action in concert with that of another power." Except for the treaty and the statute enacted pursuant to it, "there might soon be no birds for any power to deal with." Accordingly, the federal government had authority to reach this matter through a treaty, and Congress could adopt regulations in furtherance of the treaty. Justices Pitney and Van Devanter were of the view that the Tenth Amendment prohibited such action. *See also* FEDERALISM, p. 29; SUPREMACY CLAUSE, p. 227.

Significance   The Court held in *Missouri v. Holland* (252 U.S. 416: 1920) that, while a treaty is subject to "prohibitory" limitations found in the Constitution, the treaty and any statute enacted pursuant to it will prevail over the reserve clause of the Tenth Amendment. Prior to any treaty, Congress had unsuccessfully attempted to regulate the hunting of migratory birds through the interstate commerce power. The effort was voided on the ground that this was a subject matter left to the states to govern. The treaty approach offered a means by which the state sovereignty limitation precluding a commerce clause statute could be bypassed. Indeed, *Missouri v. Holland* gives the Congress a power in the presence of a treaty that it did not have without the treaty. And in this instance, through the treaty power, Congress was able to reach a domestic policy area previously seen as reserved to the states. Holmes, however, saw this as possible in the presence of a recognizable "national interest" that demanded national action. Another reason that the claim of usurpation of state power was subordinated here flows from the distinction between domestic and foreign policy making. The federal role in the latter is comprehensive, and states have never been seen as possessing any role in the conduct of foreign relations. Moving the statutory basis for the regulation of birds from the commerce clause to a properly concluded treaty, an instrument of foreign policy, had to reverse the outcome.

Title to Submerged Tidelands

United States v. California, 332 U.S. 19, 67 S.Ct. 1658, 91 L.Ed. 1889 (1947)   Held that states do not possess ownership rights to coastal waters and the marginal lands under them. The issue in *United States v. California* was whether states held title to land beneath the ocean within the "three-mile limit." The issue arose because oil was discovered off the California coast that made this land invaluable. Presuming it had title to the land, California leased oil drilling rights to various private oil companies. The federal government asserted that it possessed "paramount rights" over this land and sought to enjoin the states from interference. In a 6–2 decision (Justice Jackson not participating), the Court ruled in favor of the United States.

The opinion of the Court was delivered by Justice Black. The "crucial question," he said, was not "merely who owns the bare legal title to the lands under the marginal sea." Rather, the federal government had asserted rights "transcending those of a mere property owner." These rights were asserted in "two capacities." One capacity is the "right and responsibility" to do what is necessary to protect the nation from "dangers to the security and tranquility of its people incident to the fact that the United States is located immediately adjacent to the ocean." The United States also appeared in its capacity as a "member of the family of nations." In that capacity, the federal government is responsible for conducting "relations with other nations." To fulfill its obligations, the federal government must have power, "unencumbered by state commitments," to determine what (if any) agreements will exist regarding "control and use of the marginal sea and the land under it." California countered by claiming it owned all resources under the three-mile limit "incident to those elements of sovereignty which it exercises in that water area." California also claimed title by virtue of the "equal footing" doctrine. The original thirteen states had common law title to such submerged lands at the time the Union was established. California was admitted to that Union "on an equal footing" with all other states. The Court rejected these contentions. Black said that, at the time of independence, there was "no settled international custom or understanding . . . that each nation owned a three-mile belt along its borders." When this nation was formed, the "idea of a three-mile belt over which a littoral nation could exercise rights of ownership was but a nebulous suggestion." Neither did anything in English charters show a "purpose to set apart a three-mile ocean belt for colonial or state ownership." Black noted that soon after independence "our statesmen became interested in establishing national dominion" over these lands to "protect our neutrality." It was because of these efforts that the concept of a three-mile limit took more definite shape. That the "political agencies" of this country both "claim and exercise broad dominion and control" over the three-mile marginal belt is "now a settled fact." This assertion of national dominion over the three-mile belt is "binding upon this Court." The three-mile rule is but a "recognition of the necessity that a government next to the sea must be able to protect itself from dangers incident to its location." The ocean, including the belt, are of "vital consequence" to the nation in its desire to "engage in commerce" and "live in peace." Peace and world commerce are the "paramount responsibilities of the nation." Accordingly, the federal government has "paramount rights in and power over" this area. Justices Reed and Frankfurter dissented, saying that the states retained sovereign control over the three-mile marginal lands. *See also* ADMISSION OF NEW STATES, p. 575; FEDERALISM, p. 29.

Significance   The Court held that states have no claim to title of marginal offshore lands in *United States v. California* (332 U.S. 19: 1947). In doing so, the Court distinguished this case from *Pollard v. Hagan* (3 Howard 212: 1845), where the equal footing doctrine was used to preclude federal claims to submerged lands under navigable waters within a state. The Court held that since other states had title to these lands at the time the Union began, a state admitted later must be accorded equivalent jurisdiction over territory within it. This argument was conversely applied in *United States v. Texas* (339 U.S. 707: 1950). Prior to admission, Texas had been an independent entity and could make a more compelling case for title to offshore lands. The

Court held, however, that the equal footing doctrine precluded "special limitation" of the paramount powers of the United States. Thus, when Texas joined the Union, it relinquished some sovereignty, including title to submerged offshore land. The matter of title to these offshore lands became a major political issue in the 1952 political campaigns. The Republican Congress enacted the Submerged Lands Act of 1953, which ceded ownership of undersea lands to the states out to the three-mile limit or to other "historic" boundaries that might apply to a particular state. Congressional resolution of the "tideland oil" matter in this way was upheld by the Court in *Alabama v. Texas* (347 U.S. 272: 1954).

Election Regulations

Allen v. Board of Elections, **393 U.S. 544, 89 S.Ct. 000, 22 L.Ed. 2d 1 (1969)** Upheld provisions of the Voting Rights Act of 1965 as they pertained to state election law changes. The decision actually involved three cases out of Mississippi (*Fairly v. Patterson, Bunton v. Patterson,* and *Whitley v. Williams*) and one from Virginia (*Allen*). *Allen v. State Board of Elections* involved changes in the procedure for casting write-in votes. Suits contending that the changes violated the Voting Rights Act and the equal protection clause were dismissed by a three-judge district court. The three Mississippi cases stemmed from adoption of three amendments to state law that affected local elections. The new laws: (1) changed voting for county supervisors from districts to at-large; (2) changed the formerly elective county superintendent of education to an appointive office in certain counties; and (3) made it more difficult for independent candidates to gain access to a general election ballot. A three-judge district court held that Section 5 of the Voting Rights Act requiring federal approval of these changes did not apply to these amendments. The Supreme Court reviewed these decisions and, with only Justice Black dissenting, reversed the lower courts and ruled the Voting Rights Act governed both sets of state changes.

The opinion of the Court was delivered by Chief Justice Warren. The critical issue in these cases was whether approval procedures contained in Section 5 of the statute were permissible. Section 5 required that all changes in state voting qualifications, prerequisites for voting, standards, practices, or procedures be approved by the attorney general of the United States. The states argued that the section did not cover the practices and procedures involved in their statutes, but rather was confined only to registration procedures. The Court said that it "must reject the narrow construction" proposed by the states. The act was aimed at the "subtle as well as the obvious state regulations which have the effect of denying citizens their right to vote because of their race." The act, said Warren, gives a "broad interpretation to the right to vote," and it recognized that voting includes "all action necessary to make a vote effective." A review of the legislative history reflected congressional intent to "reach any state enactment which altered the election law of a covered state in even a minor way." Given this perspective, Warren turned to the specific practices under challenge. The right to vote "can be affected by a dilution of voting power." The change to an at-large election of county supervisors was seen as nullifying the ability of some voters to elect a candidate of their choice. Changing an important office from elective to appointive sufficiently affects the power of a citizen's vote and cannot be accomplished without review. Similarly, making it more difficult for independent candidates to access a general election ballot "might undermine the effectiveness of voters who wish to elect independent candidates," and thus fall under scrutiny of Section 5. Finally, the Court did not find the change in write-in procedure necessarily discriminating, but a sufficient enough change in process to require Section 5 review.

At this point, the eight-justice majority split around the issue of whether the decision would be prospective only or require new elections in these states. A five-justice majority ruled that new elections need not take place. Justices Harlan, Marshall, and Douglas dissented on this point. Justice Black dissented from the Court's application of Section 5. In his view, the required federal review of all statutory changes was an unconstitutional interference in state affairs. He likened it to the "old Reconstruction days" when the military controlled the South and states "were compelled to make reports to military commanders of what they did." See also FEDERALISM, p. 29; FIFTEENTH AMENDMENT, p. 606; OREGON V. MITCHELL (400 U.S. 112: 1970), p. 199, 269.

Significance   The Court held that the Congress could require federal approval of state election law changes in *Allen v. State Board of Elections* (393 U.S. 544: 1969). The review requirements upheld in *Allen* were representative of a number of changes brought by the Voting Rights Act of 1965. The act substantially impinged on what had been an area of state control. The Voting Rights Act of 1965, passed based on power granted by Section 2 of the Fifteenth Amendment, sought to eliminate voter qualification based on race. The act specifically aimed at such devices as the literacy test, which had long been used to perpetuate voting discrimination. The act was operative in any political subdivision where less than half of the persons of voting age voted in the 1964 presidential election. The act was upheld by the Court in *South Carolina v. Katzenbach* (383 U.S. 301: 1966). After what the Court characterized as a century of "systematic resistance" to the proscription of the Fifteenth Amendment, Congress was acknowledged as possessing broad authority to prohibit discriminatory state voting practices. The following statement from the Court's opinion in *Katzenbach* is representative of this concept of broad federal power: "As against the reserved powers of the States, Congress may use any rational means to effectuate the constitutional prohibition of racial discrimination in voting." The relationship of federal power over voting discrimination was clearly established. One of the other devices used to reduce minority participation in elections was the poll tax. While the tax itself was never substantial, those who wished to begin to vote often had to pay accumulated unpaid taxes before becoming eligible to participate. The Twenty-fourth Amendment (ratified in 1964) outlawed the poll tax for federal elections. In *Harper v. Virginia State Board of Elections* (383 U.S. 663: 1966), the Court eliminated the poll tax as a requirement for state elections as well.

Eighteen-Year-Old Vote

Oregon v. Mitchell, **400 U.S. 112, 91 S.Ct. 260, 27 L.Ed. 2d 272 (1970)** Upheld those sections of the Voting Rights Act of 1970 lowering the minimum voting age for federal elections to 18, but held that lowering the voting age for state and local elections could not be done by statute. In addition to the voting age question, *Oregon v. Mitchell* also upheld suspension of the literacy test as a qualifying condition for either federal or state elections and abolished residency requirements for presidential and vice-presidential elections. The cases challenging these changes came to the Supreme Court on original jurisdiction, as the United States sought to enjoin certain states from noncompliance with the statute. Other suits were brought by certain states seeking injunction against enforcement. The several components of the law split the Court differently. A unanimous Court upheld suspension of the literacy test, and only Justice Harlan disagreed on the matter of the residency requirements. A five-judge majority approved the lowering of the minimum voting age for federal elections, but a different five-justice majority refused to extend that change to state and local elections.

The opinion of the Court was delivered by Justice Black, the only member of the Court on the prevailing side of each of the several questions. The major issue for each of these component questions was the nature of federal authority over elections. Black found that Article I, Sections 2 and 4 provided Congress with power sufficient to change the voting age for federal elections. Congress possesses power to set qualifications for federal elections. This power includes geographic qualification, which involves congressional district boundaries, and is a power "vastly more significant" than permitting 18-year-olds to vote in federal elections. Black said that "it cannot be seriously contended" that Congress "has less power" over the conduct of presidential elections than it has over congressional elections. But the power to alter the voting age extends no further. The Constitution was intended to "preserve to the states the power that even the Colonies had to establish and maintain their own separate and independent governments." He went on, there is "no function more essential" to this end than the determination of voter qualifications. While states must operate within express limitations contained in the Fourteenth, Fifteenth, Nineteenth, and Twenty-fourth Amendments, those provisions cannot be used to "blot out all state power leaving the 50 states little more than impotent figureheads." In upholding the ban on literacy tests, Black noted the "long history of discriminatory use of literacy tests to disfranchise voters on account of their race." Given such a history, Black said it was appropriate for Congress to enact a national ban on such tests as a means of enforcing the Civil War amendments. Finally, the residency regulations for federal elections were permissible on the same grounds as the lowering of the voting age for federal elections.

Justices Harlan, Stewart, Blackmun, and Chief Justice Burger did not think Congress was empowered to establish voter qualifications, only the manner in which federal elections were conducted, and they constituted the dissent on the 18-year age minimum for federal elections. On the other side of the issue, Justices Douglas, Brennan, Marshall, and White saw the voting age question in equal protection terms and would have allowed Congress to address the voting age for all elections by statute. Harlan was the sole dissenter on the residency requirement component. He saw voting standards as a state matter and beyond the reach of Congress even for federal elections. He saw neither the equal protection or right to travel arguments as convincing. *See also* ALLEN V. STATE BOARD OF ELECTIONS (393 U.S. 544: 1969), p. 267; FEDERALISM, p. 29.

Significance   The Court in *Oregon v. Mitchell* (400 U.S. 112: 1970) upheld provisions of the Voting Rights Act as extended in 1970. This enactment lowered the voting age to 18 for federal elections, restricted use of residency requirements, and banned literacy tests as a condition for voting. The broad federal authority possessed by Congress to address voting discrimination, as acknowledged in *South Carolina v. Katzenbach* (383 U.S. 301: 1966), was reaffirmed in *Oregon v. Mitchell*. The limited restriction on literacy tests contained in the Voting Rights Act of 1965 was extended to the entire nation in the 1970 legislation. In addition, the 1970 act limited the use of residency requirements for presidential elections. Soon thereafter, in *Dunn v. Blumstein* (405 U.S. 330: 1972), the Court held that only short-term registration periods would be permitted. The one area of qualification where the Court refused to limit state discretion was the issue of voter age, at least as it relates to state and local elections. *Oregon v. Mitchell* thus created the prospect of conducting the 1972 elections with two sets of electors. One, age 18 and above, which could vote for candidates for federal offices, and another, age 21 and above, which could participate in state and local elections as well. Congress, however, immediately adopted the Twenty-sixth Amendment, which dropped the minimum voting age to 18 for all elections. With ratification of the amendment the following year, this aspect of the *Oregon v. Mitchell* holding was negated.

Federal Intervention in State Prosecution

***Younger v. Harris*, 401 U.S. 37, 91 S.Ct. 746, 27 L.Ed. 2d 669 (1971)** Held that federal court intervention in state criminal prosecutions should occur only under the most extraordinary circumstances. *Younger v. Harris* involved a state prosecution for violation of a state syndicalism act that prohibited "advocating, teaching or aiding and abetting" criminal conduct aimed at "affecting any political change." The case upholding the California law (*Whitney v. California*, 274 U.S. 357: 1927) had been overruled by the Court in *Brandenburg v. Ohio* (395 U.S. 444: 1969). Harris sought injunction from a federal court to keep Younger, the Los Angeles County prosecutor, from prosecuting him under provisions of the now suspect state law. A three-judge U.S. district court held the syndicalism act to be unconstitutional and enjoined the prosecution. Over the single dissent of Justice Douglas, the Supreme Court reversed the lower court and lifted the restriction on the prosecution of Harris.

The opinion of the Court was delivered by Justice Black. He indicated at the beginning that a federal lawsuit to stop a state prosecution "is a serious matter." History shows few exceptions to this policy because of a desire to "permit state courts to try state cases free from interference by federal courts." Black then looked at the sources of this policy. One source was the basic doctrine of equity jurisdiction—that courts of equity "should not act," especially to restrain a prosecution when the moving party "has an adequate remedy at law" and will not "suffer irreparable injury" without relief. This doctrine was designed to protect the role of the jury from "erosion" and "avoid duplication" of legal proceedings and legal sanctions. The restraint of courts of equity is reinforced by the "notion of comity." This concept is a "proper respect for state functions." It recognizes that the nation is made up of a "Union of separate state governments" and is based on the belief that the national government "will fare best" if the states and their institutions are "left free to perform their separate functions in their separate ways." Black referred to this as "Our Federalism." One familiar with the debates surrounding establishment of the Constitution is "bound to respect those who remain loyal to the ideals and dreams of 'Our Federalism'." The concept, Black suggested, is not "blind deference" to states' rights. What is represented by the concept is a "system in which there is sensitivity to the legitimate interests of both state and national governments." Under this system, the federal government, "anxious though it may be to vindicate and protect federal rights," always attempts to do so in ways that "will not unduly interfere with the legitimate activities of the States."

Black then returned to the specifics of this case. A criminal prosecution under a statute regulating expression "usually involves imponderables and contingencies" that themselves "may inhibit" the full exercise of First Amendment rights. But "this sort of 'chilling effect' . . . should not itself justify federal intervention." Black concluded by warning that for courts to examine state statutes "on their face" and enjoin all action to enforce the statute until a state could obtain court approval for a modified version is "fundamentally at odds with the function of the federal courts in our constitutional plan." While courts possess the power of judicial review, this does not amount to "an unlimited power" to "survey the statute books and pass judgments on laws before the courts are called upon to enforce them."

Justice Douglas dissented, saying federal intervention should not be limited to situations of "bad faith" by state officials or the threat of "multiple prosecutions." While nonintervention is clearly to be the general rule, Douglas thought the federal courts should be able to counteract statutes that are "a blunderbuss by themselves" or where statutes are used aggregately that have an "overbroad sweep." *See also* ABSTENTION, p. 575; FEDERALISM, p. 29.

Significance   The Court used considerations of federalism in *Younger v. Harris* (401 U.S. 37: 1971) to restrain federal judicial intervention in a state criminal proceeding. As a matter of general rule, neither federal or state courts enjoin judicial proceedings of the other level. There is also an abstention doctrine that allows a federal court to withhold exercise of its jurisdiction on a federal constitutional issue until a state court has rendered a judgment on any state law which may have a bearing on the federal matter. The doctrine is designed to reduce conflict between federal and state courts. The Warren Court, however, redefined the relationship of federal and state courts in the case of *Dombrowski v. Pfister* (380 U.S. 479: 1965). Faced with situations where civil rights organizations were threatened with criminal prosecution for violation of syndicalism statutes, the Court held that it was reasonable for federal courts to intervene. Since the language of most of these laws was so imprecise, the Court saw threatened enforcement as having a "chilling effect" on protected rights. *Dombrowski* permitted intervention against enforcement of state statutes until a state court could make a declaratory judgment. *Younger* severely qualified the *Dombrowski* decision and did so on federalism grounds. *Younger* left very few circumstances under which federal intervention might occur.

Federal Age Discrimination Prohibition Applied to State Governments

Equal Employment Opportunity Commission v. Wyoming, **460 U.S. 226, 103 S.Ct. 1054, 75 L.Ed. 2d 18 (1983)**   Held that the Age Discrimination in Employment Act (ADEA) applies to employees of state and local governments. An employee of the Wyoming Fish and Game Department was involuntarily dismissed from employment based on a state statute that conditions employment past the age of 55 on department approval. The employee filed a complaint with the Equal Employment Opportunity Commission (EEOC) claiming that Wyoming had violated the Age Discrimination in Employment Act. The EEOC subsequently filed suit against Wyoming in district court. The suit was dismissed on the ground that the act violated the Tenth Amendment and impermissibly interfered with Wyoming's employment relationship with its own employees. On appeal, the U.S. Supreme Court reversed in a 5–4 decision.

The opinion of the Court was delivered by Justice Brennan. The Court acknowledged that imposition of federal regulations on state governments might, "if left unchecked, allow the National Government to devour the essentials of state sovereignty." To protect against such an occurrence, the Court had drawn from the Tenth Amendment an "affirmative limitation" on the exercise of commerce power. The immunity derived from the Tenth Amendment was "functional" and its purpose was "not to create a sacred province of state autonomy." Rather, it was developed to "ensure that the unique benefits" of a federal system where states enjoy a "separate and independent existence" would not be lost through "undue federal interference in certain core state functions."

Three requirements must be shown to successfully claim that exercise of the commerce power has impermissibly interfered with state functions. First, it must be demonstrated that the challenged statute "regulates the 'States as States.'" Second, the federal law must address matters that are "indisputably attributes of state sovereignty." And third, it must be "apparent" that the states' compliance with the federal regulation would "directly impair" their ability to "structure integral operations in areas of traditional governmental functions." The Court found the first requirement "plainly met" in this instance. The second requirement, that the statute addressed an "undoubted attribute of state sovereignty," posed "significantly more difficulties." But the Court refrained from resolving this issue. It found that "even if" the Wyoming policy of mandatory retirement for game wardens did involve the exercise of state sovereignty, the act did not "directly impair" Wyoming's ability to "structure integral operations in areas of traditional governmental function."

Wyoming argued that the mandatory retirement policy assured the physical preparedness of game wardens to perform their duties. The Court held, however, that the federal law did not preclude Wyoming from assessing the fitness of its wardens and dismissing those it found unfit. The Act only required that Wyoming "achieve its goals in a more individualized and careful manner." In addition, the Court said that Wyoming remains free under the ADEA to "continue to do precisely what they are doing now," if they can demonstrate that age is a "bona fide occupational qualification for the job of game warden."

Chief Justice Burger and Justices Powell, O'Connor, and Rehnquist dissented. Burger argued that no provision of the Constitution transferred from the states to the federal government the "essentially local function of establishing standards for choosing state employees." He said that the framers did not give Congress such power because Congress lacks the "means to analyze the factors that bear on this decision." Since local conditions "generally determine" how a job should be performed and who should perform it, "the authority and responsibility for making employment decisions must be in the hands of local governments," subject only to those restrictions "unmistakably contemplated by the Fourteenth Amendment." *See also* COMMERCE CLAUSE, p. 291; FEDERALISM, p. 29; *GARCIA V. SAN ANTONIO METROPOLITAN TRANSIT AUTHORITY* (469 U.S. 528: 1985), p. 275; TENTH AMENDMENT, p. 229.

Significance   The Court ruled that Congress has the power to prohibit age discrimination against state employees in *Equal Employment Opportunity Commission v. Wyoming* (75 L.Ed. 2d 18: 1983). Wyoming had argued that the Tenth Amendment precluded federal interference with state employment practices. Although the Tenth Amendment had provided the states with virtually no immunity from federal commerce regulation since the 1930s, the Court had upheld some state immunity in *National League of Cities v. Usery* (426 U.S. 833: 1976). In the *National League of Cities* decision, the Court ruled that when the state is engaged in a "traditional" or "integral" function such as managing its own employees, it is immune from federal regulations. Wyoming and other states had sought to build upon this decision and secure immunity from other than commerce clause–based regulations such as the age discrimination statute. As the Court pointed out in *EEOC v. Wyoming*, the "most tangible consequential effect" of federal regulations on the states as identified in *National League of Cities* was financial. The Court did not see the age discrimination act as having "direct or obvious negative effect on state finances." In *Hodel v. Virginia Surface Mining and Reclamation Association* (452 U.S. 264: 1981), the Court refused to extend *Usery* to federal regulations on strip mining on private property. The Court gave the *Usery* decision narrow construction, saying its application required showing each of three elements: that a federal statute regulated "States as States"; that it covered matters that were clearly "attributes of state sovereignty"; and that compliance by states would directly impair their capacity to manage "integral operations" in matters of "traditional function." The direct rejection of *Usery* came in *Garcia v. San Antonio Metropolitan Transit Authority* (469 U.S. 528: 1985), where the Court held that the minimum wage and overtime provisions of the Fair Labor Standards Act were to apply to employees of state and local governments. Both *Usery* and *Garcia* were 5–4 decisions, as was this case, and Justice Rehnquist's statement in *Garcia* that the *Usery* rationale would again "command" support of a majority of the Court may very well prove true.

Federal Wage Regulations Applied to Local Governments

Garcia v. San Antonio Metropolitan Transit Authority, **469 U.S. 528, 105 S.Ct. 1005, 83 L.Ed. 2d 1016 (1985)**   Held that the provisions of the Fair Labor Standards Act could be applied to employees of a public mass transit authority. *Garcia v. San Antonio Metropolitan Transit Authority* (SAMTA) overruled *National League of Cities v. Usery* (426 U.S. 833: 1976), a decision that had held that exercise of the federal commerce power was limited by the Tenth Amendment. SAMTA had sought a declaratory judgment from a district court that its operations were immune from application of the minimum wage and overtime requirements of the Fair Labor Standards Act (FLSA). The district court found the city-owned mass transit system to be a "traditional" governmental function and exempted SAMTA from the FLSA provisions. On appeal, the Supreme Court reversed in a 5–4 decision.

The opinion of the Court was delivered by Justice Blackmun. He reviewed the conditions that must be present before state immunity from federal regulation can occur as set forth in *Usery*. One condition is that state compliance with the federal obligation must "directly impact" the state's ability to "structure integral operations" in areas of "traditional governmental functions." The task, however, of identifying which particular state functions are immune "remains difficult." After reviewing immunity cases that attempted to distinguish between "governmental" and "proprietary" functions, the Court concluded that no reasonable standard could be developed. Furthermore, the Court indicated that any standard that revolves around the "traditional" or "integral" nature of governmental functions "inevitably invites" an unelected federal judiciary to make decisions about "which state policies it favors and which ones it dislikes." *Usery,* based on such a judgment, was thus rejected as "unsound in principle" and "unworkable in practice."

Blackmun looked to the dynamics of the political process to resolve the problem. The framers "chose to rely" on a federal system in which restraints on federal power over states "inhered principally in the workings of the National Government itself" rather than in "discrete limitations on the objects of federal authority." *Usery* imposed a substantive limitation of congressional commerce power. State interests, the Court said, "are more properly protected by procedural safeguards inherent in the structure of the federal system" rather than by "judicially created" limitations on federal power. The "fundamental" constitutional limitation imposed on the commerce power to protect the states is "one of process rather than one of result." Any substantive restraint on the exercise of the commerce power must "find its justification" in the "procedural nature of this basic limitation." Such restraint must be "tailored to compensate for possible failings" in the national political processes rather than "dictate a sacred province of state autonomy." The "principal and basic limit" on the federal commerce power is that "inherent in all congressional action—the built-in restraints that our system provides through state participation in federal governmental action." In applying this thinking to the San Antonio case, the Court found nothing in the FLSA overtime and minimum wage provisions to be "destructive" of state sovereignty or violative of any constitutional provision."

Chief Justice Burger and Justices Powell, Rehnquist, and O'Connor dissented. Powell suggested that the decision "substantially alters the federal system embodied in the Constitution." He also said that the majority position had effectively reduced the Tenth Amendment to "meaningless rhetoric" where the commerce power is involved. Justices Rehnquist and O'Connor vigorously defended the *Usery* approach and suggested that the reasoning in that case would "again command the support of a majority of the Court." *See also* COMMERCE CLAUSE, p. 291;

EQUAL EMPLOYMENT OPPORTUNITY COMMISSION V. WYOMING (460 U.S. 226: 1983), p. 273; FEDERALISM, p. 29.

Significance   The Court held in *Garcia v. San Antonio Metropolitan Transit Authority* (469 U.S. 528: 1985) that state and local governments were subject to otherwise legitimate commerce clause–based federal regulations. Prior to 1937, the Tenth Amendment effectively protected the states from the exercise of federal power, especially the commerce power. The Court, however, changed its view of the Tenth Amendment in 1937, and the amendment was relegated to secondary status. Many pieces of federal legislation, including the Fair Labor Standards Act (FLSA), were enacted and applied to states. Against a state challenge, the Court upheld application of FLSA requirements for employees of state hospitals and schools in *Maryland v. Wirtz* (392 U.S. 183: 1968). But in the *National League of Cities v. Usery* (426 U.S. 833: 1976), the Court said that the Tenth Amendment did provide the states with some immunity from federal "interference" with "traditional" functions such as the employee relationship. *Garcia* reversed *Usery,* but *Usery* had muted impact almost from the time it was decided. In *Hodel v. Virginia Surface Mining and Reclamation Association* (452 U.S. 264: 1981), the Court rejected the *Usery* reasoning in upholding federal regulations against claims that they governed private land, a function traditionally recognized as belonging to the states. The Court, however, deferred to the argument, emphasizing the effects of strip mining on interstate commerce. A more direct rejection of *Usery* came in *Equal Employment Opportunity Commission v. Wyoming* (460 U.S. 226: 1983). In this case, the Court held that federal age discrimination prohibitions could be extended to employees of state and local governments. Less than two years later, the 5–4 *Usery* decision was overturned by *Garcia,* itself a 5–4 decision. This issue is clearly unsettled.

Privileges and Immunities

Baldwin v. Montana Fish and Game Commission, 435 U.S. 371, 98 S.Ct. 1852, 56 L.Ed. 2d 354 (1978)   Upheld a state licensing system that imposed substantially higher fees on nonresidents. *Baldwin v. Montana Fish and Game Commission* involved a privileges and immunities clause challenge to a licensure system that severely disadvantaged nonresidents. In order to hunt elk, a nonresident had to purchase a combination hunting and fishing license. The fee for this combination license was in excess of $200. A Montana resident could purchase an elk-hunting license for $9. Baldwin, a Montana resident in the business of guiding hunting expeditions, and several nonresidents sought a declaratory judgment against the disparate license fee schedule as well as recovery of previously paid fees. A three-judge district court found against them, and they appealed to the Supreme Court. In a 6–3 decision, the lower court was affirmed and the privileges and immunities clause contentions rejected.

The opinion of the Court was delivered by Justice Blackmun. Before commencing his discussion, Blackmun noted that the privileges and immunities clause of Article IV had not been "precisely shaped" through the "process and wear of constant litigation and judicial interpretation." Indeed, the clause was "overshadowed" by similar language appearing in the Fourteenth Amendment. Prior cases, limited as they might be, had viewed the clause as prohibiting states from imposing "unreasonable burdens on citizens of other states" as they pursued their "common callings" within the state, owning or disposing of property or accessing the state's courts. The Court acknowledged that the clause did not absolutely preclude use of state citizenship to "distinguish among persons." A state need not, for example, open its polls to a person registered in another state nor "always apply all its laws or all its services equally to anyone merely on request. Some distinctions between residents and nonresidents "merely reflect the fact that this is a Nation composed of individual states." Some distinctions, however, are prohibited because they "hinder the formation, the purpose, or the development of a single Union." Only with regard to those "privileges" and "immunities" bearing upon the "vitality of the Nation as a single entity" must a state treat resident and nonresident equally. One way a state frustrates development of the Union would be to interfere with a nonresident as he or she "sought to engage in an essential activity or exercise of a basic right." Thus, if basic or fundamental rights are involved, the privileges and immunities clause clearly limits state policies distinguishing between resident and nonresident. Blackmun then asked whether Montana's differential access to elk hunting threatened a "basic right in a way that offends the Privileges and Immunities Clause." He said "merely to ask the question seems to provide the answer." The Court viewed elk hunting as a "recreation and a sport." Elk hunting was not a means to the nonresident's livelihood, and Montana possessed an interest in caring for the elk supply within the state. Nonresident access to Montana elk "is not basic to the maintenance or well-being of the Union." While not attempting to fully catalog what activities might be protected as basic, the Court said whatever activities may be "fundamental," under the privileges and immunities clause, "elk hunting by nonresidents . . . is not one of them."

Justice Brennan, joined by Justices White and Marshall, dissented. He rejected placing privileges and immunities questions on a fundamental right basis. He saw the Montana policy as discriminatory, and the Court's fundamental right approach did not examine the justification for that discrimination. He did not see the privileges and immunities clause as "so impotent a guarantee" that the Montana hunting licensure system "remains wholly beyond the purview" of the clause. *See also* FEDERALISM, p. 29; *HICKLIN V. ORBECK* (437 U.S. 518: 1978), p. 453; PRIVILEGES AND IMMUNITIES CLAUSE, p. 647.

Significance   The Court held that the privileges and immunities clause did not preclude a differential hunting license fee for residents and nonresidents in *Baldwin v. Montana Fish and Game Commission* (435 U.S. 371: 1978). The privileges and immunities clause was intended to prohibit discriminatory treatment by a state toward citizens of another state. Exactly what this meant in the way of protection was not specifically defined in Article IV. As the Court noted in *Baldwin*, the clause was not frequently litigated prior to the adoption of the Fourteenth Amendment. The fundamental rights doctrine used in *Baldwin* was grounded in the concept of natural rights, and it defined privileges and immunities in terms of rights that "by nature" belong to citizens. Adoption of the Fourteenth Amendment forestalled further development of the clause along natural rights lines. Indeed, the clause was given very narrow interpretation following the Civil War. Aside from use of the fundamental or basic rights doctrine as in *Baldwin*, the Court has also resolved some privileges and immunities claims based on considerations of protecting the federal system itself. *Baldwin* referred extensively to *Toomer v. Witsell* (334 U.S. 385: 1948), where the Court said that the clause prohibits discriminatory conduct where there is "no substantial reason" for it. The Court said in *Baldwin* that such unequal treatment of nonresidents must be both "reasoned" and carefully "tailored." Under the "substantial reason" test, some differential conduct can clearly be justified.

Interstate Rendition

Pacileo v. Walker, **449 U.S. 86, 101 S.Ct. 308, 66 L.Ed. 2d 304 (1980)**   Held that the rendition clause did not permit a state to inquire into prison conditions in another state as a factor leading to extradition. Walker had been apprehended in California following his escape from an Arkansas prison. The governor of Arkansas requested rendition of Walker, and the governor of California issued a warrant of arrest and rendition. The warrant was served on Walker, who then challenged the issuance of the warrant within the California courts. The superior court of the county in which Walker was being detained was ordered by the California Supreme Court to determine if the prison facility in which Arkansas proposed to confine Walker was adequate under Eighth Amendment standards. Arkansas appealed to the Supreme Court, claiming that California had no authority to make such a determination. The Supreme Court agreed in an 8–1 decision.

The reasoning of the Court was expressed in a brief *per curiam* opinion. The Court said that Article IV does not give courts of the "asylum" state authority to inquire into the prison conditions of the "demanding" state. Interstate rendition was intended to be a "summary and mandatory executive proceeding." When a governor grants extradition, that is "prima facie evidence that the constitutional and statutory requirements have been met." Once extradition has been granted, a court considering *habeas corpus* release can only consider four questions: (1) whether the extradition documents are in order "on their face"; (2) whether the petitioner has actually been charged with a crime in the demanding state; (3) whether the petitioner is the person actually named; and (4) whether the petitioner is a fugitive. The reviewing court is confined to "readily verifiable" facts. "Considerations fundamental to our federal system" require that Walker's claims be the subject of a suit initiated within the demanding state. The Court felt the California Supreme Court had "ignored" this interpretation when it directed the trial court to conduct inquiry into the Arkansas penal system. To allow "plenary review" in the asylum state on those matters that can be "fully litigated" in the charging state would "defeat the plain purposes" of the "summary and mandatory procedures" authorized by Article IV. Justice Marshall dissented, feeling that the precedents relied on by the Court were not controlling in this instance. *See also* ARTICLE IV, p. 225; FEDERALISM, p. 29.

Significance   The Court held in *Pacileo v. Walker* (449 U.S. 86: 1980) that "asylum" states may not inquire into the question of prison conditions in the "demanding" state before executing rendition of a fugitive. The rendition clause of Article IV was designed to prevent a person from avoiding prosecution by flight to another state. Most state governors see rendition as an obligation. Compliance with rendition requests is virtually automatic. It is possible, however, for governors not to comply. In *Kentucky v. Dennison* (24 Howard 66: 1861), the Court held that even though return of a fugitive is an affirmative duty of a state governor, there are no constitutional provisions by which such action may be compelled. Congress has sought to avoid this possibility by passing statutes affirming this obligation to surrender fugitives. Utilizing the commerce power, Congress has made it a federal crime to flee across state lines. A person apprehended by federal officials for interstate flight will be returned to the state of origin for prosecution of the federal offense. At that time, the person will be subject to arrest by local authorities.

Full Faith and Credit Clause

Allstate Insurance Company v. Hague, **449 U.S. 302, 101 S.Ct. 633, 66 L.Ed. 2d 521 (1981)** Upheld application of the insurance laws of one state to an automobile accident case occurring in a bordering state over claims that this violated the full faith and credit provisions of Article IV. Ralph Hague, a Wisconsin resident, was killed in a highway accident in that state. Hague was employed in Minnesota and commuted there daily. The operators of the other vehicles involved in the accident, both Wisconsin residents, did not have insurance. Hague held a policy covering three automobiles owned by him. This policy covered Hague against loss incurred from uninsured motorists, but the coverage was limited to $15,000 per vehicle. Following the accident, Hague's widow moved to and became a resident of Minnesota. She was subsequently appointed a representative of her deceased husband's estate. She filed suit in a Minnesota court seeking to collect the $15,000 on each automobile—to "stack" the coverage to allow a total claim of $45,000. The insurance company resisted, arguing that Wisconsin law should apply. No such stacking was permitted under Wisconsin law. The trial court concluded that Minnesota's "choice-of-law rules" required use of the Minnesota law, which allowed stacking. The Minnesota Supreme Court affirmed. Review was sought from the U.S. Supreme Court, which also affirmed in a 5–3 decision (Justice Stewart not participating).

The judgment of the Court was announced in an opinion by Justice Brennan. He limited the question before the Court. The Court's review did not include whether the lower court made the best choice-of-law decision. Rather, the Court's "sole function" was to determine whether the Minnesota court's choice "of its own substantive law" exceeded constitutional limitations. The Court first considered whether Minnesota had sufficient contact with the parties and the incident to create a real interest such that choice of its law was "neither arbitrary nor fundamentally unfair." The Court found three such contacts to sustain choice of the Minnesota law. Hague was a member of the Minnesota workforce. Minnesota possessed a legitimate interest in protecting the safety and well-being of its commuting nonresidents. Second, Hague's widow became a Minnesota resident prior to initiating the suit. Third, Allstate was "at all times present and doing business in Minnesota." That presence created familiarity with Minnesota laws. In the Court's view, Allstate could hardly claim "surprise that the state courts might apply forum law to litigation in which the company is involved." In addition, Allstate's presence in Minnesota gave the state an interest in "regulating the company's insurance obligations" insofar as they affected a resident and a commuting nonresident. Taken together, the Court held that Minnesota had a "significant aggregation of contacts" with the parties and the occurrence that created a substantial enough interest to permit application of Minnesota law. Neither the provisions of the due process clause nor the full faith and credit clause were violated here.

A dissent was offered by Justice Powell and joined by Chief Justice Burger and Justice Rehnquist. Powell suggested that the due process and full faith and credit clauses do not permit a state to "reach out beyond the limits imposed on them by their status as coequal sovereigns in a federal system." Accordingly, the contacts between the forum state and the litigation should not be "slight and casual." The forum state must also have a "legitimate interest in the outcome" of the suit. The dissenters felt Minnesota was lacking in both such that it was "fundamentally unfair" to Allstate to apply the Minnesota law that permitted stacking. *See also* FEDERALISM, p. 29; FULL FAITH AND CREDIT CLAUSE, p. 615.

Significance   The Court held in *Allstate Insurance Company v. Hague* (449 U.S. 302: 1981) that a state's application of its own insurance law to a suit involving an automobile accident occurring in another state did not violate provisions of the full faith and credit clause. The clause generally obligates states to recognize certain kinds of official actions taken by other states. Judicial proceedings of one state must be given effect elsewhere. Recognition of judicial decisions is generally not a problem. The clause does not require states to enforce the criminal laws of other states. Neither, as the Court held in *Nevada v. Hall* (440 U.S. 410: 1979), does the clause require a state to apply another state's law "in violation of its own legitimate public policy." Giving effect to statutes of one state in another has created more troublesome full faith and credit problems. Litigation of this kind typically occurs, as it did in the *Hague* case, when a state law of one state is used to defend against application of another state's law. The practice generally followed permits state courts to assess the governmental interests of the competing statutes and proceed accordingly. Thus in *Hague*, the case hinged on the adequacy of Minnesota's "contact" with the parties and the incident to permit reasonable application of the Minnesota law. Had there been insufficient contact, the full faith and credit clause would have required utilization of the Wisconsin law.

6. The Commerce Power

OVERVIEW

One of the motivations for calling the Constitutional Convention of 1787 was commerce. Under the Articles of Confederation, the absence of effective national power over commerce was a principal defect of the governmental structure, and the framers of the new Constitution included direct language covering commerce. Article I, Section 8 contains the commerce clause, which provides that Congress shall have the power to "regulate commerce with foreign nations, and among the several States, and with the Indian Tribes." While this constitutes an affirmative grant of power to Congress, several interpretive questions necessarily follow. Among the more critical commerce issues are what the term "commerce" includes and excludes, whether the power permits Congress to regulate incidental local aspects of interstate commerce, and what role (if any) the states might retain in regulating commercial activities. The cases in this chapter have been organized chronologically to reflect the historical evolution of responses by the Court to these and other questions.

The first commerce clause decision was the landmark case, *Gibbons v. Ogden* (9 Wheaton 1: 1824). This case provided Chief Justice John Marshall with the opportunity to establish some basic principles. Commerce was not to be narrowly interpreted. Commerce is more than interstate traffic; it is all commercial "intercourse" concerning more than one state. When commercial activity is interstate in character, it is the exclusive domain of the federal government. Marshall allowed, however, that states retain authority to control activities wholly internal to the state. The question of when such state regulation could commence was addressed in *Brown v. Maryland* (12 Wheaton 419: 1827). When items become "mixed up" with the "mass of property" of the state, they can be regulated or taxed by the state, while items remaining in their "original package" are still considered "in commerce" and immune to state regulation.

The issue of shared authority over commerce between the federal and state levels continued to occupy the Court's attention under Marshall's successor, Roger B. Taney. The pre–Civil War Court was dominated by states' rightists, and it searched for ways to define a substantial role for states in the governance of commerce. The Court struck a compromise position among the several competing views in *Cooley v. Board of Port Wardens* (12 Howard 299: 1851). It adopted a doctrine of "selective exclusiveness." Matters of a "national" character requiring uniform regulation were exclusively the province of the federal government; other matters, "local" in nature and demanding of diverse local regulation, fell exclusively to the states. Under this doctrine, the Court acted as umpire of the federal-state line of exclusivity. Late in the century, the states tended to prevail in most of the Court's judgments. In *Brown v. Houston* (114 U.S. 622: 1885), the Court returned to the "original package" doctrine to uphold a state tax on property having concluded its interstate movement. Even though the taxed item remained in its original package (a coal barge), the Court said that the commerce of an interstate order had concluded, and thus it could be taxed like other items of state property.

A new dimension was added in the decision of *United States v. E. C. Knight Company* (156 U.S. 1: 1895). Whereas Congress had not frequently exercised its commerce power during the first decade under the Constitution, the Industrial Revolution created occasion for Congress to initiate several serious business regulations. In the *Knight* case, the Court ruled that a production monopoly was outside the reach of federal commerce power because production was distinct from commerce. As a result, activities associated with production yield effects that are too remote or indirect to be regulated. The distinctions between production and commerce, and the resulting indirect commerce effect governed the Court's decisions invalidating federal regulations in three significant cases: the federal child labor law was invalidated in *Hammer v. Dagenhart* (247 U.S. 251: 1918); the National Industrial Recovery Act was voided in *Schechter Poultry Corporation v. United States* (295 U.S. 495: 1935); and the law authorizing codes for regulation of the coal industry was nullified in *Carter v. Carter Coal Company* (298 U.S. 238: 1936). The effect of these decisions was to limit exercise of the federal commerce power through judicial negation of legislative initiative.

During this same period, certain federal regulatory statutes were upheld. In *Champion v. Ames* (188 U.S. 321: 1903), the Court permitted the commerce power to be used to prohibit distribution of lottery tickets through interstate commerce. This decision and several others in the years immediately following *Champion* came relatively close to recognizing a federal police power stemming from the commerce clause. Such a power would have come at the direct expense of the state police power, but the Court's orientation during the first three decades of the twentieth century was less states' rights than laissez-faire. Two other cases are illustrative of federal regulation of intrastate activities:

Houston, East and West Texas Railway Company v. United States (234 U.S. 342: 1914) and *Stafford v. Wallace* (258 U.S. 495: 1922). In the former, the Court permitted the Interstate Commerce Commission (ICC) to reach discriminatory intrastate rail rates that burdened interstate commerce. In *Stafford*, the Court allowed federal regulation of stockyards and meat-packing establishments on the ground that, while each might be considered local or intrastate, they operated within a "stream of commerce" that had not yet ended when they received livestock. Activities, even local ones, could be reached if in the "stream" because they had a direct effect on interstate commerce.

The year 1937 brought a dramatic turnaround in the Court's interpretation of the commerce clause. Buoyed by the electoral successes of himself and the New Deal Congress, Roosevelt sought to break the impasse with the Court by proposing to enlarge it. Before the proposal emerged from the Congress, the Court acquiesced in the face of the serious political pressure. The first major commerce decision supportive of the New Deal initiatives was *National Labor Relations Board v. Jones and Laughlin Steel Corporation* (301 U.S. 1: 1937), where the Court upheld the Wagner Act, a statute that protected the right of employees to organize into unions and engage in collective bargaining. Several other decisions rendered within the next decade reflect the extent to which the Court had accepted broad new federal authority under the commerce clause. In *United States v. Appalachian Electric Power Company* (311 U.S. 377: 1940), the Court said that federal regulatory power extended to streams and rivers that are not yet navigable but have the potential to become so. *United States v. Darby Lumber Company* (312 U.S. 100: 1941) upheld the Fair Labor Standards Act, a regulation of hours and wages of employees in industries whose products entered interstate commerce. As in *Jones and Laughlin*, this constituted direct regulation of production, something not allowed under the *Knight* rule. The Agricultural Adjustment Act was upheld in *Wickard v. Filburn* (317 U.S. 111: 1942). This federal act imposed production quotas on various agricultural commodities in an effort to stabilize prices through control of market supply. Finally, the Court upheld application of the Sherman Act to the insurance industry in *United States v. South-Eastern Underwriters' Association* (322 U.S. 533: 1944).

Ever since *Cooley*, the states have been able to exercise some power over commerce. The commerce clause prohibits states from imposing "barriers" to the free flow of interstate commerce. Accordingly, the Court struck down a state price regulation on imported milk in *Baldwin v. G.A.F. Seelig, Inc.* (294 U.S. 511: 1935). Similarly, the Court struck down a state law in *Edwards v. California* (314 U.S. 160: 1941) that prohibited bringing an indigent nonresident into the state. Other state initiatives have been upheld notwithstanding their relationship to interstate commerce. In *California v. Thompson* (313 U.S. 109: 1941), the Court permitted a state to regulate transportation agents including those arranging for interstate travel. There was no federal regulation on this subject, and it was an area where local aspects could likely best be regulated in diverse local ways. In *Parker v. Brown* (317 U.S. 341: 1943), the Court allowed a state-mandated marketing monopoly for agricultural commodities produced in the state. State regulation is permissible if it is compatible with national interests. Since Congress had authorized marketing methods like those utilized by the state, the consequences of the state activity were viewed as being "encouraged" by federal law. There are subjects, however, where uniformity, even in the absence of congressional action, precludes state regulation. In *Southern Pacific Railroad Company v. Arizona* (325 U.S. 761: 1945), the Court struck down a state law limiting the length of trains operating within its boundaries. The Court also struck down a state law requiring segregated seating on all buses (including those traveling interstate) in *Morgan v. Virginia* (328 U.S. 373: 1946). The Court said the cumulative effects of such practices impermissibly impaired interstate travel. The Court also struck down a local health ordinance in *Dean Milk Company v. City of Madison* (340 U.S. 349: 1951). While health regulations are generally allowed, here the Court found the measure to be discriminatory and aimed at protecting local business from out-of-state competition. The Court also suggested that the health objectives could be accomplished through alternate means.

The broadened scope of the federal commerce power can be seen in the Court's response to two legislative efforts in the 1960s. In 1964, Congress used the commerce power to prohibit racial discrimination in "public accommodations." The Court upheld use of the commerce power to reach national social needs in *Heart of Atlanta Motel v. United States* (379 U.S. 241: 1964). In sustaining the law, the Court was highly deferential to congressional judgment that racial discrimination adversely affected interstate commerce, and that the means adopted in response were reasonable. The Court also permitted the commerce power to be used to combat criminal activity. In *Perez v. United States* (402 U.S. 44: 1971), the Court sustained provisions of the Consumer Credit Protection Act aimed at loansharking practices. The Court upheld a conviction for violation of the law even though there were no interstate aspects to the defendant's actions.

Congressional authority to regulate commerce extensively had been firmly established by the time Warren Burger became chief justice in 1969. The clear pattern of decisions of the 1960s, as seen in *Heart of Atlanta Motel* and *Perez*, was to defer to congressional judgment as to factors or activities sufficiently affecting interstate commerce to require federal legislative response. The Burger Court has not departed from this pattern. In *Goldfarb v. Virginia State Bar Association* (421 U.S. 773: 1975), the Court held that attorney fee schedules were subject to the price-fixing provisions of the Sherman Act. The Court ruled that the relationship between legal assistance and interstate real estate transactions was sufficiently close to create an effect subject to federal regulations. Against claims of Tenth Amendment violations, the Court upheld federal environmental regulations covering surface mining in *Hodel v. Virginia Surface Mining and Reclamation Association, Inc.* (452 U.S. 264: 1981). The Court said that if Congress had a rational basis for concluding that strip mining had a substantial effect on commerce, Congress could enact regulations to address these effects. Similarly, the Court upheld another federal initiative in *Federal Energy Regulatory Commission v. Mississippi* (456 U.S. 742: 1982). The state claimed that the federal law impermissibly required state utility regulatory agencies to consider federal rate structure and other regulatory standards. The Burger Court allowed the federal policy. In *White v. Massachusetts Council of Construction Employers, Inc.* (460 U.S. 204: 1983), the Court permitted a mayoral order requiring that at least half of any construction project workforce had to be city residents. The Court found the order immune from commerce clause constraints because the city was acting as a market participant rather than a market regulator. In addition, the Court found the conditions imposed by the order compatible with federal policy. When Congress requires or even encourages a state or local government to take an action, that action is not subject to the commerce clause.

More troublesome for the Burger Court have been those commerce clause issues involving state regulatory initiatives. The Burger Court has generally sought to broaden state power. This preference occasionally collides with limits imposed through the commerce clause. Three recent cases reflect those decisions in which state laws have been upheld against commerce clause challenge. In *Complete Auto Transit, Inc. v. Brady* (430 U.S. 274: 1977), the Court sustained a state tax on the "privilege of doing business" in the state. The tax was levied against all activities including those involving interstate commerce. Immunity from state taxation does not automatically flow from conducting interstate business. In order to justify a state tax, however, a state must show a "nexus" between the interstate business and the state, that the tax is fairly apportioned, does not discriminate against the interstate activities, and that the state renders services to the business in exchange for the collected tax. In *Reeves, Inc. v. Stake* (447 U.S. 429: 1980), the Court allowed a resident-only sales restriction on cement produced in a state-owned plant. The commerce clause applies to taxes or policies where the state acts as a market regulator, but not where the state acts as a market participant. Here, the state was acting in the latter capacity as it engaged in "unquestionable" services to its citizens. The Court also permitted state regulation of wholesale electricity rates in *Arkansas Electric Cooperative Corporation v. Arkansas Public Service Commission* (461 U.S. 375: 1983). While the state regulation did affect interstate commerce, the effect was not "excessive" when compared to the local benefits.

State regulations have failed to pass commerce clause scrutiny when they create excessive barriers to commerce or discriminate against interstate commerce in favor of local commerce. Such was the case in *Hunt v. Washington State Apple Advertising Commission* (432 U.S. 333: 1977). The Court held that a state regulation, applied to the grading of apples brought into the state in closed containers, impermissibly discriminated against interstate commerce. Here the Court found the regulation was designed to advantage local producers at the expense of out-of-state producers. Similarly, the Court struck down a state safety regulation that prohibited use of long double-trailers on state highways. The Court said that states will generally be permitted to impose health and safety regulations, even where those regulations burden interstate commerce. At the same time, the safety objectives must be real and not "illusory." In *Philadelphia v. New Jersey* (437 U.S. 617: 1978), the Court struck down a state prohibition on disposal of out-of-state solid waste within the state. The Court found the waste to be commerce despite its "valueless" nature, and held that a state could not respond to difficult problems by erecting barriers between itself and other states. Finally, in *Sporhase v. Nebraska Ex. Rel. Douglas* (458 U.S. 941: 1982), the Court struck down a prohibition on the taking of groundwater withdrawn from the state to another state because the state receiving the water did not have a policy providing reciprocity. The Court said that such a condition was an "explicit barrier" to the free flow of commerce.

Commerce Clause   Empowers Congress to regulate international and interstate commercial activity. The federal government under the Articles of Confederation was exceptionally weak. This condition prompted a number of "reform" efforts, the last of which was the calling of the Constitutional Convention in 1787. While there were numerous defects under the Articles, several stood out. One was the inability of the Congress to generate revenue. Federal taxing power under the Articles was dependent on the states, many of which had an interest in frustrating the exercise of power at the national level. Federal failure to raise money led to many difficulties, especially in the national defense and international relations areas. Another of the principal defects of the Articles was that it did not provide for federal supervision over international and interstate commerce. The federal government was unable to conclude international commercial agreements without the participation and concurrence of the states. As a result, American merchants were subject to punitive trade policies from abroad, and at home, states enacted discriminatory protectionist policies against one another. Congress was powerless to intervene against either problem. By 1787, states had imposed various taxes and regulations on out-of-state goods as a means of protecting local commercial interests, and there was no semblance of a free flow of commerce nationally.

These defects led the framers of the new Constitution to dramatically strengthen the authority of the national government. Among the remedial provisions of the new document was the commerce clause. The clause is located in Article I, Section 8, and says that Congress shall have the power to "regulate commerce with foreign nations, and among the several States, and with the Indian Tribes." Ratification and subsequent implementation of the new Constitution had two immediate consequences, both of which enhanced commercial activity. Congress exercised its new authority by enacting several regulations governing foreign trade. It also passed new legislation establishing licensure requirements for those engaged in coastal trade. Little action was taken in the area of interstate commerce as such, but most of the protectionist policies that had existed prior to the Constitution were repealed by the states. Without the burdensome state regulations, interstate commerce expanded considerably.

Congressional reluctance to affirmatively exercise the commerce power did not end discussion about the scope of the commerce power or what was included in the term *commerce*. Two competing views evolved. The first, advanced by Federalists such as Hamilton, saw commerce in the broadest terms. It included all commercial activities "among the states." Commerce was functionally defined for this group, and federal power over commerce was extensive and exclusive. The second view defined commerce in terms of state boundaries. Adherents of this position saw a large segment of commercial activity as local, occurring entirely within a state, and therefore necessarily beyond federal regulation.

The Court got its first opportunity to offer its view in the case of *Gibbons v. Ogden* (9 Wheaton 1: 1824), and, through Chief Justice John Marshall, adopted the broader view of the commerce power. Marshall wrote that commerce was not merely traffic, but "something more." It is "intercourse" and includes "every species of commercial intercourse." Although Marshall did not define the commerce power as exclusively federal, he confined those aspects of commerce the federal power could not reach to those "completely internal" to a state. At the same time, congressional exercise of authority over commerce did extend into states to local incidents of interstate commerce.

The commerce clause had been included in the new Constitution to address a principal defect of the governmental structure under the Articles. With the Court's decision in *Gibbons*, the clause was given broad sweep. *See also* FEDERALISM, p. 29; *GIBBONS V. OGDEN* (9 Wheaton 1: 1824), p. 294; JOHN MARSHALL, p. 530.

Significance   Marshall's interpretation of the commerce clause in *Gibbons* was expansive. Its principal effect was to protect commercial activities from the impediment of state regulation. While Marshall's interpretation of the commerce power entertained the possibility of extensive federal regulation of commerce, Marshall himself was never called upon to review congressional regulatory initiatives except for the mild coasting laws. It was sufficient for Marshall that the clause would forestall state regulation; interstate commerce would be promoted substantially by that effect alone whether Congress enacted other legislation or not. Indeed, it was not until the late nineteenth century that Congress took legislative initiative of any consequence. Rather, the prominent commerce power question facing the post-Marshall courts was to what extent (if at all) states possessed concurrent power to regulate commercial activities. It was decided in *Cooley v. Board of Port Wardens* (12 Howard 299: 1851) that the state had some concurrent power. Under the *Cooley* doctrine known as "selective exclusiveness," it was held that states retained some power over commercial matters. Where regulatory subjects require a "single, uniform rule," the commerce power is necessarily exclusively possessed by Congress. This covers most commercial matters. For matters that are local in character and demand diverse responses to meet local needs, states may exercise their police power to that end. The *Cooley* doctrine has never been replaced, and some level of state regulation has been recognized since.

Several broad propositions have emerged regarding state regulation of commerce. No state regulation may erect barriers to trade nor discriminate against interstate commerce to the advantage of local commerce. (See, for example, *Baldwin v. G.A.F. Seelig, Inc.*, 294 U.S. 511: 1935; *Hunt v. Washington State Apple Advertising Commission*, 432 U.S. 333: 1977; and *Philadelphia v. New Jersey*, 437 U.S. 617: 1978). Neither may state regulations create substantial burdens or impediments on the free flow of interstate commerce. In each case of this kind, the Court has to weigh any burden imposed by a state against the local benefits produced to determine if the state enactment is permissible. (See, for example, *Kassel v. Consolidated Freightways Corporation*, 452 U.S. 662: 1981, and *Sporhase v. Nebraska Ex. Rel. Douglas*, 458 U.S. 941: 1982). Even state taxation of interstate commerce has been held permissible so long as it is nondiscriminatory and fairly apportioned, the commercial activity taxed has a substantial "nexus" to the taxing state, and the tax fairly relates to the state's provisions of services (see *Complete Auto Transit, Inc. v. Brady*, 430 U.S. 274: 1977).

When Congress began to assume a more assertive regulatory role with enactment of such laws as the Interstate Commerce Act of 1887 and the Sherman Antitrust Act of 1890, the Court reacted by interpreting the commerce clause and its power in a very restrictive way. Driven by the doctrines of dual federalism and the dictates of laissez-faire economics, the Court defined the commerce power narrowly, thus effectively forestalling federal regulation. This was similar in character to the Court's use of substantive due process to limit state economic regulation during this same period (see Chapter 8). Key to limiting federal power was the concept of commerce as many discrete steps. Activities that came before or after actual transportation were not commerce of a kind that could be reached by federal power. Production, for example, was seen as prior to commerce, but not part of commerce itself. Immunizing production activities from federal regulation was a dramatic limitation of the commerce power. Production activities were seen as local or intrastate in character; thus the Tenth Amendment was also interposed as a barrier to the exercise of federal commerce power. While federal authority might be used to regulate local activities that produced burdensome consequences for interstate commerce, those effects had to be "direct" rather than incidental or indirect. In short, during the period from the late 1880s until 1937, the federal commerce power was severely restricted.

Prompted by the invalidation of major elements of the New Deal, President Roosevelt sought to "pack" the Court to produce more favorable decisions. Although he failed to gain formal success with his proposal, the desired decisions were soon forthcoming. The key reversal of direction on the commerce power was the decision in *National Labor Relations Board v. Jones and Laughlin Steel Corporation* (301 U.S. 1: 1937), where the Court sustained the Wagner Act. Of particular importance was the Court's abandonment of such constructs as the production-commerce distinction. The *Jones and Laughlin* decision recognized the highly integrated character of the American economy and viewed the commerce power as the appropriate means by which to institute comprehensive regulation. This new position was solidified over the succeeding years.

Recent history clearly indicates that the Court will generally defer to congressional initiatives based on the commerce clause. For example, in 1964, the Congress enacted civil rights legislation that prohibited racial discrimination in public accommodations. The enactment was an attempt to use the commerce power to address pressing social needs. The Court, in *Heart of Atlanta Motel v. United States* (379 U.S. 241: 1964), sustained the statute and suggested a very limited role for the courts in reviewing enactments based on the commerce power. The Court said that courts may only examine whether Congress has a "rational basis" for concluding that the regulated activity has a "substantial and harmful effect" on commerce and whether the means chosen to respond to the problem are "reasonable." The Burger Court has generally embraced this language (see, for example, *Hodel v. Virginia Surface Mining and Reclamation Association*, 452 U.S. 264: 1981) and is apparently prepared to maintain the pattern of deference begun in the 1930s despite a strong predisposition to support the exercise of power from the state level. It seems clear that, even with a relatively conservative Court, Congress will be able to exercise a comprehensive power over interstate commerce for the foreseeable future.

Mutual Exclusiveness

***Gibbons v. Ogden*, 9 Wheaton 1, 6 L.Ed. 23 (1824)**   Held that the commerce clause does not permit a state to grant an exclusive franchise to navigate in its waterways. In *Gibbons v. Ogden*, the state of New York granted a monopoly to navigate state waters to Robert Fulton and Robert Livingston. They, in turn, assigned the rights to operate between certain New York and New Jersey ports to Aaron Ogden. Thomas Gibbons operated two steamships licensed under a federal coasting law between New York City and Elizabethtown, New Jersey. Ogden obtained an injunction against Gibbons's use of the waterways and was sustained by the New York courts. The Supreme Court, however, overturned the state courts in a unanimous decision.

The opinion of the Court was delivered by Chief Justice Marshall. Critical to his discussion was construction of the term *commerce*. It was argued by New York that the term should be limited to "traffic, to buying and selling, or the interchange of commodities." Such an interpretation did not include navigation. In Marshall's view, this interpretation would restrict a "general term," applicable to "many objects," to one of its "significations." Commerce, he said, is "undoubtedly traffic," but it is "something more—it is intercourse." It describes the "commercial intercourse between the nations, and parts of nations." In all its "branches," commerce is regulated by "prescribing rules for carrying on that intercourse." One can "scarcely conceive" a system for regulating international commerce that "shall exclude all laws concerning navigation." The authority to regulate commerce, including navigation, was "one of the primary objects for which the people of America adopted their government." Since it was "universally admitted" that the words in Article I "comprehend every species of commercial intercourse" between the United States and foreign nations, the term *commerce* "must carry the same meaning" when referring to interactions among states.

Marshall then turned to the extent of the federal commerce power. He did not characterize the commerce power as either exclusive or permitting of regulation of intrastate commerce. As comprehensive as the word "among" might be, it "may properly be restricted to that commerce which concerns more states than one." Congressional power did not go so far as to reach commerce that was "completely internal" and did not "extend to or affect other states." Marshall did not attempt to assert that states were without power to regulate commerce even in the absence of federal regulation. Rather, he chose to strike down the New York monopoly because it was in conflict with the coasting law enacted by Congress in 1793. Implicit in his resolution of this matter was that states retained concurrent regulatory power over commerce so long as it was compatible with federal policy. Acknowledgment of concurrent power, however, did not allow a state to prevail over conflicting federal law. Rather, the state "must yield to the law of Congress" as required under the supremacy clause. It was forcefully argued in a concurring opinion by Justice Johnson that federal commerce power was exclusive, that states had no role to play in commerce regulation even in the absence of federal policy. *See also* COMMERCE CLAUSE, p. 291; CONCURRENT POWER, p. 588; EXCLUSIVE POWER, p. 600; JOHN MARSHALL, p. 530; SUPREMACY CLAUSE, p. 227.

Significance   *Gibbons v. Ogden* (9 Wheaton 1: 1824) was the Marshall Court's first noteworthy commerce clause case. One of the principal defects of the Articles of Confederation was the absence of any central authority to govern economic activity. The commerce clause both protected private business from unreasonable regulation from the state level and provided for the fostering of trade on a national scale. Two issues soon became critical: What is the "commerce" that is subject to federal control, and should the commerce power be shared to any extent with the states? As the first formal consideration of these questions by the Supreme Court, *Gibbons* became the baseline case. The definition of commerce obviously determines what can be governed by Congress under the commerce power. There were two competing views on the definition of commerce. One, advanced by Hamilton, saw the term as encompassing commercial interaction of any kind. Even transactions of a local character fell within this definition of commerce. The states' rights position was built on the interstate aspect of the transaction. Excluded from this definition were activities occurring within a state only. The Marshall Court rejected the narrower definition, which would have confined commerce to interstate "traffic." Commerce, said Marshall, is more than just traffic; it is "intercourse." The term was seen as comprehensive. Marshall said that enumerated powers like the commerce power needed to be broadly construed so as not to "cripple the government" from the outset.

The *Gibbons* decision and Marshall's choice of supporting language had the effect of drawing authority around the federal government. Having rejected the arguments of states' rightists on these issues, one might have thought Marshall would close off the state from any role in the regulation of commerce by saying the commerce power was exclusive. While recognizing that the commerce clause permitted Congress to regulate even those intrastate activities that affect interstate commerce, Marshall said that the commerce power did not extend to matters "completely internal" to a state. In other words, *Gibbons* recognizes a limited concurrent state power to regulate commerce. State regulations, however, cannot be incompatible with federal law or they are invalid on supremacy clause grounds. The full impact of the Court's decision to recognize concurrent state power is seen by examining the behavior of the Court under Chief Justice Roger B. Taney. In a number of instances, such as *New York v. Miln* (11 Peters 102: 1837), the *License Cases* (5 Howard 504: 1847), and *Cooley v. Board of Port Wardens* (12 Howard 299: 1851), the Court upheld state regulation of commerce.

Original Package Doctrine

***Brown v. Maryland*, 12 Wheaton 419, 6 L.Ed. 678 (1827)** Established the "original package" doctrine, which precludes states from regulating imported commerce as long as it remains in its original form or package. The state law under review in *Brown v. Maryland* required all importers and sellers of imported goods to possess a license issued by the state. Brown, an importer, was prosecuted for failure to have the required license. In a 6–1 decision, the Supreme Court held that a state cannot require an importer of foreign goods to have a state license as a condition of selling such merchandise.

The opinion of the Court was delivered by Chief Justice Marshall. The issue in this case was when does commerce, foreign and by implication interstate, come to an end. As long as commerce was in progress, it was subject to federal regulation. Once the commerce had concluded, items became subject to the regulatory authority of the states. Besides the commerce clause, the provision in Article I, Section 10 that says that no state shall "lay any imposts or duties on imports or exports, except what may be absolutely necessary for executing its inspection laws" without congressional approval also applied in this case. Maryland argued that this language only prohibited duties on the act of importation or exportation. Marshall rejected this narrow construction. A duty on imports, he said, "is not merely a duty on the act of importation, but is a duty on the thing imported." The general welfare was "best promoted" by placing the matter of foreign trade under the control of Congress. The rationale for this judgment would be "completely defeated" by a power to tax "the article in the hands of the importer the instant it landed, as by a power to tax it while entering the port." The Court saw no effective difference between a power to "prohibit the sale of an article," and a power to "prohibit its introduction into the country." The Court recognized that the Article I prohibition ought not be interpreted to seriously inhibit the state's power to tax. Rather, there is a time when the "prohibition ceases and the power of the state to tax commences." That point, however, is not the "instant" that articles "enter the country." Identifying the moment the prohibition ends led directly to the fashioning of the "original package" doctrine. When an importer "has so acted" on imported items that they "become incorporated and mixed up with the mass of property in the country," they have lost their "distinctive character" as an import and become subject to state regulation. But while remaining the property of the importer "in the original form or package in which it was imported," a state tax on such goods is "too plainly" a prohibited tax on imports.

Marshall then turned to the commerce issue and reviewed the "oppressed and degraded state of commerce" prior to adoption of the Constitution. The new Constitution addressed that problem by vesting extensive power with the Congress to regulate both foreign and interstate commerce. Construction of this power in any way to "impair its efficiency" would defeat that purpose. The Court saw it as "inconceivable" that the power to authorize commercial traffic, "when given in the most comprehensive terms," and with the intent that its "efficacy should be complete," should cease "at the point when its continuance is indispensable to its value." While state taxing power is "sacred," it cannot be used to "obstruct the free course of a power given to Congress." It cannot "reach and restrain" the actions of the national government "within its proper sphere." A dissent was issued by Justice

Thompson. *See also* BROWN V. HOUSTON (114 U.S. 622: 1885), p. 300; COMMERCE CLAUSE, p. 291.

Significance   The Marshall Court used *Brown v. Maryland* (12 Wheaton 419: 1827) to examine the relationship of state power and commerce protected from it under Article I. In this case, the Court held that states can regulate items in commerce, but only after they have been removed from their original package and become "mixed up" with property in the country. The doctrine was designed to keep states from regulating imported items in such a way as to interfere with interstate commerce. The doctrine was also intended to prevent states from enacting taxes on imports or exports. While such imports or items of interstate commerce cannot permanently remain free of state taxation or regulation, the original package doctrine was an attempt by Marshall to establish a practical standard to distinguish nonregulatable items from regulatable items. Under the doctrine, states could not exercise their police power while the original package remained intact. This provides a merchant with the opportunity to make an unregulated sale so long as items are in their original package. Thus, the doctrine has substantial interstate commerce implications. The imports-exports clause, also addressed by the original package formulation, was designed to keep imported goods from suffering competitive disadvantage. The clause was also included to prevent importing states from imposing taxes that ultimately would disadvantage or create additional costs for nonentry states where imported items would come to rest. This clause does not, under current interpretation, prevent a state from imposing nondiscriminatory taxes on all goods in the state irrespective of original package.

Selective Exclusiveness

Cooley v. Board of Port Wardens, **12 Howard 299, 13 L.Ed. 996 (1851)**   Upheld a state pilotage law as properly enacted under concurrent power to regulate certain aspects of interstate commerce. Involved in *Cooley v. Board of Port Wardens* was an extensive network of regulations applying to shipping in and out of Philadelphia. The regulations were established by the Board of Port Wardens acting under a state pilotage law. Cooley operated two ships that failed to pay a prescribed fee as they left Philadelphia. Cooley claimed that while the Federal government had declared through legislation in 1789 that existing state pilotage laws should remain in effect, no state law enacted subsequently should have effect. The Pennsylvania law under which the regulations were executed was enacted in 1803. Having been unsuccessful in the state courts, Cooley sought review from the United

States Supreme Court. In a 7–2 decision, the Court held that the state had concurrent power to regulate commerce in this situation.

The opinion of the Court was written by Justice Curtis. The case necessarily involved the issue of whether the regulation of commerce was to be a shared enterprise. If the Constitution excluded the states from regulating in this field, Congress "cannot regrant, or in any manner reconvey to the states that power." Thus the question brought "directly and unavoidably" was whether the grant of the commerce power to Congress "did per se deprive the state of all power to regulate pilots." Curtis saw this question as one never before decided by the Court, nor had any case "depending on all the considerations which must govern this one, come before this Court." Curtis pointed out that the grant of commerce power did not contain any terms that "expressly exclude the states from exercising an authority over its subject-matter." They could only be excluded because the "nature of the power" granted to Congress requires that a "similar authority should not exist in the states." There are powers of both kinds. Curtis mentioned the power to govern the District of Columbia as one that is exclusive. The taxing power, on the other hand, lends itself to legitimate exercise at both levels. Assessment of the commerce power is difficult because that power "embraces a vast field" containing not only "many but exceedingly various subjects, quite unlike in their nature." Some of these subjects are "imperatively demanding of a single uniform rule," and others "imperatively demanding that diversity which alone can meet the local needs of navigation." The pilotage regulations involved in this case were seen as fitting the latter category. To absolutely rule that the commerce power is or is not exclusively federal is to "lose sight of the nature of the subject." The federal law passed in 1788 that incorporated local pilotage regulations reflected the desire to leave such regulations to the states. That law manifests congressional understanding that the nature of the subject is "not such as to require exclusive legislation." Until such time as Congress should "find it necessary to exert its power" in pursuit of a uniform policy, the states were viewed as retaining the power to regulate pilots. Justices McLean and Wayne dissented from this view. *See also* COMMERCE CLAUSE, p. 291; CONCURRENT POWER, p. 588; EXCLUSIVE POWER, p. 600.

Significance   The Court adopted the doctrine of "selective exclusiveness" in *Cooley v. Board of Port Wardens* (12 Howard 299: 1851). The commerce clause clearly granted regulatory authority to the Congress. The question remained whether states have any authority to enact regulation that involves commerce. There were those who argued that no regulatory field was exclusively federal and that both Congress and the states had authority to regulate across the board, subject only to the restrictions of the supremacy clause. Others argued that the commerce field was exclusively federal, and that even in the absence of congressional action, the commerce clause precluded all state regulations. The *Cooley* decision was an attempt through the opinion of Justice Curtis to reconcile these positions.

Within the broad field of commerce regulation, there are two kinds of matters. One involves issues so clearly "national" or federal in character that uniform national regulation from Congress is required. In this instance, federal power is to be exclusive. Other issues exist, however, that are "local" in nature and require diverse local regulation. In the absence of federal law, the states are able to exercise concurrent power, thus the term *selective exclusiveness*. The regulation under review in *Cooley* was of this latter type. The *Cooley* doctrine offered a less extensive shared or concurrent role for states than a number of states' rights advocates would have preferred. At the same time, the language of the opinion stopped far short of absolute exclusivity. Under selective exclusiveness, the first function of the courts was to determine the character of the regulated activity. State regulation was not permitted if the activity regulated required national attention. If state or local regulation was possible, the courts would then proceed to consideration of whether the state or local policy discriminated impermissibly against interstate commerce in favor of domestic or local commerce. If the local regulation was not discriminatory, the courts then had to determine whether an "unreasonable burden" was placed on interstate commerce. Obviously, response to these questions was influenced by the political and economic orientations of the reviewing court.

Conclusion of Commerce

Brown v. Houston, 114 U.S. 622, 5 S.Ct. 1091, 29 L.Ed. 257 (1885)   Examined the issue of when commerce comes to an end and can be legitimately regulated by the states. *Brown v. Houston* involved the shipment of coal by barge from Pennsylvania to Louisiana. While the coal remained tied up on the barges in New Orleans awaiting sale, the state of Louisiana attempted to levy an annual tax on "movable" property. Payment of the tax was challenged on the ground that it was an impermissible regulation of interstate commerce. Brown appealed to the Supreme Court after the Louisiana courts decided against him. The Supreme Court unanimously upheld the collection of the tax.

The opinion of the Court was delivered by Justice Bradley. He cited the doctrine of "selective exclusiveness" established in *Cooley v. Board of Port Wardens* (12 Howard 299: 1851). This doctrine holds that the power of Congress to regulate commerce is exclusive "wherever the matter is national in character or admits of one uniform system or plan of regulation." Certainly states may not negatively affect "free and unrestrained intercourse and trade" between states or impose any "discriminating burden or tax" on people or products of other states. Bradley also said that so long as Congress does not act to regulate, it indicates "its will" that particular commerce "should be free and untrammeled," and that "any regulation" of that subject by a state "is repugnant to such freedom." Against that backdrop, the Court examined the state tax to determine if it constituted a restriction of the free introduction of coal into Louisiana and a subsequent "free distribution" of that commerce. Only if the tax was an "exercise of local administrative rules under the general taxing power" could it stand even if it "incidentally" affected the subjects of "interstate commerce." The tax, in the Court's view, was not "imposed on coal as a foreign product," or the product of "another state." Neither was the tax imposed "whilst [the coal] was in a state of transit" through Louisiana to "some other place of destination." Rather, the tax was imposed "after the coal had arrived at its destination and was put up for sale." The coal had "come to its place of rest" for "final disposal or use," and as such was a "commodity in the market of New Orleans." In the Court's view, the property had become a "part of the general mass of property in the state" and was taxed as such like all other property in the state. The coal was "subjected to no discrimination" in favor of Louisiana products or property of Louisiana citizens. The Court held that it could not be "seriously contended," in the absence of congressional action to the contrary, that goods produced in other states are free from taxation in a state "to which they may be carried for use or sale." Once arriving in the state of destination, items that were in commerce may be subjected to a "general tax laid alike on all property." The Court said it "fail [ed] to see how such a taxing can be deemed a regulation of commerce." The Court acknowledged that Congress could give property transported interstate a temporary exemption from state taxation, but declined to consider the conflict between such a law and state taxing power since that question was beyond the scope of this case. *See also* BROWN V. MARY-LAND (12 Wheaton 419: 1827), p. 296; COMMERCE CLAUSE, p. 291; ORIGINAL PACKAGE DOCTRINE, p. 641.

Significance   The Court held that a state may tax items transported in from other states in *Brown v. Houston* (114 U.S. 622: 1885). The items taxed, however, must have reached their final destination and have become part of the "mass of property" of the taxing state. Under the doctrine established in *Cooley*, states were permitted, in the absence of federal legislation, to regulate commerce so long as local commerce was not advantaged or interstate commerce "unreasonably burdened." One objective of the exercise of the state police power or state taxing power was to generate revenue to defray costs of services rendered by the state. The key question was whether the tax affected interstate as opposed to intrastate commerce. The decision in *Brown* sought to clarify when items in interstate commerce had become taxable. The Louisiana tax was not seen as discriminating against interstate commerce, but rather generally levied. Further, the impact on interstate commerce was diminished because the coal had ceased its interstate movement and come to be part of the property of Louisiana. *Brown* permitted taxation of the coal even if it subsequently became interstate commerce again. More typical of the period was the view that commerce could not be segmented to permit state regulation or taxation. In *Wabash, St. Louis and Pacific Railway Company v. Illinois* (118 U.S. 557: 1886), for example, the Court struck down a state charge on a portion of interstate travel occurring within the state. The Court, in *Wabash*, saw the entire rail trip as part of an integrated activity no component of which could be broken out for state regulation.

Production-Commerce Distinction

United States v. E. C. Knight Company, **156 U.S. 1, 15 S.Ct. 249, 39 L.Ed. 325 (1895)**   Held that a production monopoly was outside the reach of congressional commerce power. *United States v. E. C. Knight Company* involved a proposed purchase of the Knight Company and three other companies by the American Sugar Refining Company. The latter already had control of more than half of the refining companies in the country, and the acquisition of Knight and the others would have created a virtual monopoly on sugar production. The United States saw this as a restraint of trade prohibited by the Sherman Antitrust Act and attempted to invalidate the purchase agreements. From an adverse decision in a lower federal court, the federal government appealed. The Supreme Court, in an 8–1 decision, ruled that the monopoly existed only for the manufacture of sugar, not its subsequent shipment interstate.

The opinion of the Court was delivered by Chief Justice Fuller. The question seen as "fundamental" was whether a monopoly in manufacture, conceded to exist here, could be directly "suppressed" under the Sherman Antitrust Act. The Court resolved this question by distinguishing manufacture from commerce, and by using the concept of dual federalism. The power to protect the "lives, health and property of citizens, and to preserve good order and the public morals" is one that "originally and always" belonged to the states; it was not "surrendered" to the federal government nor directly "retained" by the Constitution. Providing relief from the "burden of monopoly" and the "evils resulting from the restraint of trade" among such citizens was "left to the States to deal with." The Court acknowledged the exclusive power of Congress to regulate interstate commerce, but that power can only apply to that which is truly "commerce." The United States argued that power to control the production of sugar was a "monopoly over a necessary of life." Enjoyment of that commodity was dependent on interstate commerce. Thus, the federal government could utilize the commerce power to "repress" such a monopoly "directly" and "set aside the instruments which have created it." The Court was concerned with the implications of such an argument. It could not be confined to "necessaries of life merely," but rather must include "all articles of general consumption." The power to control manufacture involves "in a certain sense the control of its disposition," but this is a "secondary and not a primary sense." While the exercise of such power may bring the operation of commerce into play, "it does not control it," and affects it "only incidentally and indirectly." Commerce thus "succeeds to manufacture and is not part of it." The commerce power only allows prescribing rules by which commerce is governed, and is a power "independent of the power to suppress monopoly."

Fuller concluded by indicating it was "vital" that the "independence" of the commerce power and the state police power be maintained no matter how "perplexing" the line of demarcation. One power "furnishes the strongest bond of union," while the other is "essential to the preservation of the autonomy of the States." The Court characterized the line by saying that "contracts, combinations, or conspiracies to control domestic enterprise" in manufacture, agriculture, mining, "production in all its forms, or to raise or lower prices or wages" might "unquestionably tend to restrain external as well as domestic trade." But that restraint would be an "indirect result, however inevitable and whatever its extent," and this result could not "necessarily determine the object of the contract, combination or conspiracy."

Justice Harlan dissented, saying that "each part" of trade is "under the protection of Congress." The citizenry of the United States is "entitled" to buy goods "without being controlled by an illegal combination whose business extends across the whole country." The "free course of trade" among the states "cannot coexist with such combinations." *See also* ANTITRUST LAWS, p. 579; COMMERCE CLAUSE, p. 291; FEDERALISM, p. 29; *UNITED STATES V. SOUTH-EASTERN UNDERWRITERS' ASSOCIATION* (322 U.S. 533: 1944), p. 334.

Significance   The Court held that the commerce power could not be used to regulate means of production in *United States v. E. C. Knight Company* (156 U.S. 1: 1895). Aside from issues related to the definition of commerce in cases like *Gibbons v. Ogden* (9 Wheaton 1: 1824), the principal questions relating to the commerce clause involved the extent to which states might concurrently regulate commercial activity. The Court did not review much federal legislation prior to the late nineteenth century simply because very little was enacted. Confronted with problems stemming from industrialization, Congress began to respond with aggressive regulatory legislation such as the Interstate Commerce Act and the Sherman Act. The latter was aimed at protecting commerce from the consequences of monopolies. The Sherman Act, if broadly interpreted, would have substantially recast the federal-state relationship. The Court at this time was rather heavily invested in the doctrine of dual federalism. Permitting use of the Sherman Act against Knight was perceived as creating a condition where "comparatively little of business operations and affairs would be left for state control." As the Court sought to preserve policy at the state level, the distinction between production and commerce was a natural device. Indeed, the distinction had been suggested by Congress itself, as it gave enforcement priority to marketing practices. Nonetheless, the impact of the distinction was to immunize important components of the economy from the Sherman Act and federal regulation more generally.

The Court admitted the existence of a monopoly of manufacture in the sugar industry, but since commerce "succeeds to manufacture," it could not be part of it, and the commerce power cannot be used to regulate it. The Court also used the "direct-indirect" effects rationale in *Knight*. Although the distinction suffered from lack of precision, it became another effective means for limiting the exercise of federal commerce power. As long as the consequences of an activity had only an "indirect" effect on interstate commerce, the activity could not be regulated from the federal level. Thus, in *Knight* a monopoly of manufacture did not produce a direct enough effect to warrant application of the Sherman Act.

Commerce Clause as the Basis of Federal Police Power

Champion v. Ames (The Lottery Case), **188 U.S. 321, 23 S.Ct. 321, 47 L.Ed. 492 (1903)**   Upheld a federal law regulating distribution of lottery tickets in interstate commerce. *Champion v. Ames* (also known as *The Lottery Case*) involved an 1895 federal act which stated that it is a crime to send lottery tickets in interstate commerce. This included use of the mails or the hiring of interstate carriers for this purpose. Champion was engaged in the business of interstate transportation, and among the items his company delivered were lottery tickets. He appealed from his conviction and argued that the federal commerce power did not allow Congress to enact such a regulation. In a 5–4 decision, the Supreme Court upheld his conviction.

The opinion of the Court was delivered by Justice Harlan. Champion attacked the federal legislation on several grounds. He first argued that though his company engaged in interstate commerce, that, per se, could not make specific commodities such as the tickets regulatable commerce. He also contended that the tickets in themselves had no value, and accordingly could not be commerce. He further contended that the power to regulate commerce did not include the power to prohibit commerce. Finally, he argued that to use the commerce power to reach lottery tickets was to establish a federal police power, something precluded by the Tenth Amendment. The Court rejected each of these arguments. Because express companies like Champion's engaged in the business of transporting items from state to state are "instrumentalities" of interstate commerce, they are subject to federal regulation. The Court described congressional power over such commerce as "plenary" or "complete in itself," and thus it included the power to make criminal the interstate sending of tickets as a "means of executing" the commerce regulatory power. The Court also upheld prohibitions on carrying as a legitimate form of regulation. Congress must be free to utilize whatever means it chooses to achieve its lawful ends. Here the options of Congress are like those of the state in exercising its police power. If a state may "properly take into view the evils that inhere" in lotteries when considering legislation, "why may not Congress," as it considers using the commerce power, provide that interstate commerce "shall not be polluted by the carrying of lottery tickets from one state to another?" Such action is reasonable given the plenary character of the commerce power. And such action does not interfere with the "completely internal affairs of any state." Just as a state may forbid lottery sales as a means of "guarding the morals" of its own residents, Congress may guard the people of the United States from the "widespread pestilence of lotteries" and protect interstate commerce by prohibiting the interstate transport of lottery tickets. In taking the action contained in this act, Congress only supplemented the action of those states that themselves regulated lotteries. Harlan concluded by saying that "we should hesitate long" before finding that an "evil of such appalling character," conducted through interstate commerce, "cannot be met and crushed by the only power competent to that end."

Chief Justice Fuller issued a dissent which was joined by Justices Brewer, Peckham, and Shiras. They saw this regulation as a serious usurpation of state power. To rule that Congress has a "general police power" means that the federal government "may accomplish objects not entrusted to the General Government," and to "defeat the operation of the Tenth Amendment." *See also* COMMERCE CLAUSE, p. 291; FEDERALISM, p. 29; POLICE POWER, p. 643; TENTH AMENDMENT, p. 229.

Significance   The Court said in *Champion v. Ames* (188 U.S. 321: 1903) that the commerce power could be used to preclude certain interstate commerce as well as to protect interstate commerce. *The*

Lottery Case presented two major issues. The first was whether the commerce clause provided the federal government with a form of police power. The power to govern health, safety, morals, and welfare had traditionally lodged with the states. Indeed, if it accomplished nothing else, the Tenth Amendment was viewed as "reserving" the police power exclusively to the states. Upholding a federal act that suppressed lottery traffic required the Court to recognize a police power dimension to the commerce power. The Court ruled that Congress possessed such power and could so regulate lottery traffic. A second question dealing with the means of regulation necessarily followed. The act under review in this case actually closed interstate commerce to a particular item. It was argued that Congress's power to regulate commerce did not include prohibition; the latter is simply not a kind of regulation. The Court disagreed, however, saying that prohibition was a permissible regulatory option for Congress.

The Court's decision in *The Lottery Case* soon produced numerous similar federal regulatory initiatives. For example, a regulatory tax on oleomargarine was upheld by the Court in *McCray v. United States* (195 U.S. 27: 1904). Soon after, Congress used the commerce power to enact the Food and Drug Act, which prohibited use of interstate commerce for transport of unsafe food and drugs. This enactment was upheld in *Hipolite Egg Company v. United States* (220 U.S. 45: 1911). Using *Lottery Case* reasoning, the Court also upheld the Mann Act in *Hoke v. United States* (227 U.S. 308: 1913). The act prohibited the interstate movement of women for the purpose of prostitution. Use of the commerce power to restrict access to interstate commerce seemed well established by decisions such as those mentioned, but in 1918, the Court invalidated the Federal Child Labor Act in *Hammer v. Dagenhart* (247 U.S. 251: 1918). Though heavily grounded in the doctrine of dual federalism and the production-commerce distinction, the Court also said Congress could not close the channels of commerce. The Court sidestepped *The Lottery Case* rationale by suggesting that lottery tickets were "harmful" in character while the products of child labor were not necessarily so.

Intrastate Railroad Rate Differences

Houston, East and West Texas Railway Company v. United States (The Shreveport Case), 234 U.S. 342 S.Ct. 833, 58 L.Ed. 1341 (1914) Ruled that the commerce power permits federal regulation of the local or intrastate incidents of interstate commerce. *Houston, East and West Texas Railway Company* (known as *The Shreveport Case*) involved examination of the authority of the Interstate Commerce Commission (ICC) to establish railroad rates between points within a state. The complaint brought before the ICC claimed that the railroad discriminated against interstate commerce by charging higher rates between two points that crossed state lines (Dallas to Shreveport) than for intrastate points of longer distance. The government of the state had fixed the original rates on the intrastate routes in an effort to advantage trade for cities within the state. The ICC order required elevating the intrastate rates to the same level as those previously approved for interstate points. The railroad appealed, arguing that the ICC, established by Congress under the commerce power, had no authority to regulate intrastate rates. The Supreme Court disagreed in a 7–2 decision.

The opinion of the Court was issued by Justice Hughes. He began by broadly describing the nature of congressional power to regulate interstate commerce. Its authority "necessarily embraces" the right to control those operations of interstate carriers that have a "close and substantial relation to interstate traffic." That power also includes the "maintenance of conditions" under which interstate commerce may be conducted "upon fair terms and without molestation or hinderance [*sic*]." Given that Congress has the authority to "legislate to these ends," it may attain these ends by regulating agencies of interstate commerce. That regulated carriers are also instruments of intrastate commerce "does not derogate from the complete and paramount authority" of Congress over interstate commerce. Neither does it preclude the use of federal power to "prevent the intrastate operations of such carriers from being made a means of injury to that which has been confided to Federal care." Wherever the interstate and intrastate transactions of carriers are "so related" that the "government of the one involves control of the other," it is "Congress, not the state" that is entitled to "prescribe the final and dominant rule." While Congress cannot regulate the "internal commerce of a State, as such," it does have the power to "foster and protect" interstate commerce. That permits Congress to "take all measures necessary or appropriate to that end" even though this may mean that intrastate activities of interstate carriers may be regulated.

The Court summarized the central principle around these elements: the Congress is entitled to keep the "highways" of interstate communication "open to all interstate traffic" upon "fair and equal terms." It is "undeniable" that rates that "unjustly discriminate" by favoring a person or locality are "evil," and congressional authority to address such "evil" is "clear." The nature of the protective power is such that it is "immaterial" that the discrimination "arises from intrastate rates as compared with interstate rates." The use of any "instrument" of interstate commerce in a manner that "inflicts injury" upon any part of that commerce "furnishes abundant ground for Federal intervention." Dissents were registered by Justices Lurton and Pitney. *See also* COM-MERCE CLAUSE, p. 291; FEDERALISM, p. 29; TENTH AMENDMENT, p. 229.

Significance   The Court said in *The Shreveport Case* (234 U.S. 342: 1914) that the Interstate Commerce Commission could regulate the intrastate rates of a railroad that was also an interstate carrier. There was little disagreement that the federal commerce power extended to the "channels" and "instruments" of interstate commerce. Railroads clearly fit this category. While a number of states had established regulatory commissions to address problems related to the railroads, especially excessively high rates, around the time of the Civil War, federal regulation of railroads was not forthcoming until the late 1880s. As industrialization continued and manufacturers turned to regional and even national markets, regulation of the railroads became a more pressing national matter. If regulation remained exclusively at the state level, diversity of regulation, especially over rate structures, could ultimately be destructive to interstate commerce. Congress eventually responded with the Interstate Commerce Act of 1887. The act created a regulatory agency, the ICC, with power to review established rate structures and find them unreasonable. At the same time, the act did not preclude continued rate setting by the railroads, nor did it absolutely prohibit discriminatory long- versus short-haul rates. Under the act, such rate differences did require ICC review. These aspects of the act ultimately led to situations like that in *The Shreveport Case*.

The early history of the ICC shows that rate differences were allowed as means of permitting railroads the flexibility to respond to otherwise destructive competitive practices. As the ICC sought to regulate more aggressively, the Court was reluctant to permit it to do so. Subsequently, Congress took measures to strengthen the ICC, giving it some rate-making authority. The ICC was permitted, at its own initiative, to conduct its own examination and set aside rates. The Court's response to this redefinition of ICC power was deferential. *The Shreveport Case* is representative. The intrastate rates placed an out-of-state port at a competitive disadvantage. The thrust of the ICC order in this case was that the rate differential impermissibly burdened interstate commerce. The ICC remedy for this situation was to order equalization of rates by requiring an increase in the intrastate rates. Since the interstate rates were already part of a broader rate structure, no flexibility for adjustment of interstate rates was available. Thus, when inter- and intrastate transactions of carriers are "so related" that control of one necessarily controls the other, Congress (or its agencies) and not the states are "entitled to prescribe the final and dominant rule."

Federal Regulation of Child Labor

Hammer v. Dagenhart, **247 U.S. 251, 38 S.Ct. 529, 62 L.Ed. 1101 (1918)** Ruled that the commerce power did not permit Congress to bar all goods produced by child labor from interstate commerce. The federal law at issue in *Hammer v. Dagenhart* was the Keating-Owen Act of 1916. The act provided that products of children under 14 (16 for children working in mines) were to be excluded from interstate shipment. The statute made it financially impossible to use child labor because an establishment found to employ children would be barred from placing any of its products into interstate commerce until the business ceased the practice. Dagenhart, the father of two children under the age of 16, sought to enjoin enforcement of the act against the employment of his children. He obtained such an injunction, and Hammer, a United States attorney, appealed. The injunction was upheld in a 5–4 decision.

The opinion of the Court was delivered by Justice Day. The "controlling question" was whether Congress could prohibit the interstate shipment of goods manufactured by children. The Court reviewed those cases that sustained such uses of the commerce power to prohibit interstate shipment of lottery tickets, interstate transportation of women for the purpose of "debauchery and kindred purposes," and the shipment of impure food and drugs. But each of these cases required use of interstate commerce to successfully accomplish "harmful results." The exercise of federal power in these instances "was to regulate," but that regulation could "only be accomplished by prohibiting the use of the facilities of interstate commerce to effect the evil intended." That element was "wanting" in the child labor case. The object of this regulation is the "denial of the facilities of interstate commerce" to producers employing children. The act, then, did not really regulate interstate commerce, but "aims to standardize the ages at which children may be employed." The Court proceeded to invalidate the law on two grounds. First, the Court saw commerce as "intercourse and traffic," but saw production as a discrete and previous stage. The "making of goods" itself is "not commerce," nor does the subsequent shipment of goods in interstate commerce "make their production a part thereof." Second, the statute was invalid on dual federalism grounds. The granting of the commerce power to Congress did not give the federal government authority to "control the States" in the exercise of the police power over local trade and manufacture. While it may be desirable to have a uniform law governing child labor, the federal government possesses only "enumerated" powers. Then citing the Tenth Amendment incorrectly, Day said that to the states and the people powers "not expressly delegated to the national government are reserved." To allow federal regulation of child labor would "sanction an invasion" by the federal government into a matter "purely local in its character" and over which no authority was delegated to Congress. Thus the Court found the act "repugnant" in a "twofold sense." The act not only "transcends" congressional authority over commerce, but also exerts a power "as to a local matter to which the federal authority does not extend." The "far-reaching" consequence of upholding the act would be to end "all freedom of commerce" and eliminate state control over "local matters," and, as a consequence, our system of government would be "practically destroyed."

Justice Holmes issued a dissent that was joined by Justices Brandeis, Clarke, and McKenna. He took issue with the majority's seeming selectivity. Prohibition was used as a case in point. "The notion," Holmes said, that prohibition is "any less prohibition when applied to things now thought evil I do not understand." He then suggested that a stronger consensus existed against the "evil" of child labor than against use of intoxicants. Beyond that, he did not see the act as involving anything "belonging" to the states. States may continue to regulate their "domestic affairs" and "internal commerce" as they wish. But when they "seek to send their products across the state line, they are no longer within their rights." *See also* BAILEY V. DREXEL FURNITURE COMPANY (259 U.S. 20: 1922), p. 396; CHAMPION V. AMES (188 U.S. 321: 1903), p. 304; COMMERCE CLAUSE, p. 291; FEDERALISM, p. 29; UNITED STATES V. DARBY LUMBER COMPANY (312 U.S. 100: 1941), p. 334; UNITED STATES V. E. C. KNIGHT COMPANY (156 U.S. 1: 1895), p. 302.

Significance   The Court struck down the federal child labor law in *Hammer v. Dagenhart* (247 U.S. 251: 1918), ruling that a law prohibiting commerce exceeded federal power to regulate. The Court also saw the law as impermissibly encroaching on state police power. For a number of years prior to enactment of the child labor law, it appeared that the Court had recognized the commerce clause as providing the federal government with a limited form of police power. Federal laws prohibiting interstate shipment of lottery tickets, unsafe food and drugs, and persons for immoral purposes had all been upheld. But the Court reversed itself in *Hammer*, and utilized both established and new justifications for doing so. The effect of both kinds of rationale was to minimize the scope of the federal commerce power. First, the Court said that outright prohibition was not a permissible form of regulation; regulation and prohibition differed in kind, not just degree. The Court distinguished prior decisions upholding federal regulations of this type by saying that they had been applied to items that were inherently "harmful." While nonharmful items could not be barred from interstate commerce, harmful items could be categorically banned. Second, the Court viewed the child labor law as a health and safety measure more appropriately the domain of state police power. Thus, the federal statute encroached on police power reserved to the states by the Tenth Amendment. Justice Day even went so far as to insert the word "expressly" into the Tenth Amendment as he emphasized that such power had not been delegated to Congress. Third, the Court returned to the proposition that commerce succeeds manufacture and is therefore distinct from it. Historically, those activities associated with manufacture or production had been seen as having only an intrastate character. Undeterred, the Congress sought to deal with child labor by means of a regulatory tax. The Court also invalidated this effort in *Bailey v. Drexel Furniture Company* (259 U.S. 20: 1922). The Court gradually moved away from the *Hammer* decision and its supporting rationale, and formally overruled the precedent in *United States v. Darby Lumber Company* (312 U.S. 100: 1941).

Stream of Commerce Concept

***Stafford v. Wallace*, 258 U.S. 495, 42 S.Ct. 397, 66 L.Ed. 735 (1922)** Upheld federal regulation of certain meat-packing and stockyard practices. *Stafford v. Wallace* examined provisions of the Packers and Stockyards Act of 1921 that were enacted to address a number of "discriminatory and deceptive" practices in the meat-packing business "done in interstate commerce." The "chief evil" prompting the legislation was fear of a meat-packing monopoly that would produce "unduly and arbitrarily" lowered prices to sellers and "unduly and arbitrarily" impose increases to the consumer. Thus the act permitted federal regulation of those activities leading to establishment of a monopoly or unreasonable prices and charges. Stafford unsuccessfully sought to enjoin enforcement of the act and appealed to the Supreme Court. Over the sole dissent of Justice McReynolds, the Court upheld the act (Justice Day did not participate in the decision).

The opinion of the Court was delivered by Chief Justice Taft. Key to the Court's sustaining the federal act was the "stream of commerce" concept. When products are "in stream," commerce is still in progress. In this instance, Taft said that the stockyards are "not a place of rest or final destination." Livestock continually arrives, is sold, and "moved out" to give place to the "constantly flowing traffic that presses behind." The stockyards were seen as "but a throat through which the current flows." The transactions that occur in the yards "are only incident to this current." These transactions "cannot be separated from the movement to which they contribute" and "necessarily take on its character." The stockyards and the sales occurring there are "necessary factors" in the middle of this "current of commerce." The act treats stockyards as "great national public utilities" in an attempt to "promote the flow of commerce" from producers in the West to consumers in the East. The act assumed that stockyards conducted business "affected by a public use of a national character," and thus subject to federal regulation. Taft noted that the application of the commerce clause was the result of the "natural development" of interstate commerce under "modern conditions." It was the "inevitable recognition" that the concept of "streams of commerce" captured the "very essence" of commerce among the states. While there was no dispute that businesses that are affected with a "public use" can be regulated, the stream of commerce approach permitted the Court to sustain regulation of those stockyard practices taking place between the receipt of livestock in the yards and the subsequent shipment of that same livestock interstate.

The Court concluded with a broad and deferential statement. Whatever activity amounts to "more or less constant practice, and threatens to obstruct or unduly burden the freedom of interstate commerce" is within the regulatory reach of Congress. And it is "primarily for Congress to consider and decide the fact of danger and meet it." The Court will "certainly not substitute its judgment" for that of Congress in these situations unless the "relation of the subject to interstate commerce and its effect upon it are clearly nonexistent." *See also* COMMERCE CLAUSE, p. 291; *MUNN V. ILLINOIS* (94 U.S. 113: 1877), p. 420.

Significance   The Court used the stream of commerce doctrine to sustain the Packers and Stockyards Act in *Stafford v. Wallace* (258 U.S. 495: 1922). From Marshall's early formulation that the commerce power extends to transactions that "concern more than one state," the Court has generally permitted exercise of the power to regulate those activities that "affect" interstate commerce directly. Through the effects construct, the commerce power can reach intrastate activities that are closely enough related to interstate commerce. The concept of "stream" or "flow" of commerce is one of the ways the regulation of items otherwise considered intrastate has been justified. The stream of commerce concept had its origin in *Swift and Company v. United States* (196 U.S. 375: 1905). As part of his "trust-busting" policy, Theodore Roosevelt's administration filed an antitrust suit against meat packers alleging that various sales practices occurring at different stages of operations unduly burdened interstate commerce. Justice Holmes saw these various "local activities" as more realistically a "current of commerce" having an interstate nature. This rationale was readily applicable to the Court's review of the Packers and Stockyards Act. Key to its utility as a supportive reasoning for federal regulation is the point that discrete transactions have a cumulative effect. While any one isolated transaction may not in itself be commerce, the aggregated activity is, and its continually recurring nature reinforces this conclusion.

State Prohibition on Out-of-State Milk Sale

Baldwin v. G.A.F. Seelig, Inc., 294 U.S. 511, 55 S.Ct. 497, 79 L.Ed. 1032 (1935)   Struck down a state law that imposed price regulations on milk imported from another state. *Baldwin v. Seelig, Inc.* involved a New York milk dealer who purchased milk from a producer in a neighboring state. The New York Milk Control Act established a system of minimum prices to be paid by dealers to producers. To keep prices in a "so-called" metropolitan milk district "unimpaired by competition from afar," the act allowed extension of the protective price to "that part of the supply which comes from other states." The purpose of the regulation was to prohibit sale of milk purchased from outside New York at a lower price. Seelig purchased milk from Vermont at prices below the minimum set by the New York regulation. The New York law conditioned sale of the milk in New York on payment of at least the minimum price applicable to a transaction within the state. Seelig refused to comply and was denied a state license to transact its business. Seelig, Inc. brought suit, seeking to enjoin enforcement of the New York regulation. A district court injunction to that effect was upheld by the Supreme Court in a unanimous decision.

The opinion of the Court was delivered by Justice Cardozo. He began by focusing the issue. It was not contested that New York had no authority to "project its legislation" into another state by "regulating the price to be paid in that state for milk acquired there." Neither did New York have the power to "prohibit the introduction within the territory" of milk of "wholesale quality" acquired in another state. The question in the case was whether New york could "outlaw milk so introduced" by prohibiting its sale thereafter if the price paid to out-of-state producers was "less than would be owing in like circumstances" to producers in New York. Cardozo observed, "the importer in that view may keep his milk or drink it, but sell it he may not." The Court held that "such a power," if exerted by any state, "will set a barrier to traffic between one state and another" as effective as if "customs duties equal to the price differential" had been laid upon the goods transported. Article I confers "commerce of that order" to the Congress. Imposts and duties on interstate commerce are placed outside the power of the states "without the mention of an exception." Well established by 1935 was the doctrine that a state could not "in any form or under any guise directly burden the prosecution of interstate business." If any state is allowed to "promote the economic welfare of her farmers" by guarding them against competition from cheaper prices of out-of-state goods, "the door has been opened to rivalries and reprisals that were meant to be averted" when the commerce power was delegated to the Congress. Neither the taxing power nor the police power may be used to establish an "economic barrier against competition" with products from other states. Restrictions "so contrived are an unreasonable clog upon the mobility of commerce." Cardozo concluded by saying that it is one thing for a state to "exact adherence by our importer to fitting standards of sanitation" prior to sale. It is, however, a "very different thing" to establish a "scale of prices for use in another state" and to bar the sale of goods, "whether in original packages or in others, unless the scale has been observed." See also COMMERCE CLAUSE, p. 291.

Significance   The Court used the commerce clause in *Baldwin v. Seelig, Inc.* (294 U.S. 511: 1935) to strike down a state pricing system on milk brought in from another state. From the outset of our constitutional history, states have attempted to protect enterprise in their states from competition from other states. Indeed, the first major commerce clause case, *Gibbons v. Ogden* (9 Wheaton 1: 1824), involved a restrictive state-granted steamboat franchise. This kind of "protectionism" has been consistently viewed as incompatible with the commerce clause. Such protective policies, in Cardozo's words, create an "unreasonable clog upon the mobility of commerce." In addition, they foster "rivalries and reprisals which were meant to be averted" when the interstate commerce power was lodged with the federal government. In *Hood v. DuMond* (336 U.S. 525: 1949), a case similar to *Baldwin*, the Court ruled that a state could not refuse to license a new plant whose milk was intended for out-of-state sale. The state argued that the new plant would produce excessive competition for local milk by diverting some of that supply out of state. The Court, however, said that the commerce clause does not permit the establishment of such economic barriers. The basic thrust of *Baldwin*'s antiprotectionism doctrine remains intact. Clearly, some local regulations may be imposed notwithstanding some burdensome consequences on interstate commerce. Health and safety regulations are upheld as legitimate manifestations of the police power. Even those measures, however, are subject to scrutiny as obstructions to commerce as seen in *Dean Milk Company v. Madison* (340 U.S. 349: 1951) and may be invalidated if the health or safety objectives are subterfuges for protectionism.

Commerce-Manufacture Distinction

Schechter Poultry Corporation v. United States, **295 U.S. 495, 55 S.Ct. 837, 79 L.Ed. 1570 (1935)** Held the National Industrial Recovery Act to be unconstitutional. *Schechter Poultry Corporation v. United States* developed out of a regulatory approach that featured codes established by representatives of a particular industry. The codes addressed a variety of items including wages and trade practices. The codes became effective when approved by the president and were issued in the form of an executive order. The Schechter Corporation was convicted for violations of the Live Poultry Code. Schechter challenged the conviction, arguing that such regulations were outside the reach of federal interstate commerce powers. It was also contended that the code-making process constituted an impermissible delegation of legislative power. In a unanimous decision, the Court agreed with Schechter.

The opinion of the Court was delivered by Chief Justice Hughes. The delegation of power aspects of *Schechter* are treated fully in Chapter 4. Suffice it to say here, the Court viewed the code-making process provided in the act as leaving substantive rule making to the "virtually unfettered discretion" of the president. This absence of standards for "any trade, industry or activity" constituted an impermissible delegation of the legislative function. Beyond this pervasive defect, the Court also found commerce power problems. The power to develop the codes was based on the commerce clause, but the other question was whether the transactions of Schechter Poultry Corporation subject to the codes were actually "in" interstate commerce. An associated question before the Court was whether those transactions "directly affect" interstate commerce. The Court thought not in both instances. The code provisions as applied to Schechter "did not concern" the transportation of poultry from other states to New York. Rather, Schechter purchased from markets and terminals within New York City and moved from those locations to slaughterhouses in Brooklyn for subsequent "final disposition." Neither the slaughtering nor the later sales "were transactions in interstate commerce." The Court also rejected application of the "stream" or "flow of commerce" doctrine. The "mere fact" that there may be a "constant flow of commodities" into a state does not mean that the flow "continues after the property has arrived and become commingled with the mass of property within the State." In this case, the flow of interstate commerce "had ceased," and the poultry had come to a "permanent rest" in New York.

As for effects, the Court said that Congress has "dominant authority" over operations that have a "close and substantial" relation to interstate traffic, over activities having a "direct" effect on interstate commerce.

The hours and wage violations of Schechter as well as their local sale activities simply did not "affect" interstate commerce. The Court indicated that there was a "necessary and well-established distinction between direct and indirect effects." Where interstate activities have only an indirect effect, they "remain within the domain of state power." The distinction, drawn in precision "only as individual cases arise," is "clear in principle." The government here contended that hours and wages affect prices. A slaughterhouse paying lower than code-prescribed wages or effecting savings by demanding longer hours of work heightens demand for cheaper products. All this leads to "demoralization of the price structure," something the commerce power can reach. The Court considered this argument "too much." Such an interpretation of reachable effect would allow regulation of all "processes of production and distribution that enter into cost." If the cost of doing intrastate business is a permitted object of federal regulation, the "extent of the regulation of cost would be a question of discretion and not of power." The authority of the federal government, the Court concluded, may not be "pushed to such an extreme" as to "destroy the distinction" that the clause establishes, between "commerce among the several states and the internal concerns of a state." *See also* CARTER V. CARTER COAL COMPANY (298 U.S. 238: 1936), p. 317; COMMERCE CLAUSE, p. 291; DELEGATION OF LEGISLATIVE POWER, p. 591; FEDERALISM, p. 29.

Significance   The Court struck down the National Industrial Recovery Act (NIRA) in *Schechter Poultry Corporation v. United States* (295 U.S. 495: 1935). In addition to delegation of power defects, the Court ruled that the regulatory scheme involved exceeded the boundaries of federal authority when extended to intrastate commercial transactions. The poultry code enforced against Schechter involved local marketing practices plus hours and compensation requirements for employees in the local slaughterhouse. The Court found these matters local in character because the "flow" or "stream" of interstate commerce had concluded. Since Schechter's transactions were no longer in the "flow" of commerce, its activities had to produce effects that "directly" impaired interstate commerce in order for them to be subject to federal regulatory authority. The Court saw no such "direct" effects. Rather, the effects were only indirect. The distinction between direct and indirect effects, said Hughes, was a "fundamental" one, "essential to the maintenance of our constitutional system." Undeterred by the *Schechter* decision, other New Deal initiatives aimed at economic stabilization followed immediately. Absent in these post-*Schechter* enactments were the serious delegation of power problems so prominent in the Court's invalidation of the NIRA. Subsequent legislation focused more exclusively on the commerce power, and the embattled Court of the mid-

1930s eventually altered its position. Within two years of *Schechter*, very little still qualified as a "local activity," and the utility of the "direct-indirect" effect distinction was dramatically diminished.

Indirect Effects on Commerce

***Carter v. Carter Coal Company*, 298 U.S. 238, 56 S.Ct. 855, 80 L.Ed. 1160 (1936)** Ruled that the commerce power did not permit comprehensive regulation of the coal industry by means of codes. *Carter v. Carter Coal Company* examined provisions of the Bituminous Coal Conservation Act of 1935 (also known as the Guffey Act). Congressional intention was to "stabilize" the coal industry. The legislation sought to do this by establishing codes that regulated coal prices and also incorporated labor agreements. Coal producers were prompted to accept the codes by means of a tax on coal sales, 90 percent of which was rebated to producers who complied with code provisions. Carter brought suit against his own company, whose board of directors had agreed to comply with the code under threat of the tax. The suit permitted the Court to examine the constitutionality of the Guffey Act and its code approach. The principal defects claimed by the challengers were that it constituted an improper delegation of legislative power and impermissible use of the commerce power. In a 6–3 decision, the Supreme Court agreed.

The opinion of the Court was delivered by Justice Sutherland. The discussion that follows here will focus on the Court's opinion dealing with the commerce clause challenge. The validity of the act "depends," said Sutherland, on whether it regulates interstate commerce; thus the "nature and extent of that power becomes the determinative question." Commerce is the "equivalent" of the phrase "intercourse for the purposes of trade." The power to regulate commerce "embraces the instruments by which commerce is carried on." The commerce power, however, does not apply to transactions "wholly internal" to a state. Further, simply because products of "domestic enterprise in agriculture or manufacture, . . . may ultimately become the subjects of foreign commerce," control of the "means or the encouragements" by which enterprise is "fostered and protected" is not necessarily included within the meaning of the term *foreign commerce*. That commodities produced in a state are "intended" for interstate sale and transport "does not render their production or manufacture subject to federal regulation." Incidents "leading up to and culminating in the mining of coal" do not constitute intercourse for the purposes of trade. Employment practices, wages, and hours all constitute "intercourse for the purposes of production, not trade." Extraction of coal is the "aim and completed result of local activities." Mining "brings the subject matter of commerce into existence. Commerce disposes of it." Thus, those regulations targeting aspects of production were seen as beyond federal authority.

The Court then turned to "effects on interstate commerce of coal production and distribution." The Court said that every commodity intended for interstate sale "has some effect" on interstate commerce. Key is the distinction between "direct and indirect effects," because only the former comes under the commerce power. If the commerce clause were interpreted to reach "all enterprises and transactions" having only an indirect effect, federal authority "would embrace practically all activities of the people," and state authority over its domestic matters would exist "only by sufferance" of the federal government. While the distinction between "direct" and "indirect" is "not always easy to determine," the word *direct* implies that a condition "shall operate proximately—not mediately, remotely or collaterally—to produce the effect." The distinction turns not on the "magnitude of either the cause or the effect," but entirely upon the "manner in which the effect has been brought about." The central question is what is the "relation between" the activity or condition and the effect. Based on this formulation, the Court saw the relationship of wages and working conditions as only indirectly affecting commerce in addition to being a local matter. The Court than struck down the price-fixing features as well because they were "so related to and dependent upon" the unconstitutional labor provisions.

Justice Cardozo, joined by Justices Brandeis and Stone, dissented. Cardozo said that to regulate prices of interstate transactions is to regulate "commerce itself, and not alone its antecedent conditions or its ultimate consequences." Interstate prices cannot, he said, be regulated by the state, so they must be subject to federal authority. Otherwise a "vacuum" would exist, leaving "many a public evil incidental to interstate transactions . . . without a remedy." *See also* COMMERCE CLAUSE, p. 291; FEDERALISM, p. 29; *NATIONAL LABOR RELATIONS BOARD V. JONES AND LAUGHLIN STEEL CORPORATION* (301 U.S. 1: 1937), p. 319; *SCHECHTER POULTRY CORPORATION V. UNITED STATES* (295 U.S. 495: 1935), pp. 189, 315.

Significance   The Court struck down the Bituminous Coal Act in *Carter v. Carter Coal Company* (298 U.S. 238: 1936), finding that the labor provisions regulated an element of production that had only an indirect effect on interstate commerce. Like the decision in *Schechter Poultry Corporation v. United States* (295 U.S. 495: 1935) just a year earlier, the direct-indirect effect distinction controlled the outcome in this case. *Carter* clearly reflects the extent to which the distinction could be used to limit exercise of the federal commerce power. While *Carter* contains the most extreme applications of the effects tests, it also marks the last decision in which the anti–New Deal majority would prevail. In less than a year, the Court would reverse itself on the scope and reach of the commerce power (see *National Labor Relations Board v. Jones and Laughlin Steel Corporation*, 301 U.S. 1: 1937), and the direct-indirect distinction would be abandoned. The Court in *Carter* utilized the doctrine established in *United States v. E. C. Knight Company* (156 U.S. 1: 1895) that production was distinct from commerce. The aspects of the code dealing with labor were viewed by the Court in *Carter* as having only an indirect effect on interstate commerce. The Court's refusal to view production as anything but local was absolute; there was no recognition that scale of operation was a relevant factor.

The Court's nonnegotiable position on the federal regulatory power was more generally reflected in the striking down of the code's price regulations. The Guffey Act expressly provided that the labor and price aspects of the statute were to be considered separately such that a judicially determined defect in one would not necessarily invalidate the other. The Court, however, saw the two elements as inseparable, and voided the price-fixing portion of the act. It was this categorical non-receptivity to various New Deal initiatives that ultimately provoked the attempt to "pack" the Court by increasing its size. The plan was never adopted, but shortly after its introduction, the Court modified its commerce power position. Soon thereafter, Roosevelt was able to replace several justices, thus ensuring that the Court would not return to the commerce clause positions articulated in *Carter*.

Labor Management Regulation

***National Labor Relations Board v. Jones and Laughlin Steel Corporation*, 301 U.S. 1, 57 S.Ct. 615, 81 L.Ed. 893 (1937)**
Upheld federal regulation of labor relations through the exercise of the commerce power. *National Labor Relations Board v. Jones and Laughlin Steel Corporation* considered the constitutionality of the National Labor Relations Act (NLRA) of 1935, which was also known as the Wagner Act. The act was designed to protect the rights of workers to organize into labor unions and engage in collective bargaining. The act established the National Labor Relations Board (NRLB) to adjudicate labor-management relations. Following a formal inquiry, the NLRB found Jones and Laughlin to have engaged in certain "unfair labor practices" and ordered the corporation to "cease and desist." When Jones and Laughlin refused to do so, the NLRB unsuccessfully sought

enforcement of their order from the court of appeals. The case was then taken to the Supreme Court. In a 5–4 decision, the Court upheld the act and sustained the NLRB order against Jones and Laughlin.

The opinion of the Court was delivered by Chief Justice Hughes. The act was challenged as constituting an "invasion" of state authority over local matters. It was further contended that the act regulated subjects only indirectly related to interstate commerce. Hughes began his discussion by suggesting that the Court cannot "deny effect" to regulations Congress has the power to enact. The "cardinal principle of statutory construction is to save and not destroy." The "plain duty" of the Court is to adopt an interpretation that "will save the act." Utilizing this perspective, the Court concluded that the NLRA "may be construed so as to operate within the sphere of constitutional authority." The Court noted that the act had limited scope. It did not give the NLRB authority between "all industrial employees and employers." Rather, the act reaches only what may be "deemed to burden or obstruct" interstate commerce. So qualified, it "must be construed" as contemplating the exercise of control within constitutional bounds."

The Court then examined application of the act through the NLRB to employees engaged in production. Jones and Laughlin advanced the well-established argument that production is not in itself commerce and thus only "indirectly related to interstate commerce." The Court, however, took a broader view of commerce. Bypassing the "stream of commerce" doctrine, Hughes said that congressional power to protect interstate commerce is not limited to transactions deemed an "essential part" of commercial "flow." Burdens and obstructions may come from "injurious action springing from other sources." These sources may also be reached. Even though activities may be intrastate in character "when separately considered," these activities may be regulated if they have a "close and substantial" enough relation to interstate commerce. Industrial "strife" would have a "more serious effect" on interstate commerce in the Court's view, especially in the case of a corporation like Jones and Laughlin. In view of its "far-flung" activities, it is "idle to say that the effect would be indirect or remote." Rather, the effect would be "immediate and might be catastrophic." To view the economy of the country otherwise would be to "shut our eyes to the plainest facts of our national life." Because the relationship of a "host of local enterprises" to interstate commerce may be indirect and remote, it "does not follow" that other activities are not closely enough related to make labor-management relations a "matter of urgent national concern." When industries like Jones and Laughlin "organize themselves on a national scale," making their relation to interstate commerce the "dominant factor" in their activities, their industrial relations may be regulated to protect interstate commerce from the "paralyzing consequences" of industrial conflict.

Justice McReynolds delivered a dissent that was joined by Justices VanDevanter, Sutherland, and Butler. The minority viewed the decision as a departure from the well-established principles of such cases as *Schechter* and *Carter*. They also saw the decision as reflecting the view that congressional power would extend "into almost every field of human industry." They saw the power of the federal government inappropriately applied to situations only remotely and indirectly related to interstate commerce. Such exercise of power constituted a "definite invasion" of the reserve powers of the states. *See also* CARTER V. CARTER COAL COMPANY (298 U.S. 238: 1936), p. 317; COMMERCE CLAUSE, p. 291; FEDERALISM, p. 29; *SCHECHTER POULTRY CORPORATION V. UNITED STATES* (295 U.S. 495: 1935), pp. 189, 315.

Significance   The Court upheld the National Labor Relations Act in *National Labor Relations Board v. Jones and Laughlin Steel Corporation* (301 U.S. 1: 1937). In doing so, the Court abandoned the precedents set in *Schechter Poultry Corporation v. United States* (295 U.S. 495: 1935) and *Carter v. Carter Coal Company* (298 U.S. 238: 1936). More importantly, the Court substantially rejected the distinction between direct and indirect effects on interstate commerce as a meaningful standard for assessing federal power. Instead, the Court finally recognized the highly integrated character of the American economy. Activities or factors previously viewed as isolated and local were seen as having economic effects that transcended state lines. Indeed, Hughes referred to the consequences of protracted labor disputes in the steel industry as "catastrophic" rather than remote or indirect. This, of course, permitted application of the federal commerce power.

The *Jones and Laughlin* decision is often referred to as the "switch in time" that "saved nine." At the time the Court decided this case, a proposal was before the Congress that would have increased the size of the Court. This "court-packing" proposal was precipitated by the Court's extended resistance to the New Deal initiatives. In several key 1937 cases, Chief Justice Hughes and Justice Roberts joined the three justices who had supported New Deal legislation throughout the period. This created a new majority, one ready to sustain extensive economic regulation under the commerce power. Any thought that the Wagner Act would apply only to large corporations with national markets was dispelled in a companion case to *Jones and Laughlin*, *National Labor Relations Board v. Friedman-Harry Marks Clothing Company* (301 U.S. 58: 1937). Friedman was a small clothing manufacturer. Under virtually no circumstances could its activities produce direct effect on interstate commerce, and yet the Court sustained the NLRF order. Such a decision clearly marked the end of the time when the production-commerce distinction could effectively be used to forestall federal commerce regulation.

Navigable Waters

United States v. Appalachian Electric Power Company, **311 U.S. 377, 61 S.Ct. 291, 85 L.Ed. 243 (1940)**   Held that the commerce power could be used to regulate waterways that have the potential for becoming navigable. *United States v. Appalachian Electric Power Company* involved a decision of the Federal Power Commission (FPC) not to license the construction of a hydroelectric dam by Appalachian Electric. The lower federal courts held that the FPC could not restrict construction because the river on which the dam was to be built (the New River) was not navigable. The Supreme Court ruled in a 6–2 decision (with Chief Justice Hughes not participating) that federal power could be exercised in this situation, and the Court upheld the FPC decision not to license the project.

The opinion of the Court was delivered by Justice Reed. On the matter of navigability, the Court said that "early in our history," it was determined that the commerce regulatory power "necessarily included power over navigation." Congress, thus, has authority to keep navigable waters "open and free" and provide sanctions against "any interference" with the country's waterways. Included is the authority to "forbid or license dams" in these waters. The Court characterized power over "improvements for navigation" in rivers as "absolute." If this extensive power can be applied to navigable waters, the legal tests to determine navigability become decisive. The lower court had based its judgment on navigability on the standard that waterways be "navigable in fact," that they can be used in their "ordinary condition." Using this standard, the lower courts had ruled the New River to be not navigable. The Supreme Court said that to "appraise the evidence of navigability on the natural condition only . . . is erroneous." The "availability" of the waterway for navigation must also be considered. A waterway, said Reed, that is "otherwise suitable for navigation" is not precluded from classification as such simply because "artificial aids" must be used to make it usable for commercial navigation. Neither is it necessary that these improvements be completed or even authorized. The congressional commerce power is "not to be hampered" because of the need for "reasonable improvements" to make the waterway available for traffic. In determining navigability, it is proper to consider the "feasibility of interstate use after reasonable improvements which might be made."

Furthermore, it is not necessary to navigability that the "use should be continuous."

The Court also rejected arguments made by the power company that the federal licensure requirements encroach on the state's power to control their own resources. It could not "properly be said" that the power of the federal government over its water "is limited to control for navigation." The authority of the federal government is "regulation of commerce on its waters." Navigability is "but a part of the whole." While the federal government may not increase its power by building its own dams, neither may a power company by "seeking to use a navigable waterway for power generation alone, avoid the authority of the Government over the stream." The government's authority is "as broad as the needs of commerce." Water power generation from dams is a "by-product of the general use of the rivers for commerce." The Court concluded by saying that navigable waters are "subject to national planning and control" under the commerce power granted to Congress. The license conditions involved here have "an obvious relationship to the exercise of the commerce power." Justices Roberts and McReynolds dissented from this view. *See also* COMMERCE CLAUSE, p. 291; FEDERALISM, p. 29.

Significance   The Court adopted an extremely broad definition of navigability in *United States v. Appalachian Electric Power Company* (311 U.S. 377: 1940). The broader this definition, the greater the scope of the power to regulate navigable waters. In this instance, the power was ruled to include licensure of a hydroelectric dam construction project. It was never doubted that Congress had power to regulate all channels of interstate commerce. Such power was essential to provide the protection of commerce demanded under Article I. Congress immediately acted to require federal licensure of all vessels using interstate waterways. The scope of this kind of regulatory power rests on definition of navigability, whether the commerce power includes more than just control of navigation, and the extent to which the channel of commerce concept is to be applied within a state. On the latter point, the Court said in *The Daniel Ball* (10 Wallace 557: 1871) that federal licensure requirements extended to all ships operating on waters connecting to interstate waterways or ships that carry items that move interstate even if the ship does not. The other two issues were addressed in *Appalachian Electric*. First, the Court rejected a narrow definition of navigability. The explicitly rejected standard was navigability "in fact," a test coming from *The Daniel Ball* decision. This standard required that waterways be usable as channels of commerce in their "ordinary condition." The Court said in *Appalachian* that federal regulatory power extended to any waterway capable of becoming navigable. The broadening of the standard brought with it substantially broadened federal power. The second was the Court said that the matter of navigability was only part of what was intended in the commerce power. In addition, federal power could be exercised in relation to those activities bearing any relationship to navigable waters. This included such activities as flood protection, development of watersheds, as well as the production of hydroelectric power. Thus, the *Appalachian* case, through its definition of navigability and the navigable water concept substantially extended federal regulatory power.

Fair Labor Standards Act

***United States v. Darby Lumber Company*, 312 U.S. 100, 61 S.Ct. 451, 85 L.Ed. 609 (1941)**   Held that enactment of the Fair Labor Standards Act (FLSA) was a permissible exercise of the commerce power. The act established minimum wages and maximum hours of work for employees in industries whose products were shipped in interstate commerce. Darby Lumber Company turned raw timber into finished lumber that was then shipped to customers out of state. The company was charged with numerous wage violations (both failure to pay minimum wages and failure to pay overtime for hours worked in excess of the defined maximum) as well as failure to maintain required records. Indictment against Darby was quashed by a U.S. district court, and the federal government appealed. In a unanimous decision, the Supreme Court reversed the lower court.

The opinion of the Court was delivered by Justice Stone. The Court identified two principal issues. The first was whether Congress has the power to prohibit interstate shipment of products made by employees who worked longer hours or were paid lower wages than those prescribed. The second was whether the commerce power permits regulation of the wages and hours of production employees. The Court responded by saying that, while production is "not of itself" interstate commerce, the "shipment of manufactured goods interstate is such commerce" and the prohibition of such shipment is "indubitably a regulation of the commerce." It was asserted by Darby that this statute fit none of the established categories of permissible commerce regulation. It was only "nominally" a commerce regulation in Darby's view. Rather, the real objective, made under the "guise" of a commerce regulation, was the regulation of wages and hours of production workers. The Court found Darby's contentions unpersuasive. The motive and purpose of the regulation, Stone said, is "plainly to make effective the congressional conception of public policy" that interstate commerce should not be "made the instrument of competition" in the distribution of goods "produced under substandard labor conditions." Such competition is "injurious" to commerce and to the states "from and to which the commerce flows." In addition, the Court said that the "motive and purpose" of a regulation of commerce are matters for the "legislative judgment"; these are matters over which the courts are "given no control."

The Court then turned to the validity of the wage and hour regulations. The validity of these provisions hinges on the question of whether the employment of employees under "other than the prescribed labor standards" is sufficiently related to interstate commerce so as to bring it within congressional power to regulate. The Court said the commerce power extends to intrastate activities that "affect" interstate commerce. If an effect exists, then Congress may choose the appropriate means of addressing that effect. The statute aims at the "spread of substandard labor conditions" through use of interstate commerce to undercut goods produced under "prescribed or better labor conditions." Local business may be impaired by unfair competition "made effective through interstate commerce." The wage and hour regulations are directed toward the "suppression of a . . . kind of competition" in interstate commerce that it has in effect condemned as "unfair," in a manner similar to the Clayton and National Labor Relations acts. The act reflects recognition that in "present day industry, competition by a small part may affect the whole." The legislation "aimed at the whole embraces all its parts." Thus Congress regulated what it had authority to address through a means appropriate to achieving that end.

Finally, the Court rejected the argument that the Tenth Amendment insulated wages and hours of production employees from federal regulation. The Tenth Amendment, Stone said, "states but a truism that all is retained which has not been surrendered." The amendment is merely "declaratory" of the relationship between the federal and state governments. Its role was to generally "allay fears" that the federal government would exercise powers not granted. Its function is not to deprive the national government of power to use any means in the exercise of granted power that are "appropriate and plainly adapted to the permitted end." *See also* COMMERCE CLAUSE, p. 291; FEDERALISM, p. 29; *GARCIA V. SAN ANTONIO METROPOLITAN TRANSIT AUTHORITY* (469 U.S. 528: 1985), p. 275; *HAMMER V. DAGENHART* (247 U.S. 251: 1918), p. 309.

Significance   The Supreme Court upheld, in *United States v. Darby Lumber Company* (312 U.S. 100: 1941), federal regulation of wages and hours of production workers employed by businesses whose products would subsequently reach interstate commerce. The FLSA was an outgrowth of the Court's receptivity to the Wagner Act. A number of decisions clearly indicated that production as well as wholly intrastate activities could be reached under the commerce power so long as those activities had a substantial effect on interstate commerce. The FLSA directly targeted production with its minimum wage, maximum hours, and overtime compensation provisions. In addition, the child labor language was virtually identical to that of the 1916 statute struck down on, among other things, production grounds in *Hammer v. Dagenhart* (247 U.S. 251: 1918). *Darby* formally overruled *Hammer* and its supporting rationale.

Darby had four policy consequences. First, it categorically stated that judicial inquiry into congressional "motives and purposes" for exercise of the commerce power was inappropriate. This deference gave Congress far greater latitude in judging what activities or factors required federal regulation through the commerce power. Second, the Court ruled that Congress could lawfully prohibit entry of items into interstate commerce as a form of regulation. Third, *Darby* reinforced the proposition established in *National Labor Relations Board v. Jones and Laughlin Steel Corporation* (301 U.S. 1: 1937) that production activities can be reached by the federal commerce power. Thus, the utility of the production-commerce distinction as a means of immunizing the former from federal regulatory control was negated. Finally, this and other decisions of the period effectively ended use of the dual federalism doctrine. Under this doctrine, there were areas exclusively under the control of the states. Modes of production were, until decisions like *Jones and Laughlin* and *Darby*, generally regarded as activities of an intrastate or local character. *Darby* rather categorically rejected dual federalism.

State Licensure of Interstate Bus Ticket Sellers

California v. Thompson, **313 U.S. 109, 61 S.Ct. 930, 85 L.Ed. 1219 (1941)**   Upheld a state law regulating licensure of transportation agents including those arranging for interstate travel. The statute in question in *California v. Thompson* authorized a state agency to determine the fitness of all applicants to act as transportation agents, collect a license fee, and require receipt of a bond as a prerequisite to licensure. Thompson was convicted of violation of the statute, but a state court held the law unconstitutional on commerce clause grounds. The Supreme Court reviewed and held in a unanimous decision that the state could impose these regulations.

The opinion of the Court was delivered by Justice Stone. Two considerations dominated the Court's response in this case. First, Congress had not attempted to exercise its regulatory authority in this matter.

Second, the Court adopted a view that certain local aspects of interstate commerce could be regulated by the states. The commerce clause did not "wholly withdraw from the states" the concurrent power to regulate matters of local concern that because of their "number and diversity may never be adequately dealt with by Congress."

The California regulation had several characteristics that allowed it to be sustained. It did not "prohibit" interstate commerce nor impose conditions "which restrict or obstruct" commerce. The law did not, for example, "operate to increase the costs of the transportation." It did not apply to persons actually engaged in transportation, but rather only brokers or intermediaries of that transportation. In regulating agents of commerce, it did not discriminate; the law applied to agents who "negotiate for transportation intrastate as well as interstate." The licensure requirements were not conditioned upon control over the movement of interstate traffic, but only the "good character and responsibility" of those acting as brokers. The "fraudulent" conduct of those acting as agents was seen as "peculiarly a subject of local concern" and the "appropriate subject of local regulation." In "every practical sense," such conduct is "beyond the effective reach" of Congress. Unless "some measure" of local regulation is allowed, this activity must go "largely unregulated." Citing state regulations of interstate motor vehicle traffic, the Court said that many such regulations have been upheld in the absence of "pertinent" federal legislation. If state authority has been recognized to allow regulations affecting interstate transportation, states must also be deemed to possess the power to regulate "negotiations for such transportation" where they "affect matters of local concern." This is especially true where those matters are "in other respects" already within the scope of state regulatory power and where the state regulation does not interfere with the national interest in "maintaining the free flow" of commerce and "preserving uniformity" in the regulation of such commerce. *See also* COMMERCE CLAUSE, p. 291; CONCURRENT POWER, p. 588; *COOLEY V. BOARD OF PORT WARDENS* (12 Howard 299: 1851), p. 298.

Significance   In *California v. Thompson* (313 U.S. 109: 1941), the Court permitted a state to require licenses for all travel agents including those arranging for interstate travel. Under the doctrine developed in *Cooley v. Board of Port Wardens* (12 Howard 299: 1851), the Court permitted states to regulate those aspects of commerce that demand local and diverse responses provided that Congress has not acted on the matter. These state regulations obviously had some effect on interstate commerce. So long as that effect was only incidental, the *Cooley* rule usually dictated that the state regulation be sustained. That was not always the result, however. In 1927, a state sought to require licensure of persons selling international steamship tickets. Conditions of licensure included the filing of a bond and demonstration by the applicant that he or she was a bona fide agent of a steamship company. In *DiSanto v. Pennsylvania* (273 U.S. 34: 1927), the Court ignored the statute's consumer protection objective and struck down the enactment because it imposed a "direct burden" on commerce. *Thompson* overruled the *DiSanto* holding as the Roosevelt Court sought to encourage rather than inhibit state regulation in the absence of conflicting federal regulation on the subject.

State Prohibition on Entry of Indigents

Edwards v. California, **314 U.S. 160, 62 S.Ct. 164, 86 L.Ed. 119 (1941)**   Struck down a state law that prohibited bringing an indigent person into the state. The kind of statute at issue in *Edwards v. California* was known as an "anti-Okie" law, and these could be found on the books of almost half the states in 1940. The California statute made it a misdemeanor for any "person, firm or corporation, or officer or agent thereof" who "knowingly brings or assists in bringing" into the state "any indigent person" who is not already a resident of the state. Edwards, a California resident, drove his wife's brother (Frank Duncan), a citizen of the United States and an indigent resident of Texas, from that state into California. Edwards was allegedly aware of Duncan's indigency because he knew Duncan had last been employed by WPA, the national relief agency. Edwards was also alleged to have known that Duncan had only $20 when they had left Texas and that Duncan had completely exhausted these resources by the time they arrived in California. Edwards was convicted and sentenced to a six-month jail term for his crime (a sentence subsequently suspended). On review, the Supreme Court struck down the law.

The opinion for the unanimous Court was delivered by Justice Byrnes. The Court said that the "grave and perplexing social and economic dislocation" reflected in this statute is a matter of "common knowledge and concern." The phenomenon of large numbers of people "constantly on the move" has given rise to "urgent demands upon the ingenuity of government." A large influx of migrants creates problems of "health, morals and especially finances." The Court recognized the dimensions of the problem and termed them "staggering." While the Court's role is not to pass on the "wisdom, need or appropriateness" of legislative solutions, this does not mean that there are "no boundaries to the permissible area of state legislative activity." There are limits, and "none is more certain" than the prohibition against attempts by a state to "isolate itself from difficulties common to all of them by restraining the transportation of persons and property across its borders." The California law was framed around a parochial interest. The Court said it was "difficult to conceive" a law more "squarely in conflict" with the theory that the "peoples of the several states must sink or swim together," and that in the long run the "prosperity and salvation" of the country are in "union and not division," than the statute under review in this case. The burden placed on interstate commerce is "intended and immediate"; it is the "plain and sole function" of the law. The Court further observed that the indigent nonresidents who are the "victims" of this statute are deprived of any opportunity to exert pressure on the state legislature to change the policy. Such prohibition on transportation is an "open invitation to retaliating measures," and the burdens on movement of indigent persons "become cumulative."

Finally, the Court rejected the argument that the care and responsibility for indigents is a local matter. The Court cited the magnitude of the problem as more properly placing responsibility at the federal level. To a large degree, the Court concluded, the relief of the "needy has become the common responsibility and concern of the whole nation." Accordingly, no state can close itself off from the rest of the country, especially through means that interfere with the free movement of persons across state lines. It was pointed out in concurring opinions by Justices Douglas and Jackson that the California statute also violated Duncan's privileges and immunities of citizenship. *See also* COMMERCE CLAUSE, p. 291; *HEART OF ATLANTA MOTEL V. UNITED STATES* (379 U.S. 241: 1964), p. 343; PRIVILEGES AND IMMUNITIES CLAUSE, p. 647.

Significance   In *Edwards v. California* (314 U.S. 160: 1941), the Court struck down a state prohibition against bringing an indigent nonresident person into the state. Reflected in the Court's ruling was the proposition that state regulations that create actual barriers against commerce or travel are highly suspect. Certainly state regulations that disadvantage interstate commerce as they attempt to protect local commerce from outside competition have not fared well (see, for example, *Baldwin v. G.A.F. Seelig, Inc.*, 294 U.S. 511: 1935). There are state regulations, generally those including health and safety matters, that have been permitted despite their interference with the free flow of commerce. Quarantine laws, for example, have been upheld so long as they do not interfere too broadly with commercial flow or run counter to existing federal policy.

But what of interference with the free movement of people from state to state? Several members of the Court in *Edwards* wished to resolve the case on privileges and immunities grounds. Indeed, the case of *Crandall v. Nevada* (6 Wallace 35: 1885) seemed to govern the *Edwards* situation. *Crandall* had invalidated a state statute imposing a charge against carriers for each person transported out of the state on the ground that it interfered with the privilege of citizenship covering interstate travel. The majority, however, preferred to nullify the statute on commerce grounds. In doing so, the Court also rejected arguments by California based on the ruling in *New York v. Miln* (11 Peters 102: 1837). The law at issue in *Miln* essentially screened persons coming into the state from abroad. The Court said that a state could enact "precautionary measures" against the "moral pestilence" of "paupers, vagabonds and possible convicts." This power was comparable to guarding against "physical pestilence" stemming from "unsound and infectious" imported articles. The Court pointed out in *Edwards* that no state had actually attempted exclusion of indigents since the *Miln* decision. Justice Byrnes also said for the Court that it could not be "seriously contended" that a person "without employment and without funds" constitutes a "moral pestilence." "Poverty and immorality," Byrnes said, "are not synonymous." Thus the Court did not consider itself bound by the *Miln* precedent permitting the possible exclusion of persons despite the serious impairment it had on commerce. Court decisions since *Edwards*, based largely on privileges and immunities and equal protection clauses, have firmly established a right to travel, thus extending the *Edwards* foundation.

Regulation of Agricultural Production

***Wickard v. Filburn*, 317 U.S. 111, 63 S.Ct. 82, 87 L.Ed. 122 (1942)** Upheld the wheat production and marketing quotas contained in the Agricultural Adjustment Act (AAA) of 1938. The aim of the act under review in *Wickard v. Filburn* was to stabilize farm production and farm prices. Under provisions of the act, the secretary of agriculture would establish a national acreage allotment for specific commodities (wheat in this instance). This allotment was apportioned to states and then to individual farmers in the form of production acreage quotas. Filburn operated a small farm on which he maintained some livestock including dairy cattle and poultry. He produced small amounts of wheat, part of which was used to feed his livestock and the remainder of which was made into flour for home consumption or used for seed. He attempted to market none of his wheat production. Under the quota mechanism of the act, Filburn was assigned a wheat acreage of 11.1 acres. A normal yield per acre was calculated to be 20.1 bushels. Filburn, however, grew wheat on 23 acres and produced 239 bushels of wheat more than he was allowed using the normal yield standard. Though he claimed the wheat was wholly consumed on his farm, he was subjected to a penalty on the excess production. A unanimous Court upheld the power of Congress to regulate even that production not destined for interstate commerce.

The opinion of the Court was delivered by Justice Jackson. The issue in this case was whether the commerce power allowed regulation of production that was never intended for interstate commerce. The marketing quotas, said the Court, "not only embrace" wheat that can be sold without penalty, but also "what may be consumed on the premises." Filburn asserted that this regulation of wheat produced for personal consumption did not even indirectly affect interstate commerce. The commerce power, the court responded, is "not confined" in its exercise to the regulation of such commerce. It also extends to those intrastate activities that "so affect" interstate commerce or the "exertion of the power of Congress over it." Even if Filburn's activity is "local" and thus not regarded as commerce, it may be reached by Congress if it exerts a "substantial economic effect on interstate commerce." This is true regardless of whether such an effect is what "at some earlier time" was defined as "direct or indirect."

The Court said that it is "well established" by prior decisions that the commerce power includes authority to regulate the "prices at which commodities in that commerce are dealt in and practices affecting such prices." A principal purpose of the AAA was to increase the market price of wheat through limitations on production volume. "It can hardly be denied" that a factor of such "volume and variability" as home-consumed wheat would have a "substantial influence on price and market conditions." This is so because "being in marketable condition," the home-grown wheat "overhangs the market" and may be "induced" to flow into the market by rising prices. This would have the effect of checking those price increases. Further, even if the wheat is never marketed, it "supplies a need" of the person growing it that would otherwise lead to purchases by that person on the open market. Thus the home-grown wheat "in this sense competes with wheat in commerce." The "stimulation" of commerce was recognized as a proper use of the regulatory power, and the AAA was viewed as a permissible means to that end. *See also* COMMERCE CLAUSE, p. 291; *UNITED STATES V. BUTLER* (297 U.S. 1: 1936), p. 389; *UNITED STATES V. DARBY LUMBER COMPANY* (312 U.S. 100: 1941), p. 324.

Significance   The Court upheld wheat marketing quotas in *Wickard v. Filburn* (317 U.S. 111: 1942) and, in doing so, abandoned the "direct" and "indirect" effect distinction. The Court used instead the measure of economic consequence to determine whether a local activity could be subject to federal regulation. In *Wickard*, wheat produced for home consumption was found to have sufficient relationship to market price levels that it could be regulated even though it never entered commerce as such. As in other policy areas, the Court did a dramatic turnaround on federal regulation of agriculture between 1936 and the early 1940s. In *United States v. Butler* (297 U.S. 1: 1936) the Court struck down the Agricultural Adjustment Act of 1933, the first New Deal initiative in the area of agriculture. The act sought to use the federal taxing power to regulate farm production. The Court ruled the policy unconstitutional in that it attempted to exercise federal taxing and spending power to regulate agriculture, a traditionally local rather than national activity. Prompted by the Court's decision in *NLRB v. Jones and Laughlin Steel Corporation* (301 U.S. 1: 1937), the Congress enacted the Agricultural Adjustment Act of 1938, which imposed market quotas based on the commerce power. The Court upheld the act in *Mulford v. Smith* (307 U.S. 38: 1939), ruling that the regulation was only a control on the selling of commodities through interstate commerce. The objective was not to control production as such, but the prevention of the injury of unstable prices caused by excessive flow of agricultural commodities in commerce. The full implications of this approach became evident in *Wickard*, as the Court allowed application of federal commerce power to items never intended for interstate commerce.

Concurrent Regulation of Agriculture

Parker v. Brown, **317 U.S. 341, 63 S.Ct. 307, 87 L.Ed. 315 (1943)**   Upheld a state-created monopoly that marketed all state-grown agricultural produce. *Parker v. Brown* is an example of one of the most extensive state regulations permitted by the Court against commerce clause challenge. The state of California established a policy whereby competition among agricultural producers was restricted in an attempt to stabilize distribution prices of various products. Under the program, all marketing was to be done through a state-established commission. Brown, a raisin grower, sought to enjoin implementation of the state program because he was suffering severe losses at the established prices. Since 90 per cent of California raisins are shipped out of state, he challenged the program on commerce clause grounds as well as arguing that the policy violated the Sherman Antitrust Act. He obtained an order enjoining enforcement of the program, and the state of California appealed. In a unanimous decision, the Supreme Court reversed the lower court and upheld the state program.

The opinion of the Court was delivered by Chief Justice Stone. He started out with an acknowledgment that the commerce power was not exclusive, but could be exercised concurrently. The grant of power to Congress "did not wholly withdraw" from the state authority to regulate local commerce "with respect to matters of local concern" on which

"Congress has not spoken." As long as a state regulation serves "local ends" and does not "discriminate" against interstate commerce, it may operate even though the interstate commerce is "materially" affected. Stone then referred to two standards by which state regulations are reviewed. The first he called a "mechanical" test, which revolves around when commerce begins and features the distinction between production and manufacture and commerce. Under this test, a state is free to license and tax all intrastate buying that will result, in the normal course of business, after processing and packing, in resale for interstate commerce. So long as state regulation occurs prior to "any operation of interstate commerce," it is not prohibited by the commerce clause no matter how "drastically it may affect" that interstate commerce. But the courts are not "confined to so mechanical a test." When Congress has "not so exerted its power," under the clause, state regulation of "local matters" are permissible as long as they are compatible with national interests. Such state regulations may be upheld if they legitimately exercise state police power over local matters and address matters that create "practical difficulties" for federal regulation. There may also be local regulations whose effect is to "coincide" with an established federal policy. The California law at issue in this case was seen by the Court as of this latter type. Congress had recognized the "distressed condition" of American agriculture and had authorized marketing procedures "substantially like" those in the California program. Whatever the effects of the California regulation on interstate commerce, they are effects Congress chose to "aid and encourage" through its own legislation. Neither did the Court see the impact on commerce as "greater than or substantially different in kind" from those contemplated by federally authorized subsidy programs. Thus, the Court could not say that the effect of the state policy produced incompatible effects on commerce or was outside the reserve power that permitted California to regulate domestic agricultural production. *See also* COMMERCE CLAUSE, p. 291; CONCURRENT POWER, p. 588.

Significance   The Court upheld a state marketing program in *Parker v. Brown* (317 U.S. 341: 1943) despite the program's effect on interstate commerce. Prior to 1938, regulation of agriculture had been viewed as a local matter and thus reserved to the states. Enactment of the Agricultural Adjustment Act of 1938, based on the federal commerce power, challenged that status. In *Mulford v. Smith* (307 U.S. 38: 1939), the Court upheld the statute, recognizing the substantial relationship between the marketing of agricultural commodities and interstate commerce. In addition, the justices of the liberal Roosevelt Court wished to permit states wide latitude to regulate in areas relating to commerce. Its conservative predecessors had not only limited the scope of federal commerce power, but used the commerce clause to free many commercial activities from state regulation as well. The intention of the Roosevelt Court was clearly reflected in such decisions as *California v. Thompson* (313 U.S. 109: 1941), where a state licensure requirement on travel agents was upheld. Deference to state initiatives like that in *Parker*, focusing on local factors affecting commerce, was much more likely after *Thompson*.

Parker also provides another key proposition. Under previous commerce clause precedents, states were permitted to regulate commerce only in the absence of federal action. The California policy at issue in *Parker* was upheld despite the existence of federal regulation. The Court said that so long as the federal and state regulations are complementary, they may coexist. This practice is taken one step further in *Florida Lime and Avocado Growers v. Paul* (373 U.S. 132: 1963). In this case, the Court had to decide whether the state and federal governments may use different maturity tests in determining marketability of agricultural produce. The Court said that they could. The power of a state to "reject commodities which a federal authority [the Department of Agriculture] has certified to be marketable" depends on whether the state standard "stands as an obstacle" to the accomplishment of federal objectives. The Court said that the more restrictive state standard was not such an obstacle in this instance. Unless Congress explicitly preempts such state action, the Court thought it "unreasonable to infer" that states should be deprived of their "traditional power to enforce otherwise valid regulations designed for the protection of consumers."

Insurance as Interstate Commerce

United States v. South-Eastern Underwriters' Association, **322 U.S. 533, 64 S.Ct. 1162, 88 L.Ed. 1440 (1944)**   Ruled that the insurance industry was interstate commerce and subject to provisions of the Sherman Antitrust Act. *United States v. South-Eastern Underwriters' Association* involved a federal indictment against members of an insurance organization for violation of the Sherman Act. The association was charged with fixing fire insurance premiums in a manner that produced "arbitrary and noncompetitive" rates in a multistate area. The association argued that the selling of insurance was not commerce and, thus, could not be reached by a regulation like the Sherman Act, which was based on the commerce clause. A federal district court ruled for the underwriters' association, and the United States appealed. In a 4–3 decision (with Justices Roberts and Reed not participating), the

Court reversed the lower court and held the insurance industry subject to commerce power regulation.

The opinion of the Court was delivered by Justice Black. The case presented two issues: Was the Sherman Act intended to apply to the insurance industry, and, if so, were insurance transactions commerce? Black offered an initial interpretative perspective. He suggested that, as a matter of course, courts do not construe words in the Constitution "so as to give them a meaning more narrow" than one they had in the "common parlance" of the period in which the document was written. To find that the term "commerce," as used in the commerce clause, does not include businesses like insurance "would do just that." Accordingly, an assertion that the commerce power does not reach the insurance business bears a "heavy burden." The Court then turned to the insurance business itself. The business is "concentrated in comparatively few companies." Premiums collected from policyholders throughout the country "flow into these companies for investment." As claims are filed, payments flow back to the policyholders. The result is a "continuous and indivisible stream of intercourse. The negotiation and execution of insurance contracts involves "countless documents and communications." The policyholders have their separate financial interests "blended into one assembled fund of assets" upon which all depend for payment of claims. In addition, the operating decisions made by the company to its home office concern more than the people in the state where the office is located.

Despite what seemed to be compelling reasons to find insurance to be commerce, the lower court had found precedents to the contrary (for example, *Paul v. Virginia*, 8 Wallace 183: 1869). But each of these precedents that found insurance not to be commerce was a case where the central question had been the validity of state regulations. The Court said that "legal formulae" utilized to uphold state power cannot "uncritically be accepted as trustworthy guides" to assess federal commerce regulation. These prior decisions could not, in the Court's view, be reconciled with the "many decisions" that have sustained federal regulation of commerce. While an insurance contract, "considered as a thing apart from negotiation and execution," is not interstate commerce, it does not render the Court "powerless to examine the entire transaction" of which the formal contract is but a part. From this perspective, the Court may determine if there is a "chain of events" that constitutes interstate commerce.

The Court noted the difficulty of delineating the boundary between federal and state power over commerce, but concluded the power granted to Congress in this field is "positive." It permits establishment of rules for intercourse across state lines. This is a power "essential" to "weld" the confederacy into an "indivisible Nation," and its continued existence is "equally essential to the welfare" of the country. The Court's "basic responsibility" in interpreting the Constitution is that the power to govern intercourse among the states "remains where the Constitution placed it." No business that operates across state lines is beyond the "regulatory reach" of congressional commerce power, and the Court ruled that it could not "make an exception of the business of insurance."

Chief Justice Stone and Justices Frankfurter and Jackson dissented. Their principal disagreement with the majority was departure from precedent. Stone characterized the case law holding insurance not to be commerce as both "numerous and unvarying." Jackson found the distinction between insurance and other interstate business "unrealistic, illogical and inconsistent." He would have joined the majority had the Court been "writing on a clean slate," but thought adherence to established precedent a more important priority. *See also* ANTITRUST LAWS, p. 579; COMMERCE CLAUSE, p. 291; CONCURRENT POWER, p. 588.

Significance   In *United States v. South-Eastern Underwriters' Association* (322 U.S. 533: 1944), the Court held that insurance was interstate commerce and thus subject to federal regulations on interstate commerce. With its decision in *South-Eastern Underwriters* as well as *Polish National Alliance v. National Labor Relations Board* (322 U.S. 643: 1944), the Court reversed a long-standing policy to the contrary. In *Paul v. Virginia* (8 Wallace 168: 1869), the Court had ruled that entering into insurance contracts was a local activity, and that insurance contracts could not be considered interstate commerce. The effect of *Paul* was to free the insurance industry from regulation at the federal level. While sometimes extensive regulation was developed at the state level, insurance remained immune from federal regulation into the 1940s. Without prompting from Congress, the Court abandoned the *Paul* doctrine in *Polish National Alliance*, saying that the actions of the insurance industry sufficiently affected interstate commerce to make it subject to provisions of the Wagner Act. The Court extended this ruling in *South-Eastern Underwriters* by defining insurance as commerce. These decisions were compatible with the Roosevelt Court's predisposition to substantially expand the federal commerce power. In this instance, Congress was reluctant to accept its new regulatory role for insurance, and it almost immediately enacted legislation authorizing the states to continue regulation of the insurance industry.

State Regulation of Length of Interstate Trains

Southern Pacific Railroad Company v. Arizona, **325 U.S. 761, 65 S.Ct. 1515, 89 L.Ed. 1915 (1945)**   Struck down a state law limiting the length of trains operating within the state. *Southern Pacific Railroad Company v. Arizona* involved a 1912 statute that prohibited operation of a passenger train of more than 14 cars or a freight train of more than 70 cars within the state. The state attempted to collect fines for violations of the statute from Southern Pacific. The company unsuccessfully challenged the constitutionality of the law in the state courts, and appealed. In a 7–2 decision, the Supreme Court ruled that the statute impermissibly interfered with interstate commerce.

The opinion of the Court was delivered by Chief Justice Stone. The Court has recognized, he said, that in the absence of conflicting federal regulation, there is a "residuum of power" in the states to enact laws governing matters that are "local in character and effect" and whose impact does not seriously interfere with national commerce. But from the outset of our constitutional history, the states have not been seen as having the power to "impede substantially the free flow of commerce from state to state." Neither have states had the power to regulate "those phases of national commerce" that require "national uniformity" of regulation. While Congress can define the "distribution of power" over commerce as between the federal and state levels, Stone pointed out that it was "accepted doctrine" that where Congress has not acted, it has left it to the courts to "formulate rules" whereby the commerce clause affords some protection from state regulation that is "inimical to national commerce."

The question in this case then becomes whether the burden imposed by the state safety measure is compelling enough for the Court to conclude that this situation requires uniformity of regulation. If so, the state law is invalidated even in the absence of federal legislation. The record showed that most trains in the country exceeded the Arizona limits. Thus interstate trains running through Arizona either had to change routes to go around the state, be "broken up and reconstituted" at the point of entry into Arizona, or conform to the most restrictive state law (Arizona's) from the outset. Thus, the Arizona law imposed a "serious burden on interstate commerce." If a state can so regulate train length, any and all other states may also do so. The "practical effect" of this regulation is to "control train operations beyond the boundaries of the state imposing the restriction." In the Court's view, this was a situation where regulation "prescribed by a single body" had "national authority." The Court recognized the scope of the state police power, and the legitimacy of state regulations that promote public health and safety. The need to achieve uniformity of regulation cannot be avoided by "simply invoking the . . . apologetics of the police power." In this case, the Court agreed with the trial court that the law as a safety measure "affords at most slight and dubious advantage" over unregulated trains.

Arizona also tried to defend their train limit policy by citing state laws regulating highways and highway use. While recognizing that highways may have an interstate character, the Court distinguished height, weight, and width restrictions on the grounds that states have more "extensive control" over highways than interstate railroads. Unlike railroads, highways are "built, owned and maintained by the states." The states are responsible for their "safe and economical regulation." The application of such rules to both interstate and intrastate traffic safeguards against abuse or discrimination. The differences between the train length and highway regulations illustrated, thought Stone, the breadth of factors that enter into the determination of whether the "relative weights" of state or national interests will prevail when examining the effects of such regulation on commerce. In this case, a weighing of relevant factors "makes it plain" that the state interest is "outweighed."

Justices Black and Douglas argued in dissent that elected representatives rather than courts ought to decide these matters. They would have preferred Congress to decide that a uniform policy was required and acted accordingly. *See also* COMMERCE CLAUSE, p. 291; CONCURRENT POWER, p. 588; *KASSEL V. CONSOLIDATED FREIGHTWAYS CORPORATION* (450 U.S. 662: 1981), p. 357.

Significance   The Court struck down a state train length limitation in *Southern Pacific Railroad Company v. Arizona* (325 U.S. 761: 1945) even in the absence of federal legislation on the subject. The Court concluded that the regulation of train lengths had such injurious implication for interstate commerce that the commerce clause required uniformity of regulation. Until such time as Congress directly addressed the issue, it was the Court's role to prevent states from establishing their own regulations. Typically, the Roosevelt Court was not inclined to limit state regulatory initiatives, especially those ostensibly devoted to protecting public health and safety. Nonetheless, the need for uniformity of regulation was seen as "indispensable" to the effective operation of the railroads, a key component of national commerce.

Beyond the need for uniformity, however, was the Court's review of the substance of the regulation itself in this case. Of critical importance was the "slight and dubious" advantage the Arizona law provided as a safety measure over no regulation at all. The Court made it clear that deference to state regulations would not occur simply by invoking the "apologetics" of the police power. Not lost on the Court in this case was the union sponsorship of the legislation, no doubt prompted by a genuine concern for safety, but also aware that larger numbers of shorter trains would employ more railroad workers. The message of the *Southern Pacific* ruling was that, while states would be afforded substantial latitude in establishing health and safety regulations, the Court would retain an active role in monitoring the impacts on interstate commerce even to the point of making substantive judgments about the effectiveness of state regulation in accomplishing its stated objectives.

Segregation of Interstate Buses

Morgan v. Virginia, **328 U.S. 373, 66 S.Ct. 1050, 90 L.Ed. 1317 (1946)** Held a state law requiring segregation by race on interstate buses to be unconstitutional. *Morgan v. Virginia* involved a state law that required drivers of interstate buses to assign passengers to seats according to race. Morgan, a black passenger on a bus operating between Virginia and Maryland, refused to sit where she was assigned and was convicted for violation of the statute. She appealed to the Supreme Court, which, in a 7–1 decision (Justice Jackson not participating), struck down the law.

Justice Reed delivered the opinion of the Court. He indicated that the Court was frequently required to determine whether state laws impermissibly interfere with the federal power to regulate interstate commerce. This is a difficult task as the "precise degree" of restriction on state authority "cannot be fixed generally" or even in relation to specific legislation such as that involving taxation or public health and safety. Nevertheless, said Reed, an "abstract principle" may be used as a "postulate" for determining whether a particular state regulation, absent federal law to the contrary, goes beyond the bounds of state power. The principle is that state law is invalid if it "unduly burdens" commerce in "matters where uniformity is necessary." Where uniformity is "essential for the functioning of commerce," a state may not impose a local regulation.

The state defended this enactment as an exercise of the state police power, but Reed pointed out that a state cannot avoid commerce clause restrictions "by simply invoking the convenient apologetics of the police power." Interference with interstate commerce comes from state regulations that directly "impair the usefulness" of facilities for interstate traffic. Intolerable burdens may arise from such causes as cost or delay, but also from regulations that require interstate passengers to "order their movements" in accordance with local rules. To properly evaluate the extent of the burden a local regulation imposes on commerce, related regulations of other states are useful to show whether there are "cumulative effects" that may make local regulations "impracticable." The Court found that a number of states prohibited racial segregation while others required it. Since no state can "reach beyond its own border" nor bar transportation of people across its borders, "diverse seating requirements" for the races traveling interstate will necessarily result. Since no federal legislation deals with racial separation of interstate passengers, the Court's function is to decide the issue by weighing the police power interest of the state against the need for "national uniformity" for interstate travel. It seemed "clear" to the Court that the latter interest should prevail.

Justice Burton dissented, saying that Morgan had failed to show a "serious and major burden" on the national interest in interstate commerce to warrant striking down the local regulation. He saw congressional inaction as indicating that the issue was "better met" without "uniform affirmative" regulation. *See also* COMMERCE CLAUSE, p. 291; CONCURRENT POWER, p. 588; *SOUTHERN PACIFIC RAILROAD COMPANY V. ARIZONA* (325 U.S. 761: 1945), p. 337.

Significance   The Court used the commerce clause in *Morgan v. Virginia* (328 U.S. 373: 1946) to strike down a state law requiring racial segregation on interstate buses. The suspect status of segregation and the "separate-but-equal" doctrine fashioned in *Plessy v. Ferguson* (163 U.S. 537: 1896) could be seen in the Court's handling of segregated transportation in the 1940s. Several decisions, including *Morgan*, approached the issue using interstate commerce rather than Fourteenth Amendment grounds. Under the shared governance rule of *Cooley v. Board of Port Wardens* (12 Howard 299: 1851), states can regulate commerce where local conditions demand local and diverse response. But a state cannot extend the effect of its regulations across state lines or establish regulations that unduly burden the free flow of interstate commerce. The question facing the Court in cases like *Morgan* was whether a state regulation requiring segregation of interstate bus passengers caused a serious enough burden on commerce to justify federal intervention. The Court found the burden substantial enough that a "single, uniform rule" was necessary to fully protect national travel. Under the *Cooley* doctrine, matters requiring such uniformity of regulation were the exclusive domain of the federal government whether congressional action had occurred or not.

The Court softened its demand for uniform regulation in the form of a state attempt to prohibit segregation on transportation facilities. In *Bob-Lo Excursion Company v. Michigan* (313 U.S. 28: 1948), the Court upheld a state civil rights law even though it technically affected foreign commerce (boat transportation to a Canadian island located some 15 miles from Detroit). The Court, however, saw the commerce as local despite the location of the island within Canadian boundaries. The reality of the matter, said the Court, was that Bob-Lo Island was an "amusement adjunct" of Detroit and therefore subject to local regulation. Furthermore, the Court saw the Michigan law as compatible with established federal policy governing segregation and foreign commerce.

Health Ordinance Permitting Only Local Milk Sale

Dean Milk Company v. City of Madison, **340 U.S. 349, 71 S.Ct. 295, 95 L.Ed. 329 (1951)** Struck down a local health ordinance that prohibited sale of milk in a community unless it was pasteurized and bottled at a licensed plant located within five miles of the center of the city. *Dean Milk Company v. City of Madison* involved the denial of licensure to an out-of-state company whose processing plants were outside the five-mile limit. The out-of-state company's farms and plants were licensed and regularly inspected by Illinois authorities. After failing to secure relief in the Wisconsin courts, the company appealed. In a 6–3 decision, the U.S. Supreme Court found that the local ordinance imposed an undue burden on interstate commerce.

The Court's opinion was delivered by Justice Clark. The ordinance was invalidated, but not because it conflicted with federal regulations. No "pertinent national regulation" had been passed by Congress, although laws enacted for the Dictrict of Columbia seemed to reflect congressional recognition of the new "appropriateness" of local regulation of the "sale of fluid milk." Neither was there a problem with the "avowed purpose" of the local ordinance. The Court's difficulty was with the consequences of the ordinance on interstate commerce. The regulation "in practical effect" prevents distribution of "wholesale" Illinois milk in Madison. The ordinance erects an "economic barrier" that protects a local industry against competition from outside the state. In doing so, Madison "plainly discriminates against interstate commerce." No state can do that even in the exercise of "unquestioned power" to protect the health and safety of its population if "reasonable nondiscriminatory alternatives" exist. To take the position that the ordinance is "simply valid" because it "professes to be a health measure" would mean that the commerce clause "imposes no limitations on state action" other than that contained in the due process clause.

The issue here turned on the question of whether the "discrimination inherent in the Madison ordinance" could be justified given the "character of the local interests," and the "available methods of protecting them." The Court determined that "reasonable and adequate alternatives" were available. For example, local inspection of imported milk could have been instituted. Such an approach is "readily open" to Madison, which could pass any "actual and reasonable" costs of such inspections on to importing producers and processors. There were other options that Madison's own health commissioner agreed would leave consumers "safeguarded adequately." Allowing Madison to enact a regulation "not essential for the protection of local health interests" and through which is placed a "discriminatory burden" on interstate commerce would "invite a multiplication of preferential trade areas destructive of the very purpose of the Commerce Clause." Under such circumstances, the local ordinance "must yield" to the proposition that a state may not, in its dealings with other states, "place itself in a position of economic isolation."

Justices Black, Douglas, and Minton dissented. Black pointed out that the ordinance, a "good-faith attempt to safeguard public health," did not prohibit sale of milk coming from outside the five-mile limit. Rather, the only restriction was that licensure of such milk not pasteurized in the area would not occur. The Dean Company could "easily comply" with the ordinance except for its "personal preference" to pasteurize its milk in Illinois. Further, Black felt that the courts should not invalidate a health ordinance because it believed alternative inspection methods might be effective. Such judgments were seen as legislative rather than judicial. *See also* BALDWIN V. G.A.F. SEELIG, INC. (294 U.S. 511: 1935), p. 313; COMMERCE CLAUSE, p. 291; POLICE POWER, p. 643.

Significance   The Court used the "discriminatory burden on interstate commerce" doctrine to invalidate a local health ordinance in *Dean Milk Company v. City of Madison* (340 U.S. 349: 1951). State regulation aimed at protection of the public health and welfare generally withstands constitutional scrutiny. In no area is there more consensus than when the police power reserved to the states is appropriately used to this end. The police power is not without limit, however. In *Baldwin v. G.A.F. Seelig, Inc.* (294 U.S. 511: 1935), the Court used the commerce clause to invalidate a state price regulation that erected a barrier against incoming commerce to the competitive advantage of local businesses. Justice Cardozo said in *Baldwin* that states could not impose any restriction that creates an "unreasonable clog upon the mobility of commerce." Thirty years later, the Warren Court pronounced *Baldwin* still "sound" in *Polar Ice Cream and Creamery Company v. Andrews* (375 U.S. 361: 1964) in a decision that nullified a state law requiring a company to purchase all its milk within the state and at a fixed price. The Court saw the measure as disadvantaging out-of-state milk producers. While the ordinance in *Dean* was discriminatory and invited a "multiplicity of preferential trade areas," it was a health as opposed to a price regulation. The Court made it clear in *Dean* that, while it would normally defer to health regulations, it would not do so simply because the law "professes" to protect public health. Indeed, the Court was doubtful that the interests of health were advanced by the ordinance. Certainly the health interests could be served by any one of a number of alternatives that were less burdensome to commerce. Thus, *Dean* underscores that the commerce clause stands as a limitation on the exercise of state police power, and that the Court will engage in substantive review of state regulations in determining whether the limitation should apply.

Civil Rights Act of 1964

***Heart of Atlanta Motel v. United States*, 379 U.S. 241, 85 S.Ct. 348, 13 L.Ed. 2d 258 (1964)**   Upheld Title II of the Civil Rights Act of 1964, which prohibited racial discrimination in "public accommodations." In *Heart of Atlanta Motel v. United States*, provisions of the act were applied to a motel, a large proportion of whose guests were from outside the state. A companion case, *Katzenbach v. McClung* (379 U.S. 294: 1964), examined the prohibition on discrimination in restaurants. Heart of Atlanta Motel appealed from a district court injunction against its refusal to allow black travelers to stay in its facilities. U.S. Attorney General Katzenbach appealed in the *McClung* case following a lower court judgment that the act could not be applied to McClung's restaurant. The Supreme Court unanimously affirmed in *Heart of Atlanta* and reversed in *McClung*, finding that the Congress could use the commerce power to prohibit discrimination in facilities that serve interstate travelers.

The opinions of the Court in these two cases were both delivered by Justice Clark. He said in *Heart of Atlanta* that the "determinative test" for the exercise of commerce power is "simply whether the activity sought to be regulated is commerce which concerns more states than one" and that such activity has a "real and substantial relation to the national interest." Clark then reviewed instances where congressional power to protect interstate commerce was used. The interest in protecting commerce let Congress deal with segregation in interstate carriers, prohibit white slave traffic, and regulate deceptive sales practices, to list but three examples. That Congress was legislating "against moral wrongs" in these instances "rendered its enactments no less valid." That Congress considered discrimination a "moral problem" did not "detract" from the "overwhelming evidence" of the "disruptive effect" of discrimination in interstate traffic. The commerce power is not confined to just commerce among the states, but also includes the power to regulate the "local incidents" of commerce. This includes local activities in both the states of "origin and destination" that might have a "substantial and harmful effect" on commerce. The only questions the Court can raise are whether the Congress had a "rational basis" for its finding that discrimination affected commerce and whether the means chosen to address the matter were "reasonable and appropriate." Clark added in *Katzenbach* that Congress had determined that refusal of service to travelers imposed burdens upon the "interstate flow of food and upon the movement of products generally." Where legislators, in light of the information placed before them, have "rational basis" for finding a "chosen regulatory scheme necessary to the protection of commerce, our investigation is at an end." The power of Congress in this field, Clark concluded, "is broad and sweeping." When Congress "keeps within its sphere and violates no express constitutional limitation," it has been the practice of the Court "not to interfere."

Justice Black, concurring in *McClung*, said he recognized that some "isolated and remote lunchroom" selling only local produce to exclusively local residents "may possibly" be beyond commerce clause reach. The decision in cases like these, however, rests not on the effect of only one "isolated, individual, local event," but also the effect coming from adding a single local event to "many others of a similar nature." The cumulative effect may impose a substantial burden on interstate commerce by "reducing its volume or distorting its flow." Also in concurrence, Justice Douglas indicated reluctance to "rest solely" on the commerce clause. He agreed that Congress could regulate commerce "in the interest of human rights," but would have preferred to base the act on the Fourteenth Amendment. The right of persons to travel free from discrimination "occupies a more protected position in our constitutional system than does the interstate movement of cattle, fruit, steel and coal." A decision based on the Fourteenth Amendment, in his view, would have been more direct and would have had a "more settling effect." *See also* CIVIL RIGHTS CASES (109 U.S. 3: 1883), p. 259; COMMERCE CLAUSE, p. 291.

Significance   In *Heart of Atlanta Motel v. United States* (379 U.S. 241: 1964), the Court ruled that the commerce power could be used to prohibit racial discrimination in "public accommodations" that affect interstate commerce. The Civil Rights Act of 1964 was not the first congressional act dealing with racial discrimination and public accommodations. In 1875, Congress adopted a measure that guaranteed to all persons "full and equal enjoyment" of the "accommodations, advantages, facilities and privileges of inns, public conveyances and theaters."

The act was based upon the Fourteenth Amendment. In the *Civil Rights Cases* (109 U.S 3: 1883), the Court struck down the law, saying that Congress was not empowered to regulate private acts of discrimination. The requirement that state action exist before the remedial features of the Fourteenth Amendment could be activated had the effect of substantially limiting any federal efforts to combat segregation directly through the equal protection clause.

The provisions of the Civil Rights Act of 1964 were strikingly similar to those of the enactment of 1875 struck down in the *Civil Rights Cases*. While the limiting state action doctrine of that decision remained intact, the federal commerce power had expanded dramatically over the same period. The commerce power thus presented to Congress a well-established, albeit somewhat indirect, approach for the regulation of segregation. The Court's response to this utilization of the commerce power was wholly deferential. Citing *Gibbons v. Ogden* (9 Wheaton 1: 1824), the Court saw the commerce power as "plenary" or "complete in itself." It was immaterial to the Court that the commerce power was directed toward achieving a social rather than an economic end. The Court may only inquire whether Congress rationally linked the regulated activity to protection of commerce and whether the means chosen were rationally related to the regulatory objective. Neither was the Court particularly concerned about the regulation of some intrastate incidents of commerce. The act was aimed at patterns of discrimination. Individual discriminatory conduct is part of a class of activity that is within the "total incidence" of the practice on interstate commerce.

Local Incidents of Commerce

Perez v. United States, **402 U.S. 146, 91 S.Ct. 1357, 28 L.Ed. 2d 686 (1971)**   Upheld provisions of the Consumer Credit Protection Act making it a federal crime to use "extortionate means" to collect a debt. The law under review in *Perez v. United States* was an attempt to reach loansharking practices through the federal commerce power. Perez made several loans to a businessman. None of the transactions were interstate in character. The borrower's payments were increased on several occasions, and threats against the borrower and his family occurred. Perez attempted to have his indictment for violations of the act dismissed. He argued that the federal commerce power could not reach such intrastate activity. The district court rejected the motion to dismiss, and Perez was subsequently convicted. He appealed, and in an

8–1 decision, the Supreme Court upheld the act and affirmed the conviction.

The opinion of the Court was delivered by Justice Douglas. The case raised a "substantial" constitutional question because the criminal provisions "take a long stride" toward exercising a "general Federal police power." The commerce clause reaches three "categories of problems." The first is the "misuse" of "channels" of interstate or foreign commerce, as where stolen goods are shipped through commerce. The second category is protection of the "instrumentalities" of commerce. The third includes those activities "affecting commerce." The anti-loansharking provision under review in this case fell into the third category. Congress possesses the power to regulate intrastate activities that "so affect interstate commerce" that regulation of those activities is an "appropriate means to the attainment of a legitimate end." In examining the credit transactions of Perez, the Court used a "class of activities" approach similar to that used to uphold the Civil Rights Act of 1964 in *Heart of Atlanta Motel v. United States* (379 U.S. 241: 1964). There, individual acts of discrimination were seen as burdening the right to travel through their aggregate effect. Taken together, these activities constituted a class that could be reached by Congress because of the effect of the "total incidence" of the practices on interstate commerce. Where the "class of activities" is the object of the regulation, and that class is "within the reach of federal power," the courts have no authority to "excise . . . individual instances of the class." Although exclusively intrastate, "extortionate credit transactions" could be legitimately viewed by Congress as affecting interstate commerce. Indeed, the Congress reviewed a great deal of information on this issue. That information indicated that the "loanshark racket" provides organized crime with a lucrative source of revenue, "exacts millions" from American citizens, "coerces its victims" into commissions of crime, and causes "takeover . . . of legitimate businesses" by racketeers. The Congress had "quite adequate" grounds to conclude that a relationship exists between loansharks and interstate crime.

Justice Stewart dissented, suggesting that the constitutional framers "never intended" that the federal government could "define as a crime" and prosecute such "wholly local activity." In order to do so, it must be shown that Congress could "rationally have concluded that loansharking" is a practice distinct in "some substantial respect from other local crime." Stewart was neither able to "discern" any such "rational distinction" nor did he feel it was sufficient to say that loansharking is a "national problem" or has some interstate "characteristics." *See also* CHAMPION V. AMES (188 U.S. 321: 1903), p. 304; COMMERCE CLAUSE, p. 291; *HEART OF ATLANTA MOTEL V. UNITED STATES* (379 U.S. 241: 1964), p. 343; POLICE POWER, p. 643.

Significance   The Court ruled in *Perez v. United States* (402 U.S. 146: 1971) that the commerce power could be used to make federal crimes of local loansharking practices. Exercise of the police power is generally a function of the state government. Indeed, for many, the foremost power "reserved" to the states by the Tenth Amendment is the police power. Certainly no such power was formally delegated to the national government. Yet over the years, the Court has seemed to recognize a form of police power available to Congress through the commerce clause. In cases such as *Champion v. Ames* (188 U.S. 321: 1903), the Court upheld federal laws aimed at protecting the channels of interstate commerce from particular "evils"; in *Champion* the evil was lottery tickets. *Perez* expanded federal power to local activities where no demonstrable effect on interstate commerce could be shown. As in *Heart of Atlanta Motel v. United States* (379 U.S. 241: 1964), where the 1964 Civil Rights Act was sustained, the Court used the class of activities approach. While an isolated local activity may not come under the reach of federal power, the aggregate effects of many such isolated activities may burden the free flow of commerce in such a way as to be regulated. The Court deferred to the rationality of congressional judgment that such a burdensome effect was produced by this "class" of activities. Once it is established that Congress can regulate the class, individual acts, even though they may be "trivial," cannot be "separated or excise[d]" from the regulation.

Fee Schedules for Title Searches: Price Fixing

Goldfarb v. Virginia State Bar Association, **421 U.S. 773, 95 S.Ct. 2004, 44 L.Ed. 2d 572 (1975)**   Held that fee schedules established by lawyers and bar associations were in violation of price-fixing prohibitions contained in federal antitrust laws. *Goldfarb v. Virginia State Bar Association* developed out of a class action brought by persons unable to retain a lawyer at fees lower than those published by a county bar association. The Goldfarbs alleged that the use of the minimum fee schedule constituted price fixing, a practice prohibited by the Sherman Act. A district court agreed, but held the State Bar was exempt from the Sherman Act because its actions constituted "state action." The County Bar, however, was not held immune. The Court of Appeals agreed that the State Bar was immune on state action grounds and that the County Bar was also immune because the practice of law was not "trade or commerce" under the act. In a unanimous decision (with Justice Powell not participating), the Supreme Court reversed, finding the practice of law within the reach of the antitrust law.

The opinion of the Court was delivered by Chief Justice Burger. The

Court's inquiry was divided into four "steps," each addressing a different question. First, was the County Bar engaged in price fixing? Though it was argued that the fee schedule was "merely advisory," the Court found the record to show a "fixed, rigid price floor" flowing from the "advisory" fee schedule. Lawyers who responded to the Goldfarbs' inquiries all "adhered to the fee schedule." The schedule was enforced through the "prospect of professional discipline" and a "desire . . . to comply with professional norms." This motivation was "reinforced" by assurances that other lawyers "would not compete by underbidding." The Court saw this as a "naked agreement" with a "plain" effect on prices. Since there were no alternative sources for necessary services, the Court found a pricing system that "consumers could not realistically escape." Second, the Court considered whether these activities were "in" or "affect" interstate commerce. The County Bar argued that the effects were "incidental and remote." The Court said these arguments "misconceive" the kind of transactions at issue and the role "legal services play in those transactions." The "necessary connection" between interstate transactions and the fee schedule comes because title examinations are a critical step. Given the "substantial volume" of commerce, and the "inseparability" of legal assistance for title examinations as a part of interstate real estate transactions, the effects on commerce were seen as significant. Where, "as a matter of law or practical necessity," legal services are an "integral part" of an interstate transaction, a "restraint" on those services is an effect subject to the Sherman Act. The County Bar sought exemption from the Sherman Act on "learned profession" grounds. The Court rejected this contention, saying that the "nature of an occupation," in itself, does not "provide sanctuary" from the Sherman Act. In the "modern world," lawyers play an "important part in commercial intercourse," and "anticompetitive activities" by lawyers may produce a "restraint on commerce." Finally, the State Bar argued that the fee schedule was exempted on "state action" grounds. The Virginia legislature had authorized the state's highest court to regulate the legal practice. That court had adopted "ethical codes" dealing with fees. The State Bar argued that the fee structure reports it issued were aimed at implementation of the "fee provisions of the ethical codes." The County Bar claimed that the codes "prompted" it to issue the fee schedules. The key inquiry in determining if anticompetitive activity is "state action" is whether the activity is "required by the State acting as sovereign." The Court said that anticompetitive activities "must be compelled by direction of the State." No such direction was found here. *See also* ANTITRUST LAWS, p. 579; COMMERCE CLAUSE, p. 291; FEDERALISM, p. 29.

Significance   The Court ruled in *Goldfarb v. Virginia State Bar* (421 U.S. 773: 1975) that fee schedules established by a county bar association were subject to the Sherman Antitrust Act. The various federal antitrust laws, of which the Sherman Act was the first, were designed to protect competition by regulating activities such as price-fixing that restrict competition and restrain trade. The effectiveness of these regulations has varied depending on commitment to enforcing the regulation and the Court's definition of the scope of federal regulatory authority. It was not until 1944, more than half a century after enactment of the Sherman Act, that the Court held in *United States v. South-Eastern Underwriters' Association* (322 U.S. 533: 1944) that the act could be enforced against the insurance industry. In similar fashion, the Court extended the Sherman Act to the legal service minimum fee schedules in *Goldfarb*. In doing so, the Court rejected the contention that the "nature of an occupation" in itself created immunity from the Sherman Act. Further, the Court held that the fee schedule was not exempt from the Sherman Act on state action grounds. The state action exclusion did not apply merely because the state had "prompted" an action. Rather, the conduct must be "compelled" by requirement of the state acting as "sovereign."

Thus *Goldfarb* strengthened federal regulatory power in two ways. First, it readily recognized the interstate commerce character of real estate transactions, the need for legal services to complete such transactions, and the possible effect of fee schedules on the conduct of such commerce. This was a broad interpretation facilitating application of federal power. Second, the Court was not receptive to claimed exemptions from federal regulations, a restrictive interpretation that also facilitated exercise of federal power.

State Requirement on Incoming Commerce

Hunt v. Washington State Apple Advertising Commission, 432 U.S. 333, 97 S.Ct. 2434, 53 L.Ed. 2d 383 (1977)   Invalidated a state regulation imposed on incoming interstate shipments of fruit as constituting an impermissible burden on interstate commerce. A North Carolina law required that all closed containers of apples sold in the state or shipped into the state carry no grade other than the applicable federal grade or the designation "unclassified." The Washington State Apple Advertising Commission, a state agency, operated to promote and protect the Washington state apple industry. The commission was composed of apple growers and dealers elected by those in the apple business. The agency's activities were financed by mandatory assessments on all dealers and growers in Washington. The commission sought declaratory and injunctive relief in federal court because the North Carolina law was in direct conflict with the established Washington apple grading system. A three-judge district court issued a permanent injunction against enforcement of the North Carolina law. On direct appeal, the U.S. Supreme Court unanimously affirmed the lower court (Justice Rehnquist not participating).

The opinion of the Court was delivered by Chief Justice Burger. North Carolina did not contest that their state burdened the Washington apple industry by "increasing its costs of doing business" in North Carolina markets. They argued, however, that the only burdens were "far outweighed" by the "local benefits" flowing from their regulation, which was designed to protect residents from "fraud and deception in the marketing of apples." Prior to enactment of the North Carolina regulation, apples from 13 states were shipped into the state. Seven of those states used their own grading system. This created, in North Carolina's view, a "multiplicity of inconsistent state grades," which posed "dangers of deception and confusion" in North Carolina markets. North Carolina argued it was merely trying to establish uniformity of standards that would be applied to all apples sold in closed containers "without regard to their point of origin." The Court acknowledged that not every state regulation that imposed a burden on commerce is invalid. Especially where citizens are protected in matters pertaining to the sale of food and where there is no conflicting federal legislation, there exists a "residuum of power" in the state to make laws governing local situations. When state regulation conflicts with the commerce clause's "overriding requirement of a national 'common market,'" the Court is faced with the job of "effecting an accommodation of competing national and local interests." The Court concluded that the North Carolina statute had the "practical effect" of not only "burdening interstate sales" of Washington apples, but also "discriminating against them." The discrimination "takes various forms." First, the statute's consequences of "raising the costs" of Washington growers and dealers leaves their "North Carolina counterparts unaffected." In-state producers were not forced to "alter their marketing practices," thus the increased cost to out-of-state producers tended to "shield the local apple industry" from the competition of Washington apples. Second, the statute had the effect of "stripping away" from the Washington apple industry the "competitive and economic advantages" it "earned for itself" through the "expensive inspection and grading system." The statute had no "similar impact" on the domestic industry. Third, by not allowing marketing of Washington apples using their own grading system, the North Carolina regulation had a "leveling

effect" that "insidiously operates to the advantage of local apple producers." When a demonstrated burden is found, the state must justify
its regulation both in terms of the "local benefits" flowing from it, and
the "unavailability of nondiscriminatory alternatives." Such alternatives were seen as not "readily available." Further, the challenged regulation, in the Court's view, did "remarkably little" to further the
"laudable goal" of protecting consumers with respect to Washington
apples. As a result, the regulation was found invalid. *See also* COMMERCE
CLAUSE, p. 291; CONCURRENT POWER, p. 588; *DEAN MILK COMPANY V. CITY OF
MADISON* (340 U.S. 349: 1951), p. 341; *PARKER V. BROWN* (317 U.S. 341:
1943), p. 332.

Significance   The Court used the commerce clause in *Hunt v. Washington State Apple Advertising Commission* (432 U.S. 333: 1977) to invalidate burdensome labeling requirements imposed on imported fruit.
When a state regulation imposes burdens on commerce, the Court
must render a judgment based on a balancing of commerce interests
and state regulatory interests. To a degree, this judgment must involve
a substantive assessment of a State's regulatory objectives. Thus, in
Southern Pacific Railroad Company v. Arizona (325 U.S. 761: 1945), the
Court invalidated a state law ostensibly protecting railroad worker
safety on the grounds that it did not sufficiently advance that purpose
when compared to the burden imposed on interstate commerce. A
more recent example of this balancing judgment can be seen in *Pike v.
Bruce Church* (397 U.S. 137: 1970). Here the Court invalidated a state
law prohibiting the shipment of cantaloupes out of state unless packed
in containers approved by the state. The purpose of the act was to
require quality standards by making sure that the packing of cantaloupes did not "materially misrepresent" the quality. The prohibition
on deceptive packaging, in turn, was aimed at protecting the reputation of state growers in general. To comply with the act would have
required the company to build a packing plant in the state at substantial
capital cost rather than continuing to ship cantaloupes out of state for
packing. The Court found this requirement for outgoing commerce
too burdensome. State regulations requiring that operations be performed in the home state, even when the state is pursuing a "clearly
legitimate" local interest, are seen to be "virtually per se illegal."

State Privilege Tax on Doing Business

Complete Auto Transit, Inc. v. Brady, **430 U.S. 274, 97 S.Ct. 1076,
51 L.Ed. 2d 326 (1977)**   Upheld a state tax on the "privilege of
doing business" within the state against commerce clause challenge.

Complete Auto Transit, Inc. was in the business of transporting an out-of-state manufacturer's automobiles to various places in Mississippi. The carrier was subjected to the state "privilege" tax, and it challenged the assessments on commerce clause grounds. The carrier appealed to the Supreme Court following adverse decisions in the state courts. In a unanimous decision, the Court ruled that such a privilege tax was not necessarily unconstitutional merely because it was imposed on an activity of interstate commerce.

The opinion of the Court was delivered by Justice Blackmun. The case presented what Blackmun characterized as the "perennial problem" of the validity of a state tax imposed on the "privilege of doing business" within a state. Among other things, the tax applied to business activity that involved interstate commerce. The attack on the tax was made based on the Court's ruling in *Spector Motor Service v. O'Connor* (340 U.S. 602: 1951), which had held that such "privilege" taxes could not fall on activities that are part of interstate commerce. *Spector* gave interstate commerce a "sort of 'free trade' immunity." Since that decision, however, the Court has focused on the practical effects of challenged state taxes rather than their formal language. This "practical analysis" allowed approval of many taxes that would have otherwise run "afoul" of the prohibition established in *Spector*. By the time the Court considered this case, the "Spector rule" bore no relationship to economic realities, and needed to be replaced. Like *Spector*, this case involved a "privilege" tax on activity in interstate commerce. As in *Spector*, Complete Auto made no claim that the activity taxed was not "sufficiently connected to the state" to justify the tax. Neither was there a claim that the tax was not "fairly related to benefits provided the taxpayer." Nor did Complete Auto contend that the tax "discriminates" against interstate commerce or that the tax was not "fairly apportioned."

The *Spector* rule was seen as no longer reflective of the reality that interstate commerce was immune from taxation. The philosophy underlying the rule has been "rejected," and the rule "stripped of any practical significance." The rule stands only as a "trap" for the "unwary" legislative draftsman. Had the state called its tax one on "net income" or on the "going concern value" of Complete Auto's business, it would not have triggered the *Spector* rule. No "economic consequence" necessarily follows from use of the words "privilege of doing business," and a "focus on that formalism" only "obscures" the issue of whether the tax produces a forbidden effect. "Simply put," the *Spector* doctrine did not "address the problem with which the Commerce Clause is concerned." Accordingly, the Court rejected the *Spector* doctrine and explicitly overruled the case. *See also* COMMERCE CLAUSE, p. 291; CONCURRENT POWER, p. 588; *UNITED STATES V. NEW MEXICO* (455 U.S. 720: 1982), p. 251.

Significance   The Court permitted a state to tax certain interstate business activities in *Complete Auto Transit v. Brady* (430 U.S. 274: 1977). Since the inception of the "original package" doctrine, it has been clear that state taxes cannot fall on items in commerce. Neither can taxes discriminate against interstate commerce in favor of domestic or local items or activities. At the same time, the Court has not wholly immunized interstate commerce from local taxation. The Court seemed to decide otherwise in *Spector Motor Service v. O'Connor* (340 U.S. 602: 1951) when it struck down a state tax on the privilege of doing business in the state. *Spector Motor Service* was exclusively engaged in interstate business. But the *Spector* doctrine was soon recognized as having "no relationship to economic realities," and it was overruled in *Complete Auto*. In the latter case, the Court developed standards by which to assess the constitutionality of state taxes on interstate commerce. A state tax could pass commerce clause scrutiny if the taxed activity was substantially linked to the state, and if the tax was fairly apportioned, not discriminatory against interstate commerce, and closely related to the state's provision of services. While this standard does not foreclose judicial invalidation of state taxes, it lends itself to the opposite result, a policy direction discernable in the Court's decisions since *Spector Motor Service*.

State Restriction on Incoming Commerce

Philadelphia v. New Jersey, **437 U.S. 617, 98 S. Ct. 2531, 57 L.Ed. 2d 475 (1978)**   Held that a state ban on the importation of out-of-state waste was in conflict with federal power to regulate interstate commerce. *Philadelphia v. New Jersey* developed out of an attempt by a state to limit dumping at state landfill sites to waste produced within the state. The state's waste control act prohibited the bringing of solid or liquid waste into the state. A number of landfill operators as well as cities adjoining New Jersey had waste disposal contracts. They challenged the state law as unduly burdening interstate commerce. New Jersey argued that the law promoted essential health and environmental interests and only incidentally affected interstate commerce. Philadelphia appealed from a state court decision upholding the law. The Supreme Court reversed in a 7–2 decision.

Justice Stewart issued the Court's opinion. The Court first "laid to rest" the issue of whether the wastes banned by the state were "commerce" within the meaning of the commerce clause. The Court said they were. "All objects of interstate trade merit Commerce Clause protection." None is "excluded by definition at the outset." The banning of even "valueless" items like out-of-state wastes "implicates" the commerce clause. The Court then turned to the applicability of the clause in this instance. The Court said that it has long been alert to the "evils of economic isolation and protectionism." At the same time, the Court has also recognized that "incidental burdens" on interstate commerce may be "unavoidable" where the state seeks to safeguard public health and safety. Where simple economic protectionism is produced by state regulations, a "virtually per se rule of invalidity" has evolved. The crucial issue in this case is whether the prohibition on imported waste is "basically a protectionist measure" or a regulation directed toward legitimate local health and safety concerns. The Court concluded that the New Jersey ban "falls squarely" within the area the commerce clause puts "off limits" to state regulation. It imposed on out-of-state commercial interests the "full burden of conserving the State's remaining landfill space." Crucial here was that New Jersey had attempted to "isolate itself" from a "problem common to many" by "erecting a barrier against the movement of interstate trade."

New Jersey argued that quarantine laws discriminate against out-of-state commerce, but have been regularly upheld by the courts. The Court refused to recognize this statute as similar to quarantine laws. Health endangerment is not the target of the prohibition on imported waste. The burden caused by the waste arises "after its disposal in landfill sites." At that point, "nothing distinguishes out-of-state waste from domestic waste." If one is inherently harmful, so is the other. Yet the challenged law has banned only out-of-state waste. The law thus blocks import of out-of-state waste in an "obvious effort to saddle those outside the state with the entire burden of slowing the flow of refuse" into New Jersey. Such a state policy is "clearly impermissible" under the commerce clause.

Justice Rehnquist, joined by Chief Justice Burger, dissented. They saw this regulation as governed by quarantine laws, and felt that New Jersey ought to be free to protect its citizens from health and safety problems associated with solid waste. *See also* COMMERCE CLAUSE, p. 291; POLICE POWER, p. 643; *REEVES, INC. V. STAKE* (447 U.S. 429: 1980), p. 355.

Significance   The Court held in *Philadelphia v. New Jersey* (437 U.S. 617: 1978) that a state ban on importation of solid waste from outside the state impermissibly discriminated against interstate commerce. It is well established that a state may regulate some aspects of interstate commerce. At the same time, state laws that erect "barriers against the movement of interstate trade" are highly suspect. As the Court said in this case, such state actions fall "squarely within the area put off limits to state regulation." This restriction on state power was intended to keep the channels of commerce open, and it is irrelevant that an item in the channel may not have value in itself. Aside from the economic dimen-

sions, this construction of the commerce clause is designed to prevent
states from attempting to isolate themselves from problems that transcend state lines. As the Court said in *Edwards v. California* (314 U.S.
160: 1941), while a state may gain "momentary respite from the pressure of events" by the "simple expedient of shutting its gates to the
outside world," such an approach runs counter to the theory underlying the Constitution. That document was built upon the premise that
the "people of the several states must sink or swim together." Neither
may state regulations discriminate against interstate commerce. The
New Jersey regulation did not completely ban solid waste from state
landfills. Only waste coming from outside the state was banned; thus
the burden of "slowing the flow of refuse" into New Jersey sites fell
exclusively and entirely on other states. That New Jersey did not also
prohibit waste from within the state made it impossible for the state to
defend the regulation on health grounds. This decision clearly has
great implications for future state initiatives dealing with disposal of
solid and even nuclear waste since, under its doctrine, state regulations
governing waste disposal must also pass commerce clause scrutiny.

Limitations on Sales to State Residents

***Reeves, Inc. v. Stake*, 447 U.S. 429, 100 S.Ct. 2271, 65 L.Ed. 2d
244 (1980)** Upheld a state policy of confining sales of state-
produced cement to residents of the state. *Reeves, Inc. v. Stake* involved
litigation brought by a Wyoming concrete distributor. After being
supplied with cement for more than 40 years by South Dakota's state-
owned cement plant, supplies were cut off because of a cement shortage. During the period of shortage, the State Cement Commission
confined sales of the plant to state residents. The Wyoming distributor
sought an injunction against the resident preference policy on commerce clause grounds. The district court enjoined the sales restriction,
finding the "hoarding" policy incompatible with the "national free
market" safeguarded by the commerce clause. The Court of Appeals
reversed, however, and the issue was taken to the Supreme Court. In a
5–4 decision, the Court permitted the state restriction.

The Court's opinion was delivered by Justice Blackmun. The key
question was whether South Dakota was involved in the kind of activity
with which the commerce clause is concerned. The clause was intended
to bar state regulations "inhibiting" interstate trade. In the absence of
congressional action, the clause does not preclude a state from participating in the marketplace as distinct from a market regulator.
Blackmun characterized this distinction as making "good sense and
sound law." The clause was historically directed at "regulatory and

taxing actions" taken by a state in its "sovereign capacity." The Court found "no indication" of an intention to "limit the ability" of the "States themselves" to operate "freely in the free market." The Court found that South Dakota "unquestionably fits the 'market participant' label." Reeves, Inc. argued that since South Dakota had long "exploited the interstate market, it could not withdraw at its own discretion. The Court rejected this contention and assessed the South Dakota "residents only" policy as though it had been enforced from the outset. To invalidate the policy would "interfere significantly" with the state's capacity to "structure relations exclusively with its own citizens." Also threatened would be the state's ability to fashion "effective and creative" programs in the future aimed at solving "local problems and distributing government largesse." A "healthy regard" for federalism and effective government "renders us reluctant to risk these results."

The Court also rejected several other contentions. First, the Court said the South Dakota policy was "protectionist" only in the "sense" that it limited "benefits generated" by a state for its own residents who "fund the state treasury" and for whom the state was "created." While "protectionist in a loose sense," this policy reflected the "essential and patently unobjectionable" purpose of state government to "serve the citizens of the State." Second, the Court said this policy was not an impermissible "hoarding" of resources. Cement is not a "natural resource," but the "end-product of a complex process." The policy neither prohibited establishment of other plants in the state nor restricted access to the materials needed for production of cement. Third, though the policy may give South Dakota suppliers a competitive edge in out-of-state markets, the regulation would have created even more severe commerce clause problems if it had barred or inhibited out-of-state sales as a means of addressing the cement shortage. The Court said that the "competitive plight" of out-of-state suppliers was, at least in part, a result of their own state's failure to provide or attract supply sources or enter into contractual agreement with South Dakota to guard against shortage.

Justice Powell issued a dissent joined by Justices Brennan, White, and Stevens. They saw the policy as the kind of "economic protectionism" the commerce clause was "intended to prevent." They argued that the application of the clause should hinge on the "nature" of the governmental activity involved. The clause is "not directly relevant" if the activity is an "integral operation in areas of traditional government functions." If, on the other hand, the state "enters the private market," it may "not evade the constitutional policy against economic balkanization." *See also* COMMERCE CLAUSE, p. 291; FEDERALISM, p. 29; *GARCIA V. SAN ANTONIO METROPOLITAN TRANSIT AUTHORITY*

(469 U.S. 528: 1985), p. 275; *WHITE V. MASSACHUSETTS COUNCIL OF CONSTRUC-TION EMPLOYERS* (460 U.S. 204: 1983), p. 366.

Significance   The Court held in *Reeves, Inc. v. Stake* (447 U.S. 429: 1980) that when a state or local government enters the market as a participant, it is not subject to the restraints of the commerce clause. The market regulation–participant distinction first developed in *Hughes v. Alexandria Scrap Corporation* (426 U.S. 794: 1976). In that case, the Court reviewed a state law attempting to encourage recycling of abandoned cars by offering a bounty for every state-titled car converted into scrap. A subsequent change in the law involving ownership documentation imposed stricter requirements on out-of-state than in-state scrap processors, a change that facilitated the selling of cars to in-state processors. The Court upheld the law, saying that nothing in the "purpose of the Commerce Clause" keeps a state from participating in the marketplace and favoring its own citizens as it does so. Similar reasoning was applied to a mayoral executive order in *White v. Massachusetts Council of Construction Employers, Inc.* (460 U.S. 204: 1983) requiring a proportion of local residents in any construction work force on city projects. Typically, the Court has not permitted states to impose "protectionist" policies that disadvantage interstate commerce. Protectionism assumes a different form when used by a state acting as a market participant. It was not protectionism for a "non-governmental" purpose, but rather used to limit benefits to state taxpayers, persons whom the "State was created to serve." The Court also saw the resident sales restriction on cement as analogous to a limitation on the use of "state educational institutions, energy generated by a state-run plant, police and fire protection, and agricultural improvement and business development programs." While these are "protectionist" in a "loose sense," the Court saw these activities as "essential and patently unobjectionable" to the purpose of state government and refused to use the commerce clause to interfere with them.

Ban on Double-Trailer Trucks

Kassel v. Consolidated Freightways Corporation, 450 U.S. 662, 101 S.Ct. 1309, 67 L.Ed. 2d 580 (1981)   Invalidated a state regulation prohibiting the use of 65-foot double-trailer trucks within the state. *Kassel v. Consolidated Freightways Corporation of Delaware* involved a challenge to state highway use regulations. Iowa permitted 55-foot single-trailer trucks and 60-foot double-trailer trucks on its highways, but 65-foot double trailers were prohibited. Consolidated

Freightways, an ICC-licensed carrier serving 48 states, was unable to use its longer double-trailer trucks in Iowa and filed suit challenging the state policy as burdensome to interstate commerce. Iowa argued that the policy reasonably protected highway safety and was a legitimate exercise of the state police power. A U.S. district court determined that 60- and 65-foot double-trailer trucks were comparably safe, and that the state regulation was an unwarranted obstruction of interstate commerce. Iowa appealed following an adverse review by the U.S. court of appeals. The U.S. Supreme Court, in a 6–3 decision, also held against the state regulation.

Justice Powell delivered the opinion of the Court. The Court offered several propositions against which the case was reviewed. The commerce clause can limit exercise of state power "even without congressional implementation." At the same time, the clause does not invalidate all state regulation of commerce. A state's power to regulate commerce is "never greater" than in matters "traditionally of local concern." Regulations that "touch upon safety," particularly those involving highway safety, are ones the Court "has been most reluctant to invalidate." If safety justifications are not "illusory," the Court will not "second guess" legislative judgment about their importance as compared to associated burdens on commerce. But the mere "incantation" of public health or safety purpose "does not insulate a state law" from commerce clause challenge. Using these principles, the Court concluded that the Iowa statute impermissibly burdened interstate commerce.

Iowa failed to present "any persuasive evidence" that 65-foot double trailers were less safe than 55-foot singles or 60-foot doubles. In addition, the restriction on double trailers put Iowa "out of step" with all other midwestern and western states. This "substantially burdens" the interstate flow of goods by trucks. While Iowa was not persuasive in support of its safety rationale (statistical evidence supported the conclusion that 65-foot doubles were "at least as safe" as singles and shorter doubles), Consolidated Freightways was able to demonstrate the burdensome consequences of the Iowa law. Companies wishing to use 65-foot double trailers must either route them around Iowa or detach the double trailer and send them through Iowa separately. These options engender both "inefficiency and added expense." In addition, the Iowa law may "aggravate rather than ameliorate" the highway safety problem. It results in more trucks carrying the same quantity of goods through the state or in the same number of large trucks driving more miles in order to bypass Iowa. Iowa's safety interest was thus seen as "illusory," and the regulation as impairing "significantly" the federal interest in "efficient and safe interstate transportation." As a result, the Iowa law could not be "harmonized with the Commerce Clause."

Though deference is traditionally accorded to a state's "safety judgment," the Court concluded that deference was "not warranted" in this instance.

Justice Rehnquist, joined by Chief Justice Burger and Justice Stewart, dissented. They argued that the Court may only undertake a limited commerce clause review of state safety regulations. Such laws carry a strong "presumption of validity" and, in this case, reflected a rational judgment by the state that sufficiently advanced legitimate safety interests. *See also* COMMERCE CLAUSE, p. 291; POLICE POWER, p. 643; SOUTHERN PACIFIC RAILROAD COMPANY V. ARIZONA (325 U.S. 761: 1945), p. 337.

Significance   The Court used the commerce clause in *Kassel v. Consolidated Freightways Corporation* (450 U.S. 662: 1981) to strike down a regulation prohibiting access to state highways for 65-foot double-trailer trucks. States are able to regulate commerce where objects of regulation seem to require local and diverse attention. The commerce clause precludes state regulation where uniform national policy is required to keep interstate commerce from being excessively burdened. An example of an impermissible state regulation is the train length limitation struck down in *Southern Pacific Railroad Company v. Arizona* (325 U.S. 761: 1945). Roads and highways have typically been viewed as local in character. In *Southern Pacific*, the Court distinguished railroads from highways and indicated that state regulatory prerogatives are "far more extensive" in the latter. Unlike railroads, highways are "built, owned and maintained by the state or its municipal subdivision," and the state is "responsible for their safe and economical administration." Illustrative of this position was *South Carolina State Highway Department v. Barnwell Brothers, Inc.* (303 U.S. 177: 1938), where a state width and weight regulation for trucks was upheld even though it was more stringent than any adjacent state's regulation. In addition to finding highways "peculiarly of local concern," the regulation fell on all trucks; it did not attempt to advantage state truckers at the expense of out-of-state truckers.

But state regulations that too greatly burden interstate commerce are precluded. In *Morgan v. Virginia* (328 U.S. 373: 1946), the Court struck down a state law requiring segregated seating of passengers on interstate buses. Just three years prior to *Kassel*, the Court struck down a similar double-trailer prohibition in *Raymond Motor Transportation, Inc. v. Rice* (434 U.S. 429: 1978). In both instances, the Court examined the safety rationale supporting the state regulation and concluded that the state had "failed to present any persuasive evidence" that the law sufficiently advanced public safety to overcome the "substantial burdens" imposed on the "interstate flow of goods by trucks."

Limitations on Strip Mining

Hodel v. Virginia Surface Mining and Reclamation Association, Inc., 452 U.S. 264, 101 S.Ct. 2352, 69 L.Ed. 2d 1 (1981) Upheld a federal environmental protection law against claims it was an improper use of the commerce power as well as an impermissible encroachment on state authority. *Hodel v. Virginia Surface Mining and Reclamation Association* examined provisions of the Surface Mining Control and Reclamation Act of 1977, which established a national program of regulations designed to protect the environment from the "adverse effects of surface coal mining." An association of coal producers, some member oil companies, and some individual landowners challenged the act in federal court. A U.S. district court enjoined enforcement of the act, primarily on Tenth Amendment grounds. On appeal, the Supreme Court unanimously reversed the lower court ruling that there were no due process, just compensation, Tenth Amendment, or commerce clause violations.

That portion of Justice Marshall's opinion of the Court examining the commerce clause issues is summarized here. The association claimed that the "principal goal" of the challenged act was the regulation of private land. The association saw the issue in the case as whether "land as such" is subject to commerce regulation, and whether land can be regarded as "in commerce." The Court did not accept either the association's "framing of the question" or its proposed answers. Rather, when asked to determine if a federal enactment is valid under the commerce clause, the task is "relatively narrow." The Court must "defer to a congressional finding" that a regulated activity affects interstate commerce if there is "any rational basis for such a finding." Once the rational basis of the finding is established, the "only remaining question" is whether Congress chose means "reasonably adapted" to the permitted end. The judicial task is "at an end" once the Court decides that Congress acted "rationally" in choosing a "particular regulatory scheme." In reviewing the commerce power, it is established that the power extends beyond "channels" and "instrumentalities" of commerce and includes "activities affecting commerce." Even activity that is "purely intrastate" may be regulated where the activity, "combined with like conduct by others similarly situated," affects interstate commerce. Simply classifying an activity as "local" does not resolve the issue of whether Congress can regulate it. Congress, thus, may regulate the "conditions under which goods are shipped in interstate commerce" where the "local activity of producing these goods itself affects interstate commerce."

In this case, Congress "rationally determined" that regulation of surface coal mining is required to protect commerce from the adverse consequences of that activity. The act is a response to a congressional determination that mining and reclamation standards are "essential" in order to ensure that competition among coal distributors from different states will not be used to "undermine the ability of the several states to improve and maintain adequate standards" for the mining of coal in their respective states. The prevention of this kind of "destructive" interstate competition is a "traditional role" for the commerce power. The association also challenged the means adopted in the act, claiming that they were "redundant or unnecessary." The association claimed that existing federal law "adequately" addressed the federal interest in "controlling the environmental effects" of surface mining. The Court said that the effectiveness of current law in dealing with a problem identified by Congress was a "matter committed to legislative judgment." The final commerce issue was whether the act contravened limitations imposed through the Tenth Amendment. Among other things, there must be a showing that the challenged statute regulates the "States as States" in order to invalidate commerce clause–based legislation on Tenth Amendment grounds. The Court held that the association had failed to make that showing in this case. *See also* COMMERCE CLAUSE, p. 291; FEDERALISM, p. 29; TENTH AMENDMENT, p. 229.

Significance The Court upheld provisions of the Surface Mining and Reclamation Act as a legitimate exercise of the commerce power in *Hodel v. Virginia Surface Mining and Reclamation Association* (452 U.S. 264: 1981). Challenge of the act was based on the contention that the federal government could not so regulate private land. Rather, it was argued that land regulation had been reserved to the states by the Tenth Amendment. *Hodel* was one of the many cases filed following the Court's decision in *National League of Cities v. Usery* (426 U.S. 833: 1976), the first case in almost 40 years where the Tenth Amendment prevailed against the exercise of the federal commerce power. The effect of *Usery* was limited and short-lived, however. As is reflected in *Hodel*, for the *Usery* limitation on the commerce power to apply, it would have to be shown, among other things, that the challenged federal law regulated the states "as States." The coal producers failed to make that showing in *Hodel*; the act was seen as directly regulating private mining activities and not the states as sovereign entities. The *Usery* decision was subsequently overruled in *Garcia v. San Antonio Metropolitan Transit Authority* (469 U.S. 528: 1985). Actually, *Hodel* exhibited substantive deference to congressional determination of undesirable consequences caused by the regulated activity. So long as the congressional findings are "rational," the Court inquiry is at an end. Here the Court found the record sufficiently supportive of the judgment that surface mining "adversely affected" interstate commerce and the public welfare more generally.

The *Hodel* decision can be seen as clear recognition that environmental protection may be pursued through exercise of the federal commerce power.

Regulation of Energy Supplies

***Federal Energy Regulatory Commission v. Mississippi*, 456 U.S. 742, 102 S.Ct. 2126, 72 L.Ed. 2d 532 (1982)**   Upheld provisions of the Public Utility Regulatory Policies Act (PURPA) of 1978. Challenged in the case of *Federal Energy Regulatory Commission v. Mississippi* were two entire titles and a section of another title (Titles I and III and Section 210 of Title II) of PURPA as exceeding the scope of the federal commerce power as well as encroaching on state sovereignty. Titles I and III required state regulatory commissions to "consider federal rate design and regulatory standards" as well as follow certain procedures when acting on these standards. Section 210 of Title II sought to encourage development of cogeneration and small power production facilities by allowing the Federal Energy Regulatory Commission (FERC) to exempt certain power facilities from certain state regulation. Mississippi and its utility regulatory commission sought declaratory judgment against the act. The district court found for Mississippi. In a 5–4 decision, the Supreme Court upheld the act.

The opinion of the Court was delivered by Justice Blackmun. The opinion first addressed the commerce clause challenge and represented the view of the entire court. The Court rejected the contention that "nothing in the Commerce Clause justifies federal regulation of even the intrastate operations of public utilities." Such an argument "misapprehends the proper role of the courts" in reviewing the validity of federal enactments based on Congress's "plenary powers." Courts may invalidate commerce clause legislation "only" if there is "no rational basis" for a congressional determination that the regulated activity "affects interstate commerce" or that there is no "reasonable connection" between means and ends. The claim by Mississippi that PURPA was "facially unconstitutional" because it did not "regulate commerce" disregards "entirely" the specific congressional finding to the contrary. The Court's inquiry into whether the finding had a "rational basis" showed "ample support for Congress' conclusions." Congress was aware of the magnitude of the problem, the need for promoting "conservation and more efficient use of energy resources." It was also aware that "domestic oil production had lagged behind demand," and of the increasing national dependence on foreign oil. It was familiar with the supply shortages of natural gas and that the electricity utility industry had been "beset by numerous problems."

Congress "naturally concluded" that the energy problem was "national in scope" and that national standards governing retail sales, conservation, and efficient uses of resources were needed. This included policy aimed at development of "cogeneration and small power production facilities" as a means of conserving energy.

The Court concluded that it was "difficult to conceive of a more basic element of interstate commerce than electric energy." The Court further concluded that Congress's choice of means were "reasonably adapted" to this legitimate end. The Court's function is not to inquire into whether the means chosen were the "wisest choice." Rather, it is "sufficient" that Congress was not "irrational" in concluding that these regulations were an appropriate response to an end permitted by the Constitution.

Where the Court split was over the claim that PURPA encroached on state sovereignty. Blackmun said for the majority that Congress could have "pre-empted" this field entirely. The act should not be invalidated because, "out of deference to state authority," Congress adopted a "less intrusive scheme" that allowed states to continue regulating in this field on the condition that they "consider suggested federal standards." In dissent, Justice Powell found troublesome the PURPA requirement that "prescribes administration and judicial procedures" the states "must follow" in deciding whether to adopt the proposed standards." Justice O'Connor, joined by Chief Justice Burger and Justice Rehnquist, also dissented on Tenth Amendment grounds. O'Connor called the consequences of PURPA "antithetical to the values of federalism and inconsistent with our constitutional history." The commerce power may be used only in limited ways. It cannot be used to "conscript state utility commissions into the national bureaucratic army." *See also* COM-MERCE CLAUSE, p. 291; FEDERALISM, p. 29; *HODEL V. VIRGINIA SURFACE MINING AND RECLAMATION ASSOCIATION* (452 U.S. 264: 1981), p. 360; TENTH AMENDMENT, p. 229.

Significance   The Court upheld a federal law in *Federal Energy Regulatory Commission v. Mississippi* (456 U.S. 742: 1982) that required state utility regulatory agencies to consider adoption of certain federal rate structures and other regulatory standards. The issue splitting the Court in this and other recent commerce clause issues is federalism. Several members of the Burger Court have seen some commerce clause–based enactments as infringing on state sovereignty. PURPA was one such enactment. In 1976, the Court ruled in *National League of Cities v. Usery* (426 U.S. 833) that federal wage and hour requirements added to the Fair Labor Standards Act by Congress in 1974 could not be extended to employees of state and local governments. This ruling had major implications for the federal commerce power, but subsequent decisions (see especially, *Hodel v. Virginia Surface Mining and Reclamation Association*, 452 U.S. 264: 1981, and *Garcia v. San Antonio Metropolitan Transit Authority*, 469 U.S. 528: 1985) have replaced *Usery* as an operative doctrine.

Nonetheless, the persistence of the Burger Court minority keeps the issue open. The majority, albeit a narrow one, has maintained an essentially deferential position on the federal commerce power. As in *Hodel* and other recent cases reviewing federal initiatives, the Court has allowed Congress to determine what activities ought to be regulated and the means appropriate to do so. The Court is not, according to Justice Blackmun, to review whether the "means chosen by Congress represent the wisest choice." It is sufficient that the Court find that Congress was not "irrational" in concluding that regulated activity was "essential to protect interstate commerce." It appears that the Burger Court majority deference to congressional judgment on exercise of the commerce power will continue to face strong opposition from a minority that feels many commerce regulations too extensively interfere with state authority.

Prohibition on Withdrawal of Groundwater

***Sporhase v. Nebraska Ex. Rel. Douglas*, 458 U.S. 941, 102 S.Ct. 3456, 73 L.Ed. 2d 1254 (1982)**   Struck down a state law that prohibited the withdrawal of groundwater to another state. *Sporhase v. Nebraska Ex. Rel. Douglas* involved a commerce clause challenge of a Nebraska statute that forbid the pumping of groundwater to another state without a permit. A permit for the withdrawal of groundwater was not given unless the state to which the water was transported granted reciprocal rights to bring groundwater from that state into Nebraska. Sporhase and others owned contiguous tracts of lands in Nebraska and Colorado. The latter did not provide reciprocity for the extraction and transporting of groundwater. Nebraska obtained an injunction from a state trial court precluding transfer of water across the border without a permit. The Nebraska Supreme Court upheld the lower court finding that groundwater was not an article of commerce. In a 7–2 decision, the U.S. Supreme Court reversed.

The opinion of the Court was delivered by Justice Stevens. The case presented three questions: whether groundwater is subject to federal regulation as an "article of commerce"; whether the Nebraska transfer restriction imposed an "impermissible burden" on commerce; and whether Congress had extended permission to the state to regulate groundwater in ways otherwise not allowed. The Court concluded that groundwater was both commerce and subject to federal regulation as such. Since water, once withdrawn from the ground, may be "freely bought and sold," it is "appropriately regarded as an article of commerce." Further, the interests of states in preserving scarce water resources have an interstate character. The agricultural markets supplied with products of irrigated farmland clearly fall within the concept of interstate commerce. The "multistate" character of the aquifer underlying the tracts of land involved in this case "confirms" that there is a "significant federal interest" in both conserving and fairly allocating this scarce resource.

The Court then turned to the second issue, whether the Nebraska restriction impermissibly burdened interstate commerce. Nebraska's objective in imposing the restriction was preservation of its groundwater sources, an "unquestionably legitimate and highly important" enterprise. That interest was advanced by placing conditions on the removal and interstate transfer of groundwater. Permits were issued if the withdrawal request was "reasonable," not "contrary to" Nebraska's conservation objectives, or otherwise "detrimental to the public welfare." The Court found none of these conditions either unreasonable or improperly burdensome to interstate commerce.

The final condition, that the state into which the water was to go grant "reciprocal rights" of withdrawing and transferring water from that state into Nebraska, was more problematic. This requirement "operates as an explicit barrier to commerce." As a result, Nebraska must show a "close fit" between the reciprocity requirement and its asserted conservation goal. The Court concluded that the requirement could not "clear this . . . hurdle." There was no evidence that the restriction was "narrowly tailored to the conservation and preservation rationale." The reciprocity element, the Court added, did not survive the "strictest scrutiny reserved for facially discriminatory legislation." Finally, the Court rejected Nebraska's claim that various federal statutes that "deferred to state water law" constituted congressional authorization to impose "otherwise impermissible burdens" on interstate commerce. Such deference does not mean that Congress "wished to remove federal constitutional constraints on such state laws."

Justices Rehnquist and O'Connor disagreed. They felt that since Nebraska recognized only a "limited right" for use of groundwater, that water could not be considered commerce. As a result, the state law could neither discriminate against nor impose burdens upon interstate commerce. *See also* COMMERCE CLAUSE, p. 291; FEDERALISM, p. 29; *PHILADELPHIA V. NEW JERSEY* (437 U.S. 617: 1978), p. 353; POLICE POWER, p. 643.

Significance   In *Sporhase v. Nebraska Ex. Rel. Douglas* (458 U.S. 941: 1982), the Court ruled that a state could not condition transfer of groundwater to another state on the existence of a comparable policy in the state of transfer. As the Court noted in *Sporhase*, water is an item of commerce, and, generally, states will be permitted to impose regulations that affect water. This includes establishment of conditions under which water may be taken from the state. Indeed, the Court said that three of the permit conditions established by Nebraska in this instance were not impermissible on their face. These conditions were that the withdrawal of water be reasonable, not in violation of operative conservation and use policies, and not detrimental to the public welfare of the state. While a state can so condition outgoing commerce, it may not erect "explicit barriers." The fourth permit condition, the existence of a reciprocal withdrawal policy in the state to which the water was going, was viewed by the Court as such an explicit barrier. This regulation is distinguished from that imposed on outgoing commerce in *Reeves, Inc. v. Stake* (447 U.S. 429: 1980). There, sales from a state-operated cement plant were limited to state residents. In this case, however, the state was acting in its role as market participant as distinct from market regulator. Only in the latter context are limitations stemming from the commerce clause applicable. *Sporhase*, then, is analogous to *Philadelphia v. New Jersey* (437 U.S. 617: 1978), where the Court used the commerce clause to invalidate a state prohibition on the transportation of waste into the state from outside. Although *Sporhase* regulated outgoing commerce while *Philadelphia v. New Jersey* dealt with incoming commerce, both were defective because each erected barriers that excessively burdened the free flow of commerce.

Requirement of Local Resident Employment Preference

White v. Massachusetts Council of Construction Employers, Inc., 460 U.S. 204, 103 S.Ct. 1042, 75 L.Ed. 2d 1 (1983)   Upheld a mayoral executive order requiring that at least half the workforce on all city construction projects consist of city residents. *White v. Massachusetts Council of Construction Employers* involved a commerce clause challenge to the residency requirement. The executive order of Boston Mayor White covered all construction projects funded "in whole or in part" by city monies or by funding the city had authority to administer. The Supreme Judicial Court of Massachusetts found the order violative of the commerce clause. The U.S. Supreme Court, however, disagreed in a 7–2 decision.

The opinion of the Court was delivered by Justice Rehnquist. In assessing this situation, the Court drew upon the "basic" distinction between states as market "participants" and states as market "reg-

ulators." The commerce clause "responds principally" to state regulatory measures or taxes that impose on "free private trade in the
national marketplace." There is "no indication" of a constitutional
"plan" to restrict the capacity of states to "operate freely in the free
market." When a state or local government "enters the market as a
participant, it is not subject to the restraints of the commerce clause." If
the city is participating in the market with its own funds, even "significant impact" on work crews composed of out-of-state residents is "not
relevant." If the city is a market participant, then the commerce clause
"establishes no barrier to conditions" the city may require for its participation. Impact on out-of-state residents "figures in the equation"
only after a finding that the city is regulating rather than participating
in the market. The same proposition applies to the contention that the
mayor's order "sweeps too broadly" creating a greater burden than is
required to accomplish the city's objectives. The scope of the order
relative to an imposed burden is not relevant to deciding whether the
clause applies here.

Finally, the Court examined the mayoral order in relation to projects
funded at least in part by federal sources. The principal issue here was
whether congressional action could permit a state or local government
to take actions that may interfere with commerce. The Court said the
commerce clause is a "grant of authority to Congress, and not a restriction on the authority of that body." Unlike state legislatures, Congress is
not limited by "any negative implications" of the clause on the exercise
of its power to appropriate funds. Where Congress authorizes or
encourages an action at the state or local level, that state or local act is
not subject to the clause. Thus if conditions imposed by Boston on
federally subsidized construction projects "are directed by Congress
then no dormant Commerce Clause issue is presented." The Court
found that the federal programs from which Boston secured funds
were intended to "encourage economic revitalization," including improvement of employment opportunities for the "poor, minorities, and
unemployed." The associated regulations for these programs show
that the mayor's order "sounds a harmonious note." Those federal
regulations "affirmatively permit the type of parochial favoritism" seen
in the executive order.

Justice Blackmun, joined by Justice White, dissented. He said that
the executive order constituted market "regulations" rather than participation. The order, in Blackmun's view, "directly impedes free private trade in the national marketplace," and thus is not "immune from
Commerce Clause scrutiny." *See also* COMMERCE CLAUSE, p. 291;
FEDERALISM, p. 29; *HICKLIN V. ORBECK* (437 U.S. 518: 1978), p. 453; *REEVES,
INC. V. STAKE* (447 U.S. 429: 1980), p. 355.

Significance   The Court held in *White v. Massachusetts Council of Construction Employers, Inc.* (460 U.S. 204: 1983) that a mayor's executive order requiring a proportion of local residents in the construction workforce for projects either funded or administered by the city did not violate the commerce clause. This case was resolved on the basis of two propositions. First, a state or local government is not subject to commerce clause limitations when it enters the market as a participant as distinct from a market regulator. The market participant-regulator distinction had its origin in *Hughes v. Alexandria Scrap Corporation* (426 U.S. 794: 1976). The Court in that case said that the commerce clause "responds principally" to state taxes and regulatory measures "impeding free private trade" in the national marketplace. On the other hand, the Court saw "no indication" of a constitutional intention to "limit the ability of the States themselves to operate freely in the free market." Thus, to the extent the city construction projects were funded out of the city treasury, the city was entitled to participant status. The market participant proposition also applies when the state acts as supplier as seen in *Reeves, Inc. v. Stake* (447 U.S. 429: 1980). Second, a state or local governmental action authorized by Congress is not subject to commerce clause limitations despite burdensome effects on interstate commerce. The Court found affirmative congressional support for the kind of policy action taken by the Boston mayor. Thus, the mayoral order could be sustained even when applied to construction projects supported by federal funds.

Though the Council of Construction Employers did not pursue privileges and immunities clause arguments at the Supreme Court level, the Court distinguished the issue in this case from that in *Hicklin v. Orbeck* (437 U.S. 518: 1978). In the latter, the Court struck down a state law requiring employment in "all work connected with gas and oil leases" to which the state was a party be "offered first to 'qualified' Alaska residents in preference to nonresidents." The Court distinguished the mayoral executive order from the "Alaska hire" law, saying that the former did not "attempt to force virtually all businesses that benefit in some way from the economic ripple effect of the decision to enter into contracts for projects to bias their employment practices" in favor of Boston residents. Even so, this issue was subordinated to the commerce clause question in *White* and resolved exclusively on those grounds.

State Regulation of Electric Rates

***Arkansas Electric Cooperative Corporation v. Arkansas Public Service Commission**, 461 U.S. 375, 103 S.Ct. 1905, 76 L.Ed. 2d 1* **(1983)**   Allowed a state to regulate a cooperative's wholesale electricity rates. *Arkansas Electric Cooperative Corporation v. Arkansas Public Service Commission* (PSC) involved commerce and supremacy clause challenges to the PSC assertion of jurisdiction over the wholesale rates charged by the cooperative to its member retailers. A state trial court ruled the PSC had no jurisdiction, but that decision was reversed by the Arkansas Supreme Court. In a 7–2 decision, the U.S. Supreme Court also upheld the jurisdiction of the PSC.

The opinion of the Court was delivered by Justice Brennan. The Court first determined that the state wholesale rate regulation did not violate the supremacy clause. The Court examined the various federal statutes and administrative regulations and found that as a matter of policy, cooperatives "engaged in sales for resale" should not be regulated at the federal level. Further, the Court found nothing to suggest that state regulation of power cooperatives, even those financed under federal programs, was preempted. Central to the Court's treatment of the commerce clause issue was the suitability of *Public Utilities Commission v. Attleboro Steam and Electric Company* (273 U.S. 83: 1927). *Attleboro* held that states could regulate only retail rather than wholesale sales of electricity. If the doctrine of *Attleboro* was applied in this case, it would require "setting aside the PSC's assertion of jurisdiction" over the cooperative. The Court found it "difficult to square" the "mechanical line" established in *Attleboro* (based on the distinction between "direct" and "indirect" effects on commerce) with the "general trend" in contemporary commerce clause cases to balance the nature of the regulation, state regulatory objectives, and the regulation's effect on the "national interest in commerce." The question, then, was whether to follow the "mechanical" *Attleboro* test or the evolving "balance of interests" test. The Court pointed out that the "formalistic distinctions" that had "once defined and controlled various corners of Commerce Clause doctrine," like the one serving as the basis of *Attleboro*, have been "explicitly abandoned" over the years. The *Attleboro* distinction between retail and wholesale was no less "anachronistic." The difficulty in "harmonizing" Attleboro with "modern Commerce Clause doctrine," Brennan said, had been apparent for a "long time." Further, the Court could see "no strong reliance interests" that would be threatened by abandoning *Attleboro*.

With the *Attleboro* rule no longer providing the "sole standard," the Court proceeded to "an analysis grounded more solidly in our modern cases." The most serious concern, that of "economic protectionism," was not involved in this case. In addition, the state regulation of wholesale sales is "well within the scope of legitimate local public interests." Notwithstanding the cooperative's link to an "interstate grid," its "basic operation" consisted of supplying from local generators to member cooperatives, all of which are located in the state. The Court recognized that the state rate regulation had an effect on commerce, but it was only "incidental." The burden imposed was "not clearly excessive in relation to the putative local benefits." While the cooperative received the power it sold from out of state, the "same is true" of most retail utilities. The "national fabric" had not, in the Court's view, been "seriously disturbed by leaving regulation of retail utility rates largely to the States." Justice White, joined by Chief Justice Burger, saw state regulation of cooperative wholesale power rates as "pre-empted," as Congress has "occupied the field of wholesale power rate regulation." *See also* COMMERCE CLAUSE, p. 291; *FEDERAL ENERGY REGULATORY COMMISSION V. MISSISSIPPI* (456 U.S. 742: 1982), p. 362; PREEMPTION DOCTRINE, p. 645; SUPREMACY CLAUSE, p. 227.

Significance   The Court held in *Arkansas Electric Cooperative Corporation v. Arkansas Public Service Commission* (461 U.S. 375: 1983) that neither the commerce nor the supremacy clause precluded state regulation of cooperative wholesale electricity rates. Power to regulate aspects of commerce has been shared since the doctrine of "selective exclusiveness" was established in *Cooley v. Board of Port Wardens* (12 Howard 299: 1851). Under that decision, some regulatory subjects would fall to the states because nonuniform regulation is appropriate. States can thus exercise authority over such subjects so long as it does not directly conflict with established federal policy. The issue for the Court then became one of deciding which subjects were of a local character and within the sphere of state power. The *Arkansas* decision reflects the contemporary trend to adjudicate cases involving the boundaries of state authority over commerce by balancing competing interests rather than by means of so-called mechanical criteria. In each case, the Court examines the nature of a state regulation, the purpose of the regulation, and the consequences of the regulation on the national commerce interest. A state law that regulates "evenhandedly" and that pursues a legitimate local public interest will be sustained so long as its effects on interstate commerce are only incidental and any burdens imposed are not "excessive in relation to local benefits being pursued." In the *Arkansas Electric Cooperative* case, the Court saw the regulation of wholesale rates as a legitimate local public interest. Further, the regulation was not established for economic "protectionist" purposes. While the state regulation did produce effects on interstate commerce, these effects were only incidental and not excessively burdensome in relation to the local objectives. Thus, it was a permissible local commerce regulation.

7. The Federal Taxing and Spending Power

Overview, 373

General Welfare Clause, 377

OVERVIEW

Congress is granted broad constitutional powers to tax and spend. Article I, Section 8 says, in part, that Congress shall have the power to "lay and collect taxes, duties, imposts and excises." The clause continues by saying that Congress also has the power to "pay the debts and provide for the common defense and general welfare of the United States." The power to raise adequate revenues and the authority to make expenditures for public activities is a fundamental element of governance. The power granted in Article I, Section 8 is extensive and intended by the framers of the Constitution to rectify the serious revenue-raising problems of the federal government under the Articles of Confederation.

Possibly the most troublesome aspect of the taxing and spending power has been definition of the general welfare clause. Congress is empowered to collect taxes and use the proceeds to provide for the "general welfare." The principal issue is whether the clause independently grants spending power or conditions the specifically enumerated powers. Even though the latter alternative has been established, there still is question as to what kinds of expenditures properly pursue a general welfare purpose. Consideration of this issue was central to the Court's decisions in *United States v. Butler* (297 U.S. 1: 1936) and *Steward Machine Company v. Davis* (301 U.S. 548: 1937). In the former, the Court struck down a congressional attempt to collect a processing tax to finance a program of paying farmers to reduce their agricultural productivity. In the *Steward Machine* case, however, the Court took a different view of the general welfare clause, and upheld the unemployment compensation spending portions of the Social Security Act.

Congressional fiscal authority extends to more than just taxation and appropriation. The Congress also has the power to borrow, regulate the money supply, and define the terms of legal tender. The ability to determine what will constitute legal tender was established by the Court in the *Legal Tender Cases* (12 Wallace 457: 1871). The Congress may also attach conditions to the receipt of federal financial assistance as held in *Lau v. Nichols* (414 U.S. 563: 1974).

373

As broad as taxing and spending authority is, there are limits to the power. Article I, Section 9 prohibits the Congress from levying a "direct" tax unless apportioned across the population. While what constitutes a direct tax has never been entirely clear, the Court seems to agree that a federal property tax or a "capitation" tax would fit the direct classification. In *Hylton v. United States* (3 Dallas 171: 1796), the Court held a federal carriage tax to be indirect because it could not be apportioned. A tax on income derived from real estate and other sources was invalidated as a direct tax in *Pollock v. Farmers' Loan and Trust Company* (158 U.S. 601: 1895). Article I, Section 8 also requires that duties, imposts, and excises "shall be uniform" throughout the United States. It was held in *Knowlton v. Moore* (178 U.S. 41: 1900) that the requirement did not demand intrinsic uniformity of tax levies, only a geographic uniformity. Finally, under terms of Article III, Section 1, Congress may not diminish judicial compensation of sitting judges during their terms. In *O'Malley v. Woodrough* (307 U.S. 277: 1939), the Court determined that this limitation did not prevent the Congress from subjecting judges to a general tax on incomes.

Congressional exercise of the taxing power is limited by such provisions as the prohibition on unapportioned direct taxes and the uniformity requirement. The Court has also considered certain other restrictions where the Congress uses the taxing power for regulatory purposes. While the Court has generally permitted Congress to regulate through the taxing power, there have been occasions when regulatory taxes did not survive judicial scrutiny.

One form of regulatory tax has been sustained on the ground that it augments the exercise of other conveyed powers. In *Veazie Bank v. Fenno* (8 Wallace 533: 1869), the Court upheld a tax on state bank notes as a means of protecting the newly established national bank and the associated policy objective of providing uniform currency. Generally, if the enactment raises revenue, the Court has been reluctant to inquire into other legislative motives. The Court said in *J. W. Hampton, Jr. and Company v. United States* (276 U.S. 394: 1928) that the presence of additional motives, such as the protective tariff in *Hampton*, does not necessarily invalidate the tax. The Court's most permissive decision upholding regulatory taxation occurred in *McCray v. United States* (195 U.S. 27: 1904). The tax involved was an excise on colored oleomargarine and was intended to protect the dairy industry from the lower price of margarine. Because it was an excise that produced revenue, the Court refused to examine any further legislative motive for the tax. Eighteen years later, the Court struck down a tax on businesses using child labor in *Bailey v. Drexel Furniture Company* (259 U.S. 20: 1922). The Court here held that even incidental revenue raising could not save a tax enacted principally and obviously to impose regulation. As in the

Butler case, the Court also found the child labor tax defective on dual federalism grounds. The Court has also allowed the Congress to regulate certain illegal activities through taxation. In *United States v. Kahriger* (345 U.S. 22: 1953), the Court permitted a tax on persons engaged in wagering. The tax law additionally required persons engaged in such activities to register with the Internal Revenue Service. The Court refused to find the registration requirements a violation of the self-incrimination protection in *Kahriger*, but reversed itself in *Marchetti v. United States* (390 U.S. 39: 1968). The consequence of *Marchetti* is that the Court will scrutinize the means Congress chooses to collect a tax even if the object or activity upon which the tax is collected is itself a permissible target.

A further limitation on taxing power stems from the concept of intergovernmental tax immunity. The premise is that neither a federal or state governmental entity is subject to taxation by the other. In *Pittman v. Home Owners' Loan Corporation* (308 U.S. 21: 1939), the Court held that federal instrumentalities could be categorically exempted from state taxation or the collection of state fees. *Graves v. New York Ex. Rel. O'Keefe* (306 U.S. 466: 1939), however, held that this immunity does not extend to the employees of federal agencies. Intergovernmental immunity does not constitute a major limitation on federal taxing power. While no federal tax could properly be levied on a fundamental state activity or state property, the Court did permit, in *New York v. United States* (326 U.S. 572: 1946), a tax on a state entity engaged in an activity not deemed fundamental to maintaining the state government.

General Welfare Clause   Provision in Article I, Section 8 authorizing Congress to collect taxes and provide for the country's "general welfare." Of all the constitutional provisions relating to congressional authority to tax and spend, the general welfare clause has produced the most discussion as to its nature and scope. The basic authority to tax comes from Article I, Section 8, which empowers Congress to "lay and collect taxes, duties, imposts and excises." That same section goes on to authorize that Congress "provide for the common defense and general welfare of the United States." The limitations on the taxing and spending power are contained in Sections 8 and 9 of Article I. One limitation is known as the uniformity requirement, which compels duties, imposts and excises to be spread at the same rate on the same subjects across the states. The definitive case on the uniformity requirement is *Knowlton v. Moore* (178 U.S. 41: 1900), which held that the requirement means geographic rather than intrinsic uniformity. The standard defined in geographic terms does not impose a significant limit on federal taxing power. A little more troublesome has been the prohibition on direct taxes unless apportioned across the states. Case law has basically confined this direct tax category to the head tax and property or land tax. The only time this limitation has interfered with federal taxing power was in *Pollock v. Farmers' Loan and Trust Company* (158 U.S. 601: 1895, p. 382), where the Court invalidated a federal income tax. The principal effect of this decision was reversed by ratification in 1913 of the Sixteenth Amendment, which permitted unapportioned tax on incomes derived from any source. Although these limitations set some boundaries on the federal taxing powers, none amount to substantial restriction of that authority.

That leaves construction of the general welfare clause. The primary question is whether the clause itself conveys a grant of taxing and spending authority over and above those otherwise conferred, or if the clause is merely summary in nature, having no effect beyond the powers Congress may exercise from enumerated sources. Advocacy of the broader interpretation of the clause came from Alexander Hamilton, who saw the clause as substantively enhancing federal taxing and spending power. So long as a tax or appropation promoted the "general welfare," it was constitutionally permissible in Hamilton's view. James Madison argued to the contrary. Congress could only tax and spend in relation to the other specified powers, but no others. Thus, for example, a levy in support of post offices was allowed because Section 8 of Article I expressly assigned Congress the function of establishment of "post offices and post roads." While advancement of education may promote the general welfare, that function was not conveyed to the federal government; thus no levies or appropriations may be made for that subject. The Hamiltonian view, if taken to its logical conclusion, would place within the Congress enormous power to reach into virtually every aspect of life. It would at least potentially have the effect of transforming enumerated powers into a broad authority of a general and unlimited character. *See also* ARTICLE I, p. 183; DIRECT TAX, p. 592; NECESSARY AND PROPER CLAUSE, p. 637; UNIFORMITY CLAUSE, p. 668.

Significance   The Court's first opportunity to carefully examine the general welfare clause came in *United States v. Butler* (297 U.S. 1: 1936). Prior to *Butler*, many appropriations had taken place that were not directly associated with an enumerated power of Congress. The *Butler* case permitted focus on the general welfare clause because the tax on food processors could not be sustained on the basis of the taxing authority alone. The levy on processors, which was to be used to compensate farmers for regulating production, could survive scrutiny only if upheld as an expenditure promoting the general welfare. The Court in *Butler* espoused the Hamiltonian view of the clause. Justice Roberts said for the *Butler* majority that the confines of the clause are "set in the clause which confers it" and not from the remainder of Article I, Section 8. In other words, the taxing and spending powers are "not limited by the direct grants of legislative power found in the Constitution." Having defined a broad taxing and spending power limited essentially only by the requirement that they shall be exercised in attempts to promote the general welfare, the *Butler* decision voided the enactment on federalism grounds. No matter how broadly the taxing and spending powers may be defined, those powers "extend only to matters of national, as distinguished from local welfare." The *Butler* Court saw agricultural regulation as a local matter, thus outside the reach of the federal taxing and spending power.

The Court changed its view soon after *Butler* and diminished the salience of dual federalism arguments. The Court began to see promotion of the general welfare in national terms. In upholding the unemployment compensation provisions of the Social Security Act in *Steward Machine Company v. Davis* (301 U.S. 548: 1937), the Court recognized the problems of the unemployed as "national in area and dimensions." There was "need from the nation" to address the plight of the unemployed. The Court rejected the contention that in meeting a condition such as post-depression unemployment and its attendant poverty, "the use of monies of the nation to relieve the unemployed and their dependents is a use for any purpose narrower than the promotion of the general welfare." The Court went on to say in *Helvering v. Davis* (301 U.S. 619: 1937), a case examining the old age benefits of the Social Security Act, that the concept of general welfare is not "static." Needs that may have been "narrow or parochial" historically may be "interwoven in our day" with the nation's well-being. With the *Steward Machine* and *Helvering* cases, the Court placed substantial discretion in the hands of Congress to determine what constituted promotion of the general welfare. Unless Congress exercises its judgment in an arbitrary way, the Court will probably not intervene. Thus through a broadened definition of the general welfare clause and a posture of judicial self-restraint by the courts, Congress is able to annually appropriate federal tax monies for use in addressing such matters as education, agriculture, unemployment, poverty, housing, and many others even though these items are not expressly delegated to Congress by Article I.

Direct Tax Limitation

***Hylton v. United States*, 3 Dallas 171, 1 L.Ed. 556 (1796)**
Upheld a federal tax on carriages against claims that the levy was a prohibited direct tax. *Hylton v. United States* provided the Court with its first opportunity to address the problematic direct tax question. Language in Article I, Section 9 provides that "no capitation, or other direct, tax shall be laid, unless in proportion to the census or enumeration herein before directed to be taken." A congressional act levied a $16 tax on carriages. Hylton obtained review from the Supreme Court, arguing that the tax was direct, and that it could not be reasonably apportioned. A unanimous Court found the tax indirect rather than direct, and thus not subject to the constitutional limitation.

The Court had not yet begun the practice of delivering an opinion of the Court by 1796. Rather, individual opinions were rendered. Three of the Court's six justices offered opinions in *Hylton*. Justice Chase determined that the annual carriage tax was a properly laid "duty." He regarded the duty as a levy against the privilege of using carriages, an expense on owning a carriage. Accordingly, he regarded the tax as indirect. He added, though not as a "judicial opinion," that the direct tax prohibition applied to only two classes of levies, "capitation or poll" taxes and taxes "on land." Chase also concluded that a tax on carriages "cannot be laid by the rule of apportionment, without very great inequality and injustice." Because the ratio of carriages to population is not equivalent in each state, an apportioned tax on carriages would yield highly disparate tax amounts. Justice Paterson also refused to decide whether the direct tax limit applied to more than a head tax or a tax on land, but commented that the direct tax prohibition was "made in favor of the southern states which had extensive tracts of territory thinly settled, and not very productive." These same states possessed "large numbers of slaves." Paterson felt the direct tax language was intended to keep Congress from enacting taxes rated "so much a head" or "so much an acre." Without the direct tax language, this region would have been "wholly at the mercy of the other states." Accordingly, Paterson did not view the carriage tax as an impermissible direct tax. Justice Iredell felt that apportioning was an absolute condition of a direct tax. If apportionment is not possible, a levy "cannot be a direct tax in the sense of the Constitution." He found it "evident" that the carriage tax could not be apportioned. Iredell used a hypothetical tax to lead to the conclusion that apportionment of a tax like that imposed on the carriages was "too manifestly absurd to be supported." The shared judgment of the Court was that the carriage tax was an indirect and therefore constitutionally imposed levy. *See also* DIRECT TAX, p. 592; GENERAL WELFARE CLAUSE, p. 377; *POLLOCK V. FARMERS' LOAN AND TRUST COMPANY* (158 U.S. 601: 1895), p. 382.

Significance   *Hylton v. United States* (3 Dallas 171: 1796) allowed the Court its first occasion to examine the direct tax prohibition of Article I, Section 9. A direct tax is one paid directly by the taxpayer to the taxing unit. While this concept seems simple enough, the Court struggled with the exact meaning of the direct tax limitation. The constitutional framers provided the Court little assistance, as the records from the discussion at the Constitutional Convention are silent on the specific meaning of the term *direct tax*. By finding the tax in *Hylton* to be a levy against the use of carriages, it was held that the tax was indirect and thus not subject to the apportionment requirement of Article I, Section 9. While not necessary for the resolution of the issue in *Hylton*, the Court expressed the view that only head and land taxes fit the direct tax category. It followed from this position that only the head and land taxes required apportionment if Congress ever wished to use them as taxing bases. Because apportionment is a complex process and because it creates inequities in payments required from individual taxpayers in the various states, it is a virtually absolute prohibition. *Hylton*, however, seemed to suggest that only head and land taxes fit the category, thus minimizing its effect as a limitation on federal taxing power. It wasn't until *Pollock v. Farmers' Loan and Trust Company* (158 U.S. 601: 1895) that the Court changed its mind on that question. The *Hylton* case is also interesting because it indicated that the Court felt it possessed the power of judicial review. Although the Court did not find the carriage tax constitutionally defective, it clearly entertained the possibility of striking the tax down if it violated the Constitution. Had the Court found otherwise and held the carriage tax to be an unapportioned direct tax, *Hylton* rather than *Marbury v. Madison* (1 Cranch 137: 1803) would have been the case of origin for judicial review.

Borrowing Power

***Legal Tender Cases (Knox v. Lee** and **Parker v. Davis)*, **12 Wallace 457, 20 L.Ed. 287 (1871)**   Upheld a federal enactment that made treasury notes legal tender for payment of debts. The *Legal Tender Cases* were actually two cases, *Knox v. Lee* and *Parker v. Davis*, joined for consideration by the Court. The decision arose out of the Civil War and attempts by the Congress to finance that effort. Article I, Section 8 authorizes Congress to coin money, regulate its value, and borrow on the credit of the United States. This language allowed the federal government to print paper money, and was even used during the Civil War to allow bills of credit, commonly known as "greenbacks," to be used as legal tender for the payment of individual indebtedness. In the case of *Hepburn v. Griswold* (8 Wallace 603: 1870), however, a seven-member Court ruled, in a 4–3 decision, that the legal tender enactments were unconstitutional at least as they applied to payments for contracted debts assumed prior to the statute. At the very time the Court was invalidating the acts in Hepburn, two new members of the Court were nominated and confirmed. Their votes were decisive in the *Legal Tender Cases*, which overruled *Hepburn* in a 5–4 decision.

Justice Strong offered the opinion of the Court. He began by weaving a background of congressional authority, joining various explicit and implied powers together. He mentioned Article I, Section 8, the power to tax, regulate money, and borrow. He also developed the necessary and proper clause, language that provides underpinning for many enumerated powers. Strong intertwined the circumstance of the Civil War emergency and the need for the government to exercise the power of "self-preservation." In other words, Strong developed a broad aggregate power position for the Congress in fiscal matters, especially at a time of national stress, even though such authority was not explicitly conveyed. In Strong's view, the existence of such power could be fairly deduced either from those enumerated substantive powers or from a combination of those provisions. Against such a background, Strong said that before the Court can invalidate the Legal Tender Acts or any other legislation produced through the exercise of these powers, it must "be convinced they were not appropriate means, or means conducive to the execution of any or all of the powers of Congress." But if the end pursued by Congress is legitimate, as the Court had found here, the Congress rather than the Court should choose the means by which to pursue that end. He thus foreclosed the means question from the Court on function grounds. It is beyond the competence of the Court to engage in identifying possible means or second-guessing the choice of means made by the legislature.

The four justices making up the *Hepburn* majority—Chief Justice Chase, and Justices Nelson, Clifford, and Field—dissented. Their disagreement with the Legal Tender Acts involved the use of greenbacks as payment for debts contracted prior to the legislation. The dissenters stressed that creditors were unfairly compelled to accept payment of debts through a medium of less value than existed at the time the debt was entered. *See also* NECESSARY AND PROPER CLAUSE, p. 637.

Significance   The *Legal Tender Cases* (12 Wallace 457: 1871) decision established broad congressional monetary power. The decision also reversed the policy established in *Hepburn v. Griswold*. Had the *Hepburn* limitation on issuance of bills of credit remained unchanged, many persons would have been financially damaged, since debt repayments using "greenbacks" had occurred several years prior to *Hepburn*. The Court's change of mind was generally welcomed. It also had the effect of substantially broadening congressional authority over fiscal matters. Much of the broad power recognized by the Court in the *Legal Tender Cases* was based on the intertwining of emergency war powers with express monetary powers set out in Article I. In *Juilliard v. Greenman* (110 U.S. 421: 1884), the Court upheld congressional authority to issue such legal tender even in the absence of a war emergency. Soon after the *Legal Tender Cases* were decided, the Court determined that Congress could not require creditors with contracts specifying payment in gold to accept greenbacks instead. The Court later ruled that such "gold clauses" in private contracts could be reached through congressional monetary powers in an aggregated decision known as the *Gold Clause Cases* (294 U.S. 240: 1935). The clear pattern of all the decisions since the *Legal Tender Cases* is that the Court has concluded that Congress possesses comprehensive fiscal authority.

Income Tax: Direct Tax

***Pollock v. Farmers' Loan and Trust Company* (rehearing), 158 U.S. 601, 15 S.Ct. 673, 39 L.Ed. 1108 (1895)**   Held that a federal tax on incomes greater than $4,000 was an impermissible direct tax. *Pollock v. Farmers' Loan and Trust Company* was in front of the Court twice in 1895, with the first decision producing a split decision. The enactment in question in *Pollock*, the Wilson-Gorman Tariff Act, was passed by Congress in 1894. It imposed a 2 percent tax on income in excess of $4,000 from various sources, including income derived from real estate and municipal bonds. The statute was challenged on the ground that it was a direct tax. Article I, Section 9 prohibits a "capitation, or other direct" tax unless in proportion to the census. Pollock was a stockholder of Farmers' Loan and Trust Company, and filed suit against the company to prevent its payment of the tax. In the first decision, the Supreme Court invalidated portions of the statute, those provisions that applied to income derived from property and municipal bonds. Because Justice Jackson did not participate, the Court was divided in its judgment. The case was reheard later the same year with a full court, and the Court found the entirety of the income tax portions of Wilson-Gorman to be unconstitutional in a 5–4 decision.

The opinion of the Court was delivered by Chief Justice Fuller. He explored the historical rationale for the direct tax limitation on the federal government. The framers had intended that the states would possess the power of direct taxation. Indeed, states were intended to possess "plenary powers of taxation." The only qualification is through the apportionment provision. Such apportioning could not reasonably occur here. Inability to apportion precludes the federal government from levying a tax on either real estate or personal property. The Court held that revenue derived from such property was similarly a forbidden direct tax. Fuller asked, "is it not an evasion of that prohibition to hold that a general unapportioned tax, imposed on all property owners . . . , is not direct?" Fuller said that there could be "only one answer unless the constitutional restriction is to be treated as utterly illusory and futile, and the object of its framers defeated." The Court dispatched the tax on incomes from municipal bonds on intergovernmental immunity grounds. Because the source of the bonds itself was immune from taxation, so too must be the proceeds from the bonds issued from that source. Finally, the Court addressed the question of whether the section of Wilson-Gorman found defective brought down the tax provisions of the law in its entirety. The Court concluded that the statute's defective provisions were so tightly integrated with the remainder of the statute that "all the provisions which are thus dependent, conditional or connected, must fall with them."

Dissents were individually offered by Justices Harlan, Brown, Jackson, and White. Harlan's was the most categorically at odds with the majority. He distinguished a tax on land from a tax on income derived from land. He did not consider the latter to be a prohibited direct tax. He also emphasized that the majority's holding departed from prior cases. He used the rationale from the carriage tax case (*Hylton v. United States*, 3 Dallas 171: 1796) to argue that apportionment was not possible. In Harlan's view, that makes the tax indirect and permissible. Harlan concluded by saying that the Court's decision "strikes at the very foundations of national authority" and tends to "reestablish that condition of helplessness in which Congress found itself during the period of the Articles of Confederation. *See also* DIRECT TAX, p. 592; GENERAL WELFARE CLAUSE, p. 377; *HYLTON V. UNITED STATES* (3 Dallas 171: 1796), p. 379; SIXTEENTH AMENDMENT, p. 651.

Significance   The Court used the direct tax limitation from Article I, Section 9 to strike down the income tax provisions of the Wilson-Gorman Act in *Pollock v. Farmers' Loan and Trust Company* (158 U.S. 601: 1895). The *Pollock* decision was a departure from previous holdings on the direct tax issue. As early as 1796, the Court said in *Hylton v. United States* (3 Dallas 171) that the only taxes clearly fitting the direct category were capitation or head and land taxes. *Pollock* also ignored a previous decision upholding an income tax. Congress had used an income tax during the Civil War, and the approach was upheld in *Springer v. United States* (102 U.S. 586: 1881). Nonetheless, the Court of the mid-1890s was under severe political pressure to reject the income tax, which was characterized as alien to the concept of laissez-faire as well as a frontal assault on wealth. Given that several of the justices were altogether unsympathetic with the policy objectives embedded in the tax proposal, it was not surprising that a majority found the use of the taxing power to be invalid. The *Pollock* case precluded the use of a federal income tax for less than two decades. In 1913, the Sixteenth Amendment was ratified. It provided that Congress may tax incomes from "whatever source derived" without any apportionment requirement. Thus, by means of constitutional amendment, the *Pollock* case was overruled.

Uniformity Clause

Knowlton v. Moore, 178 U.S. 41, 20 S.Ct. 747, 44 L.Ed. 969 (1900)   Provided the definitive decision on the meaning of the uniformity clause. The Court examined the constitutionality of a federal tax on "legacies or distributive shares of personalty passing at death" in *Knowlton v. Moore*. The uniformity clause is contained in Article I, Section 8 and requires that when Congress establishes "duties, imposts and excises," those shall be "uniform throughout the United States." The question raised in this case was whether the federal tax violated this uniformity requirement. The tax was collected from the estate of Knowlton, and suit was subsequently brought to recover the amount paid. The Supreme Court upheld the tax in a 5–3 decision with Justice Peckham not participating.

The opinion of the Court was delivered by Justice White. Before dealing with the uniformity issue, White dealt with contentions that the tax was direct and therefore impermissible. The Court found the tax indirect. White then turned to the issue of uniformity. Knowlton's estate attacked the tax on two grounds. First, the tax was not levied against legacies of less than $10,000 value. Second, the rate of tax was conditional on the relationship (or lack of such a relationship) between the recipient of some personal property and the deceased. The essence of the challenge was that the uniformity clause was violated by any levy that was not "intrinsically equal and uniform." The Court rejected this contention and concluded that the clause required only that taxes be geographically uniform. White cited historical evidence that supported the view that the intent had been to require sameness of tax method throughout the country. In other words, the uniformity clause requires that "wherever a subject is taxed anywhere, the same must be taxed everywhere throughout the United States, and at the same rate." In White's view, it was "plain that the words 'uniform throughout the United States' do not signify an intrinsic but simply a geographic uniformity." The Court also rejected a contention that even though uniformly applied across the states, uniformity was lost by virtue of differences in state law. The Court held that Congress need not accommodate dissimilarities that may exist in state laws. All the uniformity clause requires is comparable liability in each state even if diverse state conditions produce unlike amounts of tax collected.

Justice Brewer dissented because he felt that no kind of progressive tax could be constitutionally levied. Justices Harlan and McKenna also dissented, but focused their disagreement on how the $10,000 triggering threshold was to apply. *See also* DIRECT TAX, p. 592; *HYLTON V. UNITED STATES* (3 Dallas 171: 1796), p. 379; *POLLOCK V. FARMERS' LOAN AND TRUST COMPANY* (158 U.S. 601: 1895), p. 382.

Significance   The scope and character of the uniformity clause was examined in *Knowlton v. Moore* (178 U.S. 41: 1900). Congress is permitted to levy indirect taxes so long as they conform to the uniformity requirement. The provision requires that a tax be imposed at the same rate and levied against the same basis throughout the country. This geographic uniformity was a crucial guarantee to states that none would be singled out for targeted or differential taxation. The uniformity requirement was intended to be a limitation on the federal taxing power, but *Knowlton* rejected the more severe intrinsic uniformity interpretation. Such an interpretation would have sharply limited congressional capacity to exercise the taxing power. Instead, the geographic limitation can be accommodated by Congress with relative ease. It has even been argued that the uniformity requirement actually enhances federal authority in that it creates an incentive or inducement for states to establish comparable policies. The federal effort to prompt states into taking certain policy steps is reflected in such measures as the Social Security Act, considered by the Court in *Steward Machine Company v. Davis* (301 U.S. 548: 1937). In the case of *Florida v. Mellon* (273

U.S. 12: 1927), the Court rejected the contention that the uniformity requirement was not achieved because a state had no inheritance taxes while other states did. In other words, the Court did not permit Florida to be advantaged by not enacting an inheritance tax of its own. Actually, Florida lost certain revenues from a source taxed by other states without saving its residents from an inheritance tax collected at the federal level. The effect here was to create an incentive for Florida to enact a tax comparable to those existing in other states.

Federal Grant Conditions

Lau v. Nichols, **414 U.S. 563, 39 L.Ed. 2d 1, 94 S.Ct. 786 (1974)**   Held that a school district receiving federal funds can be required to establish bilingual educational programs for non-English-speaking students. The Court's ruling in *Lau v. Nichols* required San Francisco's public school system to provide non-English-speaking students with access to meaningful educational experiences. The school system, recipient of substantial federal educational grants, was targeted by a class action suit brought by non-English-speaking students of Chinese ancestry. The suit claimed violations of regulations established by the Department of Health, Education and Welfare (HEW) pursuant to provisions of the Civil Rights Act of 1964. Language in the act, particularly Section 601, bans discrimination based on race, color, or national origin in any program or activity receiving federal funding. The HEW compliance regulations required establishment of a program to respond to the language problem of the Chinese students. The Supreme Court upheld the HEW orders based on the Civil Rights Act in a unanimous decision.

The views of five members of the Court were reflected in an opinion by Justice Douglas, who began by disposing of the California Education Code provision that requires English to be the "basic language of instruction" in all public schools. He stated that children who already do not understand English "are effectively foreclosed from any meaningful education." He referred to basic English skills as at the "core" of what is taught at the public schools. To require a student to already have these skills makes a "mockery of public education." Douglas found that the Civil Rights Act of 1964 authorized HEW to issue regulations to make sure that a recipient of federal funds under its jurisdiction "conduct its activities compatibly with the provisions of the Act." Douglas also pointed out that the San Francisco school district "contractually agreed" to comply with the Civil Rights Act as a condition for award of the federal assistance. The federal government "has the power to fix the terms on which its money allotments to the States shall be dispersed." The limits on that power, "whatever" they may be, "have not been reached here."

A concurring opinion by Justice Stewart, joined by Chief Justice Burger and Justice Blackmun, expressed some reservations about whether Section 601 of the Civil Rights Act, "standing alone," was sufficient. But these justices were satisfied that the guidelines promulgated by HEW were "reasonably related" to the purposes of the Civil Rights Act. A separate concurring opinion by Blackmun, joined by Burger, stressed the size of the group of students involved here, some 1800. Blackmun wanted it understood that in another situation involving perhaps a single student or a "very few" children, the holding in *Lau* should not be regarded as "conclusive." For him, "numbers were at the heart" of the *Lau* decision. Justice White concurred in the result without issuing an individual opinion. *See also* STEWARD MACHINE COMPANY V. DAVIS (301 U.S. 548: 1937), p. 391.

Significance   In *Lau v. Nichols* (414 U.S. 563: 1974), the Court permitted Congress to impose, through executive agency regulations, stringent conditions on recipient use of federal grant assistance. *Lau* is representative of a long line of cases dealing with the question of whether Congress can regulate, through its taxing and spending authority, matters at the state and local level not otherwise subject to federal regulation. In *Steward Machine Company v. Davis* (301 U.S. 548: 1937), the Court upheld provisions of the Social Security Act that conditioned distribution of federal tax benefits to states on establishment of a satisfactory unemployment compensation system at the state level. In this case, the Court rejected the argument that the incentive for states to create their own programs was unconstitutionally coercive or that it represented abdication of the states' function. A decade later, in *Oklahoma v. Civil Service Commission* (330 U.S. 127: 1947), the Court allowed the federal government to threaten withholding of federal highway funding from a state because one of the members of the state's highway commission had engaged in political activities prohibited by the Hatch Act, a federal statute. Again the Court rejected the contention that authorization to withhold funds was a punitive or coercive action despite making compliance with the federal law a condition for receipt of the federal funds. The direction of these decisions would be absolutely unbending without the Court's decision in *National League of Cities v. Usery* (426 U.S. 833: 1976), where the Court invalidated federal wage and hour requirements for state and local employees. The rationale was that such regulations encroached on state sovereignty. The question left by *Usery* is whether the Court wishes to change course and impose immunity restrictions on federal spending power as it relates to conditional federal grants to state and local units of government.

Protective Tariffs

J. W. Hampton, Jr. and Company v. United States, **276 U.S. 394, 48 S.Ct. 348, 72 L.Ed. 624 (1928)**   Upheld the use of a protective tariff as a proper exercise of the taxing power. At issue in the case of *J. W. Hampton, Jr. and Company v. United States* was the constitutionality of the Tariff Act of 1922. The act was aimed at equalizing production costs of items made in the United States and competing foreign countries by imposing a tax or tariff on the imported goods to raise their consumer prices to those of comparable domestic goods. While the measure produced revenue, it was challenged as being principally a regulatory initiative, and thus an improper use of the taxing power. The act was also challenged on delegation of legislative power grounds, with a claim that Congress had left the executive branch with too much discretion in the implementation of the policy. J. W. Hampton, Jr. and Company imported a product subject to the tariff under provisions of the act. The company's challenge was rejected by the Court in a unanimous decision.

The Court's opinion was issued by Chief Justice Taft, who dispatched the delegation of legislative power issue before moving on to the taxing power. The Court felt that the Congress had established the objectives of the policy clearly enough to allow tariff adjustments to be made by the executive branch without forfeiting rule-making authority. On the broader question of the taxing power, Taft pointed out that the protective tariff had been used from the beginning of our constitutional history. Indeed, the very second act adopted by Congress back in 1789 was a revenue measure that had protective dimensions. In the resolution preceding the act, Congress said that the tariff was necessary for the "encouragement and protection of manufactures." Taft also noted that history would show that since 1789 a "number of customs revenue laws" had been drawn "with a motive of maintaining a system of protection." That history led Taft to conclude that "whatever we may think of the wisdom of a protection policy, we cannot hold it unconstitutional." He then limited the extent to which the Court ought to review tax measures. The decisive criterion is revenue. As long as the congressional "motive" and its "effect" are to "secure revenue for the benefit of the general government, the existence of other motives in the selection of subjects of taxes cannot invalidate congressional action." Taft stressed that taxes "do not lose their character as taxes because of the incidental motive." Simply because Congress's stating that one of its objectives is to encourage domestic industries "cannot invalidate a revenue act so framed." *See also* BAILEY V. DREXEL FURNITURE COMPANY (259 U.S. 20: 1922), p. 396; DELEGATION OF LEGISLATIVE POWER, p. 591; MCCRAY V. UNITED STATES (195 U.S. 27: 1904), p. 394; REGULATORY TAX, p. 648.

Significance   The Court upheld the use of the protective tariff in *J. W. Hampton, Jr. and Company v. United States* (276 U.S. 394: 1928). In doing so, the Court upheld the use of taxation as a means of achieving objectives beyond that of simply generating revenue. The principal rationale supporting the tariff was that it allowed Congress to regulate an activity over which it already had regulatory authority. Congress is constitutionally empowered to oversee commerce with foreign countries and possesses the power to directly regulate international trade and commerce. If Congress wishes to pursue that objective by means of a tariff, it must be permitted to do so. The Court's position on the tariff, then, closely resembled the position taken in *Veazie Bank v. Fenno* (8 Wallace 533: 1869), where the Court upheld a tax on state bank notes. Whenever a tax is used by Congress to support the exercise of another of its delegated powers, the tax is permissible even if the objective is primarily regulatory.

Agricultural Regulation through Spending

United States v. Butler, 297 U.S. 1, 56 S.Ct. 312, 80 L.Ed. 477 (1936)   Struck down the Agricultural Adjustment Act (AAA) of 1933 on taxing and spending grounds. The act reviewed in *United States v. Butler* was a federal attempt to stabilize prices of agricultural products and provide some assistance to farmers. The basic plan was to pay farmers not to produce on some of their agricultural acreage. The payments were to come from revenues raised by a tax imposed on processors of various farm commodities. In the Butler case, the secretary of agriculture ordered payment of cotton crop reduction benefits to any farmer consenting to the terms of the program. Butler, the receiver of cotton for a mill, refused to pay the processing tax. The federal government appealed from an adverse decision of the court of appeals, but the Supreme Court affirmed the lower court in a 6–3 decision.

The opinion of the Court was delivered by Justice Roberts. The *Butler* case hinged on resolution of the meaning of the general welfare clause. The Court saw the enactment as "one regulating agricultural production" with the tax being "mere incident" to that regulatory objective. The government argued that the constitutional source of such power was the language in Article I, Section 8 permitting Congress to "lay and collect taxes . . . and provide for the . . . general welfare of the United States." The government argued that the clause ought to be "construed to cover anything conducive to national welfare," a position forcefully asserted by Alexander Hamilton in the early years of our constitutional history. The Court seemed to subscribe to the broader construction, but imposed dual federalism limits on the broad power to tax and spend. The powers of taxation and appropriation "extend only to matters of a national, as distinguished from local welfare." Regulation of agricultural production was seen as a matter "beyond the powers delegated to the federal government." The AAA "invades the reserved rights of the states" and uses the tax as a "means to an unconstitutional end." Finally, the Court considered whether the taxing power could be used to raise revenue necessary to "purchase compliance which the Congress is powerless to command." In other words, the issue was federal tax money being used to pay farmers who voluntarily cooperated with the program. The Court answered in the negative, calling the program "coercion by economic pressure." The farmers' choice was viewed as "illusory" because benefits are lost by refusal. The Court defined coercion as the "power to confer or withhold unlimited benefits," and the program was impermissibly coercive. More importantly, even voluntarism would not have saved the enactment because it took the federal government beyond "constitutional limitations upon its own powers" and usurped authority reserved to the states.

A dissent was offered by Justice Stone, joined by Justices Brandeis and Cardozo, which found national general welfare ends served by the enactment. The dissent also was critical of the majority's lack of judicial restraint. Stone said it was not for the courts to remove unwise laws from the statute books, and he charged the majority with invalidating the AAA because "the use to which its proceeds are put is disapproved." See also BAILEY V. DREXEL FURNITURE COMPANY (259 U.S. 20: 1922), p. 396; GENERAL WELFARE CLAUSE, p. 377; STEWARD MACHINE COMPANY V. DAVIS (301 U.S. 548: 1937), p. 391.

Significance   While *United States v. Butler* (297 U.S. 1: 1936) seemed to resist making a limiting interpretation of the general welfare clause relative to federal taxing and spending authority, the decision used the Tenth Amendment to effectively confine its exercise by Congress. The case appeared to hinge on construction of the general welfare clause. Since the processing levy was not itself a defensible tax because it appropriated "money from one group for the benefit of another," the legitimacy of the AAA rested on the power of Congress to provide crop benefits through its power to spend for the general welfare. Debate on the meaning of the clause had begun early in our constitutional history. Alexander Hamilton had contended that the clause was an independent element of Article I, Section 8, and was a substantive grant of power in and of itself. Such an interpretation would have permitted the clause to enhance or supplement congressional taxing and spending authority. James Madison argued to the contrary, saying that the language merely qualified enumerated powers, and that the clause was not an independent and additional grant of power. The Court chose the Hamiltonian position in *Butler*, but then proceeded to restrict the broad taxing and spending powers to objectives specified in the Constitution. The purpose to which the AAA was directed encroached on the reserve powers of the states. Even with the broader Hamiltonian view of the general welfare clause, the Congress was found to be without a general welfare interest to regulate agriculture. The dual federalism barrier to such legislation was not long-lived, as the Court reversed itself in *Steward Machine Company v. Davis* (301 U.S. 548) the following year. An agricultural regulation resembling AAA was also upheld soon thereafter in *Mulford v. Smith* (307 U.S. 38: 1939).

Social Security Tax

Steward Machine Company v. Davis, **301 U.S. 548, 57 S.Ct. 883, 81 L.Ed. 1279 (1937)**   Upheld a federal tax on employers used to finance unemployment compensation costs. *Steward Machine Company v. Davis* examined the limits of federal taxing and spending by reviewing provisions of the Social Security Act of 1935. Steward Machine Company, an Alabama corporation, paid the payroll tax in compliance with the act and filed claim for a refund. The revenue generated from the tax went into the federal treasury, but credits of up to 90 percent could be earned if the employer paid taxes into a comparable state unemployment compensation fund. The Steward Machine Company challenged the act on several grounds, but primarily claimed that the payroll tax itself was not lawful and that the use of revenues to fund unemployment compensation costs illegally encroached on the reserve powers of the states. The Supreme Court decided against these contentions in a 5–4 decision.

The opinion of the Court was delivered by Justice Cardozo. The tax power challenge asserted that the tax was not a proper excise and violated the uniformity requirement. The Court decided that the tax was properly imposed on the business enterprise, which includes employment, and was thus a lawful excise. The Court also rejected the nonuniformity contention. Cardozo then turned to the dual federalism issue, which was that the tax constituted an improper coercion of the states in violation of the Tenth Amendment. In order to prevail, however, Cardozo indicated that there must be a showing that the "tax and credit provisions are weapons of coercion, destroying or impairing the autonomy of the states." Cardozo began his review of the coercion issue by "reminding" the Court of the "facts as to the problem of unemployment." The Court characterized the problem as "national in area and dimensions," and one for which states were "unable to give the requisite relief." Persuaded that an "urgent need" existed, the Court's assessment of the tax and credit approach focused on the means chosen— whether the measures "overleapt the bounds of powers." The Court found the means permissible because coercion was lacking. The Court concluded that Steward Machine Company confused "motive with coercion." Such is the nature of taxation. In the Court's view, "nothing in the case suggests the exertion of a power akin to undue influence." It simply could not be said that a state choosing to create and administer an unemployment compensation program itself was doing so only because it was coerced. Neither did the Court find that the provisions of the act precluded states from exercising their sovereign authority. The Court pointed out a "wide range of judgment given to the several states" regarding the specifics of their own programs. The Court concluded that no state had sovereign powers usurped nor did any state abdicate its authority by participating in the program.

Justices Sutherland and Van Devanter dissented in part, focusing primarily on federal-state administrative problems. Justices Butler and McReynolds issued separate and categorical dissents on Tenth Amendment grounds. *See also* GENERAL WELFARE CLAUSE, p. 377; NATIONAL LABOR RELATIONS BOARD V. JONES AND LAUGHLIN STEEL CORPORATION (301 U.S. 1: 1937), p. 319; UNIFORMITY CLAUSE, p. 668; UNITED STATES V. BUTLER (297 U.S 1: 1936), p. 389.

Significance   The Court upheld broad federal taxing and spending powers in *Steward Machine Company v. Davis* (301 U.S. 548: 1937). The decision upheld the constitutionality of the Social Security Act and effectively reversed the position taken by the Court in *United States v. Butler* (297 U.S. 1: 1936). The *Steward Machine* decision rejected *Butler* on two levels. First, the Court found the credit provisions for states to be a reasonable and cooperative approach to the meeting of a national problem. They replaced the view held in *Butler*, where structurally similar initiatives were termed "coercive" and "destructive." Second, *Steward Machine* represented a deeper change of view on the Court relative to the exercise of federal power. *Steward Machine* held that the federal taxing power is extensive and is limited only by explicit constitutional restrictions. Such a view diminished the impact of dual federalism as a limitation on federal taxing and spending power. This is the most important aspect of *Steward Machine*. Coupled with the Court's upholding of broad commerce power, the federal-state power balance was permanently changed. In a companion case to *Steward Machine*, *Helvering v. Davis* (301 U.S. 619: 1937), the Court affirmed the old age benefit provisions of the Social Security Act, saying that to protect the security of that group of citizens sufficiently promoted the general welfare.

Regulation of State Banks

Veazie Bank v. Fenno, 8 Wallace 533, 19 L.Ed. 482 (1869)
Upheld a federal regulatory tax on state bank notes. The tax allowed in *Veazie Bank v. Fenno* was justified essentially because it bore a reasonable relationship to other legitimate policy objectives of Congress. The tax in question was enacted in 1866. It imposed a tax of 10 percent on notes of state banks and banking associations. The tax was enacted as a part of a comprehensive effort to standardize currency, and Congress used the tax as a means of protecting the newly created national bank from competition from state banks and banking associations. The Veazie Bank paid the tax, but brought suit against Fenno, the tax collector, on the grounds that the Congress had inappropriately used its taxing power. The Supreme Court upheld the tax in a 5–2 decision.

The opinion of the Court was issued by Chief Justice Chase. He began his discussion by establishing an important historical perspective. Government under the Articles of Confederation had been "reduced to the verge of impotency" because it could not directly generate revenues. The "leading object" in the adoption of the Constitution was to relieve the federal government from this condition and confer "ample power" to levy taxes. Judicial review of the legislative exercise of the taxing power must, then, allow Congress to make the "fullest" use of the power. Furthermore, Chase indicated that courts should not prescribe "limitations upon the exercise of [Congress's] acknowledged powers." Courts may not invalidate a tax simply because the tax is burdensome or even oppressive. Having established a broad power of taxation vested in the Congress, Chase then explored the congressional authority to regulate the monetary system. Attempting to establish a uniform currency was within the authority of Congress under its power to regulate the circulation of money. As a principal element of the uniform currency objective, the Congress legitimately created a national bank. Congress was entitled to protect that bank either directly or indirectly. It chose the latter in the form of taxing state bank notes, the principal competition for the national bank. Once the Congress established the policy objective of providing a uniform currency, a legitimate legislative goal, Congress was to employ any necessary and proper means to that end. Attempting to restrain the use of the state bank notes through the tax was a constitutional exercise of power. Without having done so, Chase felt the congressional attempt to "secure a sound and uniform currency for the country must be futile."

Justice Nelson offered a dissent that was joined by Justice Davis. The dissenters argued that the federal government was without authority to establish a national bank. They saw the states as the unit with the power to create banks, and that any banks established at the state level must be free of federal interference, especially destructive taxation. *See also* BAILEY V. DREXEL FURNITURE COMPANY (259 U.S. 20: 1922), p. 396; *J. W. HAMPTON, JR. AND COMPANY V. UNITED STATES* (276 U.S. 394: 1928), pp. 191, 388; REGULATORY TAX, p. 648.

Significance The Court permitted Congress to use the taxing power as a means of advancing the exercise of another legislative power in *Veazie Bank v. Fenno* (8 Wallace 533: 1869). Of all the arguments used to justify a regulatory tax, the most generally accepted is when the tax is used to support the exercise of another delegated or implied power. Congress possesses express authority to control the currency. Protection of the national bank established by Congress to that end permits the levy of the regulatory tax against competing state bank notes. Those taxes may even be destructive, as was the case in *Veazie Bank*. The Court has generally allowed this kind of tax because Congress has the authority to reach this subject by other powers. In the case of the state bank notes, the congressional power to regulate currency would have permitted an outright prohibition on the issuance of the bank notes. Congress chose to impose the tax. The Court simply deferred to the legislative selection of means.

Regulatory Tax: Food Product

McCray v. United States, 195 U.S. 27, 24 S.Ct. 769, 49 L.Ed. 78 (1904) Upheld a congressional act levying a tax on artificially colored oleomargarine. The tax involved in *McCray v. United States* taxed oleomargarine colored yellow to resemble butter at a rate of ten cents per pound, while uncolored margarine was assessed at only one-quarter cent per pound. The taxing measure was designed to protect the interests of the dairy industry from the competitive advantage enjoyed by oleomargarine producers resulting from the substantially lower market price. The federal government attempted to collect the higher tax from McCray on a shipment of colored oleomargarine.

McCray contested the tax on the ground that regulation of oleomargarine was a state prerogative, and that Congress had no authority to levy a tax on it. The Supreme Court, however, upheld the tax in a 6–3 decision.

The opinion of the Court was delivered by Justice White. The opinion was a classic statement of judicial self-restraint. It had been asserted by McCray that "lawful power" used for an "unlawful purpose" was not constitutionally permissible. McCray was asking the Court to restrain the abusive exercise of the taxing power. The Court thought such review exceeded the authority of the judiciary. White said that the remedy for abusive exercise of legislative power "lies not in the abuse of the judicial authority of its functions." To White, it was simply not the Court's proper role to examine the motive or purpose of the exercise of lawful congressional power. Recourse to legislative abuse lies with the electorate rather than the courts. White acknowledged that when courts review an act "within a granted power," the "scope and effect" of the enactment must be considered. But the Court rejected the suggestion that the consequences arising from the lawful exercise of power be the decisive factor in making such review. The Court reiterated its position from previous cases that the taxing power conferred by the Constitution knows no limits except those expressly stated in that instrument. "Accordingly, if a tax is lawfully imposed, the exertion of that power may not be judicially restrained because of the results to arise from its exercise." The Court recognized that the Fifth and Tenth Amendments "qualify, in so far as they are applicable," all constitutional provisions, but the Court concluded that "nothing in those amendments operates to take away the grant of power to tax." Indeed, "no want of due process" could possibly result from Congress exercising conferred power to select objects upon which an excise could be imposed. White concluded by returning to the matter of judicial power, saying that the courts "may not usurp the functions of the legislative in order to control that branch of government in the performance of its lawful duties." Chief Justice Fuller and Justices Brown and Peckham dissented. *See also* BAILEY V. DREXEL FURNITURE COMPANY (259 U.S. 20: 1922), p. 396; REGULATORY TAX, p. 648.

Significance   In *McCray v. United States* (195 U.S. 27: 1904), the Court permitted Congress to regulate, by means of a tax, an object otherwise outside its reach. The Court had little trouble sustaining regulatory taxes used to support the exercise of other enumerated congressional powers. The protective tariff is such a tax. Because Congress has the power to regulate international commerce directly, it has the power to regulate through the use of the taxing power as well. *McCray* presented a quite different problem for the Court. The tax on oleomargarine was used to pursue an economic objective and therefore was a regulatory measure that was auxiliary to no other congressional power. For the Court to permit such use of the taxing power would establish virtually unlimited congressional discretion to select subjects of and objectives for taxation. On the other hand, for the Court to substantively review such taxing measures would inappropriately place the Court in the legislative arena. The Court chose the first course in resolving *McCray*. The Court refused to inquire into the "motives and purposes of Congress." Since the taxing was obviously an excise, and because it did yield some revenue, the Court concluded it was a tax imposed through the lawful exercise of congressional power. *McCray* stated the Court's clearly restraintist intentions, and Congress generally continued to employ regulatory taxes free of serious Court scrutiny, at least until *Bailey v. Drexel Furniture Company* (259 U.S. 20: 1922).

Regulatory Tax: Child Labor

Bailey v. Drexel Furniture Company, **259 U.S. 20, 42 S.Ct. 449, 66 L.Ed. 817 (1922)**   Invalidated an attempt by Congress to impose a tax on profits of companies employing children. *Bailey v. Drexel Furniture Company* reviewed the Revenue Act passed by Congress in 1919. The statute imposed a tax on, among others, mills and factories employing children under the age of sixteen for more than eight hours per day or more than six days a week. The tax amounted to 10 percent of the mill or factory's net profits. Drexel Furniture Company was found to have employed a fourteen-year-old child and was assessed the tax. The company paid the tax, but brought suit to recover the monies paid. The company was unsuccessful in the U.S. district court, and the Supreme Court concurred with the lower court in an 8–1 decision.

Chief Justice Taft delivered the opinion of the Court. The critical question was whether the measure was a tax with incidental regulatory effects or a regulation that used the tax as a penalty. The Court decided it was the latter. The act did more than simply impose a tax. It provided a "heavy exaction for a departure from a detailed and specified course of conduct." In addition, the tax imposed was not proportionate to the "extent or frequency of the departures." The tax of one-tenth of annual net business income was the same for the employment of one child for one day or any number of children for any length of time. Finally, the act excused from the tax any employer who unknowingly utilized an underaged worker. The Court suggested that "scienter is associated with penalties not with taxes." The Court concluded that "in light of the features of the act, a court must be blind not to see that the so-called tax is imposed to stop the employment of children." The regulatory effect and purpose of the statute was called "palpable." While legislation might generally be presumed valid, occasionally a law is reviewed where "proof of the contrary is found on the very face of its provisions." To find the enactment to be principally a regulation rather than a tax was crucial because regulation of child labor was not seen as a matter "entrusted to Congress." Rather, it was a subject committed by the Constitution "to the control of the States." Taft said that the Court's duty is to strike down federal laws that exceed the limits of congressional authority even if the "legislation is designed to promote the highest good." The protection of state sovereignty was a primary concern to the Court. The word *tax* could not be used indiscriminately by Congress as a way of breaking down "constitutional limitations of the powers of Congress" or as a means to "completely wipe out the sovereignty of the States." Taxes retain their character as taxes even accompanied by some incidental motive. But "there comes a time in the extension of the penalizing features of the so-called tax when it loses its character as such, and becomes a mere penalty with the characteristics of regulation and punishment." With only Justice Clarke dissenting, the Court concluded that this was such a time. *See also* HAMMER V. DAGEN-HART (247 U.S. 251: 1918), p. 309; MARCHETTI V. UNITED STATES (390 U.S. 38: 1968), p. 399; MCCRAY V. UNITED STATES (195 U.S. 27: 1904), p. 394; REGULATORY TAX, p. 648.

Significance   *Bailey v. Drexel Furniture Company* (259 U.S. 20: 1922) held that laws imposing substantial regulation and penalty through a tax may lose their character as revenue measures and be subject to other limitations on the exercise of federal legislative power. The *Bailey* decision was a complete departure from *McCray v. United States* (195 U.S. 27: 1904), in which the Court had said congressional motives were outside the scope of judicial inquiry. *McCray* permitted Congress broad discretion to pursue social and regulatory purposes through use of the taxing power. The *Bailey* decision was grounded on a distinction between tax and penalty. Where the penalty objectives are so obvious and pervasive, a tax loses its character as a tax. Once an enactment is simply a regulatory measure, it is subject to constitutional limitations that might not apply to taxes. Determination of whether a tax is punitive requires the Court to consider what Congress was trying to achieve with the law; this is inquiry into motive. This is exactly what the Court said it would not do in *McCray*. Inquiry into the motives behind the child labor tax was not especially problematic for the Court because Congress had left it little choice.

Congress had sought to regulate child labor through the commerce power in 1916, but the Court struck down the enactment in *Hammer v. Dagenhart* (247 U.S. 251: 1918). In a clumsy and transparent effort, the Congress tried to bypass *Hammer* through a tax. If the Court had upheld this tax, it would have permitted Congress to override Court interpretations of the Constitution by statute. It would have also given license to pursue through the taxing power what could not be directly accomplished through the commerce power. Instead, the Court held that the tax in *Bailey* really was not a tax, merely a regulatory scheme that violated the reserve clause and encroached on state prerogatives. Because *McCray* and *Bailey* were incompatible, the Court had opened for itself two very different ways of handling regulatory taxes. The more deferential approach to reviewing federal taxing power eventually prevailed, but not until the late 1930s.

Regulatory Tax: Wagering

***United States v. Kahriger*, 345 U.S. 22, 73 S.Ct. 510, 97 L.Ed. 754 (1952)** Upheld a federal tax on wagering against challenges that such a measure was an improper use of the taxing power. *United States v. Kahriger* also required consideration of the federal-state relationship and self-incrimination dimensions of certain registration requirements. In 1951, Congress passed the Revenue Act after the Senate had concluded a broadly scoped and nationally visible inquiry into racketeering. The act levied a 10 percent excise tax on persons engaged in accepting wagers and required that persons subject to the tax must register with the collector of internal revenue. The act was held unconstitutional by a U.S. district court, but the Supreme Court reversed that judgment in a 6–3 decision.

The opinion of the Court was delivered by Justice Reed. The Court observed that a tax "does not cease to be valid merely because it discourages or deters the activities taxed." Neither is a tax invalid because the revenue it produces may be "negligible." As long as it raises some revenue, as the wagering tax did, it remains a valid tax "regardless of its regulatory effect." Reed said that the power of Congress to tax is "extensive" and may "sometimes fall with crushing effect on businesses deemed unessential or inimical to the public welfare." If taxation is excessive, remedy is "in the hands of Congress, not the courts." The Court acknowledged that penalty provisions in tax laws that apply where regulatory requirements are not met may invalidate the statute. But generally, the Court said that "unless there are provisions extraneous to any tax need, courts are without authority to limit the exercise of the taxing power."

Justice Frankfurter dissented on dual sovereignty grounds that resembled the Court's position in *Bailey v. Drexel Furniture Company* (259

U.S. 20: 1922). He said, when "oblique use is made of the taxing power as to matters which substantively are not within the powers delegated to Congress," the Court "cannot shut its eyes to what is obviously . . . an attempt to control conduct left to the responsibility of the States." That does not change simply because Congress wrapped the legislation in the "verbal cellophane of a revenue measure." Justices Black and Douglas dissented because they regarded the registration requirements as violative of the self-incrimination protection. *See also BAILEY V. DREXEL FURNITURE COMPANY* (259 U.S. 20: 1922), p. 396; *MARCHETTI V. UNITED STATES* (390 U.S. 62: 1968), p. 399; *MCCRAY V. UNITED STATES* (195 U.S. 27: 1904), p. 394; REGULATORY TAX, p. 648.

Significance   *Kahriger v. United States* (345 U.S. 22: 1952) upheld a federal tax on wagering as a reasonable exercise of the taxing power. The wagering tax at issue in *Kahriger* is based on the taxing power principles established in *McCray v. United States* (195 U.S. 27: 1904). *McCray* was a permissive decision establishing broad congressional power to tax with little or no judicial monitoring. Soon after the *McCray* decision, Congress exercised this power to regulate the narcotics trade through taxation. Despite a vigorous dissent arguing usurpation of the state police power, the narcotics tax was upheld in *United States v. Doremus* (274 U.S. 86: 1919). The state power argument manifested itself in various cases in which expansion of federal power was attempted, and it even prevailed through the 1930s. The Court continued to allow taxation like that in *Doremus* because such levies technically generated some revenue, albeit negligible amounts. In addition, these kinds of taxes were imposed on objects or activities of questionable legality; thus the attempt through the Revenue Act of 1951 to regulate gambling by an occupational tax. Once again, *Kahriger* split the Court on federal-state grounds. The dissenters, as in the *McCray* and *Doremus* cases earlier, protested utilization of the taxing power on matters left to the states. The majority acknowledged the salience of the dual federalism argument, but reiterated that the Court should invalidate tax measures only if the enactment is "extraneous" to revenue needs. The Black-Douglas dissent, focusing on the self-incrimination problems of the registration requirements, was also significant. It introduced a potential restraint on the taxing power based on other than states' rights grounds. Indeed, Fifth Amendment defects would prove fatal in the reconsideration of the wagering tax in *Marchetti v. United States* (390 U.S. 39: 1968).

Marchetti v. United States, 390 U.S. 39, 88 S.Ct. 697, 19 L.Ed. 2d 889 (1968)   Struck down a federal wagering tax because its registration requirements violated the Fifth Amendment privilege against self-incrimination. The wagering tax at issue in *Marchetti v. United States* had been previously upheld by the Court in *United States v. Kahriger* (345 U.S. 22: 1953). The tax imposed an excise tax of 10 percent on the gross amount of all wagers accepted. The legislation contained ancillary sections designed to assure collection of the tax. One such provision required anyone subject to the tax to register each year with the local agent of the Internal Revenue Service. The statutory obligations to register and pay the occupational tax were "essentially inseparable elements of a single registration procedure." Upon registration, registrants were issued stamps indicating payment of the tax. These stamps were to be "conspicuously displayed" where the registrants conducted wagering business. Following his conviction for violations of the tax statute, Marchetti challenged the tax and the methods used to implement it. The Court struck down the act in a 7–1 decision with Justice Marshall not participating.

The opinion of the Court was authored by Justice Harlan. The Court quickly distinguished between the target of the tax and the techniques used to implement collection. Harlan said that the issue in the case "was not whether the United States may tax activities which a state or Congress has declared unlawful." He indicated that the Court has repeatedly held that the "unlawfulness of an activity does not prevent its taxation." Rather, the issue in *Marchetti* was whether the methods used in the wagering tax statute contravene the protection afforded by the self-incrimination clause. The Court noted that wagering is "an area permeated with criminal statutes." It was also true that information obtained as a "consequence of the federal wagering tax laws is readily available" to both federal and state law enforcement authorities. The Court concluded that "substantial hazards of incrimination as to past and present acts plainly stem from the requirements to register and to pay the occupational tax." The Court said that the "hazards of incrimination" as to future behavior are not "trifling or imaginary." Registrants can "reasonably expect" that registration and payment of the tax will "significantly enhance" the likelihood of prosecution for future acts, and that evidence contributing to conviction is readily obtained. While the Court did not strike down the wagering tax as such, the Court did hold that anyone properly asserting the constitutional protection against self-incrimination may not be "criminally punished" for failing to comply with the requirements of the statute. A single dissent was entered by Chief Justice Warren, who argued that gamblers ought not be protected from the registration requirements. *See also* BAILEY V. DREXEL FURNITURE COMPANY (259 U.S. 20: 1922), p. 396; REGULATORY TAX, p. 648; UNITED STATES V. KAHRIGER (345 U.S. 22: 1953), p. 398.

Significance   The Court held in *Marchetti v. United States* (390 U.S. 39: 1968) that, while the Congress might continue to impose taxes on illegal activities, the registration provisions of the wagering tax violated the constitutional protection from self-incrimination. The *Marchetti* decision overruled the holding in *United States v. Kahriger* (345 U.S. 22: 1953), which had upheld the very same registration requirements for those engaged in gambling. *Marchetti* did not disturb the highly deferential position taken in *Kahriger* regarding the taxing power generally. It makes clear, however, that Bill of Rights provisions will be stringently applied to revenue measures. The focus in these cases will not be the power to levy the tax itself, but the means chosen to collect that tax. There were two companion cases to *Marchetti*. The Court struck down an excise tax on wagers in *Grosso v. United States* (390 U.S. 62: 1968), and found the notification requirements of the National Firearms Act unconstitutional in *Haynes v. United States* (390 U.S. 85: 1968). The self-incrimination defects in the latter case were corrected by legislative amendment and subsequently upheld in *United States v. Freed* (401 U.S. 601: 1971).

Intergovernmental Immunity: Judicial Salaries

O'Malley v. Woodrough, **307 U.S. 277, 59 S.Ct. 838, 83 L.Ed. 1289 (1939)**   Upheld a tax levied against salaries of federal judges. The key issue in *O'Malley v. Woodrough* was whether the tax on judicial income constituted a reduction in judicial compensation. Article III, Section 1 states that judges shall be regularly compensated and that this compensation "shall not be diminished during their continuance in office." Woodrough was appointed to the federal bench after the income tax in question had been enacted. He sought to exclude his federal judicial salary from the statement of his annual gross income. Woodrough's return was found deficient, and he was assessed a tax on his judicial salary. He paid under protest, but later won refund of the tax in U.S. district court. O'Malley, collector of internal revenue, appealed, and the Supreme Court reversed the lower court in a 7–1 decision with Justice McReynolds not participating.

The opinion of the Court was delivered by Justice Frankfurter. This case was a reconsideration of a decision rendered in *Evans v. Gore* (253 v. 245: 1920), where the Court had ruled that even a nondiscriminatory general tax on incomes of federal judges was contrary to Article III, Section 1. Frankfurter, however, said that *Evans* misread the history that prompted the language of Article I, Section 1. Furthermore, *Evans* had met "wide and steadily growing disfavor from legal scholarship and professional opinion" according to Frankfurter. Since *Evans* had been generally "rejected," Frankfurter articulated a new position. He abandoned the argument that a general tax on income does not violate the Article III limitation. To suggest that such a tax "makes inroads upon the independence of judges" by having them carry their "aliquot share" of the cost of government is to "trivialize the great historic experience on which the framers based the safeguards of Article III." To Frankfurter, imposition of the tax on judges was no more than to recognize that "judges are also citizens." Their governmental function does not "generate an immunity from sharing with their fellow citizens" the costs of the government whose Constitution and laws they as judges are responsible for administering. *See also* ARTICLE III, p. 73; *UNITED STATES V. WILL* (449 U.S. 200: 1980), p. 85.

Significance   The Court upheld a general tax applied to judicial incomes in *O'Malley v. Woodrough* (307 U.S. 277: 1939). This case raised a special tax immunity issue. Language in Article III, Section 1 was designed to guarantee independence of the judiciary by protecting judges from having their compensation decreased during their tenure. In fairness to the *Evans* decision, that case focused on application of the tax to an already sitting judge with the finding that the tax levy was an effective reduction in salary. The Court's thinking in *Evans* did depart from historical understandings of the intention of Article III, Section 1, but was confined to the most extreme application. The Court made matters worse in *Miles v. Graham* (268 U.S. 501: 1925), when it extended the immunity of judicial salaries to those appointed after enactment of the tax. *O'Malley* explicitly reversed both *Miles* and *Evans*. More recently, federal judges have unsuccessfully claimed that salary adjustments that fail to match or exceed rates of inflation constitute a decrease in compensation. In 1980, however, in the case of *United States v. Will* (449 U.S. 200), the Supreme Court held that federal statutes that stopped or reduced previously authorized cost-of-living increases violated the diminishment of compensation provision of Article III, Section 1.

Intergovernmental Immunity: Federal Employees

Graves v. New York Ex. Rel. O'Keefe, **306 U.S. 466, 59 S.Ct. 595, 83 L.Ed. 927 (1939)**   Denied federal employees immunity from state taxation. *Graves v. New York Ex. Rel. O'Keefe* involved an attempt by New York to impose a tax on the salary of O'Keefe, an employee of the Home Owners' Loan Corporation (HOLC), a corporation of the federal government. The HOLC was itself an immune entity as an agency of the federal government, but Congress had not explicitly provided for immunity of salaries of agency employees. O'Keefe claimed that the state tax on his salary caused damage to the HOLC itself. The Supreme Court disagreed in a 7–2 decision.

The opinion of the Court was issued by Justice Stone, and it concentrated on the single issue of whether the tax on O'Keefe's salary from his job as an employee of a "corporate instrumentality" of the federal government created an "unconstitutional burden" on the federal government. The Court reviewed the concept of intergovernmental immunity and indicated that it was necessary to "forestall undue interference" through taxation between the two levels of government. The Court also acknowledged that Congress, as the legislative body embracing representation from each state, can grant immunity from state taxation to any or all of its constitutionally created instruments. In creating the HOLC, the Congress provided exemption from taxation for the instrument itself. Congress was silent, however, on employee salaries. The Court was unwilling to find immunity through implication. The Court then focused on the state income tax and found it to be a nondiscriminatory tax that was neither in form nor substance a levy against HOLC. The tax did not affect the property or income of the instrument itself, and was not paid by the corporation or from federal monies. Rather, the tax was levied against income that had become the personal property of the taxpayer. Accordingly, the Court concluded that there was no "basis for the assumption that any . . . tangible or certain economic burden is imposed" on the federal government. The effect of nondiscriminatory general taxes on the incomes of governmental employees is but the "normal incident" of our federal system. Any indirect or incidental burden that can be asserted in cases such as these is "one which the Constitution presupposes" and cannot be deemed an "implicit restriction" upon the taxing power of either federal or state governments.

A dissenting opinion was written by Justice Butler and joined by Justice McReynolds. Butler lamented the decision to allow legislatures at either level to engage in "possibly excessive or destructive taxation," a broad power not readily subject to "judicial revision." *See also* INTER-GOVERNMENTAL TAX IMMUNITY, p. 623; *NEW YORK V. UNITED STATES* (326 U.S. 572: 1946), p. 406; *PITTMAN V. HOME OWNERS' LOAN CORPORATION* (308 U.S. 21: 1939), p. 404.

Significance   The Court held in *Graves v. New York Ex. Rel. O'Keefe* (306 U.S. 466: 1939) that salaries of employees of governmental instruments are not to be immune from taxation by either the federal or state governments. This holding explicitly overruled the Court's decision in *Collector v. Day* (11 Wallace 113: 1871). *Collector* did two things. It established state immunity from federal taxation, making a reciprocity argument drawing on the Court's holding in *McCulloch v. Maryland* (4 Wheaton 316: 1819). Such an argument was flawed because the two levels do not occupy equivalent positions. A state legislature is not subject to the same political restraint as Congress when it levies a tax borne at least indirectly by the nation as a whole. The holding in *Collector* gave rise to substantial restriction of the federal taxing power on immunity grounds. This view prevailed into the 1930s, when the Court began to demand demonstration of actual interference or damage at the state level attributable to a federal tax. This approach is reflected in *University of Illinois v. United States* (289 U.S. 48: 1933), where the Court upheld collection of a tariff from a state educational institution on scientific apparatus imported from abroad. *Collector* had a second consequence that was reconsidered by *Graves*. *Collector* intertwined salaries of officers and employees and their official functions. Day was a state judge, and the Court found that a tax on his salary was a tax on the state courts. The rationale of *Graves* replaced that of *Collector* in the 1930s. The specific situation of a state employee immunity from a federal income tax was handled in *Helvering v. Gerhardt* (304 U.S. 405: 1938). There the Court held that a general federal income tax would actually have to threaten the very existence of the state government to qualify for immunity. Generally speaking, the Court has abandoned the view that a nondiscriminatory tax on salaries of public officials or employees at any level obstructs or interferes with their performance in official functions. As a result, the doctrine of intergovernmental tax immunity seldom applies to taxes imposed on salaries.

Intergovernmental Immunity: Federal Agency

***Pittman v. Home Owners' Loan Corporation*, 308 U.S. 21, 60 S.Ct. 15, 84 L.Ed. 11 (1939)**   Upheld a congressional exemption of a federal agency from taxation by the states. *Pittman v. Home Owners' Loan Corporation* (HOLC) examined a state charge imposed on every mortgage at the time it was recorded. The regulation required that stamps showing payment of the state recording tax be affixed to the mortgage. This tax collided with provisions of the Home Owners' Loan Act, which, in addition to creating the HOLC, explicitly declared the corporation to be an instrument of the United States. The mortgages on which the state recording tax was to be levied were acquired by the HOLC in their capacity as a federal agency. HOLC prevailed in the lower courts and obtained the recording of a mortgage without payment of the charge or affixing the stamps. Pittman, clerk of Baltimore's superior court, sought review. The Court held that HOLC was immune from the recording charge and tax in a unanimous decision (Justice Butler did not participate).

Chief Justice Hughes issued the opinion of the Court. He emphasized that the Maryland statute imposed a tax rather than simply collecting a reasonable registry fee. The tax was imposed on the mortgage and was "graded according to the amount of the loan." The tax was attached to the registration process as a "practical method of collection." Nor was there a question that the tax was demanded from the HOLC itself. The Court found such a levy wholly beyond the power of Maryland to enact. The key language of the Home Owners' Loan Act was the freeing of corporation "loans and income" from state or municipal taxes. In the Court's view, the critical term *loan* must be construed as "covering the entire process of lending, the debts which result therefore, and the mortgages given to the corporation as security." Since the act requires that HOLC loans be secured by a "duly recorded" mortgage, the mortgage and its "recordation were indispensable elements in the lending operations authorized by Congress." Maryland argued that the tax was not discriminatory and did not impose a burden on the HOLC. The heart of the argument was that Congress exceeded its power to grant immunity when it included such nonburdensome taxes as the one involved here. The Supreme Court disagreed. Congress possessed the authority to create the HOLC, and the Court indicated that Congress also had the power to "protect the operations thus validly authorized." The power to preserve is conveyed by the necessary and proper clause, and the Court supported its exercise in this case. See also GRAVES V. NEW YORK EX. REL. O'KEEFE (306 U.S. 466: 1939), p. 402; INTERGOVERNMENTAL TAX IMMUNITY, p. 623; NECESSARY AND PROPER CLAUSE, p. 637; NEW YORK V. UNITED STATES (326 U.S. 572: 1946), p. 406.

Significance   In *Pittman v. Home Owners' Loan Corporation* (308 U.S. 21: 1939), the Court upheld an exemption enacted by Congress against state taxation of a federal corporation. The immunity doctrine had its origin in *McCulloch v. Maryland* (4 Wheaton 316: 1819), where the Court held a federal instrumentality, the Bank of the United States, exempt or immune from state taxation. The holding in *McCulloch* was reiterated in *Osborn v. Bank of the United States* (9 Wheaton 738: 1824), where the Court permitted bank officers to bring suit against the state of Ohio to recover monies collected from the bank under a state levy. Intergovernmental immunity from taxation was intended to inhibit one party to our federal system from interfering with the functions of the other. If there were no immunity, it is possible that one level could seriously damage the operations of the other. For a time, it was argued that the immunity doctrine is wholly reciprocal, and that states were entitled to immunity equivalent to that extended to the federal government. Although this argument prevailed during the early 1900s, the Court eventually returned to the principle underlying *McCulloch*, which is that the immunity relationship is not equivalent. State taxation of federal entities, as in *Pittman*, involves "interference with the power of a government in which other citizens are equally interested with the State which imposed the taxation." Such a situation is not comparable to a federal decision to tax something at the state level because each state participated in that decision. The political process itself acts as effective restraint on congressional power in this circumstance. As a result of decisions like *Pittman*, it has been established that comprehensive immunity exists shielding federal activities from state taxation. Congress possesses ultimate authority to define the limits of that immunity.

Intergovernmental Immunity: Federal Tax on State Activity

New York v. United States, **326 U.S. 572, 66 S.Ct. 310, 90 L.Ed. 326 (1946)**   Held that state activities not essential to the state governmental function are not immune from taxation. *New York v. United States* upheld a federal revenue enactment that imposed a tax on the sale of mineral water. The state of New York had established a public corporation named the Saratoga Springs Authority. The authority, which bottled and sold mineral water, resisted payment of the tax, claiming immunity as an agency of state government. The Supreme Court found that the authority was not entitled to immunity from the tax in a 6–2 decision with Justice Jackson not participating.

Several members of the majority offered concurring opinions, but the judgment of the Court was announced in an opinion by Justice Frankfurter. He began by describing the federal taxing power as extensive, and with the exception of exports, applicable to "every subject." Levies on at least some activities of the states are permissible. Frankfurter cited, however, the difficulties with the Court's attempt to establish appropriate guidelines. To attempt to distinguish "historically recognized governmental functions of a state" from activities of a kind "pursued by private enterprise" was seen as insufficient. The defect in this approach was that it saw governmental functions in "static" terms. To define taxing power on a distinction based on what is "normal" private activity and "usual" governmental activity is an approach "too entangled in expediency to serve as a dependable legal criterion." Frankfurter preferred to take the Court in the direction of not allowing implicit immunity, and allowing Congress to impose taxes in a fashion limited essentially by fiscal and political factors. Frankfurter noted that certain state activities and property "partake of uniqueness from the point of view of intergovernmental relations." Such activities and property "constitute a class by themselves," and Frankfurter envisioned this class as presenting the minimum limitation on the federal taxing power. As long as Congress chose to "generally tax a source of revenue by whomsoever earned, and not uniquely capable of being earned only by a State," Congress is not constitutionally forbidden to levy a tax "merely because its incidence falls also on a state." Frankfurter concluded by advocating leaving the line drawing to case-by-case adjudication. For him, it was sufficient in this case to find no restriction on congressional authority to "include the States in levying a tax enacted equally from private persons upon the same subject matter."

Justice Douglas, joined by Justice Black, vigorously dissented. They urged that states ought to be able to determine for themselves which activities were legitimate in furthering their own state's interest. They saw this case as one that severely impinged on state sovereignty. If the Congress may exercise this kind of power, states will not have the "independence" presumed to flow from the Tenth Amendment, and states will be "relegated to a more servile status." *See also GRAVES V. NEW YORK EX. REL. O'KEEFE* (306 U.S. 466: 1939), p. 402; *PITTMAN V. HOME OWNERS' LOAN CORPORATION* (308 U.S. 21: 1939), p. 404.

Significance   *New York v. United States* (326 U.S. 572: 1946) reduced the impact of the immunity doctrine as a restriction on federal taxing power. Although some had felt that states were as immune from federal taxation as the federal level is from state taxation, the decision in *New York v. United States* underscored the nonequivalence of the two situations. For states to impose a tax on the federal government or any of its instrumentalities interferes with the government shared by the people of all the states. Only the residents of the state imposing the tax have any representation in the making of the state taxing decision. When a tax is imposed by the federal government, on the other hand, each of the states participates in the decision through its elected representatives. Even at its height, the immunity doctrine was not comprehensive. As early as 1905, the Court ruled in *South Carolina v. United States* (199 U.S. 437) that when a state engages in activities not "essential" to the state governmental function, those activities may be subject to federal taxation. *South Carolina v. United States* had paralleled the mineral water case in that the federal government sought to collect a tax from a state-owned liquor monopoly. Here the Court emphasized that a state could acquire and manage all forms of enterprise, thus freeing them from federal taxation. This would have the effect of striking at the heart of federal taxing power and would "practically destroy the efficiency of the national government." It is at this point that the Court confined immunity to those instrumentalities and activities of a "strictly governmental character" and said immunity does not extend to a state when it engages in "ordinary private business."

New York v. United States sharpened that language and reduced the importance of the immunity doctrine relative to contemporary taxing power. It is this doctrine, however, that still precludes tax on the proceeds from state and municipal bonds.

8. State Economic Regulation and Due Process

409

OVERVIEW

The adoption of the Fourteenth Amendment brought the prospect of additional constitutional restrictions on state power. The due process clause especially enabled the Court to engage in extensive review of state economic regulation. During a period known as substantive due process, the Court was able to forestall many state initiatives aimed at the regulation of private property interests. The due process clause guaranteed that governmental actions would not be arbitrary, unfair, or unjust. There are two kinds of due process, procedural and substantive. The former focuses on the methods by which government policies are pursued, while the latter involves the reasonableness of the policies themselves. The substantive due process approach heavily involves the Court in the scrutiny of state policy initiatives.

The Court's first opportunity to review the Fourteenth Amendment came in the *Slaughterhouse Cases* (16 Wallace 36: 1873). The Court responded with a very narrow interpretation of the Fourteenth Amendment. The Court upheld a state statute creating a slaughterhouse monopoly against claims that the regulation violated both due process and privileges and immunities of citizenship. The Court categorically refused to utilize the new amendment to interfere with the state exercise of police power. The next decade and a half saw the Court confine itself to the procedural due process approach. In *Munn v. Illinois* (94 U.S. 113: 1877), the Court permitted a state to impose rate restrictions on privately owned grain elevators. The *Munn* precedent held that states have authority to regulate property that becomes "clothed with a public interest." The following year, the Court upheld a public improvement assessment of local property in *Davidson v. New Orleans* (96 U.S. 97: 1878). Although the Court continued the procedural focus, the language in Davidson reflected a growing sensitivity to substantive aspects of challenged regulations.

The Court openly moved to the substantive approach in *Mugler v. Kansas* (123 U.S. 623: 1887). Nonetheless, the Court upheld a state regulation prohibiting the manufacture and distribution of intoxicating liquors. Three years later, the Court struck down a rate-fixing

411

statute in *Chicago, Milwaukee and St. Paul Railway Company v. Minnesota* (134 U.S. 418: 1890). Although citing certain procedural flaws in the regulating mechanism, the Court firmly established that the business was entitled to judicial determination of the reasonableness of the rates set under the statute. With substantive due process in place, the Court began several decades of using the due process clause as the principal means to insulate vested property rights from state regulation. One of the central elements of substantive due process was the concept of liberty of contract. The reasoning was that the state had no authority to interfere with an employer and an employee in their reaching an agreement on hours, wages, and conditions of employment. *Lochner v. New York* (198 U.S. 45: 1905) is a classic liberty of contract case. In *Lochner*, the Court struck down a state law limiting employment in bakeries to 10 hours per day and 60 hours per week. The Court said that such a regulation was not justified on health or safety grounds, and therefore denied both employer and employee their due process right to contract between themselves. The same liberty of contract position governed the Court's invalidation of a minimum wage enactment for women and minors in *Adkins v. Children's Hospital* (261 U.S. 525: 1923). The Court also struck down a state law authorizing a commission to resolve wage disputes and fix wages in industries affected with a public interest in *Wolff Packing Company v. Court of Industrial Relations* (262 U.S. 522: 1923).

During this period, only a few due process challenges failed. They tended to be cases where the Court was convinced of the propriety of states exercising the police power. Such areas included regulations taken to protect the public health and safety. In *Jacobson v. Massachusetts* (197 U.S. 11: 1905), the Court upheld a regulation requiring smallpox vaccinations. The specific salience of the health issue was visible in *Muller v. Oregon* (208 U.S. 412: 1908). The Court sustained a maximum hours law very much like that in *Lochner* because it applied only to women. The Court perceived a special need to protect women and their "physical well-being," and that consideration overrode the right to contract value.

The doctrine of substantive due process began to decline in the mid-1930s. The first indication came in *Nebbia v. New York* (291 U.S. 502: 1934), when the Court upheld a price restriction on the retail sale of milk. The critical case in the return to procedural due process was *West Coast Hotel Company v. Parrish* (300 U.S. 379: 1937). The Court specifically overruled *Adkins* and upheld a state minimum wage regulation. *Parrish* was an end for the liberty of contract principle, and it constituted a break from the doctrines of substantive economic due process. From that point on, the Court has generally been unwilling to impose constitutional restrictions on the exercise of state power to regulate in the economic sphere. For example, in *Williamson v. Lee Optical Company* (348 U.S. 483: 1955), the Court upheld a restriction of many aspects of visual care to ophthalmologists or optometrists. The Court deferred to the legislative judgment to regulate but noted the possibly "needless" extent of the regulation. In *Ferguson v. Skrupa* (372 U.S. 726: 1963), the Court again permitted legislative policy to control when it upheld a prohibition on the business of "debt adjusting" for everyone except attorneys.

Most of the Burger Court due process cases have not involved economic regulation. In those cases that do have economic dimensions, the Burger Court has generally followed the recent pattern of allowing states wide latitude in exercising the police power. In *Dean v. Gadsden Times Publishing Company* (412 U.S. 543: 1973), the Court upheld a requirement that employers compensate employees excused from the job for jury duty. The Court deferred to the legislative judgment that the requirement served the public political welfare. In *City of New Orleans v. Dukes* (427 U.S. 297: 1976), the Court allowed a city to prohibit pushcart vending of food in the French Quarter except for two "grandfathered" businesses. The Court held that a city may constitutionally exercise a wide range of options where regulation of the local economy is involved. Two years later, the Court permitted implementation of a landmark preservation law in *Penn Central Transportation Company v. New York City* (438 U.S. 104: 1978) even though a specific property owner was severely disadvantaged. The Court acknowledged substantial local power to preserve the city's status as a tourist, business, and cultural center. Although the deferential pattern generally remains, the Burger Court has used provisions of the Fourteenth Amendment to invalidate some state economic regulation. In *Hicklin v. Orbeck* (437 U.S. 518: 1978), the Court disallowed a state law requiring hiring preference for state residents. The law was found to violate the privileges and immunities protection. More recently, the Burger Court used the due process clause to limit state taxing power in *ASARCO, Inc. v. Idaho State Tax Commission* (458 U.S. 307: 1982). Specifically, the Court held that the due process clause precludes a state from including as taxable income those revenues coming to a business from activities having "nothing to do" with the taxing state.

Due Process Clauses   Constitutional provisions designed to ensure that laws will be reasonable both in substance and in means of implementation. Due process language is contained in two clauses of the Constitution. The Fifth Amendment prohibits deprivation of "life, liberty, or property, without due process of law." It sets a limit on arbitrary and unreasonable actions by the federal government. The Fourteenth Amendment contains parallel language aimed at the states. The Fourteenth Amendment was added to the Constitution following the Civil War and was principally designed to protect the civil rights of blacks. It contained citizenship provisions, a privileges and immunities clause, the equal protection clause, and the due process language that prohibited states from depriving persons of "life, liberty or property without due process of law." The concept of due process is difficult to precisely define, but it is generally directed at prohibiting arbitrary governmental actions.

The due process clause of the Fourteenth Amendment targets state governmental conduct. The rights protected by the due process clause can be separated into those associated with private property and those connected to persons accused of crimes. A broad array of procedural protections have been defined relative to the latter category. The result is that all states are currently required to provide virtually every procedural protection existing at the federal level through direct application of the Bill of Rights. Of more importance is the category of private property rights. From the outset of our constitutional history, property has been intertwined with the concept of liberty. The doctrine of vested rights evolved, stressing that certain rights were so critical as to be absolutely beyond governmental reach. Possession of private property was among the most important of the vested rights. Under the vested rights doctrine, the early Supreme Court protected private property interests from state regulation through frequent use of the impairment of contract clause. This approach was relatively effective, but diminished somewhat as the Court began to recognize the fuller scope of state police power. Around the middle of the nineteenth century, the vested rights doctrine began to be tied into the concept of due process of law. With the ratification of the Fourteenth Amendment, the due process clause became a means by which property rights could be defended against state regulatory initiatives. In large part, the due process clause of the Fourteenth Amendment replaced the contract clause as the basis of challenges against state regulation.

There are two kinds of due process. The first is procedural due process, which focuses on the methods or procedures by which governmental policies are executed. It guarantees fairness in imposing regulations or sanctions. Procedural due process requires that a person be formally notified of any proceeding in which he or she is a party, and that he or she be afforded an opportunity for an impartial hearing. Specific procedural rights, especially those relating to the accused, have been enumerated in the Bill of Rights. Through a process known as "incorporation," most of the Bill of Rights provisions have been applied to the states through the due process clause of the Fourteenth Amendment.

Substantive due process represents a second kind of due process. This involves the *reasonableness* of the policy content. The substantive due process approach actually precludes certain matters from the control of governmental authority, regardless of the means used.

The distinction between procedural and substantive due process directly involves the nature of judicial review. When the Court examines a policy for procedural fairness, it makes only a limited review. It does not engage in consideration of legislative motive or the wisdom of the enactment. Appraisal of the reasonableness of substance, however, allows the Court to act as an extension of the legislative process. Since most state enactments impinge on property interests, the due process clause has provided the Court with a comprehensive method by which to judge state regulatory measures. *See also* CONTRACT CLAUSE, p. 465; FIFTH AMENDMENT, p. 607; FOURTEENTH AMENDMENT, p. 612; JUDICIAL REVIEW, p. 627; PRIVILEGES AND IMMUNITIES CLAUSE, p. 647; PROCEDURAL DUE PROCESS, p. 647; SUBSTANTIVE DUE PROCESS, p. 659.

Significance   The two due process clauses have been used to challenge many governmental actions. The due process of the Fifth Amendment restricts the federal government. While utilized to some degree to contest federal economic regulation, those regulations were infrequent early in our history. As federal power was used more extensively, constitutional challenges tended to focus on the particular federal legislative power source, such as the interstate commerce power. Claims of due process violations backstopped many of these challenges, but were not featured elements. That has not been the pattern with the due process clause of the Fourteenth Amendment. This clause has provided the mechanism by which Bill of Rights guarantees have been applied to the states. The Fifth Amendment counterpart has not had to function as a conduit since the enumerated Bill of Rights protections apply directly to the federal level. Nationalization of the Bill of Rights through the due process clause of the Fourteenth Amendment increased in impact through the 1960s. The importance of the Fourteenth Amendment due process clause as the focus of state economic policy has also been extensive. Indeed, the exclusive focus of the cases in this chapter is the use of the clause to review the application of state power to regulate business and private property.

Prior to the Civil War, the vested rights issue, which dominated many of the early contract clause cases, began to enter the Court's handling of various legislative enactments through the concept of due process. The argument was that the due process clauses could be used to protect property and economic interests. Initially, the Court rejected these contentions and deferred to state legislative enactments as in the *Slaughterhouse Cases* (16 Wallace 36: 1873). In such cases, the Court opted for an entirely procedural view of due process. In subsequent cases like *Munn v. Illinois* (94 U.S. 113: 1877), the Court also emphasized the sovereign authority of state police power, which entitled states to legislate for the health, safety, morals, and the general well-being of its citizenry. Strong substantive due process dissents were entered throughout this period, and eventually that position prevailed. The substantive majority sought to strike down state legislation it considered unreasonable. The argument was that unreasonable regulation of a substantive kind was as much a deprivation or denial of due process as actions that employed arbitrary methods. Under this approach, the Court addressed itself to the wisdom of state policies. Elements of the laissez-faire economic view were drawn into due process cases in this manner. One such element was the doctrine of liberty of contract. The doctrine held that if two parties entered into a lawful agreement, the state had no authority to interfere. The liberty of contract argument was used to invalidate a number of state regulations on hours of work, as in *Lochner v. New York* (198 U.S. 45: 1905).

The period of substantive due process subsided in the 1930s at the same time the Court became more deferential to the exercise of power at the federal level. Over time, the Court essentially abandoned economic due process. At its height, however, the clause permitted the Court to perform an almost legislative role. Since most state laws touched property or contract interests, the opportunities for active intervention were great. In more recent years, the Court has generally turned its due process inquiries to noneconomic issues. At times, the activist substantive focus of earlier courts can be seen in cases involving individual freedoms and equality.

State Monopoly

Slaughterhouse Cases, **16 Wallace 36, 21 L.Ed. 394 (1873)**
Held that a state-established slaughterhouse monopoly did not violate the due process clause of the Fourteenth Amendment or impinge upon

the privileges or immunities of citizenship. The *Slaughterhouse Cases* considered aggregated challenges from a number of New Orleans butchers who sought to overturn a Louisiana statute creating a slaughterhouse monopoly. The statute regulated livestock slaughtering within the City of New Orleans and adjacent area by restricting it to a single location. The site designated by statute was the facilities of a single local corporation. The effect of the statute was to create a monopoly, although the law required that the location be accessible to any butcher upon payment of a fee. A number of butchers sought injunctive relief in the state courts without success. Appeal was made to the Supreme Court asserting several constitutional violations including due process and privileges and immunities of citizenship. The Supreme Court rejected these claims in a 5–4 decision.

The opinion of the Court was delivered by Justice Miller. He began by making three important observations. First, states have the power to "prescribe and determine the localities where the business of slaughtering" may occur. This is an aspect of the state police power that allows it to protect the public health and safety. Power of this "essential nature" should not be made vulnerable because of the Fourteenth Amendment. Second, the Court perceived only limited injury on the part of the butchers. The statute only defined the location for slaughtering, it did not prevent any butcher from doing his own slaughtering. In other words, the Court did not see the statute as depriving the butchers of the right to pursue their livelihood or even as a serious interference with that pursuit. Third, Miller expressed the view that all three of the amendments added to the Constitution after the Civil War were aimed primarily at protection of the liberties of blacks. While not to say that "no one else but the negro can share in this protection," Miller suggested that any "fair and just construction" of any part of the Civil War amendments is grounded in the "purpose which we have said was the pervading spirit of them all." All three of Miller's observations conveyed the Court's reluctance to accept the butchers' contentions.

The opinion of the Court then turned to the particular violations. Miller concentrated especially on the privileges and immunities of the citizenship issue. The Court dealt with this matter by invoking the doctrine of dual citizenship. Persons are citizens both of the United States and individual states. These are "distinct from each other." Those fundamental civil rights held by a citizen derive from state rather than federal citizenship; thus the Fourteenth Amendment can provide no protection from actions of states. The Court pointed to the inclusion of the words "United States" after reference to privileges and immunities. This was done, in the Court's view, to clearly "contradistinguish" the two types of citizenship, and the phraseology was adopted "understandingly and with a purpose." It was also clear to the Court that to adopt the position contended by the butchers would make the judiciary a "perpetual censor upon all legislation of the States." The majority concluded that this authority to nullify state initiatives was neither intended by the Congress proposing or the states ratifying the Fourteenth Amendment. The butchers also contended that their right to pursue their livelihood was property and that it had been denied without due process. The Court rejected this argument, saying that "under no construction of that provision that we have ever seen, or nay that we deem admissable, can the restraint imposed by the State of Louisiana . . . be held to be a deprivation of property within the meaning of that provision."

Chief Justice Chase, and Justices Field, Bradley, and Swayne dissented. Field saw the privileges and immunities clause as protecting rights of citizens of "all free governments," and he would have used the clause to permit the butchers to pursue their lawful livelihood without restraint. Bradley echoed Field, calling the grant of monopoly an "invasion of the right of another to choose a lawful calling, and an infringement of personal liberty." *See also* DUE PROCESS CLAUSES, p. 594; PRIVILEGES AND IMMUNITIES CLAUSE, p. 647; PROCEDURAL DUE PROCESS, p. 647; SUBSTANTIVE DUE PROCESS, p. 659.

Significance   The *Slaughterhouse Cases* (16 Wallace 36: 1873) gave the Court its first opportunity to examine the changes brought by the Civil War amendments. The stakes were extremely high because intertwined were the issues of citizenship, private property, right to work as a property right, state police power, and the nature of American federalism itself. The Court was very cognizant that to sustain the argument advanced by the butchers would be to dramatically shift the federal-state power relationship. The Court saw the Fourteenth Amendment as having no restrictive impact on the powers of states to regulate private property within their respective boundaries. Since *Slaughterhouse* was the first construction of the Fourteenth Amendment, it had inordinate precedent value. This decision was an extremely narrow interpretation of the new amendment, and it had the effect of severely muting any impact. This was especially so with regard to the privileges and immunities clause featured in the *Slaughterhouse* decision. The dual citizenship doctrine left the clause linked only to privileges and immunities of federal citizenship. The great body of economic and civil rights was held to flow from state citizenship. The Court's decision in *Slaughterhouse* virtually nullified the impact of the Fourteenth Amendment. The Court's interpretation of the privileges and immunities of state citizenship has remained virtually unaltered. While the Court has used the due process and equal protection clauses extensively in recent decades, the Court's very narrow interpretation of the privileges and immunities clause has not allowed it to have the same contemporary influence.

Procedural Due Process

***Munn v. Illinois,* 94 U.S. 113, 4 Otto 113, 24 L.Ed. 77 (1877)**
Upheld a state statute that sought to regulate privately owned grain elevators. *Munn v. Illinois* developed from legislation enacted in Illinois. The law required licensure of grain elevators and fixed maximum storage rates for elevators operating in Chicago. The statute was passed by a legislature dominated by representatives of the Grange movement, an organization of discontented farmers who felt their economic hardships were largely caused by the financial interests who controlled railroads and utilities. A number of Grange-influenced legislatures enacted various laws aimed at imposing regulations upon these enterprises. Munn was a grain warehouseman in Chicago. He and others were sued for failure to obtain a license to engage in the grain warehousing business. The warehousemen challenged the licensure and storage rate limitation on due process grounds. The Supreme Court upheld the Illinois statute in a 7–2 decision.

The opinion of the Court was delivered by Chief Justice Waite. He opened with some observations about the nature of state police power, drawing on the concept of social compact and constitutional government. People contract with one another that "all shall be governed by certain laws for the common good." While this may not allow the "whole people to control rights which are purely and exclusively private," it does authorize the enactment of laws requiring a person to "conduct himself, and so use his own property, as not unnecessarily to injure another." Such is the "very essence of government." This is the source of the police power, authority that allows regulation of personal conduct and private property when "necessary for the public good."

Waite then considered the impact of the due process clause in examining the regulation of private property. The adoption of the Fourteenth Amendment did not preclude regulation of property use or the limiting of rates charged for its use. It only prohibited regulation that deprives a property owner of due process. Inquiry into regulation is necessarily conditioned by the proposition that "when private property is 'affected with a public interest, it ceases to be *juris privati* [of private right] only'." In Waite's view, property can become "clothed with a public interest" when used in a manner to make it of public consequence, and affect the community at large. When a person uses property in such a way, he "in effect, grants to the public an interest in that use, and must submit to be controlled by the public for the common good." While a person may end the regulation by discontinuance of the public interest use, the control remains as long as the use remains. Waite then characterized those businesses that operate at the very "gateway of commerce" as so clothed with a public interest as to cease being wholly private. Waite acknowledged that reasonable compensation was due the property owners so "clothed in the public interest," but the determination of reasonableness he viewed as a legislative rather than a judicial question. Even though this power may be abused, recourse is at the polls, not in the courts. The majority also rejected the contention that the regulation interfered with federal commerce power.

Justice Field, joined by Justice Strong, dissented. Field issued a ringing statement for substantive due process. He saw the "clothed with public interest" approach as total invasion of the private property rights. To him, it was license to regulate virtually anything and everything. Indeed, property interest in a state would be "held at the mercy of a majority of its legislature." He strongly argued that the courts utilize the due process clause to safeguard private property from the ravages of state regulatory schemes. *See also* DUE PROCESS CLAUSES, p. 594; *SLAUGHTERHOUSE CASES* (16 Wallace 36: 1873), p. 417; SUBSTANTIVE DUE PROCESS, p. 659.

Significance   *Munn v. Illinois* (94 U.S. 113: 1877) provided a narrow procedural construction of the due process clause of the Fourteenth Amendment. As in the *Slaughterhouse Cases* (16 Wallace 36: 1873) before it, the Court rejected use of the Fourteenth Amendment as a mechanism for judicial interference with state regulatory initiatives. At the same time, *Munn* had slightly different consequences from *Slaughterhouse*. *Munn* reiterated a restrictive interpretation of the due process clause and upheld a regulation of private property because that property had become "clothed with a public interest." But *Munn* also seemed to suggest that a substantive approach to due process might be appropriate when businesses are subjected to unreasonable regulation. Thus, it took a slightly broader view of due process than *Slaughterhouse*. The principal thrust of *Munn*, however, was procedural. So long as businesses were properly categorized as being affected with a public interest, the substantive regulations themselves were placed outside the scope of judicial review. The dissent by Justice Field represents the "classic" substantive due process position, a view that would come to prevail little more than a decade after *Munn*.

Local Assessment for Improvements

Davidson v. New Orleans, **96 U.S. 97, 6 Otto 97, 24 L.Ed. 616 (1878)** Upheld a local property assessment levied to raise revenue for public improvement purposes. *Davidson v. New Orleans* developed out of an effort of the city to drain certain swamplands. It was decided that proceeds from a real estate assessment would be used to finance the project. A substantial assessment was levied against the Davidson estate, and the city brought suit to collect. It was contended that the assessment denied the estate property without due process. The Court disagreed in a unanimous decision.

The opinion of the Court was authored by Justice Miller, who devoted the early discussion to tracing the history of the concept of due process. He pointed out that the "prohibition against depriving the citizen or subject of his life, liberty, or property without due process of law, is not new in the constitutional history of the English race." Neither did it first become part of the United States Constitution with the adoption of the Fourteenth Amendment. He admitted, nevertheless, that the "meaning or value" of the term *due process of law* remains without the "satisfactory precision of definition" that had evolved relative to other individual rights. Miller noted that, while the due process language had appeared in the Fifth Amendment from the outset of our constitutional history, it had "rarely been invoked in the judicial forum." The due process clause of the Fourteenth Amendment, on the other hand, had existed only a "very few years" and yet the Court's docket was "crowded with cases" claiming state violations. Miller took that as "abundant evidence that there exists some strange misconception of the scope" of the due process clause. Miller said it seemed to reflect that the clause was viewed as a means to test the "abstract opinions of every unsuccessful litigant in a state court." The Court disagreed with such a view.

The Court held that the due process clause had limited application. It did not, for example, directly restrain the states from the taking of property without just compensation in quite the same way the Fifth Amendment language limits such conduct by the federal government. To the extent it does apply, it imposes restrictions on processes rather than substance. A person is entitled, as a matter of due process, to a hearing in a court of justice. The due process clause does not permit the Supreme Court to find any violations when state judicial proceedings take place. In this instance, the assessments were required to be filed in a state court before they could be collected. All affected property owners were notified of the filing and permitted an opportunity to appear and register objections to the assessment. In the Supreme Court's view, "if this be not due process of law, then the words can have no definite meaning as used in the Constitution." In sum, the Court saw due process in exclusively procedural terms and categorically refused to consider the reasonableness of the drainage assessment itself. *See also* DUE PROCESS CLAUSES, p. 594; PROCEDURAL DUE PROCESS, p. 647; SUBSTANTIVE DUE PROCESS, p. 659.

Significance　　The transition from procedural to substantive due process can be detected in *Davidson v. New Orleans* (96 U.S. 97: 1878). Due process cases like the *Slaughterhouse Cases* (16 Wallace 36: 1873) and *Munn v. Illinois* (94 US. 113: 1877) took a very narrow procedural interpretation of the due process clause. In both cases, the Court refused to use the clause to interfere with a state regulation. More importantly, the Court's opinions stressed that the reasonableness of state laws under review was not subject to judicial scrutiny. Rather, the due process clause only guaranteed procedural fairness. A vigorous minority in *Munn* argued that the due process clause required courts to examine substantive reasonableness of challenged enactments. While resolving the New Orleans assessment through a procedural due process approach, *Davidson* encouraged the advocates of substantive due process. The Court emphasized the difficulty in defining the term *due process*. The Court also saw it necessary to let the concept evolve over time. Such language allowed some members of the Court to say in *Davidson* that due process included a substantive dimension. In addition to the procedural requirements, attention must be paid to the "cause and object" of the regulation. If these substantive considerations lead the Court to conclude that the law is "arbitrary, oppressive and unjust," the Court may strike down the enactment. Within a decade of *Davidson*, the Court would fully adopt such a substantive due process orientation.

Prohibition of Alcohol

***Mugler v. Kansas*, 123 U.S. 623, 8 S.Ct. 273, 31 L.Ed. 205 (1887)**
Upheld a state prohibition on the manufacture and sale of alcoholic beverages as a proper exercise of the state police power. *Mugler v. Kansas* examined a provision of the Kansas Constitution adopted in 1880 that placed a prohibition on the production and distribution of many specified liquors. This constitutional language was supplemented by statutory sanctions the following year. Mugler owned a brewery, a facility built prior to the adoption of prohibition. He produced and sold beer after the effective date of the prohibition policy and was prosecuted and convicted. He sought review on the grounds that the state regulation denied him liberty and property without due

process of law. The Supreme Court upheld the prohibition in a decision in which only Justice Field offered even partial disagreement.

The opinion of the Court was issued by Justice Harlan. Harlan began the examination of the state policy by suggesting that deference must generally be accorded the exercise of state police power. The Court recognized that ever since the adoption of the Fourteenth Amendment, states have broad authority to "control their purely internal affairs," and in fulfilling that function, protect the "health, morals, and safety of their people." If the state possesses broad power to regulate in the public interest, the question then becomes, where in the process are the key judgments about substantive protections of the public interest made? The Court found that, as a general rule, determination of what constitutes an actual or potential injury to the public welfare is a legislative question. The Court went on to say, however, that such power is not outside the scope of judicial inquiry. Not every law "ostensibly" enacted for public health or safety reasons "is to be accepted as a legitimate exertion of the public powers of the State." There are limits "beyond which legislation cannot rightfully go." The courts cannot be "bound by mere forms, nor are they to be misled by mere pretenses." Rather, courts are "at liberty—indeed, are under a solemn duty" to examine the "substance of things" when they review claims that a legislature has "transcended the limits of its authority." Any law enacted to protect the public health, morals, or safety that has "no real or substantial relation to those objects," or is a "palpable invasion of the rights secured by the fundamental law," obligates the courts to intervene.

On the basis of these considerations, the Court looked at the prohibition policy of Kansas. It was reasonable for Kansas to regulate the perceived evils resulting from "excessive use of ardent spirits." Having established the reasonableness of the objective, the Court deferred to the method selected by the legislature to achieve that end. The Court did not feel that persons had a right to decide individually whether or not to use alcohol because that choice could have the effect of defeating the legislative objective of protecting the public from excessive use. Citizenship does not convey such a right of choice. Neither did the Court find that prohibition interfered with a "constitutional right of liberty or of property." In the Court's view, those rights are "best secured . . . by observance, on the part of all, of such regulations as are established by competent authority to promote the common good." As for the fact that prohibition was imposed after Mugler had constructed his brewery, the Court held that state power cannot be limited because property owners are affected by regulations contrary to their expectations at the time of purchase. A state can give no assurances that in the future public policy pursuing the general welfare will not change. This point was directly examined in several post–Civil War contract clause cases. *See also* DUE PROCESS CLAUSES, p. 594; PROCEDURAL DUE PROCESS, p. 647; *STONE V. MISSISSIPPI* (101 U.S. 814: 1880), p. 478; SUBSTANTIVE DUE PROCESS, p. 659.

Significance   In *Mugler v. Kansas* (123 U.S. 623: 1887), the Court upheld a state prohibition on the manufacture and sale of most liquor. At the same time, the Court clearly served notice that state police power would be substantively examined by the courts, and that it would not routinely survive judicial scrutiny simply because the state claimed the public health, morals, and safety were promoted. Indeed, the Court's decision in *Mugler* was based on its judgment that alcoholic beverages did constitute a threat to the public health and morals and could reasonably be regulated. This substantive due process approach had its origin prior to the Civil War when the contract clause became less effective as a means of protecting private property rights. There are several state cases dating back to the 1850s that defined due process in substantive as well as procedural terms. The thrust of these cases was that the clause stood as a general limitation on state power. This view could be seen in Supreme Court decisions prior to *Mugler* as well. In the first legal tender case of *Hepburn v. Griswold* (8 Wallace 603: 1870), for example, the Court struck down an act that would have required creditors to accept paper money as payment for contracted debts on due process grounds. While the legal tender policy of *Hepburn* was almost immediately reconsidered and reversed, the substantive due process evident there was to remain for a considerable time. Generally speaking, however, even with substantive due process, the Court deferred to legislative judgments regarding public health issues.

Reasonableness of Rates

Chicago, Milwaukee and St. Paul Railway Company v. Minnesota, 134 U.S. 418, 10 S.Ct. 462, 33 L.Ed. 970 (1890)   Struck down a state regulation of railroad and warehouse rates within the state. The statute at issue in *Chicago, Milwaukee and St. Paul Railway Company v. Minnesota* was enacted by the Minnesota legislature in 1887. It established a railroad and warehouse commission with the power to review rail and warehouse rates. The commission was empowered to change any rates it viewed as unequal or unreasonable. The Minnesota law did not require notice and hearing before the commission acted on any rate matter. In addition, the rate-setting power of the commission was final; there was no provision for appeal to the courts or elsewhere after the commission exercised its judgment. In this case, the commission reviewed rates for transporting milk by rail. Contingent on points of origin and destination, the original rate was either three or four cents per gallon. The commission ordered a decrease to two and one-half cents. The Minnesota courts upheld the order, and the railway company sought review from the United States Supreme Court. The Court reversed the state courts in a 6–3 decision and invalidated the law.

The opinion of the Court was issued by Justice Blatchford. Of major concern to the Court were the procedural aspects of the regulation. The Court found the commission's rate-making processes defective principally because of the absence of notice and hearing provisions, no mechanism for the appearance of company witnesses, and no means available to obtain review of commission orders. These flaws were seen as critical because the commission had authority to establish rates finally and conclusively on the basis of its own standards of equality and reasonableness. But Blatchford did not stop with the procedural questions. He proceeded to examine the matter of reasonableness of the rate order and whether the courts should have a role in reviewing substantive reasonableness. The Court held that the railway had a right to a "judicial investigation of due process of law." Access to the judiciary had for "successive ages" provided the "forms" and "machinery" for such inquiry. No commission can be "regarded as clothed with judicial functions or possessing the machinery of a court of justice." The Court held the railroad was entitled to judicial consideration of reasonableness; the "question of a rate . . . is eminently a question for judicial investigation, requiring due process of law for its determination." The court concluded by saying that if the company is not allowed to determine rates for use of its own property in the absence of an "investigation by judicial machinery," it is unconstitutionally deprived of the lawful use of its property.

Justice Bradley issued a dissent joined by Justices Gray and Lamar. Bradley contended that businesses affected with a public interest were subject to such regulation. This kind of regulation is a "legislative prerogative and not a judicial one." He vigorously disagreed that courts should get involved with determination of reasonableness. Bradley suggested that had the legislature set the rates, it would have been upheld in a manner similar to *Munn v. Illinois* (94 U.S. 113: 1877). He could see "no good reason" why the legislature could not "delegate the duty to a board of commissioners." Bradley concluded by saying that if the decisions of legislatures or their agencies become too arbitrary, "the people always have the remedy in their hands." *See also* DUE PROCESS CLAUSES, p. 594; *MUNN V. ILLINOIS* (94 U.S. 113: 1877), p. 420; PROCEDURAL DUE PROCESS, p. 647; SUBSTANTIVE DUE PROCESS, p. 659.

Significance   The Court used the case of *Chicago, Milwaukee, and St. Paul Railway Company v. Minnesota* (134 U.S. 418: 1890) to establish substantive due process as a principle of American constitutional law. Although the Court had procedural grounds on which to reject the Minnesota statute, there was clear concern over the state effort to regulate rates charged by utilities. The Court categorically said that state-imposed regulations must be substantively reasonable, and that determination of reasonableness was "eminently" a judicial question. This constitutes a complete turnaround from the doctrines fashioned in *Slaughterhouse Cases* (16 Wallace 36: 1873) and *Munn v. Illinois* (94 U.S. 113: 1877). This decision placed the Court in the position of having perpetual oversight on state policy initiatives. Those the Court did not feel were reasonable were now subject to judicial veto. The *Chicago, Milwaukee* case did not require the Court to determine whether it would review reasonableness of rates set by state legislatures directly. In *Reagan v. Farmers' Loan and Trust Company* (154 U.S. 362: 1894), the Court claimed such power although the rates, as in *Chicago, Milwaukee,* had been set by a commission. The Court acted upon this claim in *Smyth v. Ames* (169 U.S. 466: 1898) when it struck down legislatively set intrastate shipping rates. The full extent of the policy implications of this authority were quickly to become evident.

Health Regulation

***Jacobson v. Massachusetts*, 197 U.S. 11, 25 S.Ct. 358, 49 L.Ed. 643 (1905)**   Upheld a local health regulation requiring smallpox vaccination. *Jacobson v. Massachusetts* examined the nature of the state police power to protect the public health. Jacobson refused to comply with an order of the board of health, issued pursuant to authority conveyed by state legislation, to submit to vaccination against smallpox. He was found in violation of the law, and he appealed unsuccessfully through the state courts. He ultimately sought relief from the United States Supreme Court. Jacobson argued that the state police power does not permit a state to penalize a person for refusing vaccination. He contended the law was arbitrary and unreasonable and contrary to the inherent right of every citizen to care for his or her own physical well-being. The Court upheld the compulsory vaccination in a 7–2 decision.

The opinion of the Court was delivered by Justice Harlan. He began by suggesting that the police power is broad, and that states must be accorded substantial discretion to protect the public health and safety. Even constitutional liberties may not insulate a citizen from regulation in pursuit of the public health. Constitutional liberties are not absolute and do not wholly free an individual from regulation. The exercise of an individual's personal liberty cannot inflict injury on others. In considering matters of risk to the public health, legislatures properly defer to boards of health, as they are composed of persons selected "because of their fitness to determine such questions." While a board of health does not possess unlimited power, the broad public interest does require that it have power that may impinge on individual rights. Jacobson then sought to have the Court review the substance of the vaccination order itself. Jacobson essentially argued an alternative medical position regarding the effectiveness and safety of vaccinations. The Court, however, deferred to legislative judgment on this matter. Harlan said "we must assume . . . the legislature . . . was not unaware of these opposing theories, and was compelled, of necessity, to choose between them." The function of the courts does not include determining which of several alternatives "was likely to be the most effective for the protection of the public against disease."

Harlan went on to say that judicial review of legislation respecting the general welfare can occur only under two sets of circumstances. One is when the regulations enacted to protect the public health have "no real or substantial relation" to the public health. The other is when, "beyond all question, a plain, palpable invasion of rights secured by the fundamental law" takes place. The Court found neither of these two conditions present here. Harlan concluded by reiterating that the Court would not allow an individual or minority to defy a regulation aimed at protecting the community welfare. He said that the Court was unwilling to interpret the Constitution to permit a resident of a community to have the power to "dominate the majority when supported in their action by the authority of the state." Justices Brewer and Peckham dissented. *See also* DUE PROCESS CLAUSES, p. 594; *MUGLER V. KANSAS* (123 U.S. 623: 1887), p. 423; PROCEDURAL DUE PROCESS, p. 647; SUBSTANTIVE DUE PROCESS, p. 659.

Significance Jacobson v. Massachusetts (197 U.S. 11: 1905) upheld a regulation imposed for public health purposes. Even during the height of substantive due process, when the Supreme Court was invalidating state economic regulation frequently, statutes dealing with the public health and safety, morals, and welfare were generally sustained. Indeed, the Court's position seemed to presume the validity of such regulation. The deference to legislative judgments in this sphere is clearly evident in *Jacobson*. More recent regulatory initiatives like those in *Williamson v. Lee Optical Company* (348 U.S. 483: 1955) have maintained this pattern. In *Williamson*, the Court permitted a state regulation limiting many aspects of eye care exclusively to licensed ophthalmologists or optometrists. Attempts to protect public moral standards have generally received support from the Court also. State prohibition laws were typically upheld as in *Mugler v. Kansas* (123 U.S. 623: 1887). Similarly, the Court allowed states to prohibit cigarette smoking (*Austin v. Tennessee*, 179 U.S. 343: 1900) and certain kinds of tobacco advertising (*Packer Corporation v. Utah*, 285 U.S. 105: 1932). Finally, the Court has maintained a typically deferential posture on statutes seeking to promote the general welfare. Zoning ordinances have consistently fared well despite the potential for economic burden on property owners. *Village of Euclid v. Ambler Realty Company* (272 U.S. 365: 1926) is illustrative. More recently, the Burger Court upheld a landmark preservation law aimed at preserving largely aesthetic and historical interests in *Penn Central Transportation Company v. New York City* (438 U.S. 104: 1978), finding the regulation analogous to a zoning ordinance.

Liberty of Contract

Lochner v. New York, **198 U.S. 45, 25 S.Ct. 539, 49 L.Ed. 937, (1905)** Struck down a state maximum hours of work statute on the ground that it interfered with individual rights to contract services. The statute reviewed in *Lochner v. New York* forbade any employee of a bakery or other confectionery establishment from working more than 10 hours a day or 60 hours in a single week. Lochner required an employee to work beyond the 60-hour weekly limit and was found in violation of the law. Lochner sought review from the Supreme Court after the state courts had sustained his conviction. The Supreme Court reversed Lochner's conviction and invalidated the statute in a 5–4 decision.

The opinion of the Court was delivered by Justice Peckham. Before beginning his discussion of the state police power, Peckham characterized the issue involved in this case. The act was an "absolute prohibition on the employer," preventing more than 10 hours work a day in his establishment "under any circumstances." The statute necessarily "interferes with the right of contract between the employer and employees." The right to "make a contract in relation to his business" is an individual liberty protected by the Fourteenth Amendment. The right to "purchase or to sell labor" is also part of the liberty protected by the amendment. The Court saw the valid exercise of the police power as having limits, otherwise the Fourteenth Amendment would have no "efficacy" and state legislatures would have "unbounded power" to interfere with private property. Interference with liberty to enter contracts constituted an area outside the reach of the police power except for compelling reasons. The controlling question for the Court in reviewing enactments like this one was whether the act was a "fair, reasonable, and appropriate exercise of the police power." The Court found the New York act to be indefensible as a labor law. Bakers, in the Court's mind, were in no need of special protection and were "in no sense wards of the state." Accordingly, the Court held that the act could not be sustained as a measure based on public safety or moral needs.

That left justification as a health regulation. The Court found insufficient cause, however, for the state to act here, because "clean and wholesome bread does not depend on whether the baker works but ten hours a day or sixty hours a week." Neither is the occupation an "unhealthy one" to the degree which would authorize the legislation to interfere with the right to labor. For a state to exercise the police power constitutionally, there must be "more than the mere fact of the possible existence of some small amount of unhealthiness to warrant legislative interference with liberty." Simply because the state claimed to be promoting the public health will not suffice. The Court must look at the purpose of the statute as determined from the "natural and legal effect of the language employed." Protection of the public health must bear more than a "remote relation" to the law. In this case, the Court held that New York could not reasonably impose hour restrictions because no legitimate purpose was achieved by such a regulation. Rather, laws of this type are "meddlesome interferences with the rights of the individual," and they cannot be "saved from condemnation" by simply claiming police powers.

Four members of the Court, Justices Holmes, Harlan, Day, and White, disagreed. Holmes, in a notable dissent, contended that the case was "decided upon an economic theory which a large part of the country does not entertain." The Constitution was not "intended to embody a particular economic theory," whether of "paternalism" or of "laissez-faire." He suggested that the word liberty in the Fourteenth Amendment was "perverted" when used to "prevent the natural outcome of a dominant opinion" unless an assessment by a "rational and fair man" would necessarily find the enactment violative of fundamental constitutional principles. Holmes concluded that "no such sweeping condemnation can be passed upon the statute before us." *See also* ADKINS *V. CHILDREN'S HOSPITAL* (261 U.S. 525: 1923), p. 433; DUE PROCESS CLAUSES, p. 594; LIBERTY OF CONTRACT, p. 633; *MULLER V. OREGON* (208 U.S. 412: 1908), p. 431; SUBSTANTIVE DUE PROCESS, p. 659.

Significance   Lochner v. New York (198 U.S. 45: 1905) represents one of the Court's strongest statements of substantive due process. Here the Court found the New York maximum hour regulation for the baking industry to be an unreasonable and arbitrary interference with the liberty of contract. The freedom to manage one's own labor was viewed as a core element of due process protection. The Court first invalidated a state regulation on purely substantive grounds in *Allgeyer v. Louisiana* (165 U.S. 578: 1897). The state had attempted to limit the capacity of out-of-state insurance companies to insure property within the state.

The Court held that this regulation interfered with the liberty to make personal property arrangements. The following year, the Court decided on a maximum hour regulation from Utah in *Holden v. Hardy* (169 U.S. 366: 1898). The Court upheld the regulation because it applied to minors, and the Court was satisfied that the legislature had properly assessed the occupation as dangerous when hours became excessive. Thus, the regulation was sustained as a reasonable health and safety measure. Bakers, on the other hand, did not need such protection in the view of the Court. There were simply no health risks in the industry sufficient to justify encroachment on the liberty of contract. The full implications of substantive due process are clearly evident by comparing *Holden* and *Lochner*. In both cases, the Court reviewed the regulations enacted by the states, and drew their own conclusions as to the need for the regulations. Depending on the Court's findings, state laws were either sustained or invalidated. *Lochner* is a "classic" example of the substantive due process orientation.

State Maximum Hours Law

***Muller v. Oregon,* 208 U.S. 412, 28 S.Ct. 324, 52 L.Ed. 551 (1908)**   Upheld an Oregon statute that established maximum hours of work for women. *Muller v. Oregon* appeared to be a reconsideration of issues decided in *Lochner v. New York* (198 U.S. 45: 1905), but the Court distinguished the two statutes. The Oregon statute prohibited employment of women in any "mechanical establishment, factory or laundry" within the state for more than ten hours in any one day. Muller was found in violation of the statute and fined. He appealed to the United States Supreme Court after failing to prevail in the state courts. The Supreme Court unanimously upheld the regulation.

The opinion of the Court was offered by Justice Brewer. The *Lochner* case had held that a limitation on the hours of work for men was an "unreasonable, unnecessary and arbitrary interference with the right and liberty of the individual to contract in relation to his labor." Muller asserted that *Lochner* governed this case. That assumed, however, that the difference between men and women employees did not justify a different policy respecting hours of work. The Court took note of the "copious collection" of data submitted by Louis Brandeis on behalf of Oregon speaking to such a gender distinction. The data, filed in what became known as the "Brandeis brief," were viewed as "significant of a widespread belief that women's physical structure, and the functions she performs in consequence thereof, justify special legislative restricting or qualifying the conditions under which she should be permitted to toil." While these data, "technically speaking," were not seen as authoritative, the Court took "judicial cognizance" of them as a matter of general knowledge. The Court found that a woman's "physical structure" and her "maternal functions" place her at an "obvious" disadvantage while struggling for subsistence. This is "especially true when the burdens of motherhood are upon her." Protection of the "physical well-being" of women is an object of "public interest and care in order to preserve the strength and vigor of the race." The Court also noted that women have long been seen as requiring "especial care." Citing inequality in access to education, Brewer concluded that women were not yet an "equal competitor" for subsistence with men. So differentiated, a woman is "properly placed in a class by herself." Legislation pursuing such an end may be permitted although "like legislation is not necessary for men, and could not be sustained." While this statute limits a woman's contractual powers because of her distinct status from men, it is not imposed "solely for her benefit, but also for the benefit of all." *See also* DUE PROCESS CLAUSES, p. 594; LIBERTY OF CONTRACT, p. 633; *LOCHNER V. NEW YORK* (198 U.S. 45: 1905), p. 429; PROCEDURAL DUE PROCESS, p. 647; SUBSTANTIVE DUE PROCESS, p. 659; *WEST COAST HOTEL COMPANY V. PARRISH* (300 U.S. 379: 1937), p. 435.

Significance   The Court sustained a maximum hours of work law designed to protect female workers in *Muller v. Oregon* (208 U.S. 412: 1908). The decision seemed to reflect a change in outlook for the Court. As recently as *Lochner v. New York* (198 U.S. 45: 1905), the Court had been quite unreceptive to regulations of hours and wages. Such policies were incompatible with the Court's laissez-faire views generally, and specifically interfered with liberty of contract. But *Muller* seemed to depart from *Lochner* and adopt a more supportive position with regard to economic regulation. In part, the Court's response was a result of the Oregon statute's focusing on women. The Court was also influenced substantially by the nature of the case made by Oregon to support the reasonableness of the regulation. Through data submitted in the Brandeis brief, the Court became persuaded that limiting a woman's workday was justified on health as well as social grounds. In *Muller*, the Court engaged in substantive due process, but sustained the law because it found the regulation to be substantively reasonable. In *Bunting v. Oregon* (243 U.S. 426: 1917), the Court upheld a maximum hour statute covering both men and women workers. The *Bunting* decision seemed to directly overrule the *Lochner* case, although the Court's opinion did not mention *Lochner* explicitly. Such was not the case, however. The Court was to return full force to its substantive due process approach featuring the liberty of contract principle in cases like *Adkins v. Children's Hospital* (261 U.S. 525: 1923). Nonetheless, *Muller* retains a noteworthy place in our constitutional development because it introduced sociological jurisprudence through the Brandeis brief.

State Minimum Wage Law

***Adkins v. Children's Hospital,* 261 U.S. 525, 43 S.Ct. 394, 67 L.Ed. 785 (1923)**   Struck down a District of Columbia minimum wage enactment that applied to women and minors, citing Fifth Amendment due process defects. *Adkins v. Children's Hospital* examined the Minimum Wage Act of 1918. The act established a minimum wage board for the district. The board had the authority to examine wages paid to women and minors and to establish binding minimum levels of compensation where appropriate. Children's Hospital employed a number of women, including Adkins, who were paid less than the board-established minimum. These employees were laid off as a result of the board's actions. Satisfied with their wages and working conditions prior to imposition of the minimum wage order, Adkins and others brought suit seeking to forestall implementation of the act. They argued that they were constitutionally entitled to take whatever job at whatever pay they wished. The Supreme Court agreed in a 5–3 decision that invalidated the act. Justice Brandeis did not participate in the Court's decision.

The opinion of the Court was delivered by Justice Sutherland. Key for the Court was whether the statute impermissibly interfered with anyone's right to contract. This Court felt strongly that the freedom to "contract about one's affairs" was a constitutionally protected liberty. While this freedom was not absolute, "freedom of contract is, nevertheless, the general rule and restraint the exception." The Court also disengaged itself from prior cases like *Muller v. Oregon* (208 U.S. 412: 1908), which were upheld on the basis of fundamental differences between men and women. Sutherland suggested that the "ancient inequality" noted in *Muller* has "continued 'with diminishing intensity'"; the differences have come almost to the "vanishing point." The Court rejected the contention that restrictions on women's liberty of contract could be upheld when similar restraints on men would not. Sutherland then distinguished between statutes setting maximum hours and those establishing minimum wages. They have different objectives, as hour limits have a health element absent in the wage regulation. As important, hour limitations leave the parties "free to contract about wages." Sutherland called the statute a "price-fixing law" imposed upon women "who are as legally capable of contracting themselves as men."

The Court then addressed the substantive defects of the minimum wage policy. The Court saw it as a misguided attempt to protect the health and welfare of women. Sutherland said that there was "no relation between earnings and morals"; well-paid women do not "safeguard their morals more carefully than those who are poorly paid." The minimum wage law was also defective because it considered the "necessities of only one party to the contract." It forced the employer to pay a certain wage irrespective of "whether the employee is capable of earning it," or his business is able to "sustain the burden." And the act exacts an "arbitrary payment for a purpose and upon a basis having no causal connection with his business." While workers may have an "ethical right" to a living wage, the minimum wage approach was not seen as a reasonable method to achieve it. Sutherland said the law ignored the relationship of payment and service, and it placed employers in the position of underwriting the costs of extricating the employee from poverty. The employer has "neither caused nor contributed" to that poverty. Indeed, "to the extent of what he pays, he has relieved it." The Court concluded by saying that if the police power can be sustained in this situation, it could be applied anywhere a state legislature pleases. A "wrong decision does not end with itself; it is a precedent, and, with the swing of sentiment, its bad influence may run from one extremity of the arc to the other."

A dissent by Chief Justice Taft, joined by Justice Sanford, made reference to the "evils of the sweating system" and "harsh and greedy employers." Congress, in Taft's view, had the power to address those problems, and the role of the Court should not be to hold acts invalid "simply because they are passed to carry out economic views which the Court believes to be unwise or unsound." Taft also disputed the majority's distinction between wage and hour laws. Both elements, he suggested, were equally important. Neither could Taft accept the majority use of *Lochner v. New York* (198 U.S. 45: 1905), a precedent he saw overruled by *Muller*. A dissent was also registered by Justice Holmes, who developed many of the same points as Taft. Holmes also argued that the majority had transformed the due process clause "into the dogma, Liberty of Contract," a concept not explicitly mentioned in the Fourteenth Amendment. He concluded by saying that *Muller* was still operative law, and that legislatures could still take gender into account in fashioning legislation. *See also* DUE PROCESS CLAUSES, p. 594; LIBERTY OF CONTRACT, p. 633; *LOCHNER V. NEW YORK* (198 U.S. 45: 1905), p. 429; *MULLER V. OREGON* (208 U.S. 412: 1908), p. 431; SUBSTANTIVE DUE PROCESS, p. 659; *WEST COAST HOTEL COMPANY V. PARRISH* (300 U.S. 379: 1937), p. 435.

Significance   The Court engaged in substantive due process to strike down the minimum wage statute for women in *Adkins v. Children's Hospital* (261 U.S. 525: 1923). The *Adkins* decision was a resurrection of the policies articulated in *Lochner v. New York* (198 U.S. 45: 1905) two decades earlier. While the Court had been willing to sustain regulation of hours of work under some conditions, it resisted very strongly the regulation of wage levels in *Adkins*. The Court clearly regarded wages as too tightly intertwined with an individual's right to contract over his or her own labor. Limitation on hours worked might be justifiable on health or safety grounds, especially for women. But wages were a wholly distinct issue. The minimum wage law was defective primarily because it tried to promote health and morals by fixing wage levels. The relationship of income to moral standards was so tenuous in the Court's view as to be unreasonable. In addition, the Court could not sanction compelling the employer to underwrite the costs of the policy and have no assurance of a return for that cost; there were no performance guarantees applying to the quality of the employee's work. As much as any decision, *Adkins* expressed the Court's perception that the economics of laissez-faire were constitutionally protected. Through especially the liberty of contract doctrine, the Court maintained this direction until the late 1930s, and the *Adkins* case was the principal precedent. *Adkins* was expressly overruled by the Court in *West Coast Hotel Company v. Parrish* (300 U.S. 379: 1937).

West Coast Hotel Company v. Parrish, 300 U.S. 379, 57 S.Ct. 578, 81 L.Ed. 703 (1937)   Sustained a state minimum wage law for women and minors. *West Coast Hotel Company v. Parrish* represented a dramatic change in course for the Court, as it began to disengage itself from the doctrines of liberty of contract and substantive economic due process. In 1913, the state of Washington enacted legislation authorizing a commission to fix minimum wages for women and minors. Parrish was a direct reconsideration of *Adkins v. Children's Hospital* (261 U.S. 525: 1923), which had invalidated a similar federal enactment on freedom of contract grounds. Parrish, an employee of the West Coast Hotel, sought to recover wage underpayments as compared to the wage minimum established by the commission. Parrish prevailed in the state courts, and the hotel appealed. The Supreme Court upheld the lower court, however, in a 5–4 decision.

The opinion of the Court was authored by Chief Justice Hughes. He made it clear from the outset that *Adkins* was under reexamination. The "close division" in *Adkins* plus the "economic conditions which have supervened" makes "fresh consideration" of *Adkins* "not only appropriate, but we think imperative." The controlling issue was alleged deprivation of freedom of contract, a freedom West Coast Hotel claimed was protected by the due process clause of the Fourteenth Amendment. But Hughes asked, "What is this freedom?" He pointed out that the Constitution speaks of deprivation of liberty without due process, but does not explicitly mention freedom of contract. Furthermore, no liberty is "absolute and uncontrollable." Rather, liberty is safeguarded in a "social organization which requires the protection of law against the evils which menace the health, safety, morals and welfare of the people." Liberty is "necessarily subject to the restraints of due process," and reasonable regulation in relation to "its subject" that is "adopted in the interests of the community" is due process. The Washington statute provided for wage fixing only after "full consideration by representatives of employers, employees, and the public." The process protected against arbitrary and unreasonable wage levels. Neither did the statute compel payments as such. It merely set minima through the commission, and Hughes suggested that it was safe to assume that women would not be employed unless they earned those wages or if a business could not sustain the cost. The Court held that a legislature was entitled to consider women's "relatively weak" bargaining power, the evils of the "sweating system," "exploitation of workers through low wages," and the wage levels required to yield subsistence income. Deference must be accorded by the Court to legislative judgment that "evil" exists and to legislative selection of "means adopted to check it." In the Court's opinion, *Adkins* was a "departure from the true application of the principles" governing employer-employee relationships and "should be . . . overruled."

Justices Van Devanter, Butler, and McReynolds joined in Justice Sutherland's dissent. He argued that a justice was bound by his oath to uphold the Constitution according to "his own conscientious and informed conviction." To engage in self-restraint is both "ill considered and mischievous." He criticized the majority for engaging in constitutional amendment "under the guise of interpretation." He argued that the Court gave "fresh consideration" to *Adkins* on the basis of circumstances such as economic exigency. The meaning of the Constitution, he contended, "does not change with the ebb and flow of economic events." The dissenters reiterated the liberty of contract flaw with the Washington statute and suggested that *Adkins* had "properly decided" the issue. *See also* ADKINS V. CHILDREN'S HOSPITAL (261 U.S. 525: 1923), p. 433; DUE PROCESS CLAUSES, p. 594; LIBERTY OF CONTRACT, p. 633; SUBSTANTIVE DUE PROCESS, p. 659.

Significance   *West Coast Hotel Company v. Parrish* (300 U.S. 379: 1937) formally marked the abandonment of economic substantive due process. *Parrish* sustained a state minimum wage law for women and specifically adopted the rationale rejected by the Court in *Adkins v. Children's Hospital* (261 U.S. 525: 1923). Indeed, the *Parrish* decision overruled the Court's ruling of just a year before. In *Morehead v. New York Ex Rel. Tipaldo* (298 U.S. 587: 1936), the Court struck down a minimum wage law for women even though the statute had a value-of-service requirement to protect the employer from nonperformance by an employee receiving the minimum wage. As in many of the earlier hours and wage cases (including *Adkins*), the key defect was violation of liberty of contract. While employers and men could work out their own wages and hours, employers and women employees were deprived of the same opportunity.

The *Morehead* decision came in the midst of the Court's protracted battle over many New Deal policies, and it prompted a strong dissent from, among others, Justice Stone. He argued that "economic necessities" of "ruthless" competition enter wage discussions between employer and employee, and that such bargaining is not always really "free." Further, he noted that wages that are "insufficient" to the worker "do not visit its consequences on him alone." Rather, they may have profound effects on the "entire economic structure of society." Stone argued that because of their "nature and extent," these problems were "public" and demanded the exercise of broad powers to meet them. This dissenting view was turned into precedent in *Parrish*. In adopting this position, the Court sustained the exercise of state power without a public health basis, a development of major importance. *Parrish* was part of a redirection of fundamental concepts of governance, and along with simultaneous changes in the interpretation of the federal commerce power, brought virtually every aspect of economic life within the reach of governmental regulation.

State Regulation of Labor Relations

Wolff Packing Company v. Court of Industrial Relations, **262 U.S. 522, 43 S.Ct. 630, 67 L.Ed. 1103 (1923)**   Struck down a state law vesting a special court with power to settle wage disputes in designated industries "affected with a public interest." In *Wolff Packing Company v. Court of Industrial Relations*, the Court considered arguments that the statute empowering the newly created court to resolve wage disagreements, and even fix wages in certain industries, violated due process by interfering with liberty of contract. The act enumerated certain industries such as food preparation, manufacture of clothing, fuel production, utilities, and carriers of essential products, and it declared them "affected with a public interest." The Court of Industrial Relations was empowered to intervene on its own initiative or upon complaint to review wage disputes. If the court found the public interest jeopardized by a dispute, it had authority to fix wages, and otherwise proscribe industry conduct. Review of the court decision was possible after 60 days, and appeal was available from the Kansas Supreme Court. The Meat Cutters' Union filed a complaint with the court against Wolff Packing Company. The court ordered a wage increase for the meat cutters, but Wolff Company refused to comply. The order was upheld by the Kansas Supreme Court, and the Wolff Company sought review by the United States Supreme Court. The Supreme Court reversed the Kansas Court, in a unanimous decision.

The opinion of the Court was rendered by Chief Justice Taft. Two important propositions governed the Court's review of the act. First, the Court felt that, while liberty of contract is subject to some regulation, absence of restraint is the "general rule and restraint the exception." Second, the Court indicated that "mere declaration by a legislature that a business is affected with a public interest is not conclusive." Justification for regulation is "always a subject of judicial inquiry." After articulating a substantive due process approach for the Court, Taft then turned to the Kansas statute specifically. It takes more than merely making commodities for public sale and consumption to turn a business into one clothed with a public interest or having a public use. The only way a business not originally having a solely public interest nature could change its status was for its service to become services "indispensable" in nature for which the public would be subject to "exorbitant charges and arbitrary control" without regulation. Taft then discussed how difficult it was to "lay down a working rule" by which to "readily determine" when a business had become sufficiently "clothed with a public interest."

Beyond a determination of the public interest character, it was still necessary to decide what regulation "may be permissible in view of the private rights of the owner." In other words, even with a public interest dimension, would any regulation be allowed against the private property interests? The nature and extent of regulation must necessarily vary, in the Court's view, from business to business. Both of these determinations were not matters of "legislative discretion solely." In this case, the Court disagreed with the state legislature's determination of the businesses that fit the public interest category, and the specific regulation of fixing wages in industries suffering labor disputes. *See also* DUE PROCESS CLAUSES, p. 594; LIBERTY OF CONTRACT, p. 633; *MUNN V. ILLINOIS* (94 U.S. 113: 1877), p. 420; SUBSTANTIVE DUE PROCESS, p. 659; *WEST COAST HOTEL COMPANY V. PARRISH* (300 U.S. 379: 1937), p. 435.

Significance   The Court limited the power of the states to define public interest objectives in *Wolff Packing Company v. Court of Industrial Relations* (262 U.S. 522: 1923). Kansas had attempted to prevent destructive wage disputes by creating a commission that could resolve labor disputes and ultimately fix wage levels when the public welfare might be harmed by protracted conflict. Key to the exercise of such power was the designation of businesses or industries sufficiently affected with the public interest to justify state intervention. The Court unanimously held that something beyond mere legislative declaration of a public interest dimension was required. The Court went on to establish a standard by which the character of an industry was to be judged. The only industries that could warrant classification as "affected with a public interest" were those judged "indispensable," those which would subject the public to "exorbitant charges" and "arbitrary control" without regulation. Thus, *Wolff* articulated a very narrow definition of the public interest, which, of course, was consistent with this Court's substantive due process orientation.

One of the principal elements of substantive due process is the concept of liberty of contract. It was a prominent aspect of the Court's decision in *Wolff*. It was also used to deter the development of labor unions. *Wolff*, of course, could be viewed as antilabor in that the initial wage grievance filed with the Court of Industrial Relations had come from the Meat Cutters' Union. Prior to *Wolff*, the Court had used the liberty of contract rationale to nullify a federal effort to prohibit "yellow dog" contracts. Such a contract, signed by an employee as a condition of employment, states that he or she will not join a labor union. Congress had made it a crime to make such an agreement a condition of employment for interstate railroads, but the Court struck down the enactment in *Adair v. United States* (208 U.S. 161: 1908). A state prohibition on yellow dog contracts was similarly voided in *Coppage v. Kansas* (236 U.S. 1: 1915).

Local Zoning Regulations

Village of Euclid v. Ambler Realty Company, **272 U.S. 365, 47 S.Ct. 114, 71 L.Ed. 303 (1926)**   Upheld a local zoning ordinance against claims of deprivation of property without due process. *Village of Euclid v. Ambler Realty Company* examined an ordinance that designated certain lands for exclusively residential use. Ambler Realty had acquired and held property within the village limits with the intention of placing the property in industrial use. Industrial usage would have made the land of much higher value than residential use. The ordinance also forbade multiple-family units such as apartment buildings on the same lands. Some of Ambler's property was affected by the zoning restrictions. The company was able to obtain an injunction against enforcement of the ordinance, and the village appealed. The Supreme Court reversed the lower court and upheld the local zoning regulation in a 6–3 decision.

The opinion of the Court was delivered by Justice Sutherland. He began by defining the issue presented by the case and traced the history of zoning regulations. The case raised by Ambler Realty did not focus on any specific provision of the Euclid ordinance, but rather was cast against the "ordinance as an entirety." Thus, the issue before the Court was whether the village had authority to regulate private land use generally. Sutherland noted the modern origin of such regulations. They developed as urban life became more complex because of the "great increase and concentration of population." Sutherland speculated that continued, and even additional, regulations were forthcoming as the transition from rural to urban life increased. As times change, so does the "wisdom, necessity and validity" of regulation. Even regulation that might have been rejected "even a half century ago" as "arbitrary and oppressive" may be sustained given "existing conditions." He said the Court must take an adaptive approach to reviewing such regulations. While the "meaning of constitutional guarantees never varies, the scope of the application must expand or contract to meet the new and different conditions which are constantly coming within the field of their operation." An ordinance like that involved here must "find justification in some aspect of the police power, asserted for the public welfare." The line between that regulation which is legitimate and that which is not is "not capable of precise delineation." Rather, it varies with "circumstances and conditions"; it is situational. These questions cannot be resolved by giving "abstract consideration" to the effects of the regulation, but through examination of the "circumstances" and "locality."

The Court then turned to the categorical character of the regulation, that all nonresidential uses were prohibited within the zone. The Court said that the legislative objectives sought were sufficient to justify the "general rule of the ordinance" even though some industries of an "innocent character might fall within the proscribed class." The ordinance, in the Court's view, did not pass the "bounds of reason" and assume the "character of a merely arbitrary fiat." The extent to which the court was willing to defer to the exercise of police power was evidenced by the lengthy enumeration of specific benefits to be derived from zoning in relation to promotion of the public welfare. Citing such things as traffic control and fire protection, the Court rather easily handled the separation of industrial and residential areas. As for prohibitions on multiple-resident buildings, the Court found even that could be justified. Specifically, the Court noted that as one apartment "is followed by others," interference with the "free circulation of air" and "monopolizing of the rays of the sun" would occur. Increased traffic and parking problems, more neighborhood noise, and a possible deprivation of children of "quiet and open places to play" would take place. In short, Euclid's reasons for enacting such zoning regulations were "sufficiently cogent" to preclude the Court from saying the provisions were "clearly arbitrary and unreasonable," having no substantial relation to the public health, safety, morals, or general welfare. Justices

Van Devanter, Butler, and McReynolds disagreed. *See also* DUE PROCESS CLAUSES, p. 594; PROCEDURAL DUE PROCESS, p. 647; SUBSTANTIVE DUE PROCESS, p. 659.

Significance   *Village of Euclid v. Ambler Realty Company* (272 U.S. 365: 1926) sustained broad local controls on private property uses. Zoning regulations, as noted in the Court's opinion, had been upheld prior to *Euclid*, but their scope had been relatively limited. Typically, such regulations had been aimed at specific targets such as height or size limits on buildings. The Euclid ordinance was a comprehensive prohibition on all businesses and multifamily dwellings in a given geographic area. The Court was persuaded, nonetheless, of the reasonableness of the regulation to permit the restrictions on property uses. The thrust of the Court's argument was an extension of the rationale used to support earlier zoning regulations. That is, there were certain uses that would threaten the public health or welfare that needed restriction. The Court referred in *Euclid* to the law of "nuisances." Generally, the state has the power to abate or control nuisances. *Euclid* merely represented such an effort albeit on a larger scale. More recently, other purposes have been acknowledged as sufficient to allow regulation in the public interest. In *Berman v. Parker* (348 U.S. 26: 1954), the Court permitted an urban renewal project on the grounds that power may properly be exercised in pursuit of physical and aesthetic objectives. A more recent utilization of the same argument was seen in *Penn Central Transportation Company v. New York City* (438 U.S. 104: 1978), where the court upheld a city landmark preservation law. The court saw the regulation as sufficiently analogous to the zoning power to sustain the enactment.

State Price Regulation

***Nebbia v. New York*, 291 U.S. 502, 54 S.Ct. 505, 78 L.Ed. 940 (1934)**   Upheld a state pricing regulation establishing minimum prices for the retail sale of milk. The statute at issue in *Nebbia v. New York* created a Milk Control Board empowered to fix minimum prices. The statute was enacted in an attempt to counteract the effects of the depression on the milk industry. Nebbia owned a grocery store and was convicted for selling milk below the board-established minimum price. From adverse decisions in the New York state courts, Nebbia appealed to the United States Supreme Court, arguing deprivation of due process. The Supreme Court upheld his conviction, however, in a 5–4 decision.

The opinion of the Court was offered by Justice Roberts. He overviewed the issues in the case by observing that property and contract rights were not absolute, that no person may use his property to the "detriment of his fellows," and that the public possesses a fundamental right to regulate private property in the public interest. While each of these propositions may have been abstractly acknowledged by the Court in preceding economic due process cases, property interest generally prevailed nonetheless. The statements in *Nebbia* by Roberts marked the beginning of a significant policy shift toward operational recognition of these principles. The Court in *Nebbia* saw due process as requiring only that a law "shall not be unreasonable, arbitrary, or capricious," and that means chosen to pursue the objective have a "real and substantial relation to the object sought." Nebbia argued that regulation of prices was inherently unreasonable except when applied to a business affected with the public interest. Such businesses might include public utilities, those of a monopolistic character, or those dependent on public grants or franchises. He claimed the milk industry fit none of those categories. The Court agreed, but held that the exercise of the police power need not be confined to those categories. The Court found no constitutional prohibition on legislation "correcting existing maladjustments" that involve prices. The Court noted that the due process clause "makes no mention of prices any more than it speaks of business or contracts or buildings or other incidents of property." The Court rejected the notion that there is "something particularly sacrosanct about the price one may charge for what he makes or sells." The Court said that such a view was "negatived many years ago" by *Munn v. Illinois* (94 U.S. 113: 1877).

As for the businesses that might be subject to regulation, the Court said there was no "closed class" of enterprises "affected with a public interest." The phrase "affected with a public interest" means no more than that an industry, "for adequate reason, is subject to control for the public good." Determination of such reason Roberts saw as a legislative rather than judicial judgment. If the legislature determined that the unrestricted competition in the milk industry prompted or aggravated a situation detrimental to the public interest, legislative remedies such as the minimum price regulation could be pursued. Unless there is another constitutional restriction, requirements of due process allow a state to "adopt whatever economic policy may reasonably be deemed to promote public welfare." The courts are "without authority either to declare such policy, or, when it is declared by the legislative arm, to override it."

A dissent by Justice McReynolds was joined by Justices Van Devanter, Sutherland, and Butler. McReynolds refused to defer to the economic situation that precipitated the regulation. Liberty or property cannot be sacrificed when an "impatient majority" is "stirred by distressful exigency." This exigency was caused by overproduction, an "ill-advised" but nonetheless voluntary situation. No legislature can "destroy the guaranteed rights of one man with the prime purpose of enriching another, even if for the moment this may seem advantageous to the public." In McReynolds's view, "government by stable laws will pass" if rights become subject to the "caprice of the hour." *See also* DUE PROCESS CLAUSES, p. 594; *MUNN V. ILLINOIS* (94 U.S. 113: 1877), p. 420; PROCEDURAL DUE PROCESS, p. 647; SUBSTANTIVE DUE PROCESS, p. 658; *WOLFF PACKING COMPANY V. COURT OF INDUSTRIAL RELATIONS* (262 U.S. 522: 1923), p. 437.

Significance   The Court approved a state price regulation in *Nebbia v. New York* (291 U.S. 502: 1934). *Nebbia* was the beginning of the Court's disengagement from substantive due process in the economic sphere. Prior to *Nebbia*, the Court had basically placed price regulation beyond legislative control. Cases such as *Wolff Packing Company v. Court of Industrial Relations* (262 U.S. 522: 1923) and *Ribnik v. McBride* (277 U.S. 350: 1928) had either limited regulation to a small category of public utilities or viewed most business activities as so "private" as to preclude regulation. *Nebbia* substantially broadened the concept of businesses affected with a public interest. Provided that the legislature could show adequate reasons, any business could conceivably be controlled for the public welfare. Though the specific precedents of the 1920s were not formally overruled until later, *Nebbia* was followed by other decisions generally permitting price regulation. While the permanent abandonment of substantive due process did not come until 1937, *Nebbia* did represent a clear signal that private property interests would not be comprehensively safeguarded as they had for several decades previously. That state legislatures would be allowed greater discretion to act on behalf of the "public good," including response to economic emergencies like the Depression, was also evident in *Home Building and Loan Association v. Blaisdell* (290 U.S. 398: 1934, p. 479), a contract clause case. In *Blaisdell*, the Court upheld a state mortgage moratorium law as reasonably related to public need despite a limited impairment of a private contract. Soon after *Nebbia*, it could be safely said that neither the contract clause nor the due process clause effectively insulated private property from state regulation.

Optical Industry Regulation

Williamson v. Lee Optical Company, **348 U.S. 483, 75 S.Ct. 461, 99 L.Ed. 563 (1955)**   Upheld a state regulation restricting many aspects of visual care exclusively to licensed ophthalmologists or optometrists. The statute under review in *Williamson v. Lee Optical Com-*

pany prohibited opticians from fitting or duplicating lenses without a prescription from an ophthalmologist or optometrist. It also imposed restrictions on advertising optical appliances generally and prohibited retail stores from furnishing space to persons conducting eye examinations or performing visual care. In practical terms, the statute imposed severe limitations on the practice of opticians. Under the law, an optician could not fit old glasses into new frames or supply a new lens, even to duplicate a lost or broken lens, without prescription. Lee Optical Company challenged this law as an arbitrary interference with an optician's right to do business. A lower court had found portions of the statute in violation of the due process clause. Williamson, attorney general of Oklahoma, appealed on behalf of the statute. The Supreme Court reversed the lower court and sustained the regulation in a unanimous decision (Justice Harlan did not participate).

The opinion of the Court was delivered by Justice Douglas. He began by stating that deference ought generally to be afforded in such cases as this. The Oklahoma statute "may exact a needless, wasteful requirement in many cases." But it is for the "legislature, not the courts, to balance the advantages and disadvantages of the new requirement." He indicated that it is possible to supply and fit new frames without prescriptive direction, but in some cases, "directions contained in the prescription are essential" if the vision defect is to be corrected or alleviated. The state legislature could have concluded that the "frequency of occasions when a prescription is necessary was sufficient to justify this regulation." Similarly the legislature could have reasonably concluded that eye examinations were "so critical . . . for detection of latent ailments or diseases" that every change of frames or lens duplication "should be accompanied by a prescription from a medical expert." The law did allow lens duplication without a new eye examination provided the optician had an old prescription on file. This exception seemed to weaken the overall rationale underlying the regulation. Douglas responded that a law "need not be in every respect logically consistent with its aims to be constitutional."

As for the restriction on advertising, the Court sustained the regulation finding that a state could reasonably deal with all "who deal with the human eye" as members of a profession that "should use no merchandising methods for obtaining customers." Similarly, the Court sustained the restriction on space in retail stores devoted to visual care. Douglas said the regulation could "reduce the temptation of commercialism." Furthermore, location "may be an important consideration" in a legislative effort intended to "raise the treatment of the human eye to a strictly professional level." On a more general dimension, Douglas observed that the "day is gone" when the Court uses the due process clause of the Fourteenth Amendment to strike down business regulations because they "may be unwise, improvident, or out of harmony with a particular school of thought." Reiterating the direction offered in *Munn v. Illinois* (94 U.S. 113: 1877), Douglas indicated that "for protection against abuses by legislatures the people must resort to the polls, not to the courts." *See also* DUE PROCESS CLAUSES, p. 594; *FERGUSON V.SKRUPA* (372 U.S. 726: 1963), p. 445; PROCEDURAL DUE PROCESS, p. 647.

Significance   The Court sustained a state regulation limiting many aspects of visual care practice by opticians in *Williamson v. Lee Optical Company* (348 U.S. 483: 1955). *Williamson* represents two important contemporary themes. First, the Court upheld broad regulation of a particular business in *Williamson*. The decision conveyed the Court's view that the due process clause was not a bar to state policies that substantially restrict certain business practices. Indeed, the decision clearly suggested that even entry into a particular business might be legislatively proscribed. Second, *Williamson* reflected a highly deferential posture toward legislative policy initiatives. The Court acknowledged that the restrictions in *Williamson* might be regarded as both "needless" and "wasteful," but due process only requires that an enactment be reasonably related to a substantive problem within the reach of state police power. *Williamson* forcefully reiterated the view that the judiciary must avoid consideration of the wisdom or efficacy of legislative judgments in the economic, business sphere. Most decisions of the Court since *Williamson* have followed this deferential course. In *Ferguson v. Skrupa* (372 U.S. 726: 1963), for example, the Court upheld a statute that limited the business of debt adjusting to lawyers. In *North Dakota State Board v. Snyder's Drug Stores, Inc.* (414 U.S. 156: 1973), the Court unanimously upheld a state law that required a corporation operating a pharmacy to have a majority of its stock held by licensed pharmacists who are actively involved in the management of the corporation.

Prohibition of Certain Business Activities

Ferguson v. Skrupa, 372 U.S. 726, 83 S.Ct. 1028, 10 L.Ed. 2d 93 (1963)   Upheld a state statute prohibiting anyone except lawyers from engaging in the business of "debt adjusting." The statute at issue in *Ferguson v. Skrupa* defined debt adjusting as the "making of a contract, express or implied, with a particular debtor" whereby the person agrees to pay the debt adjuster on a regular basis. The adjuster then distributes the payments "among certain specified creditors." The intent of the legislation was to regulate through prohibition a business that "lends itself to grave abuses against distressed debtors, particularly in the lower income brackets." Skrupa was engaged in business as a "credit advisor," and was found in violation of the statute. He argued that his business was "useful and desirable" and not "inherently immoral or dangerous" such that the state could not declare the business "absolutely prohibited." A lower court held Skrupa's activities to be within the scope of the law, but held the statute to be an "unreasonable regulation of a 'lawful business'" in violation of the due process clause. The state was enjoined from enforcement of the regulation. Kansas appealed to the United States Supreme Court, which reversed the lower court in a unanimous decision.

The opinion of the Court was delivered by Justice Black. He set out the fundamental question for the Court as the way in which the Court ought to exercise judicial review. Prior courts had drawn on "their own views as to the morality, legitimacy and usefulness of a particular business" in order to determine whether a regulation "bears too heavily," and in doing so, violates due process. This time, however, the Court found such an approach to be inappropriate. Rather, the Constitution leaves it to "legislatures, not to courts, to decide on the wisdom and utility of legislation." Black acknowledged that "there was a time" when the Court frequently used the due process clause to "strike down laws which were thought unreasonable," that is, "unwise or incompatible with some particular economic or social philosophy." But the doctrine that prevailed in those cases "has long since been discarded." Instead, Black said, the Court has "returned to the original constitutional proposition that courts do not substitute their social and economic beliefs" for those of an elected legislature. Legislative bodies have "broad scope to experiment with economic problems," and the Court "does not sit to 'subject the State to an intolerable supervision hostile to the basic principles of our government.'" The Court viewed as now "settled" that states have power to regulate "injurious practices in their internal commercial and business affairs" as long as not specifically prohibited by the Constitution. Accordingly, Kansas "was free to decide for itself" whether or not to regulate debt adjusting. Arguments to the issue are "properly addressed to the legislature, not to us." Black concluded by emphatically stating that the Court "will not sit as a 'superlegislature to weigh the wisdom of legislation'" or "go back to the time" when the courts used due process for that purpose. *See also* DUE PROCESS CLAUSES, p. 594; PROCEDURAL DUE PROCESS, p. 647; SUBSTANTIVE DUE PROCESS, p. 659; *WILLIAMSON V. LEE OPTICAL COMPANY* (348 U.S. 483: 1955), p. 443.

Significance   A state law limiting the business of debt adjusting was upheld in *Ferguson v. Skrupa* (372 U.S. 726: 1963). The decision was wholly deferential to the legislative judgment that such regulation was necessary, resembling the procedural due process seen in *Munn v.*

Illinois (94 U.S. 113: 1877) nearly a century earlier. The Court said in *Ferguson* that the judiciary is not to "substitute their social and economic beliefs for the judgment of legislative bodies." Courts are simply not to be concerned with the "wisdom, need, or appropriateness" of state legislation. Rather, courts should permit legislatures broad latitude to "experiment with economic problems." Prohibiting persons from engaging in particular businesses is a regulation of some severity. Earlier cases such as *Adams v. Tanner* (244 U.S. 590: 1917) had held that the due process clause precludes a state from prohibiting businesses that are "useful" or not "inherently immoral or dangerous to public welfare." In *Adams*, the Court invalidated a state law prohibiting the taking of fees from persons seeking employment. But the *Ferguson* Court found that reliance on such cases as *Adams* was "mistaken." Decisions like *Adams* were based on a view that courts may draw on "their own views" regarding the "morality, legitimacy and usefulness" of a particular business. The *Ferguson* Court saw these issues as legislative questions exclusively, and said that the Kansas legislature needed to be "free to decide for itself that legislation was needed to deal with the business of debt adjusting."

Jury Duty Compensation

***Dean v. Gadsden Times Publishing Company*, 412 U.S. 543, 93 S.Ct. 2264, 37 L.Ed. 2d 137 (1973)**   Upheld a state statute requiring that an employee receive his usual compensation although excused from employment for jury duty. *Dean v. Gadsden Times Publishing Company* arose out of the newspaper's refusal to comply with the statute. Dean, a *Times* employee, instituted action in an Alabama court to recover the difference between his jury pay and his regular wages under provisions of the statute. The trial court entered a judgment for Dean, but the *Times* was able to gain a reversal in the state appellate courts on grounds that the act deprived the employer of property in violation of the due process clause. Dean sought review from the United States Supreme Court, which subsequently reversed the Alabama judgment in a unanimous decision.

In a *per curiam* opinion, the Court noted that the cases most heavily relied upon by the state appellate court had been rendered when "substantive due process was in its heyday." Central to those cases was the argument that such regulations violated liberty of contract. The Court found that rationale no longer persuasive. The Court said that most business regulations "necessarily impose financial burdens," but such is "part of the cost of our civilization." While extreme scenarios are "conjured up" when arguing that employers may be compelled to pay wages "for a period that has no relation to the legitimate end," the Alabama statute under review here does not suffer from the "infirmity" of such extremes. Rather, the statute was designed to eliminate any penalty for participating in jury service, a function fundamental to the American legal process. The Court saw the state power to act on behalf of the public interest as extensive. The public welfare is a "broad and inclusive concept." Part of it is the "moral, social, economic and physical well-being," while another part is the political and legal well-being. The police power "adequate to fix the financial burden for one is adequate for the other." The legislative judgment that jury duty should not cost the employee and should be borne by the employer may be debatable. The Court noted, however, recent cases that have debatable issues "as respects business, economic, and social affairs to legislative decision." The opinion concluded by saying that to strike down a law such as this would mark a return to the "philosophy" of precedents long since abandoned. *See also* DUE PROCESS CLAUSES, p. 594; *LOCHNER V. NEW YORK* (198 U.S. 45: 1905), p. 429; PROCEDURAL DUE PROCESS, p. 647; SUB-STANTIVE DUE PROCESS, p. 659.

Significance   The Court upheld a state statute requiring employers to compensate employees for work time spent on jury duty in *Dean v. Gadsden Times Publishing Company* (412 U.S. 543: 1973). The state court had initially held the statute involved in this case to be unconstitutional. The state court had relied on cases like *Coppage v. Kansas* (236 U.S. 1: 1915), where the Court struck down a law making it a crime for an employer to require an employee "to agree not to join or remain a member of a union during his employment." The Court repudiated *Coppage* as a decision rendered while "substantive due process was in its heyday." More representative of operative due process precedents of this kind was *Day-Brite Lighting, Inc. v. Missouri* (342 U.S. 421: 1952). *Day-Brite* upheld a law allowing employees to be compensated for up to four hours absence from their jobs on election day. The Court made it clear in *Day-Brite* that the wisdom of the policy choice was not at issue in the case. The enactment was designed to eliminate any possible disincentive for exercising the right to vote. A "broad and inclusive" concept of the public welfare allows pursuit of the political well-being of the community. This same deferential position can be readily seen in *Williamson v. Lee Optical Company* (348 U.S. 483: 1955) and *Ferguson v. Skrupa* (372 U.S. 726: 1963). In the former, the Court permitted a law limiting many aspects of vision care to licensed ophthalmologists or optometrists, while the latter confined the business of debt adjustment to attorneys. *Dean* is a Burger Court decision that continues this permissive, "hands off" view of state economic regulation.

Local Vendor Regulation

City of New Orleans v. Dukes, **427 U.S. 297, 96 S.Ct. 2513, 49 L.Ed. 2d 511 (1976)**   Sustained an amendment to a local ordinance prohibiting certain commercial activities except for some businesses covered by a "grandfather clause." The ordinance amendment in question in *City of New Orleans v. Dukes* prohibited the selling of food from pushcarts in the city's French Quarter. Exception was made for those vendors who had been in business in the locality for at least eight years prior to the effective date of the amendment. Dukes, a vendor with less than the required eight years, filed suit against the city challenging validity of the ordinance and the use of the grandfather mechanism as a denial of due process. Dukes was successful in gaining a rehearing on the severability of the grandfather clause, and the city appealed. The Supreme Court sustained the ordinance, including the grandfather clause, in a unanimous decision (Justice Stevens not participating).

In a *per curiam* opinion, the Court noted that the French Quarter was the "heart" of New Orleans's "considerable tourist industry and an integral component of the city's economy." The French Quarter plays a "special role" in the city's life, and the New Orleans Home Rule Charter grants the city council power "to enact ordinances designed to preserve its distinctive charm, character, and economic vitality." The Court said that when a local economic regulation is challenged "solely" as violating the equal protection clause, the Court "consistently defers to legislative determinations" of the desirability of the classification plan. Unless the enactment "trammels fundamental personal rights" or is drawn upon an "inherent suspect distinction" such as race or religion, the Court presumes constitutionality. In such cases, the state need show only that the challenged enactment is "rationally related to a legitimate state interest." States are to be accorded "wide latitude" in the regulation of their "local economies" under the police power. The Court reiterated that the judiciary should not "sit as a superlegislature" reviewing the wisdom and desirability of legislative policy initiatives. Courts should only intervene where local economic regulation is "wholly arbitrary" or constitutes invidious discrimination."

The Court then examined the lower court finding that the grandfather clause "failed even the rationality test." The Court saw the classification as rationally related to furthering the city's interest in preserving the "appearance and custom valued by the Quarter's residents and attractive to tourists." The Court also concluded that the grandfather provision was not an arbitrary and irrational means of achieving its legislative objective. The city reasonably could have concluded that newer businesses were "less likely to have built up substantial reliance interests in continued operation in the Vieux Carre [the French Quarter]." Furthermore, the two grandfathered businesses had operated in the area for more than twenty years and had "become part of the distinctive character and charm that distinguishes the Vieux Carre." Under any construction, the Court said that the amendments did not lack "rationality" such that they constitute a denial of equal protection. *See also* DUE PROCESS CLAUSES, p. 594; *FERGUSON V. SKRUPA* (372 U.S. 726: 1963), p. 445; PROCEDURAL DUE PROCESS, p. 647; SUBSTANTIVE DUE PROCESS, p. 659; *WILLIAMSON V. LEE OPTICAL COMPANY* (348 U.S. 483: 1955), p. 443.

Significance   The Court upheld a local ordinance against both due process and equal protection challenges in *City of New Orleans v. Dukes* (427 U.S. 297: 1976). For a number of years prior to *Dukes*, the Court had generally allowed local governments wide latitude in regulating their own local economies or instituting restrictions to enhance the aesthetic and cultural features of a community. The regulation of land use through zoning ordinances had regularly been sustained. The issue in *Dukes* was technique, the use of the "grandfather" clause to create two classes of food vendors. Only one of those classes was permitted to continue operation in the French Quarter. A grandfather clause creates an exception to a regulation that allows those already doing something to continue doing so, despite a new restriction to the contrary. The grandfather clause in *Dukes* did not even include all those engaged in vending at the time of the new regulation, but only those who had been in business at least eight years. Of all the vendors in business in the French Quarter at the time of the ordinance amendment, only two were effectively "grandfathered." The court of appeals found the ordinance "exclusionary," and felt that it created a "protected monopoly" or "favored class." In finding an equal protection defect, the lower court depended on *Morey v. Doud* (354 U.S. 457: 1957), which had invalidated a law comprehensively regulating the business of selling money orders but giving exemption by name to a single company in the business. *Morey* was the "only case in the last half century" to strike down a wholly economic regulation "solely" on equal protection grounds, and the Burger Court concluded *Morey* was "erroneous." While the equal protection clause may prohibit many kinds of legislative classification, *Dukes* makes it clear that in the local economic sphere, only "invidious" and "wholly arbitrary" classification cannot "stand consistently with the Fourteenth Amendment."

Regulation through "Taking"

***Penn Central Transportation Company v. New York City,* 438 U.S. 104, 98 S.Ct. 2646, 57 L.Ed. 2d 631 (1978)** Upheld a local landmark preservation law against claims that the regulation constituted an impermissible "taking" of private property. *Penn Central Transportation Company v. City of New York* reviewed a regulation designed to maintain New York's status as a tourist, business, and cultural center by preserving designated historic landmarks and neighborhoods. The act created a commission vested with principal responsibility for implementation of the act. Pursuant to its function, the commission designated Grand Central Terminal as a "landmark." The owner of the terminal, Penn Central, unsuccessfully contested the designation. Subsequently, the owner sought commission approval, now required because of the terminal's landmark status, to construct a multistory office structure above the terminal. Penn Central submitted two plans to the commission, but both were rejected because they involved either destruction of portions of the terminal or were aesthetically incompatible in architectural design to the terminal building. Penn Central brought suit, claiming application of the law had "taken" its property without just compensation in violation of the due process clauses of the Fifth and Fourteenth Amendments. Although the trial court agreed with Penn Central, the New York appeals courts reversed and sustained the regulation. The United States Supreme Court affirmed the appellate judgment in a 6–3 decision.

The opinion of the Court was delivered by Justice Brennan. He said the issue of what constitutes "taking" had proved to be a question of "considerable difficulty" for the courts over the years. Certainly the Court had been "unable to develop any 'set formula' for determining when 'justice and fairness'" require compensation for injuries caused by public action. The Court had generally recognized, however, that governments may "execute laws or programs that adversely affect recognized economic values." Brennan specifically pointed to land use regulations that have "destroyed or adversely affected recognized real property interests." He referred to zoning laws as the "classic example." Use restrictions must serve a substantial public purpose, but if such purpose can be shown, regulations are generally sustained. Brennan also indicated that restrictions designed to "enhance the quality of life by preserving the character and desirable aesthetic features of a city" have been generally upheld. The Court rejected the contention that the landmark law arbitrarily singled out Grand Central Terminal for different treatment or "reverse spot" zoning. The Court also disagreed that because some property owners were more severely impacted than others, a "taking" requiring compensation had necessarily occurred.

Legislation designed to promote the general welfare "commonly burdens some more than others." Neither could Penn Central show that it was "solely burdened" or "unbenefitted" by the landmark law. Finally, the Court considered the specific claim that Penn Central was deprived of the gainful use of the "superadjacent air space." The landmark law did not interfere with the "present uses" of the terminal nor prevent Penn Central from making a "reasonable return" on its investment. Furthermore, administration of the law did not preclude all uses of the airspace above the terminal. Penn Central had submitted only two proposals. While both had been rejected, that did not necessarily mean that each and every proposal would meet the same fate. On balance, the Court found the law substantially related to promotion of the general welfare and not a "taking" for which Penn Central was constitutionally entitled to compensation.

Justice Rehnquist offered a dissent joined by Chief Justice Burger and Justice Stevens. The dissenters found the zoning analogy applicable only in the "most superficial sense." Zoning regulations are at least "partially offset" because similar restrictions are applied to neighboring properties. The selective character of the landmark law clearly distinguished it from general zoning ordinances. In addition, Rehnquist noted that, with the landmark designation, any modification to the terminal had to be approved by the commission. Rehnquist argued that Penn Central had no certainty that some proposal for modification might be approved. For the dissenters, Penn Central had suffered a "taking" of their property and were subject to the eminent domain requirement of just compensation. *See also* CITY OF NEW ORLEANS V. DUKES (427 U.S. 297: 1976), p. 449; DUE PROCESS CLAUSES, p. 594; EMINENT DOMAIN, p. 599; *VILLAGE OF EUCLID V. AMBLER REALTY COMPANY* (272 U.S. 365: 1926), p. 439.

Significance   The Court upheld a local landmark preservation ordinance in *Penn Central Transportation Company v. New York City* (438 U.S. 104: 1978). The law had been challenged on the ground that implementation of the regulation constituted a "taking" of private property without "just compensation." As long as governmental actions are generally proper, their effects may impair property values or uses without constituting a taking of property in a legal sense. Going back to *Village of Euclid v. Ambler Realty Company* (272 U.S. 365: 1926), the Court had sustained comprehensive zoning regulations on land uses. Much more recently, the Court reiterated *Euclid* in *Agins v. City of Tiburin* (447 U.S. 255: 1980), where local planned development and open space zones limited the number of single-family units that could be built on a five-acre tract. Instances of the Court's reluctance to specifically find an impermissible "taking" are relatively numerous. In *Goldblatt v.*

Hempstead (369 U.S. 590: 1962), for example, the Court upheld a ban on excavation below the water table of a community that would adversely affect a sand and gravel mining business. Because the restriction served a "substantial public purpose," the Court held that no compensable taking had occurred. And in *Hodel v. Virginia Surface Mining and Reclamation Association, Inc.* (452 U.S. 264: 1981) and *Hodel v. Indiana* (452 U.S. 314: 1981), the Court held that a federal act requiring restoration after mining operations did not constitute a taking of private property.

Residency Requirement for Employment

***Hicklin v. Orbeck*, 437 U.S. 518, 98 S.Ct. 2482, 57 L.Ed. 2d 397 (1978)**   Struck down a state statute that attempted to reserve jobs in the oil and gas development industry for qualified state residents. The law, known as "Alaska Hire," at issue in *Hicklin v. Orbeck,* required that all contracts and agreements relating to Alaskan oil and gas development within the state contain a preference commitment that qualified residents of Alaska be hired before nonresidents. A period of one year was required to establish Alaskan residency. Hicklin and other nonresidents, unable to find jobs as a result of the regulation, filed suit claiming violations of both the privileges and immunities and equal protection clauses. The Alaska Supreme Court struck down the residency requirement, but upheld the general preference policy. The United States Supreme Court invalidated the preference in a unanimous decision.

The opinion of the Court was delivered by Justice Brennan. He isolated the privileges and immunities issue as the "principal" challenge and reviewed the scope and nature of the clause. It was intended to establish a "norm of comity" that is to "prevail among the states with respect to their treatment of each other's residents." The clause places citizens of each state "upon the same footing" with citizens of other states. Brennan noted the strong support of case law for the nonresidents' claim that the privileges and immunities clause prevents a state from discriminating against "nonresidents seeking to ply their trade, practice their occupation, or pursue a common calling within the State." While the clause does not preclude "disparity of treatment" where there are "valid independent reasons for it," it does prohibit discrimination where there is "no substantial reason for the discrimination beyond the mere fact that they are citizens of other states." To justify a discrimination, a state would have to demonstrate that "noncitizens constitute a peculiar source of the evil at which the statute is aimed." Here, the state failed to show that "Alaska Hire" was reasonably related to Alaska's uniquely high unemployment and that nonresidents were a peculiar cause of the problem. To the contrary, the Court saw the trial court record as showing that Alaska's problem was caused by lack of education and training and "geographical remoteness" from job opportunities rather than nonresident competition.

The Court then responded to Alaska's contention that because the gas and oil industry toward which the act is directed is "owned" by the state, this in itself is sufficient justification for the discrimination. Ownership does not "completely remove" a law from prohibitions of the privileges and immunities clause. Rather, ownership is only one factor to be considered in evaluating the statute. It was found "not dispositive" here, a judgment that stemmed from the broad scope of activity within the "ambit of Alaska Hire." By attempting to "force virtually all businesses that benefit in some way" from the "economic ripple effect" of development of gas and oil resources, the state's "proprietary interest" was "attenuated." Finally, the Court noted that the commerce clause "circumscribes a state's ability to prefer its own citizens" in the use of natural resources found within the state, but destined for interstate commerce. The Alaskan gas and oil were "bound for out-of-state consumption," and they were commodities of "profound national importance." *See also* COMMERCE CLAUSE, p. 291; DUE PROCESS CLAUSES, p. 594; PRIVILEGES AND IMMUNITIES CLAUSE, p. 647.

Significance   The Court struck down a resident preference requirement for employment in *Hicklin v. Orbeck* (437 U.S. 518: 1978). The principal focus of the decision was the privileges and immunities language found in Article IV, Section 2, which says, "The citizens of each state shall be entitled to all privileges and immunities of citizens in the several states." Pre–Civil War interpretations of the clause cast the protection around "fundamental" rights such as unimpaired passage through a state, access to courts, and the right to vote. The function of the clause was limited by the adoption of the Fourteenth Amendment and its provisions on citizenship and the privileges and immunities that flow from citizenship. In early post–Civil War decisions like the *Slaughterhouse Cases* (16 Wallace 36: 1873), the scope of Article IV, Section 2 was greatly narrowed. Nonetheless, the clause has some contemporary impact. In *Toomer v. Witsell* (334 U.S. 385: 1948), a case involving discriminatory out-of-state commercial fishing fees, the Court said that Article IV, Section 2 prohibits a state from differential treatment of nonresidents for no "substantial reason." Mere nonresidence in itself was viewed as wholly insufficient. Rather, the clause was seen as establishing a "norm of comity" that protects basic equality of treatment. This equality is not absolute, and if "substantial reason" can be demonstrated, a state may still engage in some discrimination, such as in higher nonresident tuition rates charged at state universities. As reflected in *Hicklin,* however, the commerce and equal protection clauses seem to protect citizenship interests even more effectively than the privileges and immunities language. *Hicklin* referred to the "reinforcing" relationship between these two clauses that "stems from their common origin in the Fourth Article of the Articles of Confederation and their shared vision of federalism." Those comments are especially noteworthy in that no commerce clause challenge was made to "Alaska Hire," and its inclusion in the *Hicklin* opinion was completely at the Court's initiative.

State Tax on Nondomiciled Subsidiary

ASARCO, Inc. v. Idaho State Tax Commission, **458 U.S. 307, 102 S.Ct. 3103, 73 L.Ed. 2d 787 (1982)**   Held that a state may not tax corporate income generated by a subsidiary having no direct connection to the state. The central concept at issue in *ASARCO, Inc. v. Idaho State Tax Commission* was the principle of unitary business. Idaho attempted to levy a tax on the income of all out-of-state corporations doing business in Idaho. Included within the taxable income calculated by Idaho were certain intangible incomes (such as dividend and interest payments) that the corporation received from subsidiaries having no other connection to Idaho. ASARCO appealed from an adverse judgment by the Idaho Supreme Court, which had upheld the unitized treatment of the subsidiaries and had included the various types of intangible income as "business" income. The United States Supreme Court initially remanded the case for reconsideration, but the Idaho Supreme Court retained its original judgment. The United States Supreme Court reviewed the case on appeal and reversed the state court in a 6–3 decision.

The opinion of the Court was delivered by Justice Powell. The general principle applying in a case like this is that a state "may not tax value earned outside its borders." The controlling question is whether the taxing power exerted "bears fiscal relation to protection, opportunities, and benefits given by the state." Key to determining tax liability is the "unitary business" principle. A state tax would not violate due process limitations if levied on out-of-state activities "so long as the intrastate and extrastate activities formed part of a single unitary business." Where business activities have "nothing to do" with the recipient of income in the taxing state, "due process considerations might well preclude apportioning a tax" because there would be no "underlying unitary business."

Idaho did not dispute the unitary business principle as a necessary prerequisite to imposing a tax on the intangible income involved here. Rather, it urged the Court to expand the unitary business concept to cover the ASARCO relationship to its subsidiaries. Idaho proposed that "corporate purpose" should define unitary business. Under the Idaho proposal, intangible income would be considered part of a unitary business if the property is "acquired, managed or disposed of for purposes relating or contributing to the taxpayer's business." In the Court's view, however, such a definition "would destroy the concept." Any operation "in some sense" can be said to fit such a definition. When taken to its logical boundary, the unitary business limitation "becomes no limitation at all." Even when "less ambitious" interpretations are used, the result is "simply arbitrary." Due process standards do not permit use of a standard that allows a state to tax income derived from activities having "nothing to do" with operations within the taxing state. If such a tax were allowed, the principle that the "state has given anything for which it can ask return" would not be true. Powell concluded by saying that while the subsidiaries "add to the riches" of ASARCO, they are "discrete business enterprises." As a result, there is "no rational relationship" between the intangible income at issue here and the "intrastate values of the enterprise." The Idaho attempt to tax this income may be characterized as an "effort to reach profits earned elsewhere under the guise of legitimate taxation." The due process clause "bars such an effort" to levy a tax on something not properly within its "reach."

Justices Blackmun and Rehnquist joined in a dissent authored by Justice O'Connor. They felt the Court had "groundlessly" struck down an "eminently reasonable" assertion of state taxing power. They thought the decision too severely limited state capability to develop fairly distributed business taxes. More "dismaying" to the dissenters was the Court's "reliance" on the due process clause to invalidate the tax. To have used the commerce clause instead would have permitted Congress to shape a uniform approach to the taxation by states of interstate business. The majority did not feel resolution of this issue on due process ground foreclosed subsequent congressional action and noted that in a footnote. *See also* DUE PROCESS CLAUSES, p. 594.

Significance   In *ASARCO, Inc. v. Idaho State Tax Commission* (458 U.S. 307: 1982), the Supreme Court decided that due process is denied if a state taxes income received by a business wholly outside the state. States, of course, are free to tax subjects and activities completely internal to the state. Limitations of state taxing power begin when the state levies affect other states, interstate commerce, and foreign commerce. There are many cases dealing with these issues, some of which were developed in Chapters 5 and 6. *ASARCO* is a little different in that the Court chose to feature the due process clause in its disposition of the case even though interstate elements were present. Here the Court used the unitary business doctrine to consider the broader principle of whether Idaho was taxing a value earned outside its borders. The Court concluded that because ASARCO and its subsidiaries were not unitary, it was a violation of due process to tax revenues generated by activities of the latter. There were simply no benefits afforded by Idaho to these subsidiaries for which taxes might properly be levied. The Court saw the due process clause as a bar to taxing anything (certain business income in this case) not properly within the reach of the state. More typically, cases of this kind are adjudicated on commerce clause grounds, but *ASARCO* and several other cases indicate that the Burger Court is not unwilling to limit state taxing power on due process grounds.

9. The Contract Clause

459

OVERVIEW

States are prohibited from passing any law "impairing the obligation of contracts." The language appears in Article I, Section 10, along with prohibitions on bills of attainder, *ex post facto* laws, and state legal tender enactments. The basic thrust of these provisions was to protect the vested right of possession of private property from interference through state legislation. Early construction of the contract clause was substantially influenced by Chief Justice John Marshall, who expanded the scope dramatically. The need for this expansive view of the clause was prompted in part by a pre-Marshall Court decision in *Calder v. Bull* (3 Dallas 386: 1798) that limited application of the *ex post facto* clause to retroactive criminal enactments. This clause had been seen as a mainstay in the protection of property interests from state regulation. The withholding of its applicability to private property and contract rights in *Calder* turned Marshall toward the contract clause.

The first contract case was *Fletcher v. Peck* (6 Cranch 87: 1810), the case involving the Yazoo land fraud scandal. In *Fletcher*, the Court invalidated a state statute rescinding a bribe-induced land grant, holding that a grant is a contract notwithstanding the circumstances surrounding its origin. The decision greatly expanded the contract clause's scope by making it applicable to public as well as private contracts. Two years later, the Marshall Court used the clause to protect a grant of tax immunity in *New Jersey v. Wilson* (7 Cranch 164: 1812). The *Wilson* decision held the tax exemption to be a perpetually protected contract, and additionally had the effect of using the contract clause as a means by which to limit state power to levy taxes. The Marshall Court expanded the scope of the clause one step further in *Trustees of Dartmouth College v. Woodward* (4 Wheaton 518: 1819) by bringing private corporations under the protection of the clause. At this point, the Marshall Court had succeeded in fashioning a comprehensive means for the protection of private property interests through the contract clause.

The modification of contract clause doctrine began before Marshall himself left the Court. In *Ogden v. Saunders* (12 Wheaton 213: 1827),

461

the Court upheld a state bankruptcy law that applied to contracted indebtedness occurring after the passage of the statute. Constriction of the clause continued with the Taney Court. In the decision of *Charles River Bridge Company v. Warren Bridge Company* (11 Peters 420: 1837), the Taney Court held that public grants receiving contract clause protection must be strictly interpreted. This decision meant that state power could not be restricted through a grant or contract and certainly not implicitly.

Charles River Bridge marked the beginning of the decline of the contract clause as a virtually absolute way of protecting property rights from the exercise of state power. With greater frequency, the Court upheld the exercise of state police power against claims of contract impairment. In *Stone v. Mississippi* (101 U.S. 814: 1880), for example, the Court permitted a state to prohibit lotteries only two years after granting a 25-year lottery franchise. The Court held that no contract can grant away the fundamental police power of a state.

The full extent of the contract clause decline is reflected in the Court's decision in *Home Building and Loan Association v. Blaisdell* (290 U.S. 398: 1934). The Court upheld a state enactment calling for a moratorium on mortgage payments in an effort to mute some of the effects of the economic depression. The *Blaisdell* decision held that states have the power to protect the public interest from adverse effects of emergencies, and this authority must prevail over interests set forth in contracts.

The *Blaisdell* case brought the contract clause a full 180 degrees from the early decisions of the Marshall Court. The reversal had occurred because the Court moved away from viewing the clause as providing absolute protection from the exercise of state power. Indeed, the Court's retreat from the Marshall Court's position on contract inviolability was the proposition that state police power cannot be diminished by contract provisions. Furthermore, the addition of the Fourteenth Amendment to the Constitution brought with it a due process clause that provided a far more promising method by which private property interests could challenge state regulations.

Contract cases continue to come before the Supreme Court despite the diminished status of the clause. In most of these cases, the Court has maintained the nonrestrictive approach of *Blaisdell*. In *City of El Paso v. Simmons* (379 U.S. 497: 1965), the Court used a balancing test to review impairment claims, and held that a state could modify the process by which forfeited lands could be recovered. Similarly, in *Energy Reserves Group, Inc. v. Kansas Power and Light Company* (459 U.S. 400: 1983), the Court found that state regulation of natural gas prices did not impair a previously entered contract. Nonetheless, the Burger Court has occasionally used the contract clause to limit certain state actions. In *United*

States Trust Company v. New Jersey (431 U.S. 1: 1977), the Court did not permit a state to redirect funds previously obligated for payment of bonds. The Court seemed to suggest that it would review much more carefully those contract cases where states were attempting to alter their own contractual obligations. Finally, in *Allied Structural Steel Company v. Spannaus* (438 U.S. 234: 1978), the Court held that a pension funding statute failed to address a pressing enough public problem to warrant "severe" interference with a company's contractual relationship to its employees. Generally, however, the contract clause is not often invoked to limit the exercise of state police power.

Contract Clause   Provision in Article I, Section 10 prohibiting enactment of state legislation that impairs contractually protected interests. Article I of the Constitution defines the legislative functions and sets out the powers conveyed and limitations imposed on the Congress. In Section 10, the Constitution spells out some limitations that apply to the states. Section 10 covers several areas and says:

> No State shall enter into any Treaty, Alliance or Confederation; grant Letters of Marque or Reprisal; coin Money; emit Bills of Credit; make any Thing but gold and silver Coin a Tender in Payment of Debts; pass any Bill of Attainder, ex post facto Law, or Law impairing the Obligation of Contracts, or grant any Title of Nobility.

The first several items contained in Section 10 pertain to the conduct of foreign affairs, prerogatives the states necessarily had to relinquish at the time the government was established under the Constitution. The remaining elements, including the contract clause, were designed to protect private property rights.

Provisions for protecting property rights are stronger under the Constitution than under the Articles of Confederation which it replaced. This language was included to protect the interests of creditors primarily because a great deal of legislation was enacted by the states during the period under the Articles. Indeed, Madison attributed the push for a constitutional convention to the "evil" of state legislative interference with private property rights. Insolvency laws, statutes permitting the use of paper money to pay debts, and legislative reversals of court judgments in property cases became common under the Articles as state legislatures attempted to ease the severe economic hardships suffered by many debtors. Among the class suffering some of the most extreme burdens were farmers, and they used their considerable political influence to control many state legislatures. The constitutional provisions prohibiting the states from coining money, allowing bills of credit, using paper money to pay debts, passing bills of attainder or *ex post facto* laws or laws impairing obligations of contract were a package of restrictions on state authority that were collectively intended to safeguard creditor interests.

The property-related clauses of Article I, Section 10 were a product of the doctrine of vested rights. This doctrine is a natural law derivative that holds that certain individual rights are so preeminent as to be outside the reach and control of government. Foremost among these rights was the possession of private property. The doctrine of vested rights not only precluded governmental interference with private property, but defined the role of government in terms of protecting these vested rights as its primary responsibility.

The scope and resulting impact of the contract clause has varied widely throughout our constitutional history. At the outset, the clause ranked behind the *ex post facto* clause as the principal means of forestalling state interference with property interests. But in *Calder v. Bull* (3 Dallas 386: 1798), the Court restricted use of the *ex post facto* provision by holding that the clause applied only to laws that "extend to criminal, and not to civil cases." Interpretation of the contract clause was subsequently carefully developed to fill the void created by the *Calder* decision. Expansion of the scope and the role of the contract clause occurred during the tenure of Chief Justice John Marshall, but it began to decline in significance thereafter. The characteristics of the clause at its height and in its present state of diminished importance are outlined below. *See also* ARTICLE I, p. 183; BILL OF ATTAINDER, p. 582; DUE PROCESS CLAUSES, p. 594; *EX POST FACTO*, p. 604.

Significance   The contract clause became a critically important instrument in the early nineteenth century under Chief Justice Marshall. There is strong evidence to suggest that the framers of the Constitution intended that contracts between private individuals could not be impaired through state action. The concept of contract was expanded by the Marshall Court to extend to public contracts, a broad definition that included franchises and corporate charters. Marshall's expansion of the clause provided the Court, intent on preserving the doctrine of vested rights, with a mechanism capable of absolutely protecting property rights. During the course of the nineteenth century, the contract clause figured prominently in Supreme Court review of state regulations. Of all state legislation struck down by the Court prior to 1889, contract clause violations were found in almost half the cases.

Even before the end of the nineteenth century, however, modification of, and retreat from, the Marshall Court position began to occur. While the Marshall Court seemed to recognize no interest paramount to property rights, subsequent courts came to recognize the importance of competing community or societal rights. As early as the case of *Charles River Bridge Company v. Warren Bridge Company* (11 Peters 420: 1837, p. 476), the Court held that state authority to act on behalf of the public good could not be taken away by implication. This view was eventually replaced by one holding that state police power was essentially inalienable, and that it could not be contracted away implicitly or explicitly. At the same time, states became more protective of their authority and placed reservation clauses into grants and corporate charters that permitted, by terms of the contract itself, subsequent change or even repeal of the contract.

As the Court began to narrow the scope of the contract clause, it became a less useful instrument through which property interests could fend off the exercise of state power. Interests that had depended on the contract clause turned to a more comprehensive, less encumbered and, therefore, more effective constitutional element: the due process clause of the Fourteenth Amendment. The addition of the due process language following the Civil War ultimately brought about the actual displacement of the contract clause as a particularly meaningful part of the Constitution.

The full extent of the decline of the contract clause is reflected in the Court's holding in *Home Building and Loan Association v. Blaisdell* (290 U.S. 398: 1934, p. 479). The *Blaisdell* decision held that states have the power to protect the public interest from the adverse effects of emergencies, and this authority must prevail over the interests set forth in contracts. Although *Blaisdell* and many subsequent contract cases undermined the relevancy of the clause, it must be recognized for its central role, particularly during the first century of our constitutional history.

Contract clause cases continue to come before the Court despite the diminished status after *Blaisdell*. In most of these cases, the Court has maintained the flexible, nonrestrictive stance taken in *Blaisdell*. Nonetheless, the Burger Court has occasionally used the contract clause to limit certain state actions. The Court has made it clear, for example, that it would scrutinize very carefully those contract cases in which states attempt to alter their own contractual obligations. The Court will also require that states demonstrate substantial public need if legislation produces "severe" interference with contract rights.

Ex Post Facto Prohibition

***Calder v. Bull*, 3 Dallas 386, 1 L.Ed. 648 (1798)**   Held that the *ex post facto* prohibition of Article I, Section 10 did not apply to civil issues. Rather, the Court interpreted the clause as prohibiting federal or state legislatures from retroactively changing liability or punishments in criminal situations. In this case, Calder had been awarded title to certain property through a judgment of a state probate court. Bull failed to appeal the probate court judgment within the prescribed time period. The state legislature, however, passed a law that granted Bull a rehearing on the matter. The second hearing reversed the result, and Calder unsuccessfully appealed in the state courts before seeking review by the United States Supreme Court. All six members of the Court held that the legislation granting a new hearing was not a prohibited *ex post facto* law.

There was no opinion of the Court. Rather, each member issued his own opinion. The justices focused on two issues, the scope of the *ex post facto* prohibition, and the matter of vested property rights. Justice Chase explored the nature of legislative power generally and the rationale for particular restrictions on that power. This led him to the *ex post facto* issue, which he defined exclusively in terms of criminal liability. An *ex post facto* law "makes an action done before the passing of a law, and which was innocent when done, criminal." So too are laws that make "a crime greater than it was" at the time of commission, inflict a greater punishment retroactively, or adjust rules of evidence to the disadvantage of defendants. Chase emphasized that not all retroactive laws are *ex post facto*. A law that "takes away or impairs rights vested, agreeably to existing law," is retroactive, and while it might be "unjust" or "oppressive," such laws are not banned. The framers, in Chase's view, did not intend to prohibit "depriving a citizen even of a vested right to property." Justice Iredell also felt the Connecticut statute was suspect, but cautioned that the Court could not pronounce such laws void "merely because it is . . . contrary to principles of natural justice." The Court should only intervene where legislatures clearly "transgress the boundaries" of the legislative authority or where legislative actions "violate a fundamental law." The Connecticut legislature did not transgress the *ex post facto* boundary in this case because the "true construction of the prohibition extends to criminal, not civil actions." The prohibition does not reach cases that "merely affect the private property of citizens." Iredell suggested that "some of the most necessary and important acts of legislation are . . . founded upon the principle that private rights must yield to public exigencies." *See also* EX POST FACTO, p. 604; WEAVER V. GRAHAM (450 U.S. 24: 1981), p. 210.

Significance   The doctrine of vested property rights was limited by the Court's decision in *Calder v. Bull* (3 Dallas 386: 1798). The vested rights doctrine is a natural law derivative and holds that certain individual rights are so preeminent as to be outside governmental reach or control. Foremost among these rights early in our history was possession of private property. The doctrine of vested rights not only precludes governmental interference with private property, but defines the role of government in terms of protecting these vested rights as its foremost responsibility and function. Just a year before *Calder*, the vested rights position was articulated in *Van Horne's Lessee v. Dorrance* (2 Dallas 304: 1795). The Court indicated that the "right of acquiring property and having it protected, is one of the natural inherent and unalienable rights of man." For a legislature to deprive a person of property rights is "contrary to the principles of social alliance in every free government."

Many saw the *ex post facto* prohibition as one of the constitutional means through which legislative initiatives at the state level might be confined. *Calder*, however, limited application of the clause to retroactive penal legislation. This was a severe blow to those most interested in protecting vested property rights. With the *ex post facto* limitation sidelined as a medium of protection for vested rights, the Court under Chief Justice Marshall seized on the contract clause in its stead, at least as a limitation against state legislative actions. The *Calder* decision is largely responsible for this change of approach. Had *Calder* been decided the other way, the *ex post facto* provision would have become the first line of defense for protecting property interests, and the contract clause would have played only a secondary role.

Public Contracts

Fletcher v. Peck, **6 Cranch 87, 3 L.Ed. 162 (1810)**   Held that the contract clause of Article I, Section 10 applied to public transactions and contracts. *Fletcher v. Peck* was the first contract clause case to come before the Supreme Court, and the Court's decision marked the first time a state statute was nullified as incompatible with the U.S. Constitution. *Fletcher v. Peck* had an unusual fact situation. By an action of the Georgia legislature, millions of acres of public lands were granted to a number of land investment companies. It was subsequently discovered that the land grants had been obtained by bribing many of the legislators. A succeeding legislature rescinded the land grants. In the interim, however, the land was sold by the companies to third parties having nothing to do with the bribery. These purchasers were now in possession of worthless land titles, and they brought suit challenging the rescinding action on impairment of contract grounds. In a unanimous decision, the Supreme Court invalidated the rescinding act.

Chief Justice Marshall spoke for the Court. He discounted the bribery issue as outside the purview of the Court. It would be "unseemly in the extreme" for the Court to "speculate on legislative motivation" when reviewing a case. Thus, the question of whether or not the Georgia legislature was "improperly influenced is not before the Court." Accordingly, it could not be argued that the "original grants were a nullity" on that ground. Marshall concluded that both the original and rescinding acts "must be judged as written." Marshall examined generally the powers of a legislature to repeal acts of previous legislatures. He concluded that legislatures are generally "competent to repeal any act which a former legislature was competent to pass." He pointed out a critical exception, however. If an act be "done under a law, a succeeding legislature cannot undo it." When a law "is in its nature a contract" and when "absolute rights have vested under that contract," a rescinding of the law cannot "divest those rights." So, as a general proposition, the rescinding action of the Georgia legislature was suspect. Further, Georgia's legislature is subject to the constitutional limitations on all legislatures found in Article I, Section 10, such as the prohibition against impairment of obligation of contracts.

Was the Georgia grant a contract? The Court agreed that it was. A contract is a compact between two or more parties, and is either "executory or executed." A contract executed is one in which the "object of contract is performed; and this... differs nothing from a grant." Since a grant was seen as a contract executed, it is contained within the impairment prohibition. Marshall also put aside the assertion that the impairment clause applied only to contracts between individuals. The "words themselves contain no such distinction." Rather, the words are "general, and are applicable to contracts of every description." *See also* BILL OF ATTAINDER, p. 582; *EX POST FACTO*, p. 604.

Significance   *Fletcher v. Peck* (6 Cranch 87: 1810) was the first important contract clause case, and it substantially broadened the protection afforded by the clause. *Fletcher* was a crucial follow-up to *Calder v. Bull* (3 Dallas 386: 1798) in terms of protecting vested property rights. *Calder* had determined that the *ex post facto* prohibition applied only to penal legislation, thus private property rights were left vulnerable to retroactive state measures. *Fletcher* held that a public grant contains an implied contract that grant provisions will not be altered or revoked by the state. The Court held that the contract clause did not distinguish between public and private contracts. On the contrary, the *Fletcher* decision said that the contract clause applied to "contracts of every description." While the framers of the Constitution may have intended to circumscribe only contracts between individuals, the effect of *Fletcher* was to make the contract clause applicable to a state's transactions. In this way, *Fletcher* established the contract clause as the principal means for defending private property interests.

The *Fletcher* decision was one of the most popular ever rendered by the Court. The decision seemed to come to the aid of those engaged in bribery and fraud. For Marshall, however, the decision was meant to establish that legislatures could not interfere with interests protected by contracts. *Fletcher* was, thus, a fundamental element of Marshall's more comprehensive objective of protecting private property rights, and it served as the foundation for expansion of contract clause protection until Marshall left the Court.

Tax Exemptions

New Jersey v. Wilson, 7 Cranch 164, 3 L.Ed. 303 (1812)   Held that the contract clause may be used to protect a state grant of tax immunity. *New Jersey v. Wilson* involved a 1758 agreement between King Charles II and the Delaware Indians to resolve Indian land claims in

New Jersey. The agreement was that the government would provide the Indians with certain land in exchange for release from all other land claims. The colonial legislature of New Jersey passed an act to "give effect to this agreement." The act also stated that the lands to be purchased for the Indians "shall not hereafter be subject to any tax, any law, usage or custom." The Indians resided on these tax-free lands until 1801, when they expressed a desire to join another part of the tribe in New York. They obtained authorization to sell their land from the New Jersey legislature. The act said nothing "respecting the privilege of exemption from taxation." The land was sold in 1802, and two years later, the legislature repealed the tax exemption by rescinding the original act of 1758. The lands were assessed and taxes demanded from the new owners. Suit was brought, claiming that repeal of the exemption was precluded by the contract clause. The Supreme Court found the act rescinding the exemption unconstitutional in a unanimous decision.

Through Chief Justice Marshall, the Court drew from *Fletcher v. Peck* (6 Cranch 87: 1810, p. 469), finding that the contract clause applied to contracts to which the state is a party as well as contracts between individual citizens. The Court's only concerns here were whether a contract existed and whether an impairment had occurred. The Court answered both questions in the affirmative. Indeed, "every requisite to the formation of a contract is found in the proceedings between the colony of New Jersey and the Indians." The agreement covered title to certain lands in exchange for withdrawal of claims to other lands with additional provisions regarding such matters as immunity from taxation. This is "certainly a contract clothed in forms of unusual solemnity." The Court went on to hold that the tax immunity, a privilege intended for the benefit of the Indians, was "annexed by the terms which create it, to the land itself, not to their persons." In the Court's view, it was to the Indians' advantage that the tax exemption was attached to the land itself because the land value would be enhanced by the immunity. Since the state did not insist that the immunity be surrendered at the time authorization to sell the land was granted to the Indians, the purchaser "succeeds, with the assent of the state, to all the rights of the Indians." With respect to this land, the purchaser stands "in their place, and claims the benefits of their contract." The Court held that the contract clause was "certainly impaired" by the enactment rescinding tax immunity, which would "annul this essential part of it." *See also* FLETCHER V. PECK (6 Cranch 87: 1810), p. 469; STONE V. MISSISSIPPI (101 U.S. 814: 1880), p. 478.

Significance   New Jersey v. Wilson (7 Cranch 164: 1812) used the contract clause to protect private property interests from the exercise of state taxing power. This decision marked an expansion of the scope of the clause begun in *Fletcher v. Peck* (6 Cranch 87: 1810). It was also part of Chief Justice Marshall's design to generally protect private property from the reach of state authority. Indeed, the effect of *Wilson* was that the state power to levy taxes is not an inalienable power, and that it may be bargained away through legislative grants. Benjamin F. Wright, a leading authority on the contract clause, has said that Marshall was so driven by his preoccupation with protecting vested property rights that "he did not even pause to consider the handicap to state financial powers that this principle might produce." Marshall softened the effect of *Wilson* slightly in *Providence Bank v. Billings* (4 Peters 514: 1830). This case held that tax exemptions such as that in *Wilson* must be explicitly contained in grants and cannot be presumed as conveyed by implication. The *Billings* qualification notwithstanding, the Court has refused to abandon *Wilson* (see such cases as *Piqua Branch of the State Bank v. Knoop,* 16 Howard 369: 1853). Maintenance of the *Wilson* doctrine has led to the placing of language in state constitutions written after *Wilson* providing limitations or outright prohibitions on legislative grants of tax immunity.

Corporate Charters

Trustees of Dartmouth College v. Woodward, **4 Wheaton 518, 4 L.Ed. 629 (1819)**   Held that a corporate charter is a contract protected from state legislative impairment. The *Trustees of Dartmouth College v. Woodward* involved a contest for governance of the college. The trustees of the college, a group of private persons, based their claim of governing authority on a 1769 charter from King George III. In 1816, the legislature of New Hampshire enacted a law that amended the original charter and gave control over trustee selection and the college's governance structure to the state. In an attempt to regain control, the original trustees brought suit in the state courts against Woodward, one of the state-appointed trustees. They were unsuccessful. However, the United States Supreme Court reversed the state courts in a 5–1 decision.

The opinion of the Court was delivered by Chief Justice Marshall. The Court divided the case into two questions: whether the charter conferred by the king was a constitutionally protected contract, and if so, did the legislative enactments of New Hampshire constitute impairment of the contract's obligations. The Court determined that the charter was a protected contract. Dartmouth College was established by the donors through the charter to be a "private eleemosynary" institution. The donors used this medium of incorporation to ensure

Dartmouth's future private status. The charter included establishment of a perpetual succession of persons as trustees to act on behalf of the original donors. Simply because government allowed the property to be used in this way does not give the government the "consequent right substantially to change that form, or to vary the purposes to which the property is applied." The Court concluded that the "character of civil institutions does not grow out of their incorporation, but out of the manner in which they are formed, and the objects for which they are created." In this instance, the interests and intentions of the donors are represented by the corporation. The corporation is "the assignee of their rights, stands in their place, and distributes their bounty, as they would themselves have distributed it had they been immortal." Government must encourage such donations to education, and one "great inducement to these gifts, is the conviction felt by the giver, that the disposition he makes of them is immutable." Accordingly, the charter involved here was seen as a "contract within the letter of the Constitution, and within its spirit also."

Moving to the matter of impairment, the Court concluded that the legislative acts did impair the charter provisions. The "whole power of governing the college is transferred from trustees appointed according to the will of the founder, expressed in the charter," to the state. The "will of the state" is substituted for the "will of the donors, in every essential operation of the college." Such a change is not "immaterial" and the "charter of 1769 exists no longer." Even if the change brought about by the legislation "may be for the advantage of the college" and education more generally, it is "not according to the will of the donors, and is of that contract on the faith of which their property was given." Justice Duvall dissented, feeling that the contract clause should not extend to the charter provisions.

Significance   *Trustees of Dartmouth College v. Woodward* (4 Wheaton 518: 1819) represented the Court's most expansive interpretation of the contract clause. While the case involved an educational institution, the real consequences of *Dartmouth* fell on business corporations. The decision brought private corporations within the scope of the contract clause and seemed to fully insulate such corporations from legislative regulation. The decision more tightly joined contract and natural law concepts such that the contract clause became an impenetrable shield for private property rights. *Dartmouth* stimulated a great deal of early economic activity in this country because it created an effective protective barrier for corporations. Chief Justice Marshall and his Court sought to provide through contract clause decisions, assurances to corporations that they would have a reasonable expectation of return on their investments.

The decision also made an important assumption about charters. They were entered for the purpose of preserving particular interests. If the charter was ambiguous, Marshall felt that the benefit of the doubt ought to go to the private party rather than the state. In the *Dartmouth* case, it was governance through the private trustees as perpetual representatives of the original donor that was a decisive element in the decision. This position was subsequently modified in *Charles River Bridge Company v. Warren Bridge Company* (11 Peters 420: 1837). The corporate charter became less effective as a means of insulating private property because it was soon acknowledged, even by Marshall, that states could reserve options for future modification or even repeal of charters granted by the state. Indeed, frequent use of reservation clauses in corporate charters has been cited as one of the reasons for the decline of the importance of the contract clause.

Bankruptcy Legislation

***Ogden v. Saunders*, 12 Wheaton 213, 6 L.Ed. 605 (1827)**   Held that a state bankruptcy law covering future obligations of a debtor did not violate the contract clause. *Ogden v. Saunders* considered a state bankruptcy statute enacted soon after the War of 1812. The Constitution placed authority with the Congress to fashion bankruptcy policy, but no federal legislation had emerged. After the war, there were a number of economic conditions that created serious financial distress. Many states responded with insolvency and bankruptcy laws. The statutes were challenged by various creditors, and in *Sturges v. Crowninshield* (4 Wheaton 122: 1819), the Court invalidated laws that applied to debts contracted before passage of the statute. A number of states modified bankruptcy statutes that provided for relief from future contracted indebtedness. It was this type of prospective bankruptcy legislation that was at issue in *Ogden v. Saunders*. The Court, in a 4–3 decision, upheld the bankruptcy enactments.

The opinion of the Court was delivered by Justice Washington. The Court talked about the "universal law of all civilized nations" that absolutely required that "all men are bound to perform their contracts." There exists, however, at the time a contract is entered, a body of state law that "becomes a part of the contract, and travels with it wherever the parties may be found." While no state could pass a law that retrospectively altered any contract, prospective law did "not impair the obligation of contracts subsequently entered into." In the Court's view, it cannot be considered "unjust or oppressive to declare by law that contracts subsequently entered into, may be discharged in a way different from that which the parties have provided." Washington expressed the view that bankruptcy laws were intended as the exclusive prerogative of Congress, but noted the absence of a uniform law on bankruptcies at the federal level. The framers likely did not foresee state activity on this subject. But, given the other limitations on states regarding state interference with contracts, Washington concluded that "retrospective laws were alone in the contemplation of the convention."

A dissent was entered by Chief Justice Marshall, joined by Justices Duvall and Story. The dissenters argued that the contract clause, unlike the retroactively focused bill of attainder and *ex post facto* provisions, "relates to the civil transactions of individuals" and is "expressed in more general terms." Marshall likened the clause to that prohibiting a state from making anything but gold or silver legal tender for payment of debts. These restrictions "contemplate legislative interference with private rights, and restrain that interference." The distinction between already existing and future indebtedness was rejected by the dissenters as unpersuasive. Marshall argued that if only retroactive laws were prohibited, it would merely be a matter of time until no contracts would have been entered prior to the enactment, thus making the contract clause "so far useless."

Significance   *Ogden v. Saunders* (12 Wheaton 213: 1827) upheld state statutes providing for bankruptcy relief on contractual obligations assumed following enactment of the law. In doing so, the decision began to reverse the course set by the Marshall Court, which had dramatically expanded the protective scope of the contract clause. The state bankruptcy laws presented the Court with difficult questions about state legislative power. There was an economic panic in 1819 that produced widespread hardship. Many states acted, since no federal bankruptcy legislation existed. The Court needed to determine whether states had any authority to legislate in this area, and if so, whether such statutes necessarily impair contracts. The Court's first review of this kind of state law came in *Sturges v. Crowninshield* (4 Wheaton 122: 1819). The decision in *Sturges* held that states may enact insolvency laws in the absence of federal legislation. The Court went on, however, to say that such laws generally impaired contract obligations and were, therefore, impermissible.

The Marshall Court had spent a decade developing the contract clause as a means of protecting private property interests, so it followed that the Court would take a very negative view of state statutes that could release someone from contractual obligations. But the Court's emphasis on the retroactive aspects of the insolvency laws subsequently led to the decision in *Ogden* preserving state authority to regulate contracts prospectively. *Ogden* is the first signal of the Court's backing off the absolutist view of the protection afforded private property through the contract clause. Instead, the Court began to recognize the competing value of state police power exercised for the broader public good. While *Odgen* did not resolve that controversy, it marked the beginning of a new direction for the Court and ultimately a diminishing significance for the contract clause in our constitutional scheme.

Contract Ambiguity

***Charles River Bridge Company v. Warren Bridge Company,* 11 Peters 420, 9 L.Ed. 773 (1837)**   Established the principle that public contracts are to be interpreted strictly, and that no state interest may be contracted away implicitly. *Charles River Bridge Company v. Warren Bridge Company* involved a state grant in the form of a toll bridge franchise. By a legislative act of 1785, Massachusetts granted the Charles River Bridge Company the right to build a bridge over the Charles River and collect tolls from its use for a 40-year period. The franchise was subsequently extended to 70 years. The bridge was to replace an exclusive right that was relinquished by the holder for a fee. In 1828, the legislature authorized the Warren Bridge Company to collect tolls on its bridge. Once the second bridge was paid for, it was to become property of the state and operated without toll. This second bridge was located closely enough to the first bridge to deprive it of its toll revenues. Charles River Bridge Company unsuccessfully sought injunctive relief at the state level and brought the case to the Supreme Court. The Court affirmed the lower courts in a 5–2 decision.

The opinion of the Court was delivered by Chief Justice Taney. The crucial question was the exclusivity of the ferry franchise transferred to the Charles River Bridge Company. The matter of exclusivity was not explicitly addressed in the original bridge franchise, and the Court rejected the contention that matters of such importance can be conveyed by implication. Taney said that "no rights are taken from the public, or given to the corporation, beyond those which the words of the charter, by their natural and proper construction, purport to convey." The Court found "no words" that convey exclusivity and "none can be implied." The Court felt strongly that state prerogatives could not be restricted by implication. Taney suggested that the "object and end" of government is to "promote the happiness and prosperity of the community." It can never be "assumed" that government intended to restrict its options or "diminish its power of accomplishing the end for which it was created." The state cannot be "presumed to surrender" its power of "improvement and public accommodation" because the "whole community" has an "interest in preserving it undiminished."

The Court felt that it was "fully established" in cases like this that any contract ambiguity must "operate against the adventurers, and in favor of the public." Nothing can be claimed that is "not clearly given." Acknowledging that rights of private property must be "sacredly guarded," the Court indicated that "we must not forget that the community also have rights, and that the happiness and well-being of every citizen depends on their faithful preservation." The Court concluded by saying that it must not "take away from" any part of the state's power over its own "internal police and improvement," a power so "necessary to their well-being and prosperity."

Justice Story issued a dissent that was joined by Justice Thompson. Story rejected the position that a private grantee should be precluded from protection. In this case, Story felt the chartering of the Warren Bridge impermissibly impaired the original grant. He also suggested that the public interest was badly served by the Court's decision. He could conceive of "no surer plan to arrest all public improvements, founded on private capital and enterprise, than to make the outlay of that capital uncertain, and questionable both as to security, and as to productiveness."

Significance   The Court's decision in *Charles River Bridge Company v. Warren Bridge Company* (11 Peters 420: 1837) held that rights could not be contracted or granted by implication, and that contract ambiguities must be resolved in favor of the state. The bridge decision was a major departure from the contract clause position of the preceding Marshall Court. The earlier court had rigorously held to the view that charters issued by the states were contracts protected by the Constitution from any subsequent impairment. The decision in the bridge case did not directly confront the prior court's position in cases like *Trustees of Dartmouth College v. Woodward* (4 Wheaton 518: 1819, p. 472). Rather, the Court under Chief Justice Roger Taney sought to disengage more quietly, even though the two courts differed markedly on their views of the nature of contracts and the scope of state police power. In the bridge case, Taney used Marshall's own holding in *Providence Bank v. Billings* (4 Peters 514: 1830) to deny the injunction sought by the original franchise holder. Marshall had argued in *Billings* that state tax exemptions could be chartered away implicitly. Taney simply made the same argument for state police power more general in the bridge case. By taking this approach, Taney did not directly overrule such Marshall Court precedents as *Dartmouth*. He merely indicated that such charters must be strictly interpreted and that benefits could not be granted to the charter holder by assumption or implication. Any doubt or ambiguity that might exist in the construction of contract provisions must, in the Taney Court's view, be resolved in a way that maximizes the capacity of the state to "promote the happiness and prosperity of the community."

Contracts and State Police Power

Stone v. Mississippi, **101 U.S. 814, 25 L.Ed. 1079 (1880)**   Held that the contract clause may not impair the exercise of the state police power. *Stone v. Mississippi* involved a legislative act granting a lottery charter to a private company. In return for specified payments, the company was entitled to operate. The charter was effective for a period of 25 years. Two years after the charter had been granted, however, the state adopted a new constitution that contained a provision prohibiting lotteries. The new constitution was ratified by a statewide referendum. Pursuant to constitutional mandate, the state legislature passed a statute making it a crime to continue operation of the lottery. Stone and others appealed to the Supreme Court following their convictions in the state courts, claiming that their activities were protected by the original charter. The Supreme Court disagreed in a unanimous decision.

The opinion of the Court was delivered by Chief Justice Waite. The principal question in the case was whether Mississippi "irrevocably" bound itself by contract through the granted lottery charter. Cast in a slightly different way, the Court saw the central question as whether a legislative charter can "defeat the will of the people, authoritatively expressed," to discontinue lotteries in the state. The Court felt it could not. The legislature "cannot bargain away the police power of the state." Whatever else the police power may involve, it "extends to all matters affecting the public health or the public morals." The Court considered lotteries as "proper subjects for the exercise of this power." The police power is such that the "people themselves" cannot jeopardize or impinge upon it, "much less their servants," the legislature. The power of governing is "a trust committed by the people to the government, no part of which can be granted away." Governmental agencies, including the legislature, have substantial discretion to discharge their functions. These agencies cannot "give away nor sell the discretion of those that are to come after them." Corporations may be chartered and given privileges analogous to privileges of citizenship. But these "creatures of the government" are subject to "such rules and regulations" as may be adopted for the "preservation of health and morality."

The Court also held that the contract impairment clause relates to property rights rather than "governmental" rights. Lotteries fall into the latter category. In the Court's view, lotteries are a "species of gambling," and "wrong in their influences." Lotteries "disturb the checks and balances of a well ordered community." A society "built on such a foundation" would produce a population of "speculators and gamblers" living on the expectation of benefiting by chance. The "right to suppress them is governmental," and the police power may be exercised by those in authority "at their discretion." Anyone accepting a lottery charter did so with the "implied understanding" that the people or their constituted agencies "may resume it at any time when the public good shall require it." Certain privileges may accrue to the charter holder, but they are "subject to withdrawal at will." The charter is a permit, "good as against existing laws, but subject to future legislation and constitutional control or withdrawal."

Significance   *Stone v. Mississippi* (101 U.S. 814: 1880) held that a lottery charter was subject to the subsequent enactment of a statute prohibiting lotteries in the state. This decision reflected a view that state police power must prevail over interests covered by franchises, charters, and public grants. This view had evolved progressively since early Taney Court decisions, most notably *Charles River Bridge Company v. Warren Bridge Company* (11 Peters 420: 1837, p. 476). Following the bridge decision, however, the Court's holdings more clearly recognized the inalienability of state police power. For example, in *West River Bridge Company v. Dix* (6 Howard 507: 1848), a case much like *Charles River Bridge Company*, the Court noted the general inalienability of state police power, and upheld the exercise of eminent domain against interests protected by a corporate franchise. Similarly, in *Fertilizing Company v. Hyde Park* (97 U.S. 659: 1878), the Court upheld a local ordinance, saying that since the franchise did not exempt the holder from state power to abate nuisances, the contract was subject to the exercise of that power. *Stone* makes the point even more emphatically, and since *Stone*, the exercise of state police power has consistently prevailed against claims of impairment of previously granted charters and franchises.

Public Interest Impairment

***Home Building and Loan Association v. Blaisdell*, 290 U.S. 398, 54 S.Ct. 231, 78 L.Ed. 413 (1934)**   Held that emergency conditions may permit interests protected by contract to be adversely affected by the exercise of state power. *Home Building and Loan Association v. Blaisdell* examined the issue of the extent to which state power may be used to pursue the public interest even if contract rights were impaired. The statute in question here was the Minnesota Mortgage Moratorium law passed by the legislature in 1933 in response to the effects of the economic depression. The statute authorized state courts to grant extensions on mortgage redemption periods to allow the mortgagor to retain possession of the property and delay foreclosure sale. The act had a limited effective date. During any extension granted by a court, the interest obligation remained in effect, and the mortgage holder was free to seek redemption if payments were not received. The Home Building and Loan Association, holder of Blaisdell's mortgage, appealed from a state court judgment granting an extension to Blaisdell. The Supreme Court upheld the mortgage moratorium statute in a 5–4 decision.

The opinion of the Court was delivered by Chief Justice Hughes. It focused on the situation prompting the statute and the matter of contract impairment. The Court held that the legislature could have reasonably concluded that an economic emergency existed "which called for the exercise of the police power to grant relief." While "emergency does not create power, emergency may furnish the occasion for the exercise of power." Because the contract clause is broad and general in character, it is subject to judicial construction to "fill in the details." Judicial deliberations that take notice of special situational needs are appropriate and desirable. Hughes urged an adaptive approach to constitutional construction and suggested more flexibility be permitted in weighing the interests of individual contract rights and the public welfare. As for the matter of impairment, the Court concluded that the impairment was limited and minimal. The contract clause precludes legislation that wholly invalidates contract obligations. This statute did not do that. The statute did not "impair the integrity of mortgage indebtedness" and the "obligation for interest remains." With the exception of the time extension, the "other conditions of redemption are unaltered."

The dissenting opinion of Justice Sutherland was joined by Justices Van Devanter, McReynolds, and Butler. It emphasized that no emergency could alter the Constitution's provisions. The Constitution "does not mean one thing at one time and an entirely different thing at another time." Thus, no exigency could allow the state to act as it did. On the matter of the impairment, Sutherland saw the case as part of "ever-advancing encroachments upon the sanctity of private and public contracts." Unlike the majority, he saw the statute as impairing the contract. If it did not alter any contract conditions, all the discussion of exigency was "immaterial." Sutherland noted that periods of financial distress occur periodically, and legislatures cannot be permitted to employ various devices to "shift the misfortune of the debtor to the shoulders of the creditor."

Significance   *Home Building and Loan Association v. Blaisdell* (290 U.S. 398: 1934) held that states may make some inroads on interests protected by contract under pressing circumstances. In some ways, *Blais-dell* is the most important contract clause decision since the Civil War. It asserted that states must have the capacity to safeguard the public interest in times of emergency. Put another way, the Court held that public needs could override contractual interests if the situation were serious enough. Such a proposition was directly at odds with the Marshall Court view of a century earlier and seemingly the obvious meaning of the constitutional language itself. The *Blaisdell* majority, however, were convinced that the state had established prerogatives with respect to protecting the "good of all," and use of reasonable measures by the state was reserved and "read into all contracts."

The Court did not altogether abandon the contract clause in *Blais-dell*. In fact, the Court enumerated several factors it considered significant in reviewing claims of contract clause infringement. Certainly the critical factor is the nature of the emergency. In addition, the remedy pursued by the state must be broadly aimed and designed to protect a "basic societal interest." Finally, there were certain limiting elements of the mortgage moratorium measure. The statute was effective for only a limited period of time. It was also a carefully defined or "tailored" statute that imposed "reasonable" adjustments on the contractual relationships. These factors have been cited often in subsequent contract cases. Although the contract clause has occasionally been invoked to strike down state enactments, the relevance of the clause was substantially diminished by the Court's decision in *Blaisdell*.

Balancing Test for Impairment

***City of El Paso v. Simmons*, 379 U.S. 497, 85 S.Ct. 577, 13 L.Ed. 2d 446 (1965)**   Upheld a state-imposed time limit for the process of recovering forfeited property, a process that had previously operated under statutory provisions free of any time restrictions. *City of El Paso v. Simmons* examined a change in the manner by which forfeited land may be recovered. The land in question had been sold by the state in 1910 under statutory provisions that called for the forfeiture of title in the event of nonpayment of interest under the sales contract. The statute also permitted reinstatement of claim to the land by paying the full amount of the interest due. This statute was changed in 1941 and limited the reinstatement period to five years from the date of forfeiture. The land involved here was forfeited on July 21, 1947. Simmons applied for reinstatement accompanied by checks for the unpaid interest on July 23, 1952, or two days past the five-year time limit, The application was denied, and the state sold the land to the city of El Paso. Simmons brought suit, claiming the 1941 statute should not be applied to his contract and that he should have been able to reinstate at any time, provided he fully paid the interest due. The United States court of appeals agreed with Simmons, but the Supreme Court reversed that holding in an 8–1 decision.

The opinion of the Court was delivered by Justice White. The Court disagreed with the court of appeals that the reinstatement provision conferred a "vested right which is not subject to legislative alteration." The Court noted that the contract clause does not impose an absolute prohibition, and that the state "continues to possess authority to safeguard the vital interest of the people." The Court said that it "does not matter" that legislation pursuing the public interest "has the result of modifying or abrogating contracts already in effect." The statutory change imposing the reinstatement time limit was intended to "restore confidence in the stability and integrity of land titles and enable the state to protect and administer its property." The unlimited reinstatement policy prompted excessive speculation and produced numerous delinquencies. In the Court's view, the contract clause "does not render Texas powerless to take effective and necessary measures" to deal with the problem. Contract clause decisions have never given a "law which imposes unforeseen advantages or burdens on a contracting party constitutional immunity against change." The Court felt that laws that restrict a party to "those gains reasonably to be expected from the contract" are not subject to contract clause attack "notwithstanding that they technically alter an obligation of a contract." The Court pointed out that the five-year limitation still allowed defaulting purchasers with a "bona fide interest" in their lands a "reasonable time to reinstate." Texas did not need to allow defaulting purchasers with a "speculative interest" to remain in "endless default while retaining a cloud on title." The amendment was a "mild" measure and "hardly burdensome" to the purchaser who wanted to "adhere to his contract of purchase."

Justice Black dissented and was critical of the Court's "balancing away" the contract clause protection. Black suggested that the contract clause was included in the same section of the Constitution with language forbidding bills of attainder and *ex post facto* laws. These provisions were included because the framers believed that persons "should not have to act at their peril, fearing always that the state might change its mind and alter the legal consequences of their past acts so as to take away their lives, their liberty, or their property."

Significance   *City of El Paso v. Simmons* (379 U.S. 497: 1965) upheld a state modification for reinstating claims to forfeited land as a permissible process change. The change imposed a time limit for filing reinstatement claims of title to forfeited property. In deciding this case, the Court employed a balancing test whereby it weighed the necessity and reasonableness of the change against the claims of impairment.

Such a test reflected the Court's growing preference to allow states a substantial degree of flexibility in exercising police power. Rather than taking the contract clause at a literal level, the Court in cases like *Simmons* considered the state's purpose in enacting the original statute and its rationale for the subsequent modification. The Court recognized the state's need for "restoring the stability and integrity of land titles" as sufficiently important to the public interest to allow alteration. Balanced against the claim of impairment of a contractual "promise" of no time limit as provided in the original statute, the Court found that the modification did not impair a right warranting contract clause protection. The Court also said that, in these situations, it must "respect the wide discretion on the part of the legislature in determining what is and what is not necessary." This kind of deference provides the states with substantial flexibility in determining what is necessary for the public interest.

Impairment of Pension Agreement

Allied Structural Steel Company v. Spannaus, **438 U.S. 234, 98 S.Ct. 2716, 57 L.Ed. 2d 727 (1978)**   Struck down a state enactment because it impaired a private company's employment contracts in an impermissible manner. *Allied Structural Steel Company v. Spannaus* also set forth several factors by which contemporary contract clause claims might be reviewed. This case involved a pension plan of a company operating in Minnesota. Under the plan, all employees could receive a pension upon retirement at age 65, regardless of time of service. Under certain conditions, the pension plan vested prior to age 65. The company was the "sole contributor to the pension fund" and was virtually free from any restrictions or sanctions with regard to contributions, distribution of fund assets, and continuation of the plan. The State of Minnesota then enacted a statute requiring all employers of 100 or more employees and having a private pension plan to be subject to a "pension funding charge" if the plan was discontinued or if a Minnesota office was closed. The charge was assessed against pension funds insufficient to cover full pensions for all employees of at least ten years service. Subsequently, Allied Structural Steel closed its Minnesota office. Several employees who had not yet vested under the company plan were entitled to benefits under the statute. Minnesota notified the company that it owed a pension funding charge. The company brought suit claiming that the act impermissibly impaired its obligations as contained in its own pension agreement. The Supreme Court found that the statute as applied to the company violated the contract clause in a 5–3 decision with Justice Blackmun not participating.

The opinion of the Court was delivered by Justice Stewart. The Court began by acknowledging that the act "substantially altered" the company's contractual relationship with its employees. That in itself did not "inexorably" lead to a contract clause violation. The Court saw the clause as nonabsolute and indicated that it was not the "draconian provision that its words might seem to imply." At the same time, if the clause is to "retain any meaning at all," there must be "some limits" on state police power affecting contracts. The Court pointed to several factors found significant by the Court in reviewing the mortgage moratorium statute in *Home Building and Loan Association v. Blaisdell* (290 U.S. 398: 1934). First, an emergency existed that needed immediate attention. Second, the statute was designed to protect a "basic societal interest, not a favored group." Third, the relief afforded by the statute was carefully "tailored" to address the emergency and the "imposed conditions were reasonable." Fourth, the act was of limited duration.

The Court then examined these factors in terms of the pension funding statute. The pension act had a "severe" effect on the company's contractual obligation, and none of the *Blaisdell* factors were found to exist. The act did not respond to a bona fide emergency nor "was it necessary to meet an important general social problem." Neither did the enactment "operate in an area already subject to state regulation" at the time the original obligation was undertaken by the company. Finally, the effects of the state policy were not temporary, but rather "worked a severe, permanent and immediate" change in the company's contractual relationships "irrevocably and retroactively."

Justice Brennan, joined by Justices White and Marshall, dissented. They saw the act as merely imposing "new, additional obligations on a particular class of persons" in a manner similar to "all positive social legislation." The dissenters would have preferred to assess the statute on the basis of the due process clause of the Fourteenth Amendment rather than in terms of contract impairment. *See also* HOME BUILDING AND LOAN ASSOCIATION V. BLAISDELL (290 U.S. 398: 1934), p. 479; UNITED STATES TRUST COMPANY V. NEW JERSEY (431 U.S. 1: 1977), p. 485.

Significance   The Court's decision in *Allied Structural Steel Company v. Spannaus* indicates that the contract clause may still be used to protect private contractual relationships. *Spannaus* made clear that the contract clause retains some contemporary meaning and under which circumstances it would be used as a restriction on state police power. Differentiation from the *Blaisdell* case was key in this case. The Minnesota pension protection enactment was not prompted by a sufficiently urgent situation, nor was it designed to protect broad social interests. Absent these factors, the state is less able to impair contractual obligations. State interference with contracts is also more likely to gain the Court's approval if it is "carefully tailored," imposes only "reasonable" changes, and has an effect of only a short or limited time. The Minnesota statute at issue here had none of these characteristics. The Court also suggested one further criterion. It noted that the field of employee pensions was not a policy area "subject to state regulation" at the time the company fashioned its own pension plan. The conclusion is that if a state is going to impose "severe, permanent and immediate" changes on contractual obligations and relationships, it must be acting in a policy area where the exercise of state police power is well established. Compare the Court's judgment on this matter in the context of employee pensions with that taken in *Energy Reserves Group, Inc. v. Kansas Power and Light Company* (459 U.S. 400: 1983), where the regulation applied to natural gas pricing.

State Termination of Contract to Which It Is a Party

United States Trust Company v. New Jersey, **431 U.S. 1, 97 S.Ct. 1505, 52 L.Ed. 2d 92 (1977)**   Held that the contract clause can be invoked when a state attempts to modify a contract to which the state itself is a party. *United States Trust Company v. New Jersey* involved an interstate agreement entered into by New Jersey in 1962. The agreement prohibited the Port Authority of New York and New Jersey from subsidizing mass transit by using funds pledged to support bonds issued by the authority. In 1974, the legislatures of the two states concurrently repealed the agreement, citing the national energy crisis and the need to expand mass transportation. United States Trust Company was a bond holder of the Port Authority and brought suit claiming repeal of the agreement to be a violation of the contract clause. The Supreme Court agreed in a 4–3 decision with Justices Powell and Stewart not participating.

The opinion of the Court was delivered by Justice Blackmun. The Court began by citing *Home Building and Loan Association v. Blaisdell* (290 U.S. 398: 1934) and indicating that the prohibition against contract impairment is not an "absolute one" and cannot be "read with literal exactness like a mathematical formula." Finding a "technical impairment" is a "preliminary step" in determining whether the impairment is permissible. The Court recognized that states must possess "broad power to adopt general regulatory measures." One cannot avoid such regulation simply by making private contractual agreements. At the same time, private contracts cannot be subject to "unlimited modification under the police power." Regulations must be both necessary and reasonable to permit adjustment of contracted interests. When a state impairs a contract to which it is a party, the normal deference to legislative judgment is not appropriate because "self interest is at stake." The Court observed that a state could "reduce its financial obligations" whenever it wanted to spend monies for other public purposes, in which case the contract clause "would provide no protection at all." A state cannot refuse to meet legitimate financial obligations "simply because it would prefer to spend the money to promote the public good rather that the private welfare of its creditors." The original agreement can only be altered if the impairment is both reasonable and necessary.

The Court proceeded to examine the necessity of the impairment on "two levels." It found that total repeal of the agreement was not "essential," as a "less drastic modification" would have been sufficient. In addition, the state could have achieved the goal of improving mass transit by "alternative means." A state is not "completely free to consider impairing the obligations of its own contracts on a par with other policy alternatives." A state cannot "impose a drastic impairment" when an "evident and more moderate course would serve its purpose equally well." Thus, under these circumstances, the repeal was not reasonable or necessary.

Justice Brennan issued a dissent that was joined by Justices Marshall and White. The dissenters felt the repeal was a lawful exercise of the police power. They felt the decision "remolds" the contract clause into a "potent instrument" for overseeing policy decisions of state legislatures. In addition, the dissenters saw the decision as "creating a constitutional safe haven for property rights embodied in a contract" and thought it "substantially distorts modern constitutional jurisprudence governing regulation of private economic interests." In the dissenters' view, the Court may only review contract impairments to make certain that state enactments are not "plainly unreasonable and arbitrary." *See also* ALLIED STRUCTURAL STEEL COMPANY V. SPANNAUS (438 U.S. 234: 1978), p. 483; HOME BUILDERS AND LOAN ASSOCIATION V. BLAISDELL (290 U.S. 398: 1934), p. 479.

Significance   The Court held in *United States Trust Company v. New Jersey* (431 U.S. 1: 1977) that a state must clearly demonstrate reasonableness and necessity when it alters a contract to which it is a party. This decision is a useful contemporary barometer of the relevance of the contract clause. The Court indicated that deference will generally be accorded legislative judgments as to what constitutes reasonable and necessary regulation vis-à-vis contractual interests. This is a position very consistent with the thrust of such cases as *Home Building and Loan Association v. Blaisdell* (290 U.S. 398: 1934). *Blaisdell* appeared to say that the contract clause was no longer a serious barrier to states acting in the public interest. But *United States Trust* said something a little different.

This decision revealed that the Court has not written the contract clause out of the Constitution, especially where states engage in unilateral alteration of contracts to which they are themselves a party. The Court concluded that the normal deference cannot apply when a "State's self-interest is at stake." That self-interest makes the state unable to fairly umpire the necessity and reasonableness of proposed legislative enactments that affect contract interests. The *United States Trust* decision clearly defines at least one kind of contract clause issue where heightened judicial scrutiny remains.

State Regulation of a Utility

Energy Reserves Group, Inc. v. Kansas Power and Light Company, 459 U.S. 400, 103 S.Ct. 697, 74 L.Ed. 2d 569 (1983)   Upheld state regulation of natural gas prices against claims of contract impairment. *Energy Reserves Group, Inc. v. Kansas Power and Light Company* involved a complex fact situation intertwining a private contract, a federal statute, and a state law. Kansas Power and Light (KPL) entered into two intrastate gas supply contracts with Energy Reserves Group, Inc. (ERG) in 1975. The contracts included a price escalator provision that increased the contract price for gas to a level fixed by governmental authority. There was also a price redetermination clause that gave ERG the option to have the price of gas adjusted no more than once every two years. Price increases of either kind required approval of the Kansas Corporation Commission before they could be passed on to consumers. In 1979, the Kansas legislature imposed price controls on the intrastate gas market under provisions of the new Natural Gas Policy Act, which extended federal price regulation of intrastate gas but permitted states to establish maximum prices for the first sale of gas produced in a state. The Kansas statute did not allow use of federal ceiling prices or use of other Kansas contract prices in applying the escalator or redetermination clauses. ERG notified KPL that prices would be raised in 1978 using the governmental price escalator clause. KPL did not pay the higher prices, and ERG attempted to terminate their contracts because the utility failed to use either the escalator or redetermination methods to increase prices. The Kansas courts held that the Kansas law did not constitute a violation of the contract clause. It also held that ERG was not automatically entitled to a price increase under terms of the federal act. The Supreme Court affirmed unanimously.

The opinion of the Court was authored by Justice Blackmun. He outlined the several criteria involved in reviewing contract clause claims such as this. The "threshold inquiry" involves whether the enactment impairs a contractual relationship. If so, the severity of the impairment "increases the level of scrutiny to which the legislation will be subjected." If impairment exists, the state regulation must have a "significant and legitimate public purpose." If such purpose is identified, the next inquiry is whether the adjustment of contract "rights and responsibilities" is reasonable and appropriate to that end. In determining impairment in this case, the Court noted that the parties are "operating in a heavily regulated industry," and that state authority to regulate natural gas prices is well established. Thus, ERG "knew its contractual rights were subject to alteration by state price regulation." The "very existence" of the escalator and redetermination clauses "indicates that the contracts were structured against the background of regulated gas prices." The Court concluded that ERG's "reasonable expectation" under the contracts had not been impaired.

Justice Blackmun then proceeded to discuss the legitimacy of the Kansas policy even though impairment had not been found. He indicated that the statute was based on and prompted by "significant and legitimate state interests." Kansas could reasonably have concluded that higher gas prices would cause hardships and then move to relieve those burdens. In addition to acting toward a "legitimate public purpose," the Court concluded that the means chosen to pursue these purposes were reasonable. Finally, the Court noted that the Kansas statute was a "temporary measure" that would expire when federal regulations terminated. In sum, the Court found no constitutional defect in the statute.

Chief Justice Burger and Justices Powell and Rehnquist chose not to comment on the legitimacy of the state interests as against the contracts. They felt the conclusion of no impairment was "dispositive," and that consideration of whether a violation would exist with impairment was "unnecessary." *See also* ALLIED STRUCTURAL STEEL COMPANY V. SPANNAUS (438 U.S. 234: 1978), p. 483.

Significance   *Energy Reserves Group, Inc. v. Kansas Power and Light Company* (459 U.S. 400: 1983) upheld a state regulation of natural gas prices that displaced contractually established price levels and price adjusting mechanisms. This decision is a direct outgrowth of the Court's holding in *Home Building and Loan Association v. Blaisdell* (290 U.S. 398: 1934, p. 479), in which the nonabsolute character of the contract clause was strongly asserted. An impairment of a contract does not, under the *Blaisdell* holding, "inexorably" produce a constitutional violation. The severity of the impairment must be scrutinized and viewed against the "significance and legitimacy" of the public purpose of the impairing action. The importance of *Energy Reserves Group* is that it pointed out two related factors that bear on this comparative consideration. The first is whether the area was already subject to substantial governmental regulation at the time the contract was entered. Prior regulation tends to suggest that the necessity to act on behalf of the public interest was already established. Second, what were the expectations of the parties to the contract? In other words, what did they expect the contract to protect? Given the heavy involvement of the government in natural gas pricing in this case, the contracting parties could not have reasonably expected insulation from further regulation, especially in the area of price controls. *Energy Reserves Group* clearly shows that states will not be prevented from regulation, particularly if utilities are involved, because the Court appears likely to presume the legitimacy of the public purpose served by such regulation.

10. *Leading Supreme Court Justices*

Hugo L. Black (1937–1971)   Hugo L. Black was born in a rural area of Alabama in 1886. His family settled in the community of Ashland, where Black received his early education. After attending Birmingham Medical College for a year, Black changed career direction and decided to pursue the law. He enrolled at the University of Alabama Law School at the age of 18. Upon graduation, he returned to Ashland and began his private practice. Shortly thereafter, Black moved to Birmingham and developed a practice around labor and personal injury law. For a time, Black served as a police court judge on a part-time basis. From 1915 to 1917, Black was the elected county prosecutor in Jefferson County, Alabama. After a brief period in the service during World War I, he resumed his private practice. In 1926, Black successfully ran for the United States Senate. He was to serve almost two full terms in that body before his appointment to the Supreme Court. During his tenure, Black was strongly supportive of the New Deal, especially employment regulations. Indeed, the Fair Labor Standards Act of 1938 had provisions much like those contained in an hours of work measure introduced by Black some five years earlier. Black was also highly supportive of President Franklin Roosevelt's "court-packing" proposal.

When the retirement of Justice Willis Van Devanter created a vacancy on the Court in 1937, Black had all the credentials sought by Roosevelt. Black was confirmed by the Senate by a 63–16 vote a little more than a month after his nomination. A month after confirmation, it was reported in the media that Justice Black had been a member of the Ku Klux Klan while in private practice in the early 1920s. Black responded in a national radio broadcast in which he acknowledged his association with the Klan, but indicated that he had long since resigned from the organization. The controversy soon subsided, and Black commenced a long and distinguished career on the Court. Black resigned from the Court in September 1971 after suffering a severe stroke. He died just eight days later. Black was replaced on the Court by Lewis F. Powell. *See also* SOUTHERN PACIFIC RAILROAD COMPANY V. ARIZONA (325 U.S. 761: 1945), p. 337; UNITED STATES V. SOUTH-EASTERN UNDERWRITERS' ASSOCIATION (322 U.S. 533: 1944), p. 334; YOUNGSTOWN SHEET AND TUBE COMPANY V. SAWYER (343 U.S. 579: 1952), p. 146.

Significance   Hugo L. Black was an intellectual power on the Supreme Court for 34 years. He was a self-made legal scholar of limitless energy and tenacity. Mild-mannered in personality, Black never forgot his modest origins and relentlessly sought to use the law to protect individual rights, especially for the poor and powerless. Such protection did not carry over to property rights, however, as can be seen in Black's response to economic regulation issues. He saw the federal commerce power over the economy as complete and unrestricted. He said in *United States v. South-Eastern Underwriters' Association* (322 U.S. 533: 1944) that a "heavy burden" rests with anyone asserting that the "plenary power" over commerce does not cover any particular local business activity where there may be a "chain of events which becomes interstate commerce." *South-Eastern Underwriters* involved bringing the insurance industry within the reach of the Sherman Antitrust Act. Black had a particularly strong impact in the field of antitrust, where he wrote numerous and powerful opinions.

At the same time, Black generally supported state regulatory initiatives. He rejected the view of substantive due process and felt the courts ought not to examine the reasonableness of legislative regulations, state or federal. Illustrative is his dissent in *Southern Pacific Railroad Company v. Arizona* (325 U.S. 761: 1945). Representatives, he said, "elected by the people to make their laws," as distinct from the courts, "can best determine the policies which govern the people." It was simply not for the courts to decide whether the state law regulating lengths of trains was a reasonable policy choice. A more comprehensive deference to legislative authority can be seen in the steel seizure case, *Youngstown Sheet and Tube Company v. Sawyer* (343 U.S. 579: 1952). Black concluded that no president had the authority to seize control of a segment of private industry without explicit congressional approval. The legislative judgment must prevail in all such situations regardless of the gravity of the emergency.

Black was better known, however, for his handling of civil liberties issues. He believed that the Bill of Rights in its entirety must be extended to the states. His classic exposition of the total incorporation view can be found in his dissent in *Adamson v. California* (332 U.S. 46: 1947). Throughout his tenure, Black held the states to the same constitutional standards as the federal government, and generally Black was highly protective of the procedural rights of the accused. He wrote, for example, a powerful majority opinion in *Gideon v. Wainwright* (372 U.S. 335: 1963), the decision that established that states must provide indigent felony defendants with the assistance of counsel. On First Amendment issues, Black was basically an absolutist, although not from the outset. He took literally the constitutional prohibition on abridgement of free expression, and categorically rejected such balancing tests as clear and present danger. Government, in Black's view, simply had no power to regulate substantive expression. Black consistently maintained this view in the political expression and association (national security) cases of the 1950s and 1960s.

This approach carried over to nonpolitical expression cases such as obscenity. While he personally found obscenity distasteful, he uniformly voted to invalidate regulation of it. In his later years on the

Court, Black found expression featuring the context or manner of expression very troublesome. While regulation could not be content-bound, Black usually rejected the notion that persons could say anything anywhere at any time, and he generally supported time, place, and manner restrictions. He wrote the Court's opinion in *Adderley v. Florida* (385 U.S. 39: 1965) which sustained trespass convictions of persons demonstrating on jail property. It was not the substance of the message, but rather where they chose to demonstrate that allowed the restriction.

Black eventually took a strongly separationist position on establishment questions, although he wrote the majority opinion in the parochial school transportation cost reimbursement policy upheld in *Everson v. Board of Education* (330 U.S. 1: 1947). Most noteworthy in representation of his strict separationist position are his anti–released time program opinion and his majority opinion in *Engel v. Vitale* (370 U.S. 421: 1962) in the case invalidating the New York Regent's school prayer.

Harry A. Blackmun (1971–   )   Justice Harry A. Blackmun was nominated to the Supreme Court by Richard Nixon in April 1970. He replaced Justice Abe Fortas, who had resigned in May 1969. Blackmun was the third Nixon nominee for the Fortas seat, as the Senate failed to confirm two earlier nominations, Clement F. Haynsworth, Jr., of South Carolina and G. Harrold Carswell of Florida. Blackmun was confirmed by the Senate without a dissenting vote. Blackmun was born in Nashville, Illinois, in 1908, but spent most of his young life in St. Paul, Minnesota. It was in grade school that Blackmun first met Warren Burger, and the two became close friends. Blackmun did his undergraduate work as a scholarship student at Harvard University. He graduated Phi Beta Kappa, majoring in mathematics. Choosing law over medicine, Blackmun went on to Harvard Law School and graduated in 1932. While at Harvard, he took a course from Felix Frankfurter and was influenced by the Frankfurter judicial self-restraint viewpoint of constitutional adjudication.

Following law school, Blackmun returned to Minnesota, where he served 18 months as clerk to U.S. Circuit Judge John B. Sanborn. After a year on the faculty of the Mitchell College of Law in St. Paul, he entered private practice, joining a large and prestigious firm in Minneapolis. Blackmun's practice specialized in estates, taxation, and civil litigation. He continued to teach on a part-time basis during this period. In 1950 Blackmun took the position of resident legal counsel for the Mayo Clinic in Rochester, Minnesota, a post he held for the nine years immediately preceding his first judgeship.

A seat became vacant on the United States Court of Appeals for the Eighth Circuit in 1959 upon the retirement of Judge Sanborn, the judge for whom Blackmun had clerked a quarter-century earlier. Possessing the appropriate Republican credentials, Blackmun was appointed to this seat by President Eisenhower. Blackmun's record as a court of appeals judge was generally conservative and reflected commitment to self-restraint. He was also highly regarded as a legal scholar and was known for thorough and tightly crafted opinions. *See also* WARREN E. BURGER, p. 503; JUDICIAL SELF-RESTRAINT, p. 627.

Significance   It was expected that Justice Harry A. Blackmun would become a second Warren Burger on the Court. Indeed, the two were often termed the "Minnesota Twins" after Blackmun joined his longtime friend on the Court in 1971. And it is true, Blackmun has generally taken a conservative course since his appointment, but his flexibility and independence must be noted. He has shown an inclination to separate himself on certain issues from Burger and the conservative majority even to the point of joining the Court's two most liberal members, Justices Brennan and Marshall. The dominant value in most instances is judicial self-restraint. Blackmun is fundamentally committed to legislative resolution of major policy issues, even if those judgments are incompatible with his own preferences. His view of limited judicial intervention is well reflected in his dissent in *Furman v. Georgia* (408 U.S. 238: 1971), where the Court struck down the sentencing procedures of a state capital punishment law. Blackmun said that "I yield to no one in the depth of my distaste, antipathy, and, indeed, abhorrence, for the death penalty. Were I a legislator, I would vote against the death penalty." "But," he went on, "I do not sit on these cases . . . as a legislator." The judiciary "cannot allow our personal preferences as to the wisdom of legislation and congressional action to guide our judicial decision in cases such as these."

His record in rights of the accused cases is generally conservative. He has not been willing to extend the exclusionary rule beyond the trial stage in criminal cases and has subscribed to some of the Burger Court's highly critical comments on the rule itself. Neither has he favored extension of the *Miranda* rationale, and he can usually be found sustaining convictions out of which come Fourth or Fifth Amendment challenges.

There are, however, areas where Blackmun has clearly separated himself from conservative positions. Three stand out in particular: aid to parochial schools, equal protection, and abortion. Blackmun can typically be found among those opposing aid to nonpublic schools. For example, in one of his first establishment cases, *Lemon v. Kurtzman* (403 U.S. 602: 1971), Blackmun voted to strike down a state program that supplemented salaries paid to teachers of secular subjects in nonpublic schools. More recently, he opposed the state tax deduction for public and private school expenses in *Mueller v. Allen* (463 U.S. 388: 1983). Blackmun has also been at the forefront of extending First Amendment for commercial speech, a category of expression that advertises a product or service and that was previously subject to governmental regulation (see *Bigelow v. Virginia*, 421 U.S. 809: 1975; and *Virginia State Board of Pharmacy v. Virginia Citizens Consumer Council, Inc.*, 425 U.S. 748: 1976). Blackmun has also departed from the conservative bloc on a number of equal protection issues. He has frequently voted to invalidate classification schemes that discriminate against women, the poor, and illegitimate children (see, for example, *Frontiero v. Richardson*, 411 U.S. 667: 1973; *James v. Valtierra*, 402 U.S. 137: 1971; and *Weber v. Aetna Casualty and Surety Company*, 406 U.S. 164: 1972).

Blackmun's greatest impact, however, has come in the policy area of abortion rights. He authored the majority opinion in the landmark decision of *Roe v. Wade* (410 U.S. 113: 1973), which established the right to abortion. Ever since, he has been an outspoken opponent of attempts to regulate access to abortions (see, for example, *City of Akron v. Akron Center for Reproductive Health, Inc.*, 462 U.S. 416: 1983), and restrictions on public funding of abortion costs (see, for example, Blackmun's dissents in *Beal v. Doe*, 432 U.S. 438: 1977 and *Harris v. McRae*, 448 U.S. 297: 1980). In the latter instance, Blackmun forcefully argued that the poor are discriminated against in their pursuit of a protected right merely because of their poverty. While on balance Blackmun remains a conservative, he is not an ideological captive. He has clearly demonstrated an independence of thought that has resulted in his taking strong liberal positions on important Court decisions.

Joseph P. Bradley (1870–1892)   Joseph P. Bradley was born in Berne, New York, in 1813. His family lived on a small farm, and their limited financial resources forced Bradley to work hard as a boy. He was able to attend school for short periods, but spent a great deal of the time educating himself. He became acquainted with a local clergyman who was sufficiently impressed with Bradley's desire for an education that he sponsored his admission to Rutgers University. Three years later, Bradley graduated. Through contacts established at Rutgers, Bradley was able to read law in the office of the collector of the Port of Newark, New Jersey, and he was admitted to the bar in 1839. He then developed a successful practice specializing in corporate law. Among his clients were several railroads. His professional influence was enhanced in 1844 when he married the daughter of the chief justice of the New Jersey Supreme Court. Prior to the Civil War, Bradley switched his party affiliation from Whig to Republican. Late in 1860, Bradley went to Washington to attempt to broker a compromise on issues dividing the North and South. To that end, he drafted two constitutional amendments addressing various aspects of the slavery issue. When war broke out, Bradley sought election to the U.S. House as a strongly pro-Union Republican.

In 1867, Justice James Wayne died. To prevent President Johnson from replacing Wayne, the Congress reduced the size of the Court. In 1869, Congress increased the Court's size back to nine. Early in 1870, President Grant nominated Bradley to one of the vacancies (Grant appointed William Strong to the other vacancy on the same day). Bradley was confirmed by a 46–9 vote six weeks later. He served on the Court until his death early in 1892. The vacancy created by his death was filled by George Shiras. *See also* BROWN V. HOUSTON (114 U.S. 622: 1885), p. 300; CIVIL RIGHTS CASES (109 U.S. 3: 1883), p. 259; LEGAL TENDER CASES (12 Wallace 457: 1871), p. 381; SLAUGHTERHOUSE CASES (16 Wallace 36: 1873), p. 417.

Significance   Joseph P. Bradley was one of the Court's three prominent and distinguished justices during the period from the Civil War to the turn of the century, the others being Stephen Field and Samuel Miller. He was a first-rate lawyer, possessed enormous intellect, and is still highly regarded for the quality of his legal exposition. Bradley subscribed to the nationalism of the Republicans of his time, yet he was also sympathetic to the exercise of state power for the regulation of business and property. These views were tempered, however, by his extensive ties to the business community prior to his appointment. Indeed, he had earned the reputation of being one of the country's best railroad lawyers during his years of private practice. In other words, Bradley was an able man whose background provided a unique blend of sensitivities that were reflected in his 24 years on the Court.

The first issue to confront Bradley as a member of the Court was the legal tender question. It has been asserted that Bradley was put on the Court specifically for the purpose of reversing the Court's decision to invalidate the legal tender acts. There is persuasive evidence, however, that the Bradley nomination was in process long before the first legal tender decision. Nonetheless, Bradley did cast the decisive vote in the *Legal Tender Cases* (12 Wallace 457: 1871), where the Court upheld extensive federal power to regulate monetary matters.

Bradley was also confronted early in his judicial career with issues associated with the newly ratified Fourteenth Amendment. The first encounter for the Court was the *Slaughterhouse Cases* (16 Wallace 36: 1873), a group of cases that had come before Bradley in 1870 in his role as circuit judge. The Supreme Court refused to use the Fourteenth Amendment to invalidate a state-created slaughterhouse monopoly.

Bradley dissented, finding the Court's interpretation of federal authority under the amendment far too narrow and restrictive. Bradley's dissent was easily distinguished from that of Justice Field, who sought to free private property from any form of regulation through application of the due process clause. In fact, Bradley was generally supportive of state regulation of business, including railroad rates. He was responsible for aiding Chief Justice Waite in the development, in *Munn v. Illinois* (94 U.S. 113: 1877), of the powerful doctrine which permitted public regulation of property "clothed" in the public interest. *Munn* became Bradley's baseline decision on economic due process, and he vigorously resisted efforts, especially by Justice Field, to develop a substantive due process that would allow the Court to examine the substantive reasonableness of state regulations of property. By 1890, Bradley had lost this battle and had to be content issuing strong dissents against this form of judicial activism (see, for example, *Chicago, Milwaukee and St. Paul Railway Company v. Minnesota*, 134 U.S. 418: 1890).

Bradley was further distinguished from the laissez-fairists in that he supported full exercise of the federal commerce power. At the same time, he did not define commerce in such broad terms as to preclude the exercise of state regulatory power. In *Brown v. Houston* (114 U.S. 622: 1885), for example, he wrote for the Court upholding a state tax on all property within the state, even goods arriving from another state. Bradley said, once a commodity has "come to its place of rest, for final disposal or use," it becomes "part of the general mass of property in the state" and may be taxed by the state.

Although Bradley generally construed the Fourteenth Amendment broadly, there was a significant exception in the area of civil rights policy. He did not view the amendment as conferring broad power to Congress to protect civil rights. It was Bradley who authored the Court's opinion in the *Civil Rights Cases* (109 U.S. 3: 1883) striking down the Civil Rights Act of 1875. The act sought to regulate private acts of discrimination, a target Bradley thought beyond the power of Congress. Rather, said Bradley, the amendment only permitted Congress to correct discrimination to which the state was a party. Through the creation of the state action doctrine, Bradley severely restricted the utility of the Fourteenth Amendment for the protection of civil rights. With the exception of the *Civil Rights Cases*, Bradley's positions have generally withstood a century of scrutiny and remain timely, insightful, practical, and balanced.

Louis D. Brandeis (1916–1939)   Louis Brandeis was born in 1856 in Louisville, Kentucky, to Jewish parents who had emigrated from Bohemia to America in the wake of the 1848 Revolution. His father was a successful grain merchant in Louisville. Brandeis enrolled at the Harvard Law School at the age of 18. He worked hard to overcome the handicaps of being a Southerner and a Jew, but never really succeeded. Even at the time of his appointment to the Supreme Court by Woodrow Wilson in 1916, an influential segment of the Boston legal and commercial community felt the combination of an economic reformer and a Jew was too much to tolerate.

As an economic reformer, Brandeis was largely responsible for the trust-busting aspects of Wilson's New Freedom. He believed that excessive size produced economic waste. He lobbied for reform of the banking industry and was one of the draftsmen of the Federal Reserve Act, which initiated national control over the distribution of currency and credit. Brandeis strongly believed in scientific management, the efficiency-oriented program created by Frederick Winslow Taylor, even though it was opposed by labor unions whose members Brandeis wanted to liberate from their industrial slavery.

Competing impulses formed the core of Brandeis's philosophy as an associate justice of the Supreme Court. The impulses were primarily those of freedom and self-restraint. Excess size, inequities, or inefficiencies choked or stifled individual initiative, he believed, but success and accomplishment were ascribed to self-abnegation and a conservation of human resources. Brandeis found industrial laborers his "most congenial company," and regarded the industrious among them as heroes, although he was infuriated to see them smoking cigarettes.

The central theme in Brandeis's interpretation of the law was the importance of empirical observation. When confronted by a legal problem as a lawyer or as a justice, Brandeis sought to gather facts, and his great powers of organization and synthesis made fact analysis one of his special arts. *See also* OLIVER WENDELL HOLMES, p. 521; *MULLER V. OREGON* (211 U.S. 539: 1908), p. 431.

Significance   Louis D. Brandeis was a leader in the movement that sought to shift the emphasis of law from individual rights to social realities, a movement that advocated adaption of the law to changing social needs. A milestone in this aspect of his legal career was his *Muller v. Oregon* (211 U.S. 539) brief in 1908, which argued that long working hours are detrimental to the health and morals of women. This point of view began a new trend in legal thought, including the development of the "Brandeis Brief." In support of Oregon's ten-hour law for women, Brandeis offered two pages of argument and a hundred pages of supporting sociological data.

Sociological jurisprudence refuses to consider a case as merely a contest between abstract legal concepts. It rather uses a case as an opportunity to look at the sociological facts of modern life, which might indicate that the old freedom of contract doctrine is inadequate. Under the freedom of contract doctrine, employers and employees are free to buy and sell their goods or services on terms they choose, deriving this right from the Fourteenth Amendment's protection against state interference with liberty and property. Brandeis, and with him Roscoe Pound and Theodore Roosevelt, argued that the doctrine is unsound for two reasons: (1) it ignores new conceptions of the relation of property to human welfare; and (2) it exemplifies as artificial the process of judicial reasoning in which predetermined beliefs are developed "in the teeth of the actual facts." Louis D. Brandeis gave to American jurisprudence the belief that considerations of social welfare can transcend the exercise of individual rights.

William J. Brennan (1956–)   William J. Brennan, Jr., was born in Newark, New Jersey, in 1906. He received his B.S. from the Wharton School of Finance of the University of Pennsylvania in 1928. Three years later, he obtained his law degree from Harvard University. He joined a leading Newark law firm following graduation and cultivated an expertise in labor law. Brennan was one of a number of attorneys who worked on comprehensive reform on the New Jersey state court system. He left his successful private practice to accept appointment to the newly established New Jersey Superior Court in 1949. His performance was sufficiently distinguished to earn his elevation to the appellate division of the Superior Court the following year. Two years later, Brennan was named to the New Jersey Supreme Court. In 1956, Justice Sherman Minton left the United States Supreme Court. President Eisenhower gave Brennan a recess appointment in October 1956 despite Brennan's nominal Democratic party affiliation. Brennan was confirmed by the Senate the following year. *See also* BAKER V. CARR (369 U.S. 186: 1962), p. 123; THURGOOD MARSHALL, p. 533.

Significance   Justice William J. Brennan is one of the three Burger Court holdovers from the Warren Court. At the outset of his tenure on the Court, Brennan tended toward moderate positions on most issues. Through the early 1960s, Brennan could not have been characterized as a liberal or a judicial activist. Reflective of his more cautious approach is *Roth v. United States* (354 U.S. 476: 1957), a decision that established new definitional standards for obscenity. Brennan spoke for the majority, saying that the First Amendment was not intended to protect every utterance and that obscenity was not protected speech. As the Warren Court moved further into the 1960s, Brennan took more liberal positions and subscribed to greater judicial intervention to safeguard individual rights. It was Brennan who wrote for the Court in the landmark case of *Baker v. Carr* (369 U.S. 186: 1962). The decision held that legislative apportionment was an appropriate matter for judicial consideration. The decision opened the door for extensive federal court activity on the matter and resulted in comprehensive redistricting based on the "one person, one vote" standard. Brennan has consistently endorsed ongoing monitoring of legislative district populations since.

Brennan is not a literalist and has been receptive to expanding the scope of constitutional protections by inference. For example, Brennan joined the Warren Court majority in *Griswold v. Connecticut* (381 U.S. 479: 1965), the birth control case in which the Court established a constitutional "right" of privacy. Similarly, in *Plyler v. Doe* (457 U.S. 202: 1982), Brennan wrote for the Court as it brought education within the "framework of equality embodied in the Equal Protection Clause." Brennan has also subscribed to expanding equal protection coverage to such classifications as gender and wealth. With Justice Marshall, he can typically be found supporting claims of unconstitutional discrimination based on race as well as other bases.

Brennan has become the Court's most demanding justice on First Amendment issues. The free press and establishment clauses are illustrative. Brennan's opinion in *New York Times v. Sullivan* (376 U.S. 254: 1964) established some insulation for the press from libel actions. The Court held that a public official could not recover damages for defamation relating to conduct in office without proof that statements were made with "actual malice." Brennan also joined the Court majority in voting to dissolve the injunction against the *New York Times* restraining publication of the Pentagon Papers (*New York Times v. United States*, 403 U.S. 713: 1971). In addition, Brennan supported the concept of newsperson's privilege in *Branzburg v. Hayes* (408 U.S. 665: 1972). On establishment issues, Brennan has been strongly separationist. He was part of the Warren Court majority striking down both the prayer and Bible-reading exercises in public schools in the 1960s (see *Engel v. Vitale*, 370 U.S. 421: 1962; and *School District of Abington Township v. Schempp*, 374 U.S. 203: 1963). He took essentially the same position more than 20 years later as the Court invalidated Alabama's "moment of silence" policy in *Wallace v. Jaffree* (472 U.S. 38: 1985). Brennan has also consistently opposed virtually all forms of aid to nonpublic educational institutions, including state income tax deductions for all educational costs for both public and private schools (*Mueller v. Allen*, 463 U.S. 388: 1983).

Finally, Brennan has typically taken liberal positions in rights of the accused cases. Brennan fully supported the Warren Court in its extension of federal constitutional guarantees to the states, and was part of the majority in such cases as *Mapp v. Ohio* (367 U.S. 643: 1961), which applied the exclusionary rule to state criminal trials. As a member of the Burger Court, Brennan has more often been on the dissenting side of cases involving criminal rights. Reflective are his dissents in those decisions modifying *Miranda v. Arizona* (384 U.S. 436: 1966) such as *Harris v. New York* (401 U.S. 222: 1971) and *North Carolina v. Butler* (441 U.S. 369: 1979). Similarly, Brennan has categorically rejected use of the death penalty, a position that usually places him in the minority on the Burger Court. As the composition of the Court has changed beginning with the appointment of Burger, Brennan has moved from typically being among the majority to virtually always being in the minority. Nonetheless, he and Marshall continue to act as the spokesmen for liberal activism on the Burger Court.

Warren E. Burger (1969–1986)   Warren Earl Burger was born in St. Paul, Minnesota, in 1907. Unable to afford being a full-time student, Burger worked his way through the University of Minnesota and St. Paul College of Law on a part-time basis. He graduated magna cum laude from law school in 1931. He joined a firm in St. Paul and maintained a general private practice until 1953. He also retained a part-time faculty position at St. Paul College of Law during this period. At the same time, Burger became involved in Republican politics in Minnesota and worked extensively on the 1938 gubernatorial campaign of Harold Stassen. Burger continued his association with Stassen and was floor manager of Stassen's presidential bids in 1948 and 1952. It was at the 1948 Republican nominating convention that Burger met Herbert Brownell, then campaign manager for New York Governor Thomas Dewey.

In 1952, Burger shifted his support from Stassen to Eisenhower at a critical point, thus assisting Eisenhower to secure the nomination from Senator Robert Taft. Following Eisenhower's election, Brownell became United States attorney general. He proceeded to name Burger an assistant attorney general and head of the Civil Division of the Justice Department. In 1955, Eisenhower nominated Burger to a seat on the United States Court of Appeals for the District of Columbia, a position he held until his elevation to the Supreme Court in 1969. As a court of appeals judge, Burger demonstrated a clearly conservative orientation. He was particularly so on cases involving rights of those accused of crimes. Indeed, Burger was openly critical of the direction taken by the Warren Court. In 1969, Chief Justice Warren retired from the Court. President Nixon, who had emphasized the need to change the course of the Court during his presidential campaign, nominated Burger for the chief justiceship. The Senate confirmed the nomination in a 74–3 vote. Burger retired from the Court at the end of the 1985 term. *See also*

JUDICIAL SELF-RESTRAINT, p. 627; *UNITED STATES V. NIXON* (418 U.S. 683: 1974), p. 153.

Significance   Warren Burger was chosen chief justice in order to lead the Court to different policy decisions than had been issued by the Warren Court. An articulated priority of Richard Nixon's presidential campaign was to neutralize the Warren Court's expansion of rights afforded those accused of crimes. Burger has clearly performed as expected in this policy area. More generally, Nixon sought a "strict constructionist," someone whose judicial philosophy would fundamentally differ from Warren's activism. To a substantial degree, Burger has satisfied this priority as well, but not entirely. Rather, the Court and Burger himself have engaged in selective activism. Generally, however, Burger saw the Court's authority in the limited terms of a judicial conservative. In *Plyler v. Doe* (457 U.S. 702: 1982), the Court struck down a state law that denied public education to children in the country illegally. The decision was based on equal protection grounds. Burger dissented, saying that the Constitution "does not provide a cure for every social ill, nor does it vest judges with a mandate to remedy every social problem."

In the area of criminal rights, Burger has been the outspoken hardliner he was expected to be. He has supported use of capital punishment by states not only where sentencer discretion is guided, but he would have also permitted mandatory death sentences as well as use of the penalty for offenses other than murder. Burger was a consistent and vocal critic of the exclusionary rule, referring to it in *Stone v. Powell* (428 U.S. 465: 1976) as a "Draconian, discredited device." Burger has also consistently supported limiting by interpretation application of the *Miranda* doctrine (see, for example, *Harris v. New York*, 401 U.S. 222: 1971, and *North Carolina v. Butler*, 441, U.S. 369, 1979). When his Court has reversed criminal convictions, Burger was usually found in dissent. He was, on those occasions, known to offer broadly critical comment such as that in *Brewer v. Williams* (430 U.S. 387: 1977), where he said that the majority's holding "ought to be intolerable in any society which purports to call itself an organized society."

Burger also had great impact on First Amendment issues. His Court took a decidedly more accommodating position in the religion cases, and Burger led the way. He said in *Walz v. New York City Tax Commission* (397 U.S. 664: 1970) that the Court ought take a position of "benevolent neutrality" when reviewing religion cases. This position generally favors religion over nonreligion. He also wrote the Court's opinion in the case that permitted the Amish exemption from a state compulsory education law *(Wisconsin v. Yoder,* 406 U.S. 205: 1972). It was Burger who articulated new definitional standards of obscenity in

Miller v. California (413 U.S. 15: 1973), a decision that encouraged more aggressive state and local regulation of obscenity.

Likewise, Burger's equal protection record was conservative. He authored the first important busing opinion in *Swann v. Charlotte-Mecklenburg Board of Education* (402 U.S. 1: 1971), upholding the remedial authority of lower federal courts where constitutional violations are found in public education. On the other had, he invalidated a busing order in *Milliken v. Bradley* (418 U.S. 717: 1974), saying that interdistrict remedies could only be ordered when preceded by findings of interdistrict violations. This seriously limited the remedial authority of lower court judges. Burger also joined the Court's decision in *Washington v. Davis* (426 U.S. 229: 1976) requiring a showing of intent in employment discrimination cases. He also rejected use of quotas as a means of affirmative action in *Regents of the University of California v. Bakke* (438 U.S. 265: 1978). Similarly, Burger resisted extension of the equal protection clause to classifications other than race. While he occasionally supported claims of impermissible gender discrimination, for example, he rejected the view that gender is a "suspect" class or that gender classification should be subject to more demanding standards than other legislative enactments.

Burger was a highly visible chief justice. He tended to assign the majority opinion-writing task to himself in major cases. Certainly his executive privilege opinion in *United States v. Nixon* (418 U.S. 683: 1974) is illustrative. He also distinguished himself by his efforts on behalf of better judicial management and general reform of the judicial process. He was, however, unable to forge a lasting coalition of justices, even with changed personnel from that of the Warren Court, to establish a clear ideological direction for the Court.

Benjamin N. Cardozo (1932–1938)   Benjamin Nathan Cardozo was born in New York City in 1870. Cardozo's father was a judge in New York who eventually gained a seat on the state supreme court. He became entangled in the machine politics of Tammany Hall and ultimately resigned from the court rather than face impeachment. Cardozo was raised in the shadow of this situation, and from early youth was a relative isolate. Much of his schooling, for example, took the form of home instruction. Cardozo entered Columbia at the age of 15 and graduated first in his class in 1889. He earned an M.A. the following year and entered Columbia Law School, but he never completed a law degree. He was admitted to the bar in 1891 and began a lengthy appellate practice with his brother. In 1913, a challenge was mounted against Tammany Hall, and Cardozo agreed to be a reform candidate for the state supreme court. He won election and began what was to become a lifelong judicial career. Shortly after his election, he was assigned to the state court of appeals to help it clear its backlog. Although the assignment was intended to be temporary, Cardozo remained there and was elected to a full term in 1917. He later became chief judge of the court and established a national reputation. He also lectured extensively during his tenure on the state court, and his published writings and lectures became widely read and highly regarded.

In 1932, Justice Oliver W. Holmes resigned and Cardozo's name was among those suggested to President Hoover as a replacement. In unprecedented numbers, endorsements came from political figures of both parties, the legal profession, university faculty, and various other sources. Hoover hesitated, however, as two members of the Supreme Court were already from New York (Stone and Hughes). Hoover became convinced of the extent of support for Cardozo when Justice Stone offered to resign from the Court to allow Cardozo's appointment. Cardozo was confirmed by the Senate in a voice vote shortly thereafter. Cardozo served on the Court for little more than six years, but nonetheless left his mark. He died in July 1938, and the vacancy created by his death was filled by Justice Felix Frankfurter. *See also* CARTER V. CARTER COAL COMPANY (298 U.S. 238: 1936), p. 317; SCHECHTER POULTRY CORPORATION V. UNITED STATES (295 U.S. 495: 1935), pp. 189, 315.

Significance   Benjamin Cardozo joined the Court on the strength of unprecedented support. No president has ever been subjected to more breadth of pressure to name a particular person to the Court than Hoover was in Cardozo's case. Although a state appellate judge, Cardozo had a national reputation, and the acclaim he commanded made Hoover's selection of him inevitable. The high regard for his performance as a jurist was enhanced by his tenure, albeit brief, on the Supreme Court. He is also regarded as one of the country's foremost legal scholars with his work, especially *The Nature of the Judicial Process*, still viewed as classic discussion. When Cardozo joined the Court, he immediately aligned himself with the minority bloc of Justices Stone and Brandeis. Cardozo regarded Holmes as the personification of the ideal jurist. Like Holmes, Cardozo believed that the legislative branch possessed broad discretion for responding to societal needs. On reviewing legislative initiatives, courts must not inquire into the motives for legislative action or the wisdom of legislative judgment. This to Cardozo was a fundamental aspect of judicial philosophy. Accordingly, he categorically rejected the highly restrictive approach taken by his anti–New Deal colleagues. Thus Cardozo's approach to the New Deal legislation was different from that of Brandeis, who, while endorsing judicial deference to legislative judgment, also philosophically embraced the economic and political substance of the New Deal.

Cardozo saw the federal commerce power as broad and almost without fail could be found in support of its exercise. At the same time, he did not see regulation of commerce as exclusively federal. He joined the Court in striking down the Live Poultry Code in *Schechter Poultry Corporation v. United States* (295 U.S. 495: 1935) not only because of excessive delegation of legislative power to the executive, but because the application here was too far removed from interstate commerce. Although he recognized state authority over intrastate aspects of commerce, state power could be used to interfere with the free flow of interstate trade. In *Baldwin v. G.A.F. Seelig, Inc.* (294 U.S. 511: 1935), for example, he wrote for the Court, striking down a state law that imposed price regulations on milk imported from another area. Following the Court's "turnaround" prompted by the threat of "Court-packing," Cardozo became part of the majority for the brief time he remained on the Court. Cardozo was assigned the task of offering the Court's opinion in *Steward Machine Company v. Davis* (301 U.S. 548: 1937), the decision that upheld the unemployment compensation sections of the Social Security Act. Cardozo's opinion held the national taxing power to be extensive and broad and not inappropriately used to establish unemployment protection from the national level. The problem, he said, was national in scope.

Possibly Cardozo's most important opinion addressed the issue of applicability of the federal Bill of Rights to the states. In *Palko v. Connecticut* (302 U.S. 319: 1937), Cardozo suggested that some rights itemized in the Bill of Rights were "fundamental" because they were so deeply "rooted in the traditions and conscience of our people." Those protections ranked as fundamental also applied to the states through the due process clause of the Fourteenth Amendment. Though judgments as to which rights ought to be drawn through the due process language have changed, the Court has never departed from the "selective incorporation" approach set out by Cardozo. Cardozo is recognized as a great jurist, one who had substantial impact on our constitutional development despite his brief tenure on the Court.

Benjamin R. Curtis (1851–1857)

Benjamin Robbins Curtis was born in Watertown, Massachusetts, in 1809. He entered Harvard University in 1825 and graduated four years later. He entered Harvard Law School immediately following graduation, but left before receiving his degree to take over a law practice. While he built a successful practice, he did return to Harvard to complete his degree. In 1834, Curtis returned to Boston and joined a prominent firm. In 1849, he was elected to the state legislature, where he introduced a resolution to establish a commission charged with reform of state judicial procedures. Curtis himself chaired the commission, which produced significant legal reform in the state. This achievement enhanced Curtis's already substantial public reputation, and he was returned to the legislature in 1851. Curtis, like much of the Boston establishment, was a Whig and a staunch ally of Daniel Webster. In 1851, Justice Levi Woodbury died, creating a vacancy in the position on the Court informally designated for New England. Webster, secretary of state in the Fillmore adminstration, strongly urged the selection of Curtis. Fillmore submitted his name, and he was confirmed by the Senate two weeks later.

Curtis served on the Court for just six terms, a tenure shortened by the intense differences among the justices over the slavery issue. Curtis and a number of his colleagues were often at odds, but it was the *Dred Scott* case (he was one of the two justices dissenting from the Court's decision) that ultimately led to his resignation from the Court. He was replaced by Nathan Clifford. Curtis returned to Boston, where he resumed a highly successful private practice. He remained politically visible, however. He often represented clients before the Supreme Court, and although he was a Unionist, he was very critical of Lincoln's policies during the Civil War. In 1868, Curtis was one of the legal counsel to President Andrew Johnson during his impeachment proceedings. The effort to remove Johnson fell a vote short in the Senate, and he retained the presidency. He subsequently offered Curtis the position of United States attorney general, but Curtis preferred to remain in Boston. Curtis maintained his law practice until his death in 1874. *See also* COOLEY V. BOARD OF PORT WARDENS (12 Howard 299: 1851), p. 298; DRED SCOTT V. SANDFORD (19 Howard 393: 1857), p. 91.

Significance   Benjamin R. Curtis was a Boston Whig, and as such, fully embraced the nationalism and conservatism exhibited by Federalist predecessors like John Marshall. With his political ally Daniel Webster, Curtis saw the slavery issue as one that threatened the very future of the country. Preservation of the Union was paramount to Curtis. He found the positions taken by both abolitionists and freesoilers excessive and counterproductive. Like Webster, Curtis was pragmatic and willing to strike a compromise. Illustrative was his outspoken support of the Compromise of 1850 and endorsement of the Fugitive Slave Act, including uniformly vigorous enforcement of the controversial statute while discharging his circuit court duties.

It is not surprising that the case that contributed to his early retirement from the Court was *Dred Scott v. Sandford* (19 Howard 393: 1857). The case involved the citizenship status of Scott, who claimed that residence on free soil had made him free. A narrow decision based upon a recent precedent could have been rendered, but this did not happen. For a variety of reasons, the ruling was unnecessarily broad, and altogether ill-advised. Chief Justice Taney's opinion for the majority held that blacks could not be citizens and thus could not sue in federal courts. Further, Taney ruled the Missouri Compromise invalid on the ground that Congress could not regulate slaves in the territories. Curtis issued a blistering dissent, arguing that blacks had been citizens in a number of states in 1787 and therefore were citizens of the United States as well. Among the privileges of such citizenship was the ability to sue in federal court. Curtis also offered powerful support for congressional power to prohibit slavery in the territories. The dissent itself strained relations with his colleagues on the Court. Curtis aggravated the matter by releasing his dissent and a copy of Taney's opinion to the press. He took this action without informing his colleagues, and the action was generally regarded as undertaken for partisan reasons. Yet even without the irreparable internal conflict that arose out of *Dred Scott*, it is likely Curtis would not have remained on the Court much longer. He disliked the travel associated with his circuit duties, as he was kept from his family for long periods. He also missed the level of income he had commanded in private practice. *Dred Scott*, however, was the final straw.

Despite his short tenure on the Court, Curtis is highly regarded for the quality of his judgment as well as his written opinions. Illustrative of both qualities is his opinion in *Cooley v. Board of Port Wardens* (12 Howard 299: 1851). The principal issue in the case was the extent to which states possessed authority over interstate commerce. The Marshall Court had essentially seen this power as exclusively federal, while the Taney Court favored concurrent jurisdiction. Curtis forged a pragmatic compromise and developed the doctrine of selective exclusiveness. Because commerce "embraces a vast field" containing various unlike subjects, an absolute rule would "lose sight of the nature of the subjects of this power." Some subjects are "imperatively demanding of a single uniform rule," while others demand the diversity that comes from local regulation. In the former instance, federal control is exclusive. Where no such uniformity is appropriate, the states may regulate. Thus *Cooley* established a flexible approach to resolution of this troublesome commerce issue. The doctrine was the product of Curtis's pragmatism and intellectual power. It is unfortunate that circumstances did not permit Curtis to serve a more extended tenure on the Court.

William O. Douglas (1939–1975)   William O. Douglas was nominated for the Supreme Court by Franklin Roosevelt as successor to Justice Louis Brandeis in 1939. Douglas was 40 years of age at the time of his nomination, making him the youngest nominee in more than 125 years. In gaining appointment to the Supreme Court, Douglas overcame long odds. Born into extreme poverty, Douglas lost his father when only 6 years of age. Douglas also suffered from polio. Despite the obstacles, Douglas was able to work his way through Whitman College in his home state of Washington and graduate with honors. After graduation, he traveled across the country in freight cars, frequenting hobo jungles. He arrived in New York City with but six cents to his name. Douglas never lost an acute sensitivity for the poor and powerless (see, for example, his concurring opinion in the capital punishment case of *Furman v. Georgia*, 408 U.S. 238: 1972). After a short period as a schoolteacher, Douglas entered Columbia Law School, where he eventually graduated second in his class in 1925. He spent the next several years dividing his time between a private practice in which he specialized in corporate finance and part-time teaching at Columbia Law School. Douglas pursued teaching full-time in 1928, when he took a position as a member of the law faculty at Yale. There he further developed his expertise in corporate law and finance. As a recognized expert, he was asked to do some investigative work for the Securities and Exchange Commission (SEC). In 1936, Roosevelt appointed Douglas to the commission, and he became chair the following year.

During his time with the SEC, Douglas became part of the Roosevelt inner circle, and he was a natural candidate for the Supreme Court when the Brandeis seat opened. At the time of Justice Douglas's retirement in 1975, he had served on the Court more than 36 years, the longest tenure of any justice. He was replaced on the Court by Justice John Paul Stevens.

Significance   Justice William O. Douglas was an ardent New Dealer, and he was appointed primarily to solidify judicial support for the economic policies of the New Deal. From the outset, Douglas favored expanded use of federal power for regulation of the national economy. He also consistently supported initiatives from the state level that attempted to regulate economic activity. In *Southern Pacific Railroad Company v. Arizona* (325 U.S. 761: 1945), for example, he urged (in a dissenting opinion) that the Court not invalidate state regulations on commerce clause grounds without explicit direction from Congress. Regarded as the Court's expert on corporate law and finance, Douglas authored a number of opinions dealing with complex antitrust issues, securities practices, utility rate making, and other financial issues. It is his record in the area of individual rights, however, for which he will be best remembered. By the time he left the Court in 1975, Douglas had become an absolutist on the subject of individual rights.

Douglas did not immediately demonstrate such commitment to these issues. Indeed, he subscribed to use of the "clear and present danger" test in expression, and could generally be described as a "balancer." He upheld compulsory flag salute exercises over challenge by religious minorities such as the Jehovah's Witnesses in *Minersville School District v. Gobitis* (310 U.S. 586: 1940), supported state reimbursement of costs for transporting children to parochial schools in *Everson v. Board of Education* (330 U.S. 1: 1947), and wrote a highly "accommodationist" church-state majority opinion in *Zorach v. Clauson* (343 U.S. 306: 1952). Through the decade of the 1940s, it is safe to say that Justices Murphy and Rutledge rather than Douglas were the most strongly civil libertarian. Douglas's position began to change with the political expression and association cases in the 1950s. From a minority position (typically with Justice Black), Douglas wrote assertive free expression opinions in such cases as *Dennis v. United States* (341 U.S. 494: 1951) and *Adler v. Board of Education* (342 U.S. 485: 1952). As the composition of the Court changed beginning with the appointment of Chief Justice Earl Warren, Douglas became the libertarian anchor for the Court majority. Douglas became the certain vote for the whole range of civil liberties issues, from rights of the accused to equal protection, reapportionment, and, of course, the First Amendment issues. He was occasionally critical of his more moderate early positions. He took his typically absolutist position in the school prayer case of *Engel v. Vitale* (370 U.S. 421: 1962). In a concurring opinion, he rejected the accommodationist position he had been part of in *Everson*.

Several empirical analyses of the Warren and Burger Courts' decisions uniformly show Douglas as the most supportive of individual rights. Over his last 20 years on the Court, Douglas supported claims of civil liberties violations in over 98 percent of the cases. The full extent of Douglas's civil liberties position can be seen in his majority opinion in *Griswold v. Connecticut* (381 U.S. 479: 1965), where he fashioned a "right of privacy" from other constitutional provisions. In *Griswold*, Douglas introduced the concept of "penumbras" through which inferred rights "emanate" from Bill of Rights provisions and substantively enlarge the protections explicitly contained. As the Court turned more conservative under the chief justiceship of Warren Burger, Douglas returned to his original role of dissenter. To the end, Douglas steadfastly maintained the position that the protection of rights through constitutional provisions is imperative for the preservation of a free society. Notwithstanding other distinguishing contributions, Douglas's impact as a justice is best seen through his commitment to individual rights.

Stephen J. Field (1863–1897)   Stephen Johnson Field was born in Haddam, Connecticut, in 1816. He was born to an established New England family. His father was a distinguished clergyman, and in his immediate family were several members who would gain prominence during their professional lives. For example, his brother David became a well-known attorney and political figure in New York, and Field's nephew, David J. Brewer, served 21 years on the Supreme Court (eight of them with Field). Field received his undergraduate degree from Williams College in 1837. He then studied law with his brother and John Van Buren, the attorney general of New York and son of President Martin Van Buren. Field was admitted to the bar in 1841, and he entered into private practice with his brother. In 1848, Field dissolved the partnership and spent a year in Europe. He returned to the United States and moved to California, settling in the midst of the gold fields in the town of Marysville. He immediately became engaged in local political life. He served for a short time as Marysville's civil magistrate and then served a term in the California House. He was defeated in a bid for the state senate in 1851, and spent the next several years cultivating his private practice. In 1857, he was elected to the California Supreme Court, running as a Democrat. He served with distinction and was regarded as the most capable jurist in the West.

In 1863, the Congress created an additional judgeship on the Supreme Court. The political motivation was to create an opportunity for a new Unionist appointment. There was also legitimate need to establish a new circuit in the West. Field had many supporters, including Leland Stanford. He was also the unanimous choice of the California congressional delegation. In addition, his brother David had become a leading abolitionist and adviser to President Lincoln. He had influence in the selection of the new justice. Notwithstanding his Democratic credentials, Lincoln nominated Field, and he was confirmed shortly thereafter. He served more than 34 years on the Court before retiring in 1897. He died a little more than a year later. He was replaced on the Court by Joseph McKenna. *See also* LEGAL TENDER CASES (12 Wallace 457: 1871), p. 381; *MUNN V. ILLINOIS* (94 U.S. 113: 1877), p. 420; *SLAUGHTERHOUSE CASES* (16 Wallace 36: 1873), p. 417.

Significance   Stephen J. Field was chosen for the Court because his political values were compatible with Lincoln's notwithstanding their party difference. Paramount, of course, were Field's strong Union loyalties and his opposition to slavery. Field marshaled widespread political support for his selection, and he was generally regarded as the most distinguished justice on the West Coast. Predictably, Field was supportive of Lincoln's conduct of the war. He was one of the majority in the 5–4 decision in *The Prize Cases* (2 Black 635: 1865), where the Court upheld Lincoln's blockade of Confederate ports. Following the war, however, Field took the position that war and reconstructive policies must be subjected to careful judicial scrutiny. Accordingly, in *Ex Parte Milligan* (4 Wallace 2: 1866), Field was once again part of a five-justice majority ruling that even in time of war Congress did not have authority to substitute military tribunals for civil courts outside the actual war zone. He also wrote for the majority striking down a federal test oath law aimed at keeping supporters of the Confederacy from practicing law in federal court. Both decisions were heavily criticized by Republicans.

Field's far-reaching impact on the Court, however, did not stem from these matters. Though it could not have been predicted from Field's state judicial career, he was to become a classic defender of property rights and a most enthusiastic advocate of laissez-faire economics. The first real indication came in the greenback cases. In *Hepburn v. Griswold* (8 Wallace 603: 1870), Field was one of the four-justice majority (the Court had two vacancies) ruling that the greenbacks could not be used to pay debts contracted before the passage of the legal tender acts. With two new justices, the Court reconsidered the issue in the *Legal Tender Cases* (12 Wallace 457: 1871) the following year. This time, by a 5–4 vote, the Court upheld the acts. Field dissented, saying the policy permitted repudiation of debt. Such repudiation, in "any form, or to any extent, would be dishonor," and for the "commission of this public crime" there was no constitutional mandate. Field's development of the Fourteenth Amendment as the medium for judicial protection of property interests had far greater impact. His first attempt came in the *Slaughterhouse Cases* (16 Wallace 36: 1873), where the Court upheld a state-created slaughterhouse monopoly. Field dissented and utilized the privileges and immunities of citizenship clause as his foundation. He said that the privileges and immunities "designated are those which of right belong to the citizens of all free governments." Certainly included among those "must be placed the right to pursue a lawful employment in a lawful manner." In Field's view, the Fourteenth Amendment could be used to protect American citizens against "deprivation of their common rights by State legislation," and should have been used in this instance to invalidate the slaughterhouse monopoly.

It was in *Munn v. Illinois* (94 U.S. 113: 1877) that Field moved to the due process clause as a more comprehensive means of rejecting state regulation. The Court held in *Munn* that grain elevators were "clothed" with a public interest that allowed the elevators to be subjected to regulation, including rates that could be charged for their use. Field again dissented, saying that the Court's approach would leave all property "at the mercy" of state legislatures. No "magic language," he said, can "change a private business into a public one." Neither does a legislative body have the power to "fix the price which one shall receive for his property of any kind." The substantive due process concept Field argued in dissent in *Munn* was to become the view of the Court within another decade, and this view permitted the Court to protect businesses from virtually all taxes and state regulation. Coupled with a restrictive interpretation of the federal commerce power, this view placed the Court at the threshold of several decades of domination by the economic laissez-fairists by 1890. In large measure, Field had been the architect of this development. A justice of great intellect, he served almost 35 years and was responsible for a prodigious number of opinions. He was clearly a justice who had a substantial impact on American constitutional law.

Felix Frankfurter (1939–1962)   Felix Frankfurter was born in Vienna, Austria, in 1882 and emigrated to the United States in 1894. He received his undergraduate education at City College of New York, graduating in 1902. He earned his law degree from Harvard Law School in 1906 and began his career as an assistant United States attorney in New York. He subsequently became assistant to secretary of war Henry Stimson, a position he held until 1914. It was in this capacity that Frankfurter represented the federal government before the Supreme Court. He returned to Harvard Law School in 1914 as a member of the law faculty and remained there for some 25 years. Aside from extraordinary performance as a law professor, which earned him national reputation as a legal scholar, Frankfurter engaged in activities away from Harvard that established his strongly liberal credentials. He offered arguments to the Supreme Court in a variety of cases such as *Bunting v. Oregon* (243 U.S. 426: 1917) and *Adkins v. Children's Hospital* (261 U.S. 525: 1923), where he advocated upholding a state maximum hour law and a federal minimum wage law, respectively. He also was active with the NAACP and ACLU and conducted the appeals on behalf of Nicola Sacco and Bartolomeo Vanzetti, two anarchists convicted of murder. But Frankfurter was foremost a legal scholar, a recognized national authority on the federal judiciary. Frankfurter had the opportunity to leave Harvard on a number of occasions, but declined. In 1932, Frankfurter would not allow his nomination to the Massachusetts Supreme Court. The following year, he declined Franklin Roosevelt's offer to become solicitor general to remain at Harvard, although he remained a close advisor to Roosevelt during this period.

When Justice Benjamin Cardozo left the Court in 1938, Frankfurter was selected. His nomination was widely acclaimed, and he was easily confirmed by the Senate. Frankfurter served on the Court until 1962, when he resigned after suffering a stroke. He never fully recovered his health and died in early 1965. The Frankfurter position on the Court was filled by Justice Arthur Goldberg. *See also* JUDICIAL SELF-RESTRAINT, p. 627; *BAKER V. CARR* (369 U.S. 186: 1962), p. 123.

Significance   Justice Felix Frankfurter came to the Court with a national reputation as a legal scholar and advocate for liberal causes. Generally, it was the former and not the latter that manifested itself during his 23 years on the Court. He became a leading spokesman for those espousing judicial self-restraint. He felt that the judiciary must defer to the policy judgments of legislatures, a political branch of government that could be held accountable through the electoral process. Frankfurter rejected substantive review of legislative initiatives, believing that the judiciary should not substitute its policy choices for those of the elected branches. As a result, Frankfurter often could be found voting differently from what might be expected, given his pre-Court orientations. On those occasions where Frankfurter did limit legislative initiatives, he did so only for technical procedural reasons or on narrow statutory rather than constitutional grounds.

Frankfurter's self-restraint approach led him to sustain most of the economic regulation legislation coming before the Court, and in this respect, his positions were those expected of a Roosevelt appointee. His response to civil liberties issues was not similarly predictable. His practice of legislative deference in economic regulation issues carried over to regulations that affected individual rights. He rejected the "preferred position" concept for the First Amendment and engaged in balancing interests on a case-by-case basis using the broad criteria of due process. The overwhelming burden of proof always rested with those seeking judicial intervention. In *Minersville School District v. Gobitis* (310 U.S. 586: 1940), for example, Frankfurter wrote for the majority upholding compulsory flag salute laws against a free exercise of religion challenge. Frankfurter said that "conscientious scruples" do not relieve the "individual from obedience to a general law not aimed at the promotion or restriction of religious beliefs." But aside from finding the act to be a legitimate secular regulation, Frankfurter said that the "wisdom of training children in patriotic impulses . . . is not for our independent judgment." Even if the Court was "convinced of the folly of such a measure, such belief would be no proof of its unconstitutionality." What the state ought to do with the flag salute ceremonies was legitimate, and he did not see the due process clause as giving the judiciary the authority to deny the state the opportunity to attain that end. Frankfurter took a similar position on legislation affecting political expression and association, as virtually any of the Smith Act challenges in which he participated will reflect.

Frankfurter was more demanding on federal criminal cases, recognizing the Supreme Court's superintending role over the lower federal courts. He fashioned, for example, a tough delay in arraignment standard in *McNabb v. United States* (318 U.S. 332: 1943) that still serves as one critical element in assessing the admissibility of a defendant's statements in a trial. Frankfurter felt the states need not be held to the same standards in the operation of their criminal justice processes. He was reluctant to apply any of the Bill of Rights provisions protecting the accused to the states and, for example, consistently opposed requiring the exclusionary rule at the state level.

In some ways, the reapportionment cases are most reflective of Frankfurter's view of the proper function of the courts. He saw these cases as "political questions" outside the proper scope of judicial consideration. In his dissent in *Baker v. Carr* (369 U.S. 186: 1962), he observed that the Court's power is sustained by a "public confidence in its moral sanction." This confidence is "nourished by the Court's complete detachment . . . from political entanglements and by abstention from injecting itself into the clash of political forces in political settlements." In short, the judicial branch attempt to resolve substantive policy disputes was rejected by Frankfurter. Rather, in a democratic society, "appeal must be to an informed, civically militant electorate" that arouses a "popular conscience that sears the conscience of the public's representatives." Frankfurter was a dynamic personality and a master of the law. He was committed to democratic principles, and, accordingly, a limited role for an appointed federal judiciary. There are many, however, who feel that by limiting himself by self-restraint and narrow technical issues, Frankfurter kept himself from the greatness that would otherwise have been his.

John M. Harlan (1877–1911)   John Marshall Harlan was born in Boyle County, Kentucky, in 1833. Harlan's father James was a prominent political figure in the state. A leading Whig and follower of Henry Clay, James Harlan served two terms in Congress and was both state attorney general and secretary of state. He admired the political philosophy of Chief Justice John Marshall enough to name his son after him. The family political involvement caused Harlan to consider certain political issues very carefully as a young man; he strongly supported preservation of the Union as well as the institution of slavery. Harlan completed his undergraduate education at Centre College in 1850 and studied law for the next three years at Transylvania University. He further prepared himself in the law with his father and other attorneys in Frankfort. He was admitted to the bar in 1853.

Harlan was politically active although he did not have extensive service as a public official prior to his appointment to the Court. Though initially a Whig, Harlan joined the Know-Nothings prior to the war, finding both the Democrats and Republicans unacceptable. He was city attorney of Frankfort before becoming a county judge in 1858. The following year, Harlan ran for a seat in Congress, but lost by a narrow margin. He continued to be torn by his commitment to both slavery and maintenance of the Union. Neither major party embraced both positions, and Harlan chose to support the Constitutional Union party, a compromise third party in the election of 1860. The war forced Harlan to make a choice, and he chose to resist secession. He formed a local military unit and fought on the side of the Union until his father's death in 1863. Harlan then left the service and was elected attorney general of Kentucky. In 1864, Harlan actively opposed Lincoln's reelection because of fundamental disagreement with the issuance of the Emancipation Proclamation and several of Lincoln's other war measures. Harlan also opposed the postwar amendments to the Constitution to abolish slavery and establish civil and political rights for blacks. After the election, Harlan once again assessed his political future, and uneasily chose to cast his lot with the Republicans. This subjected him to the resentment of Kentuckians who used the excesses of Reconstruction to umbrella acts of violence and discrimination against blacks. It was at this point that Harlan fundamentally altered his political values, and emerged as favorable to both the Thirteenth and Fourteenth Amendments. Although defeated as a Republican gubernatorial candidate in 1871, he possessed substantial influence in the party, even to the point of being considered for the vice presidential nomination in 1872.

Harlan was instrumental in the election of Rutherford Hayes as president in 1876. He switched Kentucky's votes to Hayes at a point when the nominating convention was deadlocked, thus providing momentum for the selection of Hayes. The following year Hayes appointed Harlan to the Louisiana Reconstruction Commission to resolve disputes arising out of the state elections. Soon thereafter, Justice David Davis resigned from the Court, and Hayes nominated Harlan. He served on the Court for 34 years until his death in 1911. He was replaced on the Court by Justice Mahlon Pitney. His grandson, John Marshall Harlan, was to become a Supreme Court justice in the mid-twentieth century, serving from 1955 to 1971. *See also CIVIL RIGHTS CASES* (109 U.S. 3: 1883), p. 259; JOHN M. HARLAN (1955–1971), p. 519; *POLLOCK V. FARMERS' LOAN AND TRUST COMPANY* (158 U.S. 601: 1895), p. 382; *UNITED STATES V. E. C. KNIGHT COMPANY* (156 U.S. 1: 1895), p. 302.

Significance　　　John Marshall Harlan had a long and distinguished career as a justice. His jurisprudence, much of it articulated in a number of highly visible dissenting opinions, has long been recognized as insightful and intellectually powerful. In general, Harlan was an economic conservative and believed strongly in the free flow of commerce. This led him to support federal initiatives, especially those aimed at regulating monopolies. More generally, Harlan believed that deference ought be accorded legislative judgments in these matters and that alteration or negation of policy decisions was typically not appropriate for the judiciary. He dissented from the Court's ruling in *United States v. E. C. Knight Company* (156 U.S. 1: 1895), which held that the Sherman Act could not be applied to production monopolies because production precedes and is distinct from commerce. Harlan saw the production-commerce distinction as unrealistic, arguing that federal power had to extend to all commercial activities, including production, which might interfere with free trade. A stronger federal commerce power position can be seen in his majority opinion in *Champion v. Ames* (188 U.S. 321: 1903), the lottery regulation case. Here Harlan said the commerce power was "complete in itself." and if Congress wished to free channels of commerce from the evil of the lottery, it had the authority to do so.

His self-restraint approach separated Harlan from the Court's majority on other important economic issues. In *Pollock v. Farmers' Loan and Trust Company* (158 U.S. 601: 1895), the Court struck down a federal tax on income including income derived from real estate and municipal bonds. Harlan dissented, taking a strongly nationalistic position. He saw the decision as striking at the "very foundations of national authority" by limiting its capacity to raise revenue. He also rejected the substantive approach to due process that prevailed during this period. He dissented in such cases as *Lochner v. New York* (198 U.S. 45: 1905) and rejected the whole liberty of contract argument advanced by the laissez-faire majority.

Of all the matters before the Court during Harlan's tenure, his greatest and most long-lasting impact came from his positions on the Fourteenth Amendment. Although initially opposed to all the Civil War amendments, Harlan came to embrace them fully. Illustrative of his views are three cases in which he issued powerful and eloquent single dissents. The first is the *Civil Rights Cases* (109 U.S. 3: 1883). In this case, the Court struck down a federal law because it regulated private acts of discrimination. Harlan saw the matters regulated as legally protected rights and within the scope of federal legislative power conveyed by the Thirteenth and Fourteenth Amendments. Harlan would have used the due process clause of the Fourteenth to incorporate or apply all of the Bill of Rights provisions to the states. In *Hurtado v. California* (110 U.S. 516: 1884), Harlan expressed the view that the amendment intended to "impose upon the States the same restrictions . . . which had been imposed on the general government." Finally, there is Harlan's classic dissent in *Plessy v. Ferguson* (163 U.S. 537: 1896), where he rejected the "separate-but-equal" doctrine endorsed by the remainder of the Court. It was in this dissent that he uttered his famous observation that under the Constitution there is "no superior, dominant, ruling class of citizens. There is no caste here. Our constitution is color-blind, and neither allows nor tolerates classes among citizens." These cases clearly stand out, and based upon them, Harlan is considered by many as a great "dissenter." While many of his dissenting opinions have an almost immortal character, the reality is that Harlan was with the majority in more than 97 percent of the cases in which he participated. Nonetheless, it was his dissents that distinguished him from his colleagues of the late nineteenth century.

John M. Harlan (1955–1971)   John Marshall Harlan was born in Chicago, Illinois, in 1899. He was the grandson of John Marshall Harlan of Kentucky, who had distinguished himself on the Court around the turn of the century. Harlan graduated from Princeton University in 1920 and spent the next three years studying jurisprudence as a Rhodes Scholar at Balliol College at Oxford. He received his law degree from New York Law School the year after his return. Harlan became a member of a prestigious Wall Street law firm and handled much of the firm's litigation. During his private practice, Harlan specialized in corporate and antitrust law. Harlan was active outside the practice as well. He was extensively involved with professional organizations, especially the New York City Bar Association, for whom he chaired a committee on professional ethics and the committee reviewing judicial candidates, and he eventually served as vice president of the association. Harlan also served in several public capacities prior to appointment to the Supreme Court. Early in his career, he was an assistant United States attorney. Although he returned to his private practice, he made himself available to serve as special prosecutor in a state probe of local government corruption. In 1951, Harlan became chief counsel to the New York State Crime Commission, an entity established by Governor Thomas Dewey to investigate organized crime activities in the state. He served in this role for almost three years.

In January of 1954, Harlan was nominated to the U.S. Court of Appeals for the Second Circuit by President Dwight Eisenhower. Less than a year later, a vacancy was created on the Supreme Court by the death of Justice Robert Jackson. The nomination became entangled in the proceedings to censure Senator Joseph McCarthy and in Senate resistance to the school desegregation decision. After several months' delay, the Senate ultimately confirmed Harlan's nomination in March 1955 by a 71–11 vote. Harlan served for 16 terms before resigning in September 1971 for reasons of declining health. Harlan was replaced on the Court by Justice William Rehnquist. Harlan died in December 1971, a little more than three months after leaving the Court. *See also* FELIX FRANKFURTER, p. 514; JUDICIAL SELF-RESTRAINT, p. 627.

Significance   Justice John Marshall Harlan served as the Warren Court's voice of caution. He was generally conservative and subscribed to the self-restraint philosophy. Indeed, after Justice Felix Frankfurter's departure from the Court, Harlan became the Warren Court's principal advocate of the restraintist approach. He believed in a limited role for the courts vis-à-vis the other branches of government. The other branches were elective and thus, through the dynamics of electoral accountability, could be politically restrained. This view was reflected in Harlan's statements on judicial power issues involving, for example, the concept of standing. He dissented in the taxpayer suit of *Flast v. Cohen* (392 U.S. 83: 1968), finding the plaintiff's interest in the outcome of the suit insufficient to allow the courts to review such a major federal education expenditure. Harlan also felt that courts had no jurisdiction to intervene on the reapportionment issue. Doing so he called an "adventure in judicial experimentation" (see his dissent in *Baker v. Carr*, 369 U.S. 186: 1962). Two years later, in his dissent in *Reynolds v. Sims* (377 U.S. 533: 1964), the case establishing the one person, one vote standard for state legislatures, Harlan said it was a wrong-minded view that "every major social ill" can find its "cure" in some "constitutional principle," and that the Supreme Court should not "take the lead in promoting reform" even when the other branches do not take action.

  There were occasions when Harlan would join the liberal members of the Warren Court, but when he did so, he would confine himself to narrow and technical aspects of a case rather than the far-reaching constitutional bases. An example is his majority opinion in *Yates v. United States* (354 U.S. 298: 1957), a decision that reversed convictions of 14 state Communist party officers. The petitioners sought invalidation of the entire Smith Act as well as the establishment of the principle that abstract advocacy of forcible overthrow of the government was protected expression. Harlan's opinion focused on the evidence necessary to regulate advocacy. Since he was fundamentally committed to the preservation of the federal system he generally opposed Court intervention in state matters. Harlan categorically rejected the concept of incorporation, the extension of federal Bill of Rights protections to the states. In *Malloy v. Hogan* (378 U.S. 1: 1964), the Court applied the self-incrimination privilege to the states through the due process clause of the Fourteenth Amendment. Harlan dissented, calling the Court's approach "undiscriminating." He rejected the Court's view that different federal and state standards for such matters as the assertion of the self-incrimination privilege would be "incongruous." Harlan said "incongruity . . . is at the heart of our federal system." The "powers and responsibilities" of the two levels are "not congruent," and "under our Constitution, they are not intended to be." Rather, under the provisions of the Fourteenth Amendment, states ought only be required to achieve fundamental fairness in the actions they take.

Harlan's approach thus minimized but did not foreclose federal intervention. He joined the majority, for example, in *Gideon v. Wainwright* (372 U.S. 335: 1963), a decision that required states to provide counsel to all indigent felony defendants. As a general proposition, Harlan saw the Bill of Rights as imposing greater limitations on the federal government than on the states. Harlan was also committed to the values of adhering to prior decisions, and he resisted the creation of additional constitutional protections through inference. He did not, for example, join the Court's establishment of a "right" of privacy in *Griswold v. Connecticut* (381 U.S. 479: 1965) although he did find the state prohibition on use of contraceptives a violation of due process. Harlan typically opposed expansion of the equal protection clause to classifications other than race in a similar fashion. Harlan is highly regarded by students of the Court. He was a person of intellect, integrity, and dedication. He is known for his extraordinary analytic skills and his finely crafted opinions. He was, especially after Frankfurter's departure from the Court in 1962, the Warren Court's "conservative conscience," and one of the Court's leading advocates of judicial self-restraint.

Oliver Wendell Holmes (1902–1932)   Oliver Wendell Holmes was born into a prominent Boston family in 1841. His father was a leading physician at the Harvard Medical School and a well-known writer in addition. Holmes's mother was the daughter of a justice of the supreme judicial court of Massachusetts. After attending private school, Holmes went to Harvard College, graduating in 1861. Following graduation, Holmes was commissioned as a second lieutenant in a unit that came to be known as the Harvard Regiment. Holmes served three years and was wounded three times during the Civil War before leaving the service at the rank of captain. He chose to return to Harvard to commence his law studies. He received his LL.B. in 1866 and was admitted to the bar the following year. He established a successful practice in Boston.

During this time, Holmes taught constitutional law at Harvard, edited the *American Law Review*, and lectured regularly on the common law at the Lowell Institute in Boston. The Lowell lectures were subsequently compiled into a volume entitled *The Common Law*, a work that became internationally recognized as a major work in the field. The volume established Holmes's scholarly credentials, and he was offered a professorship of law at Harvard. A position had been endowed by Louis Brandeis, a prominent Boston attorney and later a distinguished

Supreme Court justice, with the understanding that Holmes would be the first to hold it. Holmes accepted, but with the proviso that he would be free to accept judicial appointment should that opportunity present itself. Less than a year later, he was appointed a justice on the Massachusetts Supreme Court. There Holmes served for twenty years, the last three as chief justice. Justice Horace Gray, also a Bostonian, left the Supreme Court in 1902. President Theodore Roosevelt wished to replace him with another person from that region and settled on Holmes. He was confirmed by the Senate without dissent. Holmes served on the Court for just over 29 years, retiring in 1932 at the age of 91. He died in Washington 3 years later. He was replaced on the Court by Benjamin Cardozo. *See also ADKINS V. CHILDREN'S HOSPITAL* (261 U.S. 925: 1923), p. 433; LOUIS D. BRANDEIS, p. 499; *HAMMER V. DAGENHART* (247 U.S. 251: 1918), p. 309; *LOCHNER V. NEW YORK* (198 U.S. 45: 1905), p. 429.

Significance   Oliver Wendell Holmes is commonly acknowledged as one of the two or three greatest justices ever to sit on the Court. He was certainly one of the Court's most intellectually gifted members. Holmes was an ideological conservative, and he invariably supported conservative Republican presidential candidates. Wholly divorced from his personal political orientation was his judicial philosophy, however. He was committed to democratic processes with an intensity matched by none. This led him to defer to legislative judgments no matter how objectionable he found them to be. He was convinced early in his life that the people are entitled to elect whomever they wish, and that those representatives could make whatever policy decisions their constituents would tolerate. The ultimate check on political power was the ballot box. Judicial interference with legislation was to be avoided at all costs save where Bill of Rights issues were involved.

To Holmes, the questions of whether a law was constitutional and whether it was the people's will were absolutely unrelated. His role as a jurist was only to examine the latter. This outlook completely governed his entire judicial career. The approach obviously put him at odds with those engaged in substantive review of regulatory initatives. In *Lochner v. New York* (198 U.S. 45: 1905), the Court invalidated a state maximum hours of work law for bakers. Holmes entered a vehement dissent, saying that the majority "perverted" the term "liberty" when it was used to nullify a properly enacted regulation. He scolded the Court's laissez-faire majority for its interventionism. The Fourteenth Amendment "does not enact . . . Spencer's Social Statics." The Constitution is "not intended to embody a particular economic theory, whether of paternalism . . . or of laissez-faire." He also deferred to the exercise of federal legislative power. Illustrative is the child labor case of *Hammer v. Dagenhart* (247 U.S. 251: 1918). In this decision, the Court held that the commerce power could not be used to prohibit the interstate shipment of products of child labor. Holmes again dissented, saying that once a manufacturer attempted to send products across state lines, he became subject to federal commerce power. The legislative judgment to prohibit such commerce was simply a decision on method of regulation, a matter not to be second-guessed by the judiciary. Unless a legislative body actually violated an explicit constitutional limitation, it was free to make any substantive decision, however misguided it might be.

Interference with civil liberties was one of those explicitly prohibited areas, and it was here that Holmes could support judicial intervention. Holmes derived a standard known as the "clear and present danger" test for use in cases involving claimed violation of the freedom of expression. Since free speech was an absolute right, Holmes thought it deserved maximum protection. More often than not, Holmes concluded that the government had acted unlawfully in these cases. In *Abrams v. United States* (250 U.S. 616: 1919), the majority upheld Espionage Act convictions of several "anarchists" for expression supporting the revolution in Russia. In dissent, Holmes said that all ideas must be exchanged in the "market place," and that the Court must be "eternally vigilant against attempts to check the expression of opinions we loathe" unless they so "imminently threaten" the society that intervention is "required to save the country." Later, in *Gitlow v. New York* (268 U.S. 652: 1925), Holmes again dissented, finding the abstract advocacy of Gitlow to be insufficiently dangerous. He rejected the contention that Gitlow's expression could be suppressed because it was inciting. The "only difference," Holmes observed, between the "expression of opinion and an incitement . . . is the speaker's enthusiasm for the result." Holmes did not confine himself to First Amendment freedoms. In the wiretap case of *Olmstead v. United States* (277 U.S. 438: 1928), Holmes dissented from the Court's position that wiretapping did not fall under the reasonable search protection of the Fourth Amendment. He called wiretapping a "dirty business" and said he preferred some criminal escaping rather than having prosecutions based on evidence obtained by "ignoble" means. Holmes was the prototype self-restraint justice, and a strong libertarian. He was also a justice of great stature who successfully blended judicial statesmanship and democratic principles.

Charles Evans Hughes (1910–1916; 1930–1941) Charles Evans Hughes was born in Glens Falls, New York, in 1862, the son of a Baptist clergyman. It was an expectation of the family that Hughes would follow in his father's footsteps, and in 1876, Hughes entered Madison College (now Colgate University) to begin studies for the ministry. Two years later, he transferred to Brown University, where he distinguished himself academically. He also came to the realization while at Brown that he was more interested in the legal profession than the ministry. Upon graduation, Hughes taught for a period as well as working as a clerk for a leading Wall Street law firm to earn enough money to enter law school. He entered Columbia Law School in 1882, and graduated two years later with highest honors. Hughes returned to the Wall Street firm after passing the bar, and he maintained an association with that firm for the next 20 years. At the same time, he engaged in the teaching of law, typically as a special lecturer, although he spent two years at Cornell University as a full-time member of the law faculty.

Hughes entered public life in 1905 when he became counsel to the Stevens Gas Commission, which was established to investigate gas and electric rate-making practices. The commission found various improprieties that ultimately led to substantial lowering of utility rates. Later that year, Hughes served as counsel for an investigation of state insurance practices. The inquiry exposed widespread corruption and led to dramatic reforms. It also established Hughes as a strong political figure. In 1906, Hughes became the Republican candidate for governor of New York and won the first of his two terms. In early 1910, Justice David Brewer died, and President William H. Taft nominated Hughes to fill the vacancy. Hughes served just over six years and then resigned to become the Republican presidential nominee in 1916. He was replaced on the Court by Justice John H. Clarke. Hughes lost the election to Wilson by only 23 electoral votes. He returned to private practice where he remained until joining the Harding administration in 1921 as secretary of state. Hughes returned once again to private practice in 1925 and specialized in international law. During this period, he also served as a member of the Permanent Court of Arbitration and the Court of International Justice. In 1930, Chief Justice Taft was forced to resign the chief justiceship because of ill health, and President Hoover designated Hughes as Taft's replacement. Opposition to the nomination developed in the Senate as some Senate members felt Hughes was too intimately related to corporate interests. Confirmation was achieved, however, on a 52–26 vote. After 11 years as chief justice, Hughes retired from the Court in 1941. He was succeeded by Justice Harlan F. Stone. Hughes enjoyed several years of retirement before his death in 1948 at the age of 86. *See also* HOME BUILDING AND LOAN ASSOCIATION *V. BLAISDELL* (290 U.S. 398: 1934), p. 479; NATIONAL LABOR RELATIONS BOARD V. JONES AND LAUGHLIN STEEL CORPORATION (301 U.S. 1: 1937), p. 319; THE SHREVEPORT CASE, HOUSTON EAST AND WEST TEXAS RAILWAY COMPANY V. UNITED STATES (234 U.S. 342: 1914), p. 306; WEST COAST HOTEL COMPANY V. PARRISH (300 U.S. 379: 1937), p. 435.

Significance   Charles Evans Hughes divided his 17 years of Supreme Court service into two discrete parts separated by 14 years. His 6 years as an associate justice (1910–1916) were quite unlike the 11 years of his chief justiceship (1930–1941). During the first period, the Court saw no need to alter established doctrine and found itself in basic agreement on most issues. Hughes, a superior communicator of the Court's thinking, was responsible for many of the Court's opinions during this time, typically writing for a unanimous Court. Most important of Hughes's opinions in this early time involved the federal commerce power. Foremost among the commerce clause cases were those involving use of federal authority to regulate intrastate activities. In *Houston, East and West Texas Railway Company v. United States* (234 U.S. 342: 1914), also known as the *Shreveport Case*, the Court held that the Interstate Commerce Commission had the authority to order rail carriers to adjust purely local rates to become compatible with interstate rates. Any common instrument of inter- and intrastate commerce, said Hughes, could be protected from intrastate practices that injure interstate commerce.

Hughes's second tour of duty was neither so consensual nor so tranquil. Unlike his first appointment, where his selection was regarded as the "best" choice possible, Hughes was criticized by many at the time of his second nomination as the personification of corporate wealth and influence. He was ultimately confirmed, and he became chief justice during one of the most difficult times of the Court's history. Hughes was generally conservative, but he did not strongly resist federal intervention to protect the national economy or individual rights. Thus he was clearly distinguished from the four nonnegotiable laissez-fairists who sat for most of his tenure. Hughes also wrote a disproportionate share of the Court's opinions, something that also occurred during his associate justiceship.

In the area of civil liberties, three of his opinions are of special consequence. Hughes spoke for the Court in *Near v. Minnesota* (283 U.S. 697: 1931), striking down a state "nuisance" regulation of publications found to be "malicious, scandalous or defamatory." The law, he held, imposed an impermissible prior restraint on the press. The case remains the foundation of contemporary free press doctrine. In *De-Jonge v. Oregon* (299 U.S. 353: 1937), Hughes took a broad free expression position in overturning a state conviction for participation in a meeting called to advocate criminal syndicalism. His views were frequently embraced by the Warren Court in the 1960s. Finally, he took the position in *Missouri Ex. Rel. Gaines v. Canada* (305 U.S. 337: 1938) that a state could not refuse to furnish a black student with access to professional education comparable to that available for white students.

The questions that divided this Court, however, were economic. Prior to 1937, the Court seldom ruled for government regulation, and Hughes was generally with the conservative majority. Often, however, he wrote for the Court and chose language that did not foreclose subsequent reconsideration and change. He certainly chose language different from that which would have been used by his laissez-fairist colleagues on these matters. Hughes could also be found with the liberal majority in those infrequent cases where regulation was upheld, such as in *Home Building and Loan Association v. Blaisdell* (290 U.S. 398: 1934) and *Nebbia v. New York* (291 U.S. 502: 1934). In the former case, he wrote in broad terms, indicating that interpretations of constitutional mandates and limitations had to take account of exigent circumstances and that interests of the general welfare might override all other considerations.

After a series of major reversals from the Court in 1935 and 1936, Roosevelt sought to capitalize on his electoral mandate and "pack" the Court. While this proposal was before Congress (never to emerge), the Court modified its stance. The key figures were Hughes and Justice Owen Roberts. In several critical decisions (including *West Coast Hotel Company v. Parrish*, 300 U.S. 379: 1937, and *National Labor Relations Board v. Jones and Laughlin Steel Corporation*, 301 U.S. 1: 1937), the Court abandoned prior positions on the power of federal and state government to regulate the economy. Hughes provided the Court's rationale in each of these cases. Thus Hughes presided over and was the spokesman for the Court that ushered in a fundamentally new approach to government in this country. Although a conservative, Hughes recognized that modern industrial society required an expanded role for government and acted accordingly. In the minds of some, his impact on American constitutional development is second only to that of Marshall.

Robert H. Jackson (1941–1954)   Robert Houghwout Jackson was born in Spring Creek, Pennsylvania, in 1892. Jackson's formal education was essentially confined to high school, where he distinguished himself in written and oral communication. While he subsequently attended Albany Law School for a year, Jackson studied law by the apprenticeship method through his affiliation with a law firm in Jamestown, New York. He was admitted to the bar in 1913 and embarked on a successful private practice. As a Democrat, Jackson had some contact with Franklin Roosevelt during the 1920s, but was not considered a party activist. He was offered appointment to the New York Public Service Commission by then Governor Roosevelt, but he declined. Indeed, his only public office venture was that of corporation counsel for the city of Jamestown. In 1934, Roosevelt offered Jackson appointment as general counsel to the Bureau of Internal Revenue. Jackson accepted and was to remain in Washington for the remainder of his life. Between 1936 and 1941, Jackson became in succession an assistant United States attorney general, solicitor general, and attorney general.

In 1941, Chief Justice Hughes left the Court and was replaced by Justice Stone, who was already an associate justice. Jackson was nominated by Roosevelt to fill the Stone vacancy. In 1945, Jackson took a leave from the Court to serve as chief prosecutor for the United States at the Nuremberg war crimes trials. On reflection, Jackson saw this 18 months as the most "constructive" of his legal career. It was during his service in Nuremberg that Justice Jackson and Justice Black became embroiled in a widely visible dispute. Jackson had been highly critical of Black's participation in a particular case (*Jewell Ridge Coal Corporation v. United Mine Workers of America, Local 6167*, 325 U.S. 161: 1945), but this difference had been confined to the Court. When Chief Justice Stone died, it was thought that Jackson might succeed him. The media reported that Justice Black threatened to leave the Court in that event. Fred Vinson was ultimately chosen, and Jackson released a statement from Nuremberg revealing the nature and basis of his differences with Justice Black on the *Jewell Ridge* case. However strong Jackson's case may have been on the merits of the dispute, he never fully recovered from the decision to make the conflict public. Jackson returned to the Court from Nuremberg, and remained on the Court until his death at the beginning of the 1954 term. Jackson was replaced in early 1955 by Justice John M. Harlan. *See also* UNITED STATES V. SOUTH-EASTERN UNDERWRITERS' ASSOCIATION (322 U.S. 533: 1944), p. 334; YOUNGSTOWN SHEET AND TUBE COMPANY V. SAWYER (343 U.S. 579: 1952), p. 146.

Significance   Robert H. Jackson has generally been well regarded as a legal technician. He was disciplined, a compelling advocate, and a masterful writer of opinions. Jackson never became a major intellectual or political leader on the Court, however. He was neither an activist nor a strong libertarian. Rather, he was known for his commitment to judicial self-restraint and his adherence to established precedent. These attitudes manifested themselves in several ways. As a Roosevelt New Dealer, Jackson believed that the commerce clause provided Congress with extensive regulatory prerogatives. He also believed the national economy should be free from state and local interference. Thus he frequently used the commerce clause to invalidate state regulations and taxes he saw as burdensome to the national commerce. At the same time, prior decisions might lead to contrary outcomes. In *United States v. South-Eastern Underwriters' Association* (322 U.S. 533:

1944), Jackson dissented from the Court's ruling applying the Sherman Act, a commerce clause–based enactment, to the insurance industry. The industry had been immune by virtue of a Court decision handed down soon after the Civil War. Jackson would have supported application of the antitrust law to the industry if the Court had been "considering the question for the first time and writing on a clean slate." He rejected the Court's "reversing the trend of history" and suggested the immunity remain as long as Congress wished. Jackson's deference to the legislative branch was also evident in the steel seizure case (*Youngstown Sheet and Tube Company v. Sawyer*, 343 U.S. 579: 1952). In a concurring opinion, Jackson rejected the inherent executive power arguments offered in defense of the seizure. He saw inherent power as "nebulous" and based on the "unarticulated assumption . . . that necessity knows no law." In Jackson's view, the Court had no authority to affirm such executive power in the absence of statutory foundation.

Early in his tenure on the Court, one might have placed Jackson among the civil liberties liberals. In his majority opinion in the compulsory flag salute case of *West Virginia State Board of Education v. Barnette* (319 U.S. 624: 1943), Jackson said, "If there is any fixed star in our constitutional constellation, it is that no official, high or petty, can prescribe what shall be orthodoxy in politics, nationalism, religion or other matters of opinion." This strong civil liberties statement was later evident in the establishment clause challenge in the transportation cost reimbursement and released time cases. In *Zorach v. Clauson* (343 U.S. 306: 1952), a released time case, Jackson said "the day this country ceases to be free for irreligion, it will cease to be free for religion—except for the act that can win political power."

But this strongly libertarian position did not generalize, even to other First Amendment issues, especially after Jackson's return from Nuremberg. He supported time, manner, and place restrictions on expression to protect the public order (see, for example, *Terminello v. Chicago*, 337 U.S. 1: 1949, and *Feiner v. New York*, 340 U.S. 315: 1949). He generally deferred to the exercise of government power in national security cases, especially where associational issues were involved, as with members of the Communist party (see, for example, *Dennis v. United States*, 341 U.S. 494: 1951). In the area of rights of the accused, Jackson was conservative. He resisted extending Bill of Rights protections to the states and tended not to support claims of state trial defects. He was, however, sensitive to excesses stemming from warrantless searches and was among the Court majority extending the Fourth Amendment protections to the states in *Wolf v. Colorado* (338 U.S. 25: 1949). Generally, however, Jackson did not see the Court's role as one of aggressively intervening in civil liberties matters, and his responses to those issues were generally conservative.

William Johnson (1804–1834)   William Johnson was born in Charleston, South Carolina, in 1771. His family had moved from New York to South Carolina in the early 1760s, and Johnson's father had been active in the drive for independence. Indeed, during the war, the Johnson family was exiled from Charleston when the British captured the city, and Johnson's father was actually imprisoned for a time. In 1790, Johnson graduated first in his class at Princeton University. Johnson returned to Charleston, where he read law with Charles Pinckney, a leading Federalist and adviser to President George Washington. Johnson was admitted to the bar in 1793. The following year, Johnson successfully sought election to the South Carolina legislature. He ran as a candidate of the Republican Party of Thomas Jefferson. He served three terms in the legislature and served as speaker in 1798. In 1799, Johnson was one of three persons elected by the legislature to South Carolina's Court of Common Pleas, the state's highest court.

In 1804, Justice Alfred Moore left the U.S. Supreme Court, and Johnson was nominated by Jefferson as his replacement. He was only 33 at the time of his confirmation, and he served until his death in 1834. He was replaced by James M. Wayne. Aside from his lengthy tenure as a judge, Johnson was also extremely interested in education. He was instrumental in the founding of the University of South Carolina and was the author of a two-volume biography of Nathanael Greene, a Revolutionary War general. *See also* GIBBONS V. OGDEN (9 Wheaton 1: 1824), p. 294; OGDEN V. SAUNDERS (12 Wheaton 213: 1827), p. 474.

Significance   William Johnson was the first Jeffersonian appointed to the Supreme Court. He joined a Court that had been captured by the Federalists and had become a platform for Chief Justice John Marshall. Jefferson selected Johnson not only because of his impeccable legal credentials, but because he was a loyal and articulate partisan. It was Jefferson's hope that Johnson would become an effective countervailing influence on the Court to Marshall. When Johnson joined the Court, public expression of disagreement was very difficult. Marshall had virtually ended the practice of issuing seriatim opinions. Almost every decision was unanimous, and Marshall was the sole spokesman for the Court. Johnson chafed under this situation and eventually was moved to render individual opinions. Thus Johnson became the Court's first real "dissenter," although the number of dissenting opinions he issued is small when compared to a number of more recent justices.

One point of difference between Johnson and several other members of the Marshall Court was over the matter of federal court jurisdiction. Johnson saw federal jurisdiction as much more subject to legislative control than did his Federalist colleagues, a view that tended to put the Court in a subordinate position to the Congress. Although Johnson joined the Court majority in both *Martin v. Hunter's Lessee* (1 Wheaton 304: 1816) and *Cohens v. Virginia* (6 Wheaton 264: 1821), decisions that affirmed Supreme Court jurisdiction over state court rulings, he separated himself from the full sweep of both opinions. The majority opinions in these cases held that Article III required Congress to lodge every aspect of judicial power in the federal courts. Johnson, on the contrary, felt that Congress could and had delegated some appellate jurisdiction to state courts. Notwithstanding this difference of view, Johnson joined in the Court's decision in both these cases.

Johnson's democratic predispositions were otherwise reflected in his deference to broad powers vested in the legislative branch. This attitude allowed him to join the majority in *McCulloch v. Maryland* (4 Wheaton 316: 1819) and recognize implied legislative power even though its exercise was adverse to state authority, an interest important to Jeffersonians. Indeed, Johnson's support of national power in *McCulloch* and a number of other cases was a disappointment to Jeffersonians. If nothing else, this reflected Johnson's independence of mind. His nationalistic thinking was also seen in his broad construction of the federal commerce power in *Gibbons v. Ogden* (9 Wheaton 1: 1824). There Johnson issued a separate opinion that went beyond even Marshall, and it characterized the commerce power as exclusively residing at the federal level. At the same time, Johnson was a Republican and more than any other member of the Marshall Court valued state authority. He represented this view strongly, especially over the last decade of his service on the Court. Illustrative is *Ogden v. Saunders* (12 Wheaton 213: 1827), a decision that upheld a state insolvency law (over the dissent of Marshall) against contract clause challenge.

Thus Johnson played a unique role on the early Supreme Court. He shared some of Marshall's nationalistic orientation and thus contributed to the development of federal power. At the same time, he had a Jeffersonian sensitivity for the value of state initiatives, and he could be found preserving state authority as fully as possible. Finally, he saw the legislative branch as that element of the governmental structure from which policy decisions should emanate. The legislative branch could most accurately reflect the views of the public as well as provide most effective limits on the exercise of executive and judicial power.

John Marshall (1801–1835)   John Marshall was the first long-term Chief Justice and probably had greater impact in shaping the Constitution than any other member of the Supreme Court. Marshall was born in Germantown, Virginia, in 1755. Marshall's education was not formal. Rather, he was tutored by two local clergymen and his father. This educational process was interrupted by the Revolutionary War. Marshall was involved in active combat at Valley Forge and elsewhere as a member of the Third Virginia Regiment. He left the service in 1781 at the rank of captain, although he had not been on active duty for the latter portion of that period. Marshall had little formal legal education, but he did take a short course at William and Mary. He was admitted to the bar in 1780 and developed a successful practice. In 1782, Marshall was elected to the Virginia House of Delegates. He was reelected two years later. After three years associated with a state court, Marshall returned to the House of Delegates, where he was instrumental in the ratification of the Constitution in Virginia. During this period, Marshall was the most influential Federalist in Virginia. During the presidencies of both Washington and Adams, Marshall had several opportunities to join the administrations. The need to attend to large personal investment demands led him to refuse such appointments. In 1797, he did agree to serve as a special envoy to France in what became known as the "XYZ Affair." Though the mission was largely unsuccessful, Marshall's performance was very positively regarded. In 1799, Marshall won a term to the U.S. House, but joined the Adams administration the following year as secretary of state.

In late 1800, Chief Justice Oliver Ellsworth resigned. Adams sought out John Jay, who had earlier served a brief time as chief justice, but he declined. Others were suggested to Adams, but he nominated Marshall instead. The Senate confirmed Marshall a week later, and he began a tenure that was to last more than 34 years. Over that period, Marshall was to author several hundred opinions for the Court, many of which would deal with fundamental issues of national power, contracts, and federalism. Marshall died in 1835 and was replaced as chief justice by Roger B. Taney. *See also COHENS V. VIRGINIA* (6 Wheaton 264: 1821), p. 236; *GIBBONS V. OGDEN* (9 Wheaton 1: 1824), p. 294; *MARBURY V. MADISON* (1 Cranch 137: 1803), p. 89; *MCCULLOCH V. MARYLAND* (4 Wheaton 316: 1819), p. 238; *TRUSTEES OF DARTMOUTH COLLEGE V. WOODWARD* (4 Wheaton 518: 1819), p. 472.

Significance   John Marshall had greater impact on the American Constitution and its development than any other justice. In part, his opportunity to influence this development was greater than most others as he was writing largely on a clean slate. Nonetheless, he possessed the intellectual and political skill to seize the opportunity. As a chief justice, he had extraordinary influence over the Court. Generally, the Court's decisions were unanimous even though many of the justices who sat with Marshall were appointed by Marshall's political opponents. Further, Marshall maintained a control over the substance of doctrine by authoring the Court's opinion in virtually all of the major decisions.

There were several dominant themes in Marshall's jurisprudence. First, he had a full appreciation for separation of power and had a clear sense of how judicial power fit into the balance. He sought to elevate the Court's role in this respect, most notably through his opinion in *Marbury v. Madison* (1 Cranch 137: 1803), the case in which the Court first invoked the principle of judicial review. It is, he said, "emphatically, the province and duty of the judicial department, to say what the law is."

Second, he fully subscribed to the notion of federal legislative and judicial supremacy. This theme ran through most of his landmark opinions. In doing so, other principles were drawn into the discussion. Before getting to the supremacy issue in *McCulloch v. Maryland* (4 Wheaton 316: 1819), for example, Marshall first had to consider whether Congress had authority to establish a national bank. He held that Congress possessed powers implied from those enumerated. Coupled with the necessary and proper clause, this gave Congress the choice of any and all means so long as the end was legitimate. In addition, he advocated making broad and adaptive interpretation of these powers when reviewing challenges to their exercise. "We must never forget," he said, "that it is a constitution we are expounding." Marshall proceeded to the state tax on the national bank and struck it down on supremacy grounds. While federal and state authority are each supreme within their separate spheres, the federal government must prevail where there are conflicts. This supremacy concept was also extended to judicial power. In a number of decisions, most notably *Cohens v. Virginia* (6 Wheaton 264: 1821), the Court through Marshall held that state court decisions on federal matters are subject to review by the United States Supreme Court. In order to provide compatibility and uniformity of interpretation of federal law, the Supreme Court, he asserted, must be able to review state court decisions. The cases contributed greatly to nurturing the affirmative power that might be exercised by the federal government.

Third, Marshall established a broad federal power attaching to interstate commercial activities. In *Gibbons v. Ogden* (9 Wheaton 1: 1824), Marshall nullified a state steamboat monopoly and essentially freed interstate commerce from state actions that might create impediments to the free flow of commerce. In addition, he defined commerce broadly, saying that it "undoubtedly is traffic, but it is something more—it is intercourse." By viewing commerce as encompassing virtually all commercial activity, he created a broad affirmative power at the federal level.

Finally, as an economic conservative, Marshall was interested in government's providing protection for private property. Marshall fully utilized the contract clause to this end. Illustrative is *Trustees of Dartmouth College v. Woodward* (4 Wheaton 518: 1819). The contract clause prohibits states from impairment of contract obligations, and Marshall effectively used the clause to thwart state initiatives that asserted regulatory authority over property.

A new constitutional structure was sought after only a brief period under the Articles of Confederation. This was because the Articles had vested such power with the states that the national government could not survive. Every tendency was toward disintegration of the federation. The new constitution changed those tendencies, but it was not failsafe. Marshall led the Court through a series of decisions that produced an integrative or centralizing thrust. In this manner, he shaped the nature of governance under the Constitution as no other single Supreme Court justice.

Thurgood Marshall (1967–   )   Thurgood Marshall was born in Baltimore, Maryland, in 1908. At the age of 18, he left Baltimore to attend Lincoln University, where he graduated cum laude in 1930. Marshall took his law degree from Howard University in Washington, D.C., where he graduated first in his class. It was during his time at law school that Marshall became interested in civil rights. Following a short private practice in Baltimore, Marshall was named assistant special counsel to the National Association for the Advancement of Colored People (NAACP). He became special counsel to the organization in 1938. In 1940, the NAACP made a significant structural change. It created a new and separate entity known as the NAACP Legal Defense and Educational Fund. Marshall was named director and counsel of the fund. From this position, Marshall orchestrated comprehensive challenges to the practice of racial discrimination in a variety of areas. For example, during its first decade, the fund was successful in having outlawed the racially exclusive "white primary" used in a number of southern states (*Smith v. Allwright*, 321 U.S. 649: 1944), racial segregation on interstate buses (*Morgan v. Virginia*, 328 U.S. 373: 1946), and segregative practices in various professional and graduate educational programs. The most significant initiative of the fund was the challenge to racial segregation in public education. Marshall supervised preparation for the several cases docketed by the Supreme Court on this issue and handled presentation of arguments in one of the suits. This litigation led to the Court's landmark ruling in *Brown v. Board of Education* (347 U.S. 483: 1954). Marshall's activity with the fund continued into the 1960s.

In September 1961, President John F. Kennedy nominated Marshall for the U.S. Court of Appeals for the Second Circuit. Marshall began service under recess appointment, but subsequent confirmation was held up until late 1962 by the chair of the Senate Judiciary Committee, who opposed Marshall's nomination. The Senate eventually confirmed Marshall by a 54–16 vote. President Lyndon Johnson appointed Marshall to the position of solicitor general in 1965. He was the first black to hold that position. Two years later, Johnson submitted Marshall's name to fill the Supreme Court vacancy created by the retirement of Justice Tom C. Clark. The Senate confirmed the nomination by a 69–11 vote, and Marshall became the first black to occupy the Supreme Court bench. *See also* WILLIAM J. BRENNAN, p. 501; *NEW YORK TIMES V. UNITED STATES* (403 U.S. 713: 1971), p. 148.

Significance   Thurgood Marshall came to the Supreme Court as the Warren Court period was drawing to a close. As the Court changed in composition over the next several years, Marshall found himself playing the role of liberal dissenter, often with Justice William J. Brennan. Marshall believes the federal courts must play a fundamental role in safeguarding individual rights and the interests of minorities. He would have, for example, used the equal protection clause to invalidate the use of property taxes to finance public schools (*San Antonio Independent School District v. Rodriguez*, 411 U.S. 1: 1973). He was also in the minority on the issue of Medicaid funding for abortions. He said in *Beal v. Doe* (432 U.S. 438: 1977) that the Court had a "duty to enforce the Constitution for the benefit of the poor and powerless" when the elective branches make decisions that do not do so. In general, Marshall has been dissatisfied at the Court's resistance to enlarge the scope of equal protection coverage, and has often urged that the Court subject various classification bases such as gender, wealth, age, and others to more stringent scrutiny. Marshall has also been strongly protective of voting rights. He opposed restrictions on access conditions to voting and is unyielding in his support of the one person, one vote standard for legislative apportionment and has been consistently resistant to the Burger Court's limited relation of that standard (see, for example, *Mahan v. Howell*, 410 U.S. 315: 1973).

Marshall has also taken a strongly liberal position on First Amendment matters. He generally opposes time, place, and manner restrictions, supports demonstrations, opposes any prior restraints (see, for example, his concurring opinion in *New York Times v. United States*, 403 U.S. 713: 1971), and dissented from the Court's upholding of state obscenity regulations in *Miller v. California* (413 U.S. 15: 1973). He also wrote the Court's opinion in *Stanley v. Georgia* (394 U.S. 557: 1969), which held that the First Amendment and considerations of privacy do not permit a state to make it a crime to privately possess obscene materials.

Finally, Marshall has typically taken the position that protections afforded those accused of crimes must be steadfastly maintained. He was a consistent dissenter in Burger Court decisions modifying the *Miranda* ruling and has supported retention of the exclusionary rule despite the majority's generally critical views of it. With Brennan, Marshall has taken the position that capital punishment is constitutionally impermissible under any circumstance, thus he automatically votes to reverse death sentences in every case seeking review from the Court. With the exception of certain equality cases where Justices White, Blackmun, or Powell might be drawn to a nonconservative position, Justice Marshall seems destined, at least for the foreseeable future, to represent the values of liberal activism from a minority position on the Court.

Samuel F. Miller (1862–1890)   Samuel Freeman Miller was born in Richmond, Kentucky, in 1816. His early education was intermittent. He was more interested in his job at a local pharmacy, an interest that ultimately led him to medical school at Transylvania University. He earned his M.D. in 1838 and practiced medicine in southeastern Kentucky for almost a decade. During the 1840s, Miller's attention turned to the law and politics. He studied law on his own and was admitted to the bar in 1847. He became an active emancipationist and was involved with campaigns of Whig candidates committed to that end. In 1849, Miller sought election to the state constitutional convention on a gradual emancipation platform. He withdrew in favor of a friend of the same persuasion, but the convention was overwhelmingly represented by those desiring to protect the institution of slavery. Recognizing that his minority view on this issue would handicap him both professionally and politically, Miller moved to the free state of Iowa and settled in Keokuk. He soon became one of Iowa's leading attorneys, and his practice prospered.

While initially a Whig, Miller joined the Republican party when it was organized in Iowa in 1854. He became chair of the local party organization and unsuccessfully sought election to both the state senate and the governorship. He strongly supported Lincoln's 1860 presidential bid and directed some of his own financial resources toward the equipping of Union forces when the Civil War broke out. Thus the political credentials that would lead to his appointment to the Court were in place. In 1862, Lincoln and the Congress needed to reorganize the federal courts. Three vacancies existed on the Supreme Court, and a number of newly admitted states were unrepresented in the circuit structure. Miller had many supporters in the Congress who succeeded in creating a new circuit west of the Mississippi River. That decision left Miller a virtually clear path to the nomination. Lincoln offered it, and the Senate confirmed him in less than an hour. In doing so, it made Miller the first justice appointed from a state west of the Mississippi. In the formal order, he assumed the seat made vacant by the death of Justice Peter V. Daniel.

During his tenure, he was twice considered for chief justice, but the nomination was not forthcoming. He was also spoken of as a potential presidential candidate both in 1880 and 1884, but neither developed beyond the discussion stage. In 1877, Miller was one of five justices to serve on a commission charged with resolving the presidential election of 1876 between Samuel Tilden and Rutherford B. Hayes. Miller voted with the majority and awarded the presidency to the Republican Hayes. Miller served on the Court for 28 years, leaving just prior to his death in 1890. He was replaced by Henry B. Brown. *See also* SLAUGHTERHOUSE CASES (16 Wallace 36: 1873), p. 417.

Significance   Few Court nominees marshaled support of the breadth and depth that existed for the Miller selection. His credentials were exemplary, and in the wake of such enthusiastic advocacy by so many, Lincoln was left no choice but to appoint Miller. His performance on the Court did not disappoint those who supported him; he clearly distinguished himself during his 28-year tenure. Miller could be characterized as a "progressive moderate." He was fully supportive of Lincoln and unswervingly committed to preservation of the Union and the abolition of slavery. Accordingly, he took strongly nationalistic positions on a number of critical issues during and immediately following the Civil War. He supported, for example, Lincoln's power to blockade Confederate ports in *The Prize Cases* (2 Black 635: 1863), and he took the position in *Ex Parte Milligan* (4 Wallace 2: 1866) that Congress could have empowered military commissions to try civilians during the war. Miller's nationalism was clearly visible outside the war context as well. He saw the taxing power as key to the effectiveness of the federal government, so he carefully monitored actions affecting the federal taxing power. Similarly, Miller supported broad exercise of the federal commerce power. Miller also supported use of greenbacks as legal tender, arguing that Congress should have complete discretion over credit and monetary policy (see Miller's dissent in *Hepburn v. Griswold*, 8 Wallace 603: 1870). He also deferred to congressional authority, albeit most reluctantly, by not invalidating Reconstruction in *Mississippi v. Johnson* (4 Wallace 475: 1867).

Nationalism aside, Miller had a strong appreciation for the federal system and the need to preserve the integrity of state authority. This view was reflected in Miller's narrow construction of the Fourteenth Amendment. Miller joined the Court in striking down the Civil Rights Act of 1875 in the *Civil Rights Cases* (109 U.S. 3: 1883). According to the Court, the Fourteenth Amendment could not empower Congress to regulate private discrimination. Rather, only discrimination to which the state was a party could be reached. The "state action" requirement from this decision severely reduced the impact of the Fourteenth Amendment. Miller's most important case on the amendment came ten years earlier in the *Slaughterhouse Cases* (16 Wallace 36: 1873). The case involved challenge to the creation of a slaughterhouse monopoly by state law. A number of adversely affected butchers attempted to have the Court invalidate the state law as a denial of due process (among other things) under the Fourteenth Amendment. To have done so would have taken the Court into the protection of property characteristic of substantive due process. While the more laissez-faire justices embraced this approach several years later, Miller fought vigorously against it, beginning with *Slaughterhouse*. His majority opinion substantially limited the reach of the amendment. He saw no abridgement of federal rights and rejected all contentions that the federal courts could interfere with state regulatory initiatives on the basis of the Fourteenth Amendment. Relief in these matters must come, said Miller, from within the states.

Miller was decisive and insightful, productive and influential. He attempted to shape and steer by means of constitutional interpretation. Although his construction of the Fourteenth Amendment did not survive, Miller is generally regarded as a justice whose constitutional views have withstood the test of time and ongoing reexamination.

Sandra Day O'Connor (1981–   ) Sandra Day O'Connor was born in El Paso, Texas, in 1930. Her family owned and operated a sizeable cattle ranch located on the Arizona–New Mexico border. Much of O'Connor's youth was spent in El Paso with her grandmother because virtually no critical services, medical facilities, or schools were available in the remote area of the ranch. O'Connor finished high school at age 16 and entered Stanford University, where she graduated magna cum laude in 1950. Two years later, she obtained her law degree from Stanford. Failing to find employment in the private legal community, O'Connor worked a short time as deputy county attorney. When her husband completed law school, he joined the Army's Judge Advocate General's Corps, and the O'Connors spent three years in

Frankfurt, West Germany. During this time, O'Connor worked as a civilian attorney for the Quartermaster Corps. The two returned to the United States and settled in Phoenix, Arizona. While O'Connor attempted to maintain a private practice after the birth of their first child, she gave it up to become a full-time housewife following the birth of their second child.

O'Connor returned to her legal career in 1965, when she was appointed an assistant state attorney general. In 1969, she was appointed to complete an unexpired state Senate term. The following year, she was elected to a full term in the Senate, and in 1972 was elected Senate majority leader. She was also co-chair of the Arizona reelection campaign organization for President Nixon. In 1974, O'Connor ended her legislative career and sought election to the Maricopa County Superior Court. She won the judgeship, and it was from this position that she was named to the Arizona Court of Appeals in 1979. When Justice Potter Stewart retired from the United States Supreme Court in 1981, O'Connor was nominated by President Ronald Reagan to fill the vacancy. O'Connor was the first woman nominated for service on the Court. Some questions were raised by antiabortion groups who felt that her record was not strong enough on that issue, but no real opposition developed, and O'Connor was confirmed by the Senate in a 99–0 vote. *See also* FEDERAL ENERGY REGULATORY COMMISSION V. MISSISSIPPI (456 U.S. 742: 1982), p. 362; GARCIA V. SAN ANTONIO METROPOLITAN TRANSIT AUTHORITY (469 U.S. 528: 1985), p. 275; WILLIAM REHNQUIST, p. 542.

Significance   In 1981, Sandra Day O'Connor became the first woman to be appointed to the Supreme Court. Her appointment was in some measure at least undertaken to fulfill a campaign pledge made by Ronald Reagan, but her jurisprudence had also reflected an ideological orientation desired by Reagan. She is strongly conservative, believes in a limited role for the federal judiciary, and prefers that the legislative branch be the one from which major policy decisions must come. O'Connor is also highly protective of the authority of states. In this respect, she blended easily into the conservative majority of the Burger Court. She dissented in *Federal Energy Regulatory Commission v. Mississippi* (456 U.S. 742: 1982), which held that a federal law could require state utility regulatory agencies to adopt a certain rate structure and other regulatory standards. She said that federal power is constitutionally limited to designated established "channels" and cannot be used to "conscript" state utility regulatory commissions "into the federal bureaucratic army." In a similar fashion, she dissented in *Garcia v. San Antonio Metropolitan Transit Authority* (469 U.S. 528: 1985), a decision that extended federal minimum wage and overtime regulations to employees of a public mass transit authority. She suggested that the "true 'essence' of federalism is that the States as States have legitimate interests which the National Government is bound to respect even though its laws are supreme." For O'Connor, state autonomy is "an essential component of federalism." If this element is ignored in reviewing the exercise of federal power, then federalism "becomes irrelevant simply because the set of activities" remaining outside federal reach "may well be negligible."

O'Connor has had limited opportunity to date to respond to the abortion question, an issue around which some resistance to her nomination had surfaced. She did, however, support state and local regulations of abortion in such decisions as *City of Akron v. Akron Center for Reproductive Health* (462 U.S. 416: 1983). She has also joined the conservatives on rights of the accused issues. In *Oregon v. Elstad* (470 U.S. 298: 1985), for example, O'Connor authored the Court's opinion in a decision that allowed use of uncoerced statements made by a suspect prior to *Miranda* warnings if rights were subsequently waived following administration of the necessary warnings. She also dissented in *Tennessee v. Garner* (471 U.S. 1: 1985), a decision that disallowed use of deadly force to prevent the escape of any fleeing felony suspect, whatever the circumstances. O'Connor said that notwithstanding a suspect's interest in his life, this interest does not encompass the "right to flee unimpeded from the scene of a burglary."

O'Connor has generally taken an accommodationist position on establishment clause questions. She dissented in *Aguilar v. Felton* (473 U.S. 402: 1985), a decision that prohibited use of federal funds by local school districts to pay the salaries of employees providing remedial instruction and guidance services to parochial school students. And while she joined the majority in striking down Alabama's "moment of silence" policy for public schools in *Wallace v. Jaffree* (472 U.S. 38: 1985), she indicated that the states could provide voluntary silent prayer time in public schools so long as there was no endorsement of prayer as the preferred activity during the period of silence.

O'Connor's rare departures from the conservative bloc have occurred in gender discrimination cases. In *Mississippi University for Women v. Hogan* (458 U.S. 718: 1982), she authored the Court's opinion holding that a public university could not deny admission (in this case to a male) solely on the basis of gender. In her view, gender classification could not be allowed unless the state presented "exceedingly persuasive justification." She also cast the decisive vote in *Arizona Governing Committee for Tax Deferred Annuity and Deferred Compensation Plans v. Norris* (463 U.S. 1073: 1983), which invalidated an employer-sponsored retirement plan that provided smaller benefits to women by using gender-based actuarial tables reflecting greater longevity for women.

O'Connor replaced Potter Stewart, a member of the Court's center or "swing" group. She has consistently aligned herself with members of the conservative bloc, especially her former law school classmate, now Chief Justice William Rehnquist. Thus, the appointment of O'Connor clearly served to solidify the conservative majority on the Court for the 1980s.

Lewis F. Powell (1971–1987)   Lewis F. Powell was born in Suffolk, Virginia, in 1907. He graduated Phi Beta Kappa from Washington and Lee University in 1929. He attended law school at Washington and Lee and received his LL.B. in 1931. He also pursued legal study at Harvard University, earning an LL.M. the following year. Upon finishing at Harvard, Powell returned to Virginia and joined a prestigious Richmond firm where he continued his private practice until his nomination to the Supreme Court. He became a full partner in the firm in 1937. His practice was in corporate law, where he specialized in securities, reorganizations, mergers, and acquisitions. Among his clients were several of the largest corporations in the United States.

There was a public side to Powell as well. He had a long and extensive involvement with the American Bar Association, culminating in his serving as president of the organization in 1964 and 1965. He later led the American College of Trial Lawyers and headed the American Bar Foundation. He was widely known and highly regarded within the legal profession. Powell also became heavily involved with public education. He was president of the Richmond Board of Education for almost ten years between 1952 and 1961. This was a time of turmoil in Virginia schools generally because of the desegregation issue. While other school systems in the state were closing to demonstrate their "resistance" to desegregation, Powell was instrumental in accomplishing orderly desegregation in the Richmond schools. Powell moved to the Virginia State Board of Education in 1961, where he served until 1969.

In 1971, Justice Hugo L. Black resigned from the Court. President Richard M. Nixon nominated Powell to replace Black despite his Democratic party affiliation. The nomination was widely praised, and Powell was subsequently confirmed by the Senate with but a single vote in opposition.

Significance   Justice Lewis F. Powell believed in a limited role for the federal judiciary. As former justices like the later John M. Harlan, Powell felt the Supreme Court functioned most effectively when it proceeded cautiously and in a restrained fashion. This fundamental belief manifested itself in a variety of ways. Powell consistently supported a narrowing of access to the federal courts. In *Warth v. Seldin* (422 U.S. 490: 1975), Powell wrote for the majority in a case where a challenge to a municipal zoning decision was decided on standing grounds. Powell saw such rules of judicial self-governance like standing as necessary to keep the courts from deciding "abstract questions of wide public significance even though other governmental institutions may be more competent to address the questions."

Typical of those advocating judicial self-restraint, Powell favored legislative solutions for major policy issues. He was also highly supportive of the exercise of power at the state level. These two positions were clearly reflected in Powell's majority opinion in *San Antonio Independent School District v. Rodriguez* (411 U.S. 1: 1973). Suit had been brought challenging on equal protection grounds the system used in Texas for financing public education. In order for the financing scheme to be subject to the closest judicial scrutiny, education would have had to be seen by the Court as a fundamental right. Powell resisted, saying that it is "not the province of the Court to create substantive constitutional rights in the name of guaranteeing equal protection of the law." But more important for Powell was that this case constituted a "direct attack" on the way Texas chose to finance public education. The Court was asked to "condemn the state's judgment" in allowing local units to tax property to supply revenues for local schools. The challenge asked the Court to "intrude in an area in which it has traditionally deferred to state legislatures." The Court, said Powell, "has often admonished against such interferences with the states' fiscal policies under the equal protection clause." Similar deference to state legislative judgment was generally exhibited by Powell, as evidenced in the obscenity regulations, state restrictions on Medicaid funding for abortions, and state capital punishment statutes.

At the same time, Powell was not insensitive to individual rights nor inflexible in his restraintist approach. On occasion, he parted company with the conservative bloc on the Court (often with Justice Blackmun) and joined the moderates and liberal members. An example is *Weber v. Aetna Casualty and Surety Company* (406 U.S. 164: 1972), where the Court struck down a state law disadvantaging illegitimate children. Powell's majority opinion held that considerations of equal protection were sufficient to invalidate a state law relating to birth status where a classification scheme "is justified by no legitimate state interest." Powell was also the decisive fifth vote in *Plyler v. Doe* (457 U.S. 202: 1982), where the Court struck down a state law that denied free public education to illegal alien school-age children.

Powell's balancing approach was also clear in relation to rights of the accused. Though generally reluctant to require the states to meet the same standards as the federal government, Powell supported extension of the right to counsel to particular misdemeanor cases in *Argersinger v. Hamlin* (407 U.S. 25: 1972).

Most illustrative of Powell's willingness to engage in pragmatic balancing of competing interests is the highly visible affirmative action case of *Regents of the University of California v. Bakke* (438 U.S. 265: 1978) in which he was the decisive vote on the three component issues of the case, authoring the majority opinion. He joined the conservatives in striking down the rigid quota system involved in the admission plan, but then aligned himself with the liberals to hold that race could be a factor in admitting a minority student. Powell was one of the Court conservatives, but throughout his tenure on the Court he demonstrated an independence and flexibility that allowed him to balance competing interests in pursuit of reasonable middle-ground decisions. Powell served on the Court for 16 years, resigning in 1987.

William H. Rehnquist (1971–)   William H. Rehnquist was born in 1924 in Milwaukee, Wisconsin, where he lived until his World War II service in the Air Force. He then entered Stanford University, where he graduated with "great distinction" in 1948 earning both baccalaureate and masters degrees. He earned a second M.A. in political science from Harvard University in 1950. He returned to Stanford and graduated first in his law school class in 1952. Upon completing law school, Rehnquist went to Washington, D.C., as a law clerk for Justice Robert Jackson. Following his clerkship, Rehnquist established a successful private practice in Phoenix, Arizona. He became heavily involved in Republican politics in the state from the outset, and he aligned himself with the conservative element of the state party.

Rehnquist was extensively involved with the 1964 presidential campaign of Arizona Senator Barry Goldwater. Through the campaign, he met Richard Kleindienst, who was later to serve as deputy attorney general in the Nixon Administration. On Kleindienst's recommendation, Rehnquist was appointed assistant attorney general and named to head the Justice Department's office of legal counsel. Among Rehnquist's responsibilities was to review all constitutional law questions involved in Nixon's executive orders and matters relating to the executive branch generally. Rehnquist was often utilized as the administration's spokesman on a broad range of issues. He frequently appeared before congressional committees representing the more conservative and controversial policy positions of the Nixon Administration. He defended the Cambodian invasion as a proper exercise of executive power, for example, and supported extensive presidential privilege to withhold information from Congress, as well as such crime control policies as "no knock" entries for searches, electronic surveillance, and the mass arrest of antiwar protesters.

In 1971, Justices Black and Harlan left the Court. A number of names surfaced as possible nominees, but Nixon ultimately chose Rehnquist (to replace Harlan) and Lewis Powell (to replace Black), neither of whom had been publicly discussed. The Rehnquist nomination prompted substantial opposition from various civil rights and civil liberties groups because of his outspoken conservatism on a wide variety of issues. His nomination was eventually confirmed in the Senate by a 68–26 vote. In 1986, President Ronald Reagan nominated Rehnquist to succeed Warren Burger as chief justice, again giving rise to lengthy debate before Senate confirmation. *See also* SANDRA DAY O'CONNOR, p. 537.

Significance   Justice William Rehnquist became the Burger Court's most outspoken conservative member. He has consistently seen the Court as having a highly limited role in fashioning policy. Even in matters that affect individual rights, Rehnquist has emphatically rejected an interventionist function for the courts. Rather, he has argued that policy decisions must emanate from the elected branches, especially the legislative. He has also taken a highly deferential position on initiatives coming from the states. Several selected cases are illustrative. His narrow view of federal judicial power can be seen in his dissent in *Weber v. Aetna Casualty and Surety Company* (406 U.S. 164: 1972). The Court invalidated a state law discriminating against illegitimate children because the law violated a "fundamental" though unenumerated right. Rehnquist saw only those rights explicitly contained in the Bill of Rights as protected.

This narrow approach is also reflected in Rehnquist's resistance to expanding the scope and coverage of the equal protection clause. He examines legislative classifications through the rational basis test, a deferential and relaxed standard, rather than placing them under "strict" judicial scrutiny. He was, for example, the only member of the Court voting to uphold different benefit requirements based on gender for military personnel (*Frontiero v. Richardson*, 411 U.S. 677: 1973), saying that Congress could "reasonably have concluded" that because husbands are typically the "breadwinners" and wives the "dependent partners," different procedures for demonstrating dependency could be used. Neither has Rehnquist been receptive to claimed procedural violations in criminal prosecutions. He has opposed extension of the exclusionary rule, supported capital punishment, and written opinions supporting police search power. He said in *United States v. Robinson* (414 U.S. 218: 1973) that an officer's decision to search an arrestee is "necessarily a quick ad hoc judgment" and the Fourth Amendment does not require it to "be broken down in each instance into an analysis of each step in the search."

Rehnquist is best known for his deference to legislative judgments. In *Rostker v. Goldberg* (453 U.S. 57: 1981), he wrote for the majority, which upheld the "male only" draft registration. He said that the gender-based classification was not "unthinkingly" or "reflexively" reached by Congress, nor was it a "byproduct of a traditional way of thinking about women." Congress was entitled to "focus on the question of military need rather than 'equity,'" and it was reasonable to conclude that males and females were not similarly situated with respect to combat duty. This deference to legislative judgment is often coupled with a strong predisposition to sustain exercise of state authority.

More than any member of the Burger Court, Rehnquist supported state initiatives and usually favored the states in conflicts with the federal level. Examples are numerous. He argued in *Roe v. Wade* (410 U.S. 113: 1973) that states should have the authority to impose restrictions on abortions, including prohibition. Subsequently, he has generally supported state legislation aimed at limiting access to abortion and disallowing use of public monies to underwrite the costs of abortions. He has consistently upheld state capital punishment laws and dissented from the Court's holding in *Coker v. Georgia* (433 U.S. 584: 1977), where the death penalty for the crime of rape was found excessive. He felt that states had broad discretion to act to deter crime, including use of the death penalty to that end. Rehnquist also supported a state statutory rape law which permitted prosecution of men but not women. He said that because the most serious consequences of teenage pregnancies fall almost exclusively on the female, a legislature is "well within its authority when it elects to punish the participant who, by nature, suffers few of the consequences of his conduct." (*Michael M. v. Superior Court*, 450 U.S. 464: 1981). Similarly, he supported new guidelines for the regulation of obscenity that permitted greater regulatory control at the state level.

Rehnquist's position regarding federal-state disputes is most clearly revealed in two cases involving application of the Fair Labor Standards Act to state and municipal employees. Rehnquist authored the majority opinion in *National League of Cities v. Usery* (426 U.S. 833: 1976), which held the state and local units immune from the federal wage and hours restrictions in the FLSA. Rehnquist used the Tenth Amendment to effectively insulate certain aspects of state sovereignty from congressional impairment. The *Usery* decision was reversed in *Garcia v. San Antonio Metropolitan Transit Authority* (469 U.S. 528: 1985). In dissent, Rehnquist said that he was confident that the *Usery* position would "again command the support of a majority of this Court." Rehnquist clearly served as the Burger Court's conservative anchor, and his relative youth means that he will be a major ideological force on the Court for many years to come. His selection as chief justice adds to his potential to influence the Court in the direction of conservative judicial policy making.

Wiley B. Rutledge (1943–1949)   Wiley Blount Rutledge was born in Cloverport, Kentucky, in 1894. The son of a fundamentalist minister, Rutledge spent his youth in a number of locations in North Carolina, Kentucky, and Tennessee. He began his undergraduate career at Marysville College but completed his degree work at the University of Wisconsin. Rutledge wished to enter law school at Wisconsin, but was unable to for financial reasons. Instead, he moved to Bloomington, Indiana, where taught at the local high school while attending Indiana Law School. He contracted tuberculosis, however, and was hospitalized for a lengthy period. He spent the next three years in Albuquerque, New Mexico, where he taught and had administrative responsibilities for the board of education. Having fully recovered his health, Rutledge moved to Boulder, Colorado, where he resumed his law studies. He received his LL.B. from the University of Colorado in 1922. He spent two years in private practice in Boulder before taking a faculty appointment at the University of Colorado Law School, the first of a number of academic positions Rutledge was to hold. In 1926, he went to Washington University, where he became dean of the Law School in 1930. Five years later, Rutledge became dean of the University of Iowa College of Law.

He was an enthusiastic supporter of President Franklin Roosevelt and the New Deal, and he was highly vocal in his criticism of the Supreme Court decisions invalidating many of the essential elements of it. These views plus his endorsement of the "Court-packing" plan caught the eye of the Roosevelt Administration, and he was subsequently nominated to the U.S. Court of Appeals for the District of Columbia in 1939. When Justice James Byrnes left the Court to become Roosevelt's administrator of domestic economic wartime regulations in late 1942, Rutledge was nominated to fill the vacancy and was easily confirmed by the Senate. Rutledge served on the Court for a little more than six years until his untimely death in 1949. Sherman Minton was nominated by President Harry Truman to fill his vacancy. *See also* IN RE YAMASHITA (327 U.S. 1: 1946), p. 171.

Significance   During his ten years on the federal bench, Justice Wiley B. Rutledge was the classic judicial liberal. He consistently voted to sustain broad construction of congressional taxing and commerce powers and the use of those powers to expand the federal regulatory role over the economy. Notable was his support of federal regulatory agencies, especially the National Labor Relations Board. At the same time, Rutledge was highly suspicious of the exercise of governmental power when it affected individual rights. With Justices Murphy, Black, and Douglas, Rutledge constituted a powerful civil libertarian coalition that could generally be expected to support claims of constitutional violations. Rutledge felt that states must fully adhere to all the guarantees set forth in the Bill of Rights. He even argued that full implementation of the Bill of Rights might be insufficient to achieve a full measure of justice. Rutledge believed that there may be occasions where the courts need to find due process lacking even in the absence of specific Bill of Rights provisions. This extreme position, termed "total incorporation plus" by Henry J. Abraham, was advocated most aggressively by Justices Murphy and Rutledge (see Murphy's dissent in *Adamson v. California* (332 U.S. 46: 1947). Rutledge demanded the full range of protections for those accused of criminal conduct. In his tenure on the Court, he did not vote to sustain a single criminal conviction raising assistance of counsel issues, and he strongly advocated requiring the exclusionary rule in state criminal proceedings.

On First Amendment issues, Rutledge subscribed to the "preferred position" doctrine, which required the judiciary to demand more of legislation intruding on these protected areas. The strongest statement of the doctrine may have come in Rutledge's majority opinion in *Thomas v. Collins* (323 U.S. 516: 1945), where he said that "any attempt" to limit First Amendment liberties must be supported by "clear public interest, threatened not doubtfully or remotely," by clear and present danger. The connection between the restriction and "evil" to be regulated, "which in other contexts might support legislation against attack on due process grounds, will not suffice. These rights rest on firmer foundation." He concluded that only the "gravest abuses endangering paramount interests give occasion for permissible limitation." This doctrine was clearly evident in Rutledge's free exercise of religion views (see, for example, *Murdock v. Pennsylvania*, 319 U.S. 105: 1943) and his strict separationist establishment position (see, for example, his dissent in *Everson v. Board of Education*, 330 U.S. 1: 1947).

There are those who contend, however, that Rutledge's strongest libertarian opinion was his dissent in *In Re Yamashita* (327 U.S. 1: 1946). Yamashita, a Japanese general charged with war crimes, was convicted by a special military commission. On appeal, the Court held that Yamashita possessed no constitutional rights, and that the case was subject to review only within the military. Rutledge disagreed most strenuously, saying that constitutional protections apply to all persons "whether citizens, aliens, alien enemies or enemy belligerents." No trial "vitiated" by the absence of these due process safeguards can "withstand constitutional scrutiny." Rutledge was certainly among the first to aggressively pursue a course of expanding the boundaries of constitutionally protected rights.

John Paul Stevens (1975–   )   John Paul Stevens was appointed to the Supreme Court in 1975 by President Gerald Ford to replace Justice William O. Douglas. Stevens was born in Chicago, Illinois, in 1920, a member of a prominent family. He received his undergraduate education at the University of Chicago, graduating in 1941. After a tour of duty in the navy, Stevens entered Northwestern University Law School. His career at Northwestern was distinguished; he served as co-editor of the *Law Review* and graduated at the top of his class. Stevens then spent almost two years as law clerk to Supreme Court Justice Wiley Rutledge. He returned to Chicago in 1948 and joined one of the leading law firms. There he developed expertise in antitrust law. Twice during his early private practice, Stevens put this expertise to use in the public arena. In 1950, he served as Republican counsel to the House Judiciary Subcommittee on Antitrust and Monopoly. Several years later, Stevens served as a member of a National Committee to Study Antitrust Laws, a panel assembled by Eisenhower's attorney general. Stevens maintained his Chicago practice throughout and added teaching to his activities; he became a part-time member of the law faculties at both Northwestern and Chicago, regularly teaching antitrust law.

Stevens was first appointed to the federal bench in 1970 when Richard Nixon nominated him for a seat on the United States Court of Appeals for the Seventh Circuit. During his tenure as a federal appellate judge, Stevens was regarded as a moderate, and a judge seemingly free of ideological orientation. He also established a reputation for clear and sound judicial opinions. When Justice Douglas retired from the Court in 1975, Ford nominated Stevens, and the nomination was unanimously confirmed by the Senate soon thereafter.

Significance   Justice John Paul Stevens was the Burger Court's most difficult member to predict. He bases his decisions on fine-line distinctions and may be positioned with either the liberal or conservative blocs depending upon the particulars of the case involved. He seems to be the least ideologically driven member of the Court and is often referred to as the "swing" or pivotal vote on the Court. Certainly no liberal or even moderate decisional outcome can occur without his vote. On balance, however, Stevens is aligned with the conservatives, although he ranks behind only Justices Brennan and Marshall as most supportive of individual rights challenges.

Stevens's fine-line drawing manifests itself in two principal ways. First, he issued more individual opinions than any other member of the Burger Court. He often feels the need to offer a concurring opinion or a separate dissent to develop a distinction. Second, Stevens can be found supporting challenges on certain issues, but not categorically as is characteristic of Brennan and Marshall. For example, Stevens deferred to state capital punishment statutes that structured or guided the judgment of judge or jury imposing sentence. At the same time, he offered the Court's rationale in *Woodson v. North Carolina* (428 U.S. 280: 1976), in which mandatory death sentences were invalidated. Stevens also joined the majority in *Coker v. Georgia* (433 U.S. 584: 1977), which found the death penalty an excessive punishment for the crime of rape. Stevens's line drawing is also evident on the abortion issue. Generally, he opposes regulation of abortion and has stood with the minority in those cases where limitation on public funding of abortion has been upheld. At the same time, he has supported state restrictions on abortions for minors, restrictions he views as impermissible if applied to adults (see, for example, *Planned Parenthood of Central Missouri v. Danforth*, 428 U.S. 52: 1976; and *H.L. v. Matheson*, 450 U.S. 398: 1981). Similarly, Stevens has generally opposed regulation of expression, yet he did not see it as "wholly immune." He supported, for example, the use of municipal zoning power to regulate the location of "adult" bookstores and theaters in *Young v. American Mini Theatres* (427 U.S. 50: 1976).

Stevens tends to take a firm separationist position in establishment cases. He has consistently opposed aid to nonpublic schools (see, for example, the recent "shared time" case, *Grand Rapids School District v. Ball*, 473 U.S. 373: 1985), and wrote the Court's opinion in *Wallace v. Jaffree* (472 U.S. 38: 1985), the decision that struck down Alabama's "moment of silence" statute. Stevens's performance on equal protection issues is generally liberal. Although criticized at the time of his nomination as insensitive to various forms of discrimination, Stevens can usually be found supporting claims of constitutional violations. Indeed, Stevens is usually positioned with Justices Brennan and Marshall on these issues except in cases where racial minorities are given preference. In such cases (see, for example, *Regents of the University of California v. Bakke*, 438 U.S. 265: 1978; and *Fullilove v. Klutznick*, 448 U.S. 448: 1980), Stevens has taken the conservative position in rejecting race as a basis for compensatory or remedial preference. Stevens has also taken a more conservative stance on issues involving rights of the accused. One of the Court's least visible members because of his ideological independence, Stevens will remain at the Court's center and the current member most likely to join the Court's liberal minority.

Potter Stewart (1959–1981)   Potter Stewart was born in Jackson, Michigan, in 1915, but his family settled and became prominent in Cincinnati, Ohio. Stewart's father was politically active and served as mayor of Cincinnati from 1938 until 1947. During his tenure as mayor, Stewart's father was the unsuccessful Republican gubernatorial candidate in 1944 and later served on the Ohio Supreme Court from 1947 until his death in 1959. Stewart's family highly valued education, and provided him with unusual opportunities. Stewart attended a prestigious eastern prep school before enrolling at Yale University. Stewart distinguished himself at Yale, graduating Phi Beta Kappa in 1937. After completing a year of graduate study at Cambridge University, Stewart returned to the United States and began law school at Yale. Following his graduation in 1941, Stewart joined a Wall Street law firm, but a lengthy tour with the navy interrupted his law career. Stewart returned to New York after the war, but soon moved back to Cincinnati and affiliated with a prominent law firm. Three years later, Stewart was elected to the Cincinnati City Council, where he served four years, the last year as vice mayor.

In April 1954, Stewart was appointed to the U.S. Court of Appeals for the Sixth Circuit by President Eisenhower. When Justice Harold H. Burton resigned from the Court in 1958, Eisenhower elevated Stewart to the Supreme Court by means of a recess appointment. The Senate confirmed the nomination the following May by a 70–17 vote. Stewart retired from the Court in 1981 after 23 years of service. He pursued an active and visible retirement until his death in late 1985. Stewart was replaced on the Court by the first woman appointee, Sandra Day O'Connor. *See also* BYRON WHITE, p. 566.

Significance   Justice Potter Stewart, a moderate Republican, played the role of the pivotal vote on the Supreme Court on two different occasions. During Stewart's first several years on the Court, he occupied the position between the liberal and conservative blocs. For example, he was the decisive vote in the legislative investigation cases involving the House Committee on Un-American Activities. In this instance, Stewart voted to uphold the legislative contempt citations imposed on witnesses who refused to testify about "subversive" activities and associations (see *Barenblatt v. United States*, 360 U.S. 109: 1959). When the liberal majority on the Court solidified after the appointment of Justice Goldberg, Stewart was more often aligned with the moderate to conservative wing and played a less pivotal role. He tended to reject the Warren Court's nationalization of the Bill of Rights and generally disagreed with broadening the scope of safeguards for the accused. He dissented in such landmark cases as *Mapp v. Ohio* (367 U.S. 643: 1961), *Miranda v. Arizona* (384 U.S. 436: 1966), and the *Gault* decision (387 U.S. 1: 1967), in which the Court applied constitutional provisions to juvenile proceedings. At the same time, Stewart wrote several majority opinions for the Warren Court that did strengthen protections of the accused. In *Robinson v. California* (370 U.S. 660: 1962), he held that it was cruel and unusual punishment to make the condition of narcotics addiction a crime. He also wrote for the Court in *Katz v. United States* (389 U.S. 347: 1967), the decision that held that electronic surveillances must be subject to Fourth Amendment restrictions. On balance, however, Stewart took the position that rights of the accused must be balanced against societal interests, and more often than the Warren Court majority, he found for the latter in criminal cases.

Stewart also had a mixed record on First Amendment issues. He took an accommodationist position in establishment cases and was the Warren Court's sole dissenter in the prayer and Bible-reading cases of the early 1960s (*Engel v. Vitale*, 370 U.S. 421: 1962; and *School District of Abington Township v. Schempp*, 374 U.S. 203: 1963). In the prayer case, Stewart did not see how the "simple" Regents prayer created an "official religion." More recently, Stewart voted to allow several state programs that extend some "aid" to nonpublic educational institutions. On the other hand, Stewart was strongly supportive of the First Amendment protection of free expression. This was especially evident in the obscenity cases of the mid-1960s and his vote in *New York Times v. Sullivan* (376 U.S. 254: 1964), which held that publications could not be subjected to libel damages for criticism of public officials and their official conduct unless deliberate malice could be shown. These positions were carried into the 1970s. Stewart found the injunction against publication of the Pentagon Papers to be an unconstitutional prior restraint, and he dissented from the Burger Court decision in *Miller v. California* (413 U.S. 15: 1973), which permitted closer governmental regulation of obscenity at the state level.

It was during the decade of the 1970s that Stewart once again became the Court's key or pivotal vote. As the composition of the Court changed under Chief Justice Burger, Stewart (and Justice White) decided cases on a closely divided Court by aligning with either the liberal Warren Court holdovers or the more conservative Nixon appointees. Illustrative of his pivotal position are the death penalty cases. Stewart wrote in *Furman v. Georgia* (408 U.S. 238: 1972) that Georgia's wholly discretionary death penalty statute permitted "freakishly" arbitrary imposition of the death sentence, and was thus cruel and unusual. He also rejected the mandatory death sentence (*Woodson v. North Carolina*, 428 U.S. 280: 1976). He was, however, part of the majority voting to sustain capital punishment laws that structured sentencer discretion (*Gregg v. Georgia*, 428 U.S. 153: 1976). Between 1971 and 1981, the Supreme Court decided 36 cases involving some aspect of capital punishment. In 24 of these cases, the Court reversed the death penalty while upholding it in 12 other cases. Stewart was the only member of the Burger Court to vote with the majority in all 36 of these cases (as compared to Burger, for example, who was with the majority in 25 or 69.4 percent of the cases, or Rehnquist who was part of the majority in only 34.6 percent of these cases).

Stewart subscribed to the value of judicial self-restraint, but he has often been called a "progressive conservative" in that he did recognize that the Court had a role in protecting individual rights. While he did not fully join the Warren Court in some of its more revolutionary decisions, neither did he categorically reject the directions pursued by that Court. He was simply more selective based on his own balancing approach, which was also clearly visible during his tenure with the Burger Court.

Harlan F. Stone (1925–1946)   Harlan Fiske Stone was born in Chesterfield, New Hampshire, in 1872. He took his B.A. and M.A. degrees from Amherst College before completing his law degree at Columbia University in 1898. During his youth, Stone became a friend of Calvin Coolidge, and the two attended Amherst together. Stone was admitted to the bar in New York, where he began a successful corporate law practice. During the period of his private practice, Stone also became a professor of law at Columbia. Eventually, he served 13 years as dean of the Columbia Law School. Coolidge succeeded to the presidency on the death of Warren Harding, and brought Stone to Washington in 1924 to replace United States Attorney General Harry Daugherty, whose tenure as head of the Justice Department had been severely damaged by the Teapot Dome scandal. Although in the position of attorney general for only a year, Stone was able to effect some substantial organizational changes in the Justice Department. In 1925, Justice Joseph McKenna left the Court and Coolidge nominated Stone as his replacement. The Senate confirmed him a month later by a 71–6 vote. Stone served as an associate justice until June 1941, when Franklin Roosevelt nominated him to be chief justice to replace Charles Evans Hughes. He was confirmed by a voice vote two days later. He served as chief justice until his death in 1946. He was succeeded as chief justice by Fred M. Vinson. *See also* CARTER V. CARTER COAL COMPANY (298 U.S. 238: 1936), p. 317; HELVERING V. GERHARDT (304 U.S. 405: 1938), p. 250; UNITED STATES V. BUTLER (297 U.S. 1: 1936), p. 389; UNITED STATES V. CAROLENE PRODUCTS COMPANY (304 U.S. 144: 1938), p. 93.

Significance   Harlan Fiske Stone was a personal friend and political ally of Calvin Coolidge. Stone had played a prominent role in the 1924 election and had served Coolidge well as attorney general. In this respect, Stone's selection was quite normal, but his on-bench performance did not square with expectations. Stone was a long-standing Republican and former corporate attorney, and it was certainly assumed by Coolidge that his decisional behavior would be dictated by these credentials. Stone's strongly independent character led him to behave otherwise. He quickly aligned himself with Justices Holmes (later Cardozo) and Brandeis, and he became a strong and consistent supporter of the Roosevelt New Deal initiatives.

Despite his Republican origins, Stone accepted the greater role for federal regulatory power that was the hallmark of the New Deal. This came not so much from his agreement with the policy, however, but rather his abiding commitment to judicial self-restraint. Several cases are representative of how these two elements merged. The first is *United States v. Butler* (297 U.S. 1: 1936). In this case, the conservative majority struck down the Agricultural Adjustment Act as an impermissible use of the federal taxing and spending power. Stone dissented and was critical of the Court's substantive veto of the enactment. A guiding principle of judicial review, said Stone, is that courts are "concerned only with the power to enact statutes, not with their wisdom." Here Stone felt the Court had engaged in disapproval of a legislative policy judgment. On construction of the scope of the federal taxing power, Stone took the position that the power was extensive. He saw the general welfare clause as enlarging the taxing power and failed to see how the majority could limit the taxing power by invoking the doctrine of state sovereignty. He offered much the same response in *Morehead v. New York Ex. Rel. Tipaldo* (298 U.S. 587: 1936), where the majority set aside a state minimum wage regulation. Here he disapproved of the Court's use of substantive due process to invalidate a state economic regulation. He said that the Fourteenth Amendment "has no more embedded in the Constitution our preference for some particular set of economic beliefs, than it has adopted, in the name of liberty, the system of theology which we may happen to approve."

Stone also viewed the federal commerce power as broad and far-reaching. Again from a minority position, he was critical of the Court's decision in *Carter v. Carter Coal Company* (298 U.S. 238: 1936), which limited the commerce power to factors that directly affected interstate commerce. The price and wage provisions of the act under review were held to be outside the reach of the commerce power. When the court changed course following the "Court-packing" episode, Stone found himself among the majority on these issues. His opinion in *United States v. Darby Lumber Company* (312 U.S. 100: 1941) reflects his view of the commerce power. The statute under review was the Fair Labor Standards Act, which attempted to regulate wages and hours of any employee working for a business whose products were shipped interstate.

Stone found this sufficiently connected to commerce interests to come within the purview of federal power. He also gave Congress discretion to "choose the means reasonably adapted to the attainment of the permitted end, even though they involve control of intrastate activities." Evident throughout the economic regulation cases, be they federal or state, was a deference to legislative judgment.

Stone saw civil liberties matters quite differently, and advocated a kind of judicial activism. He saw the Court as having an obligation to subject enactments involving civil liberties and civil rights to "more exacting judicial scrutiny." While a presumption of constitutionality exists for most legislation, that affecting commercial regulation for example, there are certain freedoms and political rights that occupy a "preferred position" in our constitutional scheme and for which the Court has a more affirmative guardianship role. (Stone's "preferred position" concept was articulated in a footnote in the case of *United States v. Carolene Products Company*, 304 U.S. 144: 1938). Generally, Stone lived by this doctrine and applied it extensively (see, for example, Stone's dissent in the flag salute case of *Minersville School District v. Gobitis*, 310 U.S. 586: 1940) for the duration of his tenure. Stone is regarded as a "great" justice because of the clarity of his thinking on the fundamental constitutional issues he confronted. Although his service as chief justice was less successful, largely because the Court during this period was so badly fragmented, Stone's contributions as a constitutional scholar to a large degree outweigh that aspect of his career.

Joseph Story (1811–1845)   A principal ally of Chief Justice John Marshall, and the youngest person ever appointed to the Supreme Court, Joseph Story was born in Marblehead, Massachusetts, in 1779. He attended a local academy for a short time, but essentially completed his precollege education on his own. He sought early admission to Harvard University, where he graduated second in his class at age 19. He then began reading law under Samuel Sewall, who would subsequently become chief justice of the Massachusetts Supreme Court. Story completed his law studies in Salem, Massachusetts, where he was admitted to the bar in 1801. He established a successful practice in Salem although it was a struggle for political reasons. Story was affiliated with the Republican-Democrats, clearly the minority party among the Federalist-dominated local bar. Story was subjected to sufficient discrimination that he considered leaving Massachusetts. His practice thrived in Salem nonetheless, and he chose to remain there.

In 1805, Story was elected to the Massachusetts legislature, where he served until his election to Congress in 1808. Story and Jefferson developed strong differences over the latter's embargo on foreign trade. The policy was eventually repealed by Congress, and Jefferson blamed Story for his defeat. In early 1811, Story returned to the Massachusetts legislature, where he was elected speaker. That same year, Justice William Cushing died, and President Madison was unsuccessful in finding a replacement until the Senate confirmed Story, Madison's fourth choice. Story served on the Court for almost 30 years until his death in 1845. He was replaced by Levi Woodbury. During his tenure as an associate justice, Story maintained an active interest in education and academic pursuits. He was elected to the Harvard Board of Overseers in 1819 and became a fellow in the Harvard Corporation in 1825. Four years later, Story moved from Salem to Cambridge to become professor of law at Harvard and was instrumental in founding the Harvard Law School. While on the Harvard faculty, Story wrote nine lengthy volumes on the law as well as countless essays and articles. *See also* CHARLES RIVER BRIDGE COMPANY V. WARREN BRIDGE COMPANY (11 Peters 420: 1837), p. 476; MARTIN V. HUNTER'S LESSEE (1 Wheaton 304: 1816), p. 234.

Significance   Although appointed by a Republican-Democratic president, Joseph Story was a personal friend of John Marshall and shared some of the nationalistic predispositions of Marshall and other Federalists. It is for this reason that many anti-Federalists like Jefferson argued against his nomination. History records Story very favorably; he is generally considered one of the several most outstanding jurists ever to serve on the Court. He did, however, prove the fears of those Republican-Democrats who contested his selection to be well founded. The first and in some respects most important indication of the direction Story was to take as a justice came in the cases that raised the issue of Supreme Court jurisdiction over state courts when constitutional issues were involved. Most noteworthy is his opinion in *Martin v. Hunter's Lessee* (1 Wheaton 304: 1816), which unequivocally established that the Supreme Court is the final constitutional authority over all other elements of government, including state courts. It was the Court's holding in this case that permitted Marshall and the remainder of the Court to fashion national authority to its fullest, particularly through use of the commerce and contract clauses. Certainly illustrative are the decisions of *Trustees of Dartmouth College v. Woodward* (4 Wheaton 518: 1819) and *McCulloch v. Maryland* (4 Wheaton 316: 1819). In the former, the Court held that a private corporate charter, even one entered prior to the establishment of the government under the Constitution, could not be altered unilaterally by a state. In this case, Story was found on the opposite side from Justice Gabriel Duvall, the Republican-Democrat appointed with Story in 1811. It had been expected that their selections would give the Jeffersonians a majority on the Court for the first time, but this result did not materialize. In

McCulloch, the Court utilized the doctrine of implied power to uphold chartering of the national bank while at the same time invalidating the state tax levied against it on supremacy grounds. *McCulloch* may have been Story's single most important statement of federal-state relations.

National politics changed dramatically during the following decade. The election of 1826 produced a Congress controlled by Jacksonians, and this was immediately reflected in some decisions from the Court. In *Ogden v. Saunders* (12 Wheaton 213: 1837), for example, the Court upheld a state insolvency law applying to prospective indebtedness over the dissents of Story and Marshall. Broader impact from Jacksonian politics was slower in developing. Indeed, it was not until Marshall was replaced by Roger Taney that the comprehensive policy change occurred. The flavor of this course change can readily be seen in *Charles River Bridge Company v. Warren Bridge Company* (11 Peters 420: 1837). There the Court held that a franchise charter did not include implicit protections from subsequent state actions that may be incompatible with the explicit provisions of the contract. Story dissented, drawing on English common law that state power could be limited by implication. In other words, Story advocated giving benefit of the doubt to the grantee rather than the state, a position clearly derived from *Dartmouth*.

Other early decisions of the Taney Court severely limited the applicability of Marshall Court decisions, and from that point on, Story was generally found on the minority side of most decisions. A significant exception was *Swift v. Tyson* (16 Peters 1: 1842), where Story wrote for a unanimous Court. In this case, Story held that federal courts need not be bound by state decisions in diversity of citizenship actions even if the case involved no federal constitutional or statutory questions. This was Story's attempt to begin developing a uniform national commercial law, and his doctrine was retained well into the twentieth century. Story was a jurist of consequence and a preeminent legal scholar. His paramount constitutional impact comes from providing the integrative and stabilizing decisions on the issue of national authority.

George Sutherland (1922–1938)   George Sutherland was born in Buckinghamshire, England, in 1862. Because of his father's conversion to the Mormon faith, Sutherland's family came to the United States and settled in the Utah Territory. Early in his life, Sutherland had learned the value of hard work and self-reliance. By the age of 12, he had left school and was at work helping support the family. At the age of 16, Sutherland had managed to save enough money to enroll at Brigham Young Academy, where he studied for three years. It was at Brigham Young that Sutherland was first introduced to the political thought of Herbert Spencer. In 1883, he undertook a year of study at the University of Michigan Law School, where he studied constitutional law under Dean Thomas M. Cooley. After a year, Sutherland returned to Provo, Utah, where he began his private practice with William King and Samuel Thurman, both of whom would themselves become prominent political figures in the state. In 1893, Sutherland moved to Salt Lake City. When Utah attained statehood three years later, Sutherland was elected to the first state senate as a Republican. Four years later, he was elected to the United States House of Representatives. He chose not to seek reelection in 1902, but was elected to the U.S. Senate in 1904, where he served two full terms.

In 1916 Sutherland failed to be renominated for the Senate. Rather than return to Utah, he remained in Washington to practice law. He also maintained close contact with then Senator Warren G. Harding. He became one of Harding's principal advisers and was one of the architects of Harding's successful presidential campaign in 1920. It was clear after Harding's election that Sutherland would eventually receive an appointment to the Court, and while he could have had virtually any job in the Harding adminstration until a vacancy occurred, Sutherland chose to take several short-term assignments abroad. In September 1922, Justice John Clarke left the Court, and Harding nominated Sutherland as his replacement. He was confirmed by the Senate on the same day. He served on the Court until 1938. The vacancy created by his retirement was filled by Stanley F. Reed. Sutherland died four years later at the age of 76. *See also* ADKINS V. CHILDREN'S HOSPITAL (261 U.S. 525: 1923), p. 433; CARTER V. CARTER COAL COMPANY (298 U.S. 238: 1936), p. 317; HOME BUILDING AND LOAN ASSOCIATION V. BLAISDELL (290 U.S. 398: 1934), p. 479; NEBBIA V. NEW YORK (291 U.S. 502: 1934), p. 441.

Significance   George Sutherland was appointed to the Court to reinforce the ranks of the economic conservatives. His Senate record was unmistakably conservative. In the last several years of his tenure in that body, he opposed the amendment allowing for an income tax, the Federal Reserve Act, establishment of the Federal Trade Commission, and the Clayton Act, to mention but a few. Sutherland fulfilled the expectations of those who had supported his selection. Indeed, Sutherland became the most effective spokesman of the portion of the Court that subscribed to the social Darwinism developed by such persons as Herbert Spencer in his *Social Statics*. First evidence came in *Adkins v. Children's Hospital* (261 U.S. 525: 1923), a case in which the Court invalidated a minimum wage law for women and children. Sutherland's majority opinion centered on interference with the liberty of employers and employees to contract about work and compensation. The right to contract was protected by the due process clauses of the Fifth and Fourteenth Amendments in Sutherland's view and, while not absolute, "legislative authority to abridge it can be justified only by the existence of exceptional circumstances." Sutherland saw due process in substantive terms and could be found in virtually every economic due process case attempting to free property from state regulation by finding enactments unreasonable and constituting a denial of due process.

Sutherland occasionally supported regulation of property against due process claims. For example, he wrote the Court's opinion in *Village of Euclid v. Ambler Realty Company* (272 U.S. 365: 1926), which upheld local zoning ordinances. There, however, Sutherland was convinced of the reasonableness of the regulation for property interests. Sutherland was also adamant in opposing state regulations that impaired obligation of contracts. In *Home Building and Loan Association v. Blaisdell* (290 U.S. 398: 1934), the Court upheld a state mortgage moratorium law that, because of the effect of the depression, allowed postponement of contracted mortgage payments. Sutherland dissented forcefully, arguing that the contact clause was not to be flexible in application. Emergencies, he argued, could not justify alteration of contracts.

Sutherland's laissez-faire orientation could also be seen in cases involving exercise of federal power. He was the ideological leader of the "Four Horsemen" (with Butler, McReynolds, and Van Devanter) who categorically opposed New Deal initiatives. Characteristic of Sutherland's views was his majority opinion in the commerce clause decision of *Carter v. Carter Coal Company* (298 U.S. 238: 1936), where the Court nullified the labor and price regulations contained in the Bituminous Coal Act of 1935. *Carter* marked the last decision in which the laissez-fairists used the direct-indirect effects distinction to invalidate the exercise of the federal commerce power.

When the Court realigned itself following the proposal to alter its size, Sutherland became part of the minority on these issues, and he left the Court soon thereafter. He must be remembered for providing effective articulation of the laissez-faire position at a time when it prevailed within the Court. Sutherland must also be remembered for his opinion in the landmark decision of *Powell v. Alabama* (287 U.S. 45: 1932), the Court's first review of the "Scottsboro" case. In *Powell*, Sutherland spoke for the Court, saying that a state could not deny assistance of counsel to indigent criminal defendants in capital cases. This case became the foundation for extending federal Bill of Rights provisions to state criminal proceedings.

William Howard Taft (1921–1930)   William Howard Taft was born in Cincinnati, Ohio, in 1857. His family had a history of public service. Both Taft's father and grandfather were attorneys and served as state trial judges. Taft's father was also President Grant's secretary of war and attorney general, and, like his son, aspired for appointment to the United States Supreme Court. Following high school, the younger Taft went to Yale University, where he graduated second in his class in 1878. He then entered Cincinnati Law School, where he earned his LL.B. in 1880. During this period, Taft also worked as a legal reporter for a Cincinnati newspaper. Upon his admission to the bar, Taft became an assistant prosecutor, where he remained for two years before establishing a private practice. In 1885, however, he returned to the public arena to serve a two-year term as assistant county solicitor. He was appointed to the Ohio Superior Court in 1887, where he remained until President Benjamin Harrison named him U.S. solicitor general in 1890. In 1892, Taft was appointed to the U.S. Court of Appeals for the Sixth Circuit, a position he held until 1900.

Throughout his life, Taft felt that he was best suited for the judiciary. It was with some reluctance that he left the court of appeals in 1900 to head a commission to establish a civil government in the Philippines. The following year, Taft was made civilian governor of the Philippines. In 1904, Taft became President Roosevelt's secretary of war. Taft became one of the key people in the Roosevelt administration and, as a result, became nationally prominent within the Republican party. He was subsequently nominated for and elected to the presidency in 1908, and he served one full term. A serious division between Taft and Roosevelt developed during Taft's first term, and the Republicans lost the White House in the election of 1912 because Roosevelt splintered the party and ran as a third-party candidate. Following his term as president, Taft taught at Yale and served a year as president of the American Bar Association. He also maintained his strong desire for appointment to the Supreme Court, although this was an impossibility throughout the terms of Woodrow Wilson. In 1920, Warren Harding was elected president, and the following year, Taft was named chief justice to replace Edward D. White. He was confirmed by the Senate the same day. He served as chief justice until 1930, when he was compelled to leave the Court for reasons of health. He was replaced by Charles Evans Hughes. Taft died in 1930 shortly after resigning his position as chief justice. See also ADKINS V. CHILDREN'S HOSPITAL (261 U.S. 525: 1923), p. 433; BAILEY V. DREXEL FURNITURE COMPANY (259 U.S. 20: 1922), p. 396; MYERS V. UNITED STATES (272 U.S. 52: 1926), p. 150; STAFFORD V. WALLACE (258 U.S. 495: 1922), p. 311.

Significance   William Howard Taft is the only person in American history to serve as both president and chief justice. There is no doubt which position he preferred. For much of his professional life, he was driven by a desire to be chief justice. It is not surprising that, once he got there, he directed his enormous energies to the institution itself. He was the first chief justice to take initiatives in the area of court management and reform. Taft was responsible for Congress's passing the Judiciary Act of 1925, legislation that modernized and centralized the federal judiciary. The act also changed some Supreme Court procedures, including providing it greater discretion over its docket. It can be accurately said that Taft was the architect of the contemporary federal judicial system. Taft has also been given principal credit for the building that houses the Court, although it was not actually begun until after his death.

Taft's leadership was not confined to external initiatives. He was also able to forge consensus within his Court by strength of personality and administrative skill. He stressed the notion of "team," and he was generally successful in establishing a cohesive Court. It is for these achievements that Taft is highly regarded as a chief justice. Taft also had extraordinary influence while chief justice on the selection of other justices to serve with him. As a former president, he was cognizant of the impact the Court could have on policy, and he wished to be sure that those selected shared his economic and political values. He saw "progressives" as subversive and used his influence to prevent their appointment. It was Taft who probably delayed the selection of Benjamin Cardozo, an eminent jurist, for more than a decade for fear that he would align himself with Justices Holmes and Brandeis, an outcome Taft wished to prevent at any cost.

Taft was not, however, the intellectual leader of his Court although he clearly subscribed to the economic conservatism of the majority. That role fell to Justices Sutherland and Van Devanter. Nevertheless, Taft wrote more than his share of opinions, a number of which are still noteworthy. Characteristic of Taft's conservative orientation is his opinion in *Bailey v. Drexel Furniture Company* (259 U.S. 20: 1922). In this case, the Court invalidated the child labor tax on Tenth Amendment grounds. The Court objected to the regulatory motive made obvious by the "penalizing features of the so-called tax." Under such circumstances, the limitations of federalism precluded Congress's reaching an improper subject by means of the taxing power. Taft was not absolutely resistant to the exercise of federal regulatory power. He wrote for the Court in *Stafford v. Wallace* (258 U.S. 495: 1922), upholding the Packers and Stockyards Act of 1921. The statute addressed monopolistic practices of packers and the impact of these practices on prices. He spoke of broad regulatory discretion residing with Congress to deal with matters still in the "stream of commerce." He also supported the exercise of federal power, albeit from a dissenting position, in *Adkins v. Children's Hospital* (261 U.S. 525: 1923). While he may have preferred to dispose of this minimum wage law for women and minors by invoking the liberty of contract doctrine, Taft argued that the power of legislators to regulate in this way had been "firmly established." In addition to precedent, Taft also suggested that the Court ought not invalidate enactments "simply because they are passed to carry out economic views which the Court believes to be unwise or unsound." Although not always willing to follow his own advice (as in *Bailey*), at least in this case Taft separated himself from the other laissez-fairists on the Court.

The opinion Taft thought his most important was *Myers v. United States* (272 U.S. 52: 1926), a separation of powers case involving presidential removal powers. Taking the position one might expect of a former president, Taft held that removal of an official is "incident to the power of appointment, not to the power of advising and consenting to appointment." The effect of the decision was to give the president unlimited and unilateral removal power of any executive officer. This doctrine was substantially modified shortly thereafter in *Humphrey's Executor v. United States* (295 U.S. 602: 1935). In a more general sense, most of the policy positions taken by Taft were short-lived. Certainly the economic conservatism of his Court did not survive the next decade. What does survive, however, is Taft's record as a judicial reformer, where his achievements are unsurpassed.

Roger B. Taney (1836–1864)   Roger Brooke Taney was born in Calvert County, Maryland, in 1777. Taney came from an established Maryland family that had origins in the state on both sides dating back to the mid-seventeenth century. At the time of Taney's birth, the family was part of the landed aristocracy, owning a large tobacco plantation in Calvert County. Following his elementary education, Taney was sent to grammar school and then received private tutoring before enrolling at Dickinson College at the age of 15. He graduated from Dickinson in 1795 at the top of his class. Taney then read law with Judge Jeremiah Chase, a member of the Maryland General Court in Annapolis. It was a quality apprenticeship as the Maryland court was highly respected. Taney was admitted to the bar in 1799. Immediately thereafter, Taney was elected to one term in the Maryland legislature as a Federalist. Defeated in his bid for reelection, Taney moved to Frederick, Maryland, where he developed a successful private practice. He remained active with the Federalist party, although he did not always subscribe to mainstream party thinking.

In 1816, Taney was elected to the state senate. He served a single term, returned to his Frederick practice, and then relocated in Baltimore. He quickly established himself as an attorney there, but he also went through a political relocation. The Federalist party had deteriorated to relative insignificance, and Taney was drawn to the Jacksonian

Democrats. He supported Jackson in the election of 1824 and chaired the Jackson organization in Maryland in 1828. In between, Taney had been chosen state attorney general, a position he held until 1831. It was in that year that he was summoned to Washington by Jackson, who was restructuring his cabinet. Taney served for two years as Jackson's attorney general and played a prominent role in the national bank controversy. Taney assisted in the formulation of Jackson's rationale for vetoing recharter of the bank. When the treasury secretary refused to implement the policy decisions of the Jackson administration, he was dismissed and replaced by Taney, who did so.

Taney served a lengthy interim (almost a year) without Senate review, but submission of his name was eventually forced, and his nomination was rejected in 1836. The previous year, Justice Gabriel Duvall had left the Court, and Jackson had nominated Taney. Senate consideration of the nomination had been indefinitely postponed. Upon the death of Chief Justice John Marshall in late 1835, Jackson again proposed Taney's name, this time as Marshall's replacement. He was confirmed three months later by a 29–15 vote. He served as chief justice for 28 years until his death in 1864. He was replaced by Salmon P. Chase. *See also CHARLES RIVER BRIDGE COMPANY V. WARREN BRIDGE COMPANY* (11 Peters 420: 1837), p. 476; *COOLEY V. BOARD OF PORT WARDENS* (12 Howard 299: 1851), p. 298; *DRED SCOTT V. SANDFORD* (19 Howard 393: 1857), p. 91.

Significance   Roger B. Taney was a states' rightist, and many felt that his appointment would bring about complete reversal of the pronational decisions of the Marshall Court. While the jurisprudence of the Taney Court differed in a number of important respects, it would be accurate to describe the Taney Court as working within the framework of Marshall Court doctrine rather than rejecting this doctrine outright. Taney clearly wanted to elevate the states as governmental entities and free them from some of the limitations attached by Marshall Court decisions, but Taney was quite restrained in pursuing this priority. While preferring to define a broad number of areas as exclusively under state authority, Taney chose to resolve many of these matters on the basis of concurrent power or the principle of dual sovereignty. This approach, in tune with Jackson's view of federal-state relations, could most readily be seen in the commerce clause area. For example, in *New York v. Miln* (11 Peters 102: 1837), the Court upheld a state law that screened persons coming into the state from abroad. The Court maintained that such a reporting law did not interfere with the federal commerce power. A decade later, in the *License Cases* (5 Howard 504: 1847), the Court upheld state licensing regulations on the sale of liquor brought in from out-of-state. While states could not regulate importation as such, a state could exercise its police power on behalf of the public health and safety once items arrived inside the state.

The balance of federal and state power endorsed by Taney can be seen in the fashioning of the "selective exclusiveness" doctrine in *Cooley v. Board of Port Wardens* (12 Howard 299: 1851). Here the Court said that the commerce power "embraces a vast field" containing many subjects "quite unlike in their nature." Some of these subjects "imperatively" demand a "single uniform rule," while others demand "diversity which alone can meet the local needs." When a subject is found to require uniform regulation, it is exclusively federal in nature. Until such time as Congress determines the need for uniform policy, the states retain authority. *Cooley* was not a decision manifesting hostility toward the exercise of federal authority, but rather a temperate compromise resolution.

The differences between Marshall and Taney can easily be seen in the contract case of *Charles River Bridge Company v. Warren Bridge Company* (11 Peters 420: 1837), and yet even there the later Court did not reject the Marshall Court ruling. In the bridge case, Taney held that a public contract must be interpreted literally and narrowly, and that no state interest may be contracted away implicitly. Diminution of state power to "promote the happiness and prosperity of the community" can never be accomplished by implication. This decision did not reverse the famous Marshall contract case of *Trustees of Dartmouth College v. Woodward* (4 Wheaton 518: 1819), but weakened it as a means of forestalling state regulation of private property. This was done by reversing the direction of benefit of the doubt. Under *Dartmouth*, all ambiguities in a contract were resolved in favor of the private interest, while the bridge decision held that any ambiguity must be resolved in favor of the state.

Finally, there is the *Dred Scott* decision (*Dred Scott v. Sandford*, 19 Howard 393: 1857). The case represents the Court's misguided attempt to resolve the slavery issue. Although each member of the Court offered a separate opinion, Taney's is generally regarded as the Court's statement in that infamous case. He was drawn into broadening the scope of the decision unnecessarily, and offered remarks about the status of blacks that unfortunately escalated an already out of control situation. While a discussion of Taney is incomplete without treatment of *Dred Scott*, the case and its injurious consequences should not receive inordinate attention. Taney believed in dual sovereignty, and that view governed all else. It was because he believed that power could be shared by federal and state governments that he sought to preserve some of Marshall's nationalism by tempering it with state authority.

Morrison R. Waite (1874–1888)   Morrison Remick Waite was born in Lyme, Connecticut, in 1816. He was born into a prominent New England family, and his father was chief justice of the Connecticut

Supreme Court. He took his undergraduate degree from Yale College, graduating in 1837. The following year, Waite moved to Ohio, settling in Maumee City. There he studied law with a leading local attorney, Samuel D. Young. He was admitted to the bar in 1839, and he established a practice in Maumee City, where he stayed until moving to Toledo in 1850. There he built a very successful practice specializing in railroad law. Three times Waite sought elective office. In 1846, he unsuccessfully ran for Congress as a Whig. Three years later, he won a seat in the state legislature. He served only a single term. In 1862, Waite again ran for the Congress, this time as a Republican. The following year, Waite declined appointment to the Ohio Supreme Court, choosing instead to serve as an adviser to the Ohio governor.

In 1871, Waite was named to the delegation representing the American compensation claims against Great Britain at the Geneva Arbitration. Waite's performance during these proceedings contributed to a substantial judgment for the United States and brought him some national recognition. Waite returned to the United States, was elected to the Ohio constitutional convention, and was selected to preside over the convention proceedings. Early in 1874, Chief Justice Salmon P. Chase died, creating a vacancy on the Supreme Court. President Grant's first three choices either declined or withdrew, fearing rejection by the Senate. Waite did not seek appointment to the Court, but he had substantial support both from inside and outside government. Feeling the volume of support, Grant yielded to political pressure and nominated Waite. During his 14 years as chief justice, he tended the responsibilities of the office conscientiously, and he is generally regarded favorably by history. He died in 1888 and was replaced as chief justice by Melville W. Fuller. *See also MUNN V. ILLINOIS* (94 U.S. 113: 1877), p. 420; *STONE V. MISSISSIPPI* (116 U.S. 307: 1886), p. 478.

Significance   Morrison Waite joined a Court that had been deeply involved with the nationalistic politics of Lincoln during the Civil War and the period immediately thereafter. Waite was successful in redirecting the court's attention and withdrawing it from the political limelight. Waite had no prior judicial experience and was the product of an ill-administered selection process by Grant. As a result, he was viewed with some suspicion and definite coolness by his colleagues as he began his tenure. Nonetheless, he "took command" and established himself as a conscientious and effective leader.

The jurisprudence of the Waite Court was essentially established the year prior to his appointment in the *Slaughterhouse Cases* (16 Wallace 36: 1873) decision. There the Court refused to use the due process clause of the Fourteenth Amendment as the basis for federal intervention against a state property regulation. This decision reflected two major themes of the Waite Court, a deference to state regulatory initiatives and a uniformly restrictive interpretation of the post–Civil War amendments. Representative of the first theme is, of course, *Munn v. Illinois* (94 U.S. 113: 1877). Waite spoke for the majority in *Munn*, and it is probably his best remembered opinion. In *Munn*, the Court upheld a state regulation on warehouse operations including rates that could be charged. Waite said that when private property is "affected with a public interest, it ceases to be *juris privati* only." Property becomes "clothed" with a public interest when it is "used in a manner to make it of public consequence." A property owner so using property "grants to the public an interest in that use," and he must "submit to be controlled by the public for the common good." *Munn* drew from Waite's sensitivity to the needs of rural interests and a view that business could not go unregulated. He was also confident that such regulation was best undertaken from the state level, the government level most effectively held accountable through the electoral process.

The state power tone of *Munn* carried over to several important contract clause opinions from Waite. Notwithstanding some acknowledged property protections, it was Waite's view that the public interest may override property and contract interests. In *Stone v. Mississippi* (101 U.S. 814: 1880), the Court upheld a state constitutional provision that negated a previously granted lottery charter. Waite said that the contract clause could not extend to governmental rights. No legislatively granted charter could "bargain away the police power of the state." Items subject to the police power such as the public health and morals require supervision that is "continuing" in nature. They are to be dealt with as the "special exigencies of the moment may require"; thus a state cannot be bound by the contract clause in a way that precludes appropriate response. Similarly, in *Stone v. Farmers' Loan and Trust Company* (116 U.S. 307: 1886), Waite held that a state may still regulate railroad rates despite charter language freeing the railroad from "all legislative control."

The other side of the states' rights theme was the narrow interpretation of the postwar amendments and the negative consequences of this on the civil rights of blacks. Illustrative is *United States v. Cruikshank* (92 U.S. 542: 1874), a decision that severely narrowed the impact of the Fifteenth Amendment on black voting rights. Waite said that the amendment did not directly grant black suffrage. Rather, it had only precluded race from being the reason for denial of suffrage, and that the right to vote was still a state matter. In similar fashion, the Court voided the Civil Rights Act of 1875 in the *Civil Rights Cases* (109 U.S. 3: 1883) and established "state action" as the threshold condition for federal "corrective" legislation. Even so, Waite came to the Court at a time when there was little consensus on a number of fundamental issues. While he did not offer great leadership or profound legal insights, he was a moderate personality who had a moderating influence on the Court, and he was able to establish much-needed stability.

Earl Warren (1954–1969)   Earl Warren was nominated for chief justice by President Eisenhower in 1953 and confirmed unanimously by the Senate in early 1954. Eisenhower was later to call the appointment the "biggest damn-fool mistake I ever made." Warren came to the Court with no previous judicial experience, but he had extraordinary political and executive credentials.

Warren was born in Los Angeles in 1891 to Norwegian immigrant parents and was reared in central California. He earned his undergraduate and law degrees from the University of California, graduating from law school in 1914. After a short period in private practice, Warren became the deputy city attorney of Oakland. He was elected Alameda County district attorney in 1925 and established a reputation as a vigorous prosecutor. Warren was elected California attorney general in 1938, and four years later was elected governor. He was reelected governor in 1946 and 1950. His nominations in 1938 and 1946 were a reflection of his enormous electoral appeal. Although he was a Republican, he gained both the Republican and Democratic nominations in those years through California's cross-filing system.

Warren's image changed over the course of his three terms as governor. He was initially regarded as a conservative. He took a hard line on crime, publicly denounced "leftist radicals," and was enthusiastic in his support of the Japanese relocation. After the war, however, he came to be regarded as a progressive. He proposed a comprehensive medical insurance program for California and liberalized state pension and welfare benefits.

Warren sought national office twice. He was the Republican vice presidential nominee in 1948, running with Thomas E. Dewey. Four years later, Warren failed in his attempt to secure the Republican presidential nomination, but his support at a crucial point of the convention enabled Eisenhower to gain the nomination over Senator Robert A. Taft. Many regard that critical support of Eisenhower's candidacy as the act which later won Warren nomination as chief justice. Warren retired from the Court in 1969 and died in 1974.

Significance   Under Earl Warren's leadership, the Supreme Court restructured the relationship of the states to the Bill of Rights, greatly expanded the rights afforded to those accused of criminal conduct, liberalized the right to vote, broke the stalemate on legislative malapportionment, and extended the coverage available through the Thirteenth and Fourteenth Amendments.

Warren is not regarded as a great legal scholar, nor as a sophisticated judicial philosopher. He is, however, generally acknowledged as a great chief justice. He possessed unusual leadership skills and an uncommon political sense. He was able to orchestrate change. His political career was marked by decisive and forceful action, and Warren was able to transfer a sense of urgency for action to his colleagues on the Court. He seemed able to focus the Court, enabling it to make its landmark decisions, while at the same time keeping the Court on a clear, long-term course.

Warren had a generally libertarian view of public law and individual rights, but the values of equality and fairness stood out over the rest. Several of his opinions are representative. His opinion in *Brown v. Board of Education* (1954), the landmark school segregation case, is probably his most far-reaching one, but his concern for procedural, as well as substantive, fairness was demonstrated through his opinions in such cases as *Miranda v. Arizona* (384 U.S. 436: 1966), which involved custodial interrogation of criminal suspects, and *Reynolds v. Sims* (377 U.S. 533: 1964), which required apportionment of both houses of state legislatures on a one person-one vote basis. Earl Warren presided over a Court that dramatically altered American constitutional history.

Byron White (1962–)   Byron R. White was born in Fort Collins, Colorado, in 1917. White went to the University of Colorado on scholarship and graduated Phi Beta Kappa and first in his class in 1938. He also distinguished himself in athletics, winning ten varsity letters over his undergraduate career. He achieved recognition as an all-American football player. Combined achievements as a scholar-athlete earned White a Rhodes scholarship, and he attended Oxford in 1939 and 1940. It was while in England that White first met John F. Kennedy. White began law school at Yale upon his return from England. He also pursued a professional football career with great success. His educational and athletic pursuits were interrupted by the war, and a tour as a naval officer. White then returned to his legal education and completed his law degree in 1946. He then clerked for Supreme Court Chief Justice Fred Vinson. It was during this time that he renewed his acquaintance with John Kennedy, who was then serving his first term in Congress. White returned to Colorado in 1947 and joined a prominent Denver firm, specializing in corporate law.

Thirteen years later, then–Senator Kennedy sought the presidency.

White joined the campaign, first working in securing the Democratic nomination for Kennedy, then playing a major role in the general election campaign organization. Following Kennedy's election, White was named deputy attorney general. For the next 15 months, he recruited Justice Department staff and had extensive responsibility for supervising the operations of the department. Specifically, he monitored antitrust and civil rights suits as well as provided evaluation of judicial nominees for the Kennedy Administration. In March 1962, Justice Charles Whitaker resigned from the Court, and White was nominated to replace him. The Senate confirmed his nomination two weeks later. *See also* POTTER STEWART, p. 549.

Significance   Justice Byron R. White was President John F. Kennedy's first appointment to the Court (he also appointed Arthur Goldberg). It was expected that White would take a solidly liberal course, but that has not occurred. From the outset, White has approached constitutional issues in a fashion independent of ideology. Indeed, White's Court career of more than 20 years defies easy classification ideologically. During the period of Warren's tenure as chief justice, White typically aligned himself with the center to conservative members—Justices Stewart, Clark, and Harlan. Especially revealing is White's record on rights of the accused questions. During the 1950s, White resisted extending certain provisions of the Bill of Rights to the states. His dissents in *Robinson v. California* (370 U.S. 660: 1962) and *Malloy v. Hogan* (378 U.S. 1: 1964), opposing incorporation of the cruel and unusual punishment and self-incrimination clauses, respectively, are representative. He also disagreed with the Warren Court majorities in two landmark decisions involving custodial interrogation of suspects, *Escobedo v. Illinois* (378 U.S. 478: 1954) and *Miranda v. Arizona* (384 U.S. 436: 1966).

More recently, White was among the Burger Court majority, which limited the scope of the *Miranda* protection (see, for example, *Harris v. New York*, 401 U.S. 222: 1971). Similarly, White has tended to support the law enforcement position on Fourth Amendment questions. White was with the majority in upholding the stop and frisk practice in *Terry v. Ohio* (392 U.S. 1: 1968) and dissented in *Chimel v. California* (395 U.S. 752: 1969), where the Court limited the scope of warrantless searches incidental to lawful arrests. White also supports use of the death penalty by the states. In *Furman v. Georgia* (408 U.S. 238: 1972), White was among the majority that struck down the wholly discretionary use of capital punishment. With Stewart, he found that the changes in procedures following *Furman* met the demands of the Eighth Amendment.

Neither has White been a leading libertarian on First Amendment issues. He was among the Burger Court majority in *Miller v. California*

(413 U.S. 15: 1973), in which the Warren Court standards for obscenity regulation were redefined to permit greater governmental control. White also wrote for the Court in *Zurcher v. Stanford Daily* (436 U.S. 547: 1978), allowing the search of a newspaper office for evidence pertaining to a criminal investigation. He also voted with the majority in *Branzburg v. Hayes* (408 U.S. 665: 1972), which required journalists to disclose sources to grand juries. White's establishment clause record is essentially accommodationist, especially in the school aid cases. He was with the majority in *Lynch v. Donnelly* (79 L.Ed. 2d 604: 1984), where the Court ruled that a municipality could include a nativity scene in its annual holiday display. White has generally supported state initiatives to regulate abortion. In fact, White dissented with Justice Rehnquist in *Roe v. Wade* (410 U.S. 113: 1973), arguing that an inferred right of privacy was insufficient to preclude state prohibition of abortion.

On the other hand, White has been a liberal activist on questions involving equal protection. Generally aligned with Justices Brennan and Marshall, he has consistently supported those claiming racial discrimination. White has also been receptive to extending the equal protection clause to other classes. In *Frontiero v. Richardson* (411 U.S. 667: 1973), White supported the designation of gender classification as "suspect," thus invoking strict judicial scrutiny. More recently he opposed the "male only" draft registration policy upheld in *Rostker v. Goldberg* (453 U.S. 57: 1981). Similarly, he has taken a strong position on economic discrimination in *San Antonio Independent School District v. Rodriguez* (411 U.S. 1: 1963). The "swing" position of White and Stewart was dramatic during the decade of the 1970s. The retirement of Stewart in 1981 and the subsequent appointment of Justice O'Connor solidified the conservative bloc sufficiently to reduce White's previously often decisive role.

Edward D. White (1894–1921)   Edward Douglass White was born in Thibodaux, Louisiana, in 1845. White's family had settled in Louisiana after having left Pennsylvania in the early nineteenth century. Having established a large and prosperous farm, White's father turned to public life. After serving four years as a New Orleans City Court judge, White's father was elected to Congress in 1834, where he served three terms. He then was elected to a four-year term as governor before returning to the Congress for two additional terms. He died shortly after White's birth. His mother remarried and sent White off to school, first to a New Orleans convent and later to prep school in Maryland. He attended Georgetown College from 1857 to 1861 before returning to Louisiana just prior to the outbreak of the Civil War. White joined the Confederate Army, was captured in 1863 during the siege of Port Hudson, and was a prisoner of war for the duration of the conflict.

Following the war, White began reading in the law under the direction of Edward Bermudez, a prominent New Orleans attorney. At the same time, he enrolled in courses at the University of Louisiana (later Tulane University) School of Law. He was admitted to the bar in 1868. He established a successful practice in New Orleans as well as becoming politically active. He was an especially vocal critic of Reconstruction. In 1874, White was elected to the state senate as a Democrat. He supported the successful gubernatorial candidate in the election of 1877, and the following year, at the age of 33, he was named to the Louisiana Supreme Court. The subsequent governor was successful in forcing White off the Court in 1880 by having a law passed creating minimum age requirements for justices. White could not meet the new requirement and was compelled to leave the Court. Eight years later, those partisan to White regained control of state politics, and the legislature named White one of the state's U.S. senators.

In July of 1893, Justice Samuel Blatchford died, creating a vacancy on the Supreme Court. President Cleveland was unable to secure Senate confirmation for his first two choices, and in February 1894, offered White as a nominee the Senate could not reject. It did not; White was confirmed immediately. White chose to stay in the Senate following confirmation to aid in hammering out a compromise on a controversial tariff bill vital to his political constituency in Louisiana. Only after the issue had been resolved did he assume his seat as an associate justice. In 1910, Chief Justice Melville Fuller died. President Taft, himself driven by the desire for the chief justiceship, named White, then 65, to the position. It was the first time an associate justice had been elevated. When White died 11 years later, it was Taft who was chosen by Harding as his successor. *See also* ANTITRUST LAWS, p. 579; SUBSTANTIVE DUE PROCESS, p. 659.

Significance   Edward D. White was selected by President Cleveland to meet a regional representational need and to smooth relations with the Senate. White was also appointed because he shared the economic conservatism of Cleveland. He generally acted compatibly with those views throughout his lengthy tenure on the Court. White joined a Court dominated by laissez-fairists and committed to substantive due process. By this means, the Court used the concept of due process to insulate property from state regulation. In order to do so, the Court had to examine each regulation under review to determine whether it was "fair" and "reasonable." Seldom was a law found to be either. The subjective nature of this approach produced decisions that were often difficult to reconcile. White's individual pattern mirrored the Court's often uneven pattern. He joined Harlan's dissent, for example, in *Lochner v. New York* (198 U.S. 45: 1905), which invalidated a state law that established maximum hours of work for bakers. He took essentially the same position in *Muller v. Oregon* (208 U.S. 412: 1908), but was found on the opposite side of virtually the same issue in *Bunting v. Oregon* (243 U.S. 426: 1917). The nature of the substantive approach to due process required fine-line distinctions, and these often produced a zigzag line of decisions.

Besides state regulation, the Court of this period was also seized with the question of the extent of federal regulatory power under the commerce clause. This Court and White were generally resistant to the exercise of such power, but White was slightly less so than most of his colleagues. Among the more important cases of this time were those reviewing Interstate Commerce Commission judgments and applications of the antitrust laws. It was with these cases that White fashioned a novel approach termed the "rule of reason." From his early days on the Court, White had argued that the common law permitted less than full application of the Sherman Act. (See, for example, *Northern Securities Company v. United States*, 193 U.S. 197: 1904.) His view was that some "reasonable" restraint of trade could lawfully exist, and for economic reasons should exist. What constituted "reasonable" restraint was a matter for judicial determination. Although his colleagues had resisted his contentions for a number of years, White was able to develop wider support after becoming chief justice. For example, White was able to use the rule of reason to free certain previously covered practices from application of the Sherman Act. (See, for example, *Standard Oil Company v. United States*, 221 U.S. 1: 1911.)

The rule of reason was a political and pragmatic response to business regulation initiatives, and it permitted the Court to play a decisive role through the use of standards of its own design. Utilization of the rule reflects White's influence from 1911 through the end of World War I. Substantial turnover in Court membership created an opportunity for White to establish himself as the clear leader of the Court, and it was his "rule of reason" that shaped national economic policy during that period.

11. Legal Words and Phrases

Abstention   A policy designed to reduce conflict between federal and state courts. Abstention allows a federal court to withhold exercise of its jurisdiction on a federal constitutional issue until a state court has rendered a judgment on such state law as may have a bearing on the federal question. *See also* MIDDLESEX COUNTY ETHICS COMMISSION V. GARDEN STATE BAR ASSOCIATION (457 U.S. 423: 1982), p. 83.

Significance   The doctrine of abstention maintains that a federal court should not assume jurisdiction in a case until the uncertainties of state law are addressed by the appropriate state courts. Abstention by the federal court may prevent or minimize conflict by limiting federal court interference in matters that pertain primarily to state law. Abstention also permits a federal court to relinquish its jurisdiction if the federal court determines that the central issue in a case has been appropriately resolved at the state level. A particular form of abstention is known as comity. Comity is a courtesy by which one court extends deference to another in the exercise of authority. Comity is offered out of respect and goodwill rather than obligation. Like other forms of abstention, it is aimed at preventing friction between courts, both of which may have legitimate jurisdictional claims in a case.

Admiralty Jurisdiction   Power conferred by Article III to the federal courts to hear cases involving commerce on the seas and navigable inland waterways. In an effort to achieve uniformity in commercial regulation, power over all matters involving shipping on the high seas was assigned exclusively to the federal district courts by the Judiciary Act of 1789. Congress later expanded this to include all the nation's navigable waters.

Significance   Exercise of admiralty jurisdiction usually occurs in cases where particular actions on the high seas or waterways are litigated. Examples of this kind of case include confiscations, forfeitures, torts, and criminal prosecutions for conduct occurring on a vessel. A related group of cases, sometimes referred to as maritime cases, involves contractual or other relationships including seaman wage and compensation matters.

Admission of New States   Power conferred by Article IV, Section 3 to the Congress. The power to govern admission of new states is comprehensive and is limited only by the provision that no new state "shall be formed or erected within an existing state or by joining two or more states without consent of the states involved." The process of admission involves persons, through their territorial legislatures, petitioning Congress for authorization to develop a state constitution. Once the constitution is drafted and approved by the residents of the territory, the draft is submitted to Congress for approval. Upon approval, Congress passes a resolution of statehood. The resolution is subject to presidential veto like any other bill. Unlike a statute, a statehood resolution may not be repealed. *See also* ARTICLE IV, p. 225.

Significance   With so much territory to the west of the original states, the framers thought it necessary to provide for a process for the admission of new states. Vermont and Kentucky joined the original thirteen states almost immediately. Thirty-five states have been added since 1792. Twenty-eight of those states were developed as territories. Each petitioned for statehood in the manner described above. Five other states were created from existing states with their consent. Texas entered statehood from the status of an independent republic, while California became a state after being ceded from Mexico. Admission of states is a political process, and Congress may make its decisions on political bases. Under provision of the Northwest Ordinance of 1787, any state added to the Union must have "equal footing" with the original states. This status equivalence was reflected in the Court's holding in *Coyle v. Smith* (221 U.S. 559: 1911). Congress had tried to make admission of a state conditional. The state agreed but subsequently failed to honor the condition. The Court held that no such condition could be enforced against a new state.

Adversary Proceeding   A legal contest that involves a real contest between two opposing parties. In an adversary proceeding, formal notice is served on the party against whom an action has been filed to allow that party an opportunity to respond. An adversary proceeding is different from an ex parte proceeding, where only one party appears. An adversary proceeding also differs from a summary proceeding, where no significant fact dispute exists and where the court may hasten and simplify the resolution of an issue. *See also* ADVISORY OPINION, p. 577; CASE OR CONTROVERSY, p. 583.

Significance   An adversary proceeding forces a plaintiff and defendant in a legal action to contest each other with evidence gathered in support of their respective cases. The system is generally regarded as the most effective means of the evaluation of evidence. The adversary system also features a diffusion of power among its principal participants, such as judge, prosecutor, jury, and defense counsel. Each actor helps to produce a check and balance effect, thus safeguarding against arbitrary or abusive judgments.

Advisory Opinion   A response by a judge or court to a legal question posed outside a bona fide case or controversy. An advisory opinion is a reply to an abstract or hypothetical question. It has no binding effect unless it is legally accepted by the requesting body. *See also* CASE OR CONTROVERSY, p. 583; DECLARATORY JUDGMENT, p. 590.

Significance   An advisory opinion may not be rendered by a federal court because of the constitutional provision limiting jurisdiction of federal courts to an actual case or controversy. The limitation is designed to preserve separation of powers and keep the judiciary from certain political entanglements that might adversely affect the judicial branch. Several states allow the rendering of an advisory opinion in order to clarify state legislation without the necessity of burdensome litigation.

Affirmative Action   A policy based on a classification in which one class is disadvantaged in order to remedy past discrimination suffered by another class. Affirmative action policies aimed at remedial ends are often said to engage in reverse discrimination. The constitutional question raised by such policies is whether benevolent discrimination is permissible because of its compensatory character.

Significance   Affirmative action was permitted but circumscribed by the Supreme Court in *Regents of the University of California v. Bakke* (438 U.S. 265: 1978). The Court upheld the use of race-conscious admissions policies for a state university graduate program, although it disallowed the allocation of seats on a quota basis. The Court found that recruitment of a diverse or heterogeneous student body was a substantial enough interest to allow race-conscious admissions. More extensive affirmative action was permitted in *United Steelworkers of America v. Weber* (443 U.S. 193: 1979), in which the Court allowed a private employer to give preference to unskilled black employees over white employees for training programs designed to elevate the unskilled workers to craft levels. The Court permitted the preferential treatment because prior racial discrimination had demonstrably disadvantaged black workers in the past. The use of "set-asides" was upheld by the Court as a remedial solution in *Fullilove v. Klutznick* (448 U.S. 448: 1980). A set-aside reserves a certain percentage of federal funds for minority businesses. The Court determined that Congress may allow narrowly tailored corrective actions to redress historical disadvantages.

Amending Power   Language in Article V providing the methods by which the federal Constitution can be changed. The amending power may be utilized in two ways. When two-thirds of both houses of Congress "shall deem it necessary," they may propose amendments. All twenty-six amendments to the Constitution have been initiated this way. Article V also permits the calling of a constitutional convention "on the application of the legislatures of two thirds of the several states." For a proposal of amendment to take effect, regardless of how it was initiated, it must secure the approval of the legislatures or specially called conventions of three-fourths of the states. Congress may determine which of these two modes of ratification is required as well as govern the amending process generally. Article V concludes by declaring that the two clauses contained in Article I, Section 9 pertaining to importation of slaves cannot be changed through the amendment process until 1808. Article V also precludes changing the provision that entitles each state to equal representation in the United States Senate. *See also* POLITICAL QUESTION, p. 644.

Significance   The amending power is set forth in Article V, which lodges principal responsibility for proposing constitutional changes with the Congress. The Court has historically viewed issues arising out of the amendment process as "political questions," and has seldom interfered with congressional judgments. When Congress specified a time limit for ratification of the Eighteenth Amendment, the Court upheld the action in *Dillon v. Gloss* (256 U.S. 368: 1921). When Congress failed to establish a similar restriction on the amendment proposing prohibition of child labor, the Court refused to determine a reasonable ratification period in *Coleman v. Miller* (307 U.S. 433: 1939). *Coleman* also determined that a legislature can reconsider a decision to reject an amendment and vote to ratify it so long as any established time limit has not expired. A state, however, may not rescind a previous affirmative vote even if the amendment process time limit has not elapsed.

Although this general pattern of deference remains, a recent decision involving the Equal Rights Amendment suggests that congressional power over the amending process is not so exclusive. Congress, by only a majority vote, extended the time for ratification of the ERA after the proposal had failed to gain sufficient state approvals in the originally specified period. A federal district court struck down the time extension. The Supreme Court stayed the ruling, but the original deadline passed before the Court gave the issue full consideration. In *National Organization for Women v. Idaho* (459 U.S. 809: 1982), the Court remanded the case with instructions to dismiss the complaint as moot. While all the changes to the Constitution to this point have occurred by congressional resolution, it is possible that Congress may call a national constitutional convention to consider a balanced budget amendment, if two-thirds of the states pass resolutions asking that such a convention be convened. A number of issues attend the convention approach, such as how delegates are to be selected and the scope of the convention's authority once convened.

Amicus Curiae   A person or organization submitting a brief to a court expressing views on a legal question before the court. An amicus curiae, literally meaning "friend of the court," is not an actual party to an action. He, she, or it is an interested third party who attempts to provide the court with information or arguments that may not have been offered by the actual parties. *See also* BRIEF, p. 583.

Significance   Amicus curiae participation is a common court-related interest group activity. It typically occurs in cases with substantial public interest ramifications. As the Supreme Court considered whether a woman has a constitutional right to an abortion in *Roe v. Wade* (410 U.S. 113: 1973), amicus briefs were submitted by 36 proabortion and 11 anti abortion organizations. Some of the groups filed jointly. Amicus arguments tend to focus on the broader implications of a particular case. Submission of an amicus brief is not a matter of right, however. With the exception of amicus participation by an agency of the federal government, an amicus brief may be filed only with the consent of both parties in an action, on motion to the court, or by invitation of the court.

Antitrust Laws   Statutes aimed at regulating business activities and arrangements that restrict competition and restrain trade. Typical targets of antitrust laws are combinations, monopolies, cartels, and trusts. Antitrust regulation presumes that competition best protects free enterprise. Federal power to regulate business to foster competition is based upon congressional authority over interstate and foreign commerce. Enforcement of federal antitrust laws has been lodged in the Department of Justice and the Federal Trade Commission. *See also* COMMERCE CLAUSE, p. 291.

Significance   Antitrust laws are designed to preserve competition through federal regulation. History shows that the pattern of regulating effort has been uneven. Circumstances and variability in commitment to antitrust regulation have been the principal reasons, as well as the Court's variance in defining the scope of enforcement authority. The last two decades have reflected a general relaxation of governmental regulation, and the period can be characterized as hospitable toward the development of large conglomerates and multinational corporations. The primary antitrust laws are the Sherman Act of 1890 and the Clayton Act of 1914. The former is directed at monopolies that restrain trade through control of market supplies of particular goods and services. Early interpretations of the Sherman Act such as in *United States v. E. C. Knight Company* (156 U.S. 1: 1895) severely limited the measure's regulatory impact. The Clayton Act was enacted to reinforce the Sherman Act, and it focuses on price fixing, acquisition of stock in competing companies, and development of interlocking directorates as activities that interfered with competition. The Federal Trade Commission was also established in 1914 to encourage business competition.

Appeal   A request to an appellate or superior court to review a final judgment made in an inferior or lower court. Appellate jurisdiction is the power placed in appeals courts to conduct such a review. It empowers the superior court to set aside or modify the lower-court decision. An appeals court has several options in reviewing a lower-court decision. It may affirm, which means the lower court result is correct and must stand. It may reverse or vacate, which means it sets aside the lower-court ruling. Vacated judgments are often remanded to the lower court for further consideration. If an appellate decision overrules a precedent, it supersedes the earlier decision and the authority of the decision as precedent. A party seeking appeal is typically referred to as the *appellant* or *petitioner*, while the party against whom an action has been filed is the *appellee* or *respondent*. Appellate jurisdiction is distinguished from original jurisdiction. In the former, some other court or agency must render a judgment in a case before an appeal can be sought. *See also* CERTIORARI, p. 584; EQUITY JURISDICTION, p. 600; JUDICIAL REVIEW, p. 627; ORIGINAL JURISDICTION, p. 640.

Significance   Appeals courts are generally structured on two levels. One is an intermediate court that handles cases initially, and the other is a superior or supreme court. Appellate jurisdiction is conveyed through constitutional or statutory mandate. Federal appellate jurisdiction is granted by Article III of the Constitution, which says that the Supreme Court possesses such jurisdiction "both as to law and fact, with such exceptions and under such regulations as the Congress shall make." Appeals may be undertaken as a matter of right where the appellate court, typically an intermediate appeals court, must review a case. Other appeals occur at the discretion of the appeals court. The writ of .certiorari is a discretionary route of access to the appellate jurisdiction of the United States Supreme Court. Review as a matter of right is subject to some discretion by the Supreme Court, as in the writ of appeal. The party seeking the appeal has a right to review, but the Court may reject the appeal for want of a substantial federal question.

Appointment Power   Power vested in the president by Article II, Section 2 allowing presidential nomination of ambassadors, federal judges, and "other officers" of the United States. Exercise of the appointment power is generally subject to Senate advice and consent, although certain appointments by the president may occur without such confirmation. The power to appoint has typically been viewed as an executive function in order to allow the president some degree of control over the persons involved in implementation of federal laws. With the exception of its own officers, no appointment initiatives rest with the Congress. In *Buckley v. Valeo* (424 U.S. 1: 1976), the Court struck down a section of the Federal Election Campaign Act that created a Federal Election Commission. The act provided that two of the commission's six members were to be appointed by the president, with the other four being selected by the president pro tem of the Senate and the Speaker of the House. The Court found the Article II language referring to "officers of the United States" applicable to "any appointee exercising significant authority pursuant to the laws of the United States." Such an officer can only be appointed by the president as required by the appointment clause of Article II, Section 2. *See also* BUCKLEY V. VALEO (424 U.S. 1: 1976), p. 200; HUMPHREY'S EXECUTOR V. UNITED STATES (295 U.S. 602: 1935), p. 151; MYERS V. UNITED STATES (272 U.S. 52: 1926), p. 150.

Significance   Serious constitutional questions have not developed around the use of the appointment power to select officers of the United States. The matter of removal of such officers, however, has been more troublesome. The only constitutional discussion of removal involves impeachment, and it is clear that impeachment is not to be a generally applicable removal process. The principal issue is whether a president may unilaterally remove officers, or whether the Senate needs to concur. The Court's first occasion to rule on the matter was in *Myers v. United States* (272 U.S. 52: 1926). In *Myers*, the Court accorded the president exclusive power over removals. The Court's rationale went beyond what was required to resolve the *Myers* situation. Through

Chief Justice Taft, the Court said that because the power to remove is "incident to the power of appointment, not the power of advising and consenting to appointment," removals may occur at the discretion of the president. The *Myers* decision gave presidents virtually unlimited removal power. That decision was short-lived as it was substantially altered in *Humphrey's Executor v. United States* (295 U.S. 602: 1935), where the Court distinguished between exclusively executive branch officers and those in agencies insulated from direct executive control. The *Humphrey* distinction has been maintained, which means presidential removal of other than purely executive personnel may be limited by Congress.

Apportionment   The allocation of the number of representatives a political unit may send to a legislative body. Apportionment is based upon population, and it is a requirement of equal protection that legislatures have districts of substantially equal populations. Prior to 1962 the Supreme Court had considered legislative apportionment to be a political question, a matter not subject to resolution by the judicial branch. In *Baker v. Carr* (369 U.S. 186: 1962), however, the Court held apportionment to be a justiciable issue. *See also* BAKER V. CARR (369 U.S. 186: 1962), p. 123; JUSTICIABILITY, p. 630; POLITICAL QUESTION, p. 644.

Significance   Apportionment evolved to the "one man, one vote" rule, although *Baker* itself did not establish that standard. *Baker* created a relatively stringent expectation of population equivalence for single-member legislative districts. The "one man, one vote" standard now applies to all levels of government, including local units.

Bill of Attainder   A legislative act that imposes punishment or penalty on named or identifiable individuals or groups. The Constitution forbids both Congress and state legislatures from passing bills of attainder in Article I, Sections 9 and 10. The Court held in *United States v. Brown* (381 U.S. 437: 1965) that the prohibition was designed to be an "implementation of the separation of powers, a general safeguard against legislative exercise of the judicial function, or more simply— trial by legislature." The bill of attainder prohibition was included in the Constitution to prevent the common English practice of legislatively imposing sanctions including capital punishment. Accordingly, legislative bodies are empowered to enact only general laws, leaving specific application of them to the judiciary. *See also* EX POST FACTO,

p. 604; *UNITED STATES V. BROWN* (381 U.S. 437: 1965), p. 209; *WEAVER V. GRAHAM* (450 U.S. 24: 1981), p. 210.

Significance   Bill of attainder challenges have been relatively infrequent, but legislation imposing penalties on professions "aiding" the Confederacy and more recently on members of "subversive" political organizations has been successful. The key objective of the bill of attainder limitation is to establish a clear boundary between legislative and judicial activity.

Brief   A written document presented to a court in support of a party's position on a legal question. A brief contains a statement of the facts, applicable law, and arguments drawn from the facts and the law urging a judgment compatible with the interests of the party submitting the brief. In a law school context, a brief is a short outline of a case studied by the student and prepared for recitation and review. *See also* AMICUS CURIAE, p. 579.

Significance   A brief is the medium through which legal arguments are placed before courts. Briefs are generally submitted by the parties themselves, although third-party briefs from amicus curiae may also be submitted. If a brief is compelling enough, it may secure the court's judgment and opinion.

Case or Controversy   A properly asserted legal claim made in a manner appropriate for judicial response. A case or controversy may be decided by federal courts under Article III of the Constitution. For a case to constitute a bona fide controversy sufficient to satisfy Article III requirements: (1) it must involve parties who are truly contending or adverse; (2) there must exist a recognizable legal interest arising out of a legitimate fact situation, and (3) the issue must be capable of judicial enforcement by judgment. A person bringing a claim or petitioning a court is known as a *party* or a *litigant*. The initiating party to a legal action is also called a *plaintiff* or a *petitioner*. The party against whom such action may be brought is a *defendant* or a *respondent*. Cases are named for the parties involved. The designation *et al.* is used after the first named party in a suit where there are several plaintiffs or defendants. Cases designated *in re* are proceedings that are not wholly adversarial, such as a juvenile case *in re*, or "in the matter of," John Doe. The abbreviation *ex. rel.* may be made when a legal action is initiated by the state at the instigation of a party with a private interest in the result.

See also ADVISORY OPINION, p. 577; JUSTICIABILITY, p. 630; STANDING, p. 655.

Significance   A case or controversy is a justiciable case. In *Aetna Life Insurance Company v. Haworth* (300 U.S. 227: 1937), the Supreme Court described a justiciable case as one in which the controversy is "definite and concrete, touching the legal relations of parties having "adverse legal interests." Such a controversy must also be "real and substantial, admitting of specific relief through a decree of a conclusive character." A true case or controversy is opposite from a hypothetical or abstract question upon which a court might render an advisory opinion.

Certiorari   A writ or order to a court whose decision is being challenged to send up the records of the case so a higher court can review a lower-court decision. *Certiorari* means "to be informed" and is granted to the losing party by the Supreme Court if four justices agree the writ should be issued. Until 1891 the Court was formally obliged to take all appeals that came through the federal court system or that concerned a federal question and were appealed from the highest state courts. In 1890 the Court had to deal with some 1,816 cases, a near physical impossibility for the justices. The problem of an overcrowded docket was then addressed by the Everts Act of 1891, by which Congress created three-judge circuit courts of appeals as intermediaries between the federal district courts and the Supreme Court. The act restricted the means of appeal to the Supreme Court by introducing discretionary certiorari power. Through certiorari the Court could decline to hear certain cases if a given number of justices felt they were not sufficiently important. Denial of a certiorari petition means the decision of the federal district or state circuit court is upheld. Despite the Everts Act, the Court's workload continued to expand, however. It was occasioned by major increases in population, a more extensive governmental administrative apparatus, and the widespread use of the writ of error, by which cases came to the Court by assertion of legal error committed by a court below. The Judiciary Act of 1925 largely did away with the writ of error and gave the Court even wider discretion in broad classes of cases by reaffirming the writ of certiorari. In the years following the Judiciary Act of 1925, the proportion of certiorari petitions granted by the Court never exceeded 22 percent. Certiorari is one of four ways by which appellate cases come before the Supreme Court. The others are appeal, the extraordinary writ, and certification. Certification is a process through which a lower court requests a higher court to resolve certain issues in a case while the case is still pending in the lower court. *See also* APPEAL, p. 580.

Significance   The certiorari power is the Supreme Court's principal means of keeping abreast of its work. It can also be an effective administrative tool in the hands of a skillful chief justice. When Charles Evans Hughes became chief justice in 1930, for example, he read and summarized all certiorari petitions coming to the Court. He weeded out some as easily disposable and put them on a separate list before the Saturday conference of the justices. In conference Chief Justice Hughes attempted to average only about three and one-half minutes for discussion of each certiorari petition. Since his preparation far exceeded that of the other justices, his views on whether to grant certiorari petitions were seldom challenged. Thus a chief justice, as chief administrative officer of the Court, can restrict access to the Court by his manipulation of certiorari petitions. He can also direct the Court's attention to policy areas he thinks are important, as when Chief Justice Hughes expanded the Court's scrutiny of *in forma pauperis* petitions to the point where *habeas corpus* arguments by prisoners became an important part of the Court's docket. *In forma pauperis* means "in the manner of a pauper" and refers to permission extended to an indigent to proceed with a legal action without having to pay court fees and other costs associated with litigation. The scope of the Supreme Court's certiorari jurisdiction is much broader than that afforded by any other means of access to the Court, including the writ of appeal. The writ of certiorari extends to any civil or criminal case in the federal courts of appeal regardless of the parties, the status of the case, or the amount in controversy. Any state court decision that involves the construction and application of the federal Constitution, treaties, or laws, or the determination of a federal title, right, privilege, or immunity falls within the Court's certiorari jurisdiction. Certiorari allows the Supreme Court to enter the policy-making process virtually at any point it chooses.

Citizenship   One's status as a person who owes allegiance to the United States and is entitled to all the rights and privileges guaranteed and protected by the Constitution. Citizenship is conferred by the federal courts as authorized by Congress. Since the Civil Rights Act of 1866, all persons born or naturalized in the United States are citizens of the United States. The Fourteenth Amendment reiterated that language in Section 1. The term *dual citizenship* refers to a person's status as a citizen of the United States and the state in which he or she resides, or to the holding of citizenship in two countries. *See also* PRIVILEGES AND IMMUNITIES CLAUSES, p. 647.

Significance   Citizenship is elaborated in two privileges and immunities clauses of the United States Constitution. The Constitution requires, for example, that citizens of a particular state have parity with citizens of all other states. The *Slaughterhouse Cases* (16 Wallace 36: 1873) emphasized the distinct character of federal and state citizenship. *Slaughterhouse* held that privileges and immunities conferred by state citizenship were outside federal reach through the Fourteenth Amendment. Such an interpretation took a very narrow view of the substance of federal citizenship. It covered only such things as interstate travel and voting. While subsequent decisions have extended the meaning of citizenship in the Fourteenth Amendment, *Slaughterhouse* is still controlling in that it precludes use of privileges and immunities language in protecting citizens by federal authority. Citizenship may be obtained by birth on American soil. This is known as the rule of *jus soli*. This rule applies to anyone except children of foreign sovereigns, or their ministers or adversaries during "hostile occupation." There is also the rule of *jus sanguinis* or "law of blood," which applies when children of Americans are born abroad. Aliens may also be admitted to citizenship under a process known as naturalization. Congress is empowered to establish all rules and qualifications for naturalization. Revocation of naturalized citizenship may occur following a formal denaturalization proceeding. The Court has imposed restrictions on the power of government to revoke citizenship, but there is a generally recognized right of expatriation that permits voluntary relinquishment of citizenship.

Class Action   A suit brought by several persons on behalf of a larger group whose members have the same legal interest. A class action is indicated when a group is so large that individual suits are impractical. Group suits have been used frequently in recent years and are often the means by which civil rights, consumer, and environmental questions are litigated. A class action is sometimes called a representative action. It can be brought in both federal and state courts. It must be certified by a trial court at the outset, and all class members must be made aware of the suit and given an opportunity to exclude themselves. Certification involves a determination that the asserted class actually exists and that the persons bringing the action are members of the class. *See also GULF OIL COMPANY V. BERNARD* (452 U.S. 89: 1981), p. 103.

Significance   A class action provides economy and efficiency in the adjudication of an issue. It significantly reduces the possibility of conflicting judgments resulting from numerous individual suits. Several limitations apply to a class action. In *Zahn v. International Paper Co.* (414 U.S. 291: 1973), the Supreme Court held that, to use federal diversity jurisdiction for class actions, each member of the class must have suffered an injury amounting to at least $10,000 in value. The Court also said in *Eisen v. Carlisle & Jacqueline* (417 U.S. 156: 1974) that the initiators of a class action must notify, at their own expense, all members of the class. The impact of these decisions has been to reduce the number of large consumer and environmental suits. The more numerous smaller class actions have not been adversely affected.

Collateral Estoppel   A legal principle that prohibits relitigation of an issue once a final fact judgment has been made. Collateral estoppel is based on the doctrine of *res judicata*, which means "a matter already decided."

Significance   Collateral estoppel was first developed in civil litigation. The Fifth Amendment protection from double jeopardy was held to include the right to argue or claim collateral estoppel in criminal cases in *Ashe v. Swenson* (397 U.S. 436: 1970). *Ashe* prohibited reprosecution in cases where an acquittal in a prior case was based on a fact issue introduced in the second case. Since the fact issue had been resolved in the defendant's favor initially, it could not be relitigated in another criminal prosecution. The *Ashe* decision clarified the same-offense criterion traditionally used in double jeopardy cases. The collateral estoppel doctrine prevents prosecution of different offenses if previously resolved fact questions would be reconsidered in a later case.

Compensation Clause   Prohibits Congress from reducing federal judicial salaries. The compensation clause is contained in Article III, Section 1 and provides that compensation of federal judges "shall not be diminished during their continuance in office." The clause came out of the Anglo-American tradition of an "independent" judiciary. The courts were seen as needing to be free from influence by the other branches, which might attempt to control the judiciary through the process of establishing levels of compensation. *See also* JUDICIAL IMMUNITY, p. 626; *O'MALLEY V. WOODROUGH* (307 U.S. 277: 1939), p. 401; *UNITED STATES V. WILL* (449 U.S. 200: 1980), p. 85.

Significance   The compensation clause and the provisions for life tenure for federal judges were explicit attempts in Article III to create political insulation for the federal judiciary. This independence is relatively extensive when the doctrine of judicial immunity is added to protections on tenure and compensation. The compensation clause was based on the notion that "power over a man's subsistence amounts to power over his will." The clause was invoked early in the twentieth century to protect federal judges from a generally imposed income tax. Such immunity from taxes was felt to "trivialize" the compensation clause, however, and the mistake was corrected in *O'Malley v. Woodrough* (307 U.S. 277: 1939). In *United States v. Will* (449 U.S. 200: 1980), the Court held that a previously scheduled salary increase could not be withdrawn once it had taken effect. The compensation clause does not entitle judges to salary increases, but once a salary level becomes effective, it cannot be reduced.

Concurrent Power   Authority held by both the national and state governments. Concurrent power permits both levels of government to do the same things. For example, both levels are able to levy taxes. Concurrent power is the opposite of exclusive power, which is conferred to one or the other level exclusively. The exercise of concurrent power by the states may not be in conflict with the substance of law at the national level. *See also* EXCLUSIVE POWER, p. 600; FEDERALISM, p. 29; POWER, p. 644.

Significance   The concept of concurrent power recognizes that the federal and state levels must both perform certain functions. Both must have the capacity to raise revenues, for example. Throughout our history, it has also been asserted that the commerce power is a concurrent power. Although formally assigned to the Congress in Article I, it has been argued that the power was not exclusively conferred, but rather permitted states to also regulate commerce as long as state policy did not collide with that of the national level. The Court examined this issue in *Gibbons v. Ogden* (9 Wheaton 1: 1824) and held that the commerce power was essentially exclusive. Chief Justice Marshall distinguished the commerce power from concurrent powers like taxation, which could be exercised simultaneously by state and federal levels. Nonetheless, the impact of *Gibbons* has been to allow regulation of certain areas of commerce from the state level.

Constitutional Courts   Courts established under language contained in Article III. The constitutional courts exercise the judicial power granted from the judicial article and are limited to the jurisdictional boundaries defined there. Judges of constitutional courts are protected from decreases in compensation during their service and may hold tenure "during good behavior." Constitutional courts are distinguished from legislative courts, which are established under powers conferred on Congress in Article I. Constitutional courts may not respond to any issue not in the form of a bona fide case or controversy, but may, under terms of the Declaratory Judgments Act of 1934, issue declaratory judgments. There are three principal constitutional courts: the United States Supreme Court, the United States district court, and the United States court of appeals. *See also* ARTICLE III, p. 73; DECLARATORY JUDGMENT, p. 590; *GIBBONS V. OGDEN* (9 Wheaton 1: 1824), p. 294; LEGISLATIVE COURTS, p. 630.

Significance   The constitutional courts, established under Article III mandate, are the most important federal courts. This category of court provides the basic judicial function in the United States and decides the overwhelming majority of constitutional issues entering the court system. These are the courts that were intended from the outset of our constitutional history to receive insulation from the other branches of government to ensure their functional independence and the judicial role in the checks and balances system.

Contempt   Any act that obstructs the administration of justice by a court or that brings disrespect on a court or its authority. Contempt may be direct in that it occurs in the presence of the court and constitutes a direct affront to the court's authority. Contempt may be indirect in that the behavior which demonstrates contempt may occur outside the courtroom. While some due process protections apply to contempt, it is generally a summary order through which penalties of fine or imprisonment may be directly imposed by the court. It is necessary to distinguish between criminal and civil contempt. Criminal contempt is an act of obstruction or disrespect typically occurring in the courtroom. A party who acts in an abusive manner in court is in criminal contempt. He or she may receive a fine and/or imprisonment for up to six months summarily imposed. Civil contempt results from failure to comply with the order of a court. Civil contempt is designed to coerce compliance with an order to protect the interests of the party on whose behalf the order to judgment was issued. Civil contempt ends when the desired conduct or compliance occurs. A legislative contempt power also exists. It may be used if a disturbance is created within a legislative chamber or if persons subpoenaed to appear before legislative committees refuse to testify. Congressional contempt is not summarily imposed, however.

It is handled through the standard criminal process with trial occurring in a federal district court if an indictment has been secured from a grand jury.

Significance   The contempt power provides courts with leverage to maintain courtroom decorum appropriate for judicial proceedings. Contempt enables a court to punish disruptive or disrespectful conduct, and it serves as a deterrent to such conduct. The contempt power also permits courts to compel compliance with a court order, backstopping the authority of all such orders. It constitutes an exception to the constitutionally mandated right to trial and right to trial by jury.

Declaratory Judgment   A form of relief invoked when a plaintiff seeks a declaration of his or her rights. A declaratory judgment does not involve monetary damages but is an assessment of a party's rights prior to a damage occurring. It differs from a conventional action in that no specific order is issued by the court. It differs from an advisory opinion in that parties have a bona fide controversy in a declaratory judgment proceeding, although actual injury has not yet occurred. The federal courts are empowered to render declaratory judgments by the Federal Declaratory Judgment Act of 1934. In a declaratory judgment proceeding there must be a real controversy, but the plaintiff is uncertain of his or her rights and seeks adjudication of them. As in injunctive relief, a declaratory judgment request is a petition for a court to exercise its powers of equity. No jury is permitted. The judge is asked to declare what the law is regarding the controversy. *See also* ADVISORY OPINION, p. 577.

Significance   Declaratory judgment actions are a comparatively recent development in American jurisprudence because for many years they were considered to be the equivalent of advisory opinions and because the traditional concept was that courts could only act when a plaintiff was entitled to a coercive remedy. A plaintiff may find it necessary, however, to determine if he or she is bound by contractual language that the plaintiff believes to be void or unenforceable for some reason. If the plaintiff should fail to comply, he or she is risking suit for breach of contract and consequential damages. The declaratory judgment procedure is helpful to all parties because it circumvents the necessity of a possible breach and the lengthy litigation that such action invites. Contract disputes frequently form the basis of declaratory judgments. Courts are reluctant to issue them on broad public policy issues.

Delegated Power   Authority specifically granted by the Constitution. Delegated, granted, enumerated, specific, or express power is distinguished from implied power in that it is explicitly conveyed. Delegated power is basically set forth in the first three articles of the Constitution, where the fundamental powers of the legislative, executive, and judicial branches are defined. *See also* IMPLIED POWER, p. 618; INHERENT POWER, p. 622; POWER, p. 644.

Significance   Delegated power is the foundation of constitutional government. It is explicitly enumerated placement of power. Actions taken by an agency of government must be based on a delegated power or power that can be reasonably derived or implied from delegated power. By linking governmental actions to powers granted either expressly or implicitly, power may be separated or diffused and effective limits established on that power. It emphasizes the role of the Constitution as a contract between the people and the government.

Delegation of Legislative Power   Assignment of some rule-making discretion by the legislative branch to the executive branch. Delegation of legislative power occurs because it is recognized that, as laws are applied, some discretion must exist for the enforcing agent. In some situations, Congress may intend enforcement officials to determine when and how a statute will apply or to develop key operational details during the course of administering the statute. Legislative power, however, is itself delegated by explicit constitutional language in Article I, and there is a general prohibition on redelegating such authority. Thus, it has been left to the Court to strike a balance between the practical need to delegate some legislative authority, and the prohibited reassignment of a fundamental constitutional function. The lines drawn separating permitted and prohibited delegation have considerable separation of power implications. *See also* AMERICAN TEXTILE MANUFACTURERS INSTITUTE, INC. V. DONOVAN (452 U.S. 490: 1981), p. 192; *J. W. HAMPTON, JR. AND COMPANY V. UNITED STATES* (276 U.S. 394: 1928), pp. 191, 388; LEGISLATIVE VETO, p. 632; *SCHECHTER POULTRY CORPORATION V. UNITED STATES* (295 U.S. 495: 1935), pp. 189, 315; SEPARATION OF POWERS, p. 56; *UNITED STATES V. CURTISS-WRIGHT EXPORT CORPORATION* (299 U.S. 304: 1936), p. 144.

Significance   The rationale for permitting delegation of some legislative power is persuasive. The legislative branch is simply unable to enact more than general laws. Delegation of power to administering agencies in the executive branch allows more effective development of implementation methods. In other words, the administrative experts involved with actual implementation "fill the gaps" of general policy set forth by legislation. The practice has been long recognized. In *J. W. Hampton, Jr. and Company v. United States* (276 U.S. 394: 1928), the Court permitted the executive to adjust tariffs by as much as 50 percent to maintain production cost parity between the United States and abroad. The Court held that Congress had established a policy objective, but did not continually have to adjust the tariff itself. At the same time, the legislature may not delegate too much discretion or rule-making authority and actually forfeit the basic legislative function. This is an unconstitutional delegation. The question hinges on the extent to which the legislature establishes objectives and standards prior to turning over implementation to the executive. In *Panama Refining Company v. Ryan* (293 U.S. 388: 1935), the Court invalidated a section of the National Industrial Recovery Act because it excessively delegated legislative power. More recently, the Court has been relatively permissive on delegation, particularly in the area of foreign policy. During most of this period, the Congress has monitored implementation through a device known as the legislative veto. This veto was struck down in 1983, however, because it impermissibly allowed the legislative branch to invade the executive function.

Direct Tax   A tax imposed directly on property. The Constitution prohibits the federal government from levying such a tax without meeting certain conditions. Article I, Section 9 provides that "no capitation, or other direct tax shall be laid, unless in proportion to the census of enumeration." The issue of what constitutes a direct tax has caused the Supreme Court great concern. It was decided in an early decision, *Hylton v. United States* (3 Dallas 171: 1796), that only head (capitation) and land taxes fit the direct tax category. Accordingly, only those taxes require apportionment. The apportionment requirement is difficult to meet, and it creates serious inequities. It requires that a state or its people pay a proportion of a direct tax equivalent to its proportion of the population. *See also* HYLTON V. UNITED STATES (3 Dallas 171: 1796), p. 379; POLLOCK V. FARMERS' LOAN AND TRUST COMPANY (158 U.S. 601: 1895), p. 382; SIXTEENTH AMENDMENT, p. 651.

Significance   The early decision that a prohibited direct tax was confined to head and property taxes did not severely impinge on federal taxing power. In *Pollock v. Farmers' Loan and Trust Company* (158 U.S. 601: 1895), however, the Court used the direct tax limitation to invalidate a tax on incomes derived from property and municipal bonds. The effect of *Pollock* was to seriously impair the federal government's capacity to generate revenue. The *Pollock* decision was eventually overturned by the Sixteenth Amendment which allowed Congress to tax incomes "from whatever source derived" without the apportionment requirement. While the direct tax limitation still exists, its importance has been seriously blunted by the Sixteenth Amendment.

Diversity Jurisdiction   A civil case with a plaintiff and a defendant from different states. Diversity jurisdiction deals with the problem of diversity of citizenship. The description of federal court jurisdiction in Article III of the Constitution provides that "federal judicial power shall extend to cases between citizens of different states" or between citizens and aliens. Since the Constitution did not establish inferior federal courts, and since only Congress is permitted to confer such jurisdiction, diversity jurisdiction lies wholly within the control of Congress. Diversity jurisdiction was first conferred upon lower federal courts in the Judiciary Act of 1789, but a $50 controversy had to exist before the federal courts could enforce their jurisdiction. The amount in controversy was raised to $10,000 in 1958. *See also* CASE OR CONTROVERSY, p. 583; *ERIE RAILROAD COMPANY V. TOMPKINS* (304 U.S. 64: 1938), p. 75; ORIGINAL JURISDICTION, p. 640.

Significance   Diversity jurisdiction is periodically debated in Congress among those who would abolish it altogether, those who would reduce it dramatically, and those who would retain it as it is. Proponents of abolition point to the cost to federal taxpayers, the intervention of federal courts in state law matters, and the redundancy and uncertainty that exist when a dual system of courts addresses the same issues. Opponents of change argue the possibility of home party bias against nonresidents, the value of two-system interaction, and the multiplicity of civil actions the federal courts, for procedural reasons, are better equipped to handle. Diversity jurisdiction exists where there is a diversity of citizenship or where there is an interstate aspect to a legal action. Suits below the dollar threshold that involve no substantial federal issue are conveyed to state courts. Diversity jurisdiction was established for the federal courts originally because state courts might be biased against litigants from out-of-state. The political interests of the federalists were well served by having federal court jurisdiction touch on state and local matters. Diversity of citizenship cases constitute a large portion, about 30 percent, of the current civil caseload in federal courts. The potential for substantial conflict between federal and state law litigated in federal courts under diversity jurisdiction was minimized by the Supreme Court's decision in *Erie Railroad Company v. Tompkins* (304 U.S. 64: 1938). The Court held that state statutory or common law is always to be applied in diversity cases. No federal common law exists.

Dual Federalism   A concept that views the federal and state levels of government as coequals. Dual federalism is based on the Tenth Amendment, which reserves to the states all powers not delegated to the federal government. The doctrine of dual federalism evolved under Chief Justice Roger B. Taney, a strong advocate of states' rights. Proponents of the dual federalism doctrine see the delegated power of the national government in the narrowest of terms. They view the reserve clause of the Tenth Amendment as a source of power for states through which national authority may be substantially limited. *See also* CONCURRENT POWER, p. 588; FEDERALISM, p. 29; TENTH AMENDMENT, p. 229.

Significance   The doctrine of dual federalism was a response to the national supremacy orientation of the Supreme Court under John Marshall. The doctrine gained dominance in the 1840s and remained an often-decisive factor for almost a century. From the outset, it limited the exercise of national power when areas reserved to the states were affected. *Dred Scott v. Sandford* (19 Howard 393: 1857) is an early example. Dual federalism arguments were later integrated with laissez-faire economic thought around the turn of the century to effectively bar governmental regulation of private property. The best example is *Hammer v. Dagenhart* (247 U.S. 251: 1918), where the Court struck down a federal law prohibiting the shipment in interstate commerce of any goods produced by child labor. The Court said that even the exercise of the explicitly delegated commerce power was "not intended to destroy the local power always existing and carefully reserved to the states." The Court's invalidation of the Agricultural Adjustment Act of 1933 in *United States v. Butler* (297 U.S. 1: 1936) was based at least in part on dual federalism grounds. The struggle over the New Deal initiatives ultimately led to the end of the doctrine, at least as originally advanced by Taney.

Due Process Clauses   Constitutional provisions designed to ensure that laws will be reasonable both in substance and in means of implementation. Due process language is contained in two clauses of the Constitution of the United States. The Fifth Amendment prohibits deprivation of "life, liberty, or property, without due process of law." It sets a limit on arbitrary and unreasonable actions by the federal government. The Fourteenth Amendment contains parallel language aimed at the states. Due process requires that actions of government occur through ordered and regularized processes. It subjects those processes to constitutional and statutory limits in the protection of individual rights. There are two kinds of due process. The first is *procedural due process*, which focuses on the methods or procedures by which governmental policies are executed. It guarantees fairness in the processes by which government imposes regulations or sanctions. Procedural due process requires that a person be formally notified of any proceeding in which he or she is a party, and that he or she be afforded an opportunity for an impartial hearing. Additional procedural rights have been enumerated in the Bill of Rights. Through the process of incorporation, most Bill of Rights protections have been applied to the states through the due process clause of the Fourteenth Amendment. *Substantive due process* represents the second kind of due process. It involves the reasonableness of policy content. Policies may deny substantive due process when they do not rationally relate to legitimate legislative objectives or when they are impermissibly vague. *See also* FIFTH AMENDMENT, p. 607; FOURTEENTH AMENDMENT, p. 612; INCORPORATION, p. 620; PROCEDURAL DUE PROCESS, p. 647; SUBSTANTIVE DUE PROCESS, p. 659.

Significance   Due process is an evolving concept that undergoes continuing adjustment and refinement. The two due process clauses provide the Supreme Court an ongoing opportunity to consider and define the legal contours of fairness. The heart of the matter is reasonableness. If the substance of a government policy, or the procedures used to implement it, are adjudged to be arbitrary and unreasonable, the Court can nullify the policy or practice under the due process clauses.

Eighteenth Amendment   Prohibited the manufacture, sale, or transportation of intoxicating liquors in the United States. The Eighteenth Amendment, known as the prohibition amendment, was ratified in 1919. In addition to the prohibition of manufacture, sale, and transportation, the amendment banned importation and exportation of liquor from the United States and its territories. There were two other interesting features of the Eighteenth Amendment. Section 2 said that the "Congress and the several states shall have concurrent power to enforce this article by appropriate legislation." Seldom have both the federal and state legislatures been enabled to regulate concurrently. Section 2 said that the process would become "inoperative" unless ratification took place "within seven years from the date of submission." It was the first amendment proposal which set a time limit for ratification. *See also* AMENDING POWER, p. 578; TWENTY-FIRST AMENDMENT, p. 665.

Significance　　The Eighteenth Amendment established national prohibition, a policy known to some as the "noble experiment." The amendment never gained the broad popular support necessary to make it an effective policy, and it was repealed by the Twenty-first Amendment in 1933. A number of states had regulations, some as extensive as outright prohibition, prior to adoption of the amendment. Once the amendment was ratified, federal legislation entitled the National Prohibition Act (also known as the Volstead Act) was passed under power granted by Section 2. Most states, though permitted to regulate concurrently under the amendment, deferred to the federal initiative. When the amendment was repealed, the federal legislation based on it was inoperative as well. The Twenty-first Amendment did provide the states with substantial discretion to establish their own regulation to fill, if they wished, the vacuum created by repeal of all regulations at the national level.

Eighth Amendment　　Protects the principle that one is presumed innocent until proven guilty and proscribes cruel and unusual punishments. The Eighth Amendment is divided into two clauses, the first saying, "excessive bail shall not be required, nor excessive fines imposed," the second adding, "nor cruel and unusual punishments inflicted." Like other provisions of the Bill of Rights, the Eighth Amendment originated in English common law. Centuries of English statutory law contributed to the tradition that individual liberties would be offended if an accused person were not afforded the opportunity to be "admitted to bail." The accused must be presumed innocent until trial of the facts and evidentiary proceedings prove otherwise. In 1679, for example, the Habeas Corpus Act required "persons imprisoned for bailable offenses to be set free on bail, so that the King's subjects could not longer be detained in prison in such cases where by law they are bailable." Like the language of excessive bail and fines, the language of the Eighth Amendment clause proscribing cruel and unusual punishments also comes from English law. In 1689 the English Parliament was forced to adopt a bill of rights as the result of widespread abuses of individual liberties during the reign of the Stuarts. The Bill of Rights was directly the result of the cruel punishments imposed during the days of the infamous Court of Star Chamber. A major difference between the English and the American bills of rights was that the former had only legislative standing, while the latter had constitutional weight and status. The American authors of the Eighth Amendment also chose to substitute for the words "ought to" in the English Bill of Rights the imperative words "shall not" in the American Bill of Rights. The change made the Amendment enforceable by the courts, not subject to future legislative caveats. *See also* BILL OF RIGHTS, p. 7; COMMON LAW, p. 13; CONSTITUTIONALISM, HISTORICAL DEVELOPMENT OF, p. 15; MAGNA CARTA, p. 45.

Significance   The Eighth Amendment assures that the amount of bail imposed on a criminal defendant is commensurate with the alleged offense. Presumption of guilt is not fixed before trial of the facts. The bail clause was codified in the Judiciary Act of 1789 and further elaborated in the Bail Reform Act of 1966. In *Stack v. Boyle* (342 U.S. 1: 1952), Chief Justice Fred M. Vinson, writing for the Supreme Court majority, said that "unless this right to bail before trial is preserved, the presumption of innocence, secured only after centuries of struggle, would lose its meaning." The second clause of the Eighth Amendment illustrates the dynamic and evolutionary processes at work in American constitutional law. In *Weems v. United States* (217 U.S. 349: 1910), the Supreme Court established that the cruel and unusual punishments clause of the amendment was to be interpreted in light of the social values of the time. Subsequent Courts have reiterated the *Weems* standard that the Eighth Amendment "is not fastened to the absolute but may acquire meaning as public opinion becomes enlightened by humane justice."

Electoral College   Mechanism by which the president and the vice president are selected. The electoral college was established by Article II, and it requires states to select electors equal in number to their representation in Congress. These electors cast votes on a date following the presidential election. The electors never meet as a national body, but cast their ballots from their respective states. If no candidate for president receives an absolute majority of electoral votes, the House of Representatives chooses from the top three candidates in total electoral votes. In the House process, each state delegation has a single vote. Failure to select a vice president would be resolved in the Senate. *See also* TWELFTH AMENDMENT, p. 662; TWENTY-THIRD AMENDMENT, p. 668.

Significance   The electoral college was designed to make selection of the president an indirect process. It was a hedge against the possible undesirable consequences that could occur through unrestricted participatory democracy. It was envisioned that the electors would be the established leadership from each state. The initial design of the electoral college was defective in that it did not anticipate the rapid rise of political parties and their role in presidential selection. Although contemporary electors are permitted to vote for whomever they wish, they are really persons pledged to vote for a particular party's candidates. The design of the electoral college was also flawed in a more functional way. Initially, electors were not able to separate presidential and vice-presidential candidates when casting their votes. Each would vote for two persons. The idea was that the runner-up would be the "second best" candidate and become the vice president. This procedure produced a tie between Jefferson and Burr in 1800, a result that was probably completely unintended by the electors. While the deadlock was ultimately resolved by the House in Jefferson's favor (he had been the "first" choice of virtually every elector), the defect was readily apparent. The Twelfth Amendment, adopted in 1803, required among other things that electors vote separately for president and vice president.

Eleventh Amendment   Establishes state immunity to suit by citizens of other states in federal courts. The Eleventh Amendment was added to the Constitution in 1798 and says that the "Judicial power of the United States shall not be construed to extend to any suit in law and equity, commenced or prosecuted against one of the United States by citizens of another state, or by citizens or subjects of any foreign state." *See also* CHISHOLM V. GEORGIA (2 Dallas 419: 1793), p. 230.

Significance   The Eleventh Amendment reversed the Supreme Court's decision in *Chisholm v. Georgia* (2 Dallas 419: 1793) and clarified the language contained in Article III, Section 2. The terms of Article III define federal judicial power and extend this power to cases between "a state and citizens of another state." There was some concern that this would permit citizen suits against states in federal courts. Assurances were made that this referred to cases where states would be plaintiffs rather than defendants as a state would be immune to any action filed against it without its own permission or consent. The Court, however, held in *Chisholm* that federal courts had jurisdiction over such citizen suits. The Eleventh Amendment was proposed immediately because many states had outstanding war debts and feared use of federal judicial power to collect them. The Eleventh Amendment provides only limited immunity to states. A state criminal defendant may still seek access to federal courts, claiming violation of federal constitutional rights. Similarly, an agent of a state is subject to federal judicial power if he or she violates rights protected by the federal Constitution or any federal statute.

Eminent Domain   The power of government to take control of private property. Eminent domain is an inherent power of government at both the federal and state levels. The power is limited in that property may only be taken to serve a public need. The Fifth Amendment also requires that the property holder is entitled to "just compensation." Determination of the sufficiency of public purpose and just compensation are addressed in a process known as a condemnation proceeding. *See also* DUE PROCESS CLAUSES, p. 594; *PENN CENTRAL TRANS-PORTATION COMPANY V. NEW YORK CITY* (438 U.S. 104: 1978), p. 451.

Significance   The power of eminent domain enables government to pursue programs and projects in the public interest that might otherwise be thwarted by the right to privately own property. The principal eminent domain issues have hinged on what is a public purpose, adequacy of compensation, and what constitutes a "taking" of property. A public purpose is generally regarded as a legislative judgment. It can involve developing a facility for extensive public use such as a park. But it may also involve a more limited access project such as an industrial park. The clear patten has been to defer to legislative determinations as to public purpose. On the issue of just compensation, a property owner is generally entitled to fair market value. The Court has typically reviewed only procedural matters in compensation disputes. Finally, "taking" of property may mean a literal taking of possession or the imposition of substantial restrictions on the use of property. The latter category has not often entitled the property holder to compensation (see *Penn Central Transportation Company v. New York City*, 438 U.S. 104: 1978).

En Banc   A decision or proceeding made or heard by the entire membership of a court. En banc distinguishes cases having full participation from the more typical use of only a fraction of a court's membership to hear a particular case. En banc is sometimes used in reference to state and federal intermediate appellate courts, which generally assign only three members of the larger panel to hear appeals.

Significance   The United States Supreme Court and a state's highest appellate tribunal always sit en banc. An en banc court in United States court of appeals cases is usually ordered only in highly controversial cases or in cases where one or more of the court's panels have disagreed on a major point of law.

Equity Jurisdiction	The power of a court to grant relief or remedy to a party seeking court assistance outside the principles of the common law. Equity jurisdiction permits judgments based on perceptions of fairness that supplement common law doctrines. Relief is assistance extended by a court to an injured or aggrieved party justified by these considerations. A remedy is the specific means, such as an injunction, by which a court intervenes to protect a legal right or interest through its equity jurisdiction. In *Brown v. Board of Education II* (349 U.S. 294: 1955), for example, the Supreme Court mandated that lower federal courts issue relief decrees shaped by equitable principles. The Court characterized equity as having a practical flexibility in its approach to constructing remedies. The lower courts were to reconcile public and private needs with decrees framed by perceptions of fairness and justice. A show cause proceeding is a process in equity jurisdiction with the rules of equity applying. A show cause order may be issued by a court to require a party to appear and explain why an action should not take place. Anyone opposed to the action has an opportunity to express his or her position and produce evidence in support of his or her interest. If the affected party does not appear or present acceptable reasons, the proposed show cause action will take place. The burden of proof is on the party required to show cause. *See also* APPEAL, p. 579; COMMON LAW, p. 13; INJUNCTION, p. 622.

Significance	Equity jurisdiction in the United States is placed in the same courts that possess jurisdiction over statutory and common law. In Great Britain courts of equity are structurally separate from courts having jurisdiction over legal matters. Considerations of equity in American courts protect against injustices occurring through proper but too rigid application of common law principles or where gaps exist in the common law.

Exclusive Power	Authority that is fully possessed by either the federal or state government. Exclusive power is conveyed such that it may be exercised exclusively by one level. The federal government, for example, has exclusive power over the conduct of foreign relations. That means a state has no authority to act in foreign policy matters. Exclusive power is the opposite of concurrent power, which may be exercised by both the federal and state governments. *See also* CONCURRENT POWER, p. 588; FEDERALISM, p. 29; POWER, p. 644.

Significance   The concept of exclusive power reflects the division of power between the federal and state governments. The concept holds that each level is preeminent or supreme within its own zone of authority. The federal government has exclusive power to coin money, for example, while states have exclusive power over the scope and form of local units of government within their boundaries. Time may alter the categorization of certain functions as exclusive. As circumstances change, power once considered the exclusive domain of one level may become less than exclusive. States, for example, were originally seen as possessing exclusive power over education and the protection of civil rights. The federal government, however, has assumed an ever larger role over those matters, especially the latter.

Executive Agreement   An international agreement concluded by a president outside the formal treaty-making process. Executive agreements are reached through the exercise of a president's authority as commander-in-chief as well as the discretion that falls to the executive to conduct foreign relations. There is no constitutional reference to executive agreements. These agreements may be invalidated by congressional actions and do not bind subsequent presidents. Most often, executive agreements cover such matters as immigration or international trade. *See also* TREATY POWER, p. 661; *UNITED STATES V. BELMONT* (301 U.S. 324: 1937), p. 156.

Significance   An executive agreement has the same legal status as a treaty. This was specifically decided by the Supreme Court in *United States v. Belmont* (301 U.S. 324: 1937). This was a major holding because it allowed presidents to enter into agreements that are legally comparable to treaties without having to undergo Senate review. Thus *Belmont* was an incentive for presidents to utilize the executive agreement approach. Indeed, the recent pattern shows a continuing increase in the use of such agreements, with a corresponding decline in the conclusion of new treaties. Furthermore, an executive agreement, like a treaty, displaces any state law with which it is in conflict.

Executive Immunity   Protection enjoyed by a president from criminal prosecution while in office, or civil suits brought against a president for official conduct. The extent to which a sitting president is actually insulated from criminal prosecution is unclear. While the Court has never ruled on the matter, it was assumed that President Richard Nixon was protected from prosecution in connection with the Watergate scandal and its cover-up. Any immunity from prosecution that exists while actually holding office does not remain once a president leaves the office. The president does, however, enjoy immunity from civil suits. In *Nixon v. Fitzgerald* (457 U.S. 731: 1982), the Court held that a president is absolutely free from civil claims for damages resulting from official actions taken during his tenure. The Court said that such immunity is a "functionally mandated incident of the President's unique office." Executive immunity was seen as "rooted in the constitutional tradition of the separation of powers and supported by our history." *See also* EXECUTIVE PRIVILEGE, p. 603; *MISSISSIPPI V. JOHNSON* (4 Wallace 475: 1867), p. 143; *NIXON V. FITZGERALD* (457 U.S. 731: 1982), p. 155; SPEECH OR DEBATE CLAUSE, p. 654; *UNITED STATES V. NIXON* (418 U.S. 683: 1974), p. 153.

Significance   The matter of executive privilege does have separation of powers implications. In the case of *Mississippi v. Johnson* (4 Wallace 475: 1867), the Court refused to issue an injunction against Andrew Johnson because to do so would assume certain enforcement functions reserved to the president. The Court had not had occasion to examine the matter of presidential immunity from indictment prior to President Nixon's possible prosecution. The failure of the special prosecutor to seek indictment and the subsequent pardon of Nixon by President Gerald Ford ended the possibility of the question's being resolved. The *Fitzgerald* case, however, clearly defines the matter of civil immunity. The Court extended broad immunity, concluding that it encompassed the "special nature" of the presidency and its functions, even those reaching only the "outer perimeter" of "official responsibility." The Court felt that the impeachment process, the desire of a president to secure reelection, other formal and informal checks on presidential actions, and perceptions of the stature of the office would sufficiently protect against presidential abuse. In a companion case to *Fitzgerald, Harlow and Butterfield v. Fitzgerald* (457 U.S. 800: 1982), the Court refused to extend executive immunity to presidential aides.

Executive Order   A regulation issued by the president or an executive subordinate for the purpose of giving effect to a constitutional provision or a statute. The executive order has the force of law and is one of the means by which the executive branch implements law. An executive order must be published in the *Federal Register* in order to have effect. *See also* DELEGATION OF LEGISLATIVE POWER, p. 591.

Significance   The use of executive orders has increased substantially in recent years, and that pattern will likely remain. Frequently, legislation leaves discretion to the executive branch to make adjustments necessary to effectively implement enacted policy objectives. While the executive discretion is to be generally guided by legislation, some policy modification can stem from executive orders.

Executive Privilege   An asserted power of the president to withhold information from either the legislative or judicial branches. The claim of executive privilege is based on a view of separation of powers that argues that presidents need to protect certain information in order to function effectively. There is no express constitutional provision on executive privilege. Rather, it is argued to be an implied and inherent executive power. Rationale for such a privilege includes the need to protect military, diplomatic, or national security secrets from disclosure. It is also asserted that in order to productively utilize advisers, a president must be able to keep conversations confidential to allow a full and free exchange of alternatives. *See also* EXECUTIVE IMMUNITY, p. 601; INHERENT POWER, p. 622; IMPLIED POWER, p. 618; SPEECH OR DEBATE CLAUSE, p. 654; *UNITED STATES V. NIXON* (418 U.S. 683: 1974), p. 153.

Significance   The claim of executive privilege has been asserted historically, but the issue assumed its greatest importance during the Nixon presidency, specifically during the inquiry into the Watergate episode. The specific question was whether President Nixon needed to supply subpoenaed tape recordings of White House conversations for presentation to a federal grand jury. The Court ruled on the claim of privilege in *United States v. Nixon* (418 U.S. 683: 1974). The Court did recognize the need for such a privilege, but rejected the argument that the privilege is absolute. The Court said that absent a need to "protect military, diplomatic, or sensitive national security secrets," it could not see the "interest in confidentiality of presidential communications as significantly diminished" by production of the subpoenaed tapes in the instance of the Watergate probe. Indeed, as a general proposition, the interests of protecting the integrity of the criminal justice process outweigh confidentiality interests except in limited national security situations. Another aspect of the privilege involves presidential records once a president has left office. In *Nixon v. Administrator of General Services* (433 U.S. 425: 1977), the Court upheld provisions of a federal statute requiring President Nixon's presidential records and documents to be screened, with only those of a personal and private nature being returned to him.

Executive Veto Power   Executive power to disapprove of bills passed by the legislature. The executive veto power is found in the presentment clause of Article I, Section 7. It says that before a bill becomes a law, it must be "presented to the President." The president may sign a bill, which formally concludes the law-making process. The president may also veto the bill and return it to the house of origin along with the reasons for not signing it. A third option for a president is to neither sign nor veto a bill, in which case it becomes law after ten congressional working days. Congress has three options in response to a veto. It may let the vetoed measure die. It may accommodate the president and repass the legislation with sufficient change to obtain presidential support. Or it may choose to confront the president's objections and try to override the veto by repassing the legislation with a minimum two-thirds roll-call vote in each house. The president does not possess item veto power, which would allow striking individual items of appropriations. Rather, the president must approve or veto each bill as a whole. At the end of every congressional session, there are some measures that are killed by pocket veto. That occurs when a bill is left unsigned by the president in the last ten days before the adjournment of the legislature. *See also* ARTICLE I, p. 183; LEGISLATIVE VETO, p. 632.

Significance   The executive veto power is provided in Article I, the legislative article. The location of this power clearly communicates the framers' intention that the president play a regular and substantial role in the law-making process. The veto power was not extensively used prior to the Civil War, as most early presidents felt that the veto ought to be reserved for bills viewed as unconstitutional. Use of the veto increased dramatically after the Civil War as the scope of the power was broadened. Presidents began to veto legislation as an expression of disapproval, and the exercise of the power took on new meaning in the context of executive-legislative relations. The Congress knows that mustering a two-thirds vote in both houses is very difficult, especially when the votes are individually recorded. Indeed, only a very small proportion of vetoes are successfully overridden. More likely is legislative-executive negotiation focusing on issues that may bring a veto in efforts to avoid actual use of the veto power.

Ex Post Facto   A law that retroactively proscribes particular conduct. Sections 9 and 10 of Article I preclude both Congress and state legislatures from enacting *ex post facto* laws. The *ex post facto* prohibition is intended to prevent abusive or vindictive exercise of legislative power and to assure "fair warning" of the effects of legislation. It may also have been prompted by a desire to insulate loans, but an early Court decision, *Calder v. Bull* (3 Dallas 386: 1798), held that the *ex post facto* provision applied only to laws affecting criminal conduct. *See also* BILL OF ATTAINDER, p. 582; *UNITED STATES V. BROWN* (381 U.S. 437: 1965), p. 209; *WEAVER V. GRAHAM* (450 U.S. 24: 1981), p. 210.

Significance   An *ex post facto* violation can occur in several ways. No legislative body may pass a law that makes criminal any conduct occurring prior to the passage of the law. Neither may a law redefine a statute to make previous conduct a more serious or aggravated violation. The *ex post facto* prohibition also precludes retroactively increasing the severity of punishment for criminal conduct. No law may alter evidentiary rules in a way that makes successful prosecution more likely or diminishes any legal protections a person may exercise. In sum, the *ex post facto* provision prohibits any legislative action that retroactively disadvantages a person in a criminal context.

Fair Labor Standards Act   A federal law that first established national wage and hours of work standards. The Fair Labor Standards Act (FLSA) was based on congressional power to regulate interstate commerce and applied to any employee directly involved in such commerce or in the production of items for interstate commerce. The act defined the minimum wage at 25 cents an hour. The maximum work week was set at 40 hours with work in excess requiring time and a half wages. The act also closed interstate commerce to products of firms violating the wage requirements or using child labor. The scope and application of the act has broadened substantially since its enactment in 1938. *See also* COMMERCE CLAUSE, p. 291; *UNITED STATES V. DARBY LUMBER COMPANY* (312 U.S. 100: 1941), p. 324.

Significance   The Fair Labor Standards Act was enacted to address workplace conditions by establishing national standards for wages and hours. In addition, the act intended to challenge the Court's decision in *Hammer v. Dagenhart* (247 U.S. 251: 1918) that regulation of child labor was beyond the reach of federal commerce power. The act was upheld by the Court in *United States v. Darby Lumber Company* (312 U.S. 100: 1941) and has been expanded since. For example, the act was amended in 1963 by the Equal Pay Act, which required equal pay for equal work irrespective of gender. In 1976, however, the Court held in *National League of Cities v. Usery* (426 U.S. 833:1976) that the FLSA could not be applied to employees of state and local governments. This decision was reversed in *Garcia v. San Antonio Metropolitan Transit Authority* (469 U.S. 528: 1985), when the Court decided that the FLSA applied to employees of a city-owned and -operated transit system.

Fairness Doctrine   A Federal Communications Commission policy that requires the holder of a broadcast license to afford a reasonable amount of air time to issues of public significance and to replies by persons of differing viewpoints from those expressed by the station. The fairness doctrine, also known as the equal time provision, is enforced by the Federal Communications Commission through its licensure authority.

Significance   The fairness doctrine has been upheld by the Supreme Court against First Amendment challenge in *Red Lion Broadcasting Company, Inc. v. Federal Communications Commission* (395 U.S. 367: 1969). The Court distinguished the broadcast medium from the print medium, saying the fairness doctrine was necessary for broadcasting because of the scarcity of access to the airwaves and because licensees could otherwise monopolize the medium.

Federal Question   The jurisdiction to hear cases involving issues related to the United States Constitution, federal laws, or treaties. A federal question is one involving judicial powers conferred in Article III of the Constitution.

Significance   A federal question must be shown by parties wishing to access the federal courts. Their case or controversy must be within the power of the federal courts to adjudicate. An exception can occur when citizens of two different states are adversaries in a legal action. The Supreme Court frequently refuses to review cases because it believes a substantial federal question is not present.

Fifteenth Amendment   A post–Civil War amendment added to the Constitution in 1870. The Fifteenth Amendment provides that "the right of the citizens of the United States to vote shall not be denied or abridged by the United States or by any State on account of race, color, or previous condition of servitude." A second section of the amendment empowered Congress to pass appropriate enforcement legislation. The Fifteenth Amendment did not extend the right to vote per se, but prohibited racial discrimination in voting. *See also* FOURTEENTH AMENDMENT, p. 612; THIRTEENTH AMENDMENT, p. 660.

Significance   The Fifteenth Amendment left control over voting to the states, which placed qualifications for voting within the purview of state legislatures. Early decisions of the Supreme Court acknowledged that federal power could be exercised if citizens were denied the opportunity to vote in state elections on racial grounds. It was not until the Second World War, however, that the Supreme Court used the Fifteenth Amendment to reach the more sophisticated discriminatory techniques used in several states, such as the white primary and qualifying tests. Congressional initiatives based on the Fifteenth Amendment did not appear until the Voting Rights Act of 1965. The Voting Rights Act abolished such devices as the literacy test and poll tax by which people had been disqualified from voting since Reconstruction. It reaffirmed the Twenty-fourth Amendment, ratified in 1964, specifying that the right of citizens to vote "shall not be denied or abridged by the United States or by any State by reason of failure to pay any poll tax or other tax." The act also provided for extensive federal supervison of elections and required that any new voter eligibility criterion be reviewed by the attorney general prior to its implementation. The Supreme Court unanimously upheld the Voting Rights Act in *South Carolina v. Katzenbach* (383 U.S. 301: 1966), saying an aggressive and inventive legislative approach was appropriate given nearly a century of systematic resistance to the Fifteenth Amendment. The Court's ruling in *Katzenbach* clearly established broad federal power over voting practices in the United States.

Fifth Amendment   Provides protections for persons in the criminal process, particularly that no one shall be deprived of life, liberty, or property, without due process of law. The Fifth Amendment was an American adaptation of elements of the English common law tradition. In contrast to the language of the Fourth Amendment, whose etiology was based on specific colonial experiences with the British use of the general warrant, the language of the Fifth Amendment was based on what Blackstone referred to as "universal maxims." The Fifth Amendment contains five separate clauses: (1) "No person shall be held to answer for a capital, or otherwise infamous crime, unless on a presentment or indictment of a Grand Jury, except in cases arising in the land or naval forces, or in the Militia, when in actual service in time of War or public danger." The language is Madison's. He drew heavily from Blackstone and tried to incorporate the rule from English common law that no case could be prosecuted until a duly sworn grand jury had attested that grounds existed for such prosecution. The exception clause regarding land or naval forces and the militia attempts to avoid potential conflicts between civilian and military tribunals. (2) "nor shall any person be subject for the same offence to be twice put in jeopardy of life or limb." Blackstone said it was a "universal maxim of the common law of England that no man is to be brought into jeopardy of his life more than once for the same offence." This principle of "non bis in idem" was based initially on a holding in twelfth-century English courts that, if a person were tried for violation of an ecclesiastical canon, he could not be tried for the same infraction in the civil courts. (3) " . . . nor shall be compelled in any criminal case to be a witness against himself." The origins of this clause were in the practices of the English Star Chamber Court, where persons even suspected of some offense were interrogated before any formal accusation had been made. The English system of justice at the time was redolent with forced confessions. The early American knowledge of and determination to reform this system was reflected in the Virginia Bill of Rights. (4) " . . . nor be deprived of life, liberty, or property, without due process of law." Hamilton argued persuasively that insertion of the phrase "due process" would remove any doubt it was "the process and proceedings of the courts of justice" being addressed. Thus the *courts* would interpret the legitimate rights of citizens, not legislative bodies, which would presumably enact legislation to "disfranchise or deprive" citizens of *any* right. Because of the clause's general thrust and applicability, the Supreme Court historically has been reluctant to give it precise definition. (5) " . . . nor shall private property be taken for public use, without just compensation." The founding fathers considered property rights to be absolute and inherent. Again, this holding is based in English common law dating from the Magna Carta. *See also* BILL OF RIGHTS, p. 7; COMMON LAW, p. 13; JOHN LOCKE, p. 43; MAGNA CARTA, p. 45.

Significance   The Fifth Amendment has been the basis of more Supreme Court decisions than any other article of the Bill of Rights or of the Constitution itself. The broad and dramatic interpretations of the due process clause after passage of the Fourteenth Amendment in 1868 make it the linchpin of American constitutional law. The Fifth Amendment's provision proscribing self-incrimination has become one of the foremost privileges incurring to citizens of the United States. The fact that the Supreme Court can review on both substantive and procedural due process grounds under the Fifth and Fourteenth Amendments gives the Supreme Court unparalleled power in modern democratic governments. Although due process, in Daniel Webster's words, fundamentally may only provide that a court "hear before it condemns," it has in American practice been elaborated to provide a series of checkpoints for the courts to assure the preservation of a distinctly American tradition, that it is better for the guilty to go free than for one innocent person to be deprived of life, liberty, or property.

First Amendment   Protects personal belief and opinion and action stemming from personal belief and opinion. The First Amendment to the Constitution of the United States was adopted in 1791. It addresses four basic freedoms its authors deemed imperative to a free society functioning within a democratic government. Those freedoms are (1) freedom of religion, (2) freedom of speech, (3) freedom of the press, and (4) the dual right to assemble peaceably and to petition the government. Freedom of religion is protected by two provisions; one prohibits the establishment of religion, and the other ensures the free exercise of religion. By implication a right of association also flows from the First Amendment. Although these rights may or may not be absolute, it has generally been held by the Supreme Court that a balance is required between First Amendment freedoms and the powers of a government to govern effectively. The primary issues that have occupied the Court are those requiring line drawing between protected and unprotected activity. Each First Amendment clause will now be taken in turn.

The establishment clause was included because the drafters remembered the colonial experience with European state churches. At minimum the clause prohibits government from showing favoritism to a particular church or sect. The Supreme Court, however, has construed the prohibitions more broadly. It has attempted to create standards by which it can distinguish church and state involvements that are forbidden from those that are not. For a policy to withstand the limitations imposed by the clause, a legislative enactment must have a secular purpose, it must have a primary effect that neither advances nor inhibits religion, and it must not excessively entangle church and state authorities. The neutral position to be occupied by the state applies both to spiritual practices such as devotional exercises and to the allocation of public monies for the benefit of religion.

The free exercise clause prevents the government from interfering with religious practices. The clause absolutely protects a person's right to believe. The line-drawing problem exists when some kind of conduct is required in addition to belief. As Justice Felix Frankfurter observed in the first flag salute case, conscientious scruples are insufficient to relieve an individual from "obedience to general law not aimed at the promotion or restriction of religious belief." Thus, a law that has a legitimate secular purpose may impinge upon the ability of a person to act out religious beliefs. More recently the Court has required that regulations that do interfere with religious practices can only do so in the absence of an alternative to the accomplishment of the legitimate secular objective.

The Court did not have occasion to consider the free speech provision until shortly after World War I. The first important free speech case, *Schenck v United States* (249 U.S. 47: 1919) held that the First Amendment would not protect a person who falsely shouted "Fire!" in a crowded theatre and thus caused a panic. The authors of the First Amendment, however, were not as concerned with an utterance such as "Fire!" as they were with normal political and social expression. The problems of interpretation for the Court have come largely because the right of expression requires that there be a receiver of speech. There must be communication. Even if the participants in a communication exchange are of limited numbers, there might arise circumstances in which governmental intervention is appropriate. The key is determining *when* that intervention might be justified. The interests of those wishing to express themselves must be weighed against the public interest. That balancing process is complex and has given rise to a typology of expression that distinguishes speech that requires no additional conduct, speech that does require additional conduct, and speech that occurs through symbolism. The Court has fashioned various standards by which it can separate protected from unprotected communication within each of these categories.

The fundamental freedom of the press is also included within the First Amendment. The framers of the Constitution believed that liberty could not be maintained without a free press, which was a check on government. If the press is truly free, it can criticize all branches of the government, public employees, and, particularly, public policy. The doctrine of a free press means the press must be free from government control, printing what it desires without fear of censorship or prior restraint. There are many related issues the framers did not anticipate, however. Since radio and television were unknown in the late eighteenth century, the framers did not anticipate the power of electronic news media. Interference with the rights of those accused of crimes and the fairness of their trials could not be jeopardized in 1791 by prejudicial publicity broadcast over the airwaves. Neither were certain questions of obscenity and commercial speech perceived at the beginning of the American constitutional era. The Supreme Court has had to address each of these issues as they have developed in American history, all the while trying to balance the freedoms mandated in the First Amendment with other individual rights.

The enunciated right of peaceful assembly contains elements of expression found both in the right of free speech and in the right of association. In recent years assembly rights have been associated with the civil rights movements of the 1960s, with anti–Viet Nam demonstrations in the late 1960s and early 1970s, and with other political assemblies. Once again the Court has had to balance peaceful assembly against the protection of other rights, including private property rights and state property rights. Assembly cases usually involve marching, picketing, demonstrating, petition gathering, and similar activities. While free speech may be protected, associated conduct may be subject to regulation by the state. Not only is government interested in protecting property rights, it is also interested in maintaining public order. The essential rule is that government may impose restrictions on the time, place, and the manner in which an expression may occur through assembly.

The First Amendment does not expressly protect the right of association. It is drawn from the free speech, peaceful assembly, and right to petition clauses of the First Amendment. While free speech focuses on one's right to express his or her views, the association right focuses on one's right to join a group, and be present at group meetings, but not necessarily to express oneself directly. It is the right to be a member of a group while the group expresses itself without regard to whether an individual member agrees with the group or not. *See also* BILL OF RIGHTS, p. 7; CONSTITUTION OF THE UNITED STATES OF AMERICA, p. 19; NATURAL LAW AND NATURAL RIGHTS, p. 50.

Significance   The First Amendment was conceived as a constraint on the power of central government. With the exception of the Alien and Sedition Acts of 1798, Congress enacted little legislation that found its way to the Supreme Court on First Amendment challenge until World War I. See, for example, *Schenck v. United States* (249 U.S. 47: 1919). Soon thereafter the Court was involved in a series of decisions that extended the various components of the First Amendment to the states through the Fourteenth Amendment, a process known as incorporation. Movement toward such an incorporation policy was evident in *Meyer v. Nebraska* (262 U.S. 390: 1923), in which the Court struck down a state statute prohibiting the teaching of German to any pre–ninth-grade student in either public or private school. In *Meyer*, the Court held that the term "liberty" included, among other things, the right to "acquire useful knowledge" and engage in "common occupations of life," such as teaching. The Court said the Nebraska statute arbitrarily and unreasonably interfered with that liberty to the degree that due process protections of the Fourteenth Amendment had been violated. The free speech protection was formally extended in *Gitlow v. New York* (268 U.S. 652: 1925), with the Court holding that freedom of speech was "among the fundamental personal rights and 'liberties' protected by the Fourteenth Amendment from impairment by the states." In *Near v. Minnesota* (283 U.S. 697: 1931), the Court said that it is "no longer open to doubt that the liberty of the press . . . is within the liberty safeguarded by the due process clause of the Fourteenth Amendment from invasion by state action." The right of assembly was incorporated in *DeJonge v. Oregon* (299 U.S. 353: 1937). The Court referred to the right of "peaceable assembly" as a right "cognate" and "equally fundamental" to those of free speech and press. It is a right that "cannot be denied without violating those fundamental principles of liberty and justice which lie at the base of all civil and political institutions— principles which the Fourteenth Amendment embodies in the general terms of its due process clause." The free exercise of religion clause was absorbed in *Cantwell v. Connecticut* (310 U.S. 296: 1940), with the Court saying the Fourteenth Amendment has "rendered the legislatures of the states as incompetent as Congress to enact such laws." The remaining element of the First Amendment, the establishment clause, was made applicable to the states in *Everson v. Board of Education* (330 U.S. 1: 1947). The Court held that the clause must be extended to the states because it "reflected in the minds of early Americans a vivid mental picture of conditions and practices which they fervently wished to stamp out to preserve liberty for themselves and their posterity." The result of these decisions is that the safeguards residing within the First Amendment stand against unreasonable actions by both national and state governments in circumscribing personal belief and opinion.

Fourteenth Amendment   A post–Civil War amendment added to the Constitution in 1868. The Fourteenth Amendment was designed to expand the Thirteenth Amendment as the basis for federal civil rights authority. The Amendment was also aimed at forcing Southern compliance with newly established political rights for blacks. The provisions of Section I constitute the heart of the amendment. It begins by declaring that "all persons born or naturalized in the United States, and subject to the jurisdiction thereof, are citizens of the United States and the State wherein they reside." This language reversed the citizenship holding in *Dred Scott v. Sandford* (19 Howard 393: 1857). The privileges and immunities provision then follows. This provision was intended to combat the effects of the Black Codes and allow federal authority to be used to protect and advance the civil rights of black citizens. The *Slaughterhouse Cases* decision (16 Wallace 36: 1873) neutralized this thrust through use of the dual citizenship concept. Dual citizenship allowed the Supreme Court to ascribe civil and political rights of major consequence to the states. Section I also says that no state shall deprive any person of life, liberty, or property without due process of law. The due process clause ultimately allowed the Court to apply most Bill of Rights guarantees to the states in a process known as incorporation. The clause also enabled the Court to engage in a substantive review of state policies, particularly those regulating private property rights. Section I concludes by saying that no state shall deny to any person within its jurisdiction the equal protection of laws. The function of this provision was to prohibit unjustified classifications that might discriminate unreasonably.

Section 5 empowers Congress "to enforce by appropriate legislation, the provisions of this article." Early attempts to do so were unsuccessful because the Court held that congressional power might only be used in a remedial fashion in cases where the state was itself an active participant in impermissible discrimination. The state action requirement survives, although the scope of federal legislative power conferred by the Fourteenth Amendment has been expanded considerably. *See also* DUE PROCESS CLAUSES, p. 594; INCORPORATION, p. 620; PRIVILEGES AND IMMUNITIES CLAUSE, p. 647; STATE ACTION, p. 657.

Significance   The Fourteenth Amendment brought a federal presence to the protection of civil rights, but early interpretations of the amendment preserved a dominant role for the states in this policy area. Only recently has the amendment produced major changes, primarily through expanded construction of the due process and equal protection clauses. The Fourteenth Amendment has now become the cornerstone of civil rights policy and the principal means by which Bill of Rights guarantees have been extended to the states. Its importance in protecting the basic rights of Americans relates to the fact that, contrary to the beliefs of the founding fathers, the main threats to the people's liberties have come from state and local governments rather than from the national government.

Fourth Amendment   Safeguards American citizens from unreasonable searches and seizures. The Fourth Amendment was included in the Bill of Rights as the direct result of the British imposition in the American colonies of writs of assistance. These general warrants allowed for arbitrary searches and seizures of persons and property. They proliferated in the years immediately preceding the American Revolution when they were issued to seize contraband smuggled into the colonies in violation of acts of Parliament imposing duties and tariffs on imports. The framers insisted on specific language to ensure that probable cause existed to issue a warrant. It said that name, place, and things sought must be identified. Further, the warrant must issue from a neutral magistrate who would be a disinterested third party between the individual citizen and the law enforcement officer seeking the warrant. Yet the Fourth Amendment only extended to the federal government in early American history. After passage of the Fourteenth Amendment in 1868, coverage of the Fourth Amendment could be extended through the Fourteenth Amendment's due process clause.

The modern nationalization of the Fourth Amendment was dramatically interpreted by the Warren Court in such cases as *Mapp v. Ohio* (367 U.S. 643: 1961), *Ker v. California* (374 U.S. 23: 1963), and *Chimel v. California* (395 U.S. 752: 1969). The direction changed, however, with more conservative appointments to the Court. Decisions of the Burger Court gradually moved from limiting the scope of permissible searches and seizures to limiting the scope of rights of criminal defendants, including the parameters of permissibility. In 1973, for example, the Burger Court upheld full searches of individuals lawfully arrested for traffic violations without the existence of evidence of probable cause (*United States v. Robinson*, 414 U.S. 218: 1973). Thus specific abuses under the Fourth Amendment are reinterpreted over time. *See also* BILL OF RIGHTS, p. 7.

Significance   The Fourth Amendment established an absolute right against threat of unreasonable intrusion by agents and officials of the newly formed American government. The clamor for the Fourth Amendment, as well as the other nine amendments in the Bill of Rights, came out of the state constitutional ratifying conventions. The delegates to the Maryland convention said, for example, that the adoption of the Fourth Amendment was necessary because "a free people" must be provided a constitutional check effective to "safeguard our citizens" against the issuance of general warrants. In making their arguments, many of the states relied heavily on the language of Sir William Blackstone's *Commentaries on the Laws of England*, Volume IV, in which general warrants were declared to be illegal. Elements of Blackstone's language found their way into both the Constitution and the Bill of Rights. The English constitution did forbid the issuance of general writs. In 1766 Parliament expressly declared all general warrants for search and seizure illegal, but abuses of both common and statutory law were prevalent in Great Britain and in the American colonies in the late eighteenth century. Just prior to the American Revolution, members of Parliament were in fact debating the abuses of the general warrant process. Among the discussants were Sir Edward Coke, Sir Matthew Hale, and especially Lord Camden, who found the general warrant wholly outside the spirit of the English constitution. Lord Camden was quoted by a justice of the United States Supreme Court as late as 1886, when Joseph P. Bradley wrote in *Boyd v. United States* (116 U.S. 616: 1886) that Camden's exposition expressed "the true doctrine on the subject of searches and seizures." It furnished "the true criteria of the reasonable and unreasonable character of such searches." The true doctrine and the true criteria are settled in American jurisprudence as the sanctity of a citizen's home and person. Hopefully the fundamental values safeguarded by the framers' prohibition against unreasonable searches and seizures will far outlast changing historical circumstances.

Full Faith and Credit Clause   Provision in Article IV that obliges states to recognize several kinds of actions taken in other states. The clause states that "full faith and credit shall be given in each state to the public acts, records, and judicial proceedings of every other state." The clause does not extend to criminal proceedings, but only civil issues. The clause guarantees that interests protected by such means as wills and contracts will be recognized in all other states. The clause does obligate a state to honor state judicial decisions from other states. *See also* ARTICLE IV, p. 225.

Significance   The full faith and credit clause was designed to promote amicable relationships among the states. The clause both protects legal rights and preserves legal obligations as people move from state to state. This has become especially important as the mobility of the American population has increased. Recognition of judicial decision is generally not a problem, although questions concerning legal residence, such as in divorce actions, were an exception during the period when there existed great diversity in state laws governing them. The clause does not require states to enforce each other's criminal laws. Furthermore, in *Nevada v. Hall* (440 U.S. 410: 1979), the Court held that the clause does not "require a state to apply another state's law in violation of its own legitimate public policy."

Fundamental Right   Protection extended to a right expressly stated or implied in the Constitution. A fundamental right occupies a preferred position in American jurisprudence. It receives demanding review by the courts. If classificatory legislation affects a fundamental right, for example, the legislation is subject to the standards of strict scrutiny. The state must demonstrate that a compelling need is served by any enactment impinging on a fundamental right. *See also* RIGHT, p. 648.

Significance   A fundamental right may be expressly provided in the Constitution or it may have evolved to a preferred status. Fundamental rights include the right to interstate travel, participation in the political process, opportunity to adjudicate legal issues, privacy, personal autonomy, and abortion. Such services as public welfare assistance and public medical care have not been viewed by the Supreme Court as fundamental rights. Residence requirements used as a condition of receiving welfare assistance or medical care have been struck down as impermissible restrictions on the fundamental right of unhindered interstate movement.

Guarantee Clause   Provision in Article IV in which the federal government assures the states that each will retain a "republican form of government." The guarantee clause requires federal intervention, on request of the state, in the event of domestic violence or insurrection. The clause also limits a state's options as to the organizational form its state government may take. By requiring a "republican" form of government, the Constitution precludes a state from direct participatory democracy. *See also* LUTHER V. BORDEN (7 Howard 1: 1849), p. 121; POLITICAL QUESTION, p. 644.

Significance   The guarantee clause does not define what constitutes a "republican form" of government. Since a republican government is not directly democratic but rather operates through elected representatives, it is safe to conclude that any state whose electoral processes are threatened may invoke the clause. Neither does Article IV specify how the federal government is to implement the guarantee clause. The federal courts, however, are not to be involved in enforcement. In *Luther v. Borden* (7 Howard 1: 1849), the Court held such issues to be "political questions" and, therefore, not appropriate for judicial determination. The Court saw Congress as the appropriate place for such decisions to be made. Indeed, more than 50 years prior to *Luther*, the Congress had formally delegated this function to the president.

Habeas Corpus   A Latin term meaning "you have the body." *Habeas corpus* was a procedure in English law designed to prevent governmental misconduct, especially the improper detention of prisoners. Its primary purpose was to force jailers to bring a detained person before a judge who would examine the adequacy of the detention. If the judge found the person improperly in custody, he could order the prisoner's release through a writ of *habeas corpus*. A writ is an order from a court requiring the recipient of the order to do what the order commands. In American law the preliminary hearing functions as a point of examination into the propriety of pretrial detention as well as into the charges brought against an accused person. Article I, Section 9 of the United States Constitution provides that the "privilege of the Writ of Habeas Corpus shall not be suspended, unless when in Cases of Rebellion or Invasion the Public Safety may require it." President Lincoln attempted to suspend the writ early in the Civil War, but it was determined in *Ex*

Parte Merryman (17 Fed. Cas. No. 9487: 1861) that suspension was entirely a congressional prerogative. Congress subsequently authorized President Lincoln to suspend the writ of *habeas corpus* at his discretion. This action was challenged and was eventually decided by the Supreme Court in *Ex Parte Milligan* (4 Wallace 2: 1866). A unanimous Court said the president could not suspend *habeas corpus* under any circumstances. A five-member majority held that Congress did not have the power either. There has been no subsequent attempt to suspend *habeas corpus* in the United States.

Significance   *Habeas corpus* today involves, *inter alia*, federal court review of state criminal convictions. After the Fourteenth Amendment was ratified, Congress enlarged *habeas corpus* to include persons already convicted and in custody in the states. These prisoners could apply for a writ of *habeas corpus* if they believed a violation of the Constitution or federal statutes had occurred in their cases. The allegations of violations were limited to jurisdictional issues at the time, but this apparently insignificant change began a transformation of the traditional concept of *habeas corpus*. It eventually turned *habeas corpus* into a virtual substitute for the conventional appeals process. Several Supreme Court decisions have expanded the *habeas corpus* remedy. *Frank v. Mangum* (237 U.S. 309: 1915) held that *habeas corpus* review existed when states failed to provide an effective means for convicted prisoners to pursue alleged violations of their federal constitutional rights. *Brown v. Allen* (344 U.S. 443: 1953) said that federal courts could reexamine a prisoner's constitutional allegations even if the state had provided corrective processes. The defendant had only to exhaust the processes. In *Fay v. Noia* (372 U.S. 391: 1963), the Court determined that even if all state processes are not utilized, a defendant can access the federal courts through a *habeas corpus* application. The number of state prisoners seeking *habeas corpus* relief in the early 1940s was slightly over one hundred annually. By the early 1970s there were over eight thousand applications per year. The Burger Court was critical of this trend. It frequently expressed disapproval of *habeas corpus* being taken "far beyond its historical bounds and in disregard of the writ's central purpose." (See *Schneckloth v. Bustamonte*, 412 U.S. 218: 1973.) In its most significant response to the issue to date, the Court held in *Stone v. Powell* (428 U.S. 465: 1972) that the *habeas corpus* remedy is not available to state prisoners, at least those pursuing Fourth Amendment search violations, when the defendant had been afforded a full and fair opportunity to press the allegations in a state court. While *habeas corpus* still provides substantial access for state as well as federal prisoners, the scope of the remedy in the state proceedings has been reduced in the last decade.

Impeachment   Part of a process that may lead to the removal of a civil officer from office. Impeachment at the federal level is an accusation made by the House of Representatives. Adoption of articles of impeachment sends the matter to the Senate for trial on the charges or articles. Reference to impeachment is contained in Articles I and II. The House has "sole" power over impeachment, while the Senate has "sole" power to try. Article II broadly defines grounds for impeachment as conviction of "treason, bribery or other high crimes and misdemeanors." The impeachment process is initiated by referral of the matter to either a standing or ad hoc committee of the House. Impeachment articles move from the committee to the full House, and they may be adopted by a simple majority vote. The House then appoints persons to present the case to the Senate. If the president is to be tried in the Senate, the chief justice of the United States presides. The person is convicted on charges considered individually by a two-thirds vote of the Senate. Conviction will likely result in removal from office, and it disqualifies the person from holding office subsequently. The pardon power cannot be applied to impeachment. While no other penalty attaches to impeachment itself, the impeached person may be prosecuted for any criminal conduct that may have been found in the impeachment inquiry. *See also* ARTICLE I, p. 183; ARTICLE II, p. 139.

Significance   The impeachment process is political rather than legal in nature. The grounds for removal may be defined by the legislative branch. It is apparent that conduct sufficient to remove an official need not be criminal. The process has seldom been used. The only actual removals from office (four times) involved members of the federal judiciary. President Andrew Johnson came within a single vote of impeachment in 1867. More recently, President Richard Nixon resigned the presidency in August of 1974 following initiation of impeachment proceedings in the House.

Implied Power   Authority not expressly conveyed in the Constitution or in statutes but inferred as stemming from expressly authorized grants of power. Implied power necessarily flows from expressed power and provides the means for the achievement of expressed power.

Significance   Implied power was first treated by the Supreme Court in *McCulloch v. Maryland* (4 Wheaton 316: 1819). At issue was the authority of Congress to establish a national bank, clearly not one of the enumerated powers of Article I of the Constitution. Chief Justice

Marshall nonetheless upheld creation of the bank on implied power grounds. The Court decided that the necessary and proper clause of Article I, Section 8 gave Congress wide discretion in the selection of methods by which it could carry out its policy judgments. Chief Justice Marshall said that if the objective sought by Congress is itself permissible, any means plainly adopted to that end were also permitted unless specifically prohibited by the Constitution. *McCulloch* thus established broad implied power as an aspect of legislative power. Inherent power is distinguished from implied power in that inherent power is authority beyond that expressly conferred or reasonably inferred. Implied power must be drawn from expressly granted power by reasonable inference.

Impoundment   Refusal by a chief executive to spend monies previously appropriated by the legislative branch. The practice of impoundment has been used over the years as presidents have withheld some portion of authorized funds from programs they did not fully support. This was done pursuant to presidents' general responsibility to develop and administer federal budgets. The Congressional Budget Reform and Impoundment Control Act of 1974 limited the president's ability to impound funds. *See also* DELEGATION OF LEGISLATIVE POWER, p. 591; LEGISLATIVE VETO, p. 632; *TRAIN V. CITY OF NEW YORK* (420 U.S. 35: 1975), p. 160.

Significance   The impoundment question is a manifestation of the larger issue of who controls the expenditures of federal funds. The Budget Act of 1921 vests the executive with substantial budget authority. While Congress retains the broad power of appropriation, it has been argued that appropriations only establish broad spending priorities. Occasional impoundment actions by presidents did not produce conflicts of any consequence with Congress. President Richard Nixon sought to impound on an unprecedented scale. These actions precipitated the impound control legislation of 1974. The Court's decision in *Train v. City of New York* (420 U.S. 35: 1975) indicated that the president was left no discretion to impound under the specific statute involved there, but the Court left the broader question of impound power unresolved. The 1974 legislation requires congressional concurrence for impounds, but the effectiveness of that requirement became unclear with the Court's decision in *Immigration and Naturalization Services v. Chadha* (462 U.S. 919: 1983), which invalidated the legislative veto.

In Camera   Means "in chambers" but refers to any kind of proceeding in which a judge conducts court business in private. *In camera* proceedings are held in a judge's chambers or any other location closed off to spectators.

Significance   *In camera* refers to the private review of written materials by a judge. The materials may be in the possession of one party who does not want to disclose them to an opposing party. The judge reviews the materials to determine if they are legally admissible. If they are, the materials are then disclosed to the other side.

Incorporation   The extent to which the federal Bill of Rights acts as a limitation on state governments. Incorporation was originally defined in *Barron v. Baltimore* (7 Peters 243: 1833). Through Chief Justice Marshall, the Supreme Court held that the Bill of Rights constrained only "the government created by the instrument," the federal government, and not the "distinct governments," the states. *Barron* was controlling until ratification of the Fourteenth Amendment in 1868. The Fourteenth Amendment reopened the question of incorporation beginning with *Gitlaw v. New York* (268 U.S 656: 1925) because the Court clearly directed its proscriptions to the states. Several schools of thought developed about how to resolve the matter. The most sweeping recommendation was to apply all Bill of Rights provisions to the states through the due process clause of the Fourteenth Amendment. The clause prohibits a state from denying liberty without due process. Those advocating total incorporation viewed the term *liberty* as an all-inclusive shorthand for each of the rights enumerated in the Bill of Rights. The approach was vigorously advocated by the first Justice John Marshall Harlan and by Justice Hugo L. Black, but it has never prevailed. A second opinion rejected any structural linkage of due process to the Bill of Rights and held simply that the due process clause required states to provide fundamental fairness. Due process is assessed under this standard by criteria of immutable principles of justice, or, as suggested by Justice Benjamin N. Cardozo in *Palko v. Connecticut* (302 U.S. 319: 1937), elements implicit in the concept of ordered liberty. Application of such standards would occur on a case-by-case basis. The third opinion is a hybrid of the first two and is known as selective incorporation. The selective approach resembles the fundamental fairness position in that it does not view as identical those rights contained in the Bill of Rights and those rights fundamental to fairness. Unlike the fundamental fairness approach, however, the selective view holds that rights expressly contained in the Bill of Rights, if adjudged fundamental, are incorporated through the Fourteenth

Amendment and are applicable at the state level regardless of the circumstances of a particular case. If the self-incrimination provision of the Fifth Amendment were determined to be fundamental, for example, it would apply in full to any state case bringing whatever substantive standards it preferred into federal courts. The selective approach created an honor roll of Bill of Rights provisions, some viewed as fundamental and wholly incorporated and a few others as less important and not worthy of incorporation. *See also* BILL OF RIGHTS, p. 7; FEDERALISM, p. 29.

Significance   Incorporation focuses on the degree to which Bill of Rights guarantees apply to the states. The question became important soon after ratification of the Fourteenth Amendment and remained unresolved for many years. The Supreme Court finally settled on the selective incorporation approach, which allowed the Warren Court to apply most Bill of Rights safeguards to the states. The Warren Court added many provisions to the list developed under the preceding fundamental fairness doctrine. The only Bill of Rights provisions that have not been incorporated are the grand jury requirement of the Fifth Amendment and the excessive bail and fine clause of the Eighth Amendment.

Independent Regulatory Commission   A regulatory agency outside the executive branch with power to fashion rules for specified segments of the economy. The independent regulatory commissions are quasi-judicial and quasi-legislative in character. That means they are empowered to conduct fact finding in a fashion not unlike a trial court. They then establish regulations for the particular area over which they have jurisdiction, hence the quasi-rule-making character. These rules are as binding as a statute. There are ten such commissions including the Consumer Product Safety Commission, Federal Communications Commission, Federal Energy Regulatory Commission, Federal Maritime Commission, Federal Power Commission, Federal Reserve Board, Federal Trade Commission, Interstate Commerce Commission, National Labor Relations Board, and the Securities and Exchange Commission. Each of these agencies is composed of five to eleven members. *See also FEDERAL POWER COMMISSION V. NATURAL GAS PIPELINE COMPANY* (315 U.S. 575: 1942), pp. 95, 362.

Significance   The independent regulatory commissions possess substantial power over economic policy. These agencies were established in an effort to provide effective regulation of highly complex segments of the nation's economy. The theory was that these commissions would be able to focus sufficiently and develop the level of expertise necessary to effectively regulate an industry. The commissioners are independent in that members cannot be removed except for cause. Members are appointed for set terms by the president with the advice and consent of the Senate. The terms are lengthy and staggered so that continuity is maintained. History will generally show that the Supreme Court exercises considerable restraint in reviewing the actions of these regulatory commissions.

Inherent Power   Authority that does not come from any specific constitutional provision. Inherent power is derived from the sovereignty of a country and permits the government, typically through the executive, to act on behalf of the national interest and security even without explicit authorization. The occasion for the exercise of such power usually arises out of foreign rather than domestic policy situations. Inherent power is a problem because its lack of express or implied constitutional underpinnings leave unattended the scope and extent of such powers. *See also* IN RE NEAGLE (135 U.S. 1: 1890), p. 141; POWER, p. 644; WAR POWERS, p. 673; *YOUNGSTOWN SHEET AND TUBE COMPANY V. SAWYER* (343 U.S. 579: 1952), p. 146.

Significance   Conceptually, inherent power runs counter to the principle of government authority defined and limited by specific constitutional language. But the claim to inherent or prerogative power predates American constitutional history. It is premised on the need to preserve the state from outside threats. Action taken to that end must be appropriate whether formally authorized or not. The Court's treatment of presidential claims to inherent power have been mixed. In *In Re Neagle* (135 U.S. 1: 1890), the Court held that a president need not have specific legislative authorization to act to preserve the "peace of the United States." Rather, power that inheres in the executive office was sufficient to empower the protective action taken.

On the other hand, the Court rejected President Truman's assertion of inherent power in the famous steel seizure incident. In *Youngstown Sheet and Tube Company v. Sawyer* (343 U.S. 579: 1952), the Court held that Congress had provided means by which national interest labor disputes were to be handled. Failure to include seizure in its legislation thus precluded the president from using that technique.

Injunction   A writ or order prohibiting a party from acting in a particular way or requiring a specific action by a party. A writ of injunction allows a court to minimize injury to a person or group until the matter can otherwise be resolved, or an injunction may prevent injury altogether. An injunction was used in the *Pentagon Papers* cases to keep the *New York Times* and the *Washington Post* from publishing sensitive Defense Department documents. (See *New York Times v. United States*, 403 U.S. 713: 1971). Failure to comply with an injunction is a contempt of court. Once issued, an injunction may be annulled or quashed. *See also* EQUITY JURISDICTION, p. 600.

Significance   An injunction may be temporary or permanent. Temporary injunctions, known as interlocutory injunctions, are used to preserve a situation until the issue is resolved through normal processes of litigation. A permanent injunction may be issued upon completion of full legal proceedings. School segregation cases such as *Brown v. Board of Education I* (347 U.S. 483: 1954) characteristically were cases in which injunctions were sought. An injunction is an example of a court's exercising its equity jurisdiction as opposed to its legal jurisdiction.

Intergovernmental Tax Immunity   A limit on the taxing power that exempts property and instruments of federal and state government from taxation by the other. The doctrine of intergovernmental tax immunity contributes to the effective operation of a federal-state system. The doctrine had its origin in *McCulloch v. Maryland* (4 Wheaton 316: 1819), where the Court held that states may not subject federal entities to taxation. It was argued that, without such immunity, the taxing power of one level could be used to impair or disrupt functions of the other level. Immunity was subsequently extended to federal taxation of state entities and functions in the late nineteenth century and was even held to shield salaries of governmental officials and employees from taxation by the other level. *See also GRAVES V. NEW YORK EX. REL. O'KEEFE* (306 U.S. 466: 1939), p. 402; *PITTMAN V. HOME OWNERS' LOAN CORPORATION* (308 U.S. 21: 1939), p. 404.

Significance   The doctrine of intergovernmental tax immunity limits taxing power by shielding federal or state governments and their instrumentalities from taxation by the other. The federal and state levels do not have parity in the application of the doctrine. Since states are represented in the making of taxing decisions by the federal government, Congress has generally been less limited by the immunity doctrine than the states. Congress may categorically exempt federal entities from state taxation or collection of state fees (see *Pittman v. Home Owners' Loan Corporation*, 308 U.S. 21: 1939). It was held in *Graves v. New York Ex. Rel. O'Keefe* (306 U.S. 466: 1939) that this immunity does not extend to employees of federal agencies. While no federal tax may be levied on fundamental state activities or property, the Court held in *New York v. United States* (326 U.S. 572: 1946) that taxes could be laid on activities not deemed fundamental to maintaining state government or its functions. The major issues involving the principle of inter-governmental tax immunity today relate to the possibility of a federal tax on lucrative state lottery operations, and the ending of immunity for state and local bonds if the money borrowed has been used to foster private business activities.

Interposition   A theory that suggests that a state may interpose itself between its citizens and the federal government to insulate the former from enforcement of federal law. The theory of interposition holds that a state may judge the constitutionality of national actions and can nullify those actions by placing its sovereignty between the federal government and its citizens. The notions of interposition and nullification present the most extreme states' rights position. *See also* FEDERALISM, p. 29; SECESSION, p. 649; SUPREMACY CLAUSE, p. 227.

Significance   Interposition was first advanced by Madison and Jefferson in the Kentucky and Virginia Resolutions, which took aim at the infamous Alien and Sedition Acts. The theory of interposition was premised on the view that when the federal government acted beyond the limits granted by the Constitution, states must have the authority to interpose to "arrest the progress of evil" and that nullification was the appropriate remedy. John C. Calhoun used the concept of nullification as the basis of his fight against the tariffs. Interposition was also utilized by the South just prior to the Civil War as well as during the 1950s in response to the Supreme Court's equal protection decisions. Arguments on behalf of interposition have been rejected by the courts as incompatible with the supremacy clause of Article VI.

Interstate Compact   An agreement between two or more states. The interstate compact has often been utilized to address problems involving more than one state in lieu of turning these problems over to the federal government. Interstate compacts have typically been used for such matters as natural resource conservation, pollution control, and transportation. The agreement between New York and New Jersey establishing the Port of New York Authority to regulate harbor facilities is a good example of an interstate compact.

Significance   Interstate compacts may be effectively used to respond to regional matters or problems. Article I, Section 10 contains language that imposes limitations on interstate agreements. The Article I provision says that states cannot enter into treaties with foreign counties or agreements with another state "without the consent of Congress." The requirement was intended to keep states from undermining the Union through series of interstate agreements. Congressional consent need not take any particular form, and such consent is generally not difficult to obtain. All compacts must conform to relevant constitutional limitations. Once an agreement has been approved by Congress, it is binding on the states' officials and cannot be revoked unilaterally.

Interstate Rendition   Return of a fugitive to the state in which the person allegedly committed a crime. Interstate rendition is an obligation required of the states by language in Article IV, Section 2. This section provides that a fugitive found in another state shall, "on demand of the executive authority of the state from which he fled, be delivered up, to be removed to the state having jurisdiction of the crime." A federal statute enacted in 1793 reiterated this obligation. The term *extradition* is often used interchangeably with *rendition*. Extradition, however, actually refers to return of fugitives from one nation to another. Extradition requires the existence of a formal treaty establishing the mechanism for the return of fugitives. *See also* ARTICLE IV, p. 225.

Significance   Interstate rendition is designed to prevent a person from avoiding prosecution by fleeing from one state to another. Most state governors view rendition as an obligation, and compliance is virtually automatic. Refusal to comply is possible, however. In *Kentucky v. Dennison* (24 Howard 66: 1861), the Court held that, while return of a fugitive was a governor's duty, there are no means by which execution of this duty can be compelled. In the mid-1930s, Congress used its commerce power to make it a federal crime to flee across state lines. If the person is arrested by federal agents for interstate flight, he or she is returned to the original state for prosecution of the federal offense, thus making the prisoner accessible by local authorities.

Irreparable Injury   A wrong or damage that has no sufficient remedy. An irreparable injury is the kind of injury for which monetary compensation is not adequate, or it is an injury that cannot be corrected or repaired. The possibility of an irreparable injury is one of the conditions precedent to granting an injunction. Plaintiffs often aver to the court that the type of injury they have suffered, or will suffer if the court does not intervene, is, or will be irreparable. *See also* EQUITY JURISDICTION, p. 600; INJUNCTION, p. 622.

Significance   Irreparable injury must be demonstrated before many courts will grant injunctive relief. A potential irreparable injury might be media disclosure of military secrets or an unauthorized disposal of chemical waste into the environment. A case can be made in either instance to enjoin such activity because recovery from the harm caused might be impossible.

Judicial Activism   An approach to appellate decision making associated with activist behavior by members of the United States Supreme Court. Judicial activism sees the appellate courts as playing an affirmative policy role. Judicial activists are inclined to find constitutional violations, and they sometimes invalidate legislative and executive policy initiatives. *See also* JUDICIAL SELF-RESTRAINT, p. 627; JUSTICIABILITY, p. 630; PREFERRED POSITION DOCTRINE, p. 645.

Significance   Judicial activism is sometimes described as legislation by justices to achieve policy outcomes compatible with their own social priorities. A judicial activist will find more issues appropriate for judicial response than will an apostle of judicial self-restraint. An example of judicial activism was the Warren Court's judgment that legislative apportionment is a justiciable issue in *Baker v. Carr* (369 U.S. 186: 1962), and the Court's subsequent formulation of the one person-one vote districting standard. Critics of this form of activism felt the Court had encroached on legislative prerogatives. Activism need not coincide with a liberal policy orientation. Classic examples of judicial activism can be found in the 1930s, when the Court struck down numerous pieces of New Deal legislation in the interest of preserving laissez-faire economic doctrine. The judicial activist sees the Court as appropriately and legitimately asserting itself in the policy-making process even if its policy objectives differ from those of the legislative and executive branches. Justices William O. Douglas and William J. Brennan, and Chief Justice Earl Warren, have generally been considered to be the leading proponents of judicial activism.

Judicial Immunity   Insulates judges from civil suits for actions done in performance of their judicial function. The doctrine of judicial immunity was intended to protect judges from fearing civil lawsuits from unhappy litigants. It was felt that threat of suit might intimidate judges from making controversial or difficult decisions. The doctrine was aimed at serving the public interest by having judges who could function with "independence" and "without fear of consequences." *See also* COMPENSATION CLAUSE, p. 587; *STUMP V. SPARKMAN* (435 U.S. 349: 1978), p. 87.

Significance   The Court first established the doctrine of judicial immunity in *Bradley v. Fisher* (13 Wallace 335: 1872). The immunity doctrine created in that case was extensive and applied to actions even when they might be "in excess of their justifications" or "maliciously or corruptly" motivated. Only acts that are "non-judicial" are not covered by the immunity doctrine. This broad definition as well as some criteria for determination of "judicial" acts was incorporated into the Court's recent decision in *Stump v. Sparkman* (435 U.S. 349: 1978).

Judicial Review   The power of a court to examine the actions of the legislative and executive branches and declare them unconstitutional. Judicial review may also find a statute or action compatible with the federal or state constitution. The power of judicial review was discussed extensively at the Constitutional Convention of 1787, but it was not included in the Constitution as an expressly delegated judicial function. The Supreme Court first asserted the power in the case of *Marbury v. Madison* (I Cranch 137: 1803) under the leadership of Chief Justice John Marshall. *See also* JUDICIAL ACTIVISM, p. 626; JUDICIAL SELF-RESTRAINT, p. 627; *MARBURY V. MADISON* (1 Cranch 137: 1803), p. 89.

Significance   Judicial review was established in *Marbury* when the Supreme Court determined that a section of the Judiciary Act of 1789 unconstitutionally expanded the original jurisdiction of the Court. The Court asserted that it must, under such circumstances, be able to void enactments that conflict with the Constitution. Chief Justice Marshall considered judicial review to be "the very essence of judicial duty." The arguments for judicial review became so firmly rooted in American jurisprudence that the doctrine became one of the principal means by which courts participate in the shaping of public policy.

Judicial Self-Restraint   A philosophy and style of judicial decision making that minimizes the extent to which judges apply their personal views to the legal judgments they render. Judicial self-restraint is particularly useful in analyzing the behavior of the United States Supreme Court. The term describes a self-imposed limitation seen by the judges who practice it as the decision-making approach most compatible with democratic principles. It is opposite from judicial activism. *See also* JUDICIAL ACTIVISM, p. 626; JUSTICIABILITY, p. 630.

Significance   Judicial self-restraint holds that courts should defer to the policy judgments made by the elected branches of government. Judges who adhere to the philosophy of restraint impose a more restrictive definition of justiciability and adhere more strictly to judicial precedent. Self-restraint does not necessarily coincide with a conservative policy orientation. Exercise of self-restraint by deferring to a legislative enactment mandating establishment of a minimum wage or an aggressive Equal Employment Opportunity Commission program, for example, might yield a liberal policy result. Judicial self-restraint is a perception of the judicial role that limits the exercise of judicial power and views the legislative and executive branches as the appropriate sources of major policy initiatives. Among the leading advocates of judicial self-restraint in the history of the Supreme Court are Justices Felix Frankfurter and the second Justice John Marshall Harlan.

Judiciary Act of 1789   A federal law that created the lower federal court system. The Judiciary Act of 1789 was based upon the power conveyed to Congress by the judicial article (III). The act provided that the Supreme Court would consist of six justices. It also established general jurisdiction trial courts in each state called district courts. Each district court was allocated one judgeship. Three circuit courts were also established, with each composed of two Supreme Court justices and one district court judge. This structuring of the circuit courts required Supreme Court justices to travel to those locations where the courts would sit, a practice known as "riding the circuit." Finally, the act defined in great detail the jurisdiction of the newly created courts as well as a number of jurisdictional matters regarding the appellate jurisdiction of the Supreme Court. *See also* JUDICIAL REVIEW, p. 627.

Significance   The Judiciary Act of 1789 has been changed numerous times since its enactment, but the principal element of the act was its reflection of the position of federal supremacy. That thrust clearly remains. One of the act's sections (25), for example, tied state courts directly to federal appellate power, at least where state court judgments failed to recognize federal supremacy. Thus the act represented a political victory for the Federalists. The Judiciary Act of 1801 increased the size of the lower courts to provide the Federalists with a place for the "midnight judges," those appointed to the federal courts in advance of the incoming Jefferson administration. The act also altered lower-court jurisdiction, solidifying the opportunity for the Federalist-controlled judiciary to withstand the loss of the White House and Congress to the Republicans. The Circuit Court of Appeals Act of 1891 established the courts of appeal and finally ended the "circuit-riding" practice.

Jurisdiction   The power of a court to act, including its authority to hear and to decide cases. Jurisdiction defines the boundaries within which a particular court may exercise judicial power. Judicial power is specifically conveyed through the definition of jurisdiction. The jurisdiction of federal courts is described in Article III of the Constitution in the case of the Supreme Court, and in acts of Congress in the case of the lower federal courts. A limitation on jurisdiction is that it may extend only to issues that Article III specifies as lying within the judicial power of the United States. Federal judicial power may extend to classes of cases defined in terms of substance and party as well as to cases in law and equity stemming directly from the federal Constitution, federal statutes, treaties, or cases falling into the admiralty and maritime category. Federal judicial power also extends to cases involving specified parties. Regardless of the substance of the case, federal jurisdiction includes actions (1) where the federal government itself is a party; (2) between two or more states; (3) between a state and a citizen of another state; (4) between citizens of different states; (5) between a state and an alien; (6) between a citizen of a state and an alien; and (7) where foreign ambassadors are involved.

State constitutions and statutes usually define the jurisdiction of state courts. They often do so in terms of the amount of money sued for in civil actions and the maximum punishment allowed in criminal actions. Jurisdiction also refers to the location of the parties and the court. A court located in a particular county may be the only court that has jurisdiction in a lawsuit involving two residents of that county, or it may be the only court that has jurisdiction to hear a criminal case when the crime occurred within that county. The concept of location of jurisdiction is technically a question of venue, however, and not one of jurisdiction. If the power of a court is questioned on the basis of location, it is usually because the court lacks the proper venue. If an issue is properly before a court, a judgment may be rendered. A judgment is the final ruling of a court on a matter properly before it. The judgment of a court may also be called its decision or decree. Judgment on occasion also refers to the reasoning underlying a decision, but more typically the rationale of a decision is called the opinion. One such judgment may be to dismiss, which is to dispose of a case with no further consideration of it. A court may also issue a stay, which suspends some action or proceeding until a further event transpires. *See also* APPEAL, p. 580; DIVERSITY JURISDICTION, p. 593; EQUITY JURISDICTION, p. 600; ORIGINAL JURISDICTION, p. 640.

Significance   Jurisdiction conveys authority to courts to act in particular cases, to, in effect, "say the law." Federal court jurisdiction is defined in provisions of the Constitution and federal statutes. Jurisdiction routes particular kinds of issues or parties to the appropriate judicial forum. While the authority of courts may overlap to some degree, the lines of differentiation are usually quite clear. The independence of federal and state court jurisdictions was designed to maintain the respective sovereignty of the two levels of government.

Justiciability　The appropriateness of an issue for resolution by judicial action. Justiciability refers to a question that may properly come before a court for decision. Justiciability differs from jurisdiction in that the latter involves the question of whether a court possesses the power to act. Justiciability presumes that the power to act exists, but it focuses on whether it is proper or reasonable to exercise that power. A court may have jurisdiction over a case, but it may find the question involved to be nonjusticiable. *See also* ADVISORY OPINION, p. 577; CASE OR CONTROVERSY, p. 583; JURISDICTION, p. 629; POLITICAL QUESTION, p. 644; STANDING, p. 655.

Significance　Justiciability considerations come in the form of real or bona fide cases as opposed to controversies raising abstract or hypothetical issues. A justiciable issue satisfies all requirements of standing, and it is not more appropriately resolved by the legislative or executive branches. Justiciability allows the courts to limit or expand the extent to which judicial power is exercised. It directly affects the functional relationship of the courts to the legislative and executive branches. To be justiciable, a question must involve an actual controversy in which one party can show harm or damage.

Legislative Courts　A court created by Congress under power contained in Article I. A legislative court is distinguished from a constitutional court, which is established from power granted by the judicial article (Article III). A legislative court may function as a court, but is also designed to fulfill functions that may not be wholly judicial in character. They are established to perform administrative functions typically in addition to or through their assigned judicial duties. Courts that fit this category are the United States Tax Court, the Court of Claims, the Court of International Trade, and the Court of Military Appeals. *See also* CONSTITUTIONAL COURTS, p. 588; ADVISORY OPINION, p. 577.

Significance　The legislative courts are highly specialized. They have been established by Congress in exercise of the Article I power to "constitute tribunals inferior to the Supreme Court" as well as the implied congressional power derived from the necessary and proper clause. Unlike constitutional courts, legislative courts may render advisory opinions, which are rulings on legal issues in absence of a real case. Judges of legislative courts also differ from judges of constitutional courts in that they are not entitled to the tenure safeguards available to Article III judges. While not required to do so, Congress has extended life tenure to most legislative court judges. Issues have arisen concerning the creation of legislative courts. In 1982, for example, the Supreme Court invalidated a law that established a new bankruptcy court system as a legislative court on the ground that the nature of the new court's work required Article III constitutional status.

Legislative Investigations   A power exercised by Congress and state legislatures that permits the gathering of information. Such information collecting is justified as an integral part of the law-making function. The authority to conduct legislative investigations is not expressly given to legislatures, but is implied from Article I of the U.S. Constitution generally, and from the necessary and proper clause more specifically. Given the deliberative character of the legislative function, an auxiliary power to inform itself is certainly defensible. Legislative bodies gather most of their information through the committee process, and special committees may be formed exclusively for the purpose of conducting an inquiry. Legislative committees may compel witnesses to testify or produce particular materials. Refusal to cooperate may result in witnesses being cited for legislative contempt. *See also* BARENBLATT V. UNITED STATES (360 U.S. 109: 1959), p. 187; EXECUTIVE PRIVILEGE, p. 603; MCGRAIN V. DAUGHERTY (273 U.S. 135: 1927), p. 185; NECESSARY AND PROPER CLAUSE, p. 637; WATKINS V. UNITED STATES (354 U.S. 178: 1957), p. 186.

Significance   The power to conduct legislative investigations is extensive and firmly established, but limitations do exist. Legislative investigations are confined by the principles of separation of power. Investigations may not take legislatures into fields expressly directed to the other branches. In addition, investigations must have a legislative purpose and reflect a genuine interest in legislating on the subject under inquiry. The legislative power to investigate upheld in *McGrain v. Daugherty* (273 U.S. 135: 1927) was very broad, and the Court was very deferential to legislative motives in the gathering of information. Subsequent decisions narrowed the power to investigate because particular practices, particularly those of the House Committee on Un-American Activities (HUAC), encroached on constitutional rights of witnesses. In *Watkins v. United States* (354 U.S. 178: 1957), the Court insisted that compelled testimony be directly related to a specific legislative purpose and that questions posed of witnesses be pertinent to that purpose. Under *Watkins*, legislative authorizations for committee investigations must be focused and clear. Committees may not pursue vague objectives nor engage in probes that "expose for the sake of exposure." In a few cases, the Court determined that legislative inquiries pressed too deeply on the associational memberships of witnesses, thus infringing on First Amendment protections. Generally, however, witness protections have been procedural, as through the self-incrimination safeguard. The Court has been largely supportive of legislative investigations, anchoring its review in the deferential legitimate legislative purpose standard. Legislative information gathering involving the executive branch raises separation of power issues. On occasion, presidents have invoked executive privilege, claiming they cannot be required to present material or have executive branch officials appear. The Court has recognized a limited executive privilege involving legislative inquiries, but not judicial proceedings.

Legislative Veto   A device whereby Congress may review and possibly terminate orders or regulations of the executive branch issued to implement legislation. The legislative veto is a means by which Congress may directly supervise the executive or enforcement function. The veto technique has been used increasingly since its introduction in the 1930s. The legislative veto has been utilized in a variety of ways, but the War Powers Resolution is a well-known example. The resolution provides that a president may not commit troops to foreign soil combat without an endorsement of that action by concurrent resolution of Congress. Other issues, such as executive reorganization and impoundment of appropriated funds, have been reached by the legislative veto. The legislative veto was declared unconstitutional by the Supreme Court in the case of *Immigration and Naturalization Service v. Chadha* (462 U.S 919: 1983). *See also* ARTICLE I, p. 183; DELEGATION OF LEGISLATIVE POWER, p. 591; *IMMIGRATION AND NATURALIZATION SERVICE V. CHADHA* (462 U.S. 919: 1983) p. 213; IMPOUNDMENT, p. 619; SEPARATION OF POWERS, p. 56.

Significance   The legislative veto was a practice with fundamental separation of power implications. The proponents of the veto argue that it is an effective means by which Congress can delegate authority to an administration while maintaining some degree of control over the policy area in which the delegation occurred. Critics, on the other hand, claim the veto preempts the executive role and allows Congress to both enact and enforce laws. The *Chadha* decision viewed the veto mechanism as essentially legislative in character. As a result, it is subject to the Article I requirement of presentment to the president for consent or rejection. Since a president or administrative agency is not presented with items subjected to legislative veto, the practice was held to be unconstitutional. The full impact of the *Chadha* decision on the legislative veto is problematical because a great many laws passed by Congress since the 1930s provide for the use of the legislative veto technique.

Liberty of Contract   A doctrine used to free private agreements from governmental regulation. The doctrine of liberty or freedom of contract was a primary element of substantive due process in which the judiciary closely scrutinized the reasonableness of legislative enactments. The liberty of contract concept holds that individuals have a right to contract about their personal affairs. This includes the right of employers and employees to enter agreements about wages, hours, and conditions of work. The doctrine was used in the employment context to strike down minimum wage and maximum hour laws as an impermissible interference with the right to contract. *See also* DUE PROCESS CLAUSES, p. 594; *LOCHNER V. NEW YORK* (198 U.S. 45: 1905), p. 429; SUBSTANTIVE DUE PROCESS, p. 659.

Significance   The liberty of contract doctrine was drawn from the Court's interpretation of the due process clause of the Fourteenth Amendment. The Court viewed the term *liberty* in that clause as meaning not only freedom from such actions as arbitrary detention by a state, but also freedom for a person to fully enjoy "all his faculties." This included the right to enter any and all lawful contractual arrangements in furtherance of that end. The liberty of contract doctrine was derived from laissez-faire economics as well, and it was extensively used by the Court to strike down regulatory state legislation. In *Lochner v. New York* (198 U.S. 45: 1905), for example, the Court struck down a maximum hours law. The Court said the hour limit interfered with the employer's right to "make contracts in relation to his business," while the employee lost his right to sell his labor through an agreement with his employer.

Mandamus   An extraordinary writ issued by a court under its equity jurisdiction to require a public official to perform a specified official act. Mandamus is an affirmative command calling for an action to occur. A command preventing an action from occurring is an injunction.

Significance   A writ of mandamus can only be issued to compel performance of a nondiscretionary or ministerial function in an instance where the plaintiff has a legal right to the performance of the function. A mandamus may be directed by a higher court to a lower court to require an action that a party has a legal right to expect. Failure to comply with a command issued through a writ of mandamus constitutes contempt of court.

Martial Law   Military rule over civilians. Martial law involves the military taking over normal civil functions of government in response to some kind of emergency. Martial law usually brings the operation of military courts or tribunals in place of civil courts, and the suspension of the writ of *habeas corpus*. The Constitution does not expressly assign the power to declare martial law, but it is implied within the president's commander-in-chief powers. *See also* EX PARTE MILLIGAN (4 Wallace 2: 1866), p. 163; HABEAS CORPUS, p. 616; WAR POWERS, p. 673.

Significance   Martial law involves the suspension of civil authority, and the assumption of basic governmental functions by the military. Federal martial law may be invoked by the president, but Congress alone, under provisions of Article I, Section 7, is empowered to suspend the writ of *habeas corpus*. Instances of federal martial law are minimal, although Lincoln resorted to it during the Civil War. Subsequent to the war, the Supreme Court held that Lincoln did not have unilateral authority to require civilians to be tried by military commissions in areas outside the actual theater of war (see *Ex Parte Milligan*, 4 Wallace 2: 1866). Similarly, in *Duncan v. Kahanamoku* (327 U.S. 304: 1946), the Court ruled that the territorial governor did not have authority to close civilian courts in favor of military tribunals.

Mootness (Moot Question)   A case in which the courts can no longer provide a party any relief because the dispute has been resolved or has ceased to exist. A moot case is no longer a real controversy, and Article III of the Constitution requires that cases before courts be bona fide controversies. *See also* ADVISORY OPINION, p. 577; *DEFUNIS V. ODEGAARD* (416 U.S. 312: 1974), p. 119; JUSTICIABILITY, p. 630; STANDING, p. 655.

Significance   Mootness is the absence of an active question. The matter is therefore nonjusticiable. When the Supreme Court refused to address the reverse discrimination issue in *DeFunis v. Odegaard* (416 U.S. 312: 1974) on grounds of mootness, it said the controversy was no longer definite and concrete. The case no longer touched "the legal relations of parties having adverse interests." Exceptions to the mootness threshold involve situations where time is too limited to litigate an issue fully, and where a likelihood exists that the question will reoccur. Abortion cases qualify for an exception to the mootness rule, for example, because no appellate court can ever get an abortion issue prior to a pregnancy running to full term. The Court observed in *Roe v Wade* (410 U.S. 113: 1973) that appellate review would forever be foreclosed by mootness because a pregnancy would not last beyond the trial stage. Saying the law should not be that rigid, the Court acknowledged the need for the exception if issues are "capable of repetition, yet evading review. If the courts responded routinely to cases that had become moot, they would constantly be engaged in rendering advisory opinions.

National Industrial Recovery Act   Federal legislation designed to counteract the economic crisis brought on by the Depression. The National Industrial Recovery Act (NIRA) was enacted in 1933. It was intended to establish the federal government as the principal coordinating agency for economic recovery. The objectives of Congress as stated in the legislation were heightened production, lowered unemployment, stabilization of wages and prices, and promotion of fair business competition. The law noted the national dimensions of the economic distress brought about by the Depression and claimed the interstate commerce power as the basis of the enactment. The act sought to establish agreements from virtually every sector of the economy. These agreements, covering wages, prices, business practices, and production, were to take the form of industry codes. The substance of the codes was provided by industrial associations. Proposed code provisions for each trade or industry were submitted to the president. Approval by the president converted the proposals into executive orders enforceable against all members of a particular industry. If a trade association was not forthcoming with a proposed code, the president was authorized to have a code drafted. The president was granted broad enforcement power through licensure and other means. *See also* DELEGATION OF LEGISLATIVE POWER, p. 591; *SCHECHTER POULTRY CORPORATION V. UNITED STATES* (295 U.S. 495: 1935), pp. 189, 315.

Significance   The National Industrial Recovery Act was novel in concept and extremely broad in its scope. The code approach to economic recovery inserted the government into almost every aspect of American economic life. The act also conveyed extensive rule-making authority to the president. The content of each industrial code was developed through the executive rather than the legislative branch.

Ultimately, it was this vast delegation of legislative power that was the constitutional undoing of the act. In *Schechter Poultry Corporation v. United States* (295 U.S. 495: 1935), the Court held that Congress had too extensively delegated legislative discretion in the NIRA. The Court also found some of the codes fashioned under NIRA to be outside the reach of congressional commerce power in that they applied to activities occurring after commerce had concluded. By the time the Court invalidated the NIRA in *Schechter*, the approach had been essentially abandoned as ineffective. Nonetheless, the NIRA represents an interesting example of legislative experimentation.

National Labor Relations Act   Federal enactment protecting the right of workers to organize labor unions and engage in collective bargaining. The *National Labor Relations Act*, known as the Wagner Act, was enacted in 1935. It defined conduct that constituted unfair labor practices. This is conduct Congress established as impermissible interference with the right to organize and bargain. The act established the National Labor Relations Board (NLRB) with authority to not only adjudicate claimed violations of the act, but also require employers found in violation to cease and desist from such conduct. The statute was based on the congressional power to regulate interstate commerce. The constitutionality of the act was upheld in *National Labor Relations Board v. Jones and Laughlin Steel Corporation* (301 U.S. 1: 1937). *See also* COMMERCE CLAUSE, p. 291; FAIR LABOR STANDARDS ACT, p. 605; *NATIONAL LABOR RELATIONS BOARD V. JONES AND LAUGHLIN STEEL CORPORATION* (301 U.S. 1: 1937), p. 319.

Significance   The National Labor Relations Act is generally regarded as the magna carta of the labor movement. Subsequent to its passage, the size and influence of labor unions increased dramatically. The Court's decisions in the wake of *Jones and Laughlin* were supportive of NLRB authority over virtually any activity that "affects" interstate commerce. Perception that the act disproportionately protected the interests of labor ultimately led to the enactment of the Labor-Management Relations Act of 1947 (more commonly known as the Taft-Hartley Act). Taft-Hartley retained many of the employee provisions of NLRA, but prohibited such things as closed shop agreements, secondary boycotts, and political campaign contributions. The act also had provisions allowing injunctive remedies in strikes affecting the national interest. Finally, the act imposed regulations on union leadership positions, e.g., officers could not be members of the Communist party, and unions were required to file reports covering use of union funds.

Necessary and Proper Clause   Provision that permits Congress to select the methods by which it exercises its authority. The necessary and proper clause, found at the end of Article I, Section 8, states that Congress has the power to "make all laws which shall be necessary and proper for carrying into execution the foregoing powers, and all other powers vested by this Constitution." The clause permits the Congress substantial flexibility in choosing the means to carry out delegated power. The clause is the foundation of the concept of implied powers. *See also* DELEGATED POWER, p. 591; IMPLIED POWER, p. 618; *MCCULLOCH V. MARYLAND* (4 Wheaton 316: 1819), p. 238.

Significance   The necessary and proper clause, sometimes known as the elastic clause, has provided Congress with the flexibility it needs to address new situations. The phrase has been broadly interpreted so that Congress now possesses a relatively wide range of implied as well as delegated authority. The major impetus in the evolution of the clause was provided by the Court's decision in *McCulloch v. Maryland* (4 Wheaton 316: 1819), where it upheld establishment of the national bank. Power to do so was seen as implied from the necessary and proper clause plus extensive congressional authority over fiscal matters generally. Acknowledgment of implied power derived from explicitly delegated power plus the necessary and proper clause greatly increased power available to the national government.

Nineteenth Amendment   Granted women's suffrage. The Nineteenth Amendment was added to the Constitution in 1920. The amendment says that the "right of citizens of the United States to vote should not be denied or abridged by the United States or by any state on account of sex." Section 2 empowers Congress to "enforce this article by appropriate legislation." *See also* AMENDING POWER, p. 578.

Significance   The Nineteenth Amendment culminated a long struggle for women's suffrage. The movement for suffrage dated back to the 1850s and developed substantial support by the early twentieth century. A number of states had extended either full or partial voting rights to women prior to the adoption of the amendment. The amendment was challenged soon after ratification in *Leser v. Garnett* (258 U.S. 130: 1922). It was contended that the electorate had been expanded by amendment to the federal Constitution, an action that impermissibly impinged upon state sovereignty. The Court found otherwise, saying that the proposal was a reasonable use of the federal amending process. The Court also refused to review a contention made in *Leser* that there were procedural flaws in the ratification actions of two states. The addition of women to the electorate has not dramatically changed electoral politics in this country. With the limited exception of some specific questions associated with the women's movement itself, few issues have split the electorate on gender lines.

Ninth Amendment   Retained for the people all rights not otherwise itemized in the Constitution. The Ninth Amendment says that the "enumeration in the Constitution, of certain rights, shall not be construed to deny or disparage others retained by the people." At the time the Constitution was adopted, the natural law concept provided the foundation of the prevailing political thought. It was believed that certain rights were beyond governmental interference. While the Bill of Rights protected specified rights, the Ninth Amendment guaranteed that those natural rights not itemized were to be preserved and retained as well. *See also* AMENDING POWER, p. 578; NATURAL LAW AND NATURAL RIGHTS, p. 50.

Significance   The Ninth Amendment spoke to the protection of fundamental or natural law rights not enumerated in the Constitution. The amendment has only seldom been before the Supreme Court. As the emphasis turned to protected rights and the concept of due process, less attention was paid to natural rights as such. One interesting exception occurred in 1965 in the case of *Griswold v. Connecticut* (381 U.S. 479). The Court ruled in *Griswold* that a state law prohibiting use of contraceptives was unconstitutional because it violated the right to personal privacy. The Court argued that the right was within the "penumbra" or shadow that emanates from the specific guarantees of the Bill of Rights. The Court argued that, taken together, various protections created a sphere of privacy. The penumbras creating the right of privacy came from the Third Amendment protection from having to quarter soldiers, the Fourth Amendment protection from unreasonable searches and seizures, and the Fifth Amendment privilege against self-incrimination. The Ninth Amendment was suggested as a principal contributor. This penumbra approach, while utilizing the Ninth Amendment in *Griswold*, also diminishes the prospect of the Ninth Amendment's receiving much attention on its own. So long as the Court can reach rights implicitly protected under these penumbras, there is little need to cultivate the protection that might be afforded by the Ninth Amendment. The amendment is certainly general enough to be amenable to a broad range of interpretations, and it has the potential to develop into a more substantial source of constitutional discussion.

Obiter Dictum Remarks contained in a court's opinion that are incidental to the disposition of the case. *Obiter dictum* or *obiter dicta*, sometimes simply called *dictum* or *dicta*, are normally directed at issues upon which no formal arguments have been heard. The positions represented by *obiter dicta* are therefore not binding on later cases. *Dicta* are not considered to be precedent and should be distinguished from the *ratio decidendi*, which provides the basis of the court's ruling.

Significance *Obiter dicta* can be found in *Myers v. United States* (272 U.S. 52: 1926), for example, in which the Supreme Court held that Congress could not require Senate consent for presidential removal of postmasters. Postmasters are generally viewed as executive branch subordinates serving exclusively at the pleasure of the president. Chief Justice Taft offered the opinion, however, that removal power was incident to the power to appoint, as distinguished from the power to advise and consent. As a general proposition presidents could remove anyone appointed by them, including members of quasi-judicial agencies such as regulatory commissions. *Myers* did not require disposition of that question to settle the case. Thus the remarks of the chief justice went beyond those necessary to resolve a case or controversy and were therefore *dicta*.

Opinion of the Court The statement of a court which specifies its decision in a case and expresses the reasoning upon which the decision was based. The opinion of the court summarizes the principles of law that apply in a given case and represents the views of the majority of a court's members. Occasionally the opinion of a court may reflect the views of less than a majority of its members (for example, in a 4–3 decision) and is then called a plurality opinion. Trial courts also issue opinions, both written and oral.

Significance The opinion of the court is the means by which the legal principles of a decision are transmitted. The opinion of the court contains the *ratio decidendi*, which is the rationale for the judgment and the principal item of precedent value. The opinion of the court is not the only statement that may be issued in a particular case, however. A concurring opinion may be issued by a member of a court who agrees with the outcome of a case but who uses different reasons for reaching a decision. In *Coker v. Georgia* (433 U.S. 584: 1977), for example, the Supreme Court ruled that the death penalty could not be imposed for the offense of rape. The majority felt the death penalty was excessive for the specific crime involved. Justice Brennan agreed that Coker's sentence ought to be vacated but expressed in a concurring opinion that the death penalty is a cruel and unusual punishment under any circumstance. A dissenting opinion, on the other hand, is an opinion by a member of a court who disagrees with the majority opinion of the court. A dissent may be joined by other members of a court's minority. It may focus on only one element of a court's decision and may be a disagreement in part. A dissenting opinion that attracts other members of a court may serve as an encouragement to litigants to bring subsequent cases raising similar legal arguments. A court may also issue a *per curiam* opinion. *Per curiam* is a Latin term meaning "by the court." It is an opinion that is either unsigned or authored by the judges collectively. A *per curiam* opinion is sometimes used to announce a court's holding summarily without discussion of the rationale. Individual members of a court frequently enter individual concurring or dissenting opinions on such occasions. See, for example, *Furman v. Georgia* (408 U.S. 238: 1972), and *New York Times v. United States* (403 U.S. 713: 1971). Opinions are occasionally important for what they do not say. *Sub silentio* means "under silence" and refers to something that occurs without notice being taken of it. Sometimes an appeals court will overrule a precedent without explicitly acknowledging the precedent it overruled. The precedent is therefore replaced *sub silentio*.

Original Jurisdiction   The authority of a court initially to hear and determine a legal question. Original jurisdiction is vested with trial courts rather than appellate courts, although Article III of the Constitution extends limited original jurisdiction to the United States Supreme Court. The original jurisdiction of the Supreme Court is limited to "all cases affecting ambassadors, other public Ministers and Consuls, and those in which a State shall be a Party" (Article III, Section 2). Various trial courts are assigned specific original jurisdiction defined in terms of subject matter or party. Original jurisdiction in civil cases is often divided on the basis of the monetary value of the action. In criminal matters, certain courts may be assigned misdemeanor cases while others adjudicate felonies. A misdemeanor is a minor criminal offense generally punishable by imprisonment in local jails and/or a fine. A felony is a criminal offense for which punishment may be death or imprisonment for more than a year. Since the United States district court is the only trial court of broad jurisdiction, it has original jurisdiction over both federal felonies and misdemeanors. *See also* APPEAL, p. 580; DIVERSITY JURISDICTION, p. 593; EQUITY JURISDICTION, p. 600; JURISDICTION, p. 629.

Significance   Original jurisdiction establishes which court will first respond to a case or controversy. Original jurisdiction is particularly important because comparatively few cases are appealed from courts of first instance. Appeals typically involve only questions of law because ordinarily questions of fact (e.g., whether the defendant was guilty of the crime) are resolved with finality by the court of original jurisdiction.

Original Package Doctrine   Rule that exempts items from state taxing power so long as those items remain in their original shipping package. The original package doctrine was initially developed to keep states from taxing foreign imports, but it was subsequently extended to items shipped in interstate commerce. This limitation is an extension of the federal government's authority over interstate commerce as well as authority from Article I, Section 10 that prohibits states, without congressional approval, from laying "any imposts or duties on imports or exports, except what may be absolutely necessary for executing its inspection laws." *See also* BROWN V. MARYLAND (12 Wheaton 419: 1827), p. 296; COMMERCE CLAUSE, p. 291.

Significance   The original package doctrine was introduced by Chief Justice John Marshall in *Brown v. Maryland* (12 Wheaton 419: 1827). The doctrine was developed to keep the states from interfering with the free flow of commerce by exercising their taxing powers. While such commerce cannot remain forever free of taxation by states, the doctrine defines the point at which items may be subject to tax. Marshall said taxes could be imposed when the importer "has so acted upon the thing imported, that it has become incorporated and mixed up with the mass of property in the country." The doctrine remains in effect although the Courts said in *Michelin Tire Company v. Wages* (423 U.S. 276: 1976) that state taxes imposed on all things, both imports and domestic, were permissible provided the actual movement of the items had concluded.

Overbreadth Doctrine   A doctrine requiring that enactments proscribing certain activity must not touch conduct that is constitutionally protected. Overbreadth refers to a statute which may fail adequately to distinguish between activities that may be regulated and those that may not.

Significance   The overbreadth doctrine illustrated in *Village of Schaumburg v. Citizens for a Better Environment* (444 U.S. 620: 1980), where the Supreme Court struck down a local ordinance that required all organizations soliciting contributions door-to-door to use at least 75 percent of their receipts for charitable purposes. The purpose of the ordinance was to prevent fraudulent solicitations. The court objected to the approach because it imposed a direct and substantial limitation on organizations such as environmental education groups whose principal activities are research, advocacy, and public education. While such organizations obviously do not meet the ordinance definition of charitable, their activities are constitutionally permissible. The village's ordinance in *Schaumburg* was simply too inclusive or overbroad. Similarly, an ordinance was invalidated in *Coates v. Cincinnati* (402 U.S. 611: 1972) because the ordinance prohibited an assembly of three or more persons on public sidewalks. It subjected such assembled persons to arrest if their behavior annoyed a police officer or passerby. The ordinance made criminal what the Constitution says cannot be a crime. Neither may an enactment suffer from vagueness. Regulations must convey standards of conduct that persons of reasonable intelligence can understand. Enactments that do not clearly convey required or prohibited conduct may be invalidated as vague. Restrictions that are either overbroad or vague may have a chilling effect on expression or some other protected activity.

Pardon Power   The power to grant exemption from criminal penalty. The power to pardon is discussed in Article II, Section 2, which conveys to the president "power to grant reprieves and pardons for offenses against the United States, except in cases of impeachment." A pardon may be used in cases of individuals or groups. In the latter case, the pardon may be called *amnesty*. A pardon not only exempts persons from penalties such as imprisonment or fine, but also restores any civil rights that may have been lost with criminal conduct. The only limitation on the power is that it may not reverse the outcome of the impeachment process. *See also* EX PARTE GROSSMAN (267 U.S. 87: 1925), p. 161.

Significance   The power to pardon may completely or partially nullify the effects of a criminal conviction. When the president grants a full or complete pardon, it "blots out" the conviction so that it is as though no offense had ever been committed. A president may also grant a partial or "conditional" pardon. In the case of *Schick v. Reed* (419 U.S. 256: 1974), the Court upheld a presidential order reducing a death penalty murder conviction to a life sentence with the condition that parole could never be obtained. As seen in *Ex Parte Grossman* (267 U.S. 87: 1925), the pardon power may extend to judicial contempt situations. The Constitution only permits presidents to grant pardons for federal offenses, although most state governors possess parallel power at the state level.

Passport   A document issued by a person's government that identifies his or her citizenship and permits foreign travel. A passport is evidence that the person has authorization for international travel, and it requests foreign sovereigns to allow free and safe passage through their territory. It differs from a visa, which is an endorsement or attachment on a passport by an official of the country to be visited authorizing admission to that state. Under provision of the Passport Act and its amendments, the executive branch (through the State Department) administers passports in the United States. *See also HAIG V. AGEE* (453 U.S. 280: 1981), p. 158.

Significance   The executive branch has been granted substantial discretion by Congress to administer issuance of passports. There are some limitations on the executive, however. The Court struck down legislation permitting denial of passports to political "subversives" in *Aptheker v. Secretary of State* (378 U.S. 500: 1964). Despite the *Aptheker* holding, the State Department continued to use passports to limit travel to particular places. This authority was upheld in *Zemel v. Rusk* (381 U.S. 1: 1965), and Zemel was denied permission to travel to Cuba. This kind of travel restriction has since been abandoned. In *Haig v. Agee* (453 U.S. 280: 1981), the Court considered authority of the State Department to revoke a passport on national security grounds. Here the Court recognized executive authority to regulate through passport revocation incident to the power to conduct foreign relations.

Police Power   Authority conveyed by the reserve clause of the Tenth Amendment to the effect that powers not delegated to the federal government or otherwise prohibited are "reserved to the States respectively, or the people." The police power gives the states broad authority to regulate private behavior in the interest of public health, safety, and general welfare. It enables states and their respective local units of government to enact and enforce policies deemed appropriate to serve the public good. Pursuit of these policies may include the creation of a police force. *See also* DUE PROCESS CLAUSES, p. 594; FEDERALISM, p. 29.

Significance   The police power is comprehensive, and substantial discretion is possessed by the states for its exercise. It is limited by various provisions of the United States Constitution and the constitutions of the states, however. It must conform to the expectations of due process. Every state civil liberty case involves a contest between the exercise of police power on behalf of the interests of society and the freedom of the individual to engage in activities that differ from established norms.

Political Question   An issue that is not justiciable or not appropriate for judicial determination. A political question is one in which the substance of an issue is primarily political or involves a matter directed toward either the legislative or executive branch by constitutional language. *See also* BAKER V. CARR (369 U.S. 186: 1962), p. 123; JUSTICIABILITY, p. 630; SEPARATION OF POWERS, p. 56.

Significance   The political question doctrine is sometimes invoked by the Supreme Court not because the Court is without power or jurisdiction but because the Court adjudges the question inappropriate for judicial response. In the court's view, to intervene or respond would be to encroach upon the functions and prerogatives of one of the other two branches of government. It would constitute a breach of the principle of separation of powers. In *Luther v. Borden* (7 Howard 1: 1849), the Court was asked to rule on the status of Dorr's Rebellion in Rhode Island. The Court refused to do so, holding that the guarantee clause of Article IV had committed the issue to Congress rather than the Supreme Court. Chief Justice Taney said it is the duty of the Court "not to pass beyond its appropriate sphere of action, and to take care not to involve itself in discussions which properly belong to other forums." Justice Brennan was more precise in characterizing a political question in *Baker v. Carr* (369 U.S. 186: 1962), the first case in which the Court held legislative apportionment to be a justiciable issue. Justice Brennan described a political question as one with "a textually demonstrable constitutional commitment of the issue to a coordinate political department; or a lack of judicially discoverable and manageable standards for resolving it." He added that such questions typically require "a policy determination of a kind clearly for nonjudicial discretion." On such matters the court cannot undertake "independent resolution without expressing lack of respect due coordinate branches of the government."

Power   The authority or capacity to perform some act. Power permits the holder to act in a particular way or exercise some control over another. Constitutional power is authority conferred directly from that document. Such power may be expressed or explicitly granted, or it may be derived or implied from the language of the Constitution. Power may be assigned to a single or exclusive location, or it may be given to more than one governmental level or entity to be exercised concurrently. Power may be exercised in a variety of ways, but the ultimate means is through use of force. Authority is a slightly different concept from power in that the exercise of authority is accepted by the governed as legitimate, but the terms are generally used as synonyms. *See also* CONCURRENT POWER, p. 588; DELEGATED POWER, p. 591; EXCLUSIVE POWER, p. 600; IMPLIED POWER, p. 618; INHERENT POWER, p. 622; SOVEREIGNTY, p. 654.

Significance   Power is the means by which a governmental system operates. Elements within a structure are established and empowered to function in described ways. Power utilized in the development and implementation of domestic policy impacts on the allocation of benefits and sanctions. Most policy determinations are reached through the dynamics of power relationships. It is generally felt that concentration of power in few hands is undesirable, thus in the American governmental system, power is diffused or separated among three principal branches and between the national and state levels.

Preemption Doctrine   Holds that federal laws supersede or preempt state laws in certain policy areas. The preemption doctrine is grounded in the supremacy clause of Article VI. *See also* FEDERALISM, p. 29; *PENNSYLVANIA V. NELSON* (350 U.S. 497: 1956), p. 244.

Significance   The preemption doctrine was said to have three criteria in *Pennsylvania v. Nelson* (350 U.S. 497: 1956). First, federal regulation must be so pervasive as to allow reasonable inference that no room is left to the states. Congress may state explicitly such a preemptive interest, or the courts may interpret the intent of Congress fully to occupy the field. Second, federal regulation must involve matters where the federal interest is so dominant as to preclude implementation of state laws in the field. Third, the administration of federal laws must be endangered by conflicting state laws. The policy area involved in *Nelson* was the regulation of seditious activity. Specifically, the question was whether the federal Smith Act prohibited enforcement of the Pennsylvania Sedition Act, which proscribed the same conduct. On the basis of the criteria described, the Supreme Court concluded that Pennsylvania's statute had to give way.

Preferred Position Doctrine   Holds that legislative enactments that affect constitutionally protected rights must be scrutinized more carefully than legislation that does not. The preferred position doctrine says that certain legislative activity deserves priority consideration because it affects fundamental rights, such as free speech. Any enactment that impinges on the First Amendment must serve a compelling state interest. The burden is clearly on the state to demonstrate justification for limiting a preferred position freedom. *See also UNITED STATES V. CAROLENE PRODUCTS COMPANY* (304 U.S. 144: 1938), p. 93.

Significance   The preferred position doctrine is attributed to Justice Harlan Fiske Stone, who said in a footnote to his opinion in *United States v. Carolene Products Company* (304 U.S. 144: 1938) that a lesser presumption of constitutionality exists when legislation "appears on its face to be within a specific prohibition such as those of the first ten amendments." Bolder articulation of the doctrine soon followed in such First Amendment cases as *Murdock v. Pennsylvania* (319 U.S. 105: 1943) and *Thomas v. Collins* (323 U.S. 516: 1945).

Prior Restraint   A restriction placed on a publication before it can be published or circulated. Prior restraint typically occurs through licensure or censorship or by a full prohibition on publication. Censorship requirements involve a review of materials by the state for objectionable content. Materials that satisfy the standards of the censor may be distributed or exhibited, while materials found unacceptable may be banned.

Significance   Prior restraint poses a greater threat to free expression than after-the-fact prosecution because government restrictions are imposed in a manner that precludes public scrutiny. The First Amendment therefore has been interpreted to prohibit prior restraint in most instances. Prior restraint may be justified if the publication threatens national security, incites overthrow of the government, is obscene, or interferes with the private rights of others. Prior restraint is otherwise heavily suspect.

Privilege   A benefit possessed by a person or class having an advantage over other persons or classes by virtue of the benefit. A privilege may exempt a person from an obligation because, without the privilege, the person's office or function would be impaired.

Significance   Privilege often refers to communications that are protected because they need to be confidential. Thus, a lawyer cannot be compelled to disclose the substance of a conversation with a client unless the client waives the privilege. Executive privilege is protection afforded presidential communications, while newsperson's privilege protects against disclosure of news sources by reporters. A privilege may be waived by the person upon whom the law bestows it. Unlike a right, a privilege can be withdrawn by the grantor of that privilege if acting according to law.

Privileges and Immunities Clauses   Clauses that protect benefits flowing from one's status as a citizen. A privilege is a benefit or an advantage, while an immunity frees a person from an obligation. Certain privileges and immunities exist for a person by virtue of his or her citizenship. The United States Constitution contains two references to privileges and immunities. Article IV, Section 2 provides that the "Citizens of each State be entitled to the Privileges and Immunities of citizens in the several States." The purpose of this clause was to ensure that out-of-state citizens receive the same treatment as a state's own citizens. It protected parity across the states. The Fourteenth Amendment also provides that "No State shall make or enforce any law which shall abridge the privileges or immunities of the United States." This section of the Fourteenth Amendment was a specific response to the Black Codes, which in many Southern states had the effect of restoring pre–Civil War conditions of slavery. *See also* CITIZENSHIP, p. 585; DUE PROCESS CLAUSES, p. 594; FOURTEENTH AMENDMENT, p. 612.

Significance   The privileges and immunities clauses were severely limited by the *Slaughterhouse Cases* (16 Wallace 36: 1873), in which the Supreme Court distinguished between federal and state citizenship. The Court placed most key civil and political rights within the state citizenship category. That limited the privileges and immunities of federal citizenship to such rights as interstate travel, protection while abroad, and participation in federal elections. The protections afforded by federal citizenship through the Fourteenth Amendment have expanded substantially over the years since *Slaughterhouse*, but the expansion has taken place under the due process and equal protection clauses rather than the privileges and immunities clauses.

Procedural Due Process   A procedural review that focuses on the means by which governmental actions are executed. Procedural due process guarantees fairness in the ways by which government imposes restrictions or punishments. It demands that before any deprivation of liberty or property can occur, a person must be formally notified and provided an opportunity for a fair hearing. *See also* DUE PROCESS CLAUSES, p. 594; SUBSTANTIVE DUE PROCESS, p. 659.

Significance   Procedural due process must be accorded persons accused of crimes. It includes access to legal counsel, the ability to confront witnesses against the accused, and a trial by jury. Constitutional protection against loss of liberty or property is guaranteed in two constitutional amendments: the Fifth, which is directed at the federal government, and the Fourteenth, which is directed at the states.

Regulatory Tax   A tax used for purposes other than or secondary to revenue raising. The constitutional question involved with a regulatory tax relates to congressional motive and the extent to which regulatory intent might breach some limit on federal taxing power. Put another way, should Congress be able to regulate through taxation areas it may not be able to regulate on other constitutional grounds? Generally, the Court has held that the taxing power is not confined exclusively to the revenue-raising objective. *See also* BAILEY V. DREXEL FURNITURE COMPANY (259 U.S. 20: 1922), p. 396; J. W. HAMPTON, JR. AND COMPANY V. UNITED STATES (276 U.S. 394: 1928), pp. 191, 388; MCCRAY V. UNITED STATES (195 U.S. 27: 1904), p. 394; UNITED STATES V. KAHRIGER (345 U.S. 22: 1953), p. 398.

Significance   Virtually any levy could be considered a regulatory tax. The historical pattern has been that the Supreme Court will not examine the motives of the legislature in imposing a tax. In *McCray v. United States* (195 U.S. 27: 1904), the Court found a tax on oleomargarine to be an excise and therefore a valid exercise of the taxing power despite its intended protective character. In *J. W. Hampton, Jr. and Company v. United States* (276 U.S. 394: 1928), the Court said that the existence of nonrevenue motives does not necessarily invalidate a tax. The Court has said that taxes that augment the exercise of other express powers are appropriate. Regulation of certain illegal activities has also been upheld (see *United States v. Kahriger*, 345 U.S. 22: 1953). There have been occasions, however, when regulatory taxes have not survived judicial scrutiny. In *Bailey v. Drexel Furniture Company* (259 U.S. 20: 1922), the Court struck down a tax on profits of businesses engaged in child labor. The tax provisions were so "obviously" penalties rather than taxes that the regulatory objective supplanted all tax characteristics of the law.

Right   A power or guarantee to which a person is entitled. A right confers control of action upon an individual and provides protection for that action. *See also* BILL OF RIGHTS, p. 7; NATURAL LAW AND NATURAL RIGHTS, p. 50.

Significance   A right is legally conveyed by a constitution, statutes, or common law. It may be absolute, such as one's right to believe, or it may be conditional so that the acting out of one's beliefs will not injure other members of a political community. Rights within constitutional systems are called natural, civil, or political. A natural right is derived from the nature of man and flows from natural law. It is not dependent on manmade law. A civil right grows out of the political community, attaching to one's citizenship. Thus, every person has the right to a jury trial or equal treatment before the law. A political right protects a person's capacity to participate in his or her own governance by voting and by seeking political office.

Secession   Withdrawal by a state from the United States. Secession is the ultimate action by a state in an attempt to protect what it judges to be its sovereign interests. Secession from the Union was seen as the last resort by Southern states after the failed doctrines of interposition and nullification. It was believed that if the actions of the federal government were sufficiently oppressive, the people had the right to withdraw what power was given up to the federal government and dissolve the relationship between the two levels. *See also* FEDERALISM, p. 29; INTERPOSITION, p. 624; *TEXAS V. WHITE* (7 Wallace 700: 1869), p. 257.

Significance   The legal status of secession was resolved by the outcome of the Civil War. The Union had been maintained on the battlefield. Secession was simply not possible. The Supreme Court reiterated that position after the fact in *Texas v. White* (7 Wallace 700: 1869) and held that when Texas was admitted to the Union as a state, the relationship was "final" and "indissoluble."

Second Amendment   Preserves the militia and the right to bear arms. The Second Amendment provides that a "well regulated militia, being necessary to the security of a free state, the right of the people to keep and bear arms, shall not be infringed." The amendment was included in the initial Bill of Rights and was adopted in 1791. *See also* AMENDING POWER, p. 578.

Significance   The principal objective of the Second Amendment was to preserve the state militias. The amendment keeps Congress from disarming these bodies. The amendment reflected the feeling that militias, prepared and ready for mobilization, were an important element in maintaining the national defense. Reference to the "state" in the amendment does not mean individual states, but rather to the state in a generic sense. While arguments are advanced to the contrary, the amendment was not intended to convey a right to private ownership of weapons. Indeed, a variety of federal regulations, such as the tax and registration provisions of the National Firearms Act, have been upheld. Neither does the amendment preclude firearm regulation at the state and local levels, where restrictions as extensive as outright bans have been sustained.

Seventeenth Amendment   Provided for the popular election of United States senators. The Seventeenth Amendment altered two elements of the Constitution as originally provided in Article I, Section 3. This section directs that a state's U.S. Senate members be chosen or replaced by that state's legislature. The amendment requires that the two senators from each state be "elected by the people thereof." Section 2 of the amendment provides that vacancies in the Senate be filled by special elections called by the governor of the affected state. The state legislatures were authorized to enable the governor "to make temporary appointments until the people fill the vacancies by election." *See also* AMENDING POWER, p. 578.

Significance   The Seventeenth Amendment brought about popular election of United States senators and capped an effort of many years' duration to achieve that reform. Indeed, when the Senate concurred in proposing the amendment, many states had preference elections through which voters could influence legislative selection of the state's representatives in the Senate. Legislatures normally would defer to these expressions of preference. Since the passage of the amendment, all states have empowered their governors to make appointments for the interim lasting through the next general election, at which time the voters can elect a senator for the balance of the original unexpired term. House members have been elected from the outset under terms of Article I, Section 2. In the event of a House vacancy, a state governor is required to "issue writs of election to fill such vacancies." This language does allow interim appointments to be made if the unexpired term is close to conclusion.

Seventh Amendment   Preserves the right of jury trial for common law cases. The Seventh Amendment provides that in "suits at common law" with a "value in controversy" that exceeds $20, the "right of trial by jury shall be preserved." The amendment also says that "no fact tried by a jury" shall be "otherwise reexamined" in any court of the United States other than by rules established by common law. *See also* AMENDING POWER, p. 578; INCORPORATION, p. 620.

Significance   The purpose of the Seventh Amendment was to protect access to juries in common law cases by preserving the jury role in
such litigation. The amendment does not extend the right to jury trial,
but preserves the right in cases that were committed to juries at the time
the constitution was adopted. The language of the amendment does
not apply to equity proceedings or admiralty cases. The amendment is
also confined to federal courts, as the amendment has never been
extended to the states through the incorporation process.

Sixteenth Amendment   Enabled the federal government to levy
income taxes. The Sixteenth Amendment simply says that Congress
"shall have the power to lay and collect taxes on incomes, from whatever source derived, without apportionment, among the several states,
and without regard to any census or enumeration." The amendment
was declared ratified in 1913. Prior to adoption of this amendment, a
tax on incomes had been regarded as a direct tax, a kind of tax
prohibited by Article I, Section 9. *See also* AMENDING POWER, p. 578;
DIRECT TAX, p. 592; FEDERALISM, p. 29; *POLLOCK V. FARMERS' LOAN AND TRUST
COMPANY* (158 U.S. 601: 1895), p. 382.

Significance   The Sixteenth Amendment repealed the Supreme
Court decision in *Pollock v. Farmers' Loan and Trust Company* (158 U.S.
601: 1895), and removed constitutional limitations on the use of the
income tax. Although the Court had previously upheld an income tax
levied during the Civil War, the court in *Pollock* ruled that a tax on
incomes derived from real estate as well as municipal bonds was a
prohibited direct tax. The *Pollock* ruling prompted almost immediate
efforts to overturn it. For some, the decision seriously inhibited the
federal government's capacity to generate revenues sufficient to keep
the government solvent. For others, the *Pollock* decision was an indication that the Court had been captured by the interests of corporate
power and the privileged. Even the Court seemed to have some second
thoughts. It was presented with a number of opportunities to apply
Pollock between 1896 and 1913, but it chose to do otherwise. In *Flint v.
Stone Tracy Company* (220 U.S 107: 1911), the Court upheld a corporate
income tax, finding it to be an excise tax "measured by income, " and
thus not subject to the apportionment requirement as a direct tax.
Around this time, Congress reconsidered an income tax and added
such a tax proposal to a tariff bill. In an attempt to defeat the income tax
amendment to the legislation, the constitutional amendment was introduced. An excise tax alternative was substituted in the legislation for
the originally proposed income tax. The amendment, however, proceeded to the states, where it was ratified, to the surprise and dismay of
many of the proposers. Passage of the amendment ushered in a new

and eventually primary source of federal tax revenue. Access to this new revenue source, in turn, had an effect on the federal-state relationship in that the new taxing capability permitted the federal government to engage to a far greater degree in domestic spending programs.

Sixth Amendment   Mandates a fair trial for criminal defendants. Like the Fifth Amendment, the Sixth is based upon English common law tradition. Abuses of laws intended to safeguard the rights of criminal defendants were common in colonial America. Most of the constitutions of the first thirteen states contained language designed to correct them. The state constitutional ratifying conventions, with North Carolina taking the lead, insisted that the principle of trial by jury is one of the most fundamental rights accruing to the citizens of a democracy.

The immediate cause of such deep concern was the British practice in colonial America of sending defendants to England for trial. Colonists believed to be guilty of violating the trade laws or stamp acts, for example, were tried by the British Admiralty Court in England without benefit of a jury. On October 21, 1774, the Continental Congress declared unequivocally that "the seizing of or attempting to seize any person in America in order to transport such person beyond the sea for trial of offenses committed within the body of a county in America, being against the law, will justify, and ought to meet with, resistance and reprisal." In that part of the Declaration of Independence containing the litany of "repeated injuries and usurpations" suffered by the colonies, the following complaints appear: "For depriving us in many cases of the benefits of Trial by Jury; for transporting us beyond seas to be tried for pretended offences." The colonists also insisted that provisions of Magna Carta be remembered on the subject of speedy trials. A person accused of a crime must not be kept in prison an unreasonable period of time before trial of the facts. The founders were equally concerned that the Bill of Rights embody the English common law tradition holding that one accused of a criminal act should have available the bill of indictment containing the charges against him. The assumption implicit in this clause of the Sixth Amendment is that if a defendant is aware of the precise charges levied against him or her, an appropriate defense can be mounted.

A clause of the Sixth Amendment that did not originate in the English common law tradition was the guarantee of compulsory process. Until 1798 it was well established in the conduct of English trials that persons accused of felonies or treason were not allowed to introduce witnesses in their own behalf. After 1787 this general law was abolished in England, but there were restrictions on the number and kinds of witnesses who could be summoned. Not only did the constitutional ratifying conventions have this immediate precedent before them in 1789, they also had the American tradition that "all criminals shall have the same privileges of Witnesses as their Prosecutors." The right of compulsory process is now an unchallenged part of American criminal procedure, as is the right of access to counsel.

Prior to 1836, defendants in the English court system were allowed to access counsel only in cases where the charge was treason. The American tradition was different, however. The right to retain counsel, albeit at one's own expense, was codified in the Judiciary Act of 1789 and the Federal Crime Act of 1790. Thus, if a defendant could afford to retain counsel, his right to counsel was guaranteed. Several twentieth-century Supreme Court decisions dramatically reinterpreted this tradition. In *Powell v. Alabama* (287 U.S. 45: 1932), the Court determined that states were required to furnish counsel as an extension of the due process guarantee of the Fourteenth Amendment. In a series of subsequent decisions, assistance of counsel has been extended to all felony trials, some misdemeanor trials, and many pretrial and post-trial proceedings, including custodial interrogation. Thus the evolution of the Sixth Amendment phrase "have the Assistance of Counsel for his defence" has made legal representation an absolute constitutional guarantee. *See also* BILL OF RIGHTS, p. 7; COMMON LAW, p. 13; MAGNA CARTA, p. 45.

Significance   The Sixth Amendment provides rights that differentiate the American system of jurisprudence from many others in the modern world. That part of the Sixth Amendment guaranteeing trial by jury emerged full-blown in the Plymouth Colony in 1623, where it was required that all criminal facts to be adjudicated should be tried by a jury of twelve "honest men to be impanelled by authority, in form of a jury upon their oaths." The Plymouth tradition that these twelve persons should unanimously agree on a verdict survives in federal criminal procedures to this day, although the Supreme Court has ruled that in state actions a unanimous jury is not always necessary to convict a criminal defendant. Similarly, later interpretations of what constitutes a fair trial and a proper jury have evolved according to the due process and equal protection standards of the Fourteenth Amendment. It is now Supreme Court doctrine that impartiality in the composition of a jury must reflect at least generally the sociological makeup of the trial district's population. By the same token the idea of witness confrontation has evolved from the right of those accused of treason to confront witnesses against them under England's Treason Act of 1696, to modern rules of procedure that take strongly into account a trial's reliance on evidence and testimony brought by witnesses. The Sixth Amendment's guarantee of the right to counsel assures that all other provisions of the amendment are monitored by persons with legal knowledge. The right to counsel has been extended to every corner and aspect of the criminal procedures process: to the states, to the poor, and to persons immediately after being put in custody. In no other modern government have so many safeguards been assigned to the rights of persons accused of crimes.

Sovereignty   The supreme power of a state by which it governs. Sovereignty is the power by which a state makes and implements its laws, imposes taxes, and conducts its external relations. Sovereignty means power in the absolute sense; it is the uncontrolled power to govern. *See also* FEDERALISM, p. 29; POWER, p. 644.

Significance   Sovereignty is the source on which governmental authority is established. It is located in the person(s) or institution(s) of a state, and there exists no politically superior power within that state's boundaries. The concept was central to seventeenth-century political philosophy and remains a factor in contemporary international politics. The notion of sovereignty was countered or altered in some respects by the concept of popular sovereignty, which retains for the governed ultimate control in a political system.

Speech or Debate Clause   Grants members of Congress immunity from reprisal for comments made in the performance of their official duties. The speech or debate clause is found in Article I, Section 6 and provides that "for any speech or debate, in either House, they should not be questioned in any other place." This immunity was intended to protect legislators from intimidation, especially from other branches of government. The theory was that the legislative function would be enhanced if legislators could engage in uninhibited debate on public issues. The clause also means that members of Congress may not be held responsible for statements made in performing official congressional duties. This precludes, among other things, suits for libel, slander, or seditious statements. *See also GRAVEL V. UNITED STATES* (408 U.S. 606: 1972), p. 194; *HUTCHINSON V. PROXMIRE* (443 U.S. 111: 1979), p. 196.

Significance   Two issues, both relating to the scope of the speech or debate clause, have occupied the Court in recent years. The first is whether anyone beyond the members of Congress is protected by the clause. The Court held in *Gravel v. United States* (408 U.S. 606: 1972) that an aide to a senator was protected to the same degree as the member of Congress. Similarly, staff members of legislative committees are generally covered. The second issue involves protected activities.

Generally, the clause protects actions that relate directly to legislative business. Thus, the committee staff member is protected while researching and drafting a committee report, but that same staffer may lose protection by making copies of the report available to the media. In *Hutchinson v. Proxmire* (443 U.S. 111: 1979), the Court held that even a member of Congress is not protected from libel actions if statements made in protected speeches are disseminated to the public via newsletters or other releases. In several recent cases, the Court has more narrowly defined the legislative process so that the speech or debate clause would not impede criminal prosecutions of several members of Congress.

Standing   The requirement that a real dispute exist between the prospective parties in a suit. Standing is necessary for a federal court to proceed with a case. The concept has several important components. Federal judicial power extends to cases or controversies through Article III of the Constitution. This has been interpreted to mean that bona fide disputes must exist if judicial resolution is to be sought. The federal courts are thus unable to respond to hypothetical or friendly suits, and they cannot render advisory opinions. The adversary system demands that litigants in a suit be true adversaries. Test cases have often been used to raise certain issues and satisfy the demands of the standing requirement. A test case is a legal action designed to obtain a court's judgment on a legal question and thereby have a principle or right established or clarified. Developing a test case is a common strategy of interest groups. The National Association for the Advancement of Colored People (NAACP), for example, orchestrated various test cases involving different aspects of racial segregation in an effort to obtain favorable judgments in the courts.

Standing means that the plaintiff bringing suit must have suffered direct injury, and the injury must be protected by constitutional or statutory provisions. This means suits cannot be brought by a third party or someone indirectly related to the legal injury. Further, each suit must specify the remedy being sought from the court. The burden rests with the plaintiff to define what relief the court might order. Standing also relates to the timing of a suit. A federal court must find a suit ripe, which means all other avenues of possible relief must have been exhausted. Similarly, a case cannot access federal courts if it has been resolved or if events have made pursuit of the original remedy inappropriate. A case that is too late is considered moot because there is no longer an adversarial situation. Exceptions will be made when the limited duration of a situation or condition interferes with the litigation of the issues. Abortion cases are examples of the need for such an exception.

Significance   Standing is discussed in several important Supreme Court decisions. The matter was first raised in *Frothingham v. Mellon* (262 U.S. 447: 1923). Plaintiff Frothingham attempted to enjoin the implementation of a federal program, claiming injury by virtue of paying federal taxes. The Supreme Court denied standing and suggested that Frothingham's injury was shared by millions of others. The injury was therefore "comparatively minute and indeterminate." A plaintiff seeking judicial review of a federal statute must be able to show "direct injury as the result of its enforcement, and not merely that he suffers in some indefinite way in common with people generally." Inability to establish such injury will prevent consideration of the constitutional issue regardless of how real and pressing the issue may be. The *Frothingham* precedent lasted as an absolute barrier to judicial review of congressional spending legislation by taxpayers until *Flast v. Cohen* (392 U.S. 83: 1968). The Court held in *Flast* that a taxpayer could achieve standing by showing a nexus between the taxpayer and the challenged program. The case involved a challenge of federal aid to private elementary and secondary schools. The Warren Court found the relationship among the federal taxing power, the payment of federal taxes, and First Amendment protections adequate to produce standing. The decision immediately raised questions about judicial review of congressional spending initiatives. It distinguished between the *Frothingham* direct injury requirement and the litigant who might be acting on behalf of broader public rights.

The Burger Court has shown, however, that access is still difficult. In *United States v. Richardson* (418 U.S. 166: 1974), the Court refused to allow a taxpayer to inquire into Central Intelligence Agency appropriations. The Court said that allowing "unrestricted taxpayer standing would significantly alter the allocation of power at the national level." A second case, *Schlesinger v. Reservist's Committee to Stop the War* (418 U.S. 208: 1974), challenged the military reserve status of more than a hundred members of Congress. The Court denied standing, saying that to allow such a challenge by someone who has no concrete injury would require the Court to respond to issues in the abstract. The Court said this would create the potential for abuse of the judicial process and distortion of the role of the judiciary. Standing too easily granted would open the courts to an arguable charge of government by the judiciary.

Stare Decisis   Latin for "let the decision stand." Stare decisis holds that once a principle of law is established for a particular fact situation, courts should adhere to that principle in similar cases in the future. The case in which the rule of law is established is called a precedent.

Significance Stare decisis creates and maintains stability and predictability in the law. It creates a large body of settled usages that define common law. Precedents may be modified or abandoned if circumstances require, but the expectation is that rules from previously adjudicated cases will prevail.

State Action A requirement that limits application of the equal protection clause to situations where discriminatory conduct occurs under state authority. The state action requirement was first established by the Supreme Court in the *Civil Rights Cases* (109 U.S. 3: 1883). It placed private discrimination outside the reach of the Fourteenth Amendment. The Court held that the amendment was intended to provide relief against state enactments rather than to empower Congress "to legislate upon subjects which are within the domain of state legislation" or "create a code of municipal law for the regulation of private rights." *See also* CIVIL RIGHTS CASES (109 U.S. 3: 1883), p. 259.

Significance State action requires a judgment about whether certain kinds of conduct occur under color of state law. A court must determine if discriminatory action is situated closely enough to state authority to be treated as though it were an overt act of the state. A sufficient nexus between challenged action and state authority is generally not difficult to demonstrate, although some private discrimination remains insulated from regulation. While softening the distinctions between private and state-authorized discrimination, thus expanding the reach of the equal protection clause, recent cases have required that discriminatory *intent* must be shown in addition to injurious impact in order to establish a constitutional violation.

Statute A written law enacted by a legislative body. A statute declares, requires, or prohibits something. *See also* JUDICIAL REVIEW, p. 627.

Significance A statute is the most common means by which conduct is governed. It must be enacted by a legislative body properly exercising the authority conveyed to it. A statute is inferior to constitutional provisions, and if a statute is incompatible with a constitutional command, the statute is void. All federal statues are published in *Statutes at Large of the United States*, and those currently valid are regularly compiled and found in the United States Code.

Stream of Commerce   Concept used to link commerce power to local activities which affect interstate commerce. The stream of commerce concept applies to situations where commerce comes to rest in a place, but where that commerce has not yet reached its point of destination. Rather, the commerce remains in the "stream" or "flow" of commerce and can be reached by federal power or protected from state regulation or taxation. *See also* COMMERCE CLAUSE, p. 291; *STAFFORD V. WALLACE* (258 U.S. 495: 1922), p. 311.

Significance   The stream of commerce rationale was developed in the early 1900s as part of a general attempt to expand the scope of the federal commerce power. Concepts such as stream of commerce focused on local activities or incidents of commerce that produce an "effect" on interstate commerce. Arguments such as these began to take the commerce power beyond the specific transaction of movement across state lines. Representative of decisions utilizing the stream of commerce concept is *Stafford v. Wallace* (258 U.S. 495: 1922). In this case the Court examined the Packers and Stockyards Act of 1921, which brought regulations to bear on meat-packing monopolies that were arbitrarily influencing shipper and consumer prices. A principal target of the statute was the stockyards, where a number of undesirable practices occurred. The Court upheld the act, saying that the stream of commerce was still flowing. Stockyards are "not a place of rest or final destination." Rather, they are "but a throat" through which the "stream or current flows." Thus such concepts as stream of commerce provided the rationale by which the federal commerce power was expanded to reach a wide range of activities that affect commerce.

Subpoena   A writ issued by a court, legislative body, or administrative agency that requires a witness to appear at some formal proceeding. The recipient of a subpoena need not be a party to a lawsuit, as distinguished from a defendant in an action who may be notified of the suit by a summons to appear. Failure to appear typically subjects the recipient to a contempt citation.

Significance   The subpoena power is frequently used by judicial, legislative, and administrative bodies to obtain evidence germane to a matter before that body. In judicial proceedings, both sides may utilize the compulsory process of subpoena. A person in possession of documents or papers may be compelled to bring such material to a proceeding through a *subpoena duces tecum*.

Substantive Due Process   A substantive review focusing on the content of government policy and actions. Substantive due process is distinguished from procedural due process, which attends to the means by which policies are executed. Judicial review of the reasonableness of legislative enactments allows the Court actively to intervene in policy judgments more than it could if review were confined to procedural considerations. *See also* DUE PROCESS CLAUSES, p. 594; PROCEDURAL DUE PROCESS, p. 647.

Significance   Substantive due process represents considerable monitoring power in the hands of the courts. In *Meyer v. Nebraska* (262 U.S. 390: 1923), for example, the Supreme Court struck down a statute prohibiting the teaching of a foreign language to any pre–ninth-grade student, public or parochial. Justice McReynolds said the statute was "arbitrary and without reasonable relation to any end within the competency of the State." The use of substantive due process to invalidate economic regulations is illustrated by *Lochner v. New York* (198 U.S. 45: 1905). *Lochner* involved an attempt to limit the work week of bakers to 60 hours. The Court held that there is "no reasonable ground for interfering with the liberty of a person or the right of free contract by determining the hours of labor in the occupation of a baker." The Court made a substantive judgment that the regulation of work hours for bakers was sufficiently unreasonable to constitute a denial of due process of law. Substantive due process review also occurs when statutes are stricken for reason of vagueness. When the Court voided a city ordinance in *Coates v. Cincinnati* (40 U.S. 611: 1971), an ordinance that prohibited public annoyance by assemblies of three or more persons standing on public sidewalks, it did so because the ordinance was arbitrary. It conveyed no discernible standard of conduct. Another example of substantive due process enforcement is the striking down of state statutes prohibiting abortion. Over the years, guarantees of procedural due process have been invoked by the Supreme Court far more frequently than guarantees relating to substantive due process.

Third Amendment   Regulates the quartering of soldiers in private homes. The Third Amendment says that "no soldier shall, in time of peace be quartered in any house, without the consent of the owner, nor in time of war, but in a manner to be prescribed by law." *See also* FOURTH AMENDMENT, p. 613.

Significance   The Third Amendment forbade the involuntary quartering of troops in private homes during peacetime. The amendment was a reflection of the paramount importance of the sanctity of one's own home. Coupled with the language of the Fourth Amendment, a fundamental concern for personal privacy is established. History does not register any claimed violations of this amendment, nor has the Court examined it in litigation. There appears to be wide consensus about its provisions, and no need has arisen to consider it more carefully.

Thirteenth Amendment   A post–Civil War constitutional amendment providing that "Neither slavery nor involuntary servitude, except as a punishment for crime whereof the party shall have been duly convicted, shall exist within the United States, or any place subject to their jurisdiction." The Thirteenth Amendment gave legal effect to the Emancipation Proclamation. It also fundamentally altered the federal-state relationship in that it conferred on the federal government authority over a policy area previously residing exclusively in the states. A state could no longer permit slavery through the exercise of its own authority. The Thirteenth Amendment does not preclude military conscription, criminal sentences involving hard labor, or other similar requirements of involuntary service. The Amendment was designed to apply to black persons in the particular context of the Emancipation Proclamation. Section 2 of the Amendment empowered Congress "to enforce this article by appropriate legislation." *See also* FOURTEENTH AMENDMENT, p. 612; STATE ACTION, p. 657.

Significance   The Thirteenth Amendment gave Congress comprehensive power to legislate against racial discrimination and the denial of civil rights. Such power was incident to the power to outlaw slavery. Consistent with this view, Congress passed the Civil Rights Act of 1866, which clarified the citizenship status of freed slaves and protected certain rights such as entering into contracts and holding and conveying real property. Early Supreme Court construction of the amendment defined slavery very narrowly, however, and placed private discrimination outside the amendment's reach. Congress therefore had no occasion to exercise the limited authority conferred by Section 2. In 1968 the Supreme Court substantially modified its previous interpretations and found that the Amendment empowered Congress to do more than simply abolish the institution of slavery. In the case of *Jones v. Alfred Mayer Company* (392 U.S. 409: 1968), a case in which a litigant attempted to utilize provisions of the Civil Rights Act of 1866 against a discriminatory housing developer, the Court said the Thirteenth Amendment had granted Congress power "to determine what are the badges and the incidents of slavery" and to respond accordingly. As construed in *Jones*, the Thirteenth Amendment became a foundation stone upon which civil rights policy was established, particularly when the policy turns on what constitutes a badge or vestige of slavery. The correction of such badges and vestiges is now clearly located within the parameters of congressional power.

Tort   A private or civil injury to a person or property. A tort action must include the legal obligation of a defendant to a plaintiff, violation of that obligation, and a cause-and-effect relationship between the defendant's conduct and the injury suffered by the plaintiff.

Significance   A tort is any civil wrong except breach of contract. A lawsuit alleging the negligence of an automobile driver is a tort action, for example. An assault is a tort. So is a trespass. A Constitutional tort involves an action or inaction that allegedly violates the Constitution of the United States.

Travel, Right to   A fundamental right drawn implicitly from the Constitution of the United States. The right to travel freely from state to state is spread among all American citizens. While several origins of the right have been suggested, the Supreme Court has settled on the commerce clause as the principal source. The Court has held that the power to regulate interstate commerce encompasses people as well as commodities. *See also* FUNDAMENTAL RIGHT, p. 615; PASSPORT, p. 643.

Significance   The right to travel not only precludes denial of movement from state to state, but it also prohibits state policies that may inhibit interstate travel. In *Shapiro v. Thompson* (394 U.S. 618: 1969), for example, the Court struck down a state residency requirement for welfare eligibility. The purpose of the enactment was to deter migration of welfare-eligible persons into a state. The Court categorically condemned any interference with the right to movement, saying that all citizens must be free to travel throughout the country. They must be "uninhibited by statutes, rules, or regulations which unreasonably burden or restrain this movement." A state must demonstrate a compelling interest before imposing any regulation that affects the right to travel.

Treaty Power   Authority to enter formal agreement between two or more sovereign nations. The treaty power is set forth in Article II, Section 2, which says that the president shall have the power "to make treaties, provided two-thirds of the Senators present concur." Treaty negotiations occur under direction of the president, although the two-thirds ratification requirement, for political reasons, typically leads to involvement of congressional leaders in the development process. The Senate has power to approve or reject a treaty in its entirety, or to consent to ratification only with changes. In the latter instance, a president must agree to the Senate amendments or reservations as well as secure concurrence of the foreign power(s) involved in the agreement before it becomes effective. The supremacy clause of Article VI stipulates that treaty provisions take precedence over state constitutional and statutory law in the event of conflict. *See also* EXECUTIVE AGREEMENT, p. 601; *MISSOURI V. HOLLAND* (252 U.S. 416: 1920), p. 263; *UNITED STATES V. BELMONT* (301 U.S. 324: 1937), p. 156.

Significance   The treaty power has been frequently exercised in the conduct of American foreign relations, and the United States currently remains party to numerous bilateral and multilateral treaties. Since the 1930s, presidents have come to more often utilize the executive agreement as the principal mode of concluding international arrangements because it permits bypass of Senate review and concurrence. The legal parity of treaties and executive agreements was established in *United States v. Belmont* (301 U.S. 324: 1937). A treaty may allow Congress to exercise legislative power not otherwise available. In *Missouri v. Holland* (252 U.S. 416: 1920), the Court upheld a law passed pursuant to a treaty even though the Congress had previously been denied direct access to this same policy matter. Justice Holmes concluded that there may be matters, even of the "sharpest exigency for the national well-being" that an act of Congress "could not deal with but that a treaty followed by such an act could." The treaty power is not without limit, but is subject to any and all restrictions imposed by other language in the Constitution.

Twelfth Amendment   Clarifies the mechanics of presidential selection. The Twelfth Amendment supersedes a portion of Article II, Section 1 and calls for presidential electors to vote for president and vice president on "distinct" ballots. Prior to the amendment, electors voted for two persons. The person gaining the most votes became president, while the candidate with the next most became vice president. The Twelfth Amendment also provides that if no candidate receives a majority of the electoral vote, the determination shall be made by the House of Representatives. The House is to choose from the three persons with the most electoral votes. This was a reduction from five candidates as originally provided. The Senate determines the vice president absent a majority through the Electoral College. There is also language in the Twelfth Amendment providing for the vice president to serve as acting president either in the event no candidate has been selected by the House or upon the death or disability of the president. This provision has been altered by language in both the Twentieth and Twenty-fifth Amendments. *See also* AMENDING POWER, p. 578; TWENTIETH AMENDMENT, p. 663; TWENTY-FIFTH AMENDMENT, p. 664.

Significance   The Twelfth Amendment modifies the presidential selection process. The principal changes were in separating the balloting for president and vice president, and the reduction of the range of choice to be considered by the House if the Electoral College fails to cast a majority of its votes for one candidate. The amendment was necessitated by the advent of political parties. Originally, the College of Electors was envisioned as a group of distinguished persons who would use their independent judgment in selecting a president and vice president. With the political parties came electors pledged to a party's candidate. When the election of 1800 was deadlocked between Thomas Jefferson and Aaron Burr, it was ultimately resolved in the House, but only after great political maneuvering. To avoid this situation in the future, the Twelfth Amendment adapted the selection process to accommodate the existence of parties. The old provisions also permitted the possibility of partisan adversaries winding up as president and vice president in the same administration, an untenable situation in a vigorous two-party system.

Twentieth Amendment   Established a fixed date for the convening of congressional sessions and the beginning of presidential terms. The Twentieth Amendment was ratified in 1933. Sections 1 and 2 fix the start of new terms for the president, vice president, and Congress by establishing a constant end point to the preceding terms at January 20 and January 3, respectively. Section 3 empowers Congress to provide for the situation where neither the president nor vice president has "qualified" for office under terms established by the Twelfth Amendment. Section 4 deals with House selection of a president if no candidate receives a majority of electoral votes and what occurs in the event of the death of one of the candidates under consideration of the House. *See also* AMENDING POWER, p. 578; TWELFTH AMENDMENT, p. 662.

Significance   The Twentieth Amendment is known as the "lame duck" amendment because it reduced the period following an election in which the outgoing president continued to serve and it was aimed at eliminating congressional sessions that occurred after elections, but prior to the beginning of a new Congress. Prior to the amendment, newly elected presidents and members of Congress did not take office until the following March. This permitted defeated incumbents to continue to transact official business for several months following the election. The language of Section 3 enabled Congress to deal with presidential succession and actually created some incentives not to "qualify" anyone as president if such determination was to be made under provisions of the Twelfth Amendment. Congress has provided that succession of the president- or vice president-elect shall parallel the process governing the president and vice president as set forth in the Twenty-fifth Amendment.

Twenty-fifth Amendment   Provides procedures for dealing with presidential disability and the procedure by which a vice presidential vacancy is to be filled. The Twenty-fifth Amendment was ratified in 1967. The amendment contains four sections, the first of which provides that the "Vice President shall become President" in the event of "removal of the President from office or his death or resignation." Section 2 covers vice presidential vacancies. It provides that upon a vacancy, the president "shall nominate a Vice President who shall take office upon confirmation by a majority of both Houses of Congress." Sections 3 and 4 deal with presidential disability. The president may assume disabled status by his or her own initiative by transmitting a "written declaration that he is unable to discharge the powers and duties of his office." Until such time as the president declares in writing that he or she is able to resume presidential duties, the responsibilities of the office are to be "discharged by the Vice President as Acting President." Section 4 provides the first constitutional discussion of how presidential disability may be determined without the president's own declaration. Section 4 places the responsibility for determining incapacity with the vice president and the cabinet. They are to transmit to the president pro tem of the Senate and the Speaker of the House their "written declaration that the President is unable to discharge the powers and duties of the office." At that point, the vice president "shall immediately assume the powers and duties of the office as Acting President." Provision is made for a president's challenge of the judgment of the vice president and cabinet as to incapacity. Congress resolves such disagreements upon receipt from the president of a declaration that no disability exists. A two-thirds vote is required to sustain the judgment of disability and lodge the powers and duties of the office with the vice president. *See also* AMENDING POWER, p. 578; TWELFTH AMENDMENT, p. 662; TWENTIETH AMENDMENT, p. 663.

Significance   The Twenty-fifth Amendment speaks to presidential succession and disability and to vacancies in the vice presidency. The amendment merely formalized existing practice relative to presidential succession, but addressed the issue of vice presidential vacancies and presidential disability for the first time. Prior to the amendment, the country had experienced frequent and sometimes long periods during which the vice presidency was vacant. Succession, if necessary with the vice presidency vacant, passed to the Speaker of the House and then the president of the Senate pro tem. The year-long vacancy following Lyndon Johnson's succession of John F. Kennedy prompted proposal of the amendment. The process has been used twice since: Richard Nixon designated Gerald Ford to replace the resigned Spiro Agnew; after Ford's succession of Nixon, he nominated Nelson Rockefeller. While confirmation of Rockefeller took several months, the vacancy was eventually filled. Rockefeller's confirmation produced the unprecedented result of a president and vice president neither of whom had been elected. Presidential disability has occurred on several occasions. Prior to the amendment, there was no procedure by which disability could be determined, although several presidents had informally arranged with their own vice-presidents to act as president for the duration of any disability. The amendment formally recognized these arrangements. The amendment also anticipated disability that is less clear-cut and bypassed the need for the president to recognize his own disability.

Twenty-first Amendment   Repealed prohibition as a national policy. The Twenty-first Amendment provided that the "eighteenth article of amendment ... is hereby repealed." The amendment was adopted in 1933, just 16 years after the institution of prohibition. It was soon recognized that the social experiment of prohibition would not affect liquor consumption. It also had the negative consequence of fostering extensive criminal conduct in the production and distribution of liquor. Repeal of prohibition became an attractive political position almost from its inception. The Twenty-first Amendment also contained a second section, which enabled the states to regulate alcohol at their own discretion. Section 2 provided that the "transportation or importation into any state ... for delivery or use therein of intoxicating liquors, in violation of the law thereof, is hereby prohibited." *See also* AMENDING POWER, p. 578; EIGHTEENTH AMENDMENT, p. 595.

Significance   The Twenty-first Amendment repealed prohibition. Change in policy from that contained in the Eighteenth Amendment was inevitable. Cases arising under the Twenty-first Amendment relate to the extent to which state power may be exercised to regulate liquor. The principal limitation on such regulation comes from the commerce clause, and the Court must determine whether state regulation is reasonably compatible with that federal prerogative. Generally, state regulation based upon the discretion conveyed by this amendment has been accorded a greater presumption of validity. The importance of the Twenty-first Amendment relates not only to the fact that it ended the great social experiment of prohibition but also to the fact that it is the only amendment that was ratified by state conventions elected solely for that purpose. This procedure was not only swifter, since the country was thirsty, but obviously more democratic than ratification by state legislatures.

Twenty-fourth Amendment   Prohibits use of the poll tax as a voting requirement for federal elections. The Twenty-fourth Amendment was ratified in early 1964. The amendment provides that American citizens have a right "to vote in any primary or other election" for federal offices, and that this right "shall not be denied or abridged by the United States or any state by reason of failure to pay any poll tax or other tax." The poll tax had historically been an effective means of engaging in racial discrimination in the administration of both federal and state elections. Unsuccessful efforts to prohibit poll taxes had been made since the 1930s. Some states that had used them had discontinued doing so at their own initiative, but the practice remained alive into the 1960s. *See also* AMENDING POWER, p. 578.

Significance   The Twenty-fourth Amendment forbade use of poll or other taxes as a condition of voting in federal elections. The amendment did not absolutely foreclose use of poll taxes. While it was clear that no such tax or "milder substitute" could be used in connection with federal elections, several states attempted to retain use of the tax in state elections. The Court struck down these efforts in *Harper v. Virginia State Board of Elections* (383 U.S. 663: 1966). The Court based its decision on the equal protection clause, however, and not the Twenty-fourth Amendment.

Twenty-second Amendment   Restricted presidents to two terms in office. The Twenty-second Amendment was ratified in 1951. It provides that no person "shall be elected to the office of the President more than twice." The limitation applies to a person succeeding to the presidency or acting as president for more than two years of the term. Thus the amendment established a maximum tenure for a president of ten years. This could occur by a person's succeeding a president just into the second half of a term who then was elected to two full terms. A maximum tenure may also be just over six years if succession occurred with more than half a term remaining. President Gerald Ford, for example, could have won only one additional term as president since he succeeded President Richard Nixon with 29 months remaining in the term. *See also* AMENDING POWER, p. 578.

Significance   The Twenty-second Amendment limits the number of presidential terms. Evidence suggests that the framers of the Constitution preferred that a president remain eligible for election to other terms. When all the prominent early presidents for whom a third term was an option declined to run, a compelling precedent was established. This tradition was breached in 1940 when Franklin Roosevelt successfully sought a third term. Four years later, Roosevelt won a fourth term, but he died less than six months later. The Republicans seemed intent on preserving the two-term tradition, and when the 1946 congressional elections produced a Republican-controlled Congress, the amendment was proposed. From one perspective, the limit seems too rigid in that the country is absolutely precluded from retaining a president who has the popularity to win a third term. At the same time, the amendment prevents concentration of power within the executive branch for what amounts to an indefinite period. Indeed, there has been some discussion in recent years of establishing a single, six-year term for presidents. The concern that a president elected to a second term would be handicapped by a "lame duck" status has not been borne out.

Twenty-sixth Amendment   Allows 18-year-olds to vote in state and federal elections. The Twenty-sixth Amendment was ratified in 1971. It simply says that the "right of citizens . . . who are eighteen years or older, to vote shall not be denied or abridged by the United States or by any state on account of age." The amendment also empowers Congress to "enforce this article by appropriate legislation." *See also* AMENDING POWER, p. 578; *OREGON V. MITCHELL* (400 U.S. 112: 1970), pp. 199, 269.

Significance   The Twenty-sixth Amendment extended the franchise to 18-year-olds. The amendment reflected a general attitude that 18-year-olds had demonstrated sufficient interest and maturity to participate in the electoral process. The amendment was also ratified very quickly to negate the effects of a Supreme Court decision of the prior year. When Congress extended the Voting Rights Act in 1970, it attempted to lower the voting age in state as well as federal elections. The Supreme Court, however, decided in *Oregon v. Mitchell* (400 U.S. 112:

1970) that only federal elections could be reached by statute. The provisions of the act that applied to state and local elections were held unconstitutional. The decision left the prospect of having separate ballots for 18- to 20-year-olds beginning with the 1972 election. Proposal and ratification of the amendment remedied that problem. Expansion of the franchise to include 18- to 20-year-olds prompted the targeting of this group in voter registration drives and political campaigns, although no decided partisan advantage has occurred.

Twenty-third Amendment   Grants residents of the District of Columbia the right to vote in presidential elections. The Twenty-third Amendment was added to the Constitution in 1961. It accomplishes the purpose of allowing district voters to participate in elections for president and vice president by establishing district representation in the electoral college. The amendment says that the District of Columbia shall appoint a "number of electors of President and Vice President" equal to the number of senators and representatives to which the district would be entitled if it were a state. The amendment does require that the minimum number of electors to which the district is entitled shall not be less than that of the least populous state. *See also* TWELFTH AMENDMENT, p. 662.

Significance   The Twenty-third Amendment extends participation in presidential elections to voters in the District of Columbia. Through the formula of the amendment, the district must be assured at least three electoral votes. The amendment is also noteworthy in that it moved the hitherto largely disenfranchised people of the District of Columbia in the direction of full congressional representation.

Uniformity Clause   Provision in Article I, Section 8 that requires uniform imposition of duties, imposts, and excises. The uniformity clause limits federal taxing power by directing that such levies be "uniform throughout the United States." This provision requires that a tax be imposed at the same rate and against the same bases throughout the country. *See also* KNOWLTON V. MOORE (178 U.S. 41: 1900), p. 384.

Significance   The uniformity clause requires geographic uniformity of taxes. In *Knowlton v. Moore* (178 U.S. 41: 1900), the Court examined the question of whether any levy need be "intrinsically equal and uniform." The Court ruled that taxes need not be intrinsically equal. To have held so would have imposed a severe limitation on the federal taxing power. Rather, the Court saw the uniformity clause in exclusively geographic terms. It guaranteed to states that none would be singled out for targeted or differential taxation. Interpretation of the clause in geographic terms does not create a serious problem for the Congress in the exercise of federal taxing power.

United States Claims Court   Hears claims from private parties against the federal government. The Court of Claims was established in 1855 and renamed by the Federal Court Improvement Act of 1982. Examples of the kinds of cases heard by the Claims Court include claims arising out of governmental contracts, injuries caused by official negligence, and claims by either civilians or military personnel for back or retirement pay. A number of cases are referred directly by Congress. The court consists of 16 judges appointed by the president. The judges preside over cases individually except in cases that are congressional referrals. The court is headquartered in Washington, D.C., although it may hold court anywhere in the country. *See also* LEGISLATIVE COURTS, p. 630.

Significance   The United States Claims Court provides a means by which claims against the federal government may be determined. Since the federal government is immune from this kind of suit without its consent, these claims require an unusual process. The Claims Court is an alternative to congressional consideration of these claims. If the court finds a party entitled to an award, however, Congress must specifically appropriate the funds to pay the claim. Final judgments of the Claims Court may be appealed to the United States Court of Appeals for the Federal Circuit.

United States Courts of Appeals   The intermediate appellate courts of the federal judicial system. The United States courts of appeal were established by Congress in 1891 to provide a first appellate review of cases brought from federal trial courts and certain administrative agencies. The objective was to decrease the number of cases seeking review from the Supreme Court. These courts were first called the circuit courts of appeals. The United States is divided geographically into 12 units called judicial circuits. Each state is assigned to one of 11 circuits. The twelfth is a separate circuit for the District of Columbia. All appeals from lower courts within these geographic areas go to the court of appeals for that circuit. Territorial courts are assigned to specific circuits as well. There is also a United States Court of Appeals for the Federal Circuit, which has national jurisdiction over specialized substantive matters. *See also* ARTICLE III, p. 73; CONSTITUTIONAL COURTS, p. 588; UNITED STATES COURT OF APPEALS FOR THE FEDERAL CIRCUIT, p. 670.

Significance   The United States courts of appeals review issues of law in approximately 30,000 cases annually. The courts were established by Congress under authority from Article III to screen some of the cases for the Supreme Court. That screening function has been performed, and only a relatively small proportion of cases decided by the courts of appeals seek further review from the Supreme Court. Courts of appeals judges are appointed for life by the president on the advice and consent of the Senate. Each circuit has from 4 to 23 permanent judges depending on case demand, for a total of 144 judges. Each of the courts usually reviews cases in divisions or panels of three judges, but will occasionally sit en banc with all the judges in the circuit participating.

United States Court of Appeals for the Federal Circuit   Established in 1982 to function as the successor to the Court of Customs and Patent Appeals. The Court of Appeals for the Federal Circuit is an Article III court with national jurisdiction and hears appeals from United States district and territorial courts in patent, trademark, and copyright cases. It also hears appeals from final decisions of the United States Claims Court and the Court of International Trade. The court may also review administrative rulings of the Patent and Trademark Office, the International Trade Commission, the secretary of commerce, and the Merit System Protection Board. *See also* CONSTITUTIONAL COURTS, p. 588; UNITED STATES COURTS OF APPEALS, p. 669.

Significance   The United States Court of Appeals for the Federal Circuit is like the other courts of appeal except that it has a specialized substantive jurisdiction, and it can hear cases from across the country rather than from smaller groupings of designated states called circuits. This court has 12 circuit judges appointed by the president with the advice and consent of the Senate. Like the other courts of appeal, the court reviews cases in panels of three or more judges. While the court generally sits in Washington, D.C., it may hear cases wherever one of the other 12 courts of appeal sits.

United States Court of International Trade   A specialized legislative court created by Congress in 1926. The United States Court of International Trade was called the Customs Court until 1981. The court has trial court jurisdiction over matters arising out of tariff laws and the imposition of duties on imports. The court is composed of a chief judge and eight associates. The judges are appointed by the president with the advice and consent of the Senate. No more than five of the judges may be affiliated with any one political party. The Customs Court was given constitutional status by Congress in 1956; thus the judges have life tenure and are protected by the bar against reducing salaries. The court is headquartered in New York City, but it has authority to hear and decide cases at any major port of entry in the United States. Decisions of this court may be appealed to the United States Court of Appeals for the Federal Circuit. *See also* LEGISLATIVE COURTS, p. 630.

Significance   The Court of International Trade is the trial court for private citizens and corporations to litigate issues involving duties, valuation of imports, and regulations on imported merchandise. The Customs Court Act of 1980 changed the name of the court and defined its jurisdiction over these civil actions arising out of import transactions. The court has the power of law and equity comparable to a district court. This court relieves the district court, which would hear these cases in the absence of the district court, from hearing frequent and highly specialized matters involved with import classifications and valuation.

United States Court of Military Appeals   A legislative court established in 1950 to review all appeals from military courts martial. The Court of Military Appeals consists of three civilian judges appointed by the president for 15-year terms. The court is exclusively an appeals court to review criminal cases out of the lower military court system. The court must review all decisions involving top-level military personnel (generals or flag officers) and cases where the death penalty is invoked. It retains discretion to review any other case from the lower military justice system on petition. *See also* LEGISLATIVE COURTS, p. 630.

Significance   Establishment of the Court of Military Appeals was an outgrowth of serious concerns about the military justice system. In 1950, the Congress enacted the Uniform Code of Military Justice, which integrated many of the rights accorded civilians into the court-martial process. Creation of an appeals court composed exclusively of civilians was an important element in the tightening of the military justice system. Decisions of the Court of Military Appeals may be reviewed by the United States Supreme Court.

United States District Courts   The federal trial courts of general jurisdiction. The United States district courts are the primary federal courts of original jurisdiction, disposing of about 200,000 cases per year. The jurisdiction of the district courts, defined pursuant to Article III, includes all federal criminal cases, civil actions arising under the federal Constitution, statutes, or treaties if the amount in controversy exceeds $10,000, cases involving citizens of different states (with the same $10,000 minimum), admiralty and maritime cases, and review of certain administrative agency orders. Congress may alter the jurisdiction of the district courts. All district judges are appointed by the president with the advice and consent of the Senate and possess life tenure. *See also* ARTICLE III, p. 73; CONSTITUTIONAL COURTS, p. 588.

Significance   The United States district courts conduct the great majority of business in the federal judicial system. Each state has at least one district court with some of the larger and more populous states having as many as four. There are 89 district courts in the 50 states plus one for the District of Columbia and the Commonwealth of Puerto Rico. There are also territorial courts in Guam, the Virgin Islands, and the Northern Mariana Islands. Territorial court judges serve eight-year terms and handle, in addition to federal matters, local issues that would fall to a state court. The district courts vary in size, ranging from 1 to 27 judges depending on the caseload in each. Congress may add district court judgeships at its discretion. Currently there are more than 550 district court judges. Cases decided by the district courts may be appealed to the United States courts of appeal, although certain issues are taken to the United States Court of Appeals for the Federal Circuit.

United States Supreme Court   Highest court in the federal judicial system. The Supreme Court is the only federal court directly established by provision of Article III. It is principally an appeals court, although it has been assigned original jurisdiction over cases involving ambassadors, consuls, public ministers, and matters where a state is an actual party. The Supreme Court exercises appellate jurisdiction "with such exceptions, and under such regulations as the Congress shall make." Appellate jurisdiction has been granted to the Court through various statutes, beginning with the Judiciary Act of 1789. Congress has also conferred rule-making authority to the Court to allow it to oversee the processes used by the lower federal courts. The Court is comprised of a chief justice of the United States and eight associate justices. The size of the Court is set by Congress and has ranged from as few as five to as many as ten justices. All justices are appointed by the president with consent of the Senate. *See also* ARTICLE III, p. 73; CERTIORARI, p. 584; CONSTITUTIONAL COURTS, p. 588; JUDICIAL REVIEW, p. 627.

Significance   The Supreme Court has extensive power to make or influence the substance of public policy. Through the exercise of its power of judicial review and statutory interpretation, the Court can define the meaning of the Constitution as well as the parameters of legislative, executive, and judicial power. The Supreme Court receives its cases from two principal sources, the United States courts of appeal and state courts of last resort. With certain exceptions, the Court has control over which cases it reviews. Most cases get to the Court via the Writ of Certiorari, a writ issued wholly at the discretion of the Court. Approximately five to six thousand cases seek review annually, with only about three hundred actually receiving a full review that yields a full decision with opinion.

United States Tax Court   A specialized judicial agency that hears disputes concerning decisions of the Internal Revenue Service (IRS). The United States Tax Court was established in 1924 as an agency of the executive branch. It was originally called the United States Board of Tax Appeals. Its name and status as an Article I court of record was changed in 1969. The Tax Court has jurisdiction in under- or overpayments of income, gift, estate, and holding company surtax cases following rulings made by the IRS. In 1969, the court was given jurisdiction to redetermine excise taxes and penalties. In 1974, the court was granted power to render declaratory judgments relating to retirement plans. The court is composed of 19 judges, but frequently utilizes senior judges and special trial judges who may be assigned at the court's discretion. The court is located in Washington, D.C., but conducts trials throughout the United States. *See also* LEGISLATIVE COURTS, p. 630.

Significance   The United States Tax Court was designed to provide a means of appealing IRS decisions. Prior to 1969, this court functioned as an administrative agency, but the Tax Reform Act designated the agency as an Article I court of record. The Tax Court relieves the district courts from the large volume of suits resulting from administration of the tax code. The court is empowered to handle "small" tax claims of under $5,000 through an informal hearing process that expedites disposition of these cases. The decisions of the court other than for the small tax cases are subject to review by the courts of appeals. Decisions in small tax cases do not set legal precedents and cannot be appealed.

War Powers   Authority conveyed by the Constitution to allow for the defense of the country. War powers are discussed in several places in Articles I and II. The Congress is given sole authority to declare war.

It is empowered to provide an army and navy and establish rules and regulations governing the military. Congress also has authority to exercise the taxing and spending power to "provide for the common defense." Finally, the necessary and proper clause permits Congress to exercise great discretion in fulfilling its assigned functions. Article II establishes the president as the commander-in-chief, which lodges vast resources within the control of the executive. *See also* INHERENT POWER, p. 622.

Significance   The exercise of war powers necessarily involves the existence of a national emergency. While constitutional provisions apply "equally in war and in peace," such emergencies have generally prompted the stretching of constitutional authority to meet the demands of the crisis. Thus war powers can be viewed as not only express power, but also implied and even inherent power. The exercise of inherent power permits any action necessary to satisfactorily meet an emergency even though such action is not even indirectly authorized. The exercise of war powers, especially when based on the inherent power argument, is subject to the scrutiny of courts. The war powers are broad, and their exercise is generally met with deference by the judiciary. These powers may reach regulation of domestic activities during wartime, and may be exercised for a reasonable period of time after formal cessation of hostilities.

APPENDIX A:
THE CONSTITUTION OF THE UNITED STATES

The Constitution of the United States

PREAMBLE

We the People of the United States, in Order to form a more perfect Union, establish Justice, insure domestic Tranquility, provide for the common defence, promote the general Welfare, and secure the Blessings of Liberty to ourselves and our Posterity, do ordain and establish this Constitution for the United States of America.

ARTICLE I

SECTION 1. All legislative Powers herein granted shall be vested in a Congress of the United States, which shall consist of a Senate and House of Representatives.

SECTION 2. The House of Representatives shall be composed of Members chosen every second Year by the People of the several States, and the Electors in each State shall have the Qualifications requisite for Electors of the most numerous Branch of the State Legislature.

No Person shall be a Representative who shall not have attained to the age of twenty five Years, and been seven Years a Citizen of the United States, and who shall not, when elected, be an Inhabitant of that State in which he shall be chosen.

Representatives and direct Taxes shall be apportioned among the several States which may be included within this Union, according to their respective Numbers, which shall be determined by adding to the whole Number of free Persons, including those bound to Service for a Term of Years, and excluding Indians not taxed, three fifths of all other Persons. The actual Enumeration shall be made within three Years after the first Meeting of the Congress of the United States, and within every subsequent Term of ten Years, in such Manner as they shall by Law direct. The Number of Representatives shall not exceed one for every thirty Thousand, but each State shall have at Least one Representative; and until such enumeration shall be made, the State of New Hampshire shall be entitled to chuse three, Massachusetts eight, Rhode-Island and Providence Plantations one, Connecticut five, New York six, New Jersey four, Pennsylvania eight, Delaware one, Maryland six, Virginia ten, North Carolina five, South Carolina five, and Georgia three.

When vacancies happen in the Representation from any State, the Executive Authority thereof shall issue Writs of Election to fill such Vacancies.

The House of Representatives shall chuse their Speaker and other Officers; and shall have the sole Power of Impeachment.

SECTION 3. The Senate of the United States shall be composed of two Senators from each State, chosen by the Legislature thereof, for six Years; and each Senator shall have one Vote.

Immediately after they shall be assembled in Consequence of the first Election, they shall be divided as equally as may be into three Classes. The seats of the Senators of the first Class shall be vacated at the Expiration of the second Year, of the second Class at the Expiration of the Fourth Year, and of the third Class at the Expiration of the sixth Year, so that one third may be chosen every second Year; and if Vacancies happen by Resignation, or otherwise, during the Recess of the Legislature of any State, the Executive thereof may make temporary Appointments until the next Meeting of the Legislature, which shall then fill such Vacancies.

No Person shall be a Senator who shall not have attained to the Age of thirty Years, and been nine Years a Citizen of the United States, and who shall not, when elected, be an Inhabitant of that State for which he shall be chosen.

The Vice President of the United States shall be President of the Senate, but shall have no Vote, unless they be equally divided.

The Senate shall chuse their other Officers, and also a President pro tempore, in the Absence of the Vice President, or when he shall exercise the Office of President of the United States.

The Senate shall have the sole Power to try all Impeachments. When sitting for that Purpose, they shall be on Oath or Affirmation. When the President of the United States is tried the Chief Justice shall preside: And no Person shall be convicted without the Concurrence of two thirds of the Members present.

Judgment in Cases of Impeachment shall not extend further than to removal from Office, and disqualification to hold and enjoy any Office of honor, Trust or Profit under the United States: but the Party convicted shall nevertheless be liable and subject to Indictment, Trial, Judgment and Punishment, according to Law.

SECTION 4. The Times, Places and Manner of holding Elections for Senators and Representatives, shall be prescribed in each State by the Legislature thereof; but the Congress may at any time by Law make or alter such Regulations, except as to the Places of chusing Senators.

The Congress shall assemble at least once in every Year, and such Meeting shall be on the first Monday in December unless they shall by Law appoint a different Day.

SECTION 5. Each House shall be the Judge of the Elections, Returns and Qualifications of its own Members, and a Majority of each shall constitute a Quorum to do Business; but a smaller Number may adjourn from day to day, and may be authorized to compel the Attendance of absent Members, in such Manner, and under such Penalties as each House may provide.

Each House may determine the Rules of its Proceedings, punish its Members for disorderly Behaviour, and, with the Concurrence of two thirds, expel a Member.

Each House shall keep a Journal of its Proceedings, and from time to time publish the same, excepting such Parts as may in their Judgment require Secrecy; and the Yeas and Nays of the Members of either House on any question shall, at the Desire of one fifth of those Present, be entered on the Journal.

Neither House, during the Session of Congress, shall, without the Consent of the other, adjourn for more than three days, nor to any other Place than that in which the two Houses shall be sitting.

SECTION 6. The Senators and Representatives shall receive a Compensation for their Services, to be ascertained by Law, and paid out of the Treasury of the United States. They shall in all Cases, except Treason, Felony and Breach of the Peace, be privileged from Arrest during their Attendance at the Session of their respective Houses, and in going to and returning from the same; and for any Speech or Debate in either House, they shall not be questioned in any other Place.

No Senator or Representative shall, during the Time for which he was elected, be appointed to any civil Office under the Authority of the United States, which shall have been created, or the Emoluments whereof shall have been encreased during such time; and no Person holding any Office under the United States, shall be a Member of either House during his Continuance in Office.

SECTION 7. All Bills for raising Revenue shall originate in the House of Representatives; but the Senate may propose or concur with amendments as on other Bills.

Every Bill which shall have passed the House of Representatives and the Senate, shall, before it becomes a Law, be presented to the President of the United States; If he approve he shall sign it, but if not he shall return it, with his Objections to that House in which it shall have originated, who shall enter the Objections at large on their Journal, and proceed to reconsider it. If after such Reconsideration two thirds of that House shall agree to pass the Bill, it shall be sent, together with the Objections, to the other House, by which it shall likewise be reconsidered, and if approved by two thirds of that House, it shall become a Law. But in all such Cases the Votes of both Houses shall be determined by Yeas and Nays, and the Names of the Persons voting for and against the Bill shall be entered on the Journal of each House respectively. If any Bill shall not be returned by the President within ten Days (Sunday excepted) after it shall have been presented to him, the Same shall be a Law, in like Manner as if he had signed it, unless the Congress by their Adjournment prevent its Return, in which Case it shall not be a Law.

Every Order, Resolution, or Vote to which the Concurrence of the Senate and House of Representatives may be necessary (except on a question of Adjournment) shall be presented to the President of the United States; and before the Same shall take Effect, shall be approved by him, or being disapproved by him, shall be repassed by two thirds of the Senate and House of Representatives, according to the Rules and Limitations prescribed in the Case of a Bill.

SECTION 8. The Congress shall have Power To lay and collect Taxes, Duties, Imposts and Excises, to pay the Debts and provide for the common Defence and general Welfare of the United States; but all Duties, Imposts and Excises shall be uniform throughout the United States;

To borrow Money on the credit of the United States;

To regulate Commerce with foreign Nations, and among the several States, and with the Indian Tribes;

To establish an uniform Rule of Naturalization, and uniform Laws on the subject of Bankruptcies throughout the United States;

To coin Money, regulate the Value thereof, and of foreign Coin, and fix the Standard of Weights and Measures;

To provide for the Punishment of counterfeiting the Securities and current

Coin of the United States;

To establish Post Offices and post Roads;

To promote the Progress of Science and useful Arts, by securing for limited Times to Authors and Inventors the exclusive Right to their respective Writings and Discoveries;

To constitute Tribunals inferior to the supreme Court;

To define and punish Piracies and Felonies commited on the high Seas, and Offences against the Law of Nations;

To declare War, grant letters of Marque and Reprisal, and make Rules concerning Captures on Land and Water;

To raise and support Armies, but no Appropriation of Money to that Use shall be for a longer Term than two Years;

To provide and maintain a Navy;

To make Rules for the Government and Regulation of the land and naval Forces;

To provide for calling forth the Militia to execute the Laws of the Union, suppress Insurrections and repel Invasions;

To provide for organizing, arming, and disciplining the Militia, and for governing such Part of them as may be employed in the Service of the United States, reserving to the States respectively, the Appointment of the Officers, and the Authority of training the Militia according to the discipline pre-scribed by Congress;

To exercise exclusive Legislation in all Cases whatsoever, over such District (not exceeding ten Miles square) as may, by Cession of Particular States, and the Acceptance of Congress, become the Seat of the Government of the United States, and to exercise like Authority over all Places purchased by the Consent of the Legislature of the State in which the Same shall be, for the Erection of Forts, Magazines, Arsenals, dock-Yards, and other needful Buildings;—
And

To make all Laws which shall be necessary and proper for carrying into Execution the foregoing Powers, and all other Powers vested by this Constitu-tion in the Government of the United States, or in any Department or Officer thereof.

SECTION 9. The Migration or Importation of such Persons as any of the States now existing shall think proper to admit, shall not be prohibited by the Congress prior to the Year one thousand eight hundred and eight, but a Tax or duty may be imposed on such Importation, not exceeding ten dollars for each Person.

The Privilege of the Writ of Habeas Corpus shall not be suspended, unless when in Cases of Rebellion or Invasion the public Safety may require it.

No Bill of Attainder or ex post facto Law shall be passed.

No capitation, or other direct, Tax shall be laid, unless in Proportion to the Census of Enumeration herein before directed to be taken.

No Tax or Duty shall be laid on Articles exported from any State.

No Preference shall be given by any Regulation of Commerce or Revenue to the Ports of one State over those of another; nor shall Vessels bound to, or from, one State, be obliged to enter, clear or pay Duties in another.

No Money shall be drawn from the Treasury, but in Consequence of Appropriations made by Law; and a regular Statement and Account of the Receipts and Expenditures of all public Money shall be published from time to time.

No Title of Nobility shall be granted by the United States: And no Person holding any Office of Profit or Trust under them, shall, without the Consent of the Congress, accept of any present, Emolument, Office, or Title, of any kind whatever, from any King, Prince, or foreign State.

SECTION 10. No State shall enter into any Treaty, Alliance, or Confederation; grant Letters of Marque and Reprisal; coin Money; emit Bills of Credit; make any Thing but gold and silver Coin a Tender in Payment of Debts; pass any Bill of Attainder, ex post facto Law, or Law impairing the Obligation of Contracts, or grant any Title of Nobility.

No State shall, without the Consent of the Congress, lay any Imposts or Duties on Imports or Exports, except what may be absolutely necessary for executing it's inspection Laws: and the net Produce of all Duties and Imposts, laid by any State on Imports or Exports, shall be for the Use of the Treasury of the United States; and all such Laws shall be subject to the Revision and Controul of the Congress.

No State shall, without the Consent of Congress, lay any Duty of Tonnage, keep Troops, or Ships of War in time of Peace, enter into any Agreement or Compact with another State, or with a foreign Power, or engage in War, unless actually invaded, or in such imminent Danger as will not admit of delay.

ARTICLE II

SECTION 1. The executive Power shall be vested in a President of the United States of America. He shall hold his Office during the Term of four Years, and together with the Vice President, chosen for the same Term, be elected, as follows.

Each State shall appoint, in such Manner as the Legislature thereof may direct, a Number of Electors, equal to the whole Number of Senators and Representatives to which the State may be entitled in the Congress: but no Senator or Representative, or Person holding an Office of Trust or Profit under the United States, shall be appointed an Elector.

The Electors shall meet in their respective States, and vote by Ballot for two Persons, of whom one at least shall not be an Inhabitant of the same State with themselves. And they shall make a List of all the Persons voted for, and of the Number of Votes for each; which List they shall sign and certify, and transmit sealed to the Seat of the Government of the United States, directed to the President of the Senate. The President of the Senate shall, in the Presence of the Senate and House of Representatives, open all the Certificates, and the Votes shall then be counted. The Person having the greatest Number of Votes shall be the President, if such Number be a Majority of the whole Number of Electors appointed; and if there be more than one who have such Majority, and have an equal Number of Votes, then the House of Representatives shall immediately chuse by Ballot one of them for President; and if no Person have a Majority, then from the five highest on the list the said House shall in like Manner chuse the President. But in chusing the President, the Votes shall be taken by States, the Representation from each State having one Vote; a quorum for this Purpose shall consist of a Member or Members from two thirds of the States, and a Majority of all the States shall be necessary to a Choice. In every Case, after the Choice of the President, the Person having the greatest Number of Votes of the Electors shall be the Vice President. But if there should remain two or more who have equal Votes, the Senate shall chuse from them by Ballot the Vice President.

The Congress may determine the Time of chusing the Electors, and the Day on which they shall give their Votes; which Day shall be the same throughout the United States.

No Person except a natural born Citizen, or a Citizen of the United States, at the time of the Adoption of this Constitution, shall be eligible to the Office of President; neither shall any Person be eligible to that Office who shall not have attained to the Age of thirty five Years, and been fourteen Years a Resident within the United States.

In Case of the Removal of the President from Office, or of his Death, Resignation, or Inability to discharge the Powers and Duties of the said Office, the Same shall devolve on the Vice President, and the Congress may by Law provide for the Case of Removal, Death, Resignation or Inability, both of the President and Vice President, declaring what Officer shall then act as President, and such Officer shall act accordingly, until the Disability be removed, or a President shall be elected.

The President shall, at stated Times, receive for his Services, a Compensation, which shall neither be encreased nor diminished during the Period for which he shall have been elected, and he shall not receive within that Period any other Emolument from the United States, or any of them.

Before he enter on the Execution of his Office, he shall take the following Oath or Affirmation—"I do solemnly swear (or affirm) that I will faithfully execute the Office of President of the United States, and will to the best of my Ability, preserve, protect and defend the Constitution of the United States."

SECTION 2. The President shall be Commander in Chief of the Army and Navy of the United States, and of the Militia of the several States, when called into the actual Service of the United States; he may require the Opinion, in writing, of the principal Officer in each of the executive Departments, upon any Subject relating to the Duties of their respective Offices, and he shall have Power to grant Reprieves and Pardons for Offenses against the United States, except in Cases of Impeachment.

He shall have Power, by and with the Advice and Consent of the Senate, to make Treaties, provided two thirds of the Senators present concur; and he shall nominate, and by and with the Advice and Consent of the Senate, shall appoint Ambassadors, other public Ministers and Consuls, Judges of the supreme Court, and all other Officers of the United States, whose Appointments are not herein otherwise provided for, and which shall be established by Law: but the Congress may by Law vest the Appointment of such inferior Officers, as they think proper, in the President alone, in the Courts of Law, or in the Heads of Departments.

The President shall have Power to fill up all Vacancies that may happen during the Recess of the Senate, by granting Commissions which shall expire at the End of their next Session.

SECTION 3. He shall from time to time give to the Congress Information of the State of the Union, and recommend to their Consideration such Measures as he shall judge necessary and expedient; he may, on extraordinary Occasions, convene both Houses, or either of them, and in Case of Disagreement between them, with Respect to the Time of Adjournment, he may adjourn them to such Time as he shall think proper; he shall receive Ambassadors and other public Ministers; he shall take Care that the Laws be faithfully executed, and shall Commission all the Officers of the United States.

SECTION 4. The President, Vice President and all Civil Officers of the United States, shall be removed from office on Impeachment for, and Conviction of, Treason, Bribery, or other high Crimes and Misdemeanors.

ARTICLE III

SECTION 1. The judicial Power of the United States, shall be vested in one supreme Court, and in such inferior Courts as the Congress may from time to time ordain and establish. The Judges, both of the supreme and inferior Courts, shall hold their Offices during good Behaviour, and shall, at stated Times, receive for their Services, a Compensation, which shall not be diminished during their Continuance in Office.

SECTION 2. The judicial Power shall extend to all Cases, in Law and Equity, arising under this Constitution, the Laws of the United States, and Treaties made, or which shall be made, under their Authority; to all Cases affecting Ambassadors, other public Ministers and Consuls;—to all Cases of admiralty and maritime Jurisdiction;—to Controversies to which the United States shall be a Party;—to Controversies between two or more States;—between a State and Citizens of another State;—between Citizens of different States;—between Citizens of the same State claiming Lands under Grants of different States, and between a State, or the Citizens thereof, and foreign States, Citizens or Subjects.

In all Cases affecting Ambassadors, other public Ministers and Consuls, and those in which a State shall be Party, the supreme Court shall have original Jurisdiction. In all the other Cases before mentioned, the supreme Court shall have appellate Jurisdiction, both as to Law and Fact, with such Exceptions, and under such Regulations as the Congress shall make.

The Trial of all Crimes, except in cases of Impeachment, shall be by Jury; and such Trial shall be held in the State where the said Crimes shall have been committed; but when not committed within any State, the Trial shall be at such Place or Places as the Congress may by Law have directed.

SECTION 3. Treason against the United States, shall consist only in levying War against them, or in adhering to their Enemies, giving them Aid and Comfort. No Person shall be convicted of Treason unless on the Testimony of two Witnesses to the same overt Act, or on Confession in open Court.

The Congress shall have Power to declare the Punishment of Treason, but no Attainder or Treason shall work Corruption of Blood, or Forfeiture except during the Life of the Person attainted.

ARTICLE IV

SECTION 1. Full Faith and Credit shall be given in each State to the public Acts, Records, and judicial Proceedings of every other State. And the Congress may by general Laws prescribe the Manner in which such Acts, Records and Proceedings shall be proved, and the Effect thereof.

SECTION 2. The Citizens of each State shall be entitled to all Privileges and Immunities of Citizens in the several States.

A Person charged in any State with Treason, Felony, or other Crime, who shall flee from Justice, and be found in another State, shall on Demand of the executive Authority of the State from which he fled, be delivered up, to be removed to the State having Jurisdiction of the Crime.

No Person held to Service or Labour in one State, under the Laws thereof, escaping into another, shall, in Consequence of any Law or Regulation therein, be discharged from such Service or Labour, but shall be delivered up on Claim of the Party to whom such Service or Labour may be due.

SECTION 3. New States may be admitted by the Congress into this Union; but no new State shall be formed or erected within the Jurisdiction of any other State; nor any State be formed by the Junction of two or more States, or

Parts of States, without the Consent of the Legislatures of the States concerned as well as of the Congress.

The Congress shall have Power to dispose of and make all needful Rules and Regulations respecting the Territory or other Property belonging to the United States; and nothing in this Constitution shall be so construed as to Prejudice any Claims of the United States, or of any particular State.

SECTION 4. The United States shall guarantee to every State in this Union a Republican Form of Government, and shall protect each of them against Invasion; and on Application of the Legislature, or of the Executive (when the Legislature cannot be convened) against domestic Violence.

ARTICLE V

The Congress, whenever two thirds of both Houses shall deem it necessary, shall propose Amendments to this Constitution, or, on the Application of the Legislatures of two thirds of the several States, shall call a Convention for proposing Amendments, which, in either Case, shall be valid to all Intents and Purposes, as Part of this Constitution, when ratified by the Legislatures of three fourths of the several States, or by Conventions in three fourths thereof, as the one or the other Mode of Ratification may be proposed by the Congress; Provided [that no Amendment which may be made prior to the Year One thousand eight hundred and eight shall in any Manner affect the first and fourth Clauses in the Ninth Section of the first Article; and] that no State, without its Consent, shall be deprived of its equal Suffrage in the Senate.

ARTICLE VI

All Debts contracted and Engagements entered into, before the Adoption of this Constitution, shall be as valid against the United States under this Constitution, as under the Confederation.

This Constitution, and the Laws of the United States which shall be made in Pursuance thereof; and all Treaties made, or which shall be made, under the Authority of the United States, shall be the supreme Law of the Land; and the Judges in every State shall be bound thereby, any Thing in the Constitution or Laws of any State to the Contrary notwithstanding.

The Senators and Representatives before mentioned, and the Members of the several State Legislatures, and all executive and judicial Officers, both of the United States and of the several States, shall be bound by Oath or Affirmation, to support this Constitution; but no religious Test shall ever be required as a Qualification to any Office or public Trust under the United States.

ARTICLE VII

The Ratification of the Conventions of nine States, shall be sufficient for the Establishment of this Constitution between the States so ratifying the Same.

AMENDMENT I

[First ten amendments ratified December 15, 1791]

Congress shall make no law respecting an establishment of religion, or prohibiting the free exercise thereof; or abridging the freedom of speech, or of the press; or the right of the people peaceably to assemble, and to petition the Government for a redress of grievances.

AMENDMENT II

A well regulated Militia, being necessary to the security of a free State, the right of the people to keep and bear Arms, shall not be infringed.

AMENDMENT III

No Soldier shall, in time of peace be quartered in any house, without the consent of the Owner, nor in time of war, but in a manner to be prescribed by law.

AMENDMENT IV

The right of the people to be secure in their persons, houses, papers, and effects, against unreasonable searches and seizures, shall not be violated, and no Warrants shall issue, but upon probable cause, supported by Oath or affirmation, and particularly describing the place to be searched, and the persons or things to be seized.

AMENDMENT V

No person shall be held to answer for a capital, or otherwise infamous crime, unless on a presentment or indictment of a Grand Jury, except in cases arising in the land or naval forces, or in the Militia, when in actual service in time of War or public danger; nor shall any person be subject for the same offence to be twice put in jeopardy of life or limb; nor shall be compelled in any criminal case to be a witness against himself, nor be deprived of life, liberty, or property, without due process of law; nor shall private property be taken for public use, without just compensation.

AMENDMENT VI

In all criminal prosecutions, the accused shall enjoy the right to a speedy and public trial, by an impartial jury of the State and district wherein the crime shall have been committed, which district shall have been previously ascertained by law, and to be informed of the nature and cause of the accusation; to be confronted with the witnesses against him; to have compulsory process for obtaining witnesses in his favor, and to have the Assistance of Counsel for his defence.

AMENDMENT VII

In Suits at common law, where the value in controversy shall exceed twenty dollars, the right of trial by jury shall be preserved, and no fact tried by a jury, shall be otherwise re-examined in any Court of the United States, than according to the rules of the common law.

AMENDMENT VIII

Excessive bail shall not be required, nor excessive fines imposed, nor cruel and unusual punishments inflicted.

AMENDMENT IX

The enumeration in the Constitution, of certain rights, shall not be construed to deny or disparage others retained by the people.

AMENDMENT X

The powers not delegated to the United States by the Constitution, nor prohibited by it to the States, are reserved to the States respectively, or to the people.

AMENDMENT XI *[Ratified February 7, 1795]*

The Judicial power of the United States shall not be construed to extend to any suit in law or equity, commenced or prosecuted against one of the United States by Citizens of another State, or by Citizens or Subjects of any Foreign State.

AMENDMENT XII *[Ratified June 15, 1804]*

The Electors shall meet in their respective states and vote by ballot for President and Vice-President, one of whom, at least, shall not be an inhabitant of the same state with themselves; they shall name in their ballots the person voted for as President, and in distinct ballots the person voted for as Vice-President, and they shall make distinct lists of all persons voted for as President, and of all persons voted for as Vice-President, and of the number of votes for each, which lists they shall sign and certify, and transmit sealed to the seat of the government of the United States, directed to the President of the Senate;—The President of the Senate shall, in the presence of the Senate and House of Representatives, open all the certificates and the votes shall then be counted;—The person having the greatest number of votes for President, shall be the President, if such number be a majority of the whole number of Electors appointed; and if no person have such majority, then from the persons having the highest numbers not exceeding three on the list of those voted for as President, the House of Representatives shall choose immediately, by ballot, the President. But in choosing the President, the votes shall be taken by states, the representation from each state having one vote; a quorum for this purpose shall consist of a member or members from two-thirds of the states, and a majority of all the states shall be necessary to a choice. And if the House of Representatives shall not choose a President whenever the right of choice shall devolve upon them, before the fourth day of March next following, then the Vice-President shall act as President, as in the case of the death or other constitutional disability of the President;—The person having the greatest number of votes as Vice-President, shall be the Vice-President, if such number be a majority of the whole number of Electors appointed, and if no person have a majority, then from the two highest numbers on the list, the Senate shall choose the Vice-President; a quorum for the purpose shall consist of two-thirds of the whole number of Senators, and a majority of the whole number shall be necessary to a choice. But no person constitutionally ineligible to the office of President shall be eligible to that of Vice-President of the United States.

AMENDMENT XIII *[Ratified December 6, 1865]*

SECTION 1. Neither slavery nor involuntary servitude, except as a punishment for crime whereof the party shall have been duly convicted, shall exist within the United States, or any place subject to their jurisdiction.

SECTION 2. Congress shall have power to enforce this article by appropriate legislation.

AMENDMENT XIV *[Ratified July 9, 1868]*

SECTION 1. All persons born or naturalized in the United States and subject to the jurisdiction thereof, are citizens of the United States and of the State wherein they reside. No State shall make or enforce any law which shall abridge the privileges or immunities of citizens of the United States; nor shall any State deprive any person of life, liberty, or property, without due process of law; nor deny to any person within its jurisdiction the equal protection of the laws.

SECTION 2. Representatives shall be apportioned among the several States according to their respective numbers, counting the whole number of persons in each State, excluding Indians not taxed. But when the right to vote at any election for the choice of electors for President and Vice President of the United States, Representatives in Congress, the Executive and Judicial officers of a State, or the members of the Legislature thereof, is denied to any of the male inhabitants of such State, being twenty-one years of age, and citizens of the United States, or in any way abridged, except for participation in rebellion, or other crime, the basis of representation therein shall be reduced in the proportion which the number of such male citizens shall bear to the whole number of male citizens twenty-one years of age in such State.

SECTION 3. No person shall be a Senator or Representative in Congress, or elector of President and Vice President, or hold any office, civil or military, under the United States, or under any State, who, having previously taken an oath, as a member of Congress, or as an officer of the United States, or as a member of any State legislature, or as an executive or judicial officer of any State, to support the Constitution of the United States, shall have engaged in insurrection or rebellion against the same, or given aid or comfort to the enemies thereof. But Congress may by a vote of two-thirds of each House, remove such disability.

SECTION 4. The validity of the public debt of the United States, authorized by law, including debts incurred for payment of pensions and bounties for services in suppressing insurrection or rebellion, shall not be questioned. But neither the United States nor any State shall assume or pay any debt or obligation incurred in aid of insurrection or rebellion against the United States, or any claim for the loss or emancipation of any slave; but all such debts, obligations and claims shall be held illegal and void.

SECTION 5. The Congress shall have power to enforce, by appropriate legislation, the provisions of this article.

AMENDMENT XV *[Ratified February 3, 1870]*

SECTION 1. The right of citizens of the United States to vote shall not be denied or abridged by the United States or by any State on account of race, color, or previous condition of servitude.

SECTION 2. The Congress shall have power to enforce this article by appropriate legislation.

AMENDMENT XVI *[Ratified February 3, 1913]*

The Congress shall have power to lay and collect taxes on incomes, from whatever source derived, without apportionment among the several States, and without regard to any census or enumeration.

AMENDMENT XVII *[Ratified April 8, 1913]*

The Senate of the United States shall be composed of two Senators from each State, elected by the people thereof, for six years; and each Senator shall have one vote. The electors in each State shall have the qualifications requisite for electors of the most numerous branch of the State legislatures.

When vacancies happen in the representation of any State in the Senate, the executive authority of such State shall issue writs of election to fill such vacancies: *Provided,* That the legislature of any State may empower the executive thereof to make temporary appointments until the people fill the vacancies by election as the legislature may direct.

This amendment shall not be so construed as to affect the election or term of any Senator chosen before it becomes valid as part of the Constitution.

AMENDMENT XVIII *[Ratified January 16, 1919]*

SECTION 1. After one year from the ratification of this article the manufacture, sale, or transportation of intoxicating liquors within, the importation thereof into, or the exportation thereof from the United States and all territory subject to the jurisdiction thereof for beverage purposes is hereby prohibited.

SECTION 2. The Congress and the several States shall have concurrent power to enforce this article by appropriate legislation.

SECTION 3. This article shall be inoperative unless it shall have been ratified as an amendment to the Constitution by the legislatures of the several States, as provided in the Constitution, within seven years from the date of the submission hereof to the States by the Congress.

AMENDMENT XIX *[Ratified August 18, 1920]*

The right of citizens of the United States to vote shall not be denied or abridged by the United States or by any State on account of sex.

Congress shall have power to enforce this article by appropriate legislation.

AMENDMENT XX *[Ratified January 23, 1933]*

SECTION 1. The terms of the President and Vice President shall end at noon on the 20th day of January, and the terms of Senators and Representatives at noon on the 3d day of January, of the years in which such terms would have ended if this article had not been ratified; and the terms of their successors shall then begin.

SECTION 2. The Congress shall assemble at least once in every year, and such meeting shall begin at noon on the 3d day of January, unless they shall by law appoint a different day.

SECTION 3. If, at the time fixed for the beginning of the term of the President, the President elect shall have died, the Vice President elect shall become President. If a President shall not have been chosen before the time fixed for the beginning of his term, or if the President elect shall have failed to qualify, then the Vice President elect shall act as President until a President shall have qualified; and the Congress may by law provide for the case wherein neither a President elect nor a Vice President elect shall have qualified, declaring who shall then act as President, or the manner in which one who is to act shall be selected, and such person shall act accordingly until a President or Vice President shall have qualified.

SECTION 4. The Congress may by law provide for the case of the death of any of the persons from whom the House of Representatives may choose a President whenever the right of choice shall have devolved upon them, and for the case of the death of any of the persons from whom the Senate may choose a Vice President whenever the right of choice shall have devolved upon them.

SECTION 5. Sections 1 and 2 shall take effect on the 15th day of October following the ratification of this article.

SECTION 6. This article shall be inoperative unless it shall have been ratified as an amendment to the Constitution by the legislatures of three-fourths of the several States within seven years from the date of its submission.

AMENDMENT XXI *[Ratified December 5, 1933]*

SECTION 1. The eighteenth article of amendment to the Constitution of the United States is hereby repealed.

SECTION 2. The transportation or importation into any State, Territory or possession of the United States for delivery or use therein of intoxicating liquors, in violation of the laws thereof, is hereby prohibited.

SECTION 3. This article shall be inoperative unless it shall have been ratified as an amendment to the Constitution by conventions in the several States, as provided in the Constitution, within seven years from the date of the submission hereof to the States by the Congress.

AMENDMENT XXII *[Ratified February 27, 1951]*

SECTION 1. No person shall be elected to the office of the President more than twice, and no person who has held the office of President, or acted as President, for more than two years of a term to which some other person was elected President shall be elected to the office of the President more than once. But this Article shall not apply to any person holding the office of President when this Article was proposed by the Congress, and shall not prevent any person who may be holding the office of President, or acting as President, during the term within which this Article become operative from holding the office of President or acting as President during the remainder of such term.

SECTION 2. This Article shall be inoperative unless it shall have been ratified as an amendment to the Constitution by the legislatures of three-fourths of the several States within seven years from the date of its submission to the States by the Congress.

AMENDMENT XXIII *[Ratified March 29, 1961]*

SECTION 1. The District constituting the seat of Government of the United States shall appoint in such manner as the Congress may direct:

A number of electors of President and Vice President equal to the whole number of Senators and Representatives in Congress to which the District would be entitled if it were a State, but in no event more than the least populous State; they shall be in addition to those appointed by the States, but they shall be considered, for the purposes of the election of President and Vice President, to be electors appointed by a State; and they shall meet in the District and perform such duties as provided by the twelfth article of amendment.

SECTION 2. The Congress shall have power to enforce this article by appropriate legislation.

AMENDMENT XXIV *[Ratified January 23, 1964]*

SECTION 1. The right of citizens of the United States to vote in any primary or other election for President or Vice President, for electors for President or Vice President, or for Senator or Representative in Congress, shall not be denied or abridged by the United States or any State by reason of failure to pay any poll tax or other tax.

SECTION 2. The Congress shall have power to enforce this article by appropriate legislation.

AMENDMENT XXV *[Ratified February 10, 1967]*

SECTION 1. In case of the removal of the President from office or of his death or resignation, the Vice President shall become President.

SECTION 2. Whenever there is a vacancy in the office of the Vice President, the President shall nominate a Vice President who shall take office upon confirmation by a majority vote of both Houses of Congress.

SECTION 3. Whenever the President transmits to the President pro tempore of the Senate and the Speaker of the House of Representatives his written declaration that he is unable to discharge the powers and duties of his office, and until he transmits to them a written declaration to the contrary, such powers and duties shall be discharged by the Vice President as Acting President.

SECTION 4. Whenever the Vice President and a majority of either the principal officers of the executive departments or of such other body as Congress may by law provide, transmit to the President pro tempore of the Senate and the Speaker of the House of Representatives their written declaration that the President is unable to discharge the powers and duties of his office, the Vice President shall immediately assume the powers and duties of the office as Acting President.

Thereafter, when the President transmits to the President pro tempore of the Senate and the Speaker of the House of Representatives his written declaration that no inability exists, he shall resume the powers and duties of his office unless the Vice President and a majority of either the principal officers of the executive department or of such other body as Congress may by law provide, transmit within four days to the President pro tempore of the Senate and the Speaker of the House of Representatives their written declaration that the President is unable to discharge the powers and duties of his office. Thereupon Congress shall decide the issue, assembling within forty-eight hours for that purpose if not in session. If the Congress, within twenty-one days after receipt of the latter written declaration, or, if Congress is not in session, within twenty-one days after Congress is required to assemble, determines by two-thirds vote of both houses that the President is unable to discharge the powers and duties of his office, the Vice President shall continue to discharge the same as Acting President; otherwise, the President shall resume the powers and duties of his office.

AMENDMENT XXVI *[Ratified July 1, 1971]*

SECTION 1. The right of citizens of the United States, who are eighteen years of age or older, to vote shall not be denied or abridged by the United States or by any State on account of age.

SECTION 2. The Congress shall have power to enforce this article by appropriate legislation.

APPENDIX B: JUSTICES OF THE SUPREME COURT

Justices of the Supreme Court

	TENURE	APPOINTED BY	REPLACED
JOHN JAY*	1789–1795	Washington	
John Rutledge	1789–1791	Washington	
William Cushing	1789–1810	Washington	
James Wilson	1789–1798	Washington	
John Blair	1789–1796	Washington	
James Iredell	1790–1799	Washington	
Thomas Johnson	1791–1793	Washington	Rutledge
William Paterson	1793–1806	Washington	Johnson
JOHN RUTLEDGE	1795	Washington	Jay
Samuel Chase	1796–1811	Washington	Blair
OLIVER ELLSWORTH	1796–1800	Washington	Rutledge
Bushrod Washington	1798–1829	John Adams	Wilson
Alfred Moore	1799–1804	John Adams	Iredell
JOHN MARSHALL	1801–1835	John Adams	Ellsworth
William Johnson	1804–1834	Jefferson	Moore
Brockholst Livingston	1806–1823	Jefferson	Paterson
Thomas Todd	1807–1826	Jefferson	(new judgeship)
Gabriel Duval	1811–1835	Madison	Chase
Joseph Story	1811–1845	Madison	Cushing
Smith Thompson	1823–1843	Monroe	Livingston
Robert Trimble	1826–1828	John Q. Adams	Todd
John McLean	1829–1861	Jackson	Trimble
Henry Baldwin	1830–1844	Jackson	Washington
James Wayne	1835–1867	Jackson	Johnson
ROGER B. TANEY	1836–1864	Jackson	Marshall
Phillip P. Barbour	1836–1841	Jackson	Duval
John Catron	1837–1865	Jackson	(new judgeship)
John McKinley	1837–1852	Van Buren	(new judgeship)
Peter V. Daniel	1841–1860	Van Buren	Barbour
Samuel Nelson	1845–1872	Tyler	Thompson
Levi Woodbury	1846–1851	Polk	Story
Robert C. Grier	1846–1870	Polk	Baldwin
Benjamin R. Curtis	1851–1857	Fillmore	Woodbury
John A. Campbell	1853–1861	Pierce	McKinley
Nathan Clifford	1858–1881	Buchanan	Curtis
Noah H. Swayne	1862–1881	Lincoln	McLean
Samuel F. Miller	1862–1890	Lincoln	Daniel
David Davis	1862–1877	Lincoln	Campbell
Stephen J. Field	1863–1897	Lincoln	(new judgeship)
SALMON CHASE	1864–1873	Lincoln	Taney
William Strong	1870–1880	Grant	Grier
Joseph P. Bradley	1870–1892	Grant	Wayne
Ward Hunt	1872–1882	Grant	Nelson
MORRISON R. WAITE	1874–1888	Grant	Chase
John Marshall Harlan	1877–1911	Hayes	Davis
William B. Woods	1880–1887	Hayes	Strong
Stanley Matthews	1881–1889	Garfield	Swayne
Horace Gray	1881–1902	Arthur	Clifford
Samuel Blatchford	1882–1893	Arthur	Hunt
Lucius Q. C. Lamar	1888–1893	Cleveland	Woods
MELVILLE W. FULLER	1888–1910	Cleveland	Waite
David J. Brewer	1889–1910	Harrison	Matthews

Chief justices capitalized

continued

Justices of the Supreme Court

	TENURE	APPOINTED BY	REPLACED
Henry B. Brown	1890–1906	Harrison	Miller
George Shiras, Jr.	1892–1903	Harrison	Bradley
Howell E. Jackson	1893–1895	Harrison	Lamar
EDWARD D. WHITE	1894–1910	Cleveland	Blatchford
Rufus W. Peckham	1895–1909	Cleveland	Jackson
Joseph McKenna	1898–1925	McKinley	Field
Oliver Wendell Holmes	1902–1932	T. Roosevelt	Gray
William R. Day	1903–1922	T. Roosevelt	Shiras
William H. Moody	1906–1910	T. Roosevelt	Brown
Horace H. Lurton	1909–1914	Taft	Peckham
Charles Evans Hughes	1910–1916	Taft	Brewer
Edward D. White	1910–1921	Taft	Fuller
Willis Van Devanter	1910–1937	Taft	White
Joseph R. Lamar	1910–1916	Taft	Moody
Mahlon Pitney	1912–1922	Taft	Harlan
James McReynolds	1914–1941	Wilson	Lurton
Louis D. Brandeis	1916–1939	Wilson	Lamar
John H. Clark	1916–1922	Wilson	Hughes
WILLIAM H. TAFT	1921–1930	Harding	White
George Sutherland	1922–1938	Harding	Clarke
Pierce Butler	1922–1939	Harding	Day
Edward T. Sanford	1923–1930	Harding	Pitney
Harlan F. Stone	1925–1941	Coolidge	McKenna
CHARLES EVANS HUGHES	1930–1941	Hoover	Taft
Owen J. Roberts	1932–1945	Hoover	Sanford
Benjamin N. Cardozo	1932–1938	Hoover	Holmes
Hugo L. Black	1937–1971	F. Roosevelt	Van Devanter
Stanley F. Reed	1938–1957	F. Roosevelt	Sutherland
Felix Frankfurter	1939–1962	F. Roosevelt	Cardozo
William O. Douglas	1939–1975	F. Roosevelt	Brandeis
Frank Murphy	1940–1949	F. Roosevelt	Butler
James F. Byrnes	1941–1942	F. Roosevelt	McReynolds
HARLAN F. STONE	1941–1946	F. Roosevelt	Hughes
Robert H. Jackson	1941–1954	F. Roosevelt	Stone
Wiley B. Rutledge	1943–1949	F. Roosevelt	Byrnes
Harold H. Burton	1945–1958	Truman	Roberts
FRED M. VINSON	1946–1953	Truman	Stone
Tom C. Clark	1949–1967	Truman	Murphy
Sherman Minton	1949–1956	Truman	Rutledge
EARL WARREN	1954–1969	Eisenhower	Vinson
John M. Harlan	1955–1971	Eisenhower	Jackson
William J. Brennan	1957–	Eisenhower	Minton
Charles E. Whittaker	1957–1962	Eisenhower	Reed
Potter Stewart	1959–1981	Eisenhower	Burton
Byron R. White	1962–	Kennedy	Whittaker
Arthur J. Goldberg	1962–1965	Kennedy	Frankfurter
Abe Fortas	1965–1969	Johnson	Goldberg
Thurgood Marshall	1967–	Johnson	Clark
WARREN E. BURGER	1969–1986	Nixon	Warren
Harry A. Blackmun	1970–	Nixon	Fortas
Lewis F. Powell	1971–1987	Nixon	Black
William H. Rehnquist	1971–1986	Nixon	Harlan
John P. Stevens	1975–	Ford	Douglas
Sandra Day O'Connor	1981–	Reagan	Stewart
WILLIAM H. REHNQUIST	1986–	Reagan	Burger
Antonin Scalia	1986–	Reagan	Rehnquist

APPENDIX C:
TERM-BY-TERM COMPOSITION
OF THE SUPREME COURT

Term-by-Term Composition of the Supreme Court

The table below has been designed to represent the members of the Supreme Court on a term-by-term basis. By locating the Court Term in which a particular case was decided, the names of the justices on the Court at the time of that decision may be determined.

THE JAY COURT (1789–1794)

1789	Jay	Rutledge	Cushing	Wilson	Blair	
1790–91	Jay	Rutledge	Cushing	Wilson	Blair	Iredell
1792	Jay	Johnson	Cushing	Wilson	Blair	Iredell
1793–94	Jay	Paterson	Cushing	Wilson	Blair	Iredell

THE RUTLEDGE COURT (1795)

1795	Rutledge	Paterson	Cushing	Wilson	Blair	Iredell

THE ELLSWORTH COURT (1796–1800)

1796–97	Ellsworth	Paterson	Cushing	Wilson	Chase	Iredell
1798–99	Ellsworth	Paterson	Cushing	Washington	Chase	Iredell
1800	Ellsworth	Paterson	Cushing	Washington	Chase	Moore

THE MARSHALL COURT (1801–1835)

1801–03	Marshall	Paterson	Cushing	Washington	Chase	Moore	
1804–05	Marshall	Paterson	Cushing	Washington	Chase	Johnson	
1806	Marshall	Livingston	Cushing	Washington	Chase	Johnson	
1807–10	Marshall	Livingston	Cushing	Washington	Chase	Johnson	Todd
1811–22	Marshall	Livingston	Story	Washington	Duvall	Johnson	Todd
1823–25	Marshall	Thompson	Story	Washington	Duvall	Johnson	Todd
1826–28	Marshall	Thompson	Story	Washington	Duvall	Johnson	Trimble
1829	Marshall	Thompson	Story	Washington	Duvall	Johnson	McLean
1830–34	Marshall	Thompson	Story	Baldwin	Duvall	Johnson	McLean
1835	Marshall	Thompson	Story	Baldwin	Duvall	Wayne	McLean

THE TANEY COURT (1836–1863)

1836	Taney	Thompson	Story	Baldwin	Barbour	Wayne	McLean		
1837–40	Taney	Thompson	Story	Baldwin	Barbour	Wayne	McLean	Catron	McKinley
1841–44	Taney	Thompson	Story	Baldwin	Daniel	Wayne	McLean	Catron	McKinley
1845	Taney	Nelson	Woodbury		Daniel	Wayne	McLean	Catron	McKinley
1846–50	Taney	Nelson	Woodbury	Grier	Daniel	Wayne	McLean	Catron	McKinley

continued

Term-by-Term Composition of the Supreme Court

THE TANEY COURT (1836–1863) *Cont'd.*

1851–52	Taney	Nelson	Curtis	Grier	Daniel	Wayne	McLean	Catron	McKinley	
1853–57	Taney	Nelson	Curtis	Grier	Daniel	Wayne	McLean	Catron	Campbell	
1858–60	Taney	Nelson	Clifford	Grier	Daniel	Wayne	McLean	Catron	Campbell	
1861	Taney	Nelson	Clifford	Grier		Wayne	McLean	Catron	Campbell	
1862	Taney	Nelson	Clifford	Grier	Miller	Wayne	Swayne	Catron	Davis	
1863	Taney	Nelson	Clifford	Grier	Miller	Wayne	Swayne	Catron	Davis	Field

THE CHASE COURT (1864–1873)

1864–65	Chase	Nelson	Clifford	Grier	Miller	Wayne	Swayne	Catron	Davis	Field
1866–67	Chase	Nelson	Clifford	Grier	Miller	Wayne	Swayne		Davis	Field
1868–69	Chase	Nelson	Clifford	Grier	Miller		Swayne		Davis	Field
1870–71	Chase	Nelson	Clifford	Strong	Miller	Bradley	Swayne		Davis	Field
1872–73	Chase	Hunt	Clifford	Strong	Miller	Bradley	Swayne		Davis	Field

THE WAITE COURT (1874–1887)

1874–76	Waite	Hunt	Clifford	Strong	Miller	Bradley	Swayne		Davis	Field
1877–79	Waite	Hunt	Clifford	Strong	Miller	Bradley	Swayne		Harlan	Field
1880	Waite	Hunt	Clifford	Woods	Miller	Bradley	Swayne		Harlan	Field
1881	Waite	Hunt	Clifford	Woods	Miller	Bradley	Matthews		Harlan	Field
1882–87	Waite	Blatchford	Gray	Woods	Miller	Bradley	Matthews		Harlan	Field

THE FULLER COURT (1888–1909)

1888	Fuller	Blatchford	Gray	Lamar	Miller	Bradley	Matthews		Harlan	Field
1889	Fuller	Blatchford	Gray	Lamar	Miller	Bradley	Brewer		Harlan	Field
1890–91	Fuller	Blatchford	Gray	Lamar	Brown	Bradley	Brewer		Harlan	Field
1892	Fuller	Blatchford	Gray	Lamar	Brown	Shiras	Brewer		Harlan	Field
1893	Fuller	Blatchford	Gray	Jackson	Brown	Shiras	Brewer		Harlan	Field
1894	Fuller	White	Gray	Jackson	Brown	Shiras	Brewer		Harlan	Field
1895–97	Fuller	White	Gray	Peckham	Brown	Shiras	Brewer		Harlan	Field
1898–1901	Fuller	White	Gray	Peckham	Brown	Shiras	Brewer		Harlan	McKenna
1902	Fuller	White	Holmes	Peckham	Brown	Shiras	Brewer		Harlan	McKenna
1903–05	Fuller	White	Holmes	Peckham	Brown	Day	Brewer		Harlan	McKenna
1906–08	Fuller	White	Holmes	Peckham	Moody	Day	Brewer		Harlan	McKenna
1909	Fuller	White	Holmes	Lurton	Moody	Day	Brewer		Harlan	McKenna

continued

Term-by-Term Composition of the Supreme Court

THE WHITE COURT (1910–1920)

1910–11	White	VanDevanter	Holmes	Lurton	Lamar	Day	Hughes	Harlan	McKenna
1912–13	White	VanDevanter	Holmes	Lurton	Lamar	Day	Hughes	Pitney	McKenna
1914–15	White	VanDevanter	Holmes	McReynolds	Lamar	Day	Hughes	Pitney	McKenna
1916–20	White	VanDevanter	Holmes	McReynolds	Brandeis	Day	Clarke	Pitney	McKenna

THE TAFT COURT (1921–1929)

1921	Taft	VanDevanter	Holmes	McReynolds	Brandeis	Day	Clarke	Pitney	McKenna
1922	Taft	VanDevanter	Holmes	McReynolds	Brandeis	Butler	Sutherland	Pitney	McKenna
1923–24	Taft	VanDevanter	Holmes	McReynolds	Brandeis	Butler	Sutherland	Sanford	McKenna
1925–29	Taft	VanDevanter	Holmes	McReynolds	Brandeis	Butler	Sutherland	Sanford	Stone

THE HUGHES COURT (1930–1940)

1930–31	Hughes	VanDevanter	Holmes	McReynolds	Brandeis	Butler	Sutherland	Roberts	Stone
1932–36	Hughes	VanDevanter	Cardozo	McReynolds	Brandeis	Butler	Sutherland	Roberts	Stone
1937	Hughes	Black	Cardozo	McReynolds	Brandeis	Butler	Sutherland	Roberts	Stone
1938	Hughes	Black	Cardozo	McReynolds	Brandeis	Butler	Reed	Roberts	Stone
1939	Hughes	Black	Frankfurter	McReynolds	Douglas	Butler	Reed	Roberts	Stone
1940	Hughes	Black	Frankfurter	McReynolds	Douglas	Murphy	Reed	Roberts	Stone

THE STONE COURT (1941–1945)

1941–42	Stone	Black	Frankfurter	Byrnes	Douglas	Murphy	Reed	Roberts	Jackson
1943–44	Stone	Black	Frankfurter	Rutledge	Douglas	Murphy	Reed	Roberts	Jackson
1945	Stone	Black	Frankfurter	Rutledge	Douglas	Murphy	Reed	Burton	Jackson

THE VINSON COURT (1946–1952)

1946–48	Vinson	Black	Frankfurter	Rutledge	Douglas	Murphy	Reed	Burton	Jackson
1949–52	Vinson	Black	Frankfurter	Minton	Douglas	Clark	Reed	Burton	Jackson

continued

Term-by-Term Composition of the Supreme Court

THE WARREN COURT (1953–1968)

1953–54	Warren	Black	Frankfurter	Minton	Douglas	Clark	Reed	Burton	Jackson
1955	Warren	Black	Frankfurter	Minton	Douglas	Clark	Reed	Burton	Harlan
1956	Warren	Black	Frankfurter	Brennan	Douglas	Clark	Reed	Burton	Harlan
1957	Warren	Black	Frankfurter	Brennan	Douglas	Clark	Whittaker	Burton	Harlan
1958–61	Warren	Black	Frankfurter	Brennan	Douglas	Clark	Whittaker	Stewart	Harlan
1962–65	Warren	Black	Goldberg	Brennan	Douglas	Clark	White	Stewart	Harlan
1965–67	Warren	Black	Fortas	Brennan	Douglas	Clark	White	Stewart	Harlan
1967–69	Warren	Black	Fortas	Brennan	Douglas	Marshall	White	Stewart	Harlan

THE BURGER COURT (1969–1985)

1969	Burger	Black	Fortas	Brennan	Douglas	Marshall	White	Stewart	Harlan
1969–70	Burger	Black		Brennan	Douglas	Marshall	White	Stewart	Harlan
1970	Burger	Black	Blackmun	Brennan	Douglas	Marshall	White	Stewart	Harlan
1971	Burger	Powell	Blackmun	Brennan	Douglas	Marshall	White	Stewart	Rehnquist
1975	Burger	Powell	Blackmun	Brennan	Stevens	Marshall	White	Stewart	Rehnquist
1981	Burger	Powell	Blackmun	Brennan	Stevens	Marshall	White	O'Connor	Rehnquist

THE REHNQUIST COURT (1986–)

1986	Rehnquist	Powell	Blackmun	Brennan	Stevens	Marshall	White	O'Connor	Scalia

INDEX

In this index, references in **bold** type indicate page numbers where that particular term is defined within the text. Numbers in roman type refer to entries containing additional information about a term that the reader may wish to consult for further information.

703